# FIRST HITS

## 1946 – 1959

# FIRST HITS
## 1946 – 1959

### Brian Henson & Colin Morgan

First published in 1989 by Boxtree Limited

© Colin Morgan and Brian Henson

Charts © The Music Publishers' Association Limited 1989
This compilation of record listings and text © Brian Henson & Colin
Morgan 1989

Designed by Julia Lilauwala
Typeset by Bookworm, Manchester
Printed and bound in Great Britain
by Richard Clay Limited, Bungay, Suffolk

for Boxtree Limited
36 Tavistock Street
London WC2E 7PB

**British Library Cataloguing in Publication Data**
Henson, Brian
    First hits: the book of sheet music hits 1946–1959
    1. Great Britain. Pop music. Sheet music. 1946–1959
    I. Title II. Morgan, Colin
    780′.42′0942

    ISBN 1–85283–268–1

THIS BOOK IS DEDICATED TO

# PHILIP FARLOW

for his non-stop help and encouragement over the last
six years. Without him, we would literally never have
got started . . . or, come to that, finished.

and to

# PETER SIMPSON

for giving up so much of his valuable eating time to
solve the seemingly insoluble.

# CONTENTS

| | |
|---|---|
| *Introduction* | 9 |
| *Acknowledgements* | 11 |
| *Notes* | 13 |
| *Preface* | 15 |
| Playlist of recordings used in the very last Radio Luxembourg Top Twenty | 18 |
| 1946 | 19 |
| Song Charts | 20 |
| 1947 | 27 |
| Song Charts | 28 |
| 1948 | 37 |
| Song Charts | 39 |
| 1949 | 47 |
| Song Charts | 49 |
| 1950 | 62 |
| Song Charts | 64 |
| 1951 | 78 |
| Song Charts | 80 |
| 1952 | 96 |
| Song Charts | 98 |
| 1953 | 113 |
| Song Charts | 115 |
| 1954 | 132 |
| Song Charts | 134 |
| 1955 | 151 |
| Song Charts | 153 |
| 1956 | 169 |
| Song Charts | 170 |
| 1957 | 185 |
| Song Charts | 186 |
| 1958 | 200 |
| Song Charts | 201 |
| 1959 | 219 |
| Song Charts | 221 |
| Outstanding Feats | 241 |
| Artist Index | 247 |
| Song Index | 295 |

# INTRODUCTION

Pop songs have been part of my life for as long as I can remember. When I was a lad in short trousers, the vocal and musical talents of my parents nurtured me on the popular Victorian and Edwardian drawing-room, or parlour songs – call them what you will – of the late 1920s. Those that had survived often provided do-it-yourself entertainment when family and relatives got together. That's how it was in the home of Martha and Victor Johnson. Lovingly, we nicknamed our parents Queen and Pop.

Queen had a double talent. She was an excellent pianist and had a beautiful lyric soprano voice that would warmly caress old ballads like *I'll sing thee songs of Araby* and *Somewhere a voice is calling*. She played for herself when she sang and would accompany Pop, too, when his pleasing light baritone voice and sparkling personality gave us such gems as *Up from Somerset* and – of course – *The lost chord*. There was further variety added to the entertainment when they merged their voices in duets like *Garden of happiness* and *Come sing to me*. Despite the fact that she was an amateur, Queen was, and always remained, an excellent sight reader of piano music. She would never busk or play from memory and resisted any attempts by my father to charm her into so doing. Many's the time we heard her say –

'No, dear, you know that I can't play by ear. I must have the music.'

So, Pop must have been one of the best customers that sheet music ever had because he ensured, at all times, that Queen played from the officially published copies. In the house, the copies would always be stored either on the music rest of the piano or in a neat pile on a table at the side of the upright. That was where they were quartered and where they remained throughout the whole of my parents' lifetime together, in whatever abode they shared.

I cannot remember exactly when or why I became interested in the sheet music of the songs they performed. I must have been around the age of nine or ten when I started to look at those copies on the table by the piano. Immediately, I found them impressive and fascinating. And impressive is not a word I'm using lightly. The thick, whiter than white, parchment-like quality of the paper gave the impression to this youngster that they *were*

important documents; certainly not just popular songs for singing! The pristine whiteness of the paper served to highlight the large and vivid black print of the letters on the front covers that, consequently, shrieked out to me the song's title and its writers. Turn a front cover and on the two pages (or sheets) in front of me would be a feast of words and music, meticulously prepared and presented. Some of the songs would run to nine or ten pages of this sheer delight.

I felt so enthusiastic about what I was seeing because, despite my lack of musical knowledge, everything seemed so easy to understand. The words of the song would be in a line, stretched out across each page, every syllable perfectly co-ordinated to its vocal note in the stave above it and, likewise, to the piano accompaniment below. How different this was to the stark bareness and briefness of the pieces that we had to sing from in the school hymn book – which was, probably, the only printed music that I had seen before. In retrospect, this discovery that I had some sort of interest in songs, apart from my enjoyment of hearing them sung, must surely have been my initiation into the world of music. Certainly, my interest in the adventures of Bob Cherry and Billy Bunter, Sexton Blake, Captain Biggles and other fictional heroes from the magazines of my boyhood suddenly evaporated.

The start of the Thirties and the arrival of a radio in the Johnson household, dragged me even further away from juvenile pastimes – but not away from sheet music. The bands of Jack Payne, Harry Roy, Lew Stone and all the others who were on the air at that time simply took over my life. I tried to listen to every dance band programme, much to the consternation of my parents. I also began to try and put into practice some of the things that I heard. I think it was just before I entered my teens that I started to make my vocal presence felt around the house. Queen and Pop, poor dears, went through enormous sufferings as I wah-dah-daared and skiddlee-um-deed my own 'hot' versions of hits of the day like *You're driving me crazy* and *Happy feet*. Pop was completely unimpressed and obviously vocally affronted, judging by his oft repeated cry of –

'Edward! Stop trying to sing that foolish rubbish.'

Quite the opposite happened. I found myself getting

more and more interested. Sometimes I couldn't understand all the words of some of the songs that I was hearing. So, if I really liked them, there was only one thing to do: save my pocket money until I had enough to go out and buy the sheet music. Then, it was a dash back home to Queen and a request that she would play it for me on the piano so that I could sing it. Being a loving mother – even if she did not like the songs – she still relished the challenge of playing the modern 'rubbish' for me. Although it was a different type of music, she still made a good job of it.

My sheet music was different in other ways, too. I found that the white cover copies that had so impressed me earlier were undoubtedly in the classic, almost cultured mould compared to the ones that I was now buying. Not that I found anything wrong in that. *You're driving me crazy* and *Happy feet* were modern and light hearted after the Victoriana of *The lost chord*.

The front covers reflected that. Mine were jolly colourful, sometimes humorous. They were overtly eye catching and always carried a picture of an artiste who had performed (as featured by) the song. They were, also, much cheaper to buy. Studying the medium now, I realise why. They were cheaper because these songs had a bigger *immediate* sales potential. They were aimed at a mass market with a quick turnover. When one hit faded, another would immediately take its place. Due to the immense amount of songs that were now coming at us via radio, records and films, sheet music was becoming big business. We were obviously following the same pattern as the USA because Hoagy Carmichael is on record as saying that, in 1933, the first song that he wrote with Johnny Mercer, *Lazybones*, sold over 300,000 copies within six weeks of publication. He considered that at that time this was the most impressive sales figure that any song had achieved – and it provided a stimulus that brought the whole of Tin Pan Alley out of the Depression.

I continued to make my own contribution to those sort of sales figures. I had managed to acquire a small set of trap drums as they were then called. Now, at the family get-togethers in the front room, Queen and I were the resident 'in-house combo'. She would play from my up-to-date, sixpenny sheet music copies and I would accompany her on drums and vocals. The guests may have hated it but it was doing wonders for me, because . . .

At the age of fourteen, with two of my school chums and two other teenage, amateur musicians, I formed my own dance band. Can you believe that? A band-leader at the age of fourteen! And, the only musical knowledge that I possessed was what I had picked up from those copies of sheet music. And they continued to be my greatest ally. As I couldn't afford to buy a library of orchestrations, I had to get the band playing from my sixpenny copies. In my own musically naive and elementary way, I managed to do it. As a band, we never achieved much. But, in loving our music, we all enjoyed going nowhere. Although it did produce something worthwhile for me. Through a friend who knew about my semi-pro band-leader status, I was offered the chance of becoming a professional drummer and singer in November 1937. I took the chance. Apart from the Second World War period, I have most gratefully been in music and show business ever since.

I was not always a drummer/vocalist, however. In 1948, my drum kit became redundant when I accepted a job as an announcer on the English programmes of Radio Luxembourg. I imagined that songs and sheet music were no longer part of my life – but they were. From the time that I started to present a programme called *Top Twenty*, they became even more important and relevant to my career. Just how is one of the things that you can read about in this book.

The authors have lovingly and assiduously researched the subject of hit songs from 1946 to 1959 and come up with the most all-embracing and formidable array of data and figures that I have ever seen. They have even managed to find out some details concerning the afore-mentioned *Top Twenty* shows that I didn't know about – and I was there in Luxembourg doing the programme at the time! My congratulations to them for their diligence and energy.

An illustration on the front cover of this book reminds me that *Beloved, be faithful* was the first time my picture ever appeared on a sheet music front cover.

Brian and Colin . . . thanks for the memory.

TEDDY JOHNSON
*1 March 1989*

# ACKNOWLEDGEMENTS

The compilers would like to thank the following for their help and assistance in putting this volume together. Particularly, we are grateful to the Music Publishers' Association Limited and its secretary, Peter Dadswell, for permission to use the charts and also for help in research. Thanks, too, to Teddy Johnson and Paul Rich for their most interesting and useful recollections of the era; to Peter Foss and Stan Kitchen for their wealth of knowledge of the sheet music scene; and to the following who have helped us with information which has cleared up many problems: Mick Booth; Janice Cable of the MPA; Alan Clark; Sandy Forbes – for supplying the final pieces of the jigsaw regarding the dance band vocalists; Roy Francis; Pat Hetherington – whose hand-written lists of the Radio Luxembourg Top Twenties down the years helped no end; Patrick Howgill; Mrs Jacqueline Kavanagh and her staff, particularly Senior Researcher Neil Somerville, of the BBC Written Archives Centre at Caversham; Derek Lewis; Bill Manley; Mr & Mrs John Matley; the *Melody Maker;* Jim Palm; Paul Pelletier – for finally clearing up for us where the join between the 78 and 45 issues on the Embassy label came; the Performing Right Society; Peter Quin; Leslie Wilson; Colin Brown; Mark Fiori and Hugh Palmer.

## ILLUSTRATION ACKNOWLEDGEMENTS

We would like to thank the following companies for the use of sheet music covers: International Music Publications (Warner-Chappell Music Ltd & EMI Music Publishing Ltd), Woodford Trading Estate, Southend Road, Woodford Green, Essex IG8 8HN. Tel: 081–551 6131. (pages 96-97). Campbell Connelly & Co Ltd, 8–9 Frith Street, London W1V 5TZ. Tel: 071–434 0066. (pages 224-225). MCA Music, 139 Piccadilly, London W1V 9FH. Tel: 071-629 7211 (for 'Beloved, be faithful').

# NOTES

A total of 1,100 songs appeared in the Sheet Music Charts between 1946 and 1959. They are listed here in chronological order, i.e. in the order in which they entered the charts and are numbered accordingly for easy reference. The information for each song consists of the following: Composer/s; Publishers; date of entry (and re-entry if applicable); highest position reached; total number of weeks on the chart; all singles recordings available at the time of the song's chart life (both 78 and 45 rpm) plus a few relevant later recordings; month and year of first issue of each recording; and record numbers in full. The recordings are listed in the order in which they were released and readers who have the record companies' numerical catalogues will find occasional differences in the month of release. This is because many singles were due for release one month but were in fact 'pre-released' the previous month or even earlier in odd cases, and the catalogues have the original date of release listed. Earlier recordings which have been deleted from the catalogues before the chart entry are in general not included, while recordings released after the chart life which we felt needed inclusion have an asterisk after the number, e.g. Capitol CL.13899★. We are pleased to have been able to include, for the first time in a reference work, the Embassy label, sold by Woolworth's and pressed by Oriole Records. On all dance band recordings you will find the names of the vocalists in brackets after the band's name. Backing groups are added where applicable after the singer's name. For space reasons, we have had to draw the line at including the backing orchestras. Some are mentioned but only where they are particularly relevant, or perhaps interesting, or, more importantly, associated irrevocably with a recording. Therefore, we have to apologise to all those wonderful leaders and arrangers who created the backgrounds so magnificently. Also, again with regret, we have had to omit the piano medleys by such as Charlie Kunz, Ian Stewart and Ivor Moreton and Dave Kaye, plus other medleys by Reginald Dixon and Primo Scala, etc. Over the years the charts were subject to change as far as the number of songs listed each week were concerned. From July 1946 until the end of May 1947 they were listed alphabetically and varied between fifteen, sixteen and seventeen songs in each list. From 29 May 1947 until 19 May 1949 a Top Ten in numerical order was produced. This became the famed Top Twenty on 28 May 1949 and was produced by the Music Publishers' Association, as opposed to the earlier listings which had come from the Wholesale Music Distributors' Association, a body long since extinct. The lists were extended to a Top Twenty-Four from 10 March 1951 but these were not published in full until 1952, so here you will find the first publication of the additional four songs each week. This Top Twenty-Four continued to be produced until 16 August 1958 when the list was extended to a Top Thirty.

All the records listed herein are 78 rpm except where stated. The key is as follows:

(a) Prefix 45- signifies 45 rpm only
(b) (45) 7M, SCM, SP, MSP – EMI 45 rpm early issues (1953–56)
(c) (& 45-) after a record number indicates that both 78 and 45 rpm issues were released together. In the early days of 45 rpm it was not always the case that there was a simultaneous release of both 78 and 45 rpm issues. Where this occurs we have listed the records both as 78 and as 45 issues, with the release date for each.

Although the continental releases of the major record companies have not been included in full, a few releases are included where we felt it was necessary. The Decca group listed their issues in their annual catalogues but the EMI companies did not. All of these records were available to special order.

Finally, perhaps we should point out that none of the records listed herein is currently available in record shops, except for the few that have found their way on to albums over the years.

# PREFACE

There was a time when nearly every other household had a piano while only a few had a gramophone. This was the pre-World War Two situation when sales of sheet music were so great that they were equivalent in their own way to the record sales of today. Songs like *After the ball* and *The Lambeth Walk* brought tremendous figures of around five million each. A fairy story indeed for some of the more successful songwriters and publishers of the day, although stories abound of composers who sold their 'sheets' to the publishers literally 'for a song' in order to pay their rent or to have a square meal, while the song went on to sell thousands and make thousands for the publishers. Sheet music was much in demand during the last war, and had there not been a paper shortage, perhaps all-time records could have been set.

Charts of varying degrees of accuracy had been compiled in the United States for several decades before the war but no single chart became totally acceptable until the mid-Thirties. Five years later came the first record charts. We in Britain had tried to start a sheet music chart in October 1936 and Geraldo, one of our top bandleaders, had persuaded the BBC to let him run a fortnightly series on the National Programme under the title 'The Music Shop' which featured a listing of the Top Ten played in any order. Unfortunately for him, and perhaps for the rest of us, the music business kicked up a tremendous fuss saying that the listing hardly compared with their sales figures at all whilst also accusing the BBC of breaking its no-advertising rules. In the event, the series ran for just six months and then disappeared for ever. As a point of interest, 50 years on, Geraldo and the music industry agreed on just one thing – that *It's a sin to tell a lie* was the first No. 1.

So the Americans had an established chart and we didn't. Strange, perhaps, when you think that they have never caught on to 'the romance of the charts' as we have. The premier music paper, *Melody Maker*, published the US charts in its pages for years, albeit somewhat haphazardly with some purporting to be the 'current week' as much as two months out of date. In January 1942 the paper began to list a British 'Top Tune' Top Ten for just two months which had been provided by 'leading London collecting houses'. This chart showed *Yours, Rose O'Day* and *That lovely weekend* as No. 1s during the period. The admission that no direct sales were included in the figures could be the reason that the chart was dropped, as it could not be considered a definitive one. *Melody Maker* tried to adopt a chart again in May 1943. Titled 'Sheet Music – The Week's Best Sellers', it ran for almost five months and consisted of either 10 or 12 songs. The longest running No. 1 during this period was *Whispering grass,* with no less than 11 weeks in top place. No reason was given when the chart disappeared in September. All our attempts to trace other charts from this period have failed.

Finally on 27 July 1946 came the alphabetical listing of the week's top 15 songs here in Britain and the Sheet Music Charts had come to stay – well, for 40 years anyway. These continuous charts had begun at a time when all entertainment was booming after the war and with radio in its golden age there was plenty of airtime available. Sales of records at that time were poor in comparison with today although there were certain exceptions. Some excuse can be found in that we were seeing a transitional stage from the dance bands to the vocalists. The American bands, hard hit by the troubles with their American Society of Composers, Authors & Publishers (ASCAP), which took them out of the recording studios in the States for over a year, were never to recover their popularity, and the door opened wide to the vocal talents of the likes of Crosby, Sinatra, Lee, Como and Day, etc. Britain, with its plethora of Service bands and the American influenced bands like Geraldo's, took slightly longer to change but when singers like Steve Conway were followed by others, among them Vera Lynn, Anne Shelton and Dorothy Squires plus Donald Peers, Teddy Johnson and Jimmy Young, the days of the dance bands became numbered here, too, although strict tempo styles continued to find favour and the recordings of Victor Silvester and Joe Loss continued to sell – witness their recordings listed herein. Still the song was king and anyone could record it. Versions of each song were numerous and the record buyer paid his money and took his choice.

Tin Pan Alley, or Denmark Street, to give it its proper name, was a hive of industry. Each publisher, having signed up a song from the writers, would immediately print about a thousand copies, mark them 'Professional Copy – Not For Sale' and hand them out to any singer or bandleader they could find from the top stars down to the most humble performers. Indeed, it was not unknown for artists to go around the publishers asking for handouts of these professional copies. Should any of the really big artists show interest, the song pluggers would urge them to broadcast the song at the earliest opportunity. If, for example, Billy Cotton was going to broadcast the song one Sunday on his Band Show, the publishers would hastily print enormous stocks with his photograph on the cover ready for the expected orders on Monday morning. It was not unusual for the same sheet music to appear with different artists on the front as they each broadcast and/or recorded the song. The pluggers had their work cut out, for obviously only a small proportion of the songs could become hits. At one time publishers were so anxious to get their songs aired on the BBC that it was not unusual for them to pay 'plug money' to an artist to perform their song on such a programme as 'Music Hall' on Saturday nights. Figures of £50–£100 per broadcast were offered. Dance bands had to play a vocal title two or three times to earn a pay-off and an instrumental number four or five times. The BBC finally investigated the situation and stern measures were taken to stop it.

Lou Preager, resident at the Hammersmith Palais in London with his Orchestra, suggested a 'Write a Song' Contest to the Palais management in 1945 and it was subsequently broadcast by the BBC. There were no less than 73,852 entries in the first competition and 55 per cent of these were waltzes, with a further 20 per cent novelty songs. Half a million listeners sent in votes for the 12 songs which reached the final. Preager's vocalist, Paul Rich, sang the eventual winner, *Cruising down the river* and the song went on to become the second biggest ever sheet music seller. At first no publisher would take the song and Preager finally approached Cinephonic Music Limited and offered to pay all expenses if they would publish it. They agreed and, of course, never regretted it.

No song could be recorded without the publisher's permission and this is indicative of the lack of power of the record companies at that time. Sheet music sales of hits could reach 10,000 per *day* or more, whereas today a No. 1 sometimes touches 1,000 a week.

American songs had always been contracted to publishers here by an unofficial auction. Although some US publishers had their own outlet in the UK, most songs were leased to the highest bidders and an advance payment of £1,000 was a common figure. This was a tremendous amount in those days when each sheet would sell for 1/- (5p) or perhaps 2/- (10p). But of course what was a hit in America didn't always make it here and the publishers could not only lose their £1,000 but also money for plugging and printing. A good example of this was *Skinnie Minnie (Fishtail)*. In 1954 the publishers printed 6,000 advance copies, yet despite a recording by Alma Cogan, the song never got off the ground. At one time, once a song was signed from an American publisher, it was signed for life, but the situation slowly changed with songs being signed for limited periods only. Songs then began to change hands between publishers quite regularly. It is important to note, in the light of subsequent mergers, etc., that the publishers listed in this book are those holding the publishing rights at the time of the chart entry.

Many smaller sheet music publishers were springing up, too. With just a one-room office they would buy a song, get it printed and then ask one of the major publishers to sell and distribute the song for them. This would incur a commission of 10 per cent of the selling price of the music for the larger company but it saved the smaller company the expense of employing staff such as a trade manager, invoice clerk and packer. This explains the presence of the term 'Sole Selling Agents' on the front of many song copies.

In May 1949, when the Popular Music Committee of the Music Publishers' Association took over the compilation of the Charts, Radio Luxembourg immediately began to broadcast them, with their resident announcer, Teddy Johnson, as the first chart presenter. This 'Top Twenty' was to be made up according to the MPA charts right up to the last programme of 1959, thereby tying in nicely with the scope of this book. Radio Luxembourg and the two music papers, *Melody Maker* and *New Musical Express,* were each asked to pay the seemingly paltry sum of 25 guineas per year for the privilege of using the MPA charts

– which worked out at approximately 10/- (50p) per week!

By the early Fifties the charts were made up from returns sent in by 65 major retail outlets including Woolworth's and British Home Stores. Each of the two big chain stores had their own way of ordering. Publishers would send Woolworth's head office in Bond Street in Central London one or more copies of their new songs. If Woolworth's accepted a song, the publishers would then send a sample copy to each of the 300 Woolworth's branches and wait for the orders to roll in. All those branches would buy the song in bundles of 25 and, even in those days, the publishers would grumble how bad the business was! British Home Stores, for its part, had a buyer who would examine the songs and then send orders once a week to each publisher for the whole chain. As the Fifties drew to a close the number of returns was down to 35. The MPA would send out printed forms to retailers who would return them to the MPA's own chartered accountants who, in turn, compiled each week's chart from the figures supplied and informed the MPA. The next step was for the MPA to ring through to Luxembourg's London office and the music papers to give them the latest lists. During the early days of 1958 the publishers were complaining that the charts were too out of date when just a week old at publication, and so arrangements were made to make up the charts to the Tuesday or Wednesday prior to the music papers' publication. In order to be consistent to this book we have kept the Saturday dates throughout, but the reader should bear in mind that as from 15 March 1958 the actual dates could be reckoned to be three or four days later.

One of the compilers of this book, Colin Morgan, spent over a year of his evenings during his National Service playing his own records in the intervals between films in the Army Camp Cinema at Crookham, near Aldershot, and he recalls that in 1953 he would get requests for 'tunes' rather than artists. He remembers also that in the early weeks of his service in the spring of 1952 when he and the other new recruits were not allowed to listen to the radio that his mother would listen to Luxembourg each week and send him the Top Twenty, which he would then read out to the rest of the occupants of the barrack-room. Against the new entries she would have written a brief description – fast or slow song, waltz, novelty or whatever. Records, despite the *New Musical Express* chart beginning in November of that year, would not begin to

be a threat to the Sheet Music Charts until around 1955. Indeed, the 'Top Twenty' show on 208 was proving by far their most popular programme. Appreciative letters rolled in and presenters Pete Murray and Peter Madren took care to select the cream of the recordings available of each song, at the same time ensuring that differing versions appeared each week – an approach that always went down well with the listeners.

Publishers unfortunately have not kept records of their sales of the period but it is generally agreed that the last sheet music million sellers were in 1953 with *That doggie in the window* a possible final seven figure seller.

Over the years many traditional songs have been revived. While this has proved something of a nightmare for the compilers of this volume, the publishing situation is simple. Anyone can adapt a traditional song and get the credit – all he needs to do is to change a word here and there and then he can be credited with a new version which any publisher can take up. Readers will find this information useful when referring to songs such as *Beautiful brown eyes* and *Tom Dooley*.

Publishers would handle some 25 songs a year of which, if they were reasonably successful, some six or so would be chart entries. Every December most of these would be compiled into an album, sometimes with photographs included, and sold for around 1/6d (7½p). Usually, the writers of the songs would get no royalties at all from these albums – it was the publishers who made the killing in this most profitable of spin-offs. On occasion, the advance orders for these albums would run to 50,000 copies.

European hits were handled similarly to the American ones and lyric writers like Geoffrey Parsons specialised in replacing the original French, Italian or whatever with words for the British listener. The Peter Maurice Music Company, headed by Jimmy Phillips, would for instance, give Parsons a French song. He would take it away and return in a couple of days with the new lyric which Phillips would examine carefully and suggest changes here and there. The credits for the English lyrics on the music would then go to Geoffrey Parsons and John Turner – the latter being a pseudonym used by Jimmy Phillips.

Pseudonyms abound in music publishing just as they do in book publishing. We have not attempted to cover this aspect as it appears to be an endless source of confusion. A good example of this can be seen via the Michael Reine Music Company which was actually owned and run by

Johnny Reine – which is the real name of Johnny Johnston, leader of The Keynotes, The Johnston Brothers and The Johnston Singers. The 'Michael' came from Mrs Mickie Cox, wife of composer and fellow publisher, Desmond Cox, who started the company with Reine.

The Sheet Music Charts ceased to be printed in the *New Musical Express* after February 1965 but were produced by the MPA until the spring of 1985. Mrs Janice Cable, who started with the MPA in the early Sixties and who is still there today, was involved in the chart compilations and recalls how for a short period at that time the charts were compiled from both sheet music sales and record sales on a points system. We are grateful that this particular era is outside the scope of this book.

Today, sheet music sales of the old songs still go on. Classics like *Easter parade* and *A couple of swells,* for instance, will sell some 1,000 a year, but equally great oldies such as *You'll never know* will only realise around 150 a year. Similarly, *Stardust,* one of the most recorded songs of all time, used to sell some 500 a week in the Fifties but now has a job to reach 50 a quarter. Those wishing to buy sheet music copies of the songs in this book may be surprised to find just how many are still available. Over the intervening years many of the companies have closed or merged but the illustrations herein are arranged in such a way as to indicate which songs are controlled by three of the major British music publishing companies: Campbell Connelly & Co. Ltd.; Warner-Chappell Music Ltd. and E.M.I. Music Publishing Ltd. (which are distributed by International Music Publications), who have generously given us their permission to reproduce their covers. Their catalogues of 'oldies' are quite extensive and they will welcome your enquiries. Their song copies are of course available from good music shops, too.

Nowadays, sheet music generally is not produced until a song is in the record charts and shows every sign of going higher. It is almost unheard of for any song to have total sales of 25,000. So sheet music today is in the state that records were in 50 years ago, and while it may be all change, no one can ever deny that in its day the sheet music chart was just as vital a guide to popular music as the record chart is today.

---

### PLAYLIST OF RECORDINGS USED IN THE VERY LAST RADIO LUXEMBOURG TOP TWENTY BASED ON THE SHEET MUSIC CHARTS

Chart for week ending 19 December 1959 broadcast on Sunday, 27 December 1959

| Pos. | Title | Recording |
|---|---|---|
| 1 | Little donkey | The Beverley Sisters |
| 2 | Seven little girls sitting in the back seat | The Avons |
| 3 | What do you want? | Adam Faith |
| 4 | Snow coach | Russ Conway |
| 5 | Mary's boy child | Nina and Frederik |
| 6 | Travellin' light | Cliff Richard |
| 7 | Jingle bell rock | Max Bygraves |
| 8 | The village of St Bernadette | Anne Shelton |
| 9 | What do you want to make those eyes at me for? | Emile Ford |
| 10 | One more sunrise (Morgen) | Dickie Valentine |
| 11 | Mack the knife | Bobby Darin |
| 12 | Side saddle | Russ Conway |
| 13 | Put your head on my shoulder | Paul Anka |
| 14 | China tea | Russ Conway |
| 15 | High hopes | Frank Sinatra |
| 16 | The little white bull | Tommy Steele |
| 17 | Mr Blue | Mike Preston |
| 18 | Treble chance | Joe 'Mr Piano' Henderson |
| 19 | The three bells | The Browns |
| 20 | Heartaches by the number | Guy Mitchell |

# 1946

The table on the right refers to the songs which appear in the Sheet Music Charts beginning on 27 July 1946 and it is interesting first of all here to speculate on the titles which might have been in the chart in the first half of the year had such a chart existed. Two song hits from the film 'State Fair' amassed good sales figures – *It's a grand night for singing* and *It might as well be spring*, while *Cruising down the river* had already begun its massive progress – Cinephonic had advertised the song as far back as Christmas 1945. Indeed, it boasted a sale of 112,000 during January and went on to state that this had been achieved in just 18 days. *Chickery chick* can be traced back to February and *I can't begin to tell you* to the following month. Other memorable songs which can be recalled from the first half of the year include *Make mine music, Coax me a little bit, This heart of mine, No can do, I'll buy that dream, It's been a long, long time* and that well remembered novelty, *Ashby-de-la Zouch (Castle Abbey)*. None of these stayed around long enough to be featured on that first alphabetical chart, however, but it was not unusual for songs to be late starters as well as instant hits, like the aforementioned *Cruising down the river*. A later 1946 release, *Let it be soon,* for example, was advertised for three months before it appeared in the chart. One of the most successful hits of the year, *Bless you*, had been around since 1939 in America with, among others, a recording by the Glenn Miller Orchestra. In March, the Musicians' Union had demanded that the BBC use live music on the air, saying it should replace the use of records.

| | MOST WEEKS ON THE CHARTS **TOP SIX** (July to December only) | |
|---|---|---|
| Pos | | Wks |
| 1= | *Bless you* | 23 |
| 1= | *Primrose Hill* | 23 |
| 3 | *Down in the valley* | 20 |
| 4 | *Laughing on the outside* | 19 |
| 5 | *There's a harvest moon tonight* | 15 |
| 6 | *To each his own* | 13 |

# SONG CHARTS

## 1   BLESS YOU (for being an angel)

*Composers*: Eddie Lane & Don Baker     *Date of Entry*: 27.7.46

*Publishers*: Noel Gay Music Co. Ltd.     *Weeks on Chart*: 26

*Recordings*:

| | | |
|---|---|---|
| The Ink Spots | 9/40 | Brunswick 03040 |
| Victor Silvester and his Ballroom Orchestra | 8/46 | Columbia FB.3232 |
| Leslie A. Hutchinson – 'Hutch' | 8/46 | HMV BD.1137 |
| The Skyrockets Dance Orchestra cond. Paul Fenoulhet (Doreen Lundy) | 8/46 | HMV BD.5938 |
| Reg. Pursglove and his Music Makers | 8/46 | Regal-Zon. MR.3777 |
| Issy Bonn | 8/46 | Decca F.8647 |
| Archie Lewis with The Geraldo Strings | 9/46 | Parlophone F.2170 |
| Billy Thorburn's The Organ, the Dance Band and Me | 10/46 | Parlophone F.2176 |

## 2   CRUISING DOWN THE RIVER

*Composers*: Eily Beadell & Nell Tollerton     *Date of Entry*: 27.7.46

*Publishers*: Cinephonic Music Co. Ltd.     *Weeks on Chart*: 10

*Recordings*:

| | | |
|---|---|---|
| Lou Preager and his Orchestra (Paul Rich) | 1/46 | Columbia FB.3180 |
| Billy Thorburn's The Organ, the Dance Band and Me (Rita Williams) | 3/46 | Parlophone F.2127 |
| The Accordeon Serenaders (Rita Williams) | 3/46 | Regal-Zon. MR.3771 |
| Primo Scala and his Accordion Band (Cyril Shane) | 4/46 | Decca F.8612 |
| Russ Morgan and his Orchestra (The Skylarks) | 3/49 | Brunswick 04055★ |
| Jack Smith and The Clark Sisters | 5/49 | Capitol CL.13088★ |
| Blue Barron and his Orchestra and Chorus | 5/49 | MGM.195★ |

## 3   CHICKERY CHICK

*Composers*: Sidney Lippman & Sylvia Dee     *Date of Entry*: 27.7.46

*Publishers*: Campbell Connelly & Co. Ltd.     *Weeks on Chart*: 4

*Recordings*:

| | | |
|---|---|---|
| Carroll Gibbons and the Savoy Hotel Orpheans (Rita Williams) | 3/46 | Columbia FB.3191 |
| Joe Loss and his Orchestra (Howard Jones) | 3/46 | HMV BD.5922 |
| Harry Lester and his Hayseeds (Harry Lester) | 4/46 | Decca F.8617 |
| Ambrose and his Orchestra (Alan Dean) | 4/46 | Decca F.8620 |
| Evelyn Knight and The Jesters | 5/46 | Brunswick 03629 |

## 4   HOMESICK – THAT'S ALL

*Composer*: Gordon Jenkins     *Date of Entry*: 27.7.46

*Publishers*: Sterling Music Publishing Co. Ltd.     *Weeks on Chart*: 7

*Recordings*:

| | | |
|---|---|---|
| Ambrose and his Orchestra (Rita Marlowe) | 4/46 | Decca F.8620 |
| Geraldo and his Orchestra (Dick James) | 5/46 | Parlophone F.2143 |
| Frank Sinatra | 6/46 | Columbia DB.2216 |

## 5   I CAN'T BEGIN TO TELL YOU

*Composers*: Mack Gordon & Jimmy Monaco     *Date of Entry*: 27.7.46

*Publishers*: Chappell & Co. Ltd.     *Weeks on Chart*: 12

*Recordings*:

| | | |
|---|---|---|
| Steve Conway | 2/46 | Columbia FB.3186 |
| Len Camber | 4/46 | Columbia FB.3196 |
| Donald Peers | 4/46 | Decca F.8619 |
| Bing Crosby with Carmen Cavallaro (piano) | 5/46 | Brunswick 03624 |
| Harry James and his Music Makers (Ruth Haag) | 2/50 | Columbia DB.2646★ |

## 6   IN THE LAND OF BEGINNING AGAIN

*Composers:* Grant Clarke & George W. Meyer    *Date of Entry:* 27.7.46

*Publishers:* B. Feldman & Co.    *Weeks on Chart:* 12

*Recordings:*

| | | |
|---|---|---|
| Archie Lewis with The Geraldo Strings | 5/46 | Parlophone F.2140 |
| Peter Yorke and his Concert Orchestra (Sam Browne) | 5/46 | Columbia DB.2215 |
| Turner Layton | 5/46 | Columbia FB.3212 |
| Ambrose and his Orchestra (Rita Marlowe) | 7/46 | Decca F.8633 |
| Bing Crosby | 7/46 | Brunswick 03636 |

## 7   INTO EACH LIFE SOME RAIN MUST FALL

*Composers:* Allan Roberts & Doris Fisher    *Date of Entry:* 27.7.46

*Publishers:* Bradbury Wood Ltd.    *Weeks on Chart:* 10

*Recordings:*

| | | |
|---|---|---|
| Ella Fitzgerald and The Ink Spots | 6/45 | Brunswick 03573 |
| Charlie Barnet and his Orchestra (Kay Starr) | 5/46 | Brunswick 03626 |
| Joe Loss and his Orchestra (Howard Jones) | 6/46 | HMV BD.5931 |
| Victor Silvester and his Ballroom Orchestra | 6/46 | Columbia FB.3219 |
| Carl Barriteau and his Orchestra (Mae Cooper) | 10/46 | Decca F.8670 |

## 8   IT'S A PITY TO SAY GOODNIGHT

*Composer:* Billy Reid    *Date of Entry:* 27.7.46

*Publishers:* Peter Maurice Music Co. Ltd.    *Weeks on Chart:* 3

*Recordings:*

| | | |
|---|---|---|
| Dorothy Squires | 6/46 | Parlophone F.2146 |
| Josephine Bradley and her Ballroom Orchestra | 7/46 | Decca F.8640 |
| Ray Ventura and his Orchestra (Billy Toffel and Bob Jacqmain Vocal Quartet) | 8/46 | Decca F.8666 |
| Ella Fitzgerald and The Delta Rhythm Boys | 12/49 | Brunswick 04312★ |

## 9   LAUGHING ON THE OUTSIDE (Crying on the inside)

*Composers:* Ben Raleigh & Bernie Wayne    *Date of Entry:* 27.7.46

*Publishers:* Campbell Connelly & Co. Ltd.    *Weeks on Chart:* 19

*Recordings:*

| | | |
|---|---|---|
| Geraldo and his Orchestra (Sally Douglas) | 7/46 | Parlophone F.2158 |
| Turner Layton | 7/46 | Columbia FB.3222 |
| Joe Loss and his Orchestra (Howard Jones) | 7/46 | HMV BD.5934 |
| Dorothy Squires | 8/46 | Parlophone F.2165 |
| Issy Bonn | 8/46 | Decca F.8647 |
| Ambrose and his Orchestra (Jane Lee) | 8/46 | Decca F.8648 |
| Dinah Shore | 9/46 | Columbia DB.2228 |
| The Merry Macs | 11/46 | Brunswick 03755 |

## 10   LET BYGONES BE BYGONES

*Composer:* Joseph George Gilbert    *Date of Entry:* 27.7.46

*Publishers:* B. Feldman & Co. Ltd.    *Weeks on Chart:* 12

*Recordings:*

| | | |
|---|---|---|
| Joe Loss and his Orchestra (Chorus) | 4/46 | HMV BD.5926 |
| Lou Preager and his Orchestra (Rita Williams) | 4/46 | Columbia FB.3200 |
| Issy Bonn | 4/46 | Decca F.8618 |
| Doreen Harris | 4/46 | HMV BD.1125 |
| Billy Thorburn's The Organ, the Dance Band and Me (Harry Kaye) | 5/46 | Parlophone F.2148 |

## 11   MARY LOU

*Composer:* Dick Hurran    *Date of Entry:* 27.7.46

*Publishers:* Francis Day & Hunter Ltd.    *Weeks on Chart:* 9

*Recordings:*

| | | |
|---|---|---|
| Carroll Gibbons and the Savoy Hotel Orpheans (Denny Vaughan) | 6/46 | Columbia FB.3220 |
| The Skyrockets Dance Orchestra cond. Paul Fenoulhet (Cyril Shane) | 6/46 | HMV BD.5933 |
| Denny Dennis | 7/46 | Decca F.8638 |
| The Squadronaires dir. Jimmy Miller (Jimmy Miller and The Quads) | 8/46 | Decca F.8654 |
| Billy Cotton and his Band (Alan Breeze) | 11/46 | Rex 10233★ |

## 12 │ MONEY IS THE ROOT OF ALL EVIL

*Composers:* Joan Whitney & Alex Kramer   *Date of Entry:* 27.7.46

*Publishers:* Chappell & Co. Ltd.   *Weeks on Chart:* 10

*Recordings:*
| | | |
|---|---|---|
| The Andrews Sisters | 5/46 | Brunswick 03627 |
| The Skyrockets Dance Orchestra cond. Paul Fenoulhet (Doreen Lundy) | 6/46 | HMV BD.5933 |
| Geraldo and his Orchestra (The Geraldo Ensemble) | 7/46 | Parlophone F.2158 |
| The Squadronaires dir. Jimmy Miller (Jimmy Miller and The Quads) | 8/46 | Decca F.8654 |

## 13 │ OH, WHAT IT SEEMED TO BE

*Composers:* Bennie Benjamin, George Weiss & Frankie Carle   *Date of Entry:* 27.7.46

*Publishers:* Sun Music Publishing Co. Ltd.   *Weeks on Chart:* 7

*Recordings:*
| | | |
|---|---|---|
| Geraldo and his Orchestra (Dick James) | 5/46 | Parlophone F.2144 |
| Joe Loss and his Orchestra (Howard Jones) | 5/46 | HMV BD.5930 |
| Dick Haymes and Helen Forrest | 5/46 | Brunswick 03628 |
| Tom Henry with The Tomboys | 5/46 | Decca F.8627 |
| Frank Sinatra | 6/46 | Columbia DB.2216 |
| Ambrose and his Orchestra (Alan Dean) | 7/46 | Decca F.8634 |

## 14 │ PRIMROSE HILL

*Composers:* Charlie Chester, Ken Morris & Everett Lynton   *Date of Entry:* 27.7.46

*Publishers:* Lawrence Wright Music Co. Ltd.   *Weeks on Chart:* 24

*Recordings:*
| | | |
|---|---|---|
| Turner Layton | 8/46 | Columbia FB.3234 |
| The Skyrockets Dance Orchestra cond. Paul Fenoulhet (Cyril Shane) | 8/46 | HMV BD.5938 |
| Billy Thorburn's The Organ, the Dance Band and Me (Harry Kaye) | 8/46 | Parlophone F.2164 |
| Carl Barriteau and his Orchestra (Mae Cooper) | 10/46 | Decca F.8670 |

## 15 │ YOU CAN BE SURE OF ME

*Composers:* Joseph George Gilbert & Lewis Ilda   *Date of Entry:* 27.7.46

*Publishers:* Irwin Dash Music Co. Ltd.   *Weeks on Chart:* 7

*Recordings:*
| | | |
|---|---|---|
| Jack Simpson and his Sextet (Maureen Morton) | 7/46 | Parlophone F.2155 |
| Joe Loss and his Orchestra (Howard Jones) | 7/46 | HMV BD.5934 |

## 16 │ DAY BY DAY

*Composers:* Axel Stordahl, Sammy Cahn & Paul Weston   *Date of Entry:* 17.8.46

*Publishers:* New World Publishers Ltd.   *Weeks on Chart:* 1

*Recordings:*
| | | |
|---|---|---|
| Geraldo and his Orchestra (Dick James) | 7/46 | Parlophone F.2159 |
| Frank Sinatra | 7/46 | Columbia DB.2224 |
| Josephine Bradley and her Ballroom Orchestra | 8/46 | Decca F.8653 |
| Ted Heath and his Music (Paul Carpenter) | 8/46 | Decca F.8657 |
| Johnny Green | 8/46 | Decca F.8660 |
| The Skyrockets Dance Orchestra cond. Paul Fenoulhet (Cyril Shane) | 9/46 | HMV BD.5940★ |
| Bing Crosby with Mel Torme and The Meltones | 9/46 | Brunswick 03731★ |

## 17 │ DOWN IN THE VALLEY

*Composer:* Frank Luther   *Date of Entry:* 17.8.46

*Publishers:* Leeds Music Ltd.   *Weeks on Chart:* 26

*Recordings:*
| | | |
|---|---|---|
| The Andrews Sisters | 5/42 | Brunswick 03502 |
| Turner Layton | 10/46 | Columbia FB.3245 |
| Geraldo and his Orchestra (Archie Lewis) | 10/46 | Parlophone F.2178 |
| The Sentimentalists presented by Billy Cotton | 10/46 | Decca F.8696 |
| Lou Preager and his Orchestra (Rita Williams) | 11/46 | Columbia FB.3260 |

## 18 THERE'S A HARVEST MOON TONIGHT

| | | |
|---|---|---|
| *Composers:* Jack Denby, Muriel Watson & Sonny Miller | *Date of Entry:* 24.8.46 | |
| *Publishers:* Strauss-Miller Music Co. Ltd. | *Weeks on Chart:* 15 | |

*Recordings:*

| | | |
|---|---|---|
| The Sentimentalists presented by Billy Cotton | 8/46 | Decca F.8655 |
| Pearl Carr and The Keynotes | 7/51 | Decca F.9733★ |

## 19 DO YOU LOVE ME?

| | | |
|---|---|---|
| *Composer:* Harry Ruby | *Date of Entry:* 14.9.46 | |
| *Publishers:* Chappell & Co. Ltd. | *Weeks on Chart:* 10 | |

*Recordings:*

| | | |
|---|---|---|
| Dick Haymes | 8/46 | Brunswick 03726 |
| Beryl Davis | 8/46 | Decca F.8658 |
| Lou Preager and his Orchestra (Rita Carr) | 9/46 | Columbia FB.3238 |
| Paula Green | 9/46 | Columbia FB.3236 |
| Leslie A. Hutchinson – 'Hutch' | 9/46 | HMV BD.1141 |
| Harry James and his Orchestra (Ginnie Powell) | 11/46 | Parlophone R.3015 |

## 20 ONE-ZY, TWO-ZY (I love you-zy)

| | | |
|---|---|---|
| *Composers:* Dave Franklin & Irving Taylor | *Date of Entry:* 14.9.46 | |
| *Publishers:* Bradbury Wood Ltd. | *Weeks on Chart:* 6 | |

*Recordings:*

| | | |
|---|---|---|
| The Squadronaires dir. Jimmy Miller (The Quads) | 9/46 | Decca F.8679 |
| Jack Simpson and his Sextet (Maureen Morton) | 11/46 | Parlophone F.2181★ |

## 21 YOU ALWAYS HURT THE ONE YOU LOVE

| | | |
|---|---|---|
| *Composers:* Allan Roberts & Doris Fisher | *Date of Entry:* 14.9.46/ Wks: 2 | |
| *Publishers:* Bradbury Wood Ltd. | *Re-entry:* 7.12.46/ Wks: 13 | |

*Recordings:*

| | | |
|---|---|---|
| Charlie Barnet and his Orchestra (Kay Starr) | 5/46 | Brunswick 03626 |
| The Mills Brothers | 7/46 | Brunswick 03639 |
| Victor Silvester and his Ballroom Orchestra | 8/46 | Columbia FB.3231 |
| Billy Thorburn's The Organ, the Dance Band and Me (Rita Williams) | 8/46 | Parlophone F.2164 |
| Spike Jones and his City Slickers (Carl Grayson and Red Ingle) | 9/46 | HMV BD.1139 |
| Leslie A. Hutchinson – 'Hutch' | 10/46 | HMV BD.1143 |
| Reg. Pursglove and his Music Makers | 10/46 | Regal-Zon. MR.3778 |

(Note: This song returned to the Sheet Music Charts in 1959 – see Song No. 976.)

## 22 AND THEN IT'S HEAVEN

| | | |
|---|---|---|
| *Composers:* Eddie Seiler, Sol Marcus & Al Kaufman | *Date of Entry:* 28.9.46 | |
| *Publishers:* Campbell Connelly & Co. Ltd. | *Weeks on Chart:* 5 | |

*Recordings:*

| | | |
|---|---|---|
| Josephine Bradley and her Ballroom Orchestra | 10/46 | Decca F.8689 |
| Johnny Denis and his Novelty Swing Sextet (Johnny Denis and Billie Campbell) | 11/46 | Decca F.8706 |
| Harry James and his Orchestra (Buddy Di Vito) | 12/46 | Parlophone R.3020 |

## 23 JOHNNY FEDORA (and Alice Blue Bonnet)

| | | |
|---|---|---|
| *Composers:* Allie Wrubel & Ray Gilbert | *Date of Entry:* 28.9.46 | |
| *Publishers:* Leeds Music Ltd. | *Weeks on Chart:* 6 | |

*Recording:*

| | | |
|---|---|---|
| The Andrews Sisters | 5/46 | Brunswick 03627 |

## 24 SO WOULD I

| | |
|---|---|
| *Composers*: Jimmy Van Heusen & Johnny Burke | *Date of Entry*: 5.10.46 |
| *Publishers*: Edwin H. Morris & Co. Ltd. | *Weeks on Chart*: 7 |

*Recordings*:

| | | |
|---|---|---|
| The Skyrockets Dance Orchestra cond. Paul Fenoulhet (Cyril Shane) | 9/46 | HMV BD.5941 |
| Steve Conway | 9/46 | Columbia FB.3243 |
| Jean Cavall | 9/46 | HMV B.9495 |
| Ted Heath and his Music (Paul Carpenter) | 9/46 | Decca F.8661 |
| Scotty McHarg and Beryl Davis with The Dozen and One Lovelies | 10/46 | Decca F.8675 |
| Ray Castle (piano) | 11/46 | Columbia DB.2267 |
| Bing Crosby with Russ Morgan and his Orchestra | 7/51 | Brunswick 04747★ |

## 25 THE 'AMPSTEAD WAY

| | |
|---|---|
| *Composers*: Jimmy Van Heusen & Johnny Burke | *Date of Entry*: 5.10.46 |
| *Publishers*: Edwin H. Morris & Co. Ltd. | *Weeks on Chart*: 7 |

*Recordings*:

| | | |
|---|---|---|
| The Skyrockets Dance Orchestra cond. Paul Fenoulhet (Cyril Shane) | 9/46 | HMV BD.5941 |
| Tessie O'Shea | 9/46 | Columbia DB.2232 |
| Beryl Davis | 10/46 | Decca F.8676 |
| Josephine Bradley and her Ballroom Orchestra | 11/46 | Decca F.8700 |

## 26 TO EACH HIS OWN

| | |
|---|---|
| *Composers*: Jay Livingston & Ray Evans | *Date of Entry*: 5.10.46 |
| *Publishers*: Victoria Music Publishing Co. Ltd. | *Weeks on Chart*: 30 |

*Recordings*:

| | | |
|---|---|---|
| The Squadronaires dir. Jimmy Miller (Jimmy Miller) | 10/46 | Decca F.8688 |
| Victor Silvester and his Ballroom Orchestra | 11/46 | Columbia FB.3258 |
| The Ink Spots | 11/46 | Brunswick 03757 |
| Scotty McHarg | 11/46 | Decca F.8713 |

## 27 LET IT BE SOON

| | |
|---|---|
| *Composers*: Dick Hurran & Hugh Wade | *Date of Entry*: 19.10.46 |
| *Publishers*: Francis Day & Hunter Ltd. | *Weeks on Chart*: 17 |

*Recordings*:

| | | |
|---|---|---|
| Victor Silvester and his Ballroom Orchestra | 8/46 | Columbia FB.3232 |
| Tessie O'Shea | 9/46 | Columbia DB.2232 |
| The Skyrockets Dance Orchestra cond. Paul Fenoulhet (Doreen Lundy) | 10/46 | HMV BD.5945 |
| 'Cheerful' Charlie Chester and his Gang | 11/46 | Decca F.8701 |
| Ted Heath and his Music (Paul Carpenter) | 1/47 | Decca F.8717 |

## 28 SWEETHEART, WE'LL NEVER GROW OLD

| | |
|---|---|
| *Composers*: Jack Denby & Muriel Watson | *Date of Entry*: 19.10.46 |
| *Publishers*: Strauss-Miller Music Co. Ltd. | *Weeks on Chart*: 21 |

*Recordings*:

| | | |
|---|---|---|
| Issy Bonn | 10/46 | Decca F.8677 |
| Doreen Harris | 11/46 | HMV BD.1146 |
| Jack Simpson and his Sextet (Maureen Morton) | 12/46 | Parlophone F.2189 |
| Joe Loss and his Orchestra (Howard Jones) | 12/46 | HMV BD.5953 |
| Monte Rey | 1/47 | Columbia FB.3277 |

## 29 YOU KEEP COMING BACK LIKE A SONG

| | |
|---|---|
| *Composer*: Irving Berlin | *Date of Entry*: 19.10.46 |
| *Publishers*: Irving Berlin Ltd. | *Weeks on Chart*: 9 |

*Recordings*:

| | | |
|---|---|---|
| The Skyrockets Dance Orchestra cond. Paul Fenoulhet (Cyril Shane) | 10/46 | HMV BD.5945 |
| Leslie A. Hutchinson – 'Hutch' | 10/46 | HMV BD.1143 |
| Geraldo and his Orchestra (Dick James) | 10/46 | Parlophone F.2179 |
| Beryl Davis | 11/46 | Decca F.8695 |
| Ted Heath and his Music (Paul Carpenter) | 11/46 | Decca F.8697 |
| Bing Crosby with Quartet | 3/47 | Brunswick 03672★ |

## 30 | ALL THROUGH THE DAY

| *Composers*: Jerome Kern & Oscar Hammerstein II | *Date of Entry*: 26.10.46 |
|---|---|
| *Publishers*: Chappell & Co. Ltd. | *Weeks on Chart*: 16 |

*Recordings*:

| Frank Weir and his Orchestra (Vivien Paget) | 8/46 | Decca F.8659 |
|---|---|---|
| Geraldo and his Orchestra (Sally Douglas) | 9/46 | Parlophone F.2171 |
| Leslie A. Hutchinson – 'Hutch' | 9/46 | HMV BD.1141 |
| Frank Sinatra | 9/46 | Columbia DB.2227 |
| Dick Haymes and Helen Forrest | 10/46 | Brunswick 03741 |
| Wal Merrall | 10/46 | Decca F.8680 |
| Bing Crosby | 12/48 | Brunswick 04127★ |

## 31 | ANY TIME AT ALL

| *Composers*: Jack Gold & Dick Emerson | *Date of Entry*: 2.11.46 |
|---|---|
| *Publishers*: Macmelodies Ltd. | *Weeks on Chart*: 5 |

*Recordings*:

| The Squadronaires dir. Jimmy Miller (Doreen Stephens) | 9/46 | Decca F.8679 |
|---|---|---|
| Victor Silvester and his Ballroom Orchestra | 11/46 | Columbia FB.3259 |

## 32 | SOMEDAY YOU'LL WANT ME TO WANT YOU

| *Composer*: Jimmie Hodges | *Date of Entry*: 9.11.46 |
|---|---|
| *Publishers*: Irwin Dash Music Co. Ltd. | *Weeks on Chart*: 14 |

*Recordings*:

| Lou Preager and his Orchestra (Paul Rich) | 10/46 | Columbia FB.3250 |
|---|---|---|
| Issy Bonn | 10/46 | Decca F.8677 |
| Joe Loss and his Orchestra (Howard Jones) | 11/46 | HMV BD.5949 |
| Gene Autry | 9/48 | Regal Zon. MR.3809★ |
| The Mills Brothers | 10/49 | Brunswick 04335★ |
| Vaughn Monroe and his Orchestra (Vaughn Monroe and The Moon Men) | 12/49 | HMV B.9853★ |

(Note: This song returned to the Sheet Music Charts in 1958 – See Song No. 954).

## 33 | IT'S ALL OVER NOW

| *Composers*: Sunny Skylar & Don Marcotte | *Date of Entry*: 23.11.46 |
|---|---|
| *Publishers*: Campbell Connelly & Co. Ltd. | *Weeks on Chart*: 12 |

*Recordings*:

| Roy Fox and his Band (Bobby Joy) | 11/46 | Decca F.8714 |
|---|---|---|
| Joe Loss and his Orchestra (Elizabeth Batey) | 12/46 | HMV BD.5953 |
| Rita Williams with Orchestra | 1/47 | Columbia FB.3269 |
| Lou Preager and his Orchestra (Rita Williams) | 1/47 | Columbia FB.3273 |
| Tom Henry with The Tomboys | 1/47 | Decca F.8729 |
| Russ Morgan and his Orchestra (Russ Morgan) | 12/48 | Brunswick 04011★ |

## 34 | MAKE-BELIEVE WORLD

| *Composers*: Box, Cox & Lewis Ilda | *Date of Entry*: 23.11.46 |
|---|---|
| *Publishers*: Irwin Dash Music Co. Ltd. | *Weeks on Chart*: 2 |

*Recordings*:

| Denny Dennis | 11/46 | Decca F.8694 |
|---|---|---|
| Billy Cotton and his Band (Alan Breeze) | 1/47 | Rex 10237★ |

## 35 | THE GREEN COCKATOO

| *Composer*: Don Rellegro | *Date of Entry*: 23.11.46 |
|---|---|
| *Publishers*: Cinephonic Music Co. Ltd. | *Weeks on Chart*: 9 |

*Recordings*:

| Mantovani and his Orchestra | 10/46 | Decca F.8682 |
|---|---|---|
| Roberto Inglez and his Orchestra | 11/46 | Parlophone F.2183 |
| Reginald Dixon (organ) | 1/48 | Columbia FB.3362★ |
| Ethel Smith (organ) | 11/48 | Brunswick 03995★ |

## 36 FIVE MINUTES MORE

| | | |
|---|---|---|
| *Composers:* Jule Styne & Sammy Cahn | *Date of Entry:* 7.12.46 | |
| *Publishers:* Edwin H. Morris & Co. Ltd. | *Weeks on Chart:* 21 | |

*Recordings:*

| | | |
|---|---|---|
| Frank Sinatra | 1/47 | Columbia DB.2275 |
| Carroll Gibbons and the Savoy Hotel Orpheans (Harry Kaye) | 1/47 | Columbia FB.3272 |
| The Skyrockets Dance Orchestra cond. Paul Fenoulhet (Doreen Lundy) | 1/47 | HMV BD.5955 |
| Josephine Bradley and her Ballroom Orchestra | 1/47 | Decca F.8715 |
| Bob Crosby and his Orchestra (Bob Crosby and The Bobolinks) | 2/47 | Brunswick 03682 |
| The Squadronaires dir. Jimmy Miller (Jimmy Miller and The Quads) | 2/47 | Decca F.8747 |

## 37 LILLI MARLENE

| | | |
|---|---|---|
| *Composers:* Hans Leip & Norbert Schultze – English lyrics by Tommie Connor | *Date of Entry:* 7.12.46 | |
| *Publishers:* Peter Maurice Music Co. Ltd. | *Weeks on Chart:* 5 | |

(Notes: This song was first published in Germany in 1941 by the Apollo Music Co. It was copyrighted for this country in 1944 by the Peter Maurice Music Co. Ltd. under the Patents, Designs, Copyright and Trade Marks (Emergency) Act 1939. The recording by the 'New Mayfair Dance Orchestra' below is, in reality, by Joe Loss and his Orchestra. Recorded on 14 October 1943, it is one of four titles made by Loss on that day under the 'Mayfair' name.)

*Recordings:*

| | | |
|---|---|---|
| The New Mayfair Dance Orchestra (Sam Browne) [Titled 'Marlene'] | 11/43 | HMV BD.5821 |
| Turner Layton | 6/44 | Columbia FB.3028 |
| Geraldo and his Orchestra (Sally Douglas and Chorus) [Titled 'Lili Marlene'] | 6/44 | Parlophone F.2024 |
| Billy Cotton and his Band (Alan Breeze and Chorus) | 6/44 | Rex 10205 |
| Anne Shelton | 6/44 | Decca F.8434 |
| Marlene Dietrich | 3/46 | Brunswick 03609 |
| Chappie D'Amato and his Orchestra (Chappie D'Amato and Chorus) | 7/47 | Regal Zon. MR.3791★ |
| Lale Andersen [In German and English] | 10/48 | Decca C.16027★ |
| Bing Crosby | 7/51 | Brunswick 04742★ |

## 38 PRETENDING

| | | |
|---|---|---|
| *Composers:* Al Sherman & Martin Symes | *Date of Entry:* 7.12.46 | |
| *Publishers:* Bradbury Wood Ltd. | *Weeks on Chart:* 13 | |

*Recordings:*

| | | |
|---|---|---|
| Lou Preager and his Orchestra (Rita Williams) | 10/46 | Columbia FB.3250 |
| Victor Silvester and his Ballroom Orchestra | 10/46 | Columbia FB.3247 |
| Geraldo and his Orchestra (Archie Lewis) | 10/46 | Parlophone F.2179 |
| Doreen Harris | 11/46 | HMV BD.1146 |
| The Squadronaires dir. Jimmy Miller (Jimmy Miller) | 11/46 | Decca F.8711 |
| Bing Crosby with The Les Paul Trio | 9/47 | Brunswick 03800★ |

## 39 TILL THEN

| | | |
|---|---|---|
| *Composers:* Guy Wood, Eddie Seiler & Sol Marcus | *Date of Entry:* 7.12.46 | |
| *Publishers:* Chappell & Co. Ltd. | *Weeks on Chart:* 15 | |

*Recordings:*

| | | |
|---|---|---|
| The Mills Brothers | 7/46 | Brunswick 03639 |
| Jean Cavall | 11/46 | HMV B.9509 |
| Jimmy Leach and his New Organolians (Cyril Shane) | 11/46 | Columbia FB.3257 |
| Leslie A. Hutchinson – 'Hutch' | 11/46 | HMV BD.1151 |
| Geraldo and his Orchestra (Archie Lewis) | 11/46 | Parlophone F.2186 |
| Issy Bonn | 11/46 | Decca F.8707 |
| Victor Silvester and his Ballroom Orchestra | 12/46 | Columbia FB.3266 |

## 40 TOO MANY IRONS IN THE FIRE

| | | |
|---|---|---|
| *Composer:* Johnny S. Black | *Date of Entry:* 21.12.46 | |
| *Publishers:* Campbell Connelly & Co. Ltd. | *Weeks on Chart:* 5 | |

*Recordings:*

| | | |
|---|---|---|
| Lou Preager and his Orchestra (Paul Rich) | 11/46 | Columbia FB.3260 |
| Maurice Winnick and his Orchestra (Sam Browne) | 11/46 | HMV BD.1152 |
| Turner Layton | 12/46 | Columbia FB.3261 |
| Victor Silvester and his Ballroom Orchestra | 12/46 | Columbia FB.3265 |
| Billy Thorburn's The Organ, the Dance Band and Me | 12/46 | Parlophone F.2190 |
| Roy Fox and his Band (Jack O'Hagan and Bobby Joy) | 1/47 | Decca F.8718 |
| The Mills Brothers | 2/47 | Brunswick 03694★ |

# 1947

We continued to see alphabetical charts until week ending 31 May 1947, with six of the 22 weeks finding no chart being compiled. Again, the number of songs in each chart was variable, with seventeen on two occasions and only ten in the final alphabetical week. This seemed to lead into the first listing published in numerical order which, confusingly, appeared with a date of 29 May 1947. This Top Ten was to be compiled for the next two years – ending on 19 May 1949. *Among my Souvenirs* won the honour of being the first 'official' No. 1, although it had in fact held first place in the alphabetical list since its first inclusion three weeks earlier! Songwriter Desmond O'Connor was quoted as saying that if he wrote a song called *Zulu war chant* and added 'A' to make it *A Zulu war chant* it would most likely appear at the top of the charts. But now the alphabetical period was gone and the charts began to be regarded with some respect. But that didn't stop the time gulf between publishing and entry for some songs. *Try a little tenderness* was aired on the BBC's 'Housewives' Choice' in January but waited four months before reaching the charts. A similar time lag was felt by *Bow bells,* while *Now is the hour* and *Chi-baba, chi-baba* were almost instant hits, the latter coming in first week at No. 3. For 13 weeks of its 27-week run, *Come back to Sorrento* held second place and thereby claimed the record for the highest number of weeks spent at No. 2 without ever reaching the No. 1 spot.

| | MOST WEEKS ON THE CHARTS TOP SIX | |
|---|---|---|
| Pos | | Wks |
| 1 | *Come back to Sorrento* | 25 |
| 2 | *The anniversary song* | 24 |
| 3 | *The old lamp-lighter* | 23 |
| 4= | *April showers* | 22 |
| 4= | *Now is the hour* | 22 |
| 6= | *How lucky you are* | 19 |
| 6= | *Among my souvenirs* | 19 |

# SONG CHARTS

## 41 (If I wasn't in your dream last night) DREAM AGAIN

| | |
|---|---|
| *Composers*: Box, Cox & Kulma | *Date of Entry*: 11.1.47 |
| *Publishers*: Box & Cox (Publications) Ltd. | *Weeks on Chart*: 11 |

*Recordings*:
| | | |
|---|---|---|
| (a) Titled 'If I wasn't in your dream last night' Joe Loss and his Orchestra (Howard Jones) | 2/47 | HMV BD.5965 |
| Jack Simpson and his Sextet (Maureen Morton) | 2/47 | Parlophone F.2203 |
| (b) Titled 'Dream Again' Primo Scala and his Accordion Band (Edna Kaye) | 4/47 | Decca F.8759★ |

## 42 THE OLD LAMP-LIGHTER

| | |
|---|---|
| *Composers*: Charlie Tobias & Nat Simon | *Date of Entry*: 11.1.47 |
| *Publishers*: Irwin Dash Music Co. Ltd. | *Highest Position*: 9 *Weeks on Chart*: 23 |

*Recordings*:
| | | |
|---|---|---|
| Joe Loss and his Orchestra (Howard Jones) | 12/46 | HMV BD.5954 |
| Lou Preager and his Orchestra (Paul Rich) | 1/47 | Columbia FB.3273 |
| Geraldo and his Orchestra (Denny Vaughan) | 1/47 | Parlophone F.2200 |
| Primo Scala and his Accordion Band (Billie Campbell) | 1/47 | Decca F.8727 |
| The Squadronaires cond. Jimmy Miller (Jimmy Miller) | 2/47 | Decca F.8747 |
| Kenny Baker with Russ Morgan and his Orchestra | 7/47 | Brunswick 03711★ |

## 43 THE ANNIVERSARY SONG

| | |
|---|---|
| *Composers*: Al Jolson & Saul Chaplin, based on 'Waves of the Danube' by Ivanovici | *Date of Entry*: 25.1.47 |
| *Publishers*: Campbell Connelly & Co. Ltd. | *Highest Position*: 4 *Weeks on Chart*: 24 |

*Recordings*:
| | | |
|---|---|---|
| Joe Loss and his Orchestra (Don Rivers) | 1/47 | HMV BD.5958 |
| Harry Davidson and his Orchestra | 1/47 | Columbia DX.1303 |
| Anne Shelton | 1/47 | Decca F.8728 |
| Al Jolson | 4/47 | Brunswick 03702 |
| Billy Cotton and his Band (Alan Breeze) | 5/47 | Rex 10238 |
| Geraldo and his Orchestra (Archie Lewis) | 5/47 | Parlophone F.2214 |
| Artie Shaw and his Orchestra | 6/47 | Parlophone R.3042 |
| Billy Thorburn's The Organ, the Dance Band and Me | 7/47 | Parlophone F.2232 |
| Jack White and his Orchestra | 7/48 | Decca F.8930★ |
| Bing Crosby | 9/48 | Brunswick 03967★ |
| Guy Lombardo and his Royal Canadians (Kenny Gardner) | 10/48 | Brunswick 03948★ |
| Dinah Shore | 12/48 | Columbia DB.2475★ |
| Vaughn Monroe and his Orchestra (Vaughn Monroe and Chorus) | 2/49 | HMV BD.6035★ |

## 44 THE STARS WILL REMEMBER (So will I)

| | |
|---|---|
| *Composers*: Don Pelosi & Leo Towers | *Date of Entry*: 25.1.47 |
| *Publishers*: B. Feldman & Co. Ltd. | *Weeks on Chart*: 18 |

*Recordings*:
| | | |
|---|---|---|
| Scotty McHarg | 11/46 | Decca F.8713 |
| Steve Conway | 11/46 | Columbia FB.3256 |
| Joe Loss and his Orchestra (Howard Jones) | 5/47 | HMV BD.5971 |
| Monte Rey | 6/47 | Columbia FB.3302★ |
| Billy Thorburn's The Organ, the Dance Band and Me (Harry Kaye) | 6/47 | Parlophone F.2223★ |
| Vera Lynn | 6/47 | Decca F.8781★ |
| Peggy Reid | 1/48 | Columbia FB.3366★ |
| Frank Sinatra | 2/48 | Columbia DB.2376★ |

## 45 GO HOME!

| | | |
|---|---|---|
| *Composers*: Carl & Roger Yale, Jimmy Lally & Joe Ferrie | | *Date of Entry*: 1.2.47 |
| *Publishers*: Yale Music Corporation Ltd. | | *Weeks on Chart*: 14 |

*Recording*:

| | | |
|---|---|---|
| Primo Scala and his Accordion Band (Edna Kaye) | 4/47 | Decca F.8759 |

## 46 APRIL SHOWERS

| | | |
|---|---|---|
| *Composers*: Louis Silvers & B.G. De Sylva | | *Date of Entry*: 15.2.47/ Pos: 2/Wks: 20 |
| *Publishers*: Chappell & Co. Ltd. | | *Re-entry*: 3.7.47/Pos: 9/Wks: 2 |

*Recordings*:

| | | |
|---|---|---|
| Steve Conway | 1/47 | Columbia FB.3270 |
| Al Jolson with orchestra directed by Carmen Dragon | 1/47 | Brunswick 03765 |
| Billy Thorburn's The Organ, the Dance Band and Me (Harry Kaye) | 2/47 | Parlophone F.2206 |
| Josephine Bradley and her Ballroom Orchestra | 2/47 | Decca F.8740 |
| Margaret Whiting | 1/49 | Capitol CL.13037★ |
| Guy Lombardo and his Royal Canadians (Jimmy Brown) | 1/49 | Brunswick 04158★ |
| Al Jolson and Guy Lombardo and his Royal Canadians | 12/49 | Columbia DB.2613★ |

## 47 MAY I CALL YOU SWEETHEART?

| | | |
|---|---|---|
| *Composers*: Muriel Watson, Jack Denby & Lewis Ilda | | *Date of Entry*: 15.2.47/ Wks: 6 |
| *Publishers*: Irwin Dash Music Co. Ltd. | | *Re-entry*: 3.5.47/Wks: 4 |

*Recordings*:

| | | |
|---|---|---|
| Issy Bonn | 4/47 | Decca F.8748 |
| Steve Conway | 4/47 | Columbia FB.3287 |
| Joe Loss and his Orchestra (Howard Jones) | 5/47 | HMV BD.5972 |
| Lou Preager and his Orchestra (Paul Rich) | 5/47 | Columbia FB.3297 |
| Victor Silvester and his Ballroom Orchestra | 6/47 | Columbia FB.3305★ |

## 48 (I love you) FOR SENTIMENTAL REASONS

| | | |
|---|---|---|
| *Composers*: Deek Watson & William Best | | *Date of Entry*: 15.2.47 |
| *Publishers*: Peter Maurice Music Co. Ltd. | | *Weeks on Chart*: 15 |

*Recordings*:

| | | |
|---|---|---|
| Dinah Shore | 1/47 | Columbia DB.2276 |
| Dorothy Squires | 1/47 | Parlophone F.2196 |
| Roy Fox and his Band (Jack O'Hagan) | 1/47 | Decca F.8718 |
| Geraldo and his Orchestra (Archie Lewis) | 1/47 | Parlophone F.2193 |
| Turner Layton | 2/47 | Columbia FB.3284 |
| Rita Williams | 2/47 | Columbia FB.3281 |
| Josephine Bradley and her Ballroom Orchestra | 4/47 | Decca F.8754 |
| Red Ingle and the Natural Seven (Buttermilk Tussie) [Titled: 'For Seventy Mental Reasons'] | 3/49 | Capitol CL.13054★ |
| Ella Fitzgerald and The Delta Rhythm Boys | 12/49 | Brunswick 04312★ |

## 49 THE THINGS WE DID LAST SUMMER

| | | |
|---|---|---|
| *Composers*: Jule Styne & Sammy Cahn | | *Date of Entry*: 15.2.47 |
| *Publishers*: Edwin H. Morris & Co. Ltd. | | *Weeks on Chart*: 8 |

*Recordings*:

| | | |
|---|---|---|
| Frank Sinatra | 2/47 | Columbia DB.2283 |
| Geraldo and his Orchestra (Carole Carr) | 2/47 | Parlophone F.2205 |
| The Sentimentalists presented by Billy Cotton | 2/47 | Decca F.8738 |
| Bing Crosby with Jimmy Dorsey and his Orchestra | 4/47 | Brunswick 03665 |

## 50 THE RICKETY RICKSHAW MAN

| | | |
|---|---|---|
| *Composer*: Ervin Drake | | *Date of Entry*: 8.3.47/ Wks: 1 |
| *Publishers*: Southern Music Publishing Co. Ltd. | | *Re-entry*: 22.3.47/ Wks: 6 |

*Recordings*:

| | | |
|---|---|---|
| Roy Fox and his Band (Beryl Templeman, Bobby Joy, Jack O'Hagan and The Cubs) | 2/47 | Decca F.8742 |
| The Skyrockets Dance Orchestra cond. Paul Fenoulhet (Cyril Shane) | 5/47 | HMV BD.5970★ |
| Geraldo and his Orchestra (Carole Carr) | 5/47 | Parlophone F.2213★ |

## 51 THE WHOLE WORLD IS SINGING MY SONG

| | | |
|---|---|---|
| *Composers*: Vic Mizzy & Mann Curtis | | *Date of Entry*: 8.3.47 |
| *Publishers*: Francis Day & Hunter Ltd. | | *Weeks on Chart*: 6 |

*Recordings*:

| | | |
|---|---|---|
| Archie Lewis with The Geraldo Strings | 2/47 | Parlophone F.2202 |
| Issy Bonn | 4/47 | Decca F.8748 |
| Roy Fox and his Band (Jack O'Hagan) | 4/47 | Decca F.8749 |
| Jimmy Dorsey and his Orchestra (Bob Carroll) | 4/47 | Brunswick 03705 |
| The Skyrockets Dance Orchestra cond. Paul Fenoulhet (Doreen Lundy) | 5/47 | HMV BD.5970★ |

## 52 ACCORDION (Accordéon)

| | | |
|---|---|---|
| *Composers*: Marcel Paul, Fred Freed & Howard Barnes | | *Date of Entry*: 15.3.47 |
| *Publishers*: Lawrence Wright Music Co. Ltd. | | *Weeks on Chart*: 2 |

*Recordings*:

| | | |
|---|---|---|
| Joe Loss and his Orchestra (Howard Jones) | 2/47 | HMV BD.5964 |
| Jack Simpson and his Sextet (Maureen Morton) | 2/47 | Parlophone F.2203 |
| Jean Cavall | 4/47 | HMV B.9542★ |
| Roy Fox and his Band (Jack O'Hagan) | 4/47 | Decca F.8749★ |
| Jimmy Leach and his New Organolians | 4/47 | Columbia FB.3289★ |

## 53 DON'T FALL IN LOVE

| | | |
|---|---|---|
| *Composers*: Eddie Lisbona & Joe Lubin | | *Date of Entry*: 15.3.47 |
| *Publishers*: Bradbury Wood Ltd. | | *Weeks on Chart*: 9 |

*Recordings*:

| | | |
|---|---|---|
| Joe Loss and his Orchestra (Elizabeth Batey) | 5/47 | HMV BD.5972 |
| Geraldo and his Orchestra (Denny Vaughan) | 5/47 | Parlophone F.2213 |
| Josephine Bradley and her Ballroom Orchestra | 6/47 | Decca F.8780★ |

## 54 HOW LUCKY YOU ARE

| | | |
|---|---|---|
| *Composers*: Eddie Cassen & Desmond O'Connor | | *Date of Entry*: 15.3.47 |
| *Publishers*: Edward Kassner Music Co. Ltd. | | *Highest Position*: 5 *Weeks on Chart*: 19 |

*Recordings*:

| | | |
|---|---|---|
| Lou Preager and his Orchestra (Rita Williams) | 4/47 | Columbia FB.3293 |
| Josephine Bradley and her Ballroom Orchestra | 6/47 | Decca F.8779 |
| Turner Layton | 7/47 | Columbia FB.3318 |
| Vera Lynn with Ambrose and his Orchestra | 10/47 | Decca F.8807★ |
| The Andrews Sisters | 11/47 | Brunswick 03823★ |

## 55 THE WORLD BELONGS TO YOU, LITTLE MAN

| | | |
|---|---|---|
| *Composers*: Don Pelosi & Leo Towers | | *Date of Entry*: 15.3.47 |
| *Publishers*: Strauss-Miller Music Co. Ltd. | | *Weeks on Chart*: 2 |

*Recordings*:

| | | |
|---|---|---|
| Vera Lynn | 1/47 | Decca F.8732 |
| Lou Preager and his Orchestra (Rita Williams) | 2/47 | Columbia FB.3282 |

## 56 OPEN THE DOOR, RICHARD

| | | |
|---|---|---|
| *Composers*: Dusty Fletcher, John Mason, Jack McVea & Don Howell | | *Date of Entry*: 29.3.47 |
| *Publishers*: Leeds Music Ltd. | | *Weeks on Chart*: 6 |

*Recordings*:

| | | |
|---|---|---|
| Ted Heath and his Music (Paul Carpenter and Dave Wilkins) | 4/47 | Decca F.8767 |
| Dusty Fletcher | 5/47 | Parlophone R.3037 |
| The Radio Revellers | 5/47 | Columbia FB.3301 |
| Geraldo and his Orchestra (Denny Vaughan and Band) | 5/47 | Parlophone F.2214 |
| Louis Jordan and his Tympany Five | 6/47 | Brunswick 03778★ |

## 57 ZIP-A-DEE-DOO-DAH

| | | |
|---|---|---|
| *Composers*: Allie Wrubel & Ray Gilbert | | *Date of Entry*: 29.3.47/ Wks: 2 |
| *Publishers*: Sun Music Publishing Co. Ltd. | | *Re-entry*: 19.4.47/ Wks: 3 |

*Recordings*:

| | | |
|---|---|---|
| Geraldo and his Orchestra (Carole Carr) | 1/47 | Parlophone F.2200 |
| Cyril Stapleton and his Orchestra (Tom Henry and Quartet) | 2/47 | Decca F.8736 |

## 58 HI-JIG-A-JIG, HI-JIG-A-JIG (Follow the band)

| | |
|---|---|
| *Composer*: Sim Simmons | *Date of Entry*: 12.4.47/ Wks: 2 |
| *Publishers*: Box & Cox Publications Ltd. | *Re-entry*: 10.5.47/ Wks: 3 |

*Recordings*:

| | | |
|---|---|---|
| Lou Preager and his Orchestra (Paul Rich) | 4/47 | Columbia FB.3293 |
| Jack Simpson and his Sextet (Maureen Morton) | 6/47 | Parlophone F.2221★ |

## 59 WHEN CHINA BOY MEETS CHINA GIRL

| | |
|---|---|
| *Composer*: Billy Reid | *Date of Entry*: 12.4.47 |
| *Publishers*: Macmelodies Ltd. | *Weeks on Chart*: 5 |

*Recordings*:

| | | |
|---|---|---|
| Dorothy Squires | 4/47 | Parlophone F.2208 |
| Lou Preager and his Orchestra (Rita Williams) | 5/47 | Columbia FB.3297 |

## 60 HEAR MY SONG, VIOLETTA

| | |
|---|---|
| *Composers*: Othmar Klose & Rudolph Luckesch with lyrics by Harry S. Pepper | *Date of Entry*: 26.4.47 |
| *Publishers*: Dix Ltd. | *Weeks on Chart*: 3 |

(Note: This song produced quite a string of recordings during its initial success in 1938 and two of these were still available in 1947 – by Jimmy Dorsey and his Orchestra [Bob Eberly] on Brunswick 03133 and by Tony Martin on Decca F.7565. You will see from the issue dates of the subsequent recordings below that all were released following the song's chart life.)

*Recordings*:

| | | |
|---|---|---|
| Tommy Dorsey and his Orchestra (Frank Sinatra) | 6/47 | HMV BD.1166★ |
| Mantovani and his Orchestra | 9/47 | Decca F.8797★ |
| Bill Johnson | 11/47 | Columbia DB.2347★ |
| Josef Locke | 11/47 | Columbia DB.2351★ |
| Archie Lewis with the Geraldo Strings | 2/48 | Parlophone F.2267★ |
| Anne Ziegler and Webster Booth | 3/49 | HMV B.9738★ |

## 61 TELL ME, MARIANNE (A media luz)

| | |
|---|---|
| *Composers*: Edgardo Donato & Bob Musel | *Date of Entry*: 26.4.47/ Wks: 1 |
| *Publishers*: Southern Music Publishing Co. Ltd. | *Re-entry*: 10.5.47/ Pos: 1 Wks: 16 |

*Recordings*:
(a) Titled 'Tell me, Marianne'

| | | |
|---|---|---|
| Monte Rey | 6/47 | Columbia FB.3302 |
| Mantovani and his Orchestra (Val Merrall) | 6/47 | Decca F.8771 |
| Joe Loss and his Orchestra (Don Rivers) | 7/47 | HMV BD.5978 |
| Rita Williams | 7/47 | Columbia FB.3320 |

(b) Titled 'A Media Luz'

| | | |
|---|---|---|
| Victor Silvester and his Ballroom Orchestra | 2/41 | Columbia FB.2567 |
| Stanley Black and his Orchestra | 6/46 | Decca F.8652 |
| Joe Loss and his Orchestra | 5/50 | HMV BD.6069★ |

## 62 GOODNIGHT (You little rascal, you)

| | |
|---|---|
| *Composer*: Art Noel | *Date of Entry*: 3.5.47 |
| *Publishers*: Francis Day & Hunter Ltd. | *Weeks on Chart*: 1 |

*Recordings*:

| | | |
|---|---|---|
| Turner Layton | 5/47 | Columbia FB.3299 |
| Anne Shelton | 6/47 | Decca F.8772★ |
| Lou Preager and his Orchestra (Rita Williams) | 6/47 | Columbia FB.3303★ |

## 63 YOU WENT AWAY AND LEFT ME

| | |
|---|---|
| *Composer*: Jennie Parker | *Date of Entry*: 3.5.47/ Pos: 7/Wks: 9 |
| *Publishers*: Box & Cox Publications Ltd. | *Re-entry*: 3.7.47/ Pos: 8/Wks: 2 |

*Recordings*:

| | | |
|---|---|---|
| Lou Preager and his Orchestra (Paul Rich) | 6/47 | Columbia FB.3304 |
| Jack Simpson and his Sextet (Peter Morton) | 6/47 | Parlophone F.2221 |
| The Sentimentalists presented by Billy Cotton | 6/47 | Decca F.8785 |
| Peggy Reid | 7/47 | Columbia FB.3313 |

## 64 HARRIETT

| | |
|---|---|
| *Composers:* Abel Baer & Paul Cunningham | *Date of Entry:* 10.5.47/<br>Pos: -/Wks: 4 |
| *Publishers:* Keith Prowse Music Publishing<br>Co. Ltd. | *Re-entry:* 5.6.47/<br>Pos: 9/Wks: 2 |

*Recordings:*

| | | |
|---|---|---|
| Geraldo and his Orchestra (Carole Carr<br>and Denny Vaughan) | 6/47 | Parlophone F.2222 |
| Billy Cotton and his Band (Alan Breeze) | 6/47 | Rex 10239 |

## 65 TRY A LITTLE TENDERNESS

| | |
|---|---|
| *Composers:* Harry Woods, James Campbell &<br>Reginald Connelly | *Date of Entry:* 10.5.47 |
| *Publishers:* Campbell Connelly & Co. Ltd. | *Highest Position:* 4<br>*Weeks on Chart:* 13 |

*Recordings:*

| | | |
|---|---|---|
| Bing Crosby | 2/41 | Columbia DB.1985 |
| Frank Sinatra | 1/47 | Columbia DB.2275 |
| Ted Heath and his Music (Paul Carpenter) | 6/47 | Decca F.8776 |
| Victor Silvester and his Ballroom<br>Orchestra | 7/47 | Columbia FB.3316 |
| Turner Layton | 7/47 | Columbia FB.3318 |
| Rita Williams | 7/47 | Columbia FB.3320 |
| The Skyrockets Dance Orchestra cond.<br>Paul Fenoulhet (Doreen Lundy) | 8/47 | HMV BD.5982 |

## 66 AMONG MY SOUVENIRS

| | |
|---|---|
| *Composers:* Edgar Leslie & Horatio Nicholls | *Date of Entry:* 17.5.47/<br>Pos: 1/Wks: 18 |
| *Publishers:* Lawrence Wright Music Co. Ltd. | *Re-entry:* 25.9.47/<br>Pos: 9/Wks: 1 |

*Recordings:*

| | | |
|---|---|---|
| Frank Sinatra [Titled 'Souvenirs'] | 3/47 | Columbia DB.2286 |
| Turner Layton [Titled 'Souvenirs'] | 5/47 | Columbia FB.3299 |
| Geraldo and his Orchestra (Denny<br>Vaughan) | 5/47 | Parlophone F.2217 |
| Bing Crosby with Russ Morgan and his<br>Orchestra | 6/47 | Brunswick 03779 |
| The Squadronaires dir. Jimmy Miller<br>(Doreen Stephens) | 6/47 | Decca F.8774 |
| Joe Loss and his Orchestra (Howard<br>Jones) | 7/47 | HMV BD.5978 |
| Victor Silvester and his Ballroom<br>Orchestra | 7/47 | Columbia FB.3315 |
| Billy Thorburn's The Organ, the Dance<br>Band and Me (Rita Williams) | 7/47 | Parlophone F.2232 |

## 67 A GAL IN CALICO

| | |
|---|---|
| *Composers:* Arthur Schwartz & Leo Robin | *Date of Entry:* 17.5.47 |
| *Publishers:* B. Feldman & Co. Ltd. | *Highest Position:* 1<br>*Weeks on Chart:* 18 |

*Recordings:*

| | | |
|---|---|---|
| Ambrose and his Orchestra (Alan Dean) | 4/47 | Decca F.8765 |
| Joe Loss and his Orchestra (Elizabeth<br>Batey) | 6/47 | HMV BD.5975 |
| Bing Crosby and The Calico Kids | 6/47 | Brunswick 03775 |
| Victor Silvester and his Ballroom<br>Orchestra | 7/47 | Columbia FB.3316 |
| Geraldo and his Orchestra (Three Boys<br>and a Girl) | 7/47 | Parlophone F.2231 |

## 68 THE PUNCH AND JUDY MAN

| | |
|---|---|
| *Composer:* Robert Addis | *Date of Entry:* 17.5.47 |
| *Publishers:* Strauss-Miller Music Co. Ltd. | *Weeks on Chart:* 2 |

*Recording:*

| | | |
|---|---|---|
| Primo Scala and his Banjo and Accordion<br>Band (Edna Kaye) | 6/47 | Decca F.8783★ |

## 69 COME BACK TO SORRENTO (Torna a Surriento)

| | |
|---|---|
| *Composers:* Ernesto De Curtis & Claude Aveling | *Date of Entry:* 29.5.47/<br>Pos: 10/Wks: 1 |
| *Publishers:* G. Ricordi & Co. (London) Ltd. | *Re-entry:* 17.7.47/<br>Pos: 2/Wks: 26 |

*Recordings:*

| | | |
|---|---|---|
| (a) Titled 'Come back to Sorrento'<br>Joe Loss and his Orchestra (Don Rivers) | 2/47 | HMV BD.5964 |
| Felix Mendelssohn and his Hawaiian<br>Serenaders | 7/47 | Columbia FB.3312 |
| Victor Silvester and his Ballroom<br>Orchestra | 8/47 | Columbia FB.3324 |
| Josef Locke | 8/47 | Columbia DB.2322 |
| Gracie Fields | 9/47 | Decca F.8805 |
| The Kingsway Symphony Orchestra<br>conducted by Camarata | 10/47 | Decca F.8820 |
| Archie Lewis with The Geraldo Strings | 2/48 | Parlophone F.2267★ |
| Vic Lewis and his Orchestra | 3/48 | Parlophone R.3097★ |
| (b) Titled 'Torna a Surriento'<br>Tito Schipa | 10/34 | HMV DA.1379 |
| Beniamino Gigli | 6/36 | HMV DA.1454 |
| Luigi Infantino | 7/47 | Columbia DB.2314 |
| Albert Sandler and his Palm Court<br>Orchestra | 9/47 | Columbia DB.2334 |
| Monte Rey | 10/47 | Columbia FB.3336 |

## 70 PEOPLE WILL SAY WE'RE IN LOVE

| *Composers:* Richard Rodgers & Oscar Hammerstein II | *Date of Entry:* 12.6.47 |
| --- | --- |
| *Publishers:* Chappell & Co. Ltd. | *Highest Position:* 1 |
| | *Weeks on Chart:* 17 |

*Recordings:*

| Alfred Drake and Joan Roberts | 5/47 | Brunswick 03718 |
| --- | --- | --- |
| Bing Crosby with Trudy Erwin and The Sportsmen Glee Club | 5/47 | Brunswick 03708 |
| Rita Williams | 5/47 | Columbia FB.3296 |
| Roberto Inglez and his Orchestra | 5/47 | Parlophone F.2219 |
| Ambrose and his Orchestra (Alan Dean) | 5/47 | Decca F.8766 |
| Ted Heath and his Music (Paul Carpenter) | 5/47 | Decca F.8768 |
| Victor Silvester and his Ballroom Orchestra | 6/47 | Columbia FB.3305 |
| Joe Loss and his Orchestra (Howard Jones) | 6/47 | HMV BD.5974 |
| Leslie A. Hutchinson – 'Hutch' | 7/47 | HMV BD.1170 |
| Geraldo and his Orchestra (Carole Carr) | 7/47 | Parlophone F.2230 |
| Frank Sinatra | 8/47 | Columbia DB.2307 |

## 71 TIME AFTER TIME

| *Composers:* Jule Styne & Sammy Cahn | *Date of Entry:* 19.6.47 |
| --- | --- |
| *Publishers:* Edwin H. Morris & Co. Ltd. | *Highest Position:* 7 |
| | *Weeks on Chart:* 2 |

*Recordings:*

| Frank Sinatra | 5/47 | Columbia DB.2296 |
| --- | --- | --- |
| Paul Carpenter | 6/47 | Deccaa F.8778 |
| Steve Conway | 8/47 | Columbia FB.3326★ |

## 72 I GOT THE SUN IN THE MORNING

| *Composer:* Irving Berlin | *Date of Entry:* 26.6.47 |
| --- | --- |
| *Publishers:* Irving Berlin Ltd. | *Highest Position:* 3 |
| | *Weeks on Chart:* 13 |

*Recordings:*

| Ethel Merman | 6/47 | Brunswick 03772 |
| --- | --- | --- |
| Joe Loss and his Orchestra (Elizabeth Batey) | 8/47 | HMV BD.5981 |
| Victor Silvester and his Ballroom Orchestra | 8/47 | Columbia FB.3325 |
| Edmundo Ros and his Rumba Band | 9/47 | Decca F.8800 |
| Betty Hutton | 7/50 | MGM.301★ |

## 73 A RAINY NIGHT IN RIO

| *Composers:* Arthur Schwartz & Leo Robin | *Date of Entry:* 26.6.47 |
| --- | --- |
| *Publishers:* B. Feldman & Co. Ltd. | *Highest Position:* 10 |
| | *Weeks on Chart:* 1 |

*Recordings:*

| Anne Shelton | 6/47 | Decca F.8772 |
| --- | --- | --- |
| Dinah Shore | 7/47 | Columbia DB.2319★ |
| Edmundo Ros and his Rumba Band (Edmundo Ros and Ensemble) | 9/47 | Decca F.8801★ |
| The Andrews Sisters | 9/47 | Brunswick 03789★ |

## 74 DEAR OLD DONEGAL

| *Composer:* Steve Graham | *Date of Entry:* 3.7.47/ Pos: 10/Wks: 2 |
| --- | --- |
| *Publishers:* Leeds Music Ltd. | *Re-entry:* 2.10.47/ Pos: 10/Wks: 3 |
| | *2nd re-entry:* 13.11.47/ Pos: 8/Wks: 2 |
| | *3rd re-entry:* 4.12.47/ Pos: 10/Wks: 1 |

*Recordings:*

| Bing Crosby and The Jesters | 11/46 | Brunswick 03753 |
| --- | --- | --- |
| The Radio Revellers | 6/47 | Columbia FB.3309 |
| Joe Loss and his Orchestra (Elizabeth Batey) | 8/47 | HMV BD.5981 |
| The Four Ramblers | 4/48 | Decca F.8868★ |
| Josef Locke | 8/48 | Columbia DB.2429★ |

## 75 DOWN THE OLD SPANISH TRAIL

| *Composers:* Kenneth Leslie-Smith & Jimmy Kennedy | *Date of Entry:* 17.7.47 |
| --- | --- |
| *Publishers:* Peter Maurice Music Co. Ltd. | *Highest Position:* 4 |
| | *Weeks on Chart:* 15 |

*Recordings:*

| The Skyrockets Dance Orchestra cond. Paul Fenoulhet (Cyril Shane) | 7/47 | HMV BD.5979 |
| --- | --- | --- |
| Monte Rey | 8/47 | Columbia FB.3321 |
| Leslie Douglas and his Orchestra (Leslie Douglas and The Skymasters) | 8/47 | Regal-Zonophone MR.3792 |
| Issy Bonn | 9/47 | Decca F.8787 |
| Roy Rogers | 10/48 | Regal-Zonophone MR.3810★ |

## 76 | MAM'SELLE

*Composers:* Mack Gordon & Edmund Goulding      *Date of Entry:* 17.7.47

*Publishers:* Francis Day & Hunter Ltd.      *Highest Position:* 5
                                             *Weeks on Chart:* 13

*Recordings:*
| | | |
|---|---|---|
| Frank Sinatra | 7/47 | Columbia DB.2321 |
| Jean Cavall | 7/47 | HMV B.9563 |
| Roberto Inglez and his Orchestra | 9/47 | Parlophone F.2238 |
| Dick Haymes | 9/47 | Brunswick 03803 |
| Jack White and his Orchestra | 7/48 | Decca F.8931★ |

## 77 | THEY SAY IT'S WONDERFUL

*Composer:* Irving Berlin      *Date of Entry:* 17.7.47

*Publishers:* Irving Berlin Ltd.      *Highest Position:* 9
                                      *Weeks on Chart:* 5

*Recordings:*
| | | |
|---|---|---|
| Ethel Merman and Ray Middleton | 6/47 | Brunswick 03771 |
| Perry Como | 6/47 | HMV BD.1167 |
| Joe Loss and his Orchestra (Howard Jones) | 6/47 | HMV BD.5975 |
| Cyril Stapleton and his Orchestra (Dick James) | 7/47 | Decca F.8775 |
| Leslie A. Hutchinson – 'Hutch' | 7/47 | HMV BD.1170 |
| Geraldo and his Orchestra (Denny Vaughan) | 7/47 | Parlophone F.2230 |
| Janet Hamilton-Smith and John Hargreaves | 8/47 | HMV B.9576 |
| Victor Silvester and his Ballroom Orchestra | 8/47 | Columbia FB.3325 |
| Frank Sinatra | 8/47 | Columbia DB.2307 |
| Bing Crosby | 9/47 | Brunswick 03794★ |
| Richard Tauber | 10/47 | Parlophone RO.20556★ |
| Carroll Gibbons and the Savoy Hotel Orpheans (Edna Kaye) | 11/47 | Columbia FB.3348★ |
| Betty Hutton and Howard Keel | 7/50 | MGM.301★ |
| Ray Anthony and his Orchestra (Ronnie Deauville) | 7/50 | Capitol CL.13336★ |

## 78 | NOW IS THE HOUR (Haere Ra)

*Composers:* Maewa Kaihau & Clement Scott      *Date of Entry:* 31.7.47

*Publishers:* Keith Prowse & Co. Ltd.      *Highest Position:* 1
                                           *Weeks on Chart:* 26

*Recordings:*
| | | |
|---|---|---|
| Gracie Fields | 9/47 | Decca F.8805 |
| Rita Williams | 10/47 | Columbia FB.3345 |
| Leslie A. Hutchinson – 'Hutch' | 11/47 | HMV BD.1181 |
| Geraldo and his Orchestra (Archie Lewis) | 11/47 | Parlophone F.2255 |
| Bing Crosby with the Ken Darby Choir | 1/48 | Brunswick 03839 |
| Felix Mendelssohn and his Hawaiian Serenaders (George Barclay and The Paradise Island Trio) | 2/48 | Columbia FB.3369★ |
| Anne Ziegler and Webster Booth | 5/48 | HMV B.9642★ |

## 79 | I BELIEVE

*Composers:* Jule Styne & Sammy Cahn      *Date of Entry:* 21.8.47

*Publishers:* Edwin H. Morris & Co. Ltd.      *Highest Position:* 5
                                              *Weeks on Chart:* 12

*Recording:*
| | | |
|---|---|---|
| Artie Shaw and his Orchestra (Mel Torme) | 9/47 | Parlophone R.3054 |

## 80 | OH! WHAT A BEAUTIFUL MORNING

*Composers:* Richard Rodgers & Oscar Hammerstein II      *Date of Entry:* 21.8.47

*Publishers:* Chappell & Co. Ltd.      *Highest Position:* 10
                                       *Weeks on Chart:* 1

*Recordings:*
| | | |
|---|---|---|
| Alfred Drake | 5/47 | Brunswick 03714 |
| Ambrose and his Orchestra (Alan Dean) | 5/47 | Decca F.8766 |
| Bing Crosby and Trudy Erwin with The Sportsmen Glee Club | 5/47 | Brunswick 03708 |
| Frank Sinatra | 6/47 | Columbia DB.2313 |
| Joe Loss and his Orchestra | 6/47 | HMV BD.5974 |
| Nelson Eddy | 7/47 | Columbia DB.2315 |
| Richard Tauber | 10/47 | Parlophone RO.20556★ |

## 81 THE LITTLE OLD MILL (went round and round)

| | |
|---|---|
| *Composers*: Don Pelosi, Lewis Ilda & Leo Towers | *Date of Entry*: 28.8.47/<br>Pos: 10/Wks: 1 |
| *Publishers*: Irwin Dash Music Co. Ltd. | *Re-entry*: 11.9.47/<br>Pos: 2/Wks: 24 |

*Recordings*:

| | | |
|---|---|---|
| Lou Preager and his Orchestra (Paul Rich) | 6/47 | Columbia FB.3303 |
| Billy Cotton and his Band (Alan Breeze) | 6/47 | Rex 10239 |
| Joe Loss and his Orchestra (Elizabeth Batey) | 7/47 | HMV BD.5977 |
| Jimmy Leach and his New Organolians | 7/47 | Columbia FB.3319 |
| Geraldo and his Orchestra (Carole Carr) | 8/47 | Parlophone F.2234 |
| The Milt Herth Trio (Bob Johnstone) | 4/48 | Brunswick 03865★ |

## 82 GUILTY

| | |
|---|---|
| *Composers*: Gus Kahn, Harry Akst & Richard P. Whiting | *Date of Entry*: 4.9.47 |
| *Publishers*: Francis Day & Hunter Ltd. | *Highest Position*: 4<br>*Weeks on Chart*: 12 |

*Recordings*:

| | | |
|---|---|---|
| Steve Conway | 6/47 | Columbia FB.3308 |
| Harry Roy and his Band (Eve Lombard) | 7/47 | Decca F.8773 |
| The Skyrockets Dance Orchestra cond. Paul Fenoulhet (Doreen Lundy) | 9/47 | HMV BD.5984 |
| Victor Silvester and his Ballroom Orchestra | 9/47 | Columbia FB.3329 |
| Peggy Reid | 9/47 | Columbia FB.3333 |
| Ella Fitzgerald | 9/47 | Brunswick 03805 |

## 83 CHI-BABA, CHI-BABA (My Bambino go to sleep)

| | |
|---|---|
| *Composers*: Mack David, Al Hoffman & Jerry Livingston | *Date of Entry*: 11.9.47 |
| *Publishers*: Sun Music Publishing Co. Ltd. | *Highest Position*: 3<br>*Weeks on Chart*: 12 |

*Recordings*:

| | | |
|---|---|---|
| Denny Dennis with The Song Pedlars | 10/47 | Decca F.8810 |
| Perry Como | 11/47 | HMV BD.1180 |
| Joe Loss and his Orchestra (Howard Jones) | 11/47 | HMV BD.5987 |
| Roberto Inglez and his Orchestra (Roberto Inglez) | 11/47 | Parlophone F.2254 |
| Geraldo and his Orchestra (Archie Lewis) | 11/47 | Parlophone F.2255 |
| Blue Barron and his Orchestra (Vocal Ensemble) | 1/48 | MGM.108 |

## 84 DANGER AHEAD! (Beware)

| | |
|---|---|
| *Composer*: Billy Reid | *Date of Entry*: 9.10.47 |
| *Publishers*: Yale Music Corporation Ltd. | *Highest Position*: 3<br>*Weeks on Chart*: 10 |

*Recordings*:

| | | |
|---|---|---|
| Leslie A. Hutchinson – 'Hutch' | 9/47 | HMV BD.1173 |
| Dorothy Squires | 10/47 | Parlophone F.2244 |
| Denny Dennis | 10/47 | Decca F.8810 |

## 85 MY FIRST LOVE, MY LAST LOVE FOR ALWAYS

| | |
|---|---|
| *Composer*: Billy Reid | *Date of Entry*: 16.10.47 |
| *Publishers*: Irwin Dash Music Co. Ltd. | *Highest Position*: 6<br>*Weeks on Chart*: 12 |

*Recordings*:

| | | |
|---|---|---|
| Oscar Rabin and his Band with Harry Davis (Diane) | 10/47 | Parlophone F.2246 |
| Dorothy Squires | 10/47 | Parlophone F.2244 |
| Joe Loss and his Orchestra (Howard Jones) | 11/47 | HMV BD.5988 |
| Lou Preager and his Orchestra (Paul Rich) | 11/47 | Columbia FB.3352 |
| The Street Singer – Arthur Tracy | 11/47 | Decca F.8811 |
| Monte Rey | 12/47 | Columbia FB.3356 |

## 86 I'LL MAKE UP FOR EVERYTHING

| | |
|---|---|
| *Composer*: Ross Parker | *Date of Entry*: 23.10.47 |
| *Publishers*: Peter Maurice Music Co. Ltd. | *Highest Position*: 2<br>*Weeks on Chart*: 21 |

*Recordings*:

| | | |
|---|---|---|
| Steve Conway | 10/47 | Columbia FB.3344 |
| Vera Lynn | 12/47 | Decca F.8826 |
| Frank Sinatra | 1/48 | Columbia DB.2365 |
| The Ink Spots | 2/48 | Brunswick 03840 |

## 87 AN APPLE BLOSSOM WEDDING

| | |
|---|---|
| *Composers*: Nat Simon & Jimmy Kennedy | *Date of Entry*: 30.10.47 |
| *Publishers*: Campbell Connelly & Co. Ltd. | *Highest Position*: 1<br>*Weeks on Chart*: 18 |

*Recordings*:
| | | |
|---|---|---|
| Lou Preager and his Orchestra (Paul Rich) | 9/47 | Columbia FB.3331 |
| Cyril Stapleton and his Orchestra (Dick James) | 10/47 | Decca F.8809 |
| Jimmy Leach and his New Organolians (Alan Dean) | 12/47 | Columbia FB.3358 |
| Kenny Baker with Russ Morgan and his Orchestra | 12/47 | Brunswick 03816 |
| The Skyrockets Dance Orchestra cond. Paul Fenoulhet (Doreen Lundy) | 12/47 | HMV BD.5992 |

## 88 BOW BELLS

| | |
|---|---|
| *Composers*: Harold Purcell & Ben Bernard | *Date of Entry*: 27.11.47 |
| *Publishers*: Edward Kassner Music Co. Ltd. | *Highest Position*: 6<br>*Weeks on Chart*: 6 |

*Recordings*:
| | | |
|---|---|---|
| The Skyrockets Dance Orchestra cond. Paul Fenoulhet (Dick James) | 9/47 | HMV BD.5984 |
| Lou Preager and his Orchestra (Paul Rich) | 10/47 | Columbia FB.3339 |
| Donald Peers with Bob Farnon and his Orchestra (ftg The Bells of St Mary-le-Bow) | 3/50 | Decca F.9375★ |

## 89 HOW ARE THINGS IN GLOCCA MORRA?

| | |
|---|---|
| *Composers*: E.Y. Harburg & Burton Lane | *Date of Entry*: 27.11.47/<br>Pos: 9/Wks: 1 |
| *Publishers*: Chappell & Co. Ltd. | *Re-entry*: 11.12.47/<br>Pos: 9/Wks: 3 |

*Recordings*:
| | | |
|---|---|---|
| Gracie Fields | 10/47 | Decca F.8808 |
| Dick Haymes | 10/47 | Brunswick 03810 |
| Bill Johnson | 11/47 | Columbia DB.2347 |
| Oscar Rabin and his Band with Harry Davis (Bob Dale) | 11/47 | Parlophone F.2248 |
| Cyril Stapleton and his Orchestra (Dick James) | 12/47 | Decca F.8822 |

## 90 PEG O' MY HEART

| | |
|---|---|
| *Composers*: Alfred Bryan & Fred Fisher | *Date of Entry*: 4.12.47 |
| *Publishers*: Ascherberg, Hopwood & Crew Ltd. | *Highest Position*: 1<br>*Weeks on Chart*: 16 |

(Note: The 1926 recording by Red Nichols and his Five Pennies on Brunswick 01019 was reissued in 1947.)

*Later Recordings*:
| | | |
|---|---|---|
| Glenn Miller and his Orchestra | 9/47 | Brunswick 03807 |
| Leslie A. Hutchinson – 'Hutch' | 11/47 | HMV BD.1181 |
| Joe Loss and his Orchestra (Howard Jones) | 11/47 | HMV BD.5987 |
| The Radio Revellers | 11/47 | Columbia FB.3349 |
| Geraldo and his Orchestra (Denny Vaughan) | 12/47 | Parlophone F.2258 |
| Lou Preager and his Orchestra (The Sunnysiders) | 12/47 | Columbia FB.3355 |
| Issy Bonn | 12/47 | Decca F.8825 |
| Victor Silvester and his Ballroom Orchestra | 12/47 | Columbia FB.3360 |
| Art Lund | 1/48 | MGM.106 |
| Eddie Heywood and his Orchestra (Eddie Heywood – piano) | 1/48 | Brunswick 03833 |
| Stan Kenton and his Orchestra | 11/49 | Capitol CL.13191★ |

## 91 SOUTH AMERICA, TAKE IT AWAY

| | |
|---|---|
| *Composer*: Harold Rome | *Date of Entry*: 18.12.47 |
| *Publishers*: B. Feldman & Co. Ltd. | *Highest Position*: 6<br>*Weeks on Chart*: 4 |

*Recordings*:
| | | |
|---|---|---|
| Edmundo Ros and his Rumba Band (Edmundo Ros) | 11/47 | Decca F.8815 |
| Bing Crosby and The Andrews Sisters | 11/47 | Brunswick 03813 |
| Joe Loss and his Orchestra (Elizabeth Batey) | 12/47 | HMV BD.5990 |
| Billy Thorburn's The Organ, the Dance Band and Me (Harry Kaye) | 1/48 | Parlophone F.2266 |
| Geraldo and his Orchestra (Archie Lewis and Ensemble) | 3/48 | Parlophone F.2279★ |

# 1948

Throughout the year a Top Ten was published – and there was no doubt which was the top song. *Galway Bay* spent no less than 39 weeks on the charts which meant, of course, that it spent those 39 weeks in the Top Ten, and this makes it the top song of all the 1,100 entries listed in these pages. Not only that, but it is the only song in the history of the Sheet Music Charts of the Forties and Fifties to have gone straight in at No. 1 – and then it spent 22 weeks there, setting up another all-time record. No less than seven songs moved into second place during its reign at the top, with *Golden earrings* having the longest spell as runner-up with eight weeks, but it was *So tired* which finally dislodged it after just one week at No. 2. It must be mentioned that 1948's second longest chart song, *The dream of Olwen,* is also the second longest Top Ten entry – and that was despite the fact that in its 38-week occupation of the Top Ten it never went higher than No. 5. But, going back to *Galway Bay,* it is rather amazing to note that prior to its 29 April first entry, a recording of it by Denis Martin was played on 'Housewives' Choice' in January. The song which entered the chart at the same time as *Galway Bay, Silver wedding waltz,* came in at No. 3 and then proceeded downwards for six weeks before going out. On no other occasion has a song come into the charts in the first week at such a high position, and then descended without ever rising again. *Near you* spent ten weeks at No. 2 behind *Tree in the meadow* and the two songs swopped places for the one week that *Near you* topped the charts. Two other

| Pos | MOST WEEKS ON THE CHARTS **TOP SIX** | Wks |
|---|---|---|
| 1 | *Galway Bay* | 36 |
| 2 | *The dream of Olwen* | 30 |
| 3 | *Near you* | 28 |
| 4 | *Golden earrings* | 24 |
| 5 | *A tree in the meadow* | 21 |
| 6= | *You can't be true, dear* | 19 |

remarkable statistics in places are noted concerning *I wonder who's kissing her now* and *Rambling rose.* The former spent ten of its 18 weeks on the chart in third place while *Rose* had 11 weeks out of 18 in eighth place. Eight months after the BBC had reacted to the plug money problems by increasing the fees paid to the dance bands while threatening to suspend any band found to be guilty of accepting the plug cash, it came to an agreement with the music publishers over the enforcing of heavy penalties for offenders. Three record labels made their first appearance in 1948 in the UK – MGM (in January) and Capitol (in December), while in between we saw the birth of the independent Esquire label. Jack Jackson broadcast the first 'Record Round Up' on Saturday, 10 January at 2.30 p.m. on the Light Programme. Two months later he was to have as guest in the studio Danny Kaye. *So tired* by Russ Morgan and his Orchestra was released in May, heard on 'Housewives' Choice' on 19 July, but took a further nine weeks to reach the charts, while *Maybe you'll be there,* an entry at the beginning of December, was heard on the radio as far back as July 1947. 'Hutch' broadcast *October twilight* on the BBC's 'Blackpool Night Out' three months before it entered the chart – but he was never to record it. 'Wait for it' note: Max C. Freedman, one of the three composers of *Heartbreaker,* didn't have another chart hit for seven years – and then came up with *Rock around the clock*!

# SONG CHARTS

## 92 THE COFFEE SONG

*Composers:* Bob Hilliard & Dick Miles

*Publishers:* Southern Music Publishing Co. Ltd.

*Date of Entry:* 1.1.48

*Highest Position:* 5
*Weeks on Chart:* 10

*Recordings:*

| | | |
|---|---|---|
| Edmundo Ros and his Rumba Band (Edmundo Ros) | 9/47 | Decca F.8800 |
| The Andrews Sisters | 9/47 | Brunswick 03789 |
| Geraldo and his Orchestra (Ensemble) | 1/48 | Parlophone F.2264 |
| Frank Sinatra | 2/48 | Columbia DB.2376 |

## 93 THE GIRL THAT I MARRY

*Composer:* Irving Berlin

*Publishers:* Irving Berlin Ltd.

*Date of Entry:* 8.1.48

*Highest Position:* 9
*Weeks on Chart:* 1

*Recordings:*

| | | |
|---|---|---|
| Ray Middleton | 6/47 | Brunswick 03773 |
| Frank Sinatra | 6/47 | Columbia DB.2313 |
| Dick Haymes | 9/47 | Brunswick 03803 |
| Bill Johnson | 2/48 | Columbia DB.2373★ |
| Howard Keel | 7/50 | MGM.302★ |
| Ray Anthony and his Orchestra (Ronnie Deauville) | 7/50 | Capitol CL.13336★ |

## 94 I WONDER WHO'S KISSING HER NOW?

*Composers:* Joseph Howard, Frank Adams & William Hough

*Publishers:* B. Feldman & Co. Ltd.

*Date of Entry:* 8.1.48

*Highest Position:* 3
*Weeks on Chart:* 18

*Recordings:*

| | | |
|---|---|---|
| Perry Como with Ted Weems and his Orchestra and Chorus | 9/47 | Brunswick 03806 |
| Danny Kaye with The Ken Darby Singers | 9/47 | Brunswick 03812 |
| Joe Loss and his Orchestra (Howard Jones) | 11/47 | HMV BD.5988 |
| Oscar Rabin and his Band with Harry Davis (Bob Dale) | 12/47 | Parlophone F.2260 |
| Perry Como with Lloyd Schaefer and his Orchestra | 1/48 | HMV BD.1190 |
| Turner Layton | 1/48 | Columbia DB.2367 |
| Victor Silvester and his Ballroom Orchestra | 2/48 | Columbia FB.3371 |

## 95 A TREE IN THE MEADOW
### (I love you till I die)

*Composer:* Billy Reid

*Publishers:* Campbell Connelly & Co. Ltd.

*Date of Entry:* 15.1.48

*Highest Position:* 1
*Weeks on Chart:* 21

*Recordings:*

| | | |
|---|---|---|
| Leslie A. Hutchinson – 'Hutch' | 1/48 | HMV B.9611 |
| Sam Browne | 1/48 | Decca F.8830 |
| Joe Loss and his Orchestra (Howard Jones) | 2/48 | HMV BD.5997 |
| Monte Rey | 2/48 | Columbia DB.2374 |
| Ivy Benson and her Girls' Band (Rita Williams) | 3/48 | Regal Zon. MR.3802 |
| Dorothy Squires | 3/48 | Parlophone R.3092 |
| Geraldo and his Orchestra (Archie Lewis) | 4/48 | Parlophone F.2283 |
| Cyril Stapleton and his Orchestra | 7/48 | Decca F.8929★ |

## 96  NEAR YOU

| | | | |
|---|---|---|---|
| *Composers*: Francis Craig & Kermit Goell | | *Date of Entry*: 15.1.48/ Pos: 1/Wks: 23 | |
| *Publishers*: Bradbury Wood Ltd. | | *Re-entry*: 1.7.48/ Pos 9/Wks: 4 | |
| | | *2nd re-entry*: 19.8.48/ Pos: 10/Wks: 1 | |

*Recordings:*

| | | |
|---|---|---|
| The Andrews Sisters | 11/47 | Brunswick 03823 |
| Jimmy Leach and his New Organolians (Alan Dean) | 2/48 | Columbia FB.3370 |
| Geraldo and his Orchestra (Archie Lewis) | 2/48 | Parlophone F.2271 |
| Victor Silvester and his Ballroom Orchestra | 3/48 | Columbia FB.3384 |
| Turner Layton | 4/48 | Columbia DB.2399 |
| Francis Craig and his Orchestra (Bob Lamm) | 4/48 | Brunswick 03876 |
| Larry Green and his Orchestra (The Trio) | 5/48 | HMV BD.1201 |

## 97  MY OWN DARBY AND JOAN

| | | |
|---|---|---|
| *Composers*: Box, Cox & Kulma | | *Date of Entry*: 15.1.48 |
| *Publishers*: Box & Cox Publications Ltd. | | *Highest Position*: 8 *Weeks on Chart*: 4 |

*Recordings:*

| | | |
|---|---|---|
| Jack Simpson and his Sextet (Betty Dale) | 10/47 | Parlophone F.2243 |
| The Sentimentalists presented by Billy Cotton | 1/48 | Decca F.8832 |
| Rita Williams | 2/48 | Columbia FB.3372 |

## 98  THE SHOEMAKER'S SERENADE

| | | |
|---|---|---|
| *Composers*: Joe Lubin & Eddie Lisbona | | *Date of Entry*: 29.1.48 |
| *Publishers*: Edward Kassner Music Co. Ltd. | | *Highest Position*: 4 *Weeks on Chart*: 13 |

*Recordings:*

| | | |
|---|---|---|
| Lou Preager and his Orchestra (Eileen Orchard) | 1/48 | Columbia FB.3368 |
| Johnny Denis and his Ranchers | 2/48 | Decca F.8844 |
| Roberto Inglez and his Orchestra | 2/48 | Parlophone F.2269 |
| The Radio Revellers | 3/48 | Columbia FB.3376 |
| The Five Smith Brothers | 4/48 | Parlophone F.2282 |
| The Squadronaires directed by Jimmy Miller (The Quads) | 7/48 | Decca F.8927★ |

## 99  SERENADE OF THE BELLS

| | | | |
|---|---|---|---|
| *Composers*: Al Urbano, Kay Twomey & Al Goodhart | | *Date of Entry*: 12.2.48/ Pos: 4/Wks 12 | |
| *Publishers*: Edwin H. Morris & Co. Ltd. | | *Re-entry*: 13.5.48/ Pos: 7/Wks: 4 | |
| | | *2nd re-entry*: 17.6.48/ Pos: 10/Wks: 2 | |

*Recordings:*

| | | |
|---|---|---|
| Geraldo and his Orchestra (Archie Lewis) | 1/48 | Parlophone F.2264 |
| Guy Lombardo and his Royal Canadians (Kenny Gardner) | 2/48 | Brunswick 03843 |
| Gracie Fields | 2/48 | Decca F.8837 |
| Jean Cavall | 4/48 | HMV B.9632 |
| Dick Haymes | 6/48 | Brunswick 03890 |
| Billy Thorburn's The Organ, the Dance Band and Me (Harry Kaye) | 6/48 | Parlophone F.2298 |

## 100  WHEN YOU WERE SWEET SIXTEEN

| | | |
|---|---|---|
| *Composer*: James Thornton | | *Date of Entry*: 26.2.48/ Pos: 3/Wks: 9 |
| *Publishers*: H. Darewski Music Publishing Co. | | *Re-entry*: 6.5.48/Pos: 10/Wks: 1 |

*Recordings:*

| | | |
|---|---|---|
| The Mills Brothers | 4/41 | Brunswick 03139 |
| Perry Como and The Satisfyers | 11/47 | HMV BD.1180 |
| Al Jolson | 12/47 | Brunswick 03821 |
| Denis Martin | 3/48 | Parlophone R.3093 |
| Archie Lewis with The Geraldo Strings | 4/48 | Parlophone F.2277 |
| Joe Loss and his Orchestra (Howard Jones) | 5/48 | HMV BD.6007 |
| Steve Conway | 5/48 | Columbia FB.3398 |
| Josef Locke | 6/48 | Columbia DB.2409★ |
| The Mills Brothers | 3/50 | Brunswick 04450★ |

## 101  ONCE UPON A WINTER-TIME

| | | |
|---|---|---|
| *Composers*: Johnny Brandon & Ray Martin | | *Date of Entry*: 4.3.48 |
| *Publishers*: Cinephonic Music Co. Ltd. | | *Highest Position*: 5 *Weeks on Chart*: 9 |

*Recordings:*

| | | |
|---|---|---|
| The Skyrockets conducted Woolf Phillips (Doreen Lundy) | 3/48 | HMV BD.6000 |
| Jack Simpson and his Sextet (Maureen Morton) | 3/48 | Parlophone F.2276 |
| Rita Williams | 5/48 | Columbia FB.3393 |
| Vera Lynn | 5/48 | Decca F.8883 |
| Paul Fenoulhet and his Orchestra (Doreen Lundy) | 5/48 | MGM.126 |
| Geraldo and his Orchestra (Amru Sani) | 6/48 | Parlophone F.2296★ |

## 102 CIVILISATION
### (Bongo, Bongo, Bongo)

| | |
|---|---|
| *Composers*: Bob Hilliard & Carl Sigman | *Date of Entry*: 11.3.48 |
| *Publishers*: Edwin H. Morris & Co. Ltd. | *Highest Position*: 3<br>*Weeks on Chart*: 15 |

*Recordings*:
| | | |
|---|---|---|
| Danny Kaye and The Andrews Sisters | 1/48 | Brunswick 03836 |
| Sy Oliver and his Orchestra (Sy Oliver) | 2/48 | MGM.117 |
| Joe Loss and his Orchestra (Elizabeth Batey) | 5/48 | HMV BD.6007 |

## 103 THE OLD POSTMAN
### (passes me by)

| | |
|---|---|
| *Composer*: Ross Parker | *Date of Entry*: 18.3.48 |
| *Publishers*: Francis Day & Hunter Ltd. | *Highest Position*: 9<br>*Weeks on Chart*: 2 |

*Recording*:
| | | |
|---|---|---|
| Sam Browne | 3/48 | Decca F.8856 |

## 104 TOO FAT POLKA

| | |
|---|---|
| *Composers*: Ross MacLean & Arthur Richardson's dance band arrangement of 'Daar Lie Die Ding' | *Date of Entry*: 25.3.48 |
| *Publishers*: Francis Day & Hunter Ltd. | *Highest Position*: 9<br>*Weeks on Chart*: 2 |

*Recordings*:
| | | |
|---|---|---|
| The Andrews Sisters | 2/48 | Brunswick 03841 |
| Arthur Godfrey | 4/48 | Columbia DB.2397 |
| Vic Lewis and his Orchestra (Vic Lewis) | 5/48 | Parlophone R.3101★ |

## 105 GOLDEN EARRINGS

| | |
|---|---|
| *Composers*: Jay Livingston, Ray Evans & Victor Young | *Date of Entry*: 1.4.48/<br>Pos: 2/Wks: 23 |
| *Publishers*: Victoria Music Publishing Co. Ltd. | *Re-entry*: 16.9.48/<br>Pos: 10/Wks: 1 |

*Recordings*:
| | | |
|---|---|---|
| Bing Crosby | 2/48 | Brunswick 03838 |
| Guy Lombardo and his Royal Canadians (Don Rodney) | 2/48 | Brunswick 03843 |
| Victor Silvester and his Ballroom Orchestra | 2/48 | Columbia FB.3374 |
| Geraldo and his Orchestra (Carole Carr) | 3/48 | Parlophone F.2279 |
| Jack Fina and his Orchestra | 5/48 | MGM.129 |

## 106 I'M MY OWN GRANDPA

| | |
|---|---|
| *Composers*: Dwight Latham & Moe Jaffe | *Date of Entry*: 8.4.48 |
| *Publishers*: Leeds Music Ltd. | *Highest Position*: 10<br>*Weeks on Chart*: 1 |

*Recordings*:
| | | |
|---|---|---|
| Guy Lombardo and his Royal Canadians (The Lombardo Trio) | 5/48 | Brunswick 03878★ |
| Phil Harris and his Orchestra (Phil Harris) [Titled 'He's his own Grandpa'] | 12/48 | HMV BD.1222★ |

## 107 TERESA

| | |
|---|---|
| *Composers*: Babe Russin & Jack Hoffman | *Date of Entry*: 15.4.48 |
| *Publishers*: Leeds Music Ltd. | *Highest Position*: 3<br>*Weeks on Chart*: 13 |

*Recordings*:
| | | |
|---|---|---|
| Dick Haymes and The Andrews Sisters | 4/48 | Brunswick 03860 |
| Joe Loss and his Orchestra (Howard Jones) | 6/48 | HMV BD.6008 |
| Jean Cavall | 6/48 | HMV B.9647 |
| Geraldo and his Orchestra (Denny Vaughan and Anne Stuart) | 6/48 | Parlophone F.2296 |
| Jimmy Leach and his New Organolians (Alan Dean) | 6/48 | Columbia FB.3400 |

## 108 THE SILVER WEDDING WALTZ

| | |
|---|---|
| *Composers*: Max & Harry Nesbitt | *Date of Entry*: 29.4.48 |
| *Publishers*: Unit Music Publishing Co. | *Highest Position*: 3<br>*Weeks on Chart*: 7 |

*Recordings*:
| | | |
|---|---|---|
| Vera Lynn | 6/48 | Decca F.8899 |
| Joe Loss and his Orchestra (Howard Jones) | 8/48 | HMV BD.6014★ |

## 109 GALWAY BAY

| Composer: Dr Arthur Colahan | Date of Entry: 29.4.48 |
| --- | --- |
| Publishers: Box & Cox Publications Ltd. | Highest Position: 1<br>Weeks on Chart: 39 |

Recordings:
(Prior to the song's popularity in the charts of 1948–49, it had been recorded by a number of notable singers, including the Irish tenor, Michael O'Higgins, on Regal Zonophone MR.3688. It was the first song to rise straight to No. 1 spot in its very first week in the Sheet Music Charts.)

| | | |
| --- | --- | --- |
| Denis Martin | 10/47 | Parlophone R.3058 |
| Robert Wilson | 1/48 | HMV B.9607 |
| Bing Crosby | 5/48 | Brunswick 03882 |
| The Sentimentalists presented by Billy Cotton | 5/48 | Decca F.8897 |
| Anne Shelton with The Wardour Singers | 6/48 | Decca F.8907 |
| Bill Johnson | 6/48 | Columbia DB.2415 |
| Jack Simpson and his Sextet (Dave Kydd) | 7/48 | Parlophone F.2299 |
| Michael O'Duffy with Duncan Morison (piano) | 9/48 | HMV B.9675 |
| Joseph McNally | 9/48 | MGM.146 |
| Josef Locke | 10/48 | Columbia DB.2447 |
| Joe Loss and his Orchestra (The Lhon D'Hoo Male Choir) | 11/48 | HMV BD.1220 |

## 110 THE WISHING WALTZ

| Composer: Art Noel | Date of Entry: 6.5.48 |
| --- | --- |
| Publishers: Noel Gay Music Co. Ltd. | Highest Position: 9<br>Weeks on Chart: 3 |

Recordings:

| | | |
| --- | --- | --- |
| Victor Silvester and his Ballroom Orchestra | 2/48 | Columbia FB.3371 |
| Rita Williams | 4/48 | Columbia FB.3390 |
| Oscar Rabin and his Band with Harry Davis | 4/48 | Parlophone F.2284 |
| Sam Browne and The Squadronaires cond. Jimmy Miller | 4/48 | Decca F.8862 |

## 111 THE DREAM OF OLWEN

| Composers: Charles Williams with lyrics added later by Winifred May | Date of Entry: 13.5.48/<br>Pos: 9/Wks: 3 |
| --- | --- |
| Publishers: Lawrence Wright Music Co. Ltd. | Re-entry: 24.6.48/<br>Pos: 9/Wks: 1<br>2nd re-entry: 8.7.48/<br>Pos: 5/Wks: 34 |

Recordings:

| | | |
| --- | --- | --- |
| Charles Williams and his Concert Orchestra (piano: Arthur Dulay) | 1/48 | Columbia DX.1433 |
| Mantovani and his Concert Orchestra (piano: Ivan Fosello) | 7/48 | Decca K.1911 |
| Philip Green and his Orchestra (piano: Arthur Sandford) | 9/48 | MGM.147 |
| The Melachrino Orchestra (piano: William Hill-Bowen) | 10/48 | HMV B.9687 |
| Frederick Ferrari | 10/48 | Parlophone R.3136 |
| Reggie Goff [Titled 'Olwen'] | 10/48 | Decca F.8997 |
| The Luton Girls' Choir with Herbert Dawson (organ) | 12/48 | Parlophone R.3156 |
| Carmen Cavallaro and his Orchestra | 6/49 | Brunswick 04097★ |
| Meredith Willson and his Orchestra (The Singing People) [Titled 'Olwen'] | 7/49 | Brunswick 04241★ |
| Tano Ferendinos (tenor) | 7/50 | HMV B.9934★ |
| John Hendrik (tenor) | 10/50 | Decca F.9533★ |
| Ronnie Ronalde | 11/50 | Columbia DB.2756★ |
| Victor Young and his Singing Strings | 4/51 | Brunswick 04687★ |

## 112 REFLECTIONS ON THE WATER

| Composer: Billy Reid | Date of Entry: 27.5.48 |
| --- | --- |
| Publishers: Peter Maurice Music Co. Ltd. | Highest Position: 6<br>Weeks on Chart: 3 |

Recordings:

| | | |
| --- | --- | --- |
| Joe Loss and his Orchestra (Howard Jones) | 4/48 | HMV BD.6004 |
| Sam Browne with The Squadronaires dir. Jimmy Miller | 5/48 | Decca F.8881 |
| Paul Fenoulhet and his Orchestra (Doreen Lundy) | 5/48 | MGM.126 |
| Dorothy Squires | 6/48 | Columbia DB.2418 |

## 113   OH! MY ACHIN' HEART

| | | |
|---|---|---|
| *Composers:* Freddy James, Little Jack Little & Jack Palmer | | *Date of Entry:* 3.6.48 |
| *Publishers:* Campbell Connelly & Co. Ltd. | | *Highest Position:* 5<br>*Weeks on Chart:* 2 |

*Recordings:*

| | | |
|---|---|---|
| Tony Martin | 12/47 | HMV B.9600 |
| Blue Barron and his Orchestra (Charles Fisher & Quartet) | 1/48 | MGM.108 |
| The Mills Brothers | 2/48 | Brunswick 03842 |
| Oscar Rabin and his Band with Harry Davis (Bob Dale) | 6/48 | Parlophone F.2297 |
| Lou Preager and his Orchestra (Paul Rich) | 6/48 | Columbia FB.3403 |

## 114   TIME MAY CHANGE

| | | |
|---|---|---|
| *Composers:* Leigh Stafford & Hugh Wade | | *Date of Entry:* 10.6.48 |
| *Publishers:* Campbell Connelly & Co. Ltd. | | *Highest Position:* 4<br>*Weeks on Chart:* 14 |

*Recordings:*

| | | |
|---|---|---|
| Anne Shelton | 6/48 | Decca F.8898 |
| Archie Lewis with The Geraldo Strings | 6/48 | Parlophone F.2294 |
| Rita Williams | 7/48 | Columbia FB.3407 |
| Joe Loss and his Orchestra (Howard Jones) | 8/48 | HMV BD.6015 |
| Jack Simpson and his Sextet (Dave Kydd) | 9/48 | Parlophone F.2309 |

## 115   NATURE BOY

| | | |
|---|---|---|
| *Composer:* eden ahbez | | *Date of Entry:* 10.6.48 |
| *Publishers:* Edwin H. Morris & Co. Ltd. | | *Highest Position:* 3<br>*Weeks on Chart:* 10 |

*Recordings:*

| | | |
|---|---|---|
| Dick Haymes and The Song Spinners | 6/48 | Brunswick 03905 |
| Dick James | 6/48 | HMV BD.1206 |
| Mantovani and his Concert Orchestra (piano: Arthur Young) | 6/48 | Decca F.8906 |
| Joe Loss and his Orchestra (Elizabeth Batey) | 7/48 | HMV BD.6012 |
| Jack White and his Orchestra | 7/48 | Decca F.8938 |
| Sarah Vaughan | 8/48 | Parlophone R.3123 |
| Turner Layton | 8/48 | Columbia DB.2434 |
| Nat 'King' Cole | 12/48 | Capitol CL.13010★ |
| Red Ingle and The Unnatural Seven (Karen Tedder and Enrohtwah) [Parody titled 'Serutan Yob'] | 12/48 | Capitol CL.13015★ |
| Nat 'King' Cole | 1/49 | Capitol CL.13028★ |

## 116   HEARTBREAKER

| | | |
|---|---|---|
| *Composers:* Frank Capano, Max C. Freedman & Morty Berk | | *Date of Entry:* 17.6.48 |
| *Publishers:* Leeds Music Ltd. | | *Highest Position:* 2<br>*Weeks on Chart:* 17 |

*Recordings:*

| | | |
|---|---|---|
| Sam Browne with The Keynotes and Primo Scala's Accordion Band | 4/48 | Decca F.8872 |
| The Merry Melody Makers | 6/48 | HMV BD.1203 |
| Victor Silvester and his Ballroom Orchestra | 7/48 | Columbia FB.3409 |
| The Andrews Sisters | 7/48 | Brunswick 03916 |

## 117   I'M LOOKING OVER A FOUR-LEAF CLOVER

| | | |
|---|---|---|
| *Composers:* Mort Dixon & Harry Woods | | *Date of Entry:* 17.6.48/<br>Pos: 4/Wks: 12 |
| *Publishers:* Francis Day & Hunter Ltd. | | *Re-entry:* 16.9.48/<br>Pos: 7/Wks: 2 |

*Recordings:*

| | | |
|---|---|---|
| Russ Morgan and his Orchestra ftg Milt Herth, organ (The Ames Brothers & Ensemble) | 4/48 | Brunswick 03877 |
| Art Mooney and his Orchestra (Ensemble) | 4/48 | MGM.122 |
| The Merry Melody Makers | 6/48 | HMV BD.1203 |
| Turner Layton | 6/48 | Columbia DB.2412 |
| Victor Silvester and his Ballroom Orchestra | 7/48 | Columbia FB.3409 |
| Al Jolson (this version includes also the song 'Baby Face') | 11/49 | Brunswick 04376★ |

## 118   DANCE, BALLERINA, DANCE

| | | |
|---|---|---|
| *Composers:* Carl Sigman & Bob Russell | | *Date of Entry:* 24.6.48/<br>Pos: 2/Wks: 16 |
| *Publishers:* Peter Maurice Music Co. Ltd. | | *Re-entry:* 21.10.48/<br>Pos: 9/Wks: 1 |

*Recordings:*

| | | |
|---|---|---|
| Enric Madriguera and his Orchestra (Don Reid) | 3/48 | Brunswick 03853 |
| Bing Crosby with The Rhythmaires | 6/48 | Brunswick 03889 |
| Jack White and his Orchestra | 6/48 | Decca F.8905 |
| Jimmy Dorsey and his Orchestra (Bob Carroll) | 6/48 | MGM.134 |
| Vaughn Monroe and his Orchestra (Vaughn Monroe) | 7/48 | HMV BD.1208 |
| Lou Preager and his Orchestra (Paul Rich) | 8/48 | Columbia FB.3413 |
| Joe Loss and his Orchestra (Howard Jones) | 9/48 | HMV BD.6017 |
| Victor Silvester and his Ballroom Orchestra | 9/48 | Columbia FB.3419 |

## 119 TOOLIE OOLIE DOOLIE (The Yodel Polka)

| | | |
|---|---|---|
| *Composers*: Vaughn Horton & Arthur Beul | *Date of Entry*: 1.7.48/ | Pos: 10/Wks: 1 |
| *Publishers*: Southern Music Publishing Co. Ltd. | *Re-entry*: 15.7.48/ | Pos: 8/Wks: 4 |

*Recordings*:

| | | |
|---|---|---|
| Johnny Denis and his Ranchers with Primo Scala and his Accordion Band | 6/48 | Decca F.8888 |
| The Andrews Sisters | 6/48 | Brunswick 03903 |
| The Five Smith Brothers | 8/48 | Parlophone F.2303 |
| Oscar Rabin and his Band with Harry Davis (Diane) | 8/48 | Parlophone F.2304 |
| Lou Preager and his Orchestra (Rusty Hurren) | 9/48 | Columbia FB.3422★ |

## 120 WOODY WOODPECKER

| | | |
|---|---|---|
| *Composers*: George Tibbles & Ramey Idriss | *Date of Entry*: 29.7.48 | |
| *Publishers*: Leeds Music Ltd. | *Highest Position*: 2 | |
| | *Weeks on Chart*: 16 | |

*Recordings*:

| | | |
|---|---|---|
| Geraldo and his Orchestra (Doreen Lundy and George Evans) | 8/48 | Parlophone F.2305 |
| Anne Shelton with The Keynotes and Alan Dean (woodpecker effects) | 9/48 | Decca F.8951 |
| Lou Preager and his Orchestra (Eileen Orchard) | 9/48 | Columbia FB.3422 |
| Danny Kaye and The Andrews Sisters with The Harmonica Gentlemen | 10/48 | Brunswick 03981 |
| Kay Kyser and his Orchestra (Gloria Wood) | 11/48 | Columbia FB.3434 |
| Mel Blanc with The Sportsmen | 11/49 | Capitol CL.13175★ |

## 121 YOU CAN'T BE TRUE, DEAR

| | | |
|---|---|---|
| *Composers*: Hans Otten, Ken Griffin & Hal Cotton | *Date of Entry*: 12.8.48/ | Pos: 2/Wks: 18 |
| *Publishers*: Chappell & Co. Ltd. | *Re-entry*: 30.12.48/ | Pos: 7/Wks: 2 |

*Recordings*:

| | | |
|---|---|---|
| Vera Lynn | 5/48 | Decca F.8883 |
| Dick Haymes with The Song Spinners | 6/48 | Brunswick 03905 |
| Dick James | 6/48 | HMV BD.1206 |
| Jack White and his Orchestra | 7/48 | Decca F.8938 |
| Oscar Rabin and his Band with Harry Davis (Bob Dale) | 8/48 | Parlophone F.2304 |
| Jerry Wayne with Ken Griffin at the organ | 9/48 | Brunswick 03941 |
| Ken Griffin (organ) | 9/48 | Brunswick 03968 |
| Dolores Gray | 10/48 | Columbia DB.2451 |

## 122 RAMBLING ROSE

| | | |
|---|---|---|
| *Composers*: Joseph McCarthy & Joe Burke | *Date of Entry*: 26.8.48/ | Pos: 6/Wks: 3 |
| *Publishers*: Irwin Dash Music Co. Ltd. | *Re-entry*: 23.9.48/ | Pos: 6/Wks: 15 |

*Recordings*:

| | | |
|---|---|---|
| The Skyrockets Dance Orchestra cond. Woolf Phillips (Doreen Lundy) | 8/48 | HMV BD.6016 |
| Lou Preager and his Orchestra (Paul Rich) | 8/48 | Columbia FB.3413 |
| George Crow and The Blue Mariners | 8/48 | Decca F.8948 |
| Perry Como with The Satisfyers | 9/48 | HMV BD.1211 |
| Billy Thorburn's The Organ, the Dance Band and Me (Harry Kaye) | 9/48 | Parlophone F.2308 |
| Benny Lee and The Keynotes | 9/48 | Decca F.8953 |
| The Five Smith Brothers | 10/48 | Parlophone F.2314 |
| Bob Eberly with Russ Morgan and his Orchestra | 10/48 | Brunswick 03976 |

## 123 SO TIRED

| | | |
|---|---|---|
| *Composers*: Russ Morgan & Jack Stuart | *Date of Entry*: 9.9.48 | |
| *Publishers*: Campbell Connelly & Co. Ltd. | *Highest Position*: 1 | |
| | *Weeks on Chart*: 19 | |

*Recordings*:

| | | |
|---|---|---|
| Russ Morgan and his Orchestra (Russ Morgan) | 5/48 | Brunswick 03892 |
| Geraldo and his Orchestra (George Evans) | 10/48 | Parlophone F.2315 |
| Reggie Goff with Felix King, his piano, and his Orchestra | 10/48 | Decca F.8995 |
| Dorothy Squires | 11/48 | Columbia DB.2455 |
| Eric Winstone and his Orchestra (Leslie Howard) | 11/48 | MGM.156 |
| Josephine Bradley and her Ballroom Orchestra | 11/48 | Decca F.8999 |
| London Piano Accordeon Band (Phil Phillips) | 12/48 | Regal-Zon. MR.3813 |

## 124 MY HAPPINESS

| | | |
|---|---|---|
| *Composers*: Betty Peterson & Borney Bergantine | *Date of Entry*: 9.9.48 | |
| *Publishers*: Chappell & Co. Ltd. | *Highest Position*: 2 | |
| | *Weeks on Chart*: 28 | |

*Recordings*:

| | | |
|---|---|---|
| Jon and Sondra Steele | 7/48 | Brunswick 03933 |
| Ella Fitzgerald with The Song Spinners | 7/48 | Brunswick 03934 |
| Rita Williams | 10/48 | Columbia FB.3423 |
| The Pied Pipers | 12/48 | Capitol CL.13011 |
| The Dorothy Morrow Ensemble (Dorothy Morrow) | 12/48 | HMV BD.1227 |
| Geraldo and his Orchestra (Doreen Lundy) | 12/48 | Parlophone F.2327 |

(Note: This returned to the Sheet Music Charts in 1959 – see No. 997.)

## 125 | WHEN YOU'RE IN LOVE

*Composers*: Desmond O'Connor, Harold Fields & Dominic John, based on 'La Golondrina' by Narciso Serradell

*Date of Entry*: 30.9.48

*Publishers*: Bradbury Wood Ltd.

*Highest Position*: 2
*Weeks on Chart*: 29

*Recordings*:

| | | |
|---|---|---|
| Monte Rey | 8/48 | Columbia DB.2432 |
| Geraldo and his Orchestra (Archie Lewis) | 8/48 | Parlophone F.2306 |
| Reggie Goff | 8/48 | Decca F.8941 |
| Ronnie Ronalde | 8/48 | Decca F.8944 |
| Joe Loss and his Orchestra (Don Rivers and Howard Jones) | 9/48 | HMV BD.6018 |
| Frederick Ferrari | 12/48 | Parlophone R.3157 |
| Josef Locke | 3/49 | Columbia DB.2502 |
| Guy Lombardo and his Royal Canadians (Kenny Gardner) | 4/49 | Brunswick 04075 |

## 126 | LA VIE EN ROSE (Take me to your heart again)

*Composers*: R.S. Louiguy & Edith Piaf. English lyrics by Frank Eyton

*Date of Entry*: 14.10.48/ Pos: 9/Wks: 1
*Re-entry*: 4.11.48/ Pos 9/Wks: 1
*2nd re-entry*: 23.12.48/ Pos: 9/Wks: 1

*Publishers*: Noel Gay Music Co. Ltd.

*Recordings*:
(a) Titled 'La vie en rose'

| | | |
|---|---|---|
| Jean Cavall, Gracie Fields | 9/48 | HMV B.9677 |
| The Melachrino Strings | 11/48 | Decca F.9031 |
| Victor Young and his Singing Strings | 10/49 | HMV B.9805★ |
| Paul Weston and his Orchestra | 1/50 | Brunswick 04427★ |
| Felix Mendelssohn and his Hawaiian Serenaders | 8/50 | Capitol CL.13346★ |
| | 3/51 | Columbia DB.2822★ |

(b) Titled 'Take me to your heart again'

| | | |
|---|---|---|
| Rita Williams | 4/48 | Columbia FB.3390 |
| Geraldo and his Orchestra (Doreen Lundy) | 10/48 | Parlophone F.2315 |
| The London Piano Accordeon Band (Phil Phillips) | 12/48 | Regal Zonophone MR.3813 |
| Victor Silvester and his Ballroom Orchestra | 12/48 | Columbia FB.3446 |
| Frederick Ferrari | 12/48 | Parlophone R.3157 |
| Peter Yorke and his Orchestra | 2/49 | Columbia DB.2496★ |

(Note: Several French versions of the song were available from the Continental lists of the various record companies, notably the Edith Piaf recording on Columbia DC.415.)

## 127 | BUTTONS AND BOWS

*Composers*: Jay Livingston & Ray Evans

*Date of Entry*: 14.10.48

*Publishers*: Victoria Music Publishing Co. Ltd.

*Highest Position*: 1
*Weeks on Chart*: 26

*Recordings*:

| | | |
|---|---|---|
| Dinah Shore and her Happy Valley Boys | 9/48 | Columbia DB.2446 |
| Gracie Fields | 10/48 | Decca F.8996 |
| Betty Garrett | 11/48 | MGM.152 |
| Evelyn Knight | 11/48 | Brunswick 03989 |
| The Dinning Sisters | 12/48 | Capitol CL.13014 |
| Geraldo and his Orchestra (Doreen Lundy) | 12/48 | Parlophone F.2326 |
| Gene Autry | 1/49 | Regal-Zon. MR.3814 |

## 128 | OCTOBER TWILIGHT

*Composers*: Henry Hadley & Guy Wood

*Date of Entry*: 28.10.48

*Publishers*: Irwin Dash Music Co. Ltd.

*Highest Position*: 10
*Weeks on Chart*: 1

*Recordings*:

| | | |
|---|---|---|
| Joe Loss and his Orchestra (Howard Jones) | 8/48 | HMV BD.6015 |
| Geraldo and his Orchestra (Archie Lewis) | 8/48 | Parlophone F.2306 |
| Steve Conway | 9/48 | Columbia FB.3416 |
| Anne Shelton | 9/48 | Decca F.8950 |

## 129 | BALLIN' THE JACK

*Composers*: Chris Smith & Jim Burris

*Date of Entry*: 18.11.48/ Pos: 9/ Wks: 4
*Re-entry*: 13.1.49/ Pos: 9/Wks: 2

*Publishers*: Francis Day & Hunter Ltd.

(Note: Although originally published as far back as 1913, earlier recorded versions of this song could be counted on one hand. The version by Jelly Roll Morton was the only one to survive in the catalogues and was actually recorded in September 1939.)

*Recordings*:

| | | |
|---|---|---|
| Jelly Roll Morton's New Orleans Jazz Band | 10/41 | HMV B.9218 |
| Vic Lewis and his Jazzmen | 11/45 | Parlophone R.2986 |
| Danny Kaye | 5/48 | Brunswick 03888 |
| Lou Preager and his Orchestra (Paul Rich and The Sunnysiders) | 10/48 | Columbia FB.3426 |
| Jimmy McPartland and his Orchestra | 11/49 | Harmony A.1009★ |

## 130 MAYBE YOU'LL BE THERE

| | | |
|---|---|---|
| *Composers*: Rube Bloom & Sammy Gallop | | *Date of Entry*: 2.12.48/ Pos: 6/Wks: 5 |
| *Publishers*: Victoria Music Publishing Co. Ltd. | | *Re-entry*: 27.1.49/ Pos: 10/Wks: 1 |

*Recordings*:

| | | |
|---|---|---|
| Paul Carpenter | 6/47 | Decca F.8778 |
| Gordon Jenkins and his Orchestra (Charles La Vere & Chorus) | 10/48 | Brunswick 03973 |
| Steve Conway and The Conway Singers | 11/48 | Columbia FB.3439 |
| Billy Butterfield and his Orchestra (Pat O'Connor) | 1/49 | Capitol CL.13034 |
| Joe Loss and his Orchestra (Howard Jones and The Loss Chords) | 2/49 | HMV BD.6032 |

## 131 THE CUCKOO WALTZ

| | | |
|---|---|---|
| *Composer*: J.E. Jonasson. Lyrics added by Alan Stranks | | *Date of Entry*: 16.12.48/ Pos: 7/Wks: 2 |
| *Publishers*: Keith Prowse & Co. Ltd. | | *Re-entry*: 6.1.49/Pos: 4/Wks: 27 |
| | | *2nd re-entry*: 6.8.49/ Pos: 18/Wks: 2 |

*Recordings*:

| | | |
|---|---|---|
| The New Mayfair Dance Orchestra | 10/38 | HMV BD.590 |
| Harry Torrani (yodel and guitar) | 3/39 | Regal Zonophone MR.2982 |
| William Star (accordion) | 8/48 | Parlophone F.3379 |
| Ken Griffin (organ) | 9/48 | Brunswick 03968 |
| Josephine Bradley and her Ballroom Orchestra | 11/48 | Decca F.9009 |
| Joe Loss and his Orchestra (Howard Jones) | 12/48 | HMV BD.6027 |
| The London Piano Accordeon Band (Phil Phillips) | 2/49 | Regal Zonophone MR.3816 |
| Toralf Tollefsen (accordion) | 2/49 | Columbia FB.3462 |
| Sydney Thompson and his Old-Tyme Dance Orchestra | 12/49 | Parlophone R.3240★ |
| Harry Davidson and his Orchestra | 3/51 | Columbia DX.1725★ |

## 132 CUANTO LE GUSTA

| | | |
|---|---|---|
| *Composers*: Gabriel Ruiz & Ray Gilbert | | *Date of Entry*: 16.12.48/ Pos: 10/Wks: 1 |
| *Publishers*: Southern Music Publishing Co. Ltd. | | *Re-entry*: 30.12.48/ Pos: 4/Wks: 11 |

*Recordings*:

| | | |
|---|---|---|
| Carmen Miranda and The Andrews Sisters | 7/48 | Brunswick 03917 |
| Jack Smith and The Clark Sisters | 12/48 | Capitol CL.13004 |
| Xavier Cugat and his Orchestra (The Trio) | 12/48 | Columbia DB.2473 |
| Joe Loss and his Orchestra (Elizabeth Batey and The Loss Chords) | 12/48 | HMV BD.6030 |
| Edmundo Ros and his Rumba Band (Edmundo Ros) [played as a March] | 12/48 | Decca F.9046 |

# 1949

The Top Ten, still supplied by the Wholesale Music Distributors' Association, continued until Thursday, 19 May. Then the Music Publishers' Association took over with a chart compiled under the auspices of its Popular Publishers' Committee, and this chart, increased in size, became the memorable Top Twenty and first appeared for Saturday, 28 May. For some unknown reason there was no No. 20 listed for 2 July. On 4 January the BBC Light Programme first broadcast a series called 'Hit Parade' which went out on Tuesdays at 8 p.m. for half an hour, beginning with Geraldo and his Orchestra (shades of 1936's 'The Music Shop') and featuring Anne Shelton, Denny Dennis and The Mitchell Men. Later the Mitchell Men became the George Mitchell Choir, Bruce Trent replaced Denny Dennis and, on 12 July, Cyril Stapleton and his Orchestra took over the bandstand. During the programme, ten songs were played including the top seven in the chart, six of which were in no special order but the No. 1 song had the final place on the show. This was the only series of the programme and lasted for most of the year. In the meantime Radio Luxembourg's Geoffrey Everitt dreamed up the Top Twenty programme despite opposition from practically everyone involved including the station's anchor man, Teddy Johnson. The feeling was that no one would want to listen to the same songs they had been listening to all week – but Everitt was right, so right that the Top Twenty show soon became the station's biggest audience puller. At the

| | MOST WEEKS ON THE CHARTS TOP SIX | |
|---|---|---|
| Pos | | Wks |
| 1 | How can you buy Killarney? | 35 |
| 2 | Forever and ever | 32 |
| 3 | Twelfth Street rag | 30 |
| 4 | The cuckoo waltz | 29 |
| 5 | The echo told me a lie | 26 |
| 6 | Lavender blue | 19 |

same time, Teddy Johnson's other very popular disc shows were beginning to draw listeners away from the BBC's output, especially on Sundays, so it must have been pleasing to the BBC that its top variety show, 'Variety Bandbox', should have been directly responsible for producing one of the big hits of the year, *Confidentially*. Reg Dixon, the programme's resident comic, wrote this song and sang it to close his act – and then had to repeat it again and again over the weeks. Another top song, *The Harry Lime theme*, was aired during a BBC spoof thriller, 'The Night of the 27th', and ceremonially 'broken' as the character was heartily sick of it. *Twelfth Street rag* was revived via the Pee Wee Hunt Orchestra recording and seemed to observers to be broadcast continually. Not so, of course, but it did manage to squeeze into an episode of 'Mrs Dale's Diary'. Perhaps it is also surprising to note that *Forever and ever* took no less than 23 weeks to reach No. 1. Billy Cotton and his Band began a Sunday morning series on the Light Programme in February and this 12-week series turned out to be the forerunner to the legendary 'Band Show' series. Half-hour long programmes of Community Singing began on 18 April at 6.30 p.m. again on the Light Programme. Conducted by Glyn Jones and introduced by John Rorke, they were eventually to inspire Parlophone to produce some recordings of the same combination under the title The London Community Singers – see Songs Nos. 148, 175 and 255. Two days after this series began, on 20 April, a British warship, HMS Amethyst, was fired on by the Chinese communist forces in the Yangtse River and this incident coincided with *On a slow boat to China*'s last appearance on the charts. Fearful of public reaction, the BBC immediately banned the song from its programmes. The composer of *Goodnight, Irene*, 64-year-old Huddie Ledbetter, died in December – just six months before the song became a chart entry in America. Meanwhile, here in Britain in October, Decca had launched the London label which, over the ensuing years, was to become a collector's dream. On 8 November a new radio series began which featured Ray Martin and his Orchestra with a young vocalist by the name of Jimmy Young – this, remember, was almost two years before his success with *Too young*. Jimmy's first song on the programme? *Is it too late*? For Jimmy it certainly was not.

# SONG CHARTS

## 133 | ON A SLOW BOAT TO CHINA

*Composer*: Frank Loesser

*Publishers*: Edwin H. Morris & Co. Ltd.

*Date of Entry*: 6.1.49

*Highest Position*: 1
*Weeks on Chart*: 16

*Recordings*:

| | | |
|---|---|---|
| The Merry Macs with The Squadronaires dir. Jimmy Miller | 12/48 | Decca F.9034 |
| Benny Goodman and his Orchestra (Al Hendrickson) | 12/48 | Capitol CL.13003 |
| Kay Kyser and his Orchestra (Harry Babbitt and Gloria Wood) | 1/49 | Columbia FB.3450 |
| Freddy Martin and his Orchestra (Glenn Hughes and The Martin Men) | 1/49 | HMV B.9716 |
| Larry Clinton and his Orchestra (Helen Lee and The Dipsy Doodlers) | 1/49 | Brunswick 04017 |
| Victor Silvester and his Ballroom Orchestra | 2/49 | Columbia FB.3457 |
| Geraldo and his Orchestra (Doreen Lundy) | 2/49 | Parlophone F.2333 |
| Billy Thorburn's The Organ, the Dance Band and Me (Harry Kaye) | 3/49 | Parlophone F.2345 |
| Maurice Chevalier | 3/49 | Decca F.9111 |

## 134 | THE HEART OF LOCH LOMOND

*Composers*: Art Noel, Fats Fisher & Charlie Forsythe

*Publishers*: Unit Music Publishing Co.

*Date of Entry*: 20.1.49

*Highest Position*: 2
*Weeks on Chart*: 16

*Recordings*:

| | | |
|---|---|---|
| Billy Thorburn's The Organ, the Dance Band and Me (Harry Kaye) | 9/48 | Parlophone F.2308 |
| The Skyrockets Dance Orchestra dir. Woolf Phillips (Sally Douglas) | 10/48 | HMV BD.6023 |
| Bill Johnson | 10/48 | Columbia DB.2450 |
| Anne Shelton | 2/49 | Decca F.9100 |
| The Star Dusters with Sy Oliver and his Orchestra | 7/49 | Brunswick 04224★ |
| Robert Wilson | 11/49 | HMV B.9839★ |

## 135 | THE MAHARAJAH OF MAGADOR

*Composers*: John Loeb & Lewis Harris

*Publishers*: Chappell & Co. Ltd.

*Date of Entry*: 27.1.49

*Highest Position*: 5
*Weeks on Chart*: 9

*Recordings*:

| | | |
|---|---|---|
| Vaughn Monroe and his Orchestra (Ziggy Talent) | 12/48 | HMV BD.6031 |
| The Squadronaires dir. Jimmy Miller (Jimmy Miller and The Quads) | 1/49 | Decca F.9067 |
| Ray Ellington and his Quartet (Ray Ellington Glee Club) | 3/49 | Parlophone R.3177 |
| Edmundo Ros and his Rumba Band (Edmundo Ros) | 3/49 | Decca F.9108 |

## 136 | A LITTLE BIRD TOLD ME

*Composer*: Harvey O. Brooks

*Publishers*: Noel Gay Music Co. Ltd.

*Date of Entry*: 3.2.49

*Highest Position*: 9
*Weeks on Chart*: 3

*Recordings*:

| | | |
|---|---|---|
| Evelyn Knight and The Star Dusters | 1/49 | Brunswick 04015 |
| Blue Lu Barker | 1/49 | Capitol CL.13033 |
| The Sentimentalists presented by Billy Cotton | 1/49 | Decca F.9053 |
| Joe Loss and his Orchestra (Elizabeth Batey) | 3/49 | HMV BD.6037★ |
| Jimmy Leach and his New Organolians (Alan Dean) | 3/49 | Columbia FB.3467★ |
| Oscar Rabin and his Band (Marion Davis) | 3/49 | Parlophone F.2344★ |

## 137 | FAR AWAY PLACES

| | | |
|---|---|---|
| *Composers*: Joan Whitney & Alex Kramer | *Date of Entry*: 24.2.49 | |
| *Publishers*: Leeds Music Ltd. | *Highest Position*: 1 | |
| | *Weeks on Chart*: 22 | |

*Recordings*:

| | | |
|---|---|---|
| Margaret Whiting with The Crew Chiefs | 1/49 | Capitol CL.13037 |
| The Sentimentalists presented by Billy Cotton | 1/49 | Decca F.9071 |
| Dinah Shore with Two in Accord | 2/49 | Columbia DB.2494 |
| Stanley Black and his Orchestra | 2/49 | Decca F.9080 |
| Bing Crosby with The Ken Darby Choir | 2/49 | Brunswick 04035 |
| Joe Loss and his Orchestra (Howard Jones) | 3/49 | HMV BD.6036 |
| The Radio Revellers | 3/49 | Columbia FB.3465 |
| Oscar Rabin and his Band (Bob Dale) | 4/49 | Parlophone F.2348 |
| Donald Peers | 4/49 | HMV B.9763 |
| Perry Como | 5/49 | HMV BD.1242 |

## 138 | ON THE 5.45

| | | |
|---|---|---|
| *Composer*: Mark Warren | *Date of Entry*: 3.3.49 | |
| *Publishers*: Strauss–Miller Music Co. Ltd. | *Highest Position*: 5 | |
| | *Weeks on Chart*: 15 | |

*Recordings*:

| | | |
|---|---|---|
| Joy Nichols and Benny Lee with The Keynotes | 3/49 | Decca F.9094 |
| Charlie Chester and The Singing Silhouettes | 5/49 | Parlophone R.3196 |
| Lou Preager and his Orchestra (Rusty Hurren) | 5/49 | Columbia FB.3486 |
| Donald Peers | 5/49 | HMV B.9772 |

## 139 | TWELFTH STREET RAG

| | | |
|---|---|---|
| *Composers*: Euday L. Bowman | *Date of Entry*: 17.3.49/ | |
| | Pos: 1/Wks: 29 | |
| *Publishers*: Chappell & Co. Ltd. | *Re-entry*: 29.10.49/ | |
| | Pos: 20/Wks: 1 | |

(Note: This old song owed its revival to the Pee Wee Hunt version issued in December 1948 which was also a massive hit in Europe. Besides the Fats Waller version listed first below, three other early recordings still survived in the catalogues: Sol Hoopii and his Novelty Five [Decca F. 7008]. Milt Herth (organ) [Brunswick 02294] and Duke Ellington and his Orchestra [Brunswick 02307])

*Other recordings*:

| | | |
|---|---|---|
| Thomas 'Fats' Waller | 11/35 | HMV BD.262 |
| Andy Kirk and his Clouds of Joy | 8/44 | Brunswick 03525 |
| The Milt Herth Trio | 10/48 | Brunswick 03978 |
| Pee Wee Hunt and his Orchestra | 12/48 | Capitol CL.13002 |
| Harry Roy and his Band | 4/49 | Parlophone F.2350 |
| Donald Peers (lyrics by Andy Razaf) | 4/49 | HMV B.9763 |
| Morton Gould and his Orchestra | 5/49 | Columbia DB.2524 |
| Victor Silvester and his Ballroom Orchestra | 5/49 | Columbia FB.3488 |
| Toralf Tollefsen (accordion) | 7/49 | Columbia FB.3497 |

## 140 | THE CRYSTAL GAZER

| | | |
|---|---|---|
| *Composer*: Frank Petch | *Date of Entry*: 24.3.49 | |
| *Publishers*: Irwin Dash Music Co. Ltd. | *Highest Position*: 10 | |
| | *Weeks on Chart*: 2 | |

*Recordings*:

| | | |
|---|---|---|
| Reggie Goff with The Stapletones | 1/49 | Decca F.9072 |
| Joe Loss and his Orchestra (Howard Jones) | 3/49 | HMV BD.6037 |
| Geraldo and his Orchestra (Denny Vaughan) | 3/49 | Parlophone F.2343 |
| Eric Winstone and his Orchestra (Julie Dawn) | 4/49 | MGM.178★ |

## 141 POWDER YOUR FACE WITH SUNSHINE (Smile! Smile! Smile!)

Composers: Stanley Rochinski & Carmen Lombardo

Date of Entry: 31.3.49

Publishers: Chappell & Co. Ltd.

Highest Position: 3
Weeks on Chart: 17

Recordings:

| | | |
|---|---|---|
| Primo Scala and his Banjo and Accordion Band (The Keynotes) | 1/49 | Decca F.9073 |
| Evelyn Knight and The Star Dusters | 2/49 | Brunswick 04033 |
| Dean Martin | 3/49 | Capitol CL.13058 |
| Victor Silvester and his Ballroom Orchestra | 4/49 | Columbia FB.3476 |
| Doris Day and Buddy Clark | 4/49 | Columbia DB.2508 |
| Blue Barron and his Orchestra (Ensemble) | 4/49 | MGM.185 |
| Donald Peers | 4/49 | HMV B.9764 |
| Joe Loss and his Orchestra (Howard Jones) | 5/49 | HMV BD.6043 |

## 142 IN A SHADY NOOK (by a babbling brook)

Composers: E.G. Nelson & Harry Pease

Date of Entry: 7.4.49

Publishers: Keith Prowse Music Publishing Co. Ltd.

Highest Position: 3
Weeks on Chart: 14

Recordings:

| | | |
|---|---|---|
| Donald Peers | 4/44 | Decca F.8418 |
| Primo Scala and his Accordion Band (The Keynotes) | 5/49 | Decca F.9139 |
| Victor Silvester and his Ballroom Orchestra | 6/49 | Columbia FB.3494 |
| Charlie Chester with The Singing Silhouettes and Edwina Carol | 7/49 | Parlophone R.3204 |

## 143 LAVENDER BLUE

Composers: Larry Morey & Eliot Daniel

Date of Entry: 14.4.49

Publishers: Sun Music Publishing Co. Ltd.

Highest Position: 1
Weeks on Chart: 25

Recordings:

| | | |
|---|---|---|
| Burl Ives | 3/49 | Brunswick 04066 |
| Jack Smith and The Clark Sisters | 3/49 | Capitol CL.13072 |
| Vera Lynn | 3/49 | Decca F.9114 |
| Joe Loss and his Orchestra (Elizabeth Batey) | 5/49 | HMV BD.6043 |
| Donald Peers | 5/49 | HMV B.9772 |
| Dinah Shore | 5/49 | Columbia DB.2529 |
| Geraldo and his Orchestra (Doreen Lundy) | 6/49 | Parlophone F.2359 |

## 144 PUT 'EM IN A BOX (Tie 'em with a ribbon)

Composers: Jule Styne & Sammy Cahn

Date of Entry: 21.4.49/
Pos: 9/Wks: 3

Publishers: Campbell Connelly & Co. Ltd.

Re-entry: 28.5.49/
Pos: 9/Wks: 5
2nd re-entry: 9.7.49/
Pos: 14/Wks: 1
3rd re-entry: 30.7.49/
Pos: 16/Wks: 1
4th re-entry: 13.8.49/
Pos: 15/Wks: 3

Recordings:

| | | |
|---|---|---|
| Doris Day | 2/49 | Columbia DB.2493 |
| Geraldo and his Orchestra (Doreen Lundy) | 2/49 | Parlophone F.2334 |
| Nat 'King' Cole Trio (Nat 'King' Cole) | 2/49 | Capitol CL.13044 |
| Danny Kaye and The Andrews Sisters with The Harmonica Gentlemen | 2/49 | Brunswick 04032 |
| Joe Loss and his Orchestra (Elizabeth Batey) | 4/49 | HMV BD.6042 |

## 145 HOW CAN YOU BUY KILLARNEY?

Composers: Hamilton Kennedy, Ted Steels, Freddie Grant (Grundland) & Gerard Morrison

Date of Entry: 28.4.49/
Pos: 7/Wks: 3

Publishers: Peter Maurice Music Co. Ltd.

Re-entry: 28.5.49/
Pos: 4/Wks: 33

Recordings:

| | | |
|---|---|---|
| Lee Lawrence | 2/49 | Decca F.9090 |
| Denis Martin | 3/49 | Parlophone R.3180 |
| Jack Simpson and his Sextet (Dave Kydd) | 4/49 | Parlophone F.2346 |
| Clive Wayne | 8/49 | HMV B.9802 |
| Josephine Bradley and her Ballroom Orchestra | 10/49 | Decca F.9252 |
| Josef Locke | 11/49 | Columbia DB.2604 |
| Bing Crosby | 1/50 | Brunswick 04425 |

## 146 | A STRAWBERRY MOON (in a blueberry sky)

| Composers: Bob Hilliard & Sammy Mysels | Date of Entry: 12.5.49 |
|---|---|
| Publishers: Yale Music Corporation Ltd. | Highest Position: 6 Weeks on Chart: 16 |

Recordings:

| | | |
|---|---|---|
| Joy Nichols and Benny Lee with The Keynotes | 3/49 | Decca F.9105 |
| Jack Smith and The Clark Sisters | 3/49 | Capitol CL.13072 |
| Donald Peers | 5/49 | HMV B.9773 |
| Blue Barron and his Orchestra (Clyde Burke & Dolores Hawkins) | 5/49 | MGM.195 |
| Geraldo and his Orchestra (Neville Williams & Chorus) | 6/49 | Parlophone F.2363 |
| Bob and Alf Pearson | 8/49 | Parlophone F.2371 |

## 147 | RED ROSES FOR A BLUE LADY

| Composers: Sid Tepper & Roy Brodsky | Date of Entry: 12.5.49 |
|---|---|
| Publishers: Lawrence Wright Music Co. Ltd. | Highest Position: 2 Weeks on Chart: 22 |

Recordings:

| | | |
|---|---|---|
| Guy Lombardo and his Royal Canadians (Don Rodney) | 5/49 | Brunswick 04078 |
| Benny Lee and The Keynotes | 5/49 | Decca F.9126 |
| Vaughn Monroe and his Orchestra (Vaughn Monroe and The Moon Men) | 6/49 | HMV BD.1247 |
| Geraldo and his Orchestra (Denny Vaughan) | 6/49 | Parlophone F.2363 |
| Paul Adam and his Mayfair Music (Frank Holmes and Vocal Quartette) | 7/49 | Regal Zonophone MR.3821 |
| Bob and Alf Pearson | 7/49 | Parlophone F.2368 |
| Victor Silvester and his Ballroom Orchestra | 7/49 | Columbia FB.3501 |

## 148 | THE WEDDING OF LILLI MARLENE

| Composers: Tommie Connor & Johnny Reine | Date of Entry: 19.5.49 |
|---|---|
| Publishers: Box & Cox Publications Ltd. | Highest Position: 1 Weeks on Chart: 23 |

(Note: The spelling of the name 'Lilli' in the title has caused some confusion, which is compounded on the sheet music. The front cover of the song shows it spelled as 'Lili', while on the back, the name is spelled as 'Lilli'.)

Recordings:

| | | |
|---|---|---|
| Anne Shelton with The Wardour Singers | 5/49 | Decca F.9148 |
| Jack Simpson and his Sextet | 6/49 | Parlophone F.2360 |
| Steve Conway | 6/49 | Columbia FB.3500 |
| Joe Loss and his Orchestra (Howard Jones) | 6/49 | HMV BD.6047 |
| Lou Preager and his Orchestra (Paul Rich) | 7/49 | Columbia FB.3506 |
| Eric Winstone and his Orchestra (Leslie Howard) | 7/49 | MGM.218 |
| John Rorke with The London Community Singers cond. Glyn Jones | 8/49 | Parlophone F.2374 |
| The Andrews Sisters | 8/49 | Brunswick 04259 |
| Gordon MacRae and The Starlighters | 8/49 | Capitol CL.13144 |

## 149 | PUT YOUR SHOES ON, LUCY

| Composer: Hank Fort | Date of Entry: 28.5.49 |
|---|---|
| Publishers: Noel Gay Music Co. Ltd. | Highest Position: 5 Weeks on Chart: 15 |

Recordings:

| | | |
|---|---|---|
| Anne Shelton with The Keynotes | 3/49 | Decca F.9102 |
| Russ Morgan and his Orchestra (Russ Morgan and The Rhythmaires) | 5/49 | Brunswick 04086 |
| The Five Smith Brothers | 6/49 | Parlophone F.2361 |
| Paul Adam and his Mayfair Music (Bette Roberts) | 6/49 | Regal Zonophone MR.3820 |
| Petula Clark | 6/49 | Columbia DB.2538 |
| Gracie Fields | 6/49 | Decca F.9166 |
| The Fontane Sisters | 7/49 | HMV BD.1253 |
| Oscar Rabin and his Band with Harry Davis (Marion Davis) | 7/49 | Parlophone F.2369 |

## 150 | IT'S MAGIC

| | | |
|---|---|---|
| *Composers*: Jule Styne & Sammy Cahn | | *Date of Entry*: 28.5.49/ Pos: 13/Wks: 5 |
| *Publishers*: Campbell Connelly & Co. Ltd. | | *Re-entry*: 30.7.49/ Pos: 17/Wks: 3 |
| | | *2nd re-entry*: 3.9.49/ Pos: 19/Wks: 1 |

*Recordings*:

| | | |
|---|---|---|
| Doris Day | 2/49 | Columbia DB.2493 |
| Geraldo and his Orchestra (Denny Vaughan) | 2/49 | Parlophone F.2334 |
| Sarah Vaughan | 2/49 | Parlophone R.3170 |
| Tony Martin | 2/49 | HMV B.9726 |
| Gordon MacRae | 2/49 | Capitol CL.13046 |
| Dick Haymes | 2/49 | Brunswick 03977 |
| Victor Silvester and his Ballroom Orchestra | 3/49 | Columbia FB.3466 |
| Ambrose and his Orchestra (Ray Burns) | 3/49 | Decca F.9112 |
| The Buddy Kaye Quintet (Artie Malvin and The Tunetimers) | 5/49 | MGM.197 |

## 151 | CANDY KISSES

| | |
|---|---|
| *Composer*: George Morgan | *Date of Entry*: 28.5.49 |
| *Publishers*: Chappell & Co. Ltd. | *Highest Position*: 5 *Weeks on Chart*: 17 |

*Recordings*:

| | | |
|---|---|---|
| Danny Kaye with The Regalaires | 5/49 | Brunswick 04087 |
| George Morgan | 5/49 | Columbia DB.2536 |
| Johnny Mercer with The Starlighters | 5/49 | Capitol CL.13106 |
| Bob Mallin | 6/49 | Parlophone F.2362 |
| The Fontane Sisters | 7/49 | HMV BD.1253 |
| Eddie Kirk | 7/49 | Capitol CL.13122 |
| Joe Loss and his Orchestra (Irene Miller) | 9/49 | HMV BD.6051 |

## 152 | BEHIND THE CLOUDS
### (are crowds and crowds of sunbeams)

| | |
|---|---|
| *Composers*: Benny Davis & B.G. de Sylva | *Date of Entry*: 28.5.49/ Pos: 15/Wks: 5 |
| *Publishers*: B. Feldman & Co. Ltd. | *Re-entry*: 16.7.49/ Pos: 15/Wks: 2 |

*Recordings*:

| | | |
|---|---|---|
| Joe Loss and his Orchestra (Irene Miller, Elizabeth Batey and Howard Jones) | 6/49 | HMV BD.6047 |
| Billy Thorburn's The Organ, the Dance Band and Me (Harry Kaye) | 9/49 | Parlophone F.2378 |

## 153 | 'A' – YOU'RE ADORABLE
### (The Alphabet Song)

| | |
|---|---|
| *Composers*: Buddy Kaye, Fred Wise & Sidney Lippman | *Date of Entry*: 28.5.49/ Pos: 4/Wks: 22 |
| *Publishers*: Campbell Connelly & Co. Ltd. | *Re-entry*: 5.11.49/ Pos: 20/Wks: 1 |

*Recordings*:

| | | |
|---|---|---|
| Larry Fotine and his Orchestra (Maralyn Marsh and Johnny Goodfellow) | 4/49 | Brunswick 04074 |
| Jo Stafford and Gordon MacRae | 5/49 | Capitol CL.13089 |
| The Buddy Kaye Quintet (Artie Malvin) | 5/49 | MGM.197 |
| Perry Como and The Fontane Sisters | 6/49 | HMV BD.1250 |
| Billy Thorburn's The Organ, the Dance Band and Me (Harry Kaye) | 7/49 | Parlophone F.2366 |
| Jimmy Leach and his New Organolians with vocal | 7/49 | Columbia FB.3505 |
| Josephine Bradley and her Ballroom Orchestra | 10/49 | Decca F.9253 |
| Red Ingle and The Natural Seven (Red Ingle and Karen Tedder) [Titled "A' – you're a-dopey-gal'] | 10/49 | Capitol CL.13166 |

## 154 | FOREVER AND EVER

| | |
|---|---|
| *Composers*: Franz Winkler & Malia Rosa | *Date of Entry*: 28.5.49 |
| *Publishers*: Francis Day & Hunter Ltd. | *Highest Position*: 1 *Weeks on Chart*: 42 |

*Recordings*:

| | | |
|---|---|---|
| The Franz Winkler Quartet [Titled 'Fliege mit mir in die Heimat'] | 7/48 | Decca C.16006 |
| Gracie Fields with The Wardour Singers | 11/48 | Decca F.9031 |
| Russ Morgan and his Orchestra (The Skylarks) with organ [Some 78s titled 'Forever and Forever'] | 3/49 | Brunswick 04064 |
| Margaret Whiting [Titled on label 'Forever and Forever'] | 4/49 | Capitol CL.13078 |
| Dinah Shore with Male Quartet | 5/49 | Columbia DB.2529 |
| Perry Como | 6/49 | HMV BD.1250 |
| Bob and Alf Pearson | 7/49 | Parlophone F.2368 |

## 155 | IT HAPPENED IN ADANO

| | |
|---|---|
| *Composers*: Don Pelosi & Harold Fields | *Date of Entry*: 28.5.49 |
| *Publishers*: Peter Maurice Music Co. Ltd. | *Highest Position*: 19 *Weeks on Chart*: 1 |

*Recordings*:

| | | |
|---|---|---|
| Ambrose and his Orchestra (Ray Burns) | 4/49 | Decca F.9116 |
| Donald Peers | 5/49 | HMV B.9773 |
| Anne Shelton | 6/49 | Decca F.9153★ |

## 156 | CLOPIN CLOPANT

**Composers:** Bruno Coquatrix, Pierre Dudan & Kermit Goell

**Date of Entry:** 28.5.49

**Publishers:** Peter Maurice Music Co. Ltd.

**Highest Position:** 20
**Weeks on Chart:** 1

Recordings:

| | | |
|---|---|---|
| Jean Cavall [In French & English] | 3/49 | HMV B.9744 |
| Georges Guetary | 4/49 | Columbia DB.2513 |
| Ambrose and his Orchestra (Ray Burns and Nadia Doré) [In French & English] | 4/49 | Decca F.9116 |
| Joe Loss and his Orchestra (Howard Jones) | 5/49 | HMV BD.6044 |
| Victor Silvester and his Ballroom Orchestra | 5/49 | Columbia FB.3489 |
| Billy Ternent and his Orchestra (Tom Henry) | 7/49 | Harmony A.1005★ |
| The Melachrino Strings | 12/49 | HMV B.9843★ |

## 157 | I'LL ALWAYS LOVE YOU

**Composers:** Frank Eyton & Noel Gay

**Date of Entry:** 4.6.49

**Publishers:** Clover Music Co. Ltd.

**Highest Position:** 16
**Weeks on Chart:** 9

Recordings:

| | | |
|---|---|---|
| The Sentimentalists presented by Billy Cotton | 10/46 | Decca F.8696 |
| Victor Silvester and his Ballroom Orchestra | 7/49 | Columbia FB.3502 |
| Petula Clark | 7/49 | Columbia DB.2551 |
| Billy Thorburn's The Organ, the Dance Band and Me (Harry Kaye) | 9/49 | Parlophone F.2378★ |
| Denny Dennis with The Keynotes | 9/49 | Decca F.9220★ |

## 158 | TILL ALL OUR DREAMS COME TRUE

**Composers:** H.C. Bonocini & Desmond O'Connor

**Date of Entry:** 4.6.49

**Publishers:** Lawrence Wright Music Co. Ltd.

**Highest Position:** 20
**Weeks on Chart:** 1

Recordings:

| | | |
|---|---|---|
| Joe Loss and his Orchestra (Howard Jones and David Griffiths) | 5/49 | HMV BD.6044 |
| Rita Williams | 5/49 | Columbia FB.3484 |
| Archie Lewis with The Luton Girls' Choir cond. Arthur E. Davies | 6/49 | Parlophone R.3202 |
| Dick James with The George Mitchell Choir | 6/49 | Decca F.9163 |

## 159 | CLANCY LOWERED THE BOOM

**Composers:** Hy Heath & Johnny Lange

**Date of Entry:** 11.6.49/
Pos: 16/Wks: 3
**Re-entry:** 9.7.49/
Pos: 15/Wks: 2
**2nd re-entry:** 30.7.49/
Pos: 17/Wks: 2

**Publishers:** Leeds Music Ltd.

Recordings:

| | | |
|---|---|---|
| Dan Dailey and The Andrews Sisters | 5/49 | Brunswick 04088 |
| Donald Peers | 6/49 | HMV B.9787 |
| Bob Mallin | 6/49 | Parlophone F.2362 |
| The Korn Kobblers cond. Stanley Fritts (Frank Saunders and The Heathertones) | 6/49 | MGM.208 |
| Petula Clark | 7/49 | Columbia DB.2551 |

## 160 | AGAIN

**Composers:** Dorcas Cochran & Lionel Newman

**Date of Entry:** 18.6.49

**Publishers:** Francis Day & Hunter Ltd.

**Highest Position:** 2
**Weeks on Chart:** 23

Recordings:

| | | |
|---|---|---|
| Vera Lynn | 3/49 | Decca F.9103 |
| Gordon Jenkins and his Orchestra (Joe Graydon and Chorus) | 5/49 | Brunswick 04082 |
| Mel Torme | 5/49 | Capitol CL.13094 |
| Clive Wayne | 8/49 | HMV B.9802 |
| Geraldo and his Orchestra (Eve Boswell) | 8/49 | Parlophone F.2376 |
| Roberto Inglez and his Orchestra | 8/49 | Parlophone R.3213 |
| Victor Silvester and his Ballroom Orchestra | 8/49 | Columbia FB.3508 |
| Doris Day | 8/49 | Columbia DB.2561 |

## 161 | RIDERS IN THE SKY (A Cowboy Legend)

**Composer:** Stan Jones

**Date of Entry:** 2.7.49

**Publishers:** Edwin H. Morris & Co. Ltd.

**Highest Position:** 1
**Weeks on Chart:** 22

Recordings:

| | | |
|---|---|---|
| Vaughn Monroe and his Orchestra (Vaughn Monroe and the Quartette) | 6/49 | HMV BD.1247 |
| Bing Crosby with the Ken Darby Singers | 6/49 | Brunswick 04098 |
| Peggy Lee with the Jud Conlon Singers | 6/49 | Capitol CL.13111 |
| Derry Falligant | 6/49 | MGM.206 |
| Burl Ives | 6/49 | Columbia DB.2555 |
| Hugh Diamond with Lew Stone and his Orchestra | 9/49 | Decca F.9210 |
| Spike Jones and his City Slickers (I.W. Harper, Sir Frederick Gas and The Sons of The Sons of the Pioneers) | 10/49 | HMV B.9816 |
| Mickey Katz and his Orchestra (Mickey Katz) [Titled 'Borscht Riders in the Sky'] | 10/51 | Capitol CL.13605★ |

## 162 | THE ECHO TOLD ME A LIE

| | |
|---|---|
| Composers: Howard Barnes, Harold Fields, Dominic John & Peter Jack | Date of Entry: 2.7.49 |
| Publishers: Chappell & Co. Ltd. | Highest Position: 8<br>Weeks on Chart: 26 |

Recordings:

| | | |
|---|---|---|
| Primo Scala and his Banjo and Accordion Band (The Keynotes) | 5/49 | Decca F.9133 |
| Paul Adam and his Mayfair Music (Bette Roberts) | 6/49 | Regal Zonophone MR.3820 |
| Geraldo and his Orchestra (Denny Vaughan and Vocal Group) | 7/49 | Parlophone F.2365 |
| Allan Jones | 10/49 | HMV B.9828 |

## 163 | BRUSH THOSE TEARS FROM YOUR EYES

| | |
|---|---|
| Composers: Oakley Haldeman, Al Trace & Jimmy Lee | Date of Entry: 2.7.49 |
| Publishers: Leeds Music Ltd. | Highest Position: 18<br>Weeks on Chart: 1 |

Recordings:

| | | |
|---|---|---|
| Evelyn Knight with The Star Dusters | 1/49 | Brunswick 04015 |
| Cyril Stapleton and his Orchestra (The Stapletones) | 1/49 | Decca F.9055 |
| Foy Willing and his Riders of the Purple Sage (Foy Willing & Trio) | 1/49 | Capitol CL.13035 |
| Lou Preager and his Orchestra (Rusty Hurren) | 2/49 | Columbia FB.3460 |
| Buddy Clark with The Modernaires and The Skylarks | 5/49 | Columbia DB.2525 |
| Billy Ternent and his Orchestra (Eve Beynon) | 7/49 | Harmony A.1006 |

## 164 | CARELESS HANDS

| | |
|---|---|
| Composers: Bob Hilliard & Carl Sigman | Date of Entry: 16.7.49 |
| Publishers: Edwin H. Morris & Co. Ltd. | Highest Position: 4<br>Weeks on Chart: 24 |

Recordings:

| | | |
|---|---|---|
| Mel Torme | 5/49 | Capitol CL.13094 |
| 'Sheriff' Johnny Denis and his Ranchers with The Cactus Kids | 5/49 | Decca F.9124 |
| Arthur 'Guitar Boogie' Smith | 5/49 | MGM.191 |
| Bob and Jeanne | 5/49 | Brunswick 04089 |
| Bing Crosby with The Ken Darby Singers | 6/49 | Brunswick 04098 |
| Tex Ritter | 7/49 | Capitol CL.13120 |
| Swing and Sway with Sammy Kaye (Don Cornell & The Three Kaydets) | 8/49 | HMV BD.1255 |
| Bob and Alf Pearson | 8/49 | Parlophone F.2371 |
| The Four Troubadours | 8/49 | Columbia DB.2562 |

## 165 | WHILE THE ANGELUS WAS RINGING (Les trois cloches)

| | |
|---|---|
| Composers: Jean Villard & Dick Manning | Date of Entry: 16.7.49/<br>Pos: 5/Wks: 19 |
| Publishers: Southern Music Publishing Co. Ltd. | Re-entry: 3.12.49/<br>Pos: 19/Wks: 1 |

Recordings:

| | | |
|---|---|---|
| Anne Shelton with The Wardour Singers | 2/49 | Decca F.9076 |
| Margaret Whiting | 3/49 | Capitol CL.13061 |
| Dick Haymes with The Jeffrey Alexander Chorus | 3/49 | Brunswick 04061 |
| Frank Sinatra | 4/49 | Columbia DB.2507 |
| Tommy Dorsey and his Orchestra (Denny Dennis) | 5/49 | HMV BD.1243 |
| Archie Lewis with The Luton Girls' Choir cond. Arthur E. Davies | 6/49 | Parlophone R.3202 |
| Josef Locke with Mixed Chorus | 6/49 | Columbia DB.2541 |
| Guy Lombardo and his Royal Canadians (Kenny Gardner) | 6/49 | Brunswick 04149 |
| Allan Jones with The Lyrian Singers | 10/49 | HMV B.9828 |

(Note: This song by French writer Jean Villard received a second English lyric by Bert Reisfeld under the title 'The Three Bells' [The Jimmy Brown Song]. The popular version of this song – by Les Compagnons de la Chanson [Columbia DB.2697] was not released until June 1950 but there had previously been issued a version by The Melody Maids [Decca F.9021] in November 1948. This song, also published by Southern, made no entry into the Sheet music charts under this title until 1959 – see Song No. 1069.)

## 166 | BEAUTIFUL EYES

| | |
|---|---|
| Composers: Frankie Adams, Leonard Rosen & Neal Madaglia | Date of Entry: 23.7.49 |
| Publishers: Leeds Music Ltd. | Highest Position: 16<br>Weeks on Chart: 1 |

Recordings:

| | | |
|---|---|---|
| Joe Loss and his Orchestra (Elizabeth Batey) | 4/49 | HMV BD.6041 |
| Larry Fotine and his Orchestra (Ensemble) | 4/49 | Brunswick 04074 |
| Art Mooney and his Orchestra (Ensemble) | 5/49 | MGM.198 |
| Billy Cotton and his Band (The Bandits) | 6/49 | Decca F.9164 |
| Victor Silvester and his Ballroom Orchestra | 7/49 | Columbia FB.3501 |
| Billy Ternent and his Orchestra (Tom Henry and Eve Beynon) | 7/49 | Harmony A.1005 |

## 167 | HAVE YOU SEEN IRENE?

*Composer*: Henry J. Thorne

*Publishers*: Clover Music Co. Ltd.

*Date of Entry*: 30.7.49

*Highest Position*: 20
*Weeks on Chart*: 1

*Recordings*:

| | | |
|---|---|---|
| Victor Silvester and his Ballroom Orchestra | 6/49 | Columbia FB.3495 |
| Dick James | 6/49 | Decca F.9163 |
| Clive Wayne | 7/49 | HMV B.9788 |
| Roberto Inglez and his Orchestra | 7/49 | Parlophone R.3206 |
| Billy Ternent and his Orchestra (Don Emsley) | 7/49 | Harmony A.1006 |

## 168 | BLUE RIBBON GAL

*Composers*: Irwin Dash & Ross Parker

*Publishers*: Irwin Dash Music Co. Ltd.

*Date of Entry*: 6.8.49/
Pos: 15/Wks: 8

*Re-entry*: 8.10.49/
Pos: 20/Wks: 1

*Recordings*:

| | | |
|---|---|---|
| Harry Gold and his Pieces of Eight (Geoff Love) | 6/49 | Decca F.9171 |
| The Radio Revellers | 7/49 | Columbia FB.3504 |
| Eric Winstone and his Orchestra | 7/49 | MGM.218 |
| Charlie Chester and Edwina Carol | 9/49 | Parlophone R.3220 |
| Peter Lind Hayes | 1/50 | Brunswick 04421★ |
| Jack Smith with The Jubalaires | 4/50 | Capitol CL.13284★ |

## 169 | EVERYWHERE YOU GO

*Composers*: Larry Shay, Joe Goodwin & Mark Fisher

*Publishers*: Chappell & Co. Ltd.

*Date of Entry*: 6.8.49/
Pos: 17/Wks: 1

*Re-entry*: 3.9.49/
Pos: 20/Wks: 1

*Recordings*:

| | | |
|---|---|---|
| Bing Crosby and Evelyn Knight with Jud Conlon's Rhythmaires | 6/49 | Brunswick 04139 |
| Jan Garber and his Orchestra (Tim Reardon) | 7/49 | Capitol CL.13124 |
| Doris Day with The Mellomen | 8/49 | Columbia DB.2561 |
| Donald Peers | 8/49 | HMV B.9808 |

## 170 | DREAMER WITH A PENNY

*Composers*: Lester Lee & Allan Roberts

*Publishers*: Magna Music Co.

*Date of Entry*: 6.8.49

*Highest Position*: 19
*Weeks on Chart*: 1

*Recordings*:

| | | |
|---|---|---|
| Margaret Whiting | 6/49 | Capitol CL.13109 |
| Charles La Vere with The Four Hits and a Miss | 9/49 | Brunswick 04278★ |

## 171 | LEICESTER SQUARE RAG

*Composer*: Harry Roy

*Publishers*: J. Norris Music

*Date of Entry*: 13.8.49

*Highest Position*: 6
*Weeks on Chart*: 24

*Recordings*:

| | | |
|---|---|---|
| Harry Roy and his Orchestra (Recorded 4/49) | 5/49 | Decca F.9145 |
| Oscar Rabin and his Band with Harry Davis | 10/49 | Parlophone F.2382 |
| Harry Roy and his Band (Recorded 10/49) | 10/49 | Parlophone F.2387 |

## 172 | I DON'T SEE ME IN YOUR EYES ANY MORE

*Composers*: Bennie Benjamin & George Weiss

*Publishers*: Campbell Connelly & Co. Ltd.

*Date of Entry*: 20.8.49

*Highest Position*: 1
*Weeks on Chart*: 24

*Recordings*:

| | | |
|---|---|---|
| The Star Dusters | 5/49 | Brunswick 04082 |
| Vera Lynn and Sam Browne | 5/49 | Decca F.9127 |
| Helen Forrest | 5/49 | MGM.190 |
| Buddy Clark | 6/49 | Columbia DB.2534 |
| Perry Como | 7/49 | HMV BD.1251 |
| Jan Garber and his Orchestra (Tim Reardon) | 7/49 | Capitol CL.13124 |

## 173 | CONFIDENTIALLY

*Composer*: Reg Dixon

*Publishers*: Chappell & Co. Ltd.

*Date of Entry*: 20.8.49

*Highest Position*: 2
*Weeks on Chart*: 28

*Recordings*:

| | | |
|---|---|---|
| Reg Dixon | 7/49 | Decca F.9192 |
| Harold Geller and his Orchestra (Anne Lenner and Bob Harvey) | 10/49 | Columbia FB.3526 |
| Clive Wayne | 10/49 | HMV B.9826 |
| Geraldo and his Orchestra (Eve Boswell) | 11/49 | Parlophone F.2385 |
| Danny Kaye with The Lee Gordon Singers | 4/50 | Brunswick 04490★ |

## 174 THE WEDDING SAMBA

| | | |
|---|---|---|
| *Composers*: Abraham Ellestein, Joseph Liebowitz & Alan Small | | *Date of Entry*: 10.9.49/ Pos: 4/Wks: 21 |
| *Publishers*: Leeds Music Ltd. | | *Re-entry*: 18.2.50/ Pos: 20/Wks: 1 |

*Recordings*:

| | | |
|---|---|---|
| Roberto Inglez and his Orchestra (Pat Hutton) | 9/49 | Parlophone R.3227 |
| Edmundo Ros and his Orchestra (Edmundo Ros) | 9/49 | Decca F.9200 |
| Lou Preager and his Orchestra | 10/49 | Columbia FB.3524 |
| Joe Loss and his Orchestra | 11/49 | HMV BD.6054 |
| Chick Rooster and The Barnyarders | 11/49 | HMV B.9837 |
| Santiago and his Music (The Kordites) | 11/49 | Harmony A.1010 |
| The Andrews Sisters and Carmen Miranda | 2/50 | Brunswick 04436 |
| Mickey Katz and his Orchestra (Jack Hilliard) | 3/50 | Capitol CL.13262★ |
| Guy Lombardo and his Royal Canadians (Kenny Gardner) | 3/50 | Brunswick 04465★ |
| Xavier Cugat and his Orchestra | 5/50 | Columbia DB.2682★ |

## 175 SAY GOODNIGHT BUT NOT GOODBYE

| | |
|---|---|
| *Composers*: F. Lilly, G. Moore & E. Cassin | *Date of Entry*: 10.9.49 |
| *Publishers*: Edward Kassner Music Co. Ltd. | *Highest Position*: 19 *Weeks on Chart*: 1 |

*Recordings*:

| | | |
|---|---|---|
| Clive Wayne with Jackie Brown (organ) | 8/49 | HMV B.9798 |
| John Rorke with The London Community Singers cond. Glyn Jones | 10/49 | Parlophone F.2381★ |
| Dorothy Squires | 11/49 | Columbia DB.2605★ |
| Dick James with The Stargazers | 11/49 | Decca F.9275★ |
| Marjorie Scott | 3/50 | Parlophone R.3265★ |

## 176 TOO-WHIT! TOO-WHOO!

| | |
|---|---|
| *Composer*: Billy Reid | *Date of Entry*: 10.9.49 |
| *Publishers*: Billy Reid Publications Ltd. | *Highest Position*: 11 *Weeks on Chart*: 10 |

*Recordings*:

| | | |
|---|---|---|
| Dorothy Squires | 9/49 | Columbia DB.2573 |
| Jack Simpson and his Sextet (Amru Sani) | 10/49 | Parlophone F.2380 |
| Lou Preager and his Orchestra (Rusty Hurren and The Sun Spots) | 10/49 | Columbia FB.3525 |
| Vera Lynn | 10/49 | Decca F.9254 |
| The Deep River Boys | 12/49 | HMV B.9851★ |

## 177 THE WINDMILL SONG

| | | |
|---|---|---|
| *Composers*: Jan Van Laar with English Lyrics by Leo Fuld & Fred F. Finklehoffe | | *Date of Entry*: 17.9.49/ Pos: 17/Wks: 3 |
| *Publishers*: Keith Prowse Music Publishing Co. Ltd. | | *Re-entry*: 15.10.49/ Pos: 19/Wks: 1 |

*Recordings*:

| | | |
|---|---|---|
| Leo Fuld [In Dutch & English] | 5/49 | Decca F.9129 |
| Primo Scala and his Banjo and Accordion Band (The Keynotes) | 5/49 | Decca F.9139 |
| Joe Loss and his Orchestra with vocal | 6/49 | HMV BD.6046 |
| Ronnie Ronalde with Vocal Quartet | 7/49 | Columbia DB.2554 |
| The Andrews Sisters | 8/49 | Brunswick 04259 |
| Ethel Smith (organ) with The Travellers | 11/49 | Brunswick 04375★ |

## 178 A SHAWL OF GALWAY GREY

| | | |
|---|---|---|
| *Composer*: Hamilton Kennedy | | *Date of Entry*: 24.9.49/ Pos: 18/Wks: 1 |
| *Publishers*: Campbell Connelly & Co. Ltd. | | *Re-entry*: 8.10.49 Pos: 11/Wks: 13 *2nd re-entry*: 21.1.50/ Pos: 20/Wks: 1 |

*Recordings*:

| | | |
|---|---|---|
| The Five Smith Brothers | 10/49 | Parlophone R.3229 |
| Steve Conway | 10/49 | Columbia DB.2586 |
| Josef Locke | 11/49 | Columbia DB.2604 |
| Bobby Wayne | 11/49 | London L.509 |
| Cyril Stapleton and his Orchestra (Bob Dale) | 11/49 | Decca F.9286 |

## 179 A ROSE IN A GARDEN OF WEEDS

| | |
|---|---|
| *Composers*: R.B. Saxe & Hubert W. David | *Date of Entry*: 1.10.49 |
| *Publishers*: Box & Cox (Publications) Ltd. | *Highest Position*: 6 *Weeks on Chart*: 35 |

*Recordings*:

| | | |
|---|---|---|
| Jack Simpson and his Sextet (Amru Sani) | 10/49 | Parlophone F.2380 |
| Donald Peers | 10/49 | HMV B.9817 |
| Denny Dennis | 10/49 | Decca F.9232 |
| Felix Mendelssohn and his Hawaiian Serenaders (George Barclay) | 12/49 | Columbia DB.2614 |
| The Five Smith Brothers | 2/50 | Parlophone R.3258 |

## 180 OUR LOVE STORY

*Composers*: Norman Newell & William Harrison

*Publishers*: Carolin Music Co. Ltd.

*Date of Entry*:1.10.49/
Pos: 14/Wks: 6
*Re-entry*: 7.1.50/
Pos: 10/Wks: 13

*Recordings*:

| | | |
|---|---|---|
| Bill Johnson | 6/49 | Columbia DB.2539 |
| Victor Silvester and his Ballroom Orchestra | 8/49 | Columbia FB.3507 |
| Dorothy Squires | 9/49 | Columbia DB.2573 |
| Vera Lynn | 9/49 | Decca F.9221 |
| Roberto Inglez and his Orchestra | 2/50 | Parlophone R.3259 |

## 181 YOU'RE BREAKING MY HEART

*Composers*: Pat Genaro & Sunny Skylar (with acknowledgements to the owners of the copyright in "'Tis the Day")

*Publishers*: Chappell & Co. Ltd.

*Date of Entry*: 8.10.49

*Highest Position*: 1
*Weeks on Chart*: 26

*Recordings*:

| | | |
|---|---|---|
| The Ink Spots | 9/49 | Brunswick 04266 |
| Russ Case and his Orchestra (The Quintones) | 10/49 | MGM.241 |
| Jan Garber and his Orchestra (Bob Grabeau) | | Capitol CL.13169 |
| Oscar Rabin and his Band with Harry Davis (Marjorie Daw) | 10/49 | Parlophone F.2382 |
| Clive Wayne | 10/49 | HMV B.9826 |
| Joe Loss and his Orchestra | 11/49 | HMV BD.6055 |
| Victor Silvester and his Ballroom Orchestra | 11/49 | Columbia FB.3530 |
| Bill Johnson | 11/49 | Columbia DB.2596 |
| Buddy Clark | 11/49 | Columbia DB.2625 |
| Reggie Goff with The Velvetones | 11/49 | Decca F.9289 |
| The Four Troubadours | 12/49 | Columbia DB.2617 |
| Allan Jones | 12/49 | HMV B.9841 |
| The Squadronaires dir. Jimmy Miller (Roy Edwards) | 12/49 | Decca F.9304 |
| Frederick Ferrari | 1/50 | Parlophone R.3246 |

## 182 BABY, IT'S COLD OUTSIDE

*Composer*: Frank Loesser

*Publishers*: Edwin H. Morris & Co. Ltd.

*Date of Entry*: 15.10.49
Pos: 15/Wks: 7
*Re-entry*: 10.12.49/
Pos: 18/Wks: 3

*Recordings*:

| | | |
|---|---|---|
| Pearl Bailey and Hot Lips Page | 8/49 | Columbia DB.2580 |
| Margaret Whiting and Johnny Mercer | 9/49 | Capitol CL.13158 |
| Dinah Shore and Buddy Clark | 10/49 | Columbia DB.2582 |
| Swing and Sway with Sammy Kaye (Don Cornell and Laura Leslie) | 10/49 | HMV B.9827 |
| Esther Williams and Ricardo Montalban | 10/49 | MGM.233 |
| Eric Winstone and his Orchestra (Julie Dawn and Leslie Howard) | 10/49 | MGM.239 |
| Ella Fitzgerald and Louis Jordan | 10/49 | Brunswick 04274 |

## 183 AM I WASTING MY TIME ON YOU?

*Composers*: Irving Bibo & Howard Johnson

*Publishers*: Lawrence Wright Music Co. Ltd.

*Date of Entry*: 22.10.49

*Highest Position*: 18
*Weeks on Chart*: 1

*Recordings*:

| | | |
|---|---|---|
| Victor Silvester and his Ballroom Orchestra | 10/49 | Columbia FB.3521 |
| The Five Smith Brothers | 10/49 | Parlophone R.3229 |
| Reggie Goff | 10/49 | Decca F.9250 |

## 184 MONDAY, TUESDAY, WEDNESDAY

*Composer*: Ross Parker

*Publishers*: Irwin Dash Music Co. Ltd.

*Date of Entry*: 22.10.49
Pos: 10/Wks: 14
*Re-entry*: 4.2.50/
Pos: 18/Wks: 2

*Recordings*:

| | | |
|---|---|---|
| Betty Driver | 10/49 | HMV B.9825 |
| Reggie Goff with The Velvetones | 10/49 | Decca F.9250 |
| Syd Dean and his Band (Jill Page and Harry Bolton) | 11/49 | Columbia FB.3533 |
| Jo Stafford and Gordon MacRae | 2/50 | Capitol CL.13258 |

## 185 THE KISS IN YOUR EYES

*Composers*: Richard Heuberger & Johnny Burke

*Publishers*: Bosworth & Co. Ltd.

*Date of Entry*: 22.10.49
Pos: 19/Wks: 3
Wks: 3
*Re-entry*: 26.11.49/
Pos: 17/Wks: 7
*2nd re-entry*: 28.1.50/
Pos: 15/Wks: 2
*3rd re-entry*: 25.2.50/
Pos: 18/Wks: 1

*Recordings*:

| | | |
|---|---|---|
| Bing Crosby | 7/48 | Brunswick 03932 |
| Harry Dawson | 12/49 | HMV B.9845 |
| Joe Loss and his Orchestra | 1/50 | HMV BD.6057 |

## 186 THE HOP SCOTCH POLKA

*Composers*: William 'Billy' Whitlock, Carl Sigman & Gene Rayburn

*Publishers*: Leeds Music Ltd.

*Date of Entry*: 12.11.49

*Highest Position*: 1
*Weeks on Chart*: 23

*Recordings*:

| | | |
|---|---|---|
| Billy Whitlock (Bell Solo) with Harry Bidgood and his Orchestra [Titled 'Scotch Hot'] | 10/49 | Decca F.9233 |
| Jan Garber and his Orchestra (Ernie Mathias and Roberta Linn) | 10/49 | Capitol CL.13169 |
| Guy Lombardo and his Royal Canadians (Kenny Gardner and The Lombardo Trio) | 10/49 | Brunswick 04281 |
| The Tanner Sisters | 11/49 | HMV B.9846 |
| Art Mooney and his Orchestra (The Art Mooney Choir) | 11/49 | MGM.246 |
| Cyril Stapleton and his Orchestra (Bob Dale and Jean Campbell) | 11/49 | Decca F.9286 |
| The Five Smith Brothers | 12/49 | Parlophone R.3239 |

## 187 THE HARRY LIME THEME

*Composer*: Anton Karas (see also note below)

*Publishers*: Chappell & Co. Ltd.

*Date of Entry*: 12.11.49

*Highest Position*: 1
*Weeks on Chart*: 26

*Recordings*:

| | | |
|---|---|---|
| Anton Karas (zither solo) | 10/49 | Decca F.9235 |
| The Cafe Vienna Quartet | 11/49 | Columbia DB.2611 |
| Lou Preager and his Orchestra | 12/49 | Columbia FB.3534 |
| Roberto Inglez and his Orchestra | 12/49 | Parlophone R.3242 |
| Victor Silvester and his Ballroom Orchestra | 1/50 | Columbia FB.3541 |
| Alvino Rey (guitar) | 1/50 | Capitol CL.13240 |
| Guy Lombardo and his Royal Canadians (guitar: Don Rodney) | 3/50 | Brunswick 04460 |
| Ethel Smith (organ) | 4/50 | Brunswick 04480 |
| Anton Karas (zither solo) | 10/54 | Decca 45-F.9235★ |

The following three versions had lyrics added. The first two were titled 'The Zither Melody', the third 'The Song Version of the Harry Lime Theme'.

| | | |
|---|---|---|
| Reggie Goff with The Velvetones (Comp: Karas, Carr, Golden) | 2/50 | Decca F.9359 |
| Donald Peers (Comp: Karas & Lord) | 2/50 | HMV B.9890 |
| The Five Smith Brothers (Comp: Karas, Golden, Carr) | 2/50 | Parlophone R.3266 |

## 188 I'LL STRING ALONG WITH YOU

*Composers*: Al Dubin & Harry Warren

*Publishers*: B. Feldman & Co. Ltd.

*Date of Entry*: 12.11.49

*Highest Position*: 5
*Weeks on Chart*: 22

(This song, first popular in 1934–5, was recorded by many artists at the time, including two versions by Dick Powell, but none remained in the catalogue at the time of its revival.)

*Recordings*:

| | | |
|---|---|---|
| Jo Stafford and Gordon MacRae | 5/49 | Capitol CL.13089 |
| Doris Day and Buddy Clark | 10/49 | Columbia DB.2584 |
| Cyril Stapleton and his Orchestra (Bob Dale) | 1/50 | Decca F.9330 |
| Donald Peers | 2/50 | HMV B.9877 |
| Jo Stafford and Gordon MacRae | 2/50 | Capitol CL.13258 |

## 189 SNOWY WHITE SNOW AND JINGLE BELLS

Composer: Billy Reid, based on a theme by Johnny Sheridan, Ralph Ruvin, Harold Irving & Dennis Berger

Date of Entry: 19.11.49

Publishers: Billy Reid Publications Ltd.

Highest Position: 3
Weeks on Chart: 9

Recordings:
| | | |
|---|---|---|
| Dorothy Squires | 11/49 | Columbia DB.2605 |
| Primo Scala and his Banjo and Accordion Band (The Keynotes) | 11/49 | Decca F.9270 |

## 190 DECEMBER

Composers: Al Rinker & Floyd Huddleston

Date of Entry: 26.11.49

Publishers: Bradbury Wood Ltd.

Highest Position: 10
Weeks on Chart: 6

Recordings:
| | | |
|---|---|---|
| Clive Wayne | 11/49 | HMV B.9840 |
| Gordon Jenkins and his Orchestra (Floyd Huddleston and Chorus) | 11/49 | Brunswick 04401 |
| Victor Silvester and his Ballroom Orchestra | 12/49 | Columbia FB.3537 |
| The Squadronaires dir. Jimmy Miller (Roy Edwards) | 12/49 | Decca F.9304 |

## 191 IS IT TOO LATE?

Composers: Leo Towers & Michael White

Date of Entry: 3.12.49

Publishers: Yale Music Corporation Ltd.

Highest Position: 11
Weeks on Chart: 16

Recordings:
| | | |
|---|---|---|
| Denny Dennis | 1/47 | Decca F.8726 |
| Vaughn Monroe and his Orchestra (Vaughn Monroe and The Moon Maids) | 9/49 | HMV BD.1259 |
| Jack Simpson and his Sextet (Amru Sani) | 11/49 | Parlophone F.2383 |
| Josephine Bradley and her Ballroom Orchestra | 3/50 | Decca F.9372 |

## 192 A SONG OF CAPRI

Composers: Mischa Spoliansky & Norman Newell

Publishers: Chappell & Co. Ltd.

Highest Position: 17
Weeks on Chart: 2

Recordings:
| | | |
|---|---|---|
| The Queen's Hall Light Orchestra conducted by Sidney Torch | 8/49 | Columbia DB.2564 |
| Geraldo and his Orchestra (Archie Lewis) | 9/49 | Parlophone F.2377 |
| Monte Rey | 9/49 | Columbia DB.2570 |
| John Hendrik | 9/49 | Parlophone R.3217 |
| Lee Lawrence | 9/49 | Decca F.9198 |
| Lou Preager and his Orchestra (Paul Rich) | 10/49 | Columbia FB.3524 |
| Harry Dawson | 12/49 | HMV B.9845 |

## 193 THE SCOTTISH SAMBA

Composers: Tommie Connor & Johnny Reine

Date of Entry: 31.12.49/
Pos: 17/Wks: 2

Publishers: Sun Music Publishing Co. Ltd.

Re-entry: 28.1.50/
Pos: 16/Wks: 2
2nd re-entry: 18.2.50/
Pos: 16/Wks: 3

Recordings:
| | | |
|---|---|---|
| Syd Dean and his Band (Harry Bolton) | 12/49 | Columbia FB.3538 |
| Edmundo Ros and his Rumba Band (Edmundo Ros) | 12/49 | Decca F.9306 |
| Roberto Inglez and his Orchestra | 2/50 | Parlophone R.3259 |
| Ethel Smith (organ) with Guy Lombardo and his Royal Canadians (The Lombardo Trio) | 5/50 | Brunswick 04500★ |

## 194 | DOWN IN THE GLEN

*Composers*: Harry Gordon & Tommie Connor  
*Date of Entry*: 31.12.49/  
Pos: 18/Wks: 1

*Publishers*: Lawrence Wright Music Co. Ltd.  
*Re-entry*: 14.1.50/  
Pos: 4/Wks: 28

*Recordings*:

| | | |
|---|---|---|
| Robert Wilson | 3/49 | HMV B.9736 |
| Sylvia Robin and Tudor Evans | 7/49 | Decca F.9173 |
| The Deep River Boys | 2/50 | HMV B.9869 |
| Denis Martin | 2/50 | Parlophone R.3254 |
| Victor Silvester and his Ballroom Orchestra | 2/50 | Columbia FB.3543 |
| The Squadronaires dir. Jimmy Miller (Firth Archer and The Squads Choir) | 2/50 | Decca F.9346 |
| Josef Locke | 3/50 | Columbia DB.2661 |
| The Luton Girls' Choir cond. Arthur E. Davies | 4/50 | Parlophone R.3276 |
| Joe Loss and his Orchestra | 4/50 | HMV BD.6066 |
| Patrick O'Hagan | 4/50 | Decca F.9378 |
| Donald Peers | 5/50 | HMV B.9907 |
| The Horsham Girls' Choir cond. C. Hall | 2/51 | Columbia DB.2812★ |

## 195 | WHY IS IT?

*Composers*: Joan Whitney & Alex Kramer  
*Date of Entry*: 31.12.49

*Publishers*: Cinephonic Music Co. Ltd.  
*Highest Position*: 10  
*Weeks on Chart*: 13

*Recordings*:

| | | |
|---|---|---|
| Dick James with Felix King, his piano, and his Orchestra | 10/49 | Decca F.9227 |
| Billy Thorburn's The Organ, the Dance Band and Me (The Stargazers) | 3/50 | Parlophone F.2403 |
| Josephine Bradley and her Ballroom Orchestra | 3/50 | Decca F.9371 |
| Monte Rey | 3/50 | Columbia DB.2650 |

# 1950

Top composer of the period covered by this book, Bob Merrill, came into the charts with a bang. His first hit, *I'd've baked a cake*, raced into the No. 1 spot to be the first of four songs of his to appear in the top spot during the Fifties out of a total of no less than 26 chart songs. On the radio front, Teddy Johnson left Radio Luxembourg after two years, and was replaced for a short while by Roger Moffat, during which time the Top Twenty presentation was shuffled about with 17 of the songs being broadcast in any order, and only the top three ending the show in reverse order. Sam Costa took over the Light Programme's regular Sunday afternoon record show, 'Record Rendezvous', and in no time at all his theme *Sam's song*, as played by Joe 'Fingers' Carr, was featuring prominently in the Top Twenty. Previous comperes of the show had been Dennis Moonan and Richard Attenborough. In late September came the memorable 'Top Score' show, featuring Stanley Black and the BBC Dance Orchestra with vocalists Diana Coupland, Marie Benson, Dick James and The Stargazers, which immediately followed the Sam Costa show on Sundays. The programmes all closed with what was called 'Top Score's Top Four', four songs which were the actual top four of the sheet music charts. The shows were introduced by Cliff Michelmore and produced by Johnnie Stewart. Two songs first broadcast in mid–49 each took six months to reach the charts – *The last mile home*, having been played by Maurice Winnick in June 1949 appeared for the first time in January 1950, while *We all have a song in our hearts* (Lew Stone July 1949) also bided its time before appearing in February 1950. And as for records, this was the first year for Oriole releases. The

| | MOST WEEKS ON THE CHARTS TOP SIX | |
|---|---|---|
| Pos | | Wks |
| 1 | *Jealous heart* | 33 |
| 2 | *My foolish heart* | 30 |
| 3 | *Down in the glen* | 28 |
| 4 | *Daddy's little girl* | 27 |
| 5 | *Bewitched* | 26 |
| 6= | *Quicksilver* | 23 |
| 6= | *If I loved you* | 23 |
| 6= | *Silver dollar* | 23 |

distinctive red label of the Polygon Record Company appeared in December, while back in June, Decca had released the first long-playing records ever to appear in Britain. Among the first eight albums in the 10″ LF series were two each by Edmundo Ros and Stanley Black and their orchestras. A printing strike during most of October had deprived readers of many publications, but the disappearance of *Melody Maker* for four weeks meant that no charts were published for the period. On 23 October, the news came of the death of Al Jolson. In America, the recording of *Goodnight Irene* by Gordon Jenkins and his Orchestra with The Weavers was No. 1 in the charts for 13 consecutive weeks thereby equalling the feat achieved by Artie Shaw's *Frenesi* (1940) and *I've heard that song before* by Harry James in 1943.

# SONG CHARTS

## 196 THE LAST MILE HOME

*Composers*: Walter Kent & Walton Farrar

*Publishers*: Leeds Music Ltd.

*Date of Entry*: 7.1.50/
Pos: 17/Wks: 1
*Re-entry*: 4.2.50/
Pos 20/Wks: 2
*2nd re-entry*: 25.2.50/
Pos: 19/Wks: 1

*Recordings*:
| | | |
|---|---|---|
| Gracie Fields | 6/49 | Decca F.9169 |
| Victor Silvester and his Ballroom Orchestra | 8/49 | Columbia FB.3507 |
| Donald Peers | 9/49 | HMV B.9809 |
| Bing Crosby with The Ken Lane Singers | 9/49 | Brunswick 04260 |
| Jo Stafford and The Starlighters | 9/49 | Capitol CL.13147 |
| Doris Day | 10/49 | Columbia DB.2584 |
| Denis Martin | 11/49 | Parlophone R.3234 |
| Bing Crosby with The Ken Lane Singers | 2/52 | Brunswick 04868★ |

## 197 DEAR HEARTS AND GENTLE PEOPLE

*Composers*: Sammy Fain & Bob Hilliard

*Publishers*: Edwin H. Morris & Co. Ltd.

*Date of Entry*: 7.1.50

*Highest Position*: 1
*Weeks on Chart*: 22

*Recordings*:
| | | |
|---|---|---|
| Dinah Shore | 12/49 | Columbia DB.2634 |
| Bing Crosby with Jud Conlon's Rhythmaires | 12/49 | Brunswick 04420 |
| Gordon MacRae | 12/49 | Capitol CL.13226 |
| Benny Strong and his Orchestra (Benny Strong) | 12/49 | Capitol CL.13236 |
| Cyril Stapleton and his Orchestra (Bob Dale) | 1/50 | Decca F.9330 |
| Victor Silvester and his Ballroom Orchestra | 2/50 | Columbia FB.3544 |
| Donald Peers | 2/50 | HMV B.9877 |
| The Radio Revellers | 2/50 | Columbia DB.2640 |
| Peter Yorke and his Concert Orchestra (Doreen Lundy) | 3/50 | Columbia DB.2649 |
| Joe Loss and his Orchestra | 3/50 | HMV BD.6062 |
| 'Sheriff' Johnny Denis and his Ranchers (The Cactus Kids) | 3/50 | Decca F.9373 |
| Geraldo and his Orchestra (Eve Boswell) | 3/50 | Parlophone F.2402 |

## 198 MULE TRAIN

*Composers*: Johnny Lange, Hy Heath & Fred Glickman

*Publishers*: Chappell & Co. Ltd.

*Date of Entry*: 14.1.50

*Highest Position*: 8
*Weeks on Chart*: 10

*Recordings*:
| | | |
|---|---|---|
| Vaughn Monroe and his Orchestra (Vaughn Monroe and The Moon Men) | 12/49 | HMV B.9857 |
| Bing Crosby | 12/49 | Brunswick 04420 |
| Gordon MacRae | 12/49 | Capitol CL.13226 |
| Tennessee Ernie | 1/50 | Capitol CL.13237 |
| Arthur 'Guitar Boogie' Smith and his Crackerjacks (Arthur Smith) | 1/50 | MGM.254 |
| Woody Herman and Nat 'King' Cole with King Cole's Muleskinners | 2/50 | Capitol CL.13229 |
| Mickey Katz and his Orchestra (Titled 'Yiddish Mule Train') | 9/50 | Capitol CL.13365★ |
| Frankie Laine | 10/52 | Oriole CB.1120★ |
| Frankie Laine | 6/54 | Mercury MB.2988★ |

## 199 JEALOUS HEART

*Composer*: Jennie Lou Carson

*Publishers*: New World Publishers Ltd.

*Date of Entry*: 14.1.50

*Highest Position*: 2
*Weeks on Chart*: 33

*Recordings*:
| | | |
|---|---|---|
| Jack Owens | 10/49 | Brunswick 04349 |
| Jan Garber and his Orchestra (Bob Grabeau) | 10/49 | Capitol CL.13201 |
| The Tanner Sisters | 11/49 | HMV B.9846 |
| Al Morgan | 11/49 | London L.500 |
| Derry Falligant with the Bob Haggart Trio | 11/49 | MGM.251 |
| The Four Troubadours | 12/49 | Columbia DB.2617 |
| Squadronaires dir. Jimmy Miller (Squads Choir, Roy Edwards, Susan Jeans) | 1/50 | Decca F.9303 |
| Oscar Rabin and his Band with Harry Davis (Marjorie Daw & Marion Davis) | 2/50 | Parlophone F.2400 |
| Joe Loss and his Orchestra | 3/50 | HMV BD.6063 |

## 200 I'VE GOT A LOVELY BUNCH OF COCONUTS

*Composer*: Fred Heatherton

*Date of Entry*: 14.1.50

*Publishers*: Box & Cox (Publications) Ltd.

*Highest Position*: 5
*Weeks on Chart*: 18

*Recordings*:

| | | |
|---|---|---|
| Primo Scala & his Banjo and Accordion Band (The Keynotes) | 5/49 | Decca F.9133 |
| Billy Cotton and his Band (Alan Breeze) | 5/49 | Decca F.9149 |
| Jack Simpson and his Sextet (Jack Simpson) | 11/49 | Parlophone F.2383 |
| Danny Kaye | 12/49 | Brunswick 04416 |
| Tommy Tucker and his Orchestra with vocal | 1/50 | MGM.257 |

## 201 SOME DAY MY HEART WILL AWAKE

*Composers*: Ivor Novello & Christopher Hassall

*Date of Entry*: 28.1.50/
Pos: 20/Wks: 1

*Publishers*: Chappell & Co. Ltd.

*Re-entry*: 11.2.50/
Pos: 17/Wks: 2

*Recordings*:

| | | |
|---|---|---|
| Vanessa Lee | 10/49 | HMV C.3918 |
| Ambrose and his Orchestra (Ray Burns) | 10/49 | Decca F.9251 |
| Bill Johnson | 11/49 | Columbia DB.2596 |
| Paul Adam and his Mayfair Music (Rita Williams) | 11/49 | Columbia FB.3532 |
| Victor Silvester and his Ballroom Orchestra | 12/49 | Columbia FB.3536 |
| Oscar Rabin and his Band with Harry Davis | 2/50 | Parlophone F.2400 |
| The Luton Girls' Choir | 6/50 | Parlophone R.3293★ |
| Anne Ziegler and Webster Booth | 11/50 | HMV B.9992★ |

## 202 WE ALL HAVE A SONG IN OUR HEARTS

*Composers*: Carl & Roger Yale

*Date of Entry*: 4.2.50

*Publishers*: 20th Century

*Highest Position*: 10
*Weeks on Chart*: 18

*Recordings*:

| | | |
|---|---|---|
| Harold Geller and his Orchestra (Bob Harvey) | 10/49 | Columbia FB.3526 |
| Geraldo and his Orchestra (Archie Lewis) | 11/49 | Parlophone F.2385 |
| Dorothy Squires | 12/49 | Columbia DB.2610 |
| Josef Locke | 1/50 | Columbia DB.2636 |
| Josephine Bradley and her Ballroom Orchestra | 3/50 | Decca F.9372 |
| Bing Crosby | 2/52 | Brunswick 04868★ |

## 203 IS IT TRUE WHAT THEY SAY ABOUT DIXIE?

*Composers*: Irving Caesar, Sammy Lerner & Gerald Marks

*Date of Entry*: 11.2.50

*Publishers*: Bradbury Wood Ltd.

*Highest Position*: 7
*Weeks on Chart*: 12

(Note: This song, first published in 1936, was recorded by many bands and artists in that period, but only one record survived from that time to the catalogues of 1950 – by Frances Langford on Brunswick 02216.)

*Later recordings*:

| | | |
|---|---|---|
| Al Jolson and The Mills Brothers | 2/49 | Brunswick 04027 |
| Phil Harris and his Orchestra (Phil Harris) | 9/49 | HMV BD.1257 |
| Al Jolson with The Lee Gordon Sisters | 11/49 | Brunswick 04379 |
| Sid Phillips and his Band | 4/50 | HMV BD.6064 |

## 204 OUT OF A CLEAR BLUE SKY

*Composers*: Gene Piller & Ruth Roberts

*Date of Entry*: 25.2.50/
Pos: 14/Wks: 7

*Publishers*: Edward Kassner Music Co. Ltd.

*Re-entry*: 22.4.50/
Pos: 19/Wks: 2

*Recordings*:

| | | |
|---|---|---|
| Primo Scala & his Banjo & Accordion Band (The Keynotes) | 2/50 | Decca F.9341 |
| Tommy Tucker and his Orchestra with vocal group | 3/50 | MGM.268 |
| Donald Peers | 4/50 | HMV B.9903 |

## 205 (Put another nickel in) MUSIC! MUSIC! MUSIC!

*Composers*: Stephan Weiss & Bernie Baum

*Date of Entry*: 4.3.50

*Publishers*: Leeds Music Ltd.

*Highest Position*: 1
*Weeks on Chart*: 13

*Recordings*:

| | | |
|---|---|---|
| Teresa Brewer with the Dixieland All Stars | 2/50 | London L.604 |
| Mickey Katz and his Orchestra (Mickey Katz) | 3/50 | Capitol CL.13262 |
| Donald Peers | 3/50 | HMV B.9899 |
| Johnny Bond and his Orchestra (Rosemary Calvin & Ensemble) | 3/50 | MGM.262 |
| Dolores Gray | 3/50 | Columbia DB.2675 |
| Joe Loss and his Orchestra | 4/50 | HMV BD.1264 |
| Carmen Cavallaro and his Orchestra (Bob Lido, the Cavaliers & Ensemble) | 4/50 | Brunswick 04472 |
| Anne Shelton | 4/50 | Decca F.9393 |
| Geraldo and his Orchestra (Nadia Doré) | 4/50 | Parlophone F.2406 |
| Victor Silvester and his Ballroom Orchestra | 4/50 | Columbia FB.3557 |

## 206 (Where are you) NOW THAT I NEED YOU?

| | | |
|---|---|---|
| *Composer*: Frank Loesser | | *Date of Entry*: 4.3.50 |
| *Publishers*: Victoria Music Co. Ltd. | | *Highest Position*: 15 |
| | | *Weeks on Chart*: 2 |

Recordings:

| | | |
|---|---|---|
| Vera Lynn | 10/49 | Decca F.9199 |
| Betty Hutton | 10/49 | Capitol CL.13195 |
| Fran Warren | 11/49 | HMV B.9835 |
| Doris Day with The Mellomen | 12/49 | Columbia DB.2612 |

## 207 BEST OF ALL

| | | |
|---|---|---|
| *Composers*: Ray Sonin & Wally Dewar | | *Date of Entry*: 11.3.50 |
| *Publishers*: Campbell Connelly & Co. Ltd. | | *Highest Position*: 11 |
| | | *Weeks on Chart*: 7 |

Recordings:

| | | |
|---|---|---|
| Steve Conway | 12/49 | Columbia DB.2616 |
| Sid Phillips and his Band (The Tanner Sisters) | 1/50 | HMV BD.6060 |
| Geraldo and his Orchestra (Eve Boswell) | 2/50 | Parlophone F.2399 |
| Vera Lynn | 2/50 | Decca F.9350 |
| Victor Silvester and his Ballroom Orchestra | 3/50 | Columbia FB.3550 |

## 208 THE FRENCH CAN-CAN POLKA

| | | |
|---|---|---|
| *Composers*: Jacques Offenbach & Jimmy Kennedy | *Date of Entry*: 18.3.50 |
| *Publishers*: Campbell Connelly & Co. Ltd. | | *Highest Position*: 6 |
| | | *Weeks on Chart*: 15 |

Recordings:

| | | |
|---|---|---|
| Billy Cotton and his Band (The Bandits) | 2/50 | Decca F.9360 |
| Ethel Smith (organ) | 4/50 | Brunswick 04479 |
| Lou Preager and his Orchestra (The Sun Spots) | 4/50 | Columbia FB.3554 |
| The Radio Revellers | 4/50 | Columbia DB.2666 |
| Billy Thorburn's The Organ, The Dance Band & Me (The Stargazers) | 5/50 | Parlophone F.2412 |

## 209 CHATTANOOGIE SHOE-SHINE BOY

| | | |
|---|---|---|
| *Composers*: Harry Stone & Jack Stapp | | *Date of Entry*: 18.3.50 |
| *Publishers*: Anglo-Pic Music Co. Ltd. | | *Highest Position*: 2 |
| | | *Weeks on Chart*: 20 |

Recordings:

| | | |
|---|---|---|
| Skitch Henderson and his Orchestra (Gregg Lawrence) | 2/50 | Capitol CL.13252 |
| Tommy Duncan and his Western All Stars | 3/50 | Capitol CL.13261 |
| Donald Peers | 3/50 | HMV B.9899 |
| Bing Crosby | 3/50 | Brunswick 04442 |
| Red Foley | 3/50 | Brunswick 04467 |
| George Towne and his Orchestra (The Satisfyers) | 3/50 | London L.609 |
| Joe Loss and his Orchestra | 4/50 | HMV BD.6065 |
| Frank Sinatra with The Jeff Alexander Choir | 4/50 | Columbia DB.2664 |
| Phil Harris and his Orchestra (Phil Harris) | 4/50 | HMV B.9895 |

## 210 WHEN THE WORLD HAS FORGOTTEN

| | | |
|---|---|---|
| *Composer*: Dave Burke | | *Date of Entry*: 25.3.50 |
| *Publishers*: Carolin Music Co. Ltd. | | *Highest Position*: 17 |
| | | *Weeks on Chart*: 1 |

Recordings:

| | | |
|---|---|---|
| Steve Conway | 10/49 | Columbia DB.2586 |
| Billy Thorburn's The Organ, the Dance Band & Me (Harry Kaye) | 11/49 | Parlophone F.2386 |
| Syd Dean and his Band (Jill Page) | 3/50 | Columbia FB.3547 |
| Vera Lynn | 4/50 | Decca F.9382* |

## 211 MY THANKS TO YOU

| | | |
|---|---|---|
| *Composers*: Norman Newell & Noel Gay | | *Date of Entry*: 25.3.50 |
| *Publishers*: Noel Gay Music Ltd. | | *Highest Position*: 13 |
| | | *Weeks on Chart*: 6 |

Recordings:

| | | |
|---|---|---|
| Steve Conway | 3/50 | Columbia DB.2669 |
| Vera Lynn | 4/50 | Decca F.9382 |
| Billy Cotton and his Band (Doreen Stephens and Alan Breeze) | 4/50 | Decca F.9399 |

## 212 If I knew you were comin' I'D'VE BAKED A CAKE

| | | |
|---|---|---|
| *Composers*: Al Hoffman, Bob Merrill & Clem Watts | | *Date of Entry*: 1.4.50 |
| *Publishers*: Chappell & Co. Ltd. | | *Highest Position*: 1 |
| | | *Weeks on Chart*: 12 |

*Recordings*:

| | | |
|---|---|---|
| Eve Young and The Homesteaders | 4/50 | London L.658 |
| Donald Peers | 4/50 | HMV B.9903 |
| Paul Adam and his Mayfair Music (Paul Adam) | 4/50 | Columbia FB.3558 |
| Art Mooney and his Orchestra (Betty Harris and the Art Mooney Choir) | 4/50 | MGM.279 |
| Ethel Merman and Ray Bolger | 4/50 | Brunswick 04491 |
| Gracie Fields and The Keynotes | 4/50 | Decca F.9405 |
| Benny Strong and his Orchestra (Benny Strong) | 4/50 | Capitol CL.13276 |
| Joe Loss and his Orchestra | 5/50 | HMV BD.6068 |
| Jack Simpson and his Sextet (Rita Williams) | 5/50 | Parlophone F.2411 |
| Josephine Bradley and her Ballroom Orchestra | 5/50 | Decca F.9431 |
| Marie Benson with Norrie's Novelties | 11/50 | Oriole CB.1026★ |

## 213 I SAID MY PAJAMAS (and put on my prayers)

| | | |
|---|---|---|
| *Composers*: Eddie Pola & George Wyle | | *Date of Entry*: 1.4.50 |
| *Publishers*: Leeds Music Ltd. | | *Highest Position*: 16 |
| | | *Weeks on Chart*: 6 |

*Recordings*:

| | | |
|---|---|---|
| Tony Martin and Fran Warren | 3/50 | HMV B.9888 |
| Margaret Whiting and Frank DeVol | 3/50 | Capitol CL.13265 |
| Ethel Merman and Ray Bolger | 4/50 | Brunswick 04456 |
| Doris Day | 4/50 | Columbia DB.2689 |

## 214 MY FOOLISH HEART

| | | |
|---|---|---|
| *Composers*: Ned Washington & Victor Young | | *Date of Entry*: 8.4.50/ Pos: 1/Wks: 29 |
| *Publishers*: Sun Music Publishing Co. Ltd. | | *Re-entry*: 4.11.50/ Pos: 19/Wks: 1 |

*Recordings*:

| | | |
|---|---|---|
| Billy Eckstine | 3/50 | MGM.264 |
| Gordon Jenkins and his Orchestra (Sandy Evans and Chorus) | 3/50 | Brunswick 04469 |
| Steve Conway | 3/50 | Columbia DB.2669 |
| Roberto Inglez and his Orchestra | 4/50 | Parlophone R.3275 |
| Victor Silvester and his Ballroom Orchestra | 4/50 | Columbia FB.3553 |
| Joe Loss and his Orchestra | 4/50 | HMV BD.6065 |
| Margaret Whiting | 4/50 | Capitol CL.13277 |
| Jean Sablon | 5/50 | HMV B.9914 |
| The Peterson Brothers with Barry Snow (Hammond Organ) | 5/50 | Decca F.9433 |
| Allan Jones | 8/50 | HMV B.9948 |

## 215 C'EST SI BON (It's so good)

| | | |
|---|---|---|
| *Composers*: Henri Betti, Jerry Seelen & Andre Hornez | | *Date of Entry*: 8.4.50 |
| *Publishers*: Peter Maurice Music Co. Ltd. | | *Highest Position*: 3 |
| | | *Weeks on Chart*: 18 |

*Recordings*:

| | | |
|---|---|---|
| Johnny Desmond with The Quintones | 3/50 | MGM.263 |
| Danny Kaye with The Lee Gordon Singers | 4/50 | Brunswick 04485 |
| Robert Clary | 4/50 | Capitol CL.13289 |
| Victor Silvester and his Ballroom Orchestra | 5/50 | Columbia FB.3559 |
| Geraldo and his Orchestra (Cyril Grantham and The Geraldtones) | 5/50 | Parlophone F.2409 |
| Jean Sablon | 5/50 | HMV B.9914 |
| Leo Fuld | 5/50 | Decca F.9434 |
| Joe Loss and his Orchestra | 6/50 | HMV BD.6070 |
| Louis Armstrong and his Orchestra (Louis Armstrong) | 4/51 | Brunswick 04674★ |

## 216 ENJOY YOURSELF (It's later than you think)

| | | |
|---|---|---|
| *Composers*: Herb Magidson & Carl Sigman | | *Date of Entry*: 15.4.50 |
| *Publishers*: Edwin H. Morris & Co. Ltd. | | *Highest Position*: 7 |
| | | *Weeks on Chart*: 12 |

*Recordings*:

| | | |
|---|---|---|
| Guy Lombardo and his Royal Canadians (Kenny Gardner and The Lombardo Trio) | 4/50 | Brunswick 04484 |
| Doris Day | 4/50 | Columbia DB.2689 |
| Jack Smith with The Jud Conlon Singers | 4/50 | Capitol CL.13284 |
| Geraldo and his Orchestra (The Geraldtones) | 5/50 | Parlophone F.2409 |
| The Hedley Ward Trio | 5/50 | HMV B.9911 |
| Benny Lee | 5/50 | Decca F.9407 |
| Joe Loss and his Orchestra | 6/50 | HMV BD.6071 |
| Donald Peers with The Cherokeys | 6/50 | HMV B.9924 |

## 217 CHERRY STONES

| | | |
|---|---|---|
| *Composer*: John Jerome | | *Date of Entry*: 15.4.50 |
| *Publishers*: John Fields Music Co. Ltd. | | *Highest Position*: 10 |
| | | *Weeks on Chart*: 11 |

*Recordings*:

| | | |
|---|---|---|
| Joy Nichols | 2/50 | Decca F.9333 |
| Anton Karas (zither) | 3/50 | Decca F.9364 |
| The Radio Revellers | 4/50 | Columbia DB.2666 |
| The Tanner Sisters with The Hedley Ward Trio | 4/50 | HMV B.9900 |
| Vera Lynn and Lee Lawrence | 6/50 | Decca F.9448 |
| Evelyn Knight with The Ray Charles Singers | 8/50 | Brunswick 04542★ |

## 218 THE OLD PIANO ROLL BLUES

*Composer*: Cy Coben

*Publishers*: Leeds Music Ltd.

*Date of Entry*: 29.4.50/
Pos: 4/Wks: 20
*Re-entry*: 30.9.50/
Pos: 19/Wks: 2

*Recordings*:

| | | |
|---|---|---|
| The Jubalaires (Titled 'That old piano roll blues') | 4/50 | Capitol CL.13278 |
| Jan Garber and his Orchestra (Ernie Mathias and Frank Macaulay) | 5/50 | Capitol CL.13285 |
| Hoagy Carmichael and Cass Daley | 5/50 | Brunswick 04495 |
| Sid Phillips and his Band (The Tanner Sisters) | 6/50 | HMV B.9921 |
| Joe Daniels and his Hot Shots | 6/50 | Parlophone F.2413 |
| Geraldo and his Orchestra (Nadia Doré and The Geraldtones) | 6/50 | Parlophone F.2415 |
| Beatrice Kay and her Kay Jammers | 6/50 | Columbia DB.2699 |
| Frankie Vaughan | 7/50 | Decca F.9465 |
| Al Jolson and The Andrews Sisters | 7/50 | Brunswick 04537 |

## 219 QUICKSILVER

*Composers*: Irving Taylor, George Wyle & Eddie Pola

*Publishers*: Edwin H. Morris & Co. Ltd.

*Date of Entry*: 6.5.50

*Highest Position*: 11
*Weeks on Chart*: 23

*Recordings*:

| | | |
|---|---|---|
| Doris Day with her Country Cousins | 3/50 | Columbia DB.2656 |
| Dolores Gray | 3/50 | Columbia DB.2660 |
| Bing Crosby and The Andrews Sisters | 3/50 | Brunswick 04454 |
| 'Sheriff' Johnny Denis and his Ranchers | 4/50 | Decca F.9397 |
| The Tanner Sisters with The Hedley Ward Trio | 5/50 | HMV B.9910 |

## 220 OH, YOU SWEET ONE (The Schnitzelbank Song)

*Composers*: Moe Jaffe & Dick Hardt

*Publishers*: Southern Music Publishing Co. Ltd.

*Date of Entry*: 6.5.50

*Highest Position*: 3
*Weeks on Chart*: 18

*Recordings*:

| | | |
|---|---|---|
| The Andrews Sisters and Russ Morgan (vcl) with his Orchestra | 9/49 | Brunswick 04262 |
| Benny Lee and Lynette Rae with The Keynotes | 5/50 | Decca F.9425 |
| Geraldo and his Orchestra (The Geraldtones) | 6/50 | Parlophone F.2415 |
| Billy Ternent and his Orchestra (Eva Beynon and Bobby Breen) | 6/50 | Columbia FB.3564 |
| Donald Peers | 7/50 | HMV B.9933 |
| Joe Loss and his Orchestra | 7/50 | HMV BD.6073 |

## 221 LET'S DO IT AGAIN

*Composers*: Desmond O'Connor & Ray Hartley

*Publishers*: Cecil Lennox Music Co. Ltd.

*Date of Entry*: 6.5.50

*Highest Position*: 4
*Weeks on Chart*: 20

*Recordings*:

| | | |
|---|---|---|
| Donald Peers with The Cherokeys | 5/50 | HMV B.9915 |
| Dick James with The Stargazers | 5/50 | Decca F.9424 |
| Marie Benson | 6/50 | Columbia DB.2707 |
| The Cherokeys with Frank Baron and his Orchestra | 7/50 | Esquire 5–002 |
| Margaret Whiting with Joe 'Fingers' Carr and the Carr Hops | 9/50 | Capitol CL.13353 |

## 222 DEARIE

*Composers*: Bob Hilliard & Dave Mann

*Publishers*: Campbell Connelly & Co. Ltd.

*Date of Entry*: 13.5.50

*Highest Position*: 2
*Weeks on Chart*: 21

*Recordings*:

| | | |
|---|---|---|
| George Towne and his Orchestra (The Satisfyers) | 3/50 | London L.609 |
| Ray Bolger and Ethel Merman | 4/50 | Brunswick 04456 |
| Jo Stafford and Gordon MacRae | 4/50 | Capitol CL.13286 |
| Guy Lombardo and his Royal Canadians (Kenny Gardner and The Lombardo Trio) | 5/50 | Brunswick 04494 |
| Mary Ellen Quartet (Mary Ellen, Bob Scott and Quartet) | 5/50 | MGM.286 |
| Lisa Kirk and Fran Warren | 6/50 | HMV B.9919 |
| The Five Smith Brothers | 6/50 | Parlophone R.3290 |
| Ted Ray and Kitty Bluett | 6/50 | Columbia DB.2698 |
| Billy Ternent and his Orchestra (Eva Beynon and Bobby Breen) | 6/50 | Columbia FB.3564 |
| Joe Loss and his Orchestra | 7/50 | HMV BD.6073 |
| Donald Peers | 7/50 | HMV B.9933 |

## 223 ME AND MY SHADOW

*Composers*: Dave Dreyer, Al Jolson & Billy Rose

*Publishers*: Francis Day & Hunter Ltd.

*Date of Entry*: 13.5.50/
Pos: 12/Wks: 16
*Re-entry*: 9.9.50/
Pos: 20/Wks: 1
*2nd re-entry*: 30.9.50/
Pos: 20/Wks: 1

*Recordings*:

| | | |
|---|---|---|
| The Sportsmen | 1/50 | Capitol CL.13239 |
| Josephine Bradley and her Ballroom Orchestra | 5/50 | Decca F.9431 |
| Rose Murphy | 5/50 | Brunswick 04493 |
| Ziggy Elman and his Orchestra | 7/50 | MGM.295 |
| Victor Silvester and his Ballroom Orchestra | 7/50 | Columbia FB.3566 |
| Bill Snyder and his Orchestra | 1/51 | London L.876★ |

## 224 | CHOO'N GUM

| Composers: Vic Mizzy & Mann Curtis | Date of Entry: 20.5.50 |
| Publishers: Chappell & Co. Ltd. | Highest Position: 18 |
| | Weeks on Chart: 3 |

Recordings:

| Teresa Brewer | 4/50 | London L.678 |
| Dean Martin | 4/50 | Capitol CL.13290 |
| The Tanner Sisters with The Hedley Ward Trio | 6/50 | HMV B.9923 |
| The Radio Revellers | 6/50 | Columbia DB.2700 |
| The Andrews Sisters | 7/50 | Brunswick 04535★ |

## 225 | I REMEMBER THE CORNFIELDS

| Composers: Martyn Mayne & Harry Ralton | Date of Entry: 3.6.50 |
| Publishers: Arcadia Music Publishing Co. Ltd. | Highest Position: 6 |
| | Weeks on Chart: 17 |

Recordings:

| Evelyn Knight | 3/50 | Brunswick 04459 |
| Margaret Eaves | 5/50 | Columbia DB.2679 |
| Dorothy Squires | 8/50 | Columbia DB.2722 |
| Donald Peers | 8/50 | HMV B.9945 |
| Eve Boswell | 8/50 | Parlophone R.3311 |
| Denis Martin | 8/50 | Parlophone R.3306 |
| Anne Shelton | 9/50 | Decca F.9477 |

## 226 | DADDY'S LITTLE GIRL

| Composers: Horace Gerlach & Bobbie Burke | Date of Entry: 3.6.50 |
| Publishers: Yale Music Corporation Ltd. | Highest Position: 5 |
| | Weeks on Chart: 27 |

Recordings:

| The Mills Brothers | 4/50 | Brunswick 04487 |
| Henry Jerome and his Orchestra (Hal Barton) | 4/50 | Decca F.9401 |
| Donald Peers with The Cherokeys | 5/50 | HMV B.9915 |
| Skitch Henderson and his Orchestra (Gregg Lawrence and Choir) | 5/50 | Capitol CL.13301 |
| Steve Conway | 6/50 | Columbia DB.2703 |
| Frankie Vaughan | 7/50 | Decca F.9465 |
| Billy Cotton and his Band (Alan Breeze and The Sentimentalists) | 9/50 | Decca F.9479 |

## 227 | TWO ON A TANDEM

| Composer: Elwyn Jones | Date of Entry: 10.6.50 |
| Publishers: Merrin Music Ltd. | Highest Position: 10 |
| | Weeks on Chart: 9 |

Recordings:

| Lou Preager and his Orchestra (Paul Rich) | 6/50 | Columbia FB.3565 |
| Billy Cotton and his Band (The Bandits) | 6/50 | Decca F.9458 |
| The Merry Macs | 9/50 | Decca F.9476★ |

## 228 | BEWITCHED

| Composers: Richard Rodgers & Lorenz Hart | Date of Entry: 10.6.50 |
| Publishers: Sterling Music Publishing Co. Ltd. | Highest Position: 1 |
| | Weeks on Chart: 26 |

Recordings:

| Eve Boswell with Geraldo and his Orchestra | 6/50 | Parlophone R.3297 |
| Mel Torme | 6/50 | Capitol CL.13322 |
| Bill Snyder, his Piano, and his Orchestra | 6/50 | Parlophone R.3302 |
| Gordon Jenkins and his Chorus and Orchestra (Bonnie Lou Williams) | 6/50 | Brunswick 04532 |
| David Rose and his Orchestra | 7/50 | MGM.297 |
| Doris Day with The Mellomen | 7/50 | Columbia DB.2706 |
| Ronald Chesney (harmonica) | 7/50 | HMV B.9947 |
| Felix King, his Piano, and his Orchestra | 7/50 | Decca F.9468 |
| Victor Silvester and his Ballroom Orchestra | 7/50 | Columbia FB.3570 |
| The Deep River Boys | 9/50 | HMV B.9960 |
| Bill Snyder, his Piano, and his Orchestra | 12/50 | London L.868 |
| Bill Snyder, his Piano, and his Orchestra | 1/53 | Parlophone (45) MSP.6005★ |

## 229 | SUNSHINE CAKE

| Composers: Johnny Burke & Jimmy Van Heusen | Date of Entry: 10.6.50/ Pos: 20/Wks: 1 |
| Publishers: Victoria Music Co. Ltd. | Re-entry: 1.7.50/ Pos: 19/Wks: 3 |

Recordings:

| Bing Crosby and Carole Richards with The Jeff Alexander Chorus | 4/50 | Brunswick 04482 |
| Benny Lee and The Keynotes | 4/50 | Decca F.9387 |
| Peggy Lee | 4/50 | Capitol CL.13280 |

## 230 THE NIGHT THE FLOOR FELL IN

*Composer*: Ken Wheeley

*Date of Entry*: 17.6.50/
Pos: 18/Wks: 3

*Publishers*: Southern Music Publishing Co. Ltd.

*Re-entry* 15.7.50/
Pos: 19/Wks: 1

*Recordings*:
| | | |
|---|---|---|
| Lou Preager and his Orchestra (Paul Rich) | 6/50 | Columbia FB.3565 |
| Billy Cotton and his Band (Alan Breeze and The Bandits) | 6/50 | Decca F.9458 |

## 231 A LOAD OF HAY

*Composers*: Lyrics and adaptation by Michael Feahy & Howard Barnes, with acknowledgements to Ethelbert Nevin

*Date of Entry*: 24.6.50

*Publishers*: John Fields Music Co. Ltd.

*Highest Position*: 14
*Weeks on Chart*: 8

*Recordings*:
| | | |
|---|---|---|
| Benny Lee and The Keynotes | 5/50 | Decca F.9423 |
| The Tanner Sisters with The Hedley Ward Trio | 6/50 | HMV B.9923 |
| The Five Smith Brothers | 6/50 | Parlophone R.3290 |
| Billy Thorburn's The Organ, the Dance Band and Me (The Stargazers) | 6/50 | Parlophone F.2420 |
| 'Sheriff' Johnny Denis and his Ranchers | 7/50 | Decca F.9462 |
| Doris Day and The Page Cavanaugh Trio | 2/54 | Columbia DB.3417★/ (45) SCM.5087★ |

## 232 SOMEWHERE AT THE END OF THE RAINDOW

*Composers*: John Willis & David Griffiths

*Date of Entry*: 1.7.50

*Publishers*: Tonic Music Co.

*Highest Position*: 16
*Weeks on Chart*: 2

*Recording*:
| | | |
|---|---|---|
| Dick James with The Stargazers | 5/50 | Decca F.9424 |

## 233 YOUR HEART AND MY HEART

*Composer*: Ross Parker

*Date of Entry*: 8.7.50/
Pos: 11/Wks: 11

*Publishers*: Lawrence Wright Music Co. Ltd.

*Re-entry*: 30.9.50/Pos: 19/Wks: 1

*Recordings*:
| | | |
|---|---|---|
| Harry Dawson | 6/50 | HMV B.9920 |
| Vera Lynn | 6/50 | Decca F.9448 |
| Victor Silvester and his Ballroom Orchestra | 7/50 | Columbia FB.3569 |
| Eve Boswell | 8/50 | Parlophone R.3311 |

## 234 IF I LOVED YOU

*Composers*: Richard Rodgers & Oscar Hammerstein II

*Date of Entry*: 8.7.50/
Pos: 8/Wks: 23

*Publishers*: Chappell & Co. Ltd.

*Re-entry*: 13.1.51/
Pos: 19/Wks: 1
*2nd re-entry*: 31.3.51/
Pos: 23/Wks: 1

*Recordings*:
| | | |
|---|---|---|
| Alan Dean | 6/50 | Decca F.9454 |
| Frank Sinatra | 6/50 | Columbia DB.2705 |
| Billy Ternent and his Orchestra (Bobby Breen) | 6/50 | Columbia FB.3563 |
| Eve Boswell | 6/50 | Parlophone R.3297 |
| Jan Clayton and John Raitt | 6/50 | Brunswick 04524 |
| Bing Crosby | 6/50 | Brunswick 04527 |
| Leo Reisman and his Orchestra (Marshall Young) | 6/50 | Brunswick 04529 |
| Roberto Inglez and his Orchestra | 7/50 | Parlophone R.3310 |
| Victor Silvester and his Ballroom Orchestra | 7/50 | Columbia FB.3567 |
| Joe Loss and his Orchestra | 7/50 | HMV BD.6072 |
| Harry Dawson | 7/50 | HMV B.9926 |
| Jo Stafford | 7/50 | Capitol CL.13344 |
| Edmund Hockridge | 1/51 | HMV B.10016 |

## 235 SILVER DOLLAR

*Composers*: Clarke Van Ness & Jack Palmer

*Date of Entry*: 22.7.50

*Publishers*: Pic Music Ltd.

*Highest Position*: 1
*Weeks on Chart*: 23

*Recordings*:
| | | |
|---|---|---|
| Eve Young and The Homesteaders | 4/50 | London L.658 |
| Sid Philips and his Band (Johnnie Eager) | 8/50 | HMV BD.6074 |
| Art Mooney and his Orchestra (The Art Mooney Choir) | 8/50 | MGM.307 |
| Marie Benson and The Stargazers | 9/50 | Columbia DB.2734 |
| The Keynotes | 9/50 | Decca F.9488 |
| The Five Smith Brothers | 10/50 | Parlophone R.3325 |

## 236 | CANDY AND CAKE

*Composer:* Bob Merrill | *Date of Entry:* 22.7.50

*Publishers:* Irwin Dash Music Co. Ltd. | *Highest Position:* 13
| *Weeks on Chart:* 12

*Recordings:*

| | | |
|---|---|---|
| The Mary Ellen Quartet (Mary Ellen, Bob Scott and Quartet) | 5/50 | MGM.286 |
| Mindy Carson | 6/50 | HMV B.9919 |
| Arthur Godfrey and The Chordettes | 6/50 | Columbia DB.2687 |
| Ray Anthony and his Orchestra (Betty Holliday) | 7/50 | Capitol CL.13343 |
| Geraldo and his Orchestra (Nadia Doré) | 8/50 | Parlophone F.2422 |
| Cyril Stapleton and his Orchestra (Jean Campbell and The Staplejacks) | 8/50 | Decca F.9470 |
| Evelyn Knight with The Lee-Gordon Singers | 8/50 | Brunswick 04542 |

## 237 | HEY! NEIGHBOUR

*Composer:* Ross Parker | *Date of Entry:* 29.7.50/ Pos: 19/Wks: 1

*Publishers:* Lawrence Wright Music Co. Ltd. | *Re-entry:* 12.8.50/ Pos: 4/Wks: 22

*Recordings:*

| | | |
|---|---|---|
| Primo Scala and his Banjo and Accordion Band (The Keynotes) | 6/50 | Decca F.9453 |
| Billy Thorburn's The Organ, the Dance Band and Me (The Stargazers) | 7/50 | Parlophone F.2417 |
| Bud Flanagan and Chesney Allen | 9/50 | Columbia DB.2725 |

## 238 | IF I WERE A BLACKBIRD

*Composer:* Delia Murphy | *Date of Entry:* 29.7.50/ Pos: 20/Wks: 1

*Publishers:* Box & Cox (Publications) Ltd. | *Re-entry:* 12.8.50/ Pos: 4/Wks: 22

*Recordings:*

| | | |
|---|---|---|
| Ronnie Ronalde | 3/50 | Columbia DB.2654 |
| Delia Murphy with Arthur Darley (guitar) | 7/50 | HMV BD.1237 |
| Anne Shelton | 10/50 | Decca F.9526 |
| Billy Cotton and his Band (Alan Breeze and Choir) | 10/50 | Decca F.9531 |
| Michael O'Duffy | 11/50 | HMV B.9990 |
| Josef Locke | 11/50 | Columbia DB.2763 |
| Stanley Black, his Piano, and his Orchestra (Dick James, The Stargazers and The George Mitchell Choir) | 11/50 | Decca F.9559 |
| Ronnie Ronalde | 1/53 | Columbia (45) SCM.5006★ |

(Note: The HMV release by Delia Murphy had been previously available in the UK on Regal Zonophone MR.3379.)

## 239 | SENTIMENTAL ME

*Composers:* Jim Morehead & Jimmy Cassin | *Date of Entry:* 5.8.50

*Publishers:* Cinephonic Music Co. Ltd. | *Highest Position:* 6
| *Weeks on Chart:* 16

*Recordings:*

| | | |
|---|---|---|
| Russ Morgan and his Orchestra (Russ Morgan and The Morganaires) | 4/50 | Brunswick 04478 |
| Ray Anthony and his Orchestra (Ronnie Deauville) | 6/50 | Capitol CL.13318 |
| The Ray-O-Vacs (Lester Harris) | 6/50 | Brunswick 04511 |
| The Squadronaires cond. Jimmy Miller (Roy Edwards and Ensemble) | 6/50 | Decca F.9455 |
| Steve Conway and The Stargazers | 9/50 | Columbia DB.2724 |
| Terry, The Irish Minstrel | 9/50 | HMV B.9959 |
| Joe Loss and his Orchestra | 10/50 | HMV BD.6075 |
| Allan Jones | 10/50 | HMV B.9975 |

## 240 | HAVE I TOLD YOU LATELY THAT I LOVE YOU?

*Composer:* Scott Wiseman | *Date of Entry:* 5.8.50

*Publishers:* Leeds Music Ltd. | *Highest Position:* 2
| *Weeks on Chart:* 23

*Recordings:*

| | | |
|---|---|---|
| Bing Crosby and The Andrews Sisters | 3/50 | Brunswick 04454 |
| Monte Rey | 9/50 | Columbia DB.2723 |
| Gene Autry | 9/50 | Columbia FB.3575 |
| The Tanner Sisters | 9/50 | HMV B.9957 |
| Tex Ritter | 9/50 | Capitol CL.13355 |
| Eddie Grant (Hammond organ) | 9/50 | Capitol CL.13362 |
| Red Foley and Judy Martin | 9/50 | Brunswick 04565 |
| Joe Loss and his Orchestra | 10/50 | HMV BD.6075 |
| Squadronaires cond. Jimmy Miller (Roy Edwards, Squads Choir) | 10/50 | Decca F.9500 |
| Lulubelle and Scotty | 10/50 | London L.833 |
| Oscar Rabin and his Band with Harry Davis (Marion Davis and Majorie Daw) | 12/50 | Parlophone F.2435 |

## 241 ONCE IN A WHILE

*Composers*: Bud Green & Michael Edwards

*Date of Entry*: 12.8.50

*Publishers*: Robbins Music Corporation Ltd.

*Highest Position*: 7
*Weeks on Chart*: 15

(Note: This song, first published in 1937, boasted many recordings on its first spell of popularity in 1937/8 of which the following three were the only ones still available at the time of its revival – Frances Langford with The Foursome – Brunswick 02563; Greta Keller – Decca F.6640; Louis Armstrong and his Orchestra – Decca F.6613.)

*Later recordings*:

| | | |
|---|---|---|
| The Dinning Sisters | 2/50 | Capitol CL.13192 |
| Felix King, his Piano, and his Orchestra | 7/50 | Decca F.9468 |
| Dinah Shore | 9/50 | Columbia DB.2728 |
| Anne Shelton | 10/50 | Decca F.9526 |
| Geraldo and his Orchestra | 11/50 | Parlophone F.2434 |
| Dorothy Squires | 12/50 | Columbia DB.2766★ |
| Reinhold Svensson and his Quintet | 3/51 | Esquire 10–114★ |

## 242 SAM'S SONG (The happy tune)

*Composers*: Lew Quadling & Jack Elliott

*Date of Entry*: 19.8.50

*Publishers*: Sterling Music Publishing Co. Ltd.

*Highest Position*: 4
*Weeks on Chart*: 23

*Recordings*:

| | | |
|---|---|---|
| Joe 'Fingers' Carr and the Carr-Hops (vcl & inst) | 7/50 | Capitol CL.13339 |
| Claire Hogan and Bobby Wayne | 7/50 | London L.693 |
| Bing and Gary Crosby | 9/50 | Brunswick 04553 |
| Toni Harper with The Four Hits and a Miss | 9/50 | Columbia DB.2738 |
| The Melodeons | 9/50 | MGM.319 |
| Oscar Rabin and his Band with Harry Davis (David Ede) | 10/50 | Parlophone F.2429 |
| The Johnny Dankworth Seven (Marion Williams) | 10/50 | Esquire 5–005 |
| Ted Heath and his Music (Dennis Lotis) | 11/50 | Decca F.9553 |

## 243 MONA LISA

*Composers*: Jay Livingston & Ray Evans

*Date of Entry*: 2.9.50

*Publishers*: New World Publishers Ltd.

*Highest Position*: 2
*Weeks on Chart*: 20

*Recordings*:

| | | |
|---|---|---|
| Nat 'King' Cole | 5/50 | Capitol CL.13308 |
| Ronald Chesney (harmonica) | 7/50 | HMV B.9947 |
| Charlie Spivak and his Orchestra (Tommy Lynn and The Stardreamers) | 7/50 | London L.710 |
| Victor Young and his Orchestra (Don Cherry and Chorus) | 7/50 | Brunswick 04546 |
| Art Lund | 8/50 | MGM.305 |
| Harry James and his Orchestra (Dick Williams) | 9/50 | Columbia DB.2731 |
| Steve Conway and The Stargazers | 10/50 | Columbia DB.2749 |
| Frederick Ferrari | 10/50 | Parlophone R.3328 |
| Oscar Rabin and his Band (Dennis Hale) | 10/50 | Parlophone F.2429 |
| Joe Loss and his Orchestra | 10/50 | HMV BD.6076 |
| Max Bygraves | 10/50 | Decca F.9532 |
| Allan Jones | 11/50 | HMV B.9989 |
| Ted Heath and his Music (Dickie Valentine) | 11/50 | Decca F.9554 |
| Raymond Girerd [in French] | 2/51 | Decca F.9613★ |
| Mickey Katz and his Orchestra (Anzio Pizza) [Parody titled 'Mona Liza'] | 4/51 | Capitol CL.13499★ |

(Note: For the reappearance of the song in 1959, see Song No. 1066.)

## 244 TZENA TZENA TZENA

*Composers*: Original melody by Issachar Miron arranged by Spencer Ross with English lyrics by Gordon Jenkins

*Date of Entry*: 2.9.50/
*Pos*: 20/Wks: 1

*Publishers*: Leeds Music Ltd.

*Re-entry*: 23.9.50/
*Pos*: 7/Wks: 11

*Recordings*:

| | | |
|---|---|---|
| Mitch Miller and his Orchestra and Chorus | 8/50 | Columbia DB.2726 |
| Gordon Jenkins and his Orchestra (The Weavers & Chorus) | 8/50 | Brunswick 04552 |
| Sid Phillips and his Band (The Tanner Sisters and Johnnie Eager) | 8/50 | HMV BD.6074 |
| The Weavers [sung in Hebrew] with Banjo, Guitar & Bass acc. | 9/50 | Brunswick 04563 |
| Edmundo Ros and his Orchestra (Edmundo Ros) | 10/50 | Decca F.9495 |

## 245 | ASHES OF ROSES

*Composers*: Harry Tobias, Lew Porter & Sidney Mitchell

*Date of Entry*: 9.9.50/
Pos: 8/Wks: 16

*Publishers*: Campbell Connelly & Co. Ltd.

*Re-entry*: 6.1.51/
Pos: 19/Wks: 1

*Recordings*:

| | | |
|---|---|---|
| Billy Thorburn's The Organ, the Dance Band and Me (The Stargazers) | 9/50 | Parlophone F.2425 |
| The Deep River Boys | 9/50 | HMV B.9960 |
| The Keynotes with The Keynotes Choir | 9/50 | Decca F.9488 |
| Art Morton and Evelyn Bell Knightingales | 9/50 | MGM.320 |
| Steve Conway and The Stargazers | 10/50 | Columbia DB.2749 |

## 246 | I ONLY HAVE EYES FOR YOU

*Composers*: Al Dubin & Harry Warren

*Date of Entry*: 16.9.50

*Publishers*: B. Feldman & Co. Ltd.

*Highest Position*: 14
*Weeks on Chart*: 10

*Recordings*:

| | | |
|---|---|---|
| Freddy Gardner (sax) with Peter Yorke and his Concert Orchestra | 6/48 | Columbia DB.2411 |
| Al Jolson | 7/49 | Brunswick 04200 |
| Al Jolson (Re-issue with a different title on reverse side) | 11/49 | Brunswick 04379 |
| George Shearing and his Trio | 4/50 | Decca F.9386 |
| Cyril Stapleton and his Orchestra (Bob Dale) | 8/50 | Decca F.9482 |
| Paul Weston and his Orchestra | 9/50 | Capitol CL.13358 |
| Geraldo and his Orchestra | 11/50 | Parlophone F.2434 |
| Roberto Inglez and his Orchestra | 11/50 | Parlophone R.3332 |
| Doris Day | 12/50 | Columbia DB.2769★ |
| Victor Silvester and his Ballroom Orchestra | 2/51 | Columbia FB.3595★ |

(Note: The Frank Sinatra version on Columbia DB.2226 – issued in 8/46 – was deleted from the catalogue before the sheet music success in 1950. The song was first recorded in 1934 with much popularity in early 1935.)

## 247 | HAPPY TIMES

*Composer*: Sylvia Fine

*Date of Entry*: 16.9.50

*Publishers*: B. Feldman & Co. Ltd.

*Highest Position*: 20
*Weeks on Chart*: 1

*Recordings*:

| | | |
|---|---|---|
| Joe Loss and his Orchestra | 5/50 | HMV BD.6068 |
| Dinah Shore | 5/50 | Columbia DB.2684 |
| Benny Lee and The Keynotes | 5/50 | Decca F.9423 |
| Jo Stafford | 5/50 | Capitol CL.13303 |
| Danny Kaye with The Lee Gordon Singers | 5/50 | Brunswick 04505 |

## 248 | GOODNIGHT, IRENE

*Composers*: Huddie 'Leadbelly' Ledbetter & John Lomax

*Date of Entry*: 23.9.50

*Publishers*: Leeds Music Ltd.

*Highest Position*: 1
*Weeks on Chart*: 20

*Recordings*:

| | | |
|---|---|---|
| Gordon Jenkins and his Orchestra (The Weavers and Chorus) | 8/50 | Brunswick 04552 |
| Frank Sinatra | 9/50 | Columbia DB.2737 |
| Jo Stafford with Trio | 9/50 | Capitol CL.13352 |
| The Tanner Sisters with The Hedley Ward Trio | 10/50 | HMV B.9980 |
| Eddie Grant (Hammond organ) | 10/50 | Capitol CL.13375 |
| Billy Thorburn's The Organ, the Dance Band and Me (The Stargazers) | 11/50 | Parlophone F.2431 |
| The Five Smith Brothers | 11/50 | Parlophone R.3341 |
| Ted Heath and his Music (Dennis Lotis) | 11/50 | Decca F.9553 |
| Huddie 'Leadbelly' Ledbetter | 12/50 | Melodisc 1151 |

## 249 | COUNT EVERY STAR

*Composers*: Bruno Coquatrix & Sammy Gallop

*Date of Entry*: 23.9.50

*Publishers*: Peter Maurice Music Co. Ltd

*Highest Position*: 12
*Weeks on Chart*: 8

*Recordings*:

| | | |
|---|---|---|
| Ray Anthony and his Orchestra (Dick Noel) | 7/50 | Capitol CL.13342 |
| Herb Jeffries | 8/50 | Columbia DB.2715 |
| Hugo Winterhalter and his Orchestra and Mixed Chorus | 8/50 | HMV B.9939 |
| Dick Haymes with Artie Shaw & his Strings and Woodwind | 9/50 | Brunswick 04557 |
| Kathran Oldfield | 10/50 | Esquire 5–004 |
| Victor Silvester and his Ballroom Orchestra | 12/50 | Columbia FB.3591★ |

## 250 | I ONLY SAW HIM ONCE

*Composers*: Joan Whitney & Alex Kramer

*Date of Entry*: 7.10.50/
Pos: 20/Wks: 1

*Publishers*: Unit Music Publishing Co.

*Re-entry*: 4.11.50/
Pos: 20/Wks: 1
*2nd re-entry*: 18.11.50/
Pos: 10/Wks: 10

*Recordings*:

| | | |
|---|---|---|
| Rosemary Clooney | 9/50 | Columbia DB.2738 |
| Billy Cotton and his Band (Doreen Stephens) | 11/50 | Decca F.9564 |

## 251 BIBBIDI-BOBBIDI-BOO (The Magic Song)

**Composers:** Al Hoffman, Jerry Livingston & Mack David

**Date of Entry:** 21.10.50

**Publishers:** Walt Disney Music Co. Ltd.

**Highest Position:** 12
**Weeks on Chart:** 6

Recordings:
| | | |
|---|---|---|
| Jimmy Durante | 10/50 | MGM.315 |
| Perry Como and The Fontane Sisters | 10/50 | HMV B.9961 |
| Ilene Woods with The Woodsmen | 10/50 | HMV B.9970 |
| Dinah Shore | 10/50 | Columbia DB.2735 |
| Sy Oliver and his Orchestra (The Aristokats and Ensemble) | 10/50 | Brunswick 04577 |
| Bing Crosby with Jud Conlon's Rhythmaires | 10/50 | Brunswick 04580 |
| Jo Stafford and Gordon MacRae | 10/50 | Capitol CL.13386 |
| Jack Berch and The Mullan Sisters | 10/50 | London L.570 |
| Joe Loss and his Orchestra | 11/50 | HMV BD.6079 |
| Ray Robbins and his Orchestra (Ray Robbins) | 11/50 | Capitol CL.13396 |
| Mickey Katz and his Orchestra (Mickey Katz) [Titled 'The Baby, the Bubbe and you'] | 2/51 | Capitol CL.13457★ |

## 252 RUDOLPH THE RED-NOSED REINDEER

**Composer:** Johnny Marks

*1950 Date of Entry:* 21.10.50/Pos: 1/ Wks: 17

**Publishers:** Chappell & Co. Ltd./ Sterling Music Publishing Co. Ltd.

*1951 Date of Entry:* 1.12.51/Pos: 19/ Wks: 5

*1952 Date of Entry:* 13.12.52/Pos: 17/ Wks: 3

*1953 Date of Entry:* 26.12.53/Pos: 24/ Wks: 1

Recordings:
| | | |
|---|---|---|
| Gene Autry with The Pinafores | 10/50 | Columbia FB.3576 |
| Bing Crosby with Jud Conlon's Rhythmaires | 10/50 | Brunswick 04581 |
| Smiley Burnette | 10/50 | Capitol CL.13388 |
| Donald Peers with Hattie Jacques as the Reindeer | 11/50 | HMV B.9984 |
| Spike Jones and his City Slickers (Rudolph and The Reindeers) [special lyrics by Maxwell] | 11/50 | HMV B.9988 |
| Sugar 'Chile' Robinson | 11/50 | Capitol CL.13393 |
| Primo Scala and his Banjo and Accordion Band (The Keynotes) | 11/50 | Decca F.9503 |
| Ken Griffin (organ) | 12/50 | Columbia DB.2780 |
| Red Foley and the Little Foleys – Shirley, Julie and Jenny | 11/51 | Brunswick 04820 |

| | | |
|---|---|---|
| Guy Lombardo and his Royal Canadians (Kenny Gardner and The Lombardo Trio) | 11/51 | Brunswick 04832 |
| Jimmy Durante | 11/52 | London L.1153 |
| Ray Martin and his Concert Orchestra | 11/53 | Columbia DB.3376 |
| Homer and Jethro (Titled 'Randolph, the Flat-nosed Reindeer') | 11/53 | HMV B.10581 |
| Ray Martin and his Concert Orchestra | 12/53 | Columbia (45) SCM.5071 |
| Jimmy Boyd | 11/54 | Philips PB.358★ |
| Billy May and his Orchestra (Alvin Stoller) | 12/54 | Capitol CL.14210 (& 45-)★ |
| The Four-in-A-Chord | 11/55 | Embassy WB.159★ |

## 253 HOME COOKIN'

**Composers:** Jay Livingston & Ray Evans

**Date of Entry:** 28.10.50

**Publishers:** Victoria Music Publishing Co. Ltd.

**Highest Position:** 18
**Weeks on Chart:** 2

Recordings:
| | | |
|---|---|---|
| Margaret Whiting and Bob Hope with The Starlighters | 8/50 | Capitol CL.13348 |
| Bing Crosby with Jud Conlon's Rhythmaires | 8/50 | Brunswick 04534 |
| Dorothy Shay | 9/50 | Columbia DB.2730 |
| Jerry Gray and his Orchestra (The Crew Chiefs) | 9/50 | Brunswick 04570 |
| Betty Garrett | 9/50 | MGM.321 |

## 254 A DREAM IS A WISH YOUR HEART MAKES

**Composers:** Al Hoffman, Jerry Livingston & Mack David

**Date of Entry:** 11.11.50

**Publishers:** Walt Disney Music Co. Ltd.

**Highest Position:** 17
**Weeks on Chart:** 1

Recordings:
| | | |
|---|---|---|
| Perry Como | 10/50 | HMV B.9961 |
| Ilene Woods | 10/50 | HMV B.9971 |
| Victor Silvester and his Ballroom Orchestra | 10/50 | Columbia FB.3577 |
| Steve Conway | 10/50 | Columbia DB.2729 |
| Sy Oliver and his Orchestra (Jack Haskell and The Aristokats) | 10/50 | Brunswick 04577 |
| The Jubalaires | 10/50 | Capitol CL.13378 |
| Joe Loss and his Orchestra | 11/50 | HMV BD.6079 |
| Mantovani and his Orchestra (Dick James) | 11/50 | Decca F.9566 |

## 255 WE'LL KEEP A WELCOME

**Composers**: Mai Jones, Lyn Joshua & James Harper

**Publishers**: Lawrence Wright Music Co. Ltd.

*Date of Entry*:
11.11.50/Pos: 14/ Wks: 2
*Re-entry*: 2.12.50/ Pos: 20/Wks: 2
*2nd re-entry*: 13.1.51/ Pos: 20/Wks: 1

*Recordings*:
| | | |
|---|---|---|
| The George Mitchell Choir with Don Lorusso (organ) | 7/49 | Decca F.9191 |
| Bill Johnson | 9/49 | Columbia DB.2574 |
| John Rorke and The London Community Singers cond. Glyn Jones | 10/49 | Parlophone F.2381 |
| The Lyrian Singers cond. Idloes Owen with narration by Tom Jones | 10/49 | HMV B.9833 |
| Dick James with The Ilford Girls' Choir | 6/51 | Decca F.9689★ |

## 256 AUTUMN LEAVES
### (Les Feuilles Mortes)

**Composers**: Joseph Kosma & Jacques Prevert. English lyrics by Johnny Mercer. Additional verse lyrics by Geoffrey Parsons

**Publishers**: Peter Maurice Music Co. Ltd.

*Date of Entry*: 11.11.50

*Highest Position*: 7
*Weeks on Chart*: 21

*Recordings*:
| | | |
|---|---|---|
| Paul Weston and his Orchestra | 5/50 | Capitol CL.13311 |
| The Melachrino Strings | 9/50 | HMV B.9952 |
| Jo Stafford | 9/50 | Capitol CL.13367 |
| Fred Hartley and his Music | 9/50 | Columbia DB.2743 |
| Alan Dean | 9/50 | Decca F.9492 |
| Mitch Miller and his Orchestra and Chorus | 11/50 | Columbia DB.2752 |
| Ray Anthony and his Orchestra (Ronnie Deauville and The Skyliners) | 11/50 | Capitol CL.13417 |
| Victor Silvester and his Ballroom Orchestra | 12/50 | Columbia FB.3590 |
| Bing Crosby | 12/50 | Brunswick 04602 |
| Steve Conway | 12/50 | Columbia DB.2775 |
| Roberto Inglez and his Orchestra | 1/51 | Parlophone R.3349 |
| Jack Pleis and his Orchestra (Bob Houston and Chorus) | 1/51 | London L.871 |
| Artie Shaw and his Orchestra | 1/51 | Brunswick 04628 |
| Carmen Cavallaro (piano) | 5/51 | Brunswick 04692★ |

## 257 ORANGE COLOURED SKY

**Composers**: Milton DeLugg & Willie Stein

**Publishers**: Edwin H. Morris & Co. Ltd.

*Date of Entry*: 18.11.50

*Highest Position*: 9
*Weeks on Chart*: 13

*Recordings*:
| | | |
|---|---|---|
| Nat 'King' Cole with his Trio and Stan Kenton and his Orchestra | 10/50 | Capitol CL.13392 |
| Doris Day with The Page Cavanaugh Trio | 11/50 | Columbia DB.2750 |
| Betty Hutton | 11/50 | HMV B.9991 |
| Danny Kaye and Patty Andrews | 11/50 | Brunswick 04609 |
| Joe Loss and his Orchestra | 12/50 | HMV BD.6083 |
| Cyril Stapleton and his Orchestra (Jean Campbell) | 12/50 | Decca F.9576 |
| Geraldo and his Orchestra (Nadia Doré) | 1/51 | Parlophone F.2443 |

## 258 CHRISTMAS IN KILLARNEY

**Composers**: John Redmond, James Cavanaugh & Frank Weldon

**Publishers**: Harms–Connelly Ltd.

*Date of Entry*: 25.11.50

*Highest Position*: 4
*Weeks on Chart*: 7

*Recordings*:
| | | |
|---|---|---|
| The Four Ramblers | 11/50 | Decca F.9558 |
| Terry, The Irish Minstrel | 12/50 | HMV B.10008 |
| Percy Faith and his Orchestra (The Shillelagh Singers) | 12/50 | Columbia DB.2793 |
| Bing Crosby with Jud Conlon's Rhythmaires | 12/51 | Brunswick 04838★ |

## 259 I TAUT I TAW A PUDDY TAT

**Composers**: Alan Livingston, Billy May & Warren Foster

**Publishers**: Harms–Connelly Ltd.

*Date of Entry*: 25.11.50

*Highest Position*: 1
*Weeks on Chart*: 14

*Recordings*:
| | | |
|---|---|---|
| Mel Blanc | 11/50 | Capitol CL.13407 |
| Benny Lee and Mary with The Stargazers | 12/50 | Decca F.9577 |

## 260 MY CHRISTMAS WISH

**Composers**: Johnny Reine & Tommie Connor

**Publishers**: Michael Reine Music Co. Ltd.

*Date of Entry*: 25.11.50

*Highest Position*: 9
*Weeks on Chart*: 6

*Recordings*:
| | | |
|---|---|---|
| Anne Shelton | 11/50 | Decca F.9551 |
| Mary Burns and her Boy Friends | 11/50 | Melodisc 1017 |

## 261 BELOVED, BE FAITHFUL

| | | |
|---|---|---|
| *Composers:* Ervin Drake & Jimmy Shirl | *Date of Entry:* 25.11.50 | |
| *Publishers:* Pickwick Music Ltd. | *Highest Position:* 1<br>*Weeks on Chart:* 22 | |

Recordings:

| | | |
|---|---|---|
| Russ Morgan and his Orchestra (The Morganaires) | 7/50 | Brunswick 04540 |
| Paul Weston and his Orchestra (The Norman Luboff Choir) | 11/50 | Columbia DB.2758 |
| Teddy Johnson | 11/50 | Columbia DB.2759 |
| Donald Peers | 11/50 | HMV B.9984 |
| Snooky Lanson and Eve Young | 12/50 | London L.751 |
| Eve Boswell | 12/50 | Parlophone R.3343 |
| Cyril Stapleton and his Orchestra (Bob Dale and The Staplejacks) | 12/50 | Decca F.9581 |
| Joe Loss and his Orchestra | 1/51 | HMV BD.6085 |
| Petula Clark | 1/51 | Polygon P.1003 |

## 262 I LEAVE MY HEART IN AN ENGLISH GARDEN

| | | |
|---|---|---|
| *Composers:* Harry Parr-Davies & Christopher Hassall | *Date of Entry:* 9.12.50/<br>Pos: 9/Wks: 23 | |
| *Publishers:* Sun Music Publishing Co. Ltd. | *Re-entry:* 26.5.51/<br>Pos: 22/Wks: 2<br>*2nd re-entry:* 21.7.51/<br>Pos: 22/Wks: 2 | |

Recordings:

| | | |
|---|---|---|
| Lee Lawrence | 12/50 | Decca F.9575 |
| Edmund Hockridge | 12/50 | HMV B.10001 |
| Webster Booth | 2/51 | HMV B.10027 |
| Ronnie Ronalde | 4/51 | Columbia DB.2839 |
| The Luton Girls' Choir | 4/51 | Parlophone R.3373 |
| The George Mitchell Choir with Don Lorusso (organ) | 5/51 | Decca F.9672 |

## 263 (Down at the) FERRY BOAT INN

| | | |
|---|---|---|
| *Composers:* Don Pelosi & Jimmy Campbell | *Date of Entry:* 9.12.50 | |
| *Publishers:* Campbell Connelly & Co. Ltd. | *Highest Position:* 4<br>*Weeks on Chart:* 20 | |

Recordings:

| | | |
|---|---|---|
| Benny Lee with The Stargazers | 12/50 | Decca F.9577 |
| The Tanner Sisters with The Hedley Ward Trio | 12/50 | HMV B.10003 |
| The Beverley Sisters | 1/51 | Columbia DB.2786 |
| Geraldo and his Orchestra (The Geraldtones) | 3/51 | Parlophone F.2453 |

## 264 ALL MY LOVE (Bolero)

| | | |
|---|---|---|
| *Composers:* Henri Contet & Paul Durand with English lyrics added in 1950 by Mitchell Parish | *Date of Entry:* 9.12.50 | |
| *Publishers:* Peter Maurice Music Co. Ltd. | *Highest Position:* 5<br>*Weeks on Chart:* 19 | |

Recordings:

| | | |
|---|---|---|
| (a) Titled 'Bolero' (Contet-Durand) | | |
| Georges Guetary | 6/49 | Columbia DB.2528 |
| Denny Dennis | 9/49 | Decca F.9220 |
| (b) Titled 'All my Love' (Durand-Parish) | | |
| Xavier Cugat and his Orchestra (Abbe Lane) | 9/50 | Columbia DB.2741 |
| Percy Faith and his Orchestra and Chorus | 11/50 | Columbia DB.2753 |
| Allan Jones | 11/50 | HMV B.9989 |
| Bing Crosby with The Jeff Alexander Chorus | 11/50 | Brunswick 04606 |
| Lester Ferguson | 12/50 | Parlophone R.3340 |
| Joe Loss and his Orchestra | 12/50 | HMV BD.6082 |
| Cyril Stapleton and his Orchestra (Bob Dale) | 12/50 | Decca F.9576 |
| Geraldo and his Orchestra (Eve Boswell) | 1/51 | Parlophone F.2443 |
| Guy Lombardo and his Royal Canadians (Bill Flanagan) | 1/51 | Brunswick 04633 |
| Eddie Grant (organ) | 1/51 | Capitol CL.13435 |
| Patti Page | 2/52 | Oriole CB.1065★ |
| Patti Page | 6/54 | Mercury MB.2953★ |
| (c) Titled 'All my Love – Bolero' | | |
| Roberto Inglez and his Orchestra | 1/51 | Parlophone R.3349 |

## 265 THE THING

| | | |
|---|---|---|
| *Composer:* Charles Randolph Grean (derived from an old English ballad, 'The Chandler's Wife') | *Date of Entry:* 16.12.50 | |
| *Publishers:* Leeds Music Ltd. | *Highest Position:* 2<br>*Weeks on Chart:* 10 | |

Recordings:

| | | |
|---|---|---|
| Phil Harris | 12/50 | HMV B.10007 |
| Phil Morrow's Music (Charles Forsythe and The Beaux and The Belles) | 12/50 | Columbia DB.2795 |
| Teresa Brewer | 12/50 | London L.873 |
| Billy Cotton and his Band (Alan Breeze and The Bandits) | 12/50 | Decca F.9583 |
| The Five Smith Brothers | 1/51 | Parlophone R.3353 |
| Danny Kaye | 1/51 | Brunswick 04635 |

## 266 THE PETITE WALTZ (La Petite Valse)

| | | |
|---|---|---|
| *Composers*: Joe Heyne, E. A. Ellington & Phyllis Claire | | *Date of Entry*: 16.12.50/ Pos: 1/Wks: 30 |
| *Publishers*: Leeds Music Ltd. | | *Re-entry*: 25.8.51/ Pos: 21/Wks: 1 |

*Recordings*:

| | | |
|---|---|---|
| Jack Pleis, his piano, and his Orchestra | 9/50 | London L.762 |
| Anne Shelton and Dick James with Anton Karas (zither) | 11/50 | Decca F.9563 |
| Billy Cotton and his Band | 11/50 | Decca F.9564 |
| Guy Lombardo and his Royal Canadians (two Pianos: Fred Kreitzer and Buddy Brennen) | 11/50 | Brunswick 04598 |
| Roberto Inglez and his Orchestra (Titled 'La Petite Waltz') | 12/50 | Parlophone R.3344 |
| Swing and Sway with Sammy Kaye | 12/50 | Columbia DB.2768 |
| Ken Griffin (organ) | 12/50 | Columbia DB.2780 |
| Joe Loss and his Orchestra | 12/50 | HMV BD.6082 |
| The Three Suns with Larry Green (piano) | 12/50 | HMV B.10000 |
| The Tanner Sisters | 12/50 | HMV B.10003 |
| Sidney Torch and his Orchestra | 1/51 | Parlophone R.3348 |
| Rawicz and Landauer (two Pianos) | 1/51 | Columbia DB.2788 |
| Eddie Grant (organ) | 1/51 | Capitol CL.13435 |
| The Joe Heyne Players, featuring Joe Heyne (piano) | 2/51 | Esquire 5–009 |
| Etienne Lorin and his Orchestra | 4/51 | Nixa BY.1581 |

## 267 SLEIGH RIDE

| | | |
|---|---|---|
| *Composer*: Leroy Anderson – lyrics added by Mitchell Parish | | *Date of Entry*: 30.12.50 |
| *Publishers*: Arcadia Music Publishing Co. Ltd. | | *Highest Position*: 7 *Weeks on Chart*: 12 |

*Recordings*:

| | | |
|---|---|---|
| Ethel Smith (organ) | 6/50 | Brunswick 04517 |
| Johnny Desmond | 11/50 | MGM.342 |
| The Madcaps (harmonicas) | 11/50 | London L.786 |
| Percy Faith and his Orchestra and Chorus | 12/50 | Columbia DB.2782 |
| The Capitol Symphonic Band cond. Louis Castellucci | 12/50 | Capitol CL.13428 |
| The Boston Promenade Orchestra cond. Arthur Fiedler | 12/50 | HMV B.9993 |
| The Three Suns | 12/50 | HMV B.10000 |
| The Andrews Sisters | 1/51 | Brunswick 04629 |
| Leroy Anderson and his 'Pops' Concert Orchestra | 2/51 | Brunswick 04652 |

## 268 (Two little men in a) FLYING SAUCER

| | | |
|---|---|---|
| *Composer*: Arthur Pitt | | *Date of Entry*: 30.12.50/ Pos: 20/Wks: 1 |
| *Publishers*: Unit Music Ltd. | | *Re-entry*: 13.1.51/ Pos: 18/Wks: 2 |

*Recordings*:

| | | |
|---|---|---|
| Phil Morrow and his Music ('Jennifer' and The Beaux and the Belles) | 12/50 | Columbia DB.2795 |
| Joe Loss and his Orchestra (The Loss Chords) | 12/50 | HMV BD.6084 |
| Billy Cotton and his Band (Alan Breeze and The Bandits) | 12/50 | Decca F.9583 |
| Ella Fitzgerald | 6/51 | Brunswick 04717★ |

# 1951

The Top Twenty became a Top Twenty-four from 10 March 1951 although the extra songs did not appear in public anywhere at the time. It was a particularly bad year as far as British songs were concerned, with less than a quarter of the chart entries coming from these shores. The top British song of the year, *Good luck, good health, God bless you*, appeared at No. 14 in the 21 July chart and was the highest placed of only four British entries that week. Our music trade was highly concerned and urged the BBC to boost the British material – approaches were also made to Jack Jackson, who was to broadcast his 'Record Round-Up' throughout the year on Saturday nights beginning at 11.15 with his familiar cry of 'Ooh, it's Saturday!' To play a record three times running was to award what one might call a Jackson 'Oscar' and guaranteed a song's success. Jack featured Jimmy Young's recording of *Too young* no less than four times in a row from 21 July – and two weeks later the song entered the sheet music charts. But this airplay created problems for Alan Freeman, the boss of the new Polygon record company. His presses couldn't get the records out quickly enough to satisfy the demand and production of all other titles stopped for a time while they caught up with the orders. The story goes that even the rival company, Decca, helped out by pressing some copies! It was a year to remember for some American singers who came to the fore with a bang – Guy Mitchell, Rosemary Clooney, Tennessee Ernie – before he added the Ford – and Frankie Laine after his transfer from

| | MOST WEEKS ON THE CHARTS TOP SIX | |
|---|---|---|
| Pos | | Wks |
| 1 | *Be my love* | 43 |
| 2 | *Good luck, good health God bless you* | 36 |
| 3 | *September song* | 32 |
| 4 | *The loveliest night of the year* | 30 |
| 5 | *The petite waltz* | 28 |
| 6 | *Mockin' bird hill* | 26 |

Mercury to Columbia. Although it is virtually certain that Jimmy Young would have had a record chart No. 1 with *Too young* had there been record charts at the time, one could just as easily speculate that two possible earlier No. 1s might have gone to another British singer, Teddy Johnson, whose *Beloved, be faithful* and *Tennessee waltz* were also big sellers and No. 1 sheet music songs at the start of the year. They prompted a guest appearance for Teddy on

'Top Score' on 10 February and he sang no less than three of his recordings including *Tennessee waltz* which was in the top four at the time. So, for all the lack of British sheet music hits, homegrown talent like Johnson and Steve Conway were leading us into the Fifties with some optimism. Bob Merrill, however, continued his domination of the sheet music charts. He had five hits during 1951 with *My truly, truly fair* gaining the highest spot at No. 2. In his first programme of the year on 6 January, Jack Jackson played seven seconds of each of the Tanner Sisters, Gordon Jenkins, Frank Sinatra and Jo Stafford recordings of *Goodnight, Irene*, followed by the parody follow-up, *Please say goodnight to the guy, Irene* by *Maharajah of Magador* vocalist, Ziggy Talent. The programme also included the first broadcast of Guy Mitchell's version of *My heart cries for you*,

thus heralding a period of extreme success for the former Al Cernick. 19 May saw the one hundredth 'Round-Up' celebrated with extracts of no less than 50 records in the usual 41 minutes of the programme including parts of three continental recordings of *The thing*. Wilfrid Thomas, having taken over 'Record Rendezvous' from Sam Costa, promptly made a hit of *Rose, Rose, I love you* by Chinese vocalist Miss Hue Lee on the show and then wrote English lyrics which created a hit disc for Frankie Laine. Thomas had obtained the Lee recording during the war and the demand from listeners after he aired it ensured that it would be issued, and Columbia are to be credited with doing just that. Many listeners sent Thomas recordings of other Chinese girls named Lee but unfortunately none turned out to be the same Lee.

# SONG CHARTS

## 269 | (It's a) MARSHMALLOW WORLD

*Composers:* Peter de Rose & Carl Sigman

*Publishers:* Edward Kassner Music Co. Ltd.

*Date of Entry:* 6.1.51/ Pos: 12/Wks: 5
*Re-entry:* 17.2.51/ Pos: 18/Wks: 1

*Recordings:*

| | | |
|---|---|---|
| Anne Shelton | 11/50 | Decca F.9552 |
| Ray Anthony and his Orchestra (Ronnie Deauville) | 11/50 | Capitol CL.13417 |
| Bing Crosby with The Lee Gordon Singers | 11/50 | Brunswick 04606 |
| Arthur Godfrey with The Chordettes and The Cherry Sisters | 12/50 | Columbia DB.2767 |
| Johnny Desmond with The Ray Charles Singers | 1/51 | MGM.351 |

## 270 | IF

*Composers:* Tolchard Evans, Robert Hargreaves & Stanley Damerell

*Publishers:* Cecil Lennox Music Co. Ltd.

*Date of Entry:* 13.1.51

*Highest Position:* 4
*Weeks on Chart:* 22

*Recordings:*

| | | |
|---|---|---|
| Frederick Ferrari | 9/50 | Parlophone R.3318 |
| Allan Jones | 10/50 | HMV B.9975 |
| Dick James | 11/50 | Decca F.9556 |
| Jo Stafford | 1/51 | Columbia DB.2792 |
| Dean Martin | 2/51 | Capitol CL.13451 |
| Jan Garber and his Orchestra (Roy Cordell) | 2/51 | Capitol CL.13454 |
| Perry Como | 2/51 | HMV B.10042 |
| Victor Silvester and his Ballroom Orchestra | 3/51 | Columbia FB.3599 |
| Geraldo and his Orchestra (Eve Boswell) | 3/51 | Parlophone F.2453 |
| Billy Eckstine | 3/51 | MGM.380 |
| Joe Loss and his Orchestra | 4/51 | HMV BD.6091 |
| The Ink Spots | 4/51 | Brunswick 04681 |
| Guy Lombardo and his Royal Canadians (Bill Flanagan) | 4/51 | Brunswick 04691 |
| Louis Armstrong and his Orchestra (Louis Armstrong) | 10/51 | Brunswick 04791★ |

## 271 | TENNESSEE WALTZ

*Composers:* Redd Stewart & Pee Wee King

*Publishers:* Campbell Connelly & Co. Ltd

*Date of Entry:* 20.1.51

*Highest Position:* 1
*Weeks on Chart:* 25

*Recordings:*

| | | |
|---|---|---|
| Anita O'Day with The All Stars | 12/50 | London L. 867 |
| Teddy Johnson | 1/51 | Columbia DB.2799 |
| Les Paul and Mary Ford | 1/51 | Capitol CL.13434 |
| The Fontane Sisters | 1/51 | HMV B.10021 |
| Tommy Tucker and his Orchestra (Don Brown and Trio) | 1/51 | MGM.357 |
| Guy Lombardo and his Royal Canadians (Kenny Gardner and The Lombardo Trio) | 1/51 | Brunswick 04633 |
| Petula Clark | 1/51 | Polygon P.1004 |
| The Johnston Brothers | 1/51 | Decca F.9606 |
| Victor Silvester and his Ballroom Orchestra | 2/51 | Columbia FB.3594 |
| Geraldo and his Orchestra | 2/51 | Parlophone F.2448 |
| Jo Stafford | 2/51 | Columbia DB.2802 |
| Donald Peers and The Merry Macs | 2/51 | HMV B.10039 |
| Billy Cotton and his Band (Rita and Joyce) | 2/51 | Decca F.9617 |
| Joe Loss and his Orchestra | 3/51 | HMV BD.6087 |
| Spike Jones and his City Slickers (Sara Berner assisted by Sir Frederick Gas) | 3/51 | HMV B.10049 |
| Patti Page | 5/51 | Oriole CB.1046 |
| Patti Page | 6/54 | Mercury MB.2944★ |

## 272 NEVERTHELESS

| | |
|---|---|
| *Composers*: Bert Kalmar & Harry Ruby | *Date of Entry*: 20.1.51 |
| *Publishers*: Chappell & Co. Ltd. | *Highest Position*: 9 |
| | *Weeks on Chart*: 15 |

*Recordings*:

| | | |
|---|---|---|
| Paul Weston and his Orchestra (The Norman Luboff Choir) | 11/50 | Columbia DB.2758 |
| Sid Phillips and his Band (Geraldine Farrar) | 11/50 | HMV BD.6077 |
| Ray Anthony and his Orchestra (Ronnie Deauville and The Skyliners) | 11/50 | Capitol CL.13397 |
| Fred Astaire, Red Skelton and Anita Ellis | 11/50 | MGM.336 |
| Ted Heath and his Music (Dennis Lotis) | 11/50 | Decca F.9554 |
| Teddy Phillips and his Orchestra (Billy Sagonn) | 11/50 | London L.773 |
| Victor Silvester and his Ballroom Orchestra | 1/51 | Columbia FB.3593 |
| Frank Sinatra | 1/51 | Columbia DB.2790 |
| The Mills Brothers | 1/51 | Brunswick 04639 |
| Ralph Flanagan and his Orchestra (Harry Prime) | 2/51 | HMV B.10024 |

## 273 JUST THE WAY YOU ARE

| | |
|---|---|
| *Composer*: Ralph Freed | *Date of Entry*: 20.1.51 |
| *Publishers*: Walt Disney Music Co. Ltd. | *Highest Position*: 17 |
| | *Weeks on Chart*: 6 |

*Recordings*:

| | | |
|---|---|---|
| Gordon MacRae with The Ewing Sisters | 11/50 | Capitol CL.13412 |
| Sy Oliver and his Orchestra (Ralph Young and The Three Beaux and a Peep) | 1/51 | Brunswick 04630 |

## 274 ME AND MY IMAGINATION

| | |
|---|---|
| *Composers*: Bob Merrill & Al Hoffman | *Date of Entry*: 20.1.51/ Pos: 20/Wks: 2 |
| *Publishers*: Campbell Connelly & Co. Ltd. | *Re-entry*: 17.2.51/ Pos: 19/Wks: 6 |

*Recordings*:

| | | |
|---|---|---|
| The Squadronaires cond. Jimmy Miller (Roy Edwards) | 10/50 | Decca F.9500 |
| Betty Brewer | 10/50 | Brunswick 04575 |
| Marie Benson | 11/50 | Columbia DB.2755 |
| The Stargazers | 11/50 | Decca F.9535 |
| Donald Peers | 12/50 | HMV B.10002 |
| Victor Silvester and his Ballroom Orchestra | 1/51 | Columbia FB.3592 |
| Dorothy Collins | 1/51 | MGM.354 |
| Guy Mitchell | 1/51 | Columbia DB.2800 |

## 275 SEPTEMBER SONG

| | |
|---|---|
| *Composers*: Kurt Weill & Maxwell Anderson | *Date of Entry*: 27.1.51 |
| *Publishers*: Sterling Music Publishing Co. Ltd. | *Highest Position*: 4 |
| | *Weeks on Chart*: 32 |

(Some earlier issues from 1946–47 had been deleted by the time the song reached the charts in 1951. The Walter Huston version was recorded on 31 October 1944.)

*Recordings*:

| | | |
|---|---|---|
| Bing Crosby | 1/47 | Brunswick 03758 |
| Josephine Bradley and her Ballroom Orchestra | 2/47 | Decca F.8740 |
| Frank Sinatra | 3/47 | Columbia DB.2286 |
| Joe Mooney and his Quartet (Joe Mooney) | 6/48 | Brunswick 03896 |
| Harry James and his Orchestra | 6/48 | Columbia DB.2414 |
| Carmen Cavallaro (piano) | 12/49 | Brunswick 04395 |
| The Sidney Bechet Circle Seven | 7/50 | Esquire 10–076 |
| The Melachrino Strings | 9/50 | HMV B.9952 |
| David Rose and his Orchestra | 9/50 | MGM.323 |
| Jo Stafford | 10/50 | Capitol CL.13372 |
| The Deep River Boys | 1/51 | HMV B.10012 |
| Walter Huston | 2/51 | Brunswick 04658 |
| Tony Martin | 2/51 | Brunswick 04655 |
| The Ronnie Scott Quartet | 5/51 | Esquire 10–125 |
| Stan Kenton and his Orchestra | 6/51 | Capitol CL.13525 |
| The Dave Brubeck Trio | 2/52 | Vogue V.2096★ |
| Billy Daniels | 5/52 | Oriole CB.1096★ |
| Billy Daniels | 6/54 | Mercury MB.2969★ |

## 276 I'LL ALWAYS LOVE YOU (Querida Mia)

| | |
|---|---|
| *Composers*: Jay Livingston & Ray Evans | *Date of Entry*: 27.1.51 |
| *Publishers*: Victoria Music Co. Ltd. | *Highest Position*: 7 |
| | *Weeks on Chart*: 19 |

*Recordings*:

| | | |
|---|---|---|
| Eileen Wilson and Don Cherry | 12/50 | Brunswick 04624 |
| Dean Martin | 12/50 | Capitol CL.13433 |
| Dinah Shore | 1/51 | Columbia DB.2787 |
| Teddy Johnson | 1/51 | Columbia DB.2799 |
| Felix King, his Piano, and his Orchestra | 2/51 | Decca F.9621 |
| Roberto Inglez and his Orchestra | 3/51 | Parlophone R.3367 |
| Lester Ferguson | 3/51 | Parlophone R.3370 |
| Harry Dawson | 5/51 | HMV B.10068 |

## 277 MY HEART CRIES FOR YOU

*Composers*: Percy Faith & Carl Sigman

*Publishers*: Edwin H. Morris & Co.Ltd.

*Date of Entry*: 3.2.51

*Highest Position*: 2
*Weeks on Chart*: 24

*Recordings*:

| | | |
|---|---|---|
| Al Morgan with The Keynotes | 12/50 | London L.877 |
| Guy Mitchell | 1/51 | Columbia DB.2800 |
| Jimmy Wakely | 1/51 | Capitol CL.13446 |
| Victor Young and his Orchestra (Louanne Hogan, Joe Graydon and Chorus) | 1/51 | Brunswick 04646 |
| Johnston Brothers | 1/51 | Decca F.9606 |
| Evelyn Knight and Red Foley | 1/51 | Brunswick 04644 |
| Gene Autry and Jo Stafford | 2/51 | Columbia DB.2802 |
| The Beverley Sisters | 2/51 | Columbia DB.2810 |
| Dinah Shore | 2/51 | HMV B.10026 |
| Donald Peers with The Merry Macs | 2/51 | HMV B.10039 |
| Bill Farrell | 2/51 | MGM.364 |
| Billy Cotton and his Band (Doreen Stephens, Alan Breeze and Ensemble) | 2/51 | Decca F.9617 |
| Eve Boswell | 3/51 | Parlophone R.3372 |
| Billy Thorburn's The Organ, the Dance Band and Me (The Lennox Three) | 3/51 | Parlophone F.2451 |
| Joe Loss and his Orchestra | 3/51 | HMV BD.6087 |

## 278 C'N I CANOE YOU UP THE RIVER?

*Composers*: Marjorie Goetschius & Edna Osser

*Publishers*: Leeds Music Ltd.

*Date of Entry*: 10.2.51

*Highest Position*: 5
*Weeks on Chart*: 15

*Recordings*:

| | | |
|---|---|---|
| Arthur Godfrey | 12/50 | Columbia DB.2767 |
| Billy Cotton and his Band (Alan Breeze and The Bandits) | 2/51 | Decca F.9619 |
| Joe Loss and his Orchestra | 4/51 | HMV BD.6089 |

## 279 PLAY A SIMPLE MELODY

*Composer*: Irving Berlin

*Publishers*: Irving Berlin Ltd.

*Date of Entry*: 10.2.51

*Highest Position*: 17
*Weeks on Chart*: 2

*Recordings*:

| | | |
|---|---|---|
| Harry Roy and his Orchestra (Johnny Green and The Keynotes) | 9/50 | Decca F.9485 |
| Jo Stafford and The Starlighters | 9/50 | Capitol CL.13352 |
| Bing and Gary Crosby | 9/50 | Brunswick 04568 |
| The Five Smith Brothers | 10/50 | Parlophone R.3325 |
| Dinah Shore | 11/50 | Columbia DB.2751 |
| Joe Loss and his Orchestra | 11/50 | HMV BD.6080 |

## 280 PATRICIA

*Composer*: Benny Davis

*Publishers*: New World Publishers Ltd.

*Date of Entry*: 24.2.51/
Pos: 12/Wks: 10
*Re-entry*: 12.5.51/
Pos: 23/Wks: 1

*Recordings*:

| | | |
|---|---|---|
| Perry Como | 1/51 | HMV B.10010 |
| Lee Lawrence | 1/51 | Decca F.9598 |
| Russ Morgan and his Orchestra (Russ Morgan) | 2/51 | Brunswick 04650 |
| Swing and Sway with Sammy Kaye (The Kaydets) | 3/51 | Columbia DB.2825 |
| Oscar Rabin and his Band with Harry Davis (Dennis Hale and The David Ede Ensemble) | 4/51 | Parlophone F.2455 |

## 281 GOOD LUCK, GOOD HEALTH, GOD BLESS YOU

*Composers*: Charles Adams & A. Le Royal

*Publishers*: Carolin Music Ltd. (Unit Music)

*Date of Entry*: 24.2.51/
Pos: 3/Wks: 34
*Re-entry*: 15.12.51/
Pos: 23/Wks: 2

*Recordings*:

| | | |
|---|---|---|
| Billy Thorburn's The Organ, the Dance Band and Me (The Stargazers) | 1/51 | Parlophone F.2442 |
| Steve Conway with The Hastings Girls' Choir | 2/51 | Columbia DB.2809 |
| Billy Cotton and his Band (Doreen Stephens, Alan Breeze and Chorus) | 2/51 | Decca F.9608 |
| Issy Bonn with The Keynotes and Charles Smart (organ) | 4/51 | Oriole CB.1043 |

## 282 TIPPERARY SAMBA

*Composers*: Tommie Connor & Johnny Reine

*Publishers*: Michael Reine Music Co.Ltd.

*Date of Entry*: 24.2.51

*Highest Position*: 16
*Weeks on Chart*: 10

*Recordings*:

| | | |
|---|---|---|
| The Four Ramblers | 1/51 | Decca F.9595 |
| Phil Morrow's Music and Singers | 4/51 | Columbia DB.2845 |
| Edmundo Ros and his Rumba Band (Edmundo Ros) | 4/51 | Decca F.9645 |
| Billy Cotton and his Band (Alan Breeze and The Bandits) | 4/51 | Decca F.9644 |

## 283 | TEASIN'

Composers: Richard Adler & Philip Springer

Publishers: Pickwick Music Ltd.

Date of Entry: 24.2.51/
Pos: 20/Wks: 1
Re-entry: 10.3.51/
Pos: 20/Wks: 6
2nd re-entry: 28.4.51/
Pos: 22/Wks: 1

Recordings:

| | | |
|---|---|---|
| The Beverley Sisters | 2/51 | Columbia DB.2810 |
| Petula Clark | 3/51 | Polygon P.1005 |
| Cyril Stapleton and his Orchestra (Jean Campbell) | 4/51 | Decca F.9646 |

## 284 | SENORA

Composers: Ramaz Idriss & George Tibbles

Publishers: Dash Music Co. Ltd.

Date of Entry: 24.2.51

Highest Position: 18
Weeks on Chart: 4

Recordings:

| | | |
|---|---|---|
| Ray Ellington and his Quartet (Ray Ellington) | 10/50 | Decca F.9496 |
| Jack Smith | 11/50 | Capitol CL.13403 |

## 285 | THE ROVING KIND

Composers: Jessie Cavanaugh & Arnold Stanton

Publishers: Leeds Music Ltd.

Date of Entry: 3.3.51

Highest Position: 2
Weeks on Chart: 17

Recordings:

| | | |
|---|---|---|
| Les Baxter and his Orchestra and Chorus (Lindy Doherty) | 2/51 | Capitol CL.13449 |
| Cyril Stapleton and his Orchestra (David Carey and The Staplejacks) | 2/51 | Decca F.9615 |
| Guy Mitchell | 2/51 | Columbia DB.2816 |
| Sid Phillips and his Band (The Tanner Sisters, Johnnie Eager and Geraldine Farrar) | 3/51 | HMV BD.1269 |
| The Weavers | 3/51 | Brunswick 04659 |

## 286 | BE MY LOVE

Composers: Nicholas Brodszky & Sammy Cahn

Publishers: Francis Day & Hunter Ltd.

Date of Entry: 10.3.51/
Pos: 2/Wks: 45
Re-entry: 2.2.52/
Pos: 24/Wks: 1

Recordings:

| | | |
|---|---|---|
| Ray Anthony and his Orchestra (Ronnie Deauville) | 2/51 | Capitol CL.13455 |
| Billy Eckstine | 2/51 | MGM.362 |
| Cyril Stapleton and his Orchestra (Bob Dale) | 2/51 | Decca F.9615 |
| Mario Lanza with the Jeff Alexander Choir | 3/51 | HMV DA.1964 |
| Victor Young and his Orchestra (Louanne Hogan, Joe Graydon and Chorus) | 4/51 | Brunswick 04693 |
| Joe Loss and his Orchestra | 4/51 | HMV BD.6091 |
| Victor Silvester and his Ballroom Orchestra | 5/51 | Columbia FB.3605 |
| Dorothy Squires | 5/51 | Columbia DB.2855 |
| Ethel Smith (organ) | 6/51 | Brunswick 04725 |
| Dany Dauberson | 6/51 | Nixa BY.1011 |
| Vic Lewis and his Orchestra | 6/51 | Esquire 5–024 |
| The Jacques Dieval Quartet | 8/51 | Nixa BY.1144 |
| Mario Lanza with the Jeff Alexander Choir | 10/52 | HMV (45) 7R.130* |

## 287 | RED SILKEN STOCKINGS

Composers: Johnny Brandon & Peter Hart

Publishers: John Fields Music Co. Ltd.

Date of Entry: 10.3.51/
Pos: 23/Wks: 1
Re-entry: 24.3.51/
Pos: 22/Wks: 1

Recordings:

| | | |
|---|---|---|
| The Stargazers with Cyril Stapleton and his Orchestra | 12/50 | Decca F.9578 |
| Sid Phillips and his Band (Betty Driver) | 2/51 | HMV BD.6086 |
| Helen Grayco | 3/51 | London L.1022 |

## 288 | SO LONG
(It's been good to know yuh)

Composer: Woody Guthrie

Publishers: Leeds Music Ltd.

Date of Entry: 10.3.51

Highest Position: 22
Weeks on Chart: 2

Recordings:

| | | |
|---|---|---|
| The Weavers and Gordon Jenkins (vocal) with orch. acc. | 1/51 | Brunswick 04636 |
| Les Baxter and his Orchestra (Lindy Doherty and Chorus) | 2/51 | Capitol CL.13449 |
| Reggie Goff with The Drifters (vocal) and his Waltztimers | 2/51 | Decca F.9614 |
| Sam Browne and his All-Star Singers | 3/51 | HMV B.10054 |
| Paul Weston and his Orchestra with The Norman Luboff Choir | 3/51 | Columbia DB.2824 |
| Joe Loss and his Orchestra | 4/51 | HMV BD.6089* |
| The Five Smith Brothers | 4/51 | Parlophone R.3378* |

## 289 | A PENNY A KISS – A PENNY A HUG

| Composers: Buddy Kaye & Ralph Care | Date of Entry: 17.3.51 |
|---|---|
| Publishers: Leeds Music Ltd. | Highest Position: 14<br>Weeks on Chart: 8 |

Recordings:

| | | |
|---|---|---|
| Teresa Brewer and Snooky Lanson | 1/51 | London L.878 |
| Tony Martin and Dinah Shore (Titled 'A Penny a kiss') | 3/51 | HMV B.10034 |
| The Andrews Sisters | 3/51 | Brunswick 04665 |
| Cyril Stapleton and his Orchestra (Dave Carey and Jean Campbell) | 4/51 | Decca F.9648 |
| Mary Mayo with The Four Chicks and a Chuck (Titled 'A Penny a kiss') | 4/51 | Capitol CL.13491 |

## 290 | MOCKIN' BIRD HILL

| Composer: Vaughn Horton | Date of Entry: 24.3.51 |
|---|---|
| Publishers: Southern Music Publishing Co.Ltd. | Highest Position: 1<br>Weeks on Chart: 26 |

Recordings:

| | | |
|---|---|---|
| Les Paul and Mary Ford | 3/51 | Capitol CL.13466 |
| Russ Morgan and his Orchestra (Russ Morgan and The Gay Sisters) | 3/51 | Brunswick 04668 |
| Donald Peers | 4/51 | HMV B.10043 |
| Primo Scala Banjo and Accordion Band (The Keynotes) | 4/51 | Decca F.9650 |
| The Tanner Sisters | 4/51 | HMV B.10071 |
| Ronnie Ronalde | 4/51 | Columbia DB.2852 |
| The Marlin Sisters and Don Miles | 4/51 | London L.851 |
| Billy Thorburn's The Organ, the Dance Band and Me (The Bobolinks) | 5/51 | Parlophone F.2460 |
| Joe Loss and his Orchestra | 5/51 | HMV BD.6093 |
| Patti Page | 6/51 | Oriole CB.1047 |
| Patti Page | 6/54 | Mercury MB.2945★ |

## 291 | SO IN LOVE

| Composer: Cole Porter | Date of Entry: 24.3.51/<br>Pos: 22/Wks: 3 |
|---|---|
| Publishers: Chappell & Co. Ltd. | Re-entry: 21.4.51/<br>Pos: 13/Wks: 10<br>2nd re-entry: 7.7.51/<br>Pos: 23/Wks: 1 |

Recordings:

| | | |
|---|---|---|
| Joe Loss and his Orchestra | 3/51 | HMV BD.6088 |
| Allan Jones | 3/51 | HMV B.10040 |
| Stanley Black and his Orchestra | 3/51 | Decca F.9632 |
| Bing Crosby | 3/51 | Brunswick 04660 |
| Gordon MacRae | 3/51 | Capitol CL. 13478 |
| Dinah Shore | 3/51 | Columbia DB.2820 |
| Steve Race (piano) with Strings | 3/51 | Columbia DB.2827 |
| Victor Silvester and his Ballroom Orchestra | 3/51 | Columbia FB.3598 |
| Lester Ferguson | 3/51 | Parlophone R.3370 |
| Patricia Morison | 4/51 | Columbia DB.2847 |
| Bill Johnson | 4/51 | Columbia DB.2849 |
| Carmen Cavallaro and his Muted Strings | 4/51 | Brunswick 04667 |
| Alan Dean with The Johnny Dankworth Seven | 6/51 | Esquire 5–023 |

## 292 | ROSE, ROSE, I LOVE YOU

| Composers: Traditional (Chinese) – English Lyrics by Wilfrid Thomas | Date of Entry: 31.3.51 |
|---|---|
| Publishers: Sterling Music Publishing Co. Ltd. | Highest Position: 2<br>Weeks on Chart: 15 |

(Notes: Recorded versions below marked as follows: (a) In Chinese. (b) English lyrics by Wilfrid Thomas. There is also a version titled 'May Kway O May Kway' – see Song No. 299 – with English Lyrics by John Turner. The only non-vocal recording, by Joe Loss, is included below as it was titled 'Rose, Rose, I love you'.)

Recordings:

| | | |
|---|---|---|
| (a) Miss Hue Lee | 3/51 | Columbia DB.2837 |
| (b) Malcolm Mitchell Trio | 4/51 | Parlophone R.3383 |
| (b) Benny Lee and The Stargazers | 5/51 | Decca F.9679 |
| Joe Loss and his Orchestra | 5/51 | HMV BD.6094 |
| (b) Frankie Laine and The Norman Luboff Choir | 6/51 | Columbia DB.2876 |
| (b) Gordon Jenkins and his Chorus and Orchestra (Frisco Ruston) | 6/51 | Brunswick 04724 |

## 293 SALOON BAR RAG

| | | |
|---|---|---|
| *Composer:* Ephraim Lifshey | | *Date of Entry:* 31.3.51 |
| *Publishers:* Sterling Music Publishing Co. Ltd. | | *Highest Position:* 23 *Weeks on Chart:* 1 |

*Recordings:*

| | | |
|---|---|---|
| Philip Green and his Band (The Beaux and the Belles) | 1/51 | Parlophone F.2444 |
| Harry Roy and his Band (Harry Roy) | 2/51 | Decca F.9610 |
| Norrie Paramor and his Rhythm | 3/51 | Columbia DB.2821 |

## 294 MARY ROSE (Bloesem van Seringen)

| | | |
|---|---|---|
| *Composers:* Scheffer, Vogel and Dunk – English Lyric by Tommie Connor | | *Date of Entry:* 7.4.51 |
| *Publishers:* Magna Music Co. Ltd. | | *Highest Position:* 8 *Weeks on Chart:* 15 |

*Recordings:*

| | | |
|---|---|---|
| Stanley Black and his Orchestra (Dick James, The Stargazers and The George Mitchell Choir) | 3/51 | Decca F.9636 |
| Denis Martin | 5/51 | Parlophone R.3392 |
| Steve Conway | 5/51 | Columbia DB.2875 |
| Larry Day | 5/51 | HMV B.10077 |
| Joe Loss and his Orchestra | 6/51 | HMV BD.6096 |

## 295 SPARROW IN THE TREE TOP

| | | |
|---|---|---|
| *Composer:* Bob Merrill | | *Date of Entry:* 7.4.51 |
| *Publishers:* Cinephonic Music Co. Ltd. | | *Highest Position:* 5 *Weeks on Chart:* 17 |

*Recordings:*

| | | |
|---|---|---|
| Reggie Goff with The Johnston Brothers | 3/51 | Decca F.9625 |
| Guy Mitchell | 3/51 | Columbia DB.2831 |
| Art Mooney and his Orchestra and Chorus (Alan Foster) | 4/51 | MGM.389 |
| Bing Crosby and The Andrews Sisters | 4/51 | Brunswick 04672 |
| Les Baxter and his Orchestra and Chorus (Lindy Doherty) | 4/51 | Capitol CL.13487 |

## 296 A RAINY DAY REFRAIN (Da-dim, Da-dom)

| | | |
|---|---|---|
| *Composers:* Heino Gaze & Eric Maschwitz | | *Date of Entry:* 14.4.51 |
| *Publishers:* Peter Maurice Music Co. Ltd. | | *Highest Position:* 14 *Weeks on Chart:* 7 |

*Recordings:*
(a) Titled 'A rainy day refrain'

| | | |
|---|---|---|
| Mindy Carson | 11/50 | HMV B.9986 |
| Vera Lynn with The Mayfair Singers | 11/50 | Decca F.9534 |
| The Andrews Sisters | 11/50 | Brunswick 04599 |
| Jan Garber and his Orchestra (Roy Cordell) | 12/50 | Capitol CL.13423 |
| Sidney Torch and his Orchestra (The Torch Singers) | 4/51 | Parlophone R.3375 |

(b) Titled 'Da-dim, da-dom, da-dim, da-dom'

| | | |
|---|---|---|
| Billy Cotton and his Band (Doreen Stephens, Rita and Joyce) | 4/51 | Decca F.9644 |

(c) Titled 'Dadim, Dadom'

| | | |
|---|---|---|
| Mary Martin and Arthur Godfrey | 3/51 | Columbia DB.2813 |

## 297 THE SHOT GUN BOOGIE

| | | |
|---|---|---|
| *Composer:* Tennessee Ernie Ford | | *Date of Entry:* 21.4.51/ Pos: 4/Wks: 21 |
| *Publishers:* Campbell Connelly & Co. Ltd. | | *Re-entry:* 29.9.51/ Pos: 22/Wks: 1 |

*Recordings:*

| | | |
|---|---|---|
| Tennessee Ernie | 2/51 | Capitol CL.13447 |
| Rosemary Clooney | 5/51 | Columbia DB.2861 |
| Billy Cotton and his Band (Alan Breeze and The Bandits) | 6/51 | Decca F.9716 |

## 298 LIFE'S DESIRE

| | | |
|---|---|---|
| *Composers:* Tolchard Evans, Stanley J. Damerell & Robert Hargreaves | | *Date of Entry:* 28.4.51 |
| *Publishers:* Cecil Lennox Ltd. | | *Highest Position:* 13 *Weeks on Chart:* 15 |

(Note: The original version of this song was recorded in 1932 by Gracie Fields on HMV B.4000 but was deleted long before the song's revival.)

*Recordings:*

| | | |
|---|---|---|
| Jimmy Young | 3/51 | Polygon P.1006 |
| Dick James | 3/51 | Decca F.9638 |
| Victor Silvester and his Ballroom Orchestra | 5/51 | Columbia FB.3605 |
| Dorothy Squires | 5/51 | Columbia DB.2855 |
| Harry Dawson | 5/51 | HMV B.10068 |
| Doris Day | 7/51 | Columbia DB.2888 |
| Bob Eberly | 7/51 | Capitol CL.13560 |
| Don Cherry | 9/51 | Brunswick 04768★ |

## 299 | MAY KWAY O MAY KWAY (Rose, Rose, I love you)

**Composers:** Traditional (Chinese) with English Lyrics by John Turner

**Publishers:** Peter Maurice Music Co. Ltd.

**Date of Entry:** 5.5.51

**Highest Position:** 16
**Weeks on Chart:** 5

(Note: For versions of the song under the title 'Rose, Rose, I love you' see Song No. 292.)

**Recordings:**

| | | |
|---|---|---|
| Petula Clark | 5/51 | Polygon P.1008 |
| Billy Cotton and his Band (Billy Cotton, Doreen Stephens and The Bandits) | 5/51 | Decca F.9687 |
| Lou Ella Robertson with The Wanderers | 6/51 | Capitol CL.13540 |

## 300 | OUR VERY OWN

**Composers:** Jack Elliott & Victor Young

**Publishers:** Bradbury Wood Ltd.

**Date of Entry:** 5.5.51/
Pos: 21/Wks: 1
**Re-entry:** 19.5.51/
Pos: 8/Wks: 20

**Recordings:**

| | | |
|---|---|---|
| Charlie Spivak and his Orchestra (Tommy Lynn) | 9/50 | London L.691 |
| Victor Young and his Orchestra (Don Cherry and Chorus) | 12/50 | Brunswick 04621 |
| Jo Stafford | 1/51 | Capitol CL.13444 |
| Victor Silvester and his Ballroom Orchestra | 4/51 | Columbia FB.3601 |
| Teddy Johnson | 4/51 | Columbia DB.2840 |

## 301 | LIST'NIN' TO THE GREEN GRASS GROW

**Composers:** Jimmy Kennedy and Guy Wood

**Publishers:** Box & Cox (Publications) Ltd.

**Date of Entry:** 5.5.51

**Highest Position:** 21
**Weeks on Chart:** 4

**Recordings:**

| | | |
|---|---|---|
| Oscar Rabin and his Band with Harry Davis (Dennis Hale and The David Ede Ensemble) | 4/51 | Parlophone F.2455 |
| Frank Cordell and his Orchestra and Chorus (Larry Day) | 4/51 | HMV B.10072 |
| Reggie Goff with The Kingpins | 4/51 | Decca F.9665 |
| The Radio Revellers | 5/51 | Columbia DB.2858 |
| The Holidays (vcl & inst) | 11/52 | Parlophone R.3614★ |

## 302 | WOULD I LOVE YOU (Love you, love you)

**Composers:** Harold Spina & Bob Russell

**Publishers:** Walt Disney Music Co. Ltd.

**Date of Entry:** 5.5.51

**Highest Position:** 8
**Weeks on Chart:** 15

**Recordings:**

| | | |
|---|---|---|
| Eve Young | 1/51 | London L.892 |
| Tony Martin | 4/51 | HMV B.10051 |
| Steve Conway | 4/51 | Columbia DB.2841 |
| Helen O'Connell | 4/51 | Capitol CL.13492 |
| Dick James | 4/51 | Decca F.9658 |
| Jerry Gray and his Orchestra (Tommy Traynor) | 4/51 | Brunswick 04680 |
| Joe Loss and his Orchestra | 5/51 | HMV BD.6093 |
| Doris Day with Harry James (trumpet) and his Orchestra | 5/51 | Columbia DB.2862 |
| Jimmy Young | 5/51 | Polygon P.1010 |
| Gordon Jenkins and his Orchestra (Bob Stevens and Chorus) | 6/51 | Brunswick 04723 |

## 304 | BEAUTIFUL BROWN EYES

There are two versions of this traditional song with only slightly differing words to distinguish them. The one which appeared in the charts was published by Pickwick Music Ltd. and described as having 'words and music by Grace Walters'. There are no recordings of this. All the recordings below relate to the other arrangement – by Arthur Smith and Alton Delmore – which was published in the UK at the same time by Campbell Connelly & Co. Ltd.

**Date of Entry:** 12.5.51
**Highest Position:** 24
**Weeks on Chart:** 1

**Recordings:**

| | | |
|---|---|---|
| Art Mooney and his Orchestra (Alan Foster, Rosetta Shaw and The Art Mooney Choir) | 4/51 | MGM.389 |
| Jimmy Wakely with The Les Baxter Chorus | 4/51 | Capitol CL.13484 |
| Billy Thorburn's The Organ, the Dance Band and Me (The Bobolinks) | 5/51 | Parlophone F.2460 |
| Rosemary Clooney | 5/51 | Columbia DB.2861 |
| Lisa Kirk | 5/51 | HMV B.10063 |
| Evelyn Knight with The Ray Charles Singers dir. by Sy Oliver | 5/51 | Brunswick 04697 |

## 304 | GIRLS WERE MADE TO TAKE CARE OF BOYS

**Composer:** Ralph Blane

**Publishers:** B. Feldman & Co. Ltd.

**Date of Entry:** 12.5.51

**Highest Position:** 24
**Weeks on Chart:** 1

**Recordings:**

| | | |
|---|---|---|
| Rose Murphy | 4/50 | HMV B.9901 |
| Jo Stafford and Gordon MacRae | 4/50 | Capitol CL.13286 |
| Billie Holiday with The Star Dusters | 9/50 | Brunswick 04558 |

## 305 WITH THESE HANDS

| Composers: Abner Silver & Benny Davis | Date of Entry: 19.5.51 |
|---|---|
| Publishers: Edward Kassner Music Co. Ltd. | Highest Position: 1<br>Weeks on Chart: 24 |

Recordings:

| | | |
|---|---|---|
| Lee Lawrence | 1/51 | Decca F.9590 |
| Nelson Eddy and Jo Stafford | 5/51 | Columbia DB.2868 |
| Victor Silvester and his Ballroom Orchestra | 7/51 | Columbia FB.3613 |
| David Hughes | 7/51 | HMV B.10104 |
| Frank Cordell and his Orchestra and Choir (Larry Day) | 8/51 | HMV B.10109 |
| Joe Loss and his Orchestra | 8/51 | HMV BD.6102 |
| Guy Lombardo and his Royal Canadians (Bill Flanagan) | 8/51 | Brunswick 04762 |
| Johnnie Ray | 9/53 | Philips PB.183★ |

## 306 YOU ARE MY DESTINY

| Composers: Sydney Baynes with new lyrics by Harry Ralton (based on 'Destiny Waltz' by Baynes, first published in 1912) | Date of Entry: 19.5.51/<br>Pos: 24/Wks: 1 |
|---|---|
| Publishers: Swan & Co. | Re-entry: 2.6.51/<br>Pos: 15/Wks: 14 |

(Note: All available recordings of 'Destiny Waltz' have been discounted in this listing due to the new lyrics and change of title of the chart song.)

Recordings:

| | | |
|---|---|---|
| Harry Dawson with The Mitchell Maids | 5/51 | Decca F.9685 |
| Lester Ferguson | 5/51 | Parlophone R.3384 |

## 307 ON TOP OF OLD SMOKY

| Composer: Traditional, arranged by Pete Seeger | Date of Entry: 26.5.51 |
|---|---|
| Publishers: Leeds Music Co. Ltd. | Highest Position: 6<br>Weeks on Chart: 20 |

Recordings:

| | | |
|---|---|---|
| Josh White and The Stargazers | 4/51 | London L.1028 |
| The Weavers and Terry Gilkyson | 5/51 | Brunswick 04700 |
| Sid Phillips and his Band (Johnnie Eager and The Song Pedlars) | 6/51 | HMV BD.6095 |
| Percy Faith and his Orchestra and Chorus with Burl Ives | 6/51 | Columbia DB.2877 |

## 308 IVORY RAG

| Composers: Lou Busch & Jack Elliott | Date of Entry: 2.6.51 |
|---|---|
| Publishers: Macmelodies Ltd. | Highest Position: 3<br>Weeks on Chart: 24 |

Recordings:

| | | |
|---|---|---|
| Joe 'Fingers' Carr (piano) and The Carr-hops | 7/50 | Capitol CL.13339 |
| Joe 'Fingers' Carr (piano) and The Carr-hops | 6/51 | Capitol CL.13532 |
| Sid Phillips and his Band (Johnnie Eager) | 7/51 | HMV BD.6100 |
| Ivor Moreton and Dave Kaye (two pianos) | 7/51 | Parlophone F.2468 |
| Norrie Paramor and his Ragmen | 8/51 | Columbia DB.2898 |
| Victor Silvester and his Ballroom Orchestra | 8/51 | Columbia FB.3614 |
| Billy Cotton and his Band (Alan Breeze and The Bandits) | 8/51 | Decca F.9741 |

## 309 MY RESISTANCE IS LOW

| Composers: Hoagy Carmichael & Harold Adamson | Date of Entry: 9.6.51 |
|---|---|
| Publishers: Edwin H. Morris & Co. Ltd. | Highest Position: 1<br>Weeks on Chart: 20 |

Recordings:

| | | |
|---|---|---|
| Hoagy Carmichael | 5/51 | Brunswick 04710 |
| Dorothy Squires | 8/51 | Columbia DB.2897 |
| Robert Farnon and his Concert Orchestra with The Johnston Singers | 2/53 | Decca F.10052★ |

## 310 THE LOVELIEST NIGHT OF THE YEAR

| Composers: Paul Francis Webster & Irving Aaronson (adapted from 'Sabre las Olas' by Juventino Rosas) | Date of Entry: 9.6.51/<br>Pos: 1/Wks: 45 |
|---|---|
| Publishers: Francis Day & Hunter Ltd. | Re-entry: 26.4.52/<br>Pos: 20/Wks: 1 |

Recordings:

| | | |
|---|---|---|
| Fred Waring and his Pennsylvanians (Gordon Goodman) | 5/51 | Brunswick 04699 |
| Ann Blyth | 5/51 | MGM.391 |
| Mario Lanza | 6/51 | HMV DA.1978 |
| Percy Faith and his Orchestra and Chorus | 6/51 | Columbia DB.2877 |
| Helen O'Connell | 6/51 | Capitol CL.13531 |
| Anne Shelton with The George Mitchell Choir | 6/51 | Decca F.9692 |
| Ethel Smith (organ) | 6/51 | Brunswick 04725 |
| Joe Loss and his Orchestra | 7/51 | HMV BD.6098 |
| Frederick Ferrari | 8/51 | Parlophone R.3422 |

## 311 I APOLOGISE

| Composers: Ed Nelson, Al Goodhart & Al Hoffman | Date of Entry: 9.6.51 |
|---|---|
| Publishers: Victoria Music Publishing Co. Ltd. | Highest Position: 4 |
| | Weeks on Chart: 21 |

(Note: Originally popular in 1931/2 with a recording by Bing Crosby which had been long deleted, the return of the song brought a reissue of the Crosby recording on Brunswick 01219 in 1951.)

Recordings:

| | | |
|---|---|---|
| Anita O'Day | 3/51 | London L.964 |
| Tony Martin | 4/51 | HMV B.10051 |
| Don Cherry | 4/51 | Brunswick 04690 |
| Champ Butler | 5/51 | Columbia DB.2865 |
| Billy Eckstine | 5/51 | MGM.390 |
| Victor Silvester and his Ballroom Orchestra | 8/51 | Columbia FB.3614 |
| Joe Loss and his Orchestra | 9/51 | HMV BD.6104 |
| Billy Eckstine | 1/53 | MGM (45) SP.1011★ |

## 312 JEZEBEL

| Composer: Wayne Shanklin | Date of Entry: 16.6.51 |
|---|---|
| Publishers: Campbell Connelly & Co. Ltd. | Highest Position: 5 |
| | Weeks on Chart: 16 |

Recordings:

| | | |
|---|---|---|
| Frankie Laine with The Norman Luboff Choir | 6/51 | Columbia DB.2876 |
| Winifred Atwell (piano) | 6/51 | Decca F.9715 |
| Joe Loss and his Orchestra (Howard Jones and The Loss Chords) | 7/51 | HMV BD.6101 |
| Billy Cotton and his Band (Alan Breeze) | 7/51 | Decca F.9736 |
| Roberto Inglez and his Orchestra | 8/51 | Parlophone R.3417 |

## 313 TOO LATE NOW

| Composers: Alan Jay Lerner & Burton Lane | Date of Entry: 30.6.51 |
|---|---|
| Publishers: New World Publishers Ltd. | Highest Position: 4 |
| | Weeks on Chart: 23 |

Recordings:

| | | |
|---|---|---|
| Jane Powell | 3/51 | MGM.370 |
| Dick Haymes | 5/51 | Brunswick 04708 |
| Dinah Shore | 6/51 | HMV B.10081 |
| Toni Arden | 6/51 | Columbia DB.2880 |
| Victor Silvester and his Ballroom Orchestra | 9/51 | Columbia FB.3617 |
| Les Howard | 9/51 | Decca F.9761 |

## 314 SMOKY MOUNTAIN BOOGIE

| Composers: Tennessee Ernie Ford & Cliffie Stone | Date of Entry: 30.6.51 / Pos: 23/Wks: 1 |
|---|---|
| Publishers: Campbell Connelly & Co. Ltd. | Re-entry: 14.7.51/ Pos: 21/Wks: 2 |
| | 2nd re-entry: 4.8.51/ Pos: 24/Wks: 2 |
| | 3rd re-entry: 25.8.51/ Pos: 23/Wks: 1 |

Recording:

| | | |
|---|---|---|
| Tennessee Ernie (Titled 'Smokey . . .') | 11/49 | Capitol CL.13211 |

## 315 THE LITTLE WHITE DUCK

| Composers: Bernard Zaritzky & Walt Barrows | Date of Entry: 7.7.51/ Pos: 21/Wks: 1 |
|---|---|
| Publishers: Southern Music Publishing Co. Ltd. | Re-entry:21.7.51/ Pos: 19/Wks: 5 |
| | 2nd re-entry: 1.9.51/ Pos: 22/Wks: 4 |

Recordings:

| | | |
|---|---|---|
| Danny Kaye | 1/51 | Brunswick 04635 |
| Guy Lombardo and his Royal Canadians (Kenny Gardner) | 4/51 | Brunswick 04691 |
| Burl Ives | 7/51 | Columbia DB.2884 |
| Candy Candido | 3/52 | Capitol CL.13695★ |

## 316 MY TRULY, TRULY FAIR

| Composer: Bob Merrill | Date of Entry: 14.7.51 |
|---|---|
| Publishers: Dash Music Co. Ltd. | Highest Position: 2 |
| | Weeks on Chart: 26 |

Recordings:

| | | |
|---|---|---|
| Dick James and The Stargazers | 6/51 | Decca F.9701 |
| Larry Cross and The Song Pedlars | 6/51 | Parlophone R.3411 |
| Guy Mitchell | 6/51 | Columbia DB.2885 |
| Frank Cordell and his Orchestra (Larry Day) | 8/51 | HMV B.10109 |
| Russ Morgan and his Orchestra (Russ Morgan and The Morganaires) | 9/51 | Brunswick 04759 |
| Ray Anthony and his Orchestra (Tommy Mercer and Ensemble) | 9/51 | Capitol CL.13563 |

## 317 UNLESS

*Composers*: Tolchard Evans, Stanley J. Damerell & Robert Hargreaves
*Publishers*: Francis Day & Hunter Ltd

*Date of Entry*: 14.7.51/ Pos: 20/Wks: 1
*Re-entry*: 28.7.51/ Pos: 6/Wks: 18
*2nd re-entry*: 12.1.52/ Pos: 24/Wks: 1

*Recordings*:

| | | |
|---|---|---|
| Dick James | 5/51 | Decca F.9666 |
| Bill Snyder, his Magic Piano, and his Orchestra (Stuart Foster) | 5/51 | London L.1075 |
| Guy Mitchell | 6/51 | Columbia DB.2871 |
| Les Baxter and his Chorus and Orchestra (Dick Beavers) | 6/51 | Capitol CL.13524 |
| Gordon Jenkins and his Chorus and Orchestra (Bob Stevens) | 6/51 | Brunswick 04724 |
| Victor Silvester and his Ballroom Orchestra | 7/51 | Columbia FB.3612 |
| Eddie Fisher | 7/51 | HMV B.10099 |
| Frederick Ferrari | 8/51 | Parlophone R.3422 |
| Louis Armstrong and his Orchestra (Louis Armstrong) | 10/51 | Brunswick 04791 |

## 318 A BEGGAR IN LOVE

*Composer*: Bob Merrill

*Publishers*: Cinephonic Music Co. Ltd.

*Date of Entry*: 14.7.51

*Highest Position*: 6
*Weeks on Chart*: 29

*Recordings*:

| | | |
|---|---|---|
| Guy Mitchell | 6/51 | Columbia DB.2871 |
| Joe Loss and his Orchestra | 7/51 | HMV BD.6099 |
| Tommy Edwards | 7/51 | MGM.413 |
| David Hughes | 7/51 | HMV B.10104 |
| Lee Lawrence | 7/51 | Decca F.9726 |

## 319 (I wish we were sweethearts) FIFTY YEARS AGO

*Composers*: Al Hoffman & Arthur Freed
*Publishers*: Campbell Connelly & Co. Ltd.

*Date of Entry*: 21.7.51/ Pos: 22/Wks: 2
*Re-entry*: 18.8.51/ Pos: 24/Wks: 1

*Recording*:

| | | |
|---|---|---|
| Benny Lee with The Stargazers | 5/51 | Decca F.9688 |

## 320 TOO YOUNG

*Composers*: Sidney Lippman & Sylvia Dee

*Publishers*: Sun Music Publishing Co. Ltd.

*Date of Entry*: 4.8.51

*Highest Position*: 1
*Weeks on Chart*: 28

*Recordings*:

| | | |
|---|---|---|
| Victor Young and his Orchestra (Louanne Hogan) | 4/51 | Brunswick 04693 |
| Nat 'King' Cole | 7/51 | Capitol CL.13564 |
| Patty Andrews | 7/51 | Brunswick 04754 |
| Jimmy Young | 7/51 | Polygon P.1013 |
| Steve Conway | 8/51 | Columbia DB.2903 |
| Toni Arden | 8/51 | Columbia DB.2906 |
| Johnny Desmond | 8/51 | MGM.419 |
| The Melachrino Strings | 9/51 | HMV B.10118 |
| The Deep River Boys | 9/51 | HMV B.10120 |
| Wally Fryer and his Perfect Tempo Dance Orchestra | 9/51 | Decca F.9747 |
| Larry Cross | 9/51 | Parlophone R.3433 |
| Billy Thorburn's The Organ, the Dance Band and Me (The Bobolinks) | 9/51 | Parlophone F.2470 |
| Victor Silvester and his Ballroom Orchestra | 9/51 | Columbia FB.3616 |
| Les Howard | 9/51 | Decca F.9761 |
| Bobby Breen | 9/51 | Nixa NY.7777 |

## 321 SWEET VIOLETS

*Composers*: Cy Coben & Charles Grean

*Publishers*: Edwin H. Morris & Co. Ltd.

*Date of Entry*: 4.8.51

*Highest Position*: 3
*Weeks on Chart*: 23

*Recordings*:

| | | |
|---|---|---|
| Larry Cross and The Song Pedlars | 8/51 | Parlophone R.3420 |
| Dinah Shore | 8/51 | HMV B.10115 |
| Jane Turzy | 9/51 | Brunswick 04763 |
| Billy Thorburn's The Organ, the Dance Band and Me (The Bobolinks) | 9/51 | Parlophone F.2470 |
| The Radio Revellers | 9/51 | Columbia DB.2922 |
| Billy Cotton and his Band (Alan Breeze and The Bandits) | 9/51 | Decca F.9760 |

## 322 CHRISTOPHER COLUMBUS (The world ain't big enough for me)

*Composer*: Terry Gilkyson

*Publishers*: Campbell Connelly & Co. Ltd.

*Date of Entry*: 11.8.51

*Highest Position*: 5
*Weeks on Chart*: 16

*Recordings*:

| | | |
|---|---|---|
| Guy Mitchell | 3/51 | Columbia DB.2831 |
| Cyril Stapleton and his Orchestra (The Stargazers) | 10/51 | Decca F.9777 |

## 323 TULIPS AND HEATHER

*Composer*: Milton Carson      *Date of Entry*: 18.8.51

*Publishers*: John Fields Music Co. Ltd.      *Highest Position*: 2
    *Weeks on Chart*: 23

*Recordings*:
| | | |
|---|---|---|
| Fred Waring and his Pennsylvanians (The Glee Club) | 5/51 | Brunswick 04699 |
| Bob and Alf Pearson | 9/51 | Parlophone F.2471 |
| Daphne and Benny Lee | 9/51 | Decca F.9734 |
| Joe Loss and his Orchestra (Rose Brennan and The Loss Chords) | 10/51 | HMV BD.6110 |
| Victor Silvester and his Ballroom Orchestra | 11/51 | Columbia FB.3622 |
| Benny Strong and his Orchestra | 3/52 | Capitol CL.13689★ |

## 324 MADEMOISELLE DE PAREE

*Composers*: Henri Contet & Paul Durand with English lyrics added by Eric Maschwitz      *Date of Entry*: 18.8.51

*Publishers*: Peter Maurice Music Co. Ltd.      *Highest Position*: 23
    *Weeks on Chart*: 1

| | | |
|---|---|---|
| (a) Titled 'Mademoiselle de Paris' (Contet–Durand) | | |
| Andre Claveau [in French] | 4/51 | Nixa BY.1402 |
| Lys Assia [in French] | 4/51 | Decca C.16156 |
| (b) Titled 'Mademoiselle de Paree' (Durand–Maschwitz) | | |
| Anne Shelton with The George Mitchell Choir | 4/51 | Decca F.9664 |
| Bing Crosby | 10/53 | Brunswick 05182★ |
| (c) Titled 'Ma'moiselle de Paris' (Durand–Maschwitz) | | |
| Dany Dauberson | 5/51 | Nixa BY.1012 |
| Teddy Johnson | 5/51 | Columbia DB.2854 |
| (d) Titled 'Mademoiselle de Paris' (lyrics by Mitchell Parish) | | |
| Danny Kaye | 5/52 | Brunswick 04922★ |

## 325 THE KENTUCKY WALTZ

*Composer*: William S. (Bill) Monroe      *Date of Entry*: 1.9.51

*Publishers*: Southern Music Publishing Co. Ltd.      *Highest Position*: 14
    *Weeks on Chart*: 23

*Recordings*:
| | | |
|---|---|---|
| Tennessee Ernie | 5/51 | Capitol CL.13517 |
| 'Sheriff' Johnny Denis and his Ranchers | 6/51 | Decca F.9710 |
| Rosemary Clooney | 8/51 | Columbia DB.2895 |
| Ernest Tubb and Red Foley | 9/51 | Brunswick 04783 |

## 326 THERE'S NO BOAT LIKE A ROWBOAT

*Composer*: Irving Gordon      *Date of Entry*: 8.9.51

*Publishers*: Bourne Music Ltd.      *Highest Position*: 14
    *Weeks on Chart*: 9

*Recordings*:
| | | |
|---|---|---|
| Pearl Carr and The Keynotes | 7/51 | Decca F.9730 |
| Perry Como and The Fontane Sisters | 8/51 | HMV B.10114 |

## 327 THE BLACK NOTE SERENADE

*Composers*: Benny Litchfield & Harry Bolton      *Date of Entry*: 8.9.51

*Publishers*: Peter Maurice Music Co. Ltd.      *Highest Position*: 24
    *Weeks on Chart*: 2

*Recordings*:
| | | |
|---|---|---|
| Petula Clark | 3/51 | Polygon P.1005 |
| Billy Thorburn's The Organ, the Dance Band and Me (The Bobolinks) | 7/51 | Parlophone F.2465 |
| Billy Cotton and his Band (The Bandits) | 7/51 | Decca F.9736 |
| Norrie Paramor and his Ragmen (Carole Newton) | 8/51 | Columbia DB.2898 |
| The Londoners | 9/51 | Decca F.9750 |
| Sid Phillips and his Band (Johnnie Eager) | 9/51 | HMV BD.6106 |

## 328 SHANGHAI

*Composers*: Bob Hilliard & Milton DeLugg      *Date of Entry*: 15.9.51

*Publishers*: Harms-Connelly Ltd.      *Highest Position*: 9
    *Weeks on Chart*: 13

*Recordings*:
| | | |
|---|---|---|
| The Billy Williams Quartette | 8/51 | MGM.418 |
| Doris Day | 9/51 | Columbia DB.2909 |
| Bing Crosby | 9/51 | Brunswick 04764 |
| Buddy Morrow and his Orchestra (Frankie Lester and Quartette) | 9/51 | HMV B.10132 |
| Bob Crosby and his Orchestra (Bob Crosby) | 9/51 | Capitol CL.13585 |
| Benny Lee | 9/51 | Decca F.9734 |
| Sid Phillips and his Band (Johnnie Eager) | 10/51 | HMV BD.6107 |
| Joe Loss and his Orchestra | 10/51 | HMV BD.6109 |
| The Malcolm Mitchell Trio | 10/51 | Parlophone R.3439 |

## 329 BECAUSE OF YOU

| Composers: Dudley Wilkinson & Arthur Hammerstein | | Date of Entry: 22.9.51 |
|---|---|---|
| Publishers: Dash Music Co. Ltd. | | Highest Position: 2 |
| | | Weeks on Chart: 28 |

Recordings:

| | | |
|---|---|---|
| Les Baxter and his Orchestra and Chorus | 6/51 | Capitol CL.13524 |
| Jan Peerce | 8/51 | HMV DB.21303 |
| Gloria de Haven and Guy Lombardo | 9/51 | Brunswick 04772 |
| Larry Cross | 9/51 | Parlophone R.3433 |
| Les Howard | 9/51 | Decca F.9757 |
| Victor Silvester and his Ballroom Orchestra | 10/51 | Columbia FB.3620 |
| Tony Bennett | 10/51 | Columbia DB.2924 |
| Jimmy Young | 10/51 | Polygon P.1018 |
| Teddy Johnson | 10/51 | Columbia DB.2944 |
| Johnny Desmond | 10/51 | MGM.434 |
| Joe Loss and his Orchestra | 11/51 | HMV BD.6112 |
| Wally Fryer and his Perfect Tempo Dance Orchestra | 11/51 | Decca F.9802 |
| Louis Armstrong (vocal and trumpet) | 12/51 | Brunswick 04837 |

## 330 I LOVE THE SUNSHINE OF YOUR SMILE

| Composers: Jimmy MacDonald & Jack Hoffman | | Date of Entry: 22.9.51/ Pos: 24/Wks: 1 |
|---|---|---|
| Publishers: New World Publishers Ltd. | | Re-entry: 6.10.51/ Pos: 2/Wks: 24 |

Recordings:

| | | |
|---|---|---|
| The Four Knights | 9/51 | Capitol CL.13587 |
| Jerry Gray and his Orchestra (Tommy Traynor and Ensemble) | 9/51 | Brunswick 04782 |
| Billy Cotton and his Band (Alan Breeze and The Bandits) | 10/51 | Decca F.9780 |
| Ken Mackintosh and his Orchestra | 11/51 | HMV BD.1276 |
| The Radio Revellers | 12/51 | Columbia DB.2976 |

## 331 WHITE WEDDING

| Composers: Peter Phillips, Johnny Sheridan & Harry Ralton | | Date of Entry: 29.9.51/ Pos: 21/Wks: 1 |
|---|---|---|
| Publishers: Arcadia Music Publishing Co. Ltd. | | Re-entry: 13.10.51/ Pos: 24/Wks: 1 |
| | | 2nd re-entry: 24.11.51/ Pos: 24/Wks: 1 |
| | | 3rd re-entry: 8.12.51/ Pos: 24/Wks: 1 |

Recordings:

| | | |
|---|---|---|
| Steve Conway | 8/51 | Columbia DB.2903 |
| Sam Browne and his All-Star Singers | 9/51 | HMV B.10130 |
| Les Howard | 9/51 | Decca F.9757 |
| Bobby Breen | 9/51 | Nixa NY.7779 |

## 332 HOW CAN I LEAVE YOU?

| Composers: Bob Musel & Ed Steiner | | Date of Entry: 29.9.51/ Pos: 24/Wks: 1 |
|---|---|---|
| Publishers: John Fields Music Co. Ltd. | | Re-entry: 20.10.51/ Pos: 22/Wks: 2 |

Recordings:

| | | |
|---|---|---|
| Vera Lynn with The Mayfair Singers | 12/50 | Decca F.9567 |
| Frederick Ferrari | 2/51 | Parlophone R.3362 |
| Jimmy Young | 7/51 | Polygon P.1013 |
| Lee Lawrence | 10/51 | Decca F.9776 |

## 333 VANITY

| Composers: Guy Wood, Jack Manus & Bernard Bierman | | Date of Entry: 6.10.51 |
|---|---|---|
| Publishers: Sun Music Publishing Co. Ltd. | | Highest Position: 16 |
| | | Weeks on Chart: 9 |

Recordings:

| | | |
|---|---|---|
| Les Baxter and his Orchestra and Chorus (Sue Allen) | 9/51 | Capitol CL.13586 |
| Tony Martin | 10/51 | HMV B.10143 |
| Adelaide Hall | 10/51 | Columbia DB.2928 |
| Hadda Brooks (vocal & piano) | 10/51 | London L.895 |
| Jimmy Young | 10/51 | Polygon P.1017 |
| Don Cherry | 10/51 | Brunswick 04793 |
| Lee Lawrence | 10/51 | Decca F.9776 |

## 334 BELLE, BELLE, MY LIBERTY BELLE

| Composer: Bob Merrill | | Date of Entry: 6.10.51 |
|---|---|---|
| Publishers: Dash Music Co. Ltd. | | Highest Position: 6 |
| | | Weeks on Chart: 20 |

Recordings:

| | | |
|---|---|---|
| Guy Mitchell | 9/51 | Columbia DB.2908 |
| Don Cherry | 10/51 | Brunswick 04779 |
| Cyril Stapleton and his Orchestra (The Stargazers) | 10/51 | Decca F.9777 |
| Frank Cordell and his Orchestra (Larry Day) | 11/51 | HMV B.10160 |

## 335 | BLOW OUT THE CANDLE

| | | |
|---|---|---|
| *Composer:* Phil Moore | *Date of Entry:* 6.10.51 | |
| *Publishers:* Chappell & Co. Ltd. | *Highest Position:* 24 | |
| | *Weeks on Chart:* 1 | |

*Recordings:*

| | | |
|---|---|---|
| Rose Murphy | 9/51 | HMV B.10129 |
| Dorothy Dandridge with orch. cond. Phil Moore (piano) | 9/51 | Columbia DB.2923 |
| The Delta Rhythm Boys | 10/51 | London L.1145 |

## 336 | LONGING FOR YOU

| | | |
|---|---|---|
| *Composers:* Walter Dana & Bernard Jansen (based on 'Waltz Dream' by Oscar Straus) | *Date of Entry:* 13.10.51 | |
| *Publishers:* Chappell & Co. Ltd. | *Highest Position:* 1 | |
| | *Weeks on Chart:* 23 | |

*Recordings:*

| | | |
|---|---|---|
| Teresa Brewer | 7/51 | London L.1069 |
| Joe Loss and his Orchestra | 10/51 | HMV BD.6108 |
| Alan Dean | 10/51 | HMV B.10141 |
| Lou Preager and his Charm of the Waltz Orchestra (Paul Rich) | 10/51 | Columbia DB.2931 |
| Les Baxter and his Chorus and Orchestra (Sue Allen) | 10/51 | Capitol CL.13593 |
| Russ Morgan and his Orchestra (Russ Morgan and The Morganaires) | 10/51 | Brunswick 04792 |
| Billy Cotton and his Band (Alan Breeze and The Bandits) | 10/51 | Decca F.9780 |
| Lester Ferguson | 11/51 | Parlophone R.3457 |
| Oscar Rabin and his Band with David Ede (Patti Forbes and Marjorie Daw) | 11/51 | Parlophone F.2476 |
| Ethel Smith (organ) | 11/51 | Brunswick 04814 |
| Teddy Johnson | 12/51 | Columbia DB.2984 |
| Vic Damone | 1/52 | Oriole CB.1062 |
| Vic Damone | 6/54 | Mercury MB.2951★ |

## 337 | IN THE COOL, COOL, COOL OF THE EVENING

| | | |
|---|---|---|
| *Composers:* Hoagy Carmichael & Johnny Mercer | *Date of Entry:* 20.10.51 | |
| *Publishers:* Victoria Music Publishing Co. Ltd. | *Highest Position:* 23 | |
| | *Weeks on Chart:* 1 | |

*Recordings:*

| | | |
|---|---|---|
| Jo Stafford and Frankie Laine | 8/51 | Columbia DB.2900 |
| Bing Crosby and Jane Wyman with The Four Hits and a Miss | 9/51 | Brunswick 04760 |
| Dean Martin | 9/51 | Capitol CL.13575 |
| The Five Smith Brothers | 10/51 | Parlophone R.3440 |
| Art Lund | 10/51 | MGM.438 |

## 338 | LULLABY OF BROADWAY

| | | |
|---|---|---|
| *Composers:* Al Dubin & Harry Warren | *Date of Entry:* 27.10.51 | |
| *Publishers:* B. Feldman & Co. Ltd. | *Highest Position:* 19 | |
| | *Weeks on Chart:* 5 | |

(Note: Only one recording from the Thirties remained in the catalogues of 1951 – that by the Boswell Sisters on Brunswick 02043.)

*Later recordings:*

| | | |
|---|---|---|
| The Andrews Sisters | 9/48 | Brunswick 04202 |
| The Brass Hats with Kenny Baker (trumpet) | 10/50 | Oriole LB.1010 |
| Benny Fields with the Jud Conlon Singers | 4/51 | MGM.386 |
| Victor Silvester and his Ballroom Orchestra | 10/51 | Columbia FB.3619 |
| Doris Day with The Norman Luboff Choir | 10/51 | Columbia DB.2933 |
| Ted Heath and his Music (Lita Roza) | 12/51 | Decca F.9813 |
| Kenny Baker and his Band | 2/52 | Parlophone R.3490★ |
| Andre Previn (piano) | 7/52 | HMV B.10296★ |

## 339 | LOVE'S ROUNDABOUT (La ronde de l'amour)

| | | |
|---|---|---|
| *Composers:* Oscar Straus, Louis Ducreaux & Harold Purcell | *Date of Entry:* 27.10.51/ Pos 23/Wks: 2 | |
| *Publishers:* Cinephonic Music Co. Ltd. | *Re-entry:* 17.11.51/ Pos: 11/Wks: 23 | |

*Recordings:*

| | | |
|---|---|---|
| Anton Walbrook | 7/51 | Parlophone R.3423 |
| Jan Rosol | 8/51 | Polygon P.1014 |
| Teddy Johnson | 9/51 | Columbia DB.2914 |
| Dany Dauberson | 9/51 | Nixa BY.1014 |
| John Cameron | 9/51 | Decca F.9753 |
| The Melachrino Orchestra | 10/51 | HMV B.10138 |
| Lou Preager and his Charm of the Waltz Orchestra | 10/51 | Columbia DB.2931 |
| Gisele MacKenzie | 1/52 | Capitol CL.13661 |
| Mantovani and his Orchestra | 1/52 | Decca F.9831 |
| Peter Kreuder (piano) and his Rhythms | 5/52 | Nixa BY.9011 |
| Robinson Cleaver (two organs) & Patricia Rossborough (piano and celeste) | 7/52 | Parlophone R.3552★ |
| Anton Walbrook | 1/53 | Parlophone (45) MSP.6002★ |

## 340 | ROSALINE

*Composers:* Johnny Reine & Tommie Connor

*Publishers:* Michael Reine Music Co. Ltd.

*Date of Entry:* 3.11.51

*Highest Position:* 4
*Weeks on Chart:* 17

*Recordings:*

| | | |
|---|---|---|
| Lee Lawrence | 10/51 | Decca F.9765 |
| Billy Cotton and his Band (Alan Breeze and The Bandits) | 10/51 | Decca F.9781 |
| Joe Loss and his Orchestra (Howard Jones and The Loss Chords) | 10/51 | HMV BD.6110 |
| Teddy Johnson | 12/51 | Columbia DB.2984 |

## 341 | ALLENTOWN JAIL

*Composer:* Irving Gordon

*Publishers:* Bourne Music Ltd.

*Date of Entry:* 3.11.51

*Highest Position:* 6
*Weeks on Chart:* 18

*Recordings:*

| | | |
|---|---|---|
| Lita Roza with Ted Heath and his Music | 7/51 | Decca F.9731 |
| Jo Stafford | 10/51 | Columbia DB.2961 |
| Joe Loss and his Orchestra | 12/51 | HMV BD.6117 |
| Frank Cordell and his Orchestra (Chorus and Stella Tanner) | 12/51 | HMV B.10183 |

## 342 | IF YOU GO (Si tu partais)

*Composers:* Michel Emer & Geoffrey Parsons

*Publishers:* Peter Maurice Music Co. Ltd.

*Date of Entry:* 3.11.51

*Highest Position:* 8
*Weeks on Chart:* 18

*Recordings:*

| | | |
|---|---|---|
| The Melachrino Orchestra | 6/51 | HMV B.10087 |
| Alan Dean | 7/51 | HMV B.10102 |
| Lester Ferguson | 10/51 | Parlophone R.3441 |
| Vera Lynn | 11/51 | Decca F.9803 |
| Victor Silvester and his Ballroom Orchestra | 2/52 | Columbia FB.3631 |

(Note: The original French recording by Edith Piaf was available on Decca C.16096.)

## 343 | I WISH I WUZ

*Composers:* Sid Kuller & Lyn Murray

*Publishers:* Peter Maurice Music Co. Ltd.

*Date of Entry:* 10.11.51

*Highest Position:* 13
*Weeks on Chart:* 14

*Recordings:*

| | | |
|---|---|---|
| Teresa Brewer | 9/51 | London L.1085 |
| Art Lund | 10/51 | MGM.438 |
| Donald Peers | 11/51 | HMV B.10158 |
| Rosemary Clooney | 11/51 | Columbia DB.2949 |
| The Beverley Sisters | 11/51 | Columbia DB.2966 |
| Roy Hogsed | 11/51 | Capitol CL.13617 |
| Gloria de Haven with The Lombardo Trio | 12/51 | Brunswick 04839 |

## 344 | AT THE END OF THE DAY

*Composer:* Donald O'Keefe

*Publishers:* Chappell & Co. Ltd.

*Date of Entry:* 10.11.51/
Pos: 21/Wks: 2
*Re-entry:* 1.12.51/
Pos: 7/Wks: 26
*2nd re-entry:* 7.6.52/
Pos: 22/Wks: 2

(Notes: Philip Green provided the backings on no less than three of the versions: by Lester Ferguson, Steve Conway and Dorothy Squires. The Gracie Fields and Lester Ferguson recordings were reissued with different songs on the reverse side of the records.)

*Recordings:*

| | | |
|---|---|---|
| Gracie Fields with The Eight Stars | 6/51 | Decca F.9713 |
| Webster Booth | 7/51 | HMV B.10092 |
| Lester Ferguson | 8/51 | Parlophone R.3419 |
| Steve Conway and The Hastings Girls' Choir | 9/51 | Columbia DB.2913 |
| Dorothy Squires | 11/51 | Columbia DB.2950 |
| Bill Kenny with Male Quartet | 1/52 | Brunswick 04849 |
| Gracie Fields with The Eight Stars | 2/52 | Decca F.9828 |
| Lester Ferguson | 6/52 | Parlophone R.3533 |
| Josef Locke | 6/52 | Columbia DB.3093 |

## 345 SOME ENCHANTED EVENING

| | | |
|---|---|---|
| *Composers*: Richard Rodgers & Oscar Hammerstein II | *Date of Entry*: 1.12.51/ Pos: 4/Wks: 22 | |
| *Publishers*: Williamson Music Inc. | *Re-entry*: 17.5.52/ Pos: 24/Wks: 1 | |

*Recordings*:

| | | |
|---|---|---|
| Wilbur Evans | 11/51 | Columbia DB.2956 |
| Fred Waring and his Pennsylvanians (The Glee Club) | 11/51 | Brunswick 04755 |
| Gordon MacRae | 11/51 | Capitol CL.13570 |
| Bing Crosby | 11/51 | Brunswick 04756 |
| Paul Weston and his Orchestra | 11/51 | Capitol CL.13573 |
| Jo Stafford | 11/51 | Capitol CL.13574 |
| Les Howard with Ted Heath and his Music | 11/51 | Decca F.9792 |
| Al Jolson | 11/51 | Brunswick 04813 |
| Carmen Cavallaro (piano) | 11/51 | Brunswick 04822 |
| Joe Loss and his Orchestra | 11/51 | HMV BD.6113 |
| Perry Como | 11/51 | HMV B.10149 |
| Eddie Calvert (trumpet) and his Orchestra | 11/51 | Columbia DB.2953 |
| Ian Stewart and his Music | 11/51 | Parlophone F.2474 |
| Victor Silvester and his Ballroom Orchestra | 11/51 | Columbia FB.3623 |
| Stanley Black and his Orchestra | 11/51 | Decca F.9791 |
| Mantovani and his Orchestra | 5/52 | Decca F.9914 |
| Perry Como | 1/53 | HMV (45) 7M.110★ |

## 346 BLACK AND WHITE RAG

| | | |
|---|---|---|
| *Composer*: George Botsford | *Date of Entry*: 1.12.51 | |
| *Publishers*: Francis Day & Hunter Ltd. | *Highest Position*: 17 *Weeks on Chart*: 13 | |

*Recordings*:

| | | |
|---|---|---|
| Graeme Bell and his Ragtime Four | 5/51 | Parlophone R.3390 |
| Winifred Atwell (piano) | 11/51 | Decca F.9790 |
| Frank Petty and his Trio | 7/52 | MGM.529★ |
| Lu Watters' Buena Jazz Band | 7/52 | Tempo Jazz Man JMB.1★ |
| Nappy Lamare and his Dixieland Band | 10/52 | Vogue V.2070★ |

## 347 SHRIMP BOATS (A-comin' – there's dancin' tonight)

| | | |
|---|---|---|
| *Composers*: Paul Mason Howard & Paul Weston | *Date of Entry*: 8.12.51 | |
| *Publishers*: Walt Disney Music Co. Ltd. | *Highest Position*: 6 *Weeks on Chart*: 14 | |

*Recordings*:

| | | |
|---|---|---|
| Jo Stafford and The Norman Luboff Choir | 12/51 | Columbia DB.2983 |
| Dolores Gray | 12/51 | Brunswick 04840 |
| Danny Scholl | 12/51 | HMV B.10187 |
| Billy Cotton and his Band (Doreen Stephens, Alan Breeze and The Bandits) | 12/51 | Decca F.9814 |
| Dick Beavers and Les Baxter | 1/52 | Capitol CL.13655 |
| Mickey Katz and his Orchestra (Mickey Katz) [Titled 'Herring Boats'] | 3/52 | Capitol CL.13705 |

## 348 SWEETHEART OF YESTERDAY

| | | |
|---|---|---|
| *Composers*: Carl Sigman & Percy Faith | *Date of Entry*: 15.12.51/ Pos: 24/ Wks: 2 | |
| *Publishers*: Cinephonic Music Co. Ltd. | *Re-entry*: 1.3.52/ Pos: 23/Wks: 1 | |

*Recordings*:

| | | |
|---|---|---|
| Guy Mitchell | 9/51 | Columbia DB.2908 |
| The Beverley Sisters | 11/51 | Columbia DB.2966 |
| Reggie Goff with The Keynotes | 11/51 | Decca F.9806 |
| Guy Lombardo and his Royal Canadians (Kenny Gardner and The Lombardo Trio) | 12/51 | Brunswick 04829 |
| The Five Smith Brothers | 12/51 | Parlophone R.3463 |
| Bobby Wayne | 1/52 | Oriole CB.1067 |
| Bobby Wayne | 6/54 | Mercury MB.2955★ |

## 349 MISTAKES

| | | |
|---|---|---|
| *Composers*: Edgar Leslie & Everett Lynton | *Date of Entry*: 29.12.51 | |
| *Publishers*: Lawrence Wright Music Co. Ltd. | *Highest Position*: 2 *Weeks on Chart*: 26 | |

*Recordings*:

| | | |
|---|---|---|
| Frankie Froba and his Boys (some 78s labelled 'Froeba') | 2/51 | Brunswick 04653 |
| Dorothy Squires | 1/52 | Columbia DB.3005 |
| The King's Men with The Pianotones | 1/52 | Decca F.9838 |
| Gwen Liddel | 1/52 | Polygon P.1036 |
| Victor Silvester and his Ballroom Orchestra | 3/52 | Columbia FB.3635 |
| Frederick Ferrari | 3/52 | Parlophone R.3500 |
| Donald Peers with Quartette | 3/52 | HMV B.10227 |
| Al Morgan with Frankie Froba and his Boys | 3/52 | Brunswick 04913 |
| The Squadronaires cond. Ronnie Aldrich (Roy Edwards) | 4/52 | Decca F.9896 |

| 350 | WHY WORRY |
|---|---|

| *Composers*: Ralph Edwards & John Sexton | *Date of Entry*: 29.12.51 |
|---|---|
| *Publishers*: Macmelodies Ltd. | *Highest Position*: 4 |
| | *Weeks on Chart*: 19 |

*Recordings*:

| Donald Peers | 1/52 | HMV B.10192 |
|---|---|---|
| Ivor Moreton and Dave Kaye [two pianos] (Val Merrall) | 2/52 | Parlophone F.2484 |
| Billy Cotton and his Band (Billy Cotton) | 2/52 | Decca F.9860 |

| 351 | I WANT TO BE NEAR YOU (You're the one, the one, the one) |
|---|---|

| *Composer*: Traditional, new lyrics by Michael Brown | *Date of Entry*: 29.12.51 |
|---|---|
| *Publishers*: Chappell & Co. Ltd. | *Highest Position*: 24 |
| | *Weeks on Chart*: 1 |

*Recordings*:

| Nellie Lutcher | 10/51 | Capitol CL.13606 |
|---|---|---|
| Percy Faith and his Orchestra (Peter Hanley and Chorus) | 11/51 | Columbia DB.2962 |
| Tex Williams | 11/51 | Capitol CL.13620 |
| The Stargazers | 11/51 | Decca F.9800 |
| Johnny Desmond with The Ray Charles Singers | 11/51 | MGM.450 |
| Ray Noble and his Orchestra (The Noblemen) | 12/51 | HMV B.10165 |

# 1952

One of 1951's big hits, *The loveliest night of the year*, finally climbed to No. 1 on 12 January after no less than 32 weeks on the charts and by doing so created an unbeaten record. Bob Merrill added another five chart hits to his ever growing list with all of them reaching the top six, and one, *There's always room at our house*, making it to the top. Vera Lynn teamed up with men and women of the Forces to record some very big hits with *Auf wiederseh'n sweetheart* and *The homing waltz* being successive No. 1 sheet music sellers. Indeed the former also made the US sheet music charts and did even better in their record listings, becoming the first-ever British record to go top in the States. The big BBC event was the launching of the Show Band directed by Cyril Stapleton. First mooted and rehearsed in March, the initial broadcast went out on Thursday, 2 October with a 45-minute show beginning at 9.15 p.m. on the Light. On 3 October the band could be heard over the Home Service wavelengths between 7 and 7.40 p.m., while the third broadcast of the week went out on Saturday evening at 10.45 p.m. immediately preceding the first Jack Jackson programme of a new series at 11.30 p.m. Three shows a week was to be the opening pattern, and so, much was heard of resident vocalists Lee Lawrence, Jean Campbell and Johnny Johnston and The Johnston Singers. The theme tune, *Just for you*, was a Johnny Johnston original which had been arranged by Robert Farnon, one of several major arrangers employed to produce the best in popular music for the shows. The first 'chart hit' to be played was *The homing waltz* –

| Pos | MOST WEEKS ON THE CHARTS TOP SIX | Wks |
|---|---|---|
| 1 | *Auf wiederseh'n sweetheart* | 32 |
| 2 | *Blue tango* | 30 |
| 3 | *The homing waltz* | 28 |
| 4= | *We won't live in a castle* | 26 |
| 4= | *Kiss of fire* | 26 |
| 6 | *Mistakes* | 25 |

well, it was No. 1 at the time. Jimmy Phillips of the Peter Maurice Music Company complained to Cyril Stapleton in early December that the Show Band had not been playing any of his material and offered to put at Stapleton's disposal all his new material with an option to play it exclusively for a while. Phillips had quite obviously realised the excellency of the Show Band and its selling potential for his music. One of the most popular singles of the year,

INTERNATIONAL MUSIC PUBLICATIONS

# I CAN'T BEGIN TO TELL YOU
Words by MACK GORDON
Music by JIMMY V. MONACO

20TH CENTURY-FOX PRESENTS

## THE DOLLY SISTERS
IN TECHNICOLOR

Starring
BETTY GRABLE
and
JOHN PAYNE
JUNE HAVER

CHAPPELL

PRICE 1/- NET

# OH BABY MINE
# I GET SO LONELY
Words and Music by Pat Ballard

RECORDED BY
ANNE SHELTON
ON H.M.V. RECORDS

1/- NET

# I LEAVE MY HEART IN
# AN ENGLISH GARDEN
FROM
EMILE LITTLER'S
NEW MUSICAL PLAY

## "Dear Miss Phoebe"

BASED ON SIR JAMES BARRIE'S
"QUALITY STREET"

MUSIC BY
HARRY PARR DAVIES
BOOK AND LYRICS BY
CHRISTOPHER HASSALL
PRODUCTION DIRECTED BY
CHARLES HICKMAN

# ...OU GO
...hel Emer • English Lyric by GEOFFREY PARSONS

Broadcast by
LES HOWARD

# I NEED YOU NOW
Words and Music by — JIMMIE CRANE and AL JACOBS

Recorded on H.M.V. B10755
by EDDIE FISHER

2/-

# IT HAPPENED
# IN ADANO
by DON PELOSI
& HAROLD FIELDS

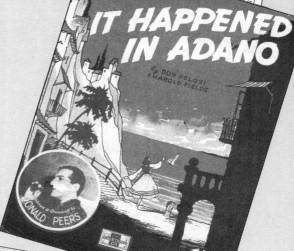

...sung & Broadcast by
DONALD PEERS

# INTO EACH LIFE
# SOME RAIN MUST FALL
WORDS AND MUSIC BY ALLAN ROBERTS & DORIS FISHER

...Ink Spots

BRADBURY WOOD LTD.
CHARING CROSS ROAD, LONDON, W.C.2
SUN MUSIC CO. INC. N.Y.C.
1/- NET

# I'D LOVE TO FALL ASLEEP
( AND WAKE UP IN YOUR ARMS )
( LE SOIR )
English words by SONNY MILLER
Original words by GÉO KOGER
Music by
LOUIS GASTÉ

Best Wishes
Line Renaud

Featured, Recorded & Broadcast by
LINE RENAUD

COPYRIGHT

LONDON, ENGLAND.
B. FELDMAN & CO. LTD.
125, 127, 129, SHAFTESBURY AVENUE, W.C.2.

# I WENT TO YOUR WEDDING
Words and Music by JESSIE MAE ROBINSON

Featured & Broadcast by
JOHN HAUXWELL

THE VICTORIA MUSIC PUBLISHING CO. LTD.,
52 MADDOX STREET, LONDON, W.1.
ST. LOUIS MUSIC CORPORATION
HILL AND RANGE SONGS, INC., BEVERLY HILLS, CAL., U.S.A.
This Edition is authorised for sale only in Great Britain (The British Isles and Eire)

1/- NET

MADE IN ENGLAND

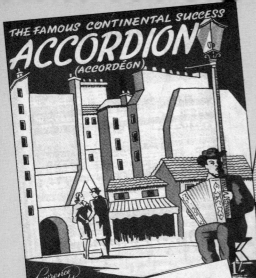

THE FAMOUS CONTINENTAL SUCCESS
# ACCORDION
(ACCORDÉON)

*Lawrence Wright*

# APRIL IN PORTUGAL
Words by
JIMMY KENNEDY
(COIMBRA)
By RAUL FERRÃO

SONG
PIANO SOLO

Broadcast by
SAM COSTA
in his BBC programme "PICK OF THE BUNCH"

# BLUE TANGO
By LEROY ANDERSON

Recorded by
LEROY ANDERSON

PIANO SOLO

2/6

# AUTUMN CONCERTO
Music by
C. BARDONI
English Lyric by
PAUL SIEGEL, JOHN TURNER
& GEOFFREY PARSONS    Italian Lyric by DANPA

Featured & Recorded on H.M.V. B.10958
by
GEORGE MELACHRINO
AND HIS ORCHESTRA

CHAPPELL & CO. LTD.
80 NEW BOND STREET

# The BLACKSMITH BLUES
Words and Music by
JACK HOLMES

Featured by
SAM BROWNE
in "RECORD TIME"

CHAPPELL & CO. LTD.
80 NEW BOND ST.
5928

# APRIL SHOWERS
Words by B.G. De SYLVA * Music by LOUIS SILVERS

COLUMBIA PICTURES
presents
## THE JOLSON STORY
LARRY    with    EVELYN
PARKS    *    KEYES
WILLIAM DEMAREST  BILL GOODWIN
in Technicolor

1867

CHAPPELL

# BLACK & WHITE RAG
BY
GEORGE BOTSFORD

WINIFRED ATWELL'S
Arrangement as Recorded on
DECCA F.9790.

2/-

FRANCIS, DAY & HUNTER LTD, 138-140, CHARING CROSS RD, LONDON W.C.2

# THE BLACK NOTE SERENADE
Words and Music by BENNY LITCHFIELD
and HARRY BOLTON

Featured & Broadcast by
SID PHILLIPS
AND HIS BAND

1/- NET

# Blow out the Candle
by PHIL MOORE

Recorded by
DOROTHY DANDRIDGE
& PHIL MOORE

CHAPPELL

# MROSE HILL

Words by
LIE CHESTER
and EVERETT LYNTON

# THE
# PURPLE PEOPLE EATER

Words and Music by
SHEB WOOLEY

Recorded by
SHEB WOOLEY
on the M.G.M. Records

2/-

# PUT YOUR SHOES ON, LUCY

By HANK FORT

Featured
and
Broadcast
by
GRACIE FIELDS

PRICE
ONE SHILLING

# PUT YOUR HEAD ON MY SHOULDER

BY PAUL ANKA

2/-
RECORDED BY
PAUL ANKA
ON COLUMBIA 45-DB 4355

SPANKA MUSIC COMPANY
Sole Selling Agents: BRON A... ...ES ROAD LONDON W C 2

# SAY YOU'RE MINE AGAIN

Words and Music by CHARLES NATHAN and DAVE HEISLER

Featured & Broadcast by
JACK NATHAN
AND HIS BAND

EDWIN H. MORRIS & CO L...
52 Maddox St. London W...

# SOMEWHERE ALONG THE WAY

Words by SAMMY GALLOP          Music by KURT ADAMS

Recorded by
NAT "KING" COLE

ROLAND'S PIANOFORTE TUTOR THE BEST IN THE WORLD
ENGLISH FINGERING          CONTINENTAL FINGERING

# SO WOULD I

Words by JOHNNY BURKE          Music by JAMES VAN HEUSEN

"London Town"
starring
SID FIELD

WITH
GRETA GYNT
AND
KAY KENDALL

Songs from the Film
SO WOULD I
YOU CAN'T KEEP A DENNIS DOWN
MY HEART GOES CRAZY

EDWIN H. MORRIS & CO., LTD
52, MADDOX STREET, LONDON, W.1.

EM 4004

# Snowflakes

WORDS & MUSIC BY MARJORIE KURTZ

Featured & Broadcast by
THE RADIO REVELLERS

MADDOX MUSIC COMPANY LTD.
52 MADDOX STREET, LONDON, W.1

1/-
MADE IN ENGLAND

8531

# THE STARS
# WILL REMEMBER
## (SO WILL I)

Words & Music by
DON PELOSI & LEO TOWERS

FEATURED BY
VERA LYNN

B. FELDMAN & CO. LTD
135-7-9 Shaftesbury Avenue, W.C.2

1/-
NET
COPYRIGHT

**WHY IS IT?**

*by*
JOAN WHITNEY
&
ALEX KRAMER

FEATURED AND BROADCAST BY
SYDNEY LIPTON
AND HIS ORCHESTRA

CINEPHONIC MUSIC CO. LTD. 100 CHARING CROSS RD. L

**VENI - VIDI - VICI**

Words by PAUL FRANCIS WEBSTER

Music by JERRY LIVINGSTON

BROADCAST & RECORDED BY
RAY MARTIN
AND HIS ORCHESTRA
ON COLUMBIA BD. 3539

DASH MUSIC CO. LTD.

HAWTHORNE MUSIC CORP. NEW YORK

**WHEN YOU'RE IN LOVE**

Words by FRANKIE LAINE, A.S.C.A.P.

Music by CARL FISCHER, A.S.C.A.P.

Broadcast & Recorded by
LEE LAWRENCE
on Decca Record F9971

CAMPBELL, CONNELLY & CO. LTD.
10 DENMARK STREET, LONDON, W.C.2
ALAMO MUSIC, INC.

**YOU CAN BE SURE OF ME**

Words & Music By JOS. GEO. GILBERT & LEWIS ILDA

IRWIN DASH MUSIC CO. LTD. 17. BERNERS St. LON

**THE WORLD BELONGS TO YOU**
**LITTLE MAN**

Featured and Broadcast by
BERTHA WILLMOTT

1/-

STRAUSS, MILLER MUSIC CO.

**The Very**
**First Christmas of All**

Words by PADDY ROBERTS

Music by PETER HART

Recorded by
RUBY MURRAY
ON COLUMBIA RECORDS

DASH MUSIC CO. LTD.

2/-

Johnnie Ray's *Cry*, was followed by a parody version, *Try*, from Stan Freberg, complete with the famous sobbing chorus that just went on and on. All light entertainment and dance music was banned from the BBC airwaves for two weeks following the death of King George VI on 6 February and, sadly, popular music in Britain lost one of its most revered figures, Steve Conway, when he died in October, aged just 31. EMI joined the microgroove field in October with the first albums but beat Decca to 45 rpm releases with the first classical issues coming the same month. The recording which was to become the renowned signature tune of the Radio Luxembourg 'Top Twenty' show, *Doodletown fifers*, played by the Sauter-Finegan Orchestra, was released in November on HMV B.10360, but perhaps the most recalled memory of that month was the first record chart compiled by the *New Musical Express*. The novelty value and interest contained in it were enormous, but it was to be just over two years – in 1955 – before it came to be regarded as a serious rival to the sheet music charts. There is also the fact that while the latter had 24 entries each week, the record chart stayed with only 12 until late 1954. The elder relation was not going to give in to its eager youngster without a fight.

# SONG CHARTS

## 352 DOWN YONDER

| | | |
|---|---|---|
| *Composer*: L. Wolfe Gilbert | | *Date of Entry*: 5.1.52 |
| *Publishers*: B. Feldman & Co. Ltd. | | *Highest Position*: 6<br>*Weeks on Chart*: 16 |

*Recordings*:

| | | |
|---|---|---|
| Spade Cooley and his Fiddlin' Friends | 11/51 | Brunswick 04812 |
| Del Wood (piano) | 11/51 | London L.1127 |
| Joe'Fingers'Carr (piano) and the Carr-hops | 11/51 | Capitol CL.13626 |
| The Frank Petty Trio | 12/51 | MGM.457 |
| Sid Phillips and his Band (Johnnie Eager) | 12/51 | HMV BD.6114 |
| Ronald Chesney (harmonica) and George Elliott (guitar) | 12/51 | HMV B.10189 |
| The Squadronaires featuring Ronnie Aldrich (piano) | 12/51 | Decca F.9818 |
| Champ Butler | 1/52 | Columbia DB.2994 |
| Oscar Rabin and his Band (David Ede and Ensemble) | 1/52 | Parlophone F.2481 |
| Ian Stewart and his Music | 2/52 | Parlophone F.2483 |
| Eddie Smith and The Chief (pianos) | 2/52 | Vogue V.9022 |

## 353 SIN (It's no sin)

| | | |
|---|---|---|
| *Composers*: George Hoven & Chester R. Shull | | *Date of Entry*: 12.1.52/<br>Pos: 23/Wks: 1 |
| *Publishers*: Edwin H. Morris & Co. Ltd. | | *Re-entry*: 26.1.52/<br>Pos: 22/Wks: 1 |

*Recordings*:

| | | |
|---|---|---|
| The Four Knights | 11/51 | Capitol CL.13622 |
| Billy Williams and his Quartette | 11/51 | MGM.451 |
| Arthur Prysock | 12/51 | Brunswick 04816 |
| Al Morgan | 12/51 | Brunswick 04835 |
| Penny Nichols | 12/51 | HMV B.10185 |
| Teddy Johnson | 12/51 | Columbia DB.2996 |
| Annette Klooger | 12/51 | Decca F.9816 |
| Eddy Howard and his Orchestra (Eddy Howard) | 12/51 | Oriole CB.1057 |
| Jimmy Young | 1/52 | Polygon P.1032 |
| The Deep River Boys | 1/52 | HMV B.10194 |
| Joe Loss and his Orchestra | 1/52 | HMV BD.6121 |
| The Beverley Sisters | 1/52 | Columbia DB.3008 |
| Ian Stewart and his Music | 2/52 | Parlophone F.2483★ |
| The Johnny Dankworth Seven (Cleo Laine) | 2/52 | Esquire 5−056★ |
| Mickey Katz and his Orchestra (Mickey Katz) | 3/52 | Capitol CL.13705★ |
| Eddy Howard and his Orchestra (Eddy Howard) | 6/54 | Mercury MB.2947★ |

## 354 THERE'S ALWAYS ROOM AT OUR HOUSE

| | | |
|---|---|---|
| *Composer*: Bob Merrill | | *Date of Entry*: 12.1.52 |
| *Publishers*: Campbell Connelly & Co. Ltd. | | *Highest Position*: 1<br>*Weeks on Chart*: 21 |

*Recordings*:

| | | |
|---|---|---|
| Guy Mitchell | 12/51 | Columbia DB.2969 |
| Annette Klooger | 12/51 | Decca F.9816 |
| Billy Cotton and his Band (Alan Breeze and The Bandits) | 1/52 | Decca F.9827 |
| Donald Peers | 2/52 | HMV B.10211 |

## 355 DOMINO

| | | |
|---|---|---|
| *Composers*: Jacques Plante, Louis Ferrari & Don Raye | | *Date of Entry*: 19.1.52 |
| *Publishers*: Leeds Music Ltd. | | *Highest Position*: 4<br>*Weeks on Chart*: 18 |

*Recordings*:

| | | |
|---|---|---|
| Charlie Kunz and his Music | 11/51 | Decca F.9797 |
| Betty Paul | 11/51 | Nixa NY.7601 |
| Mary Mayo | 12/51 | Capitol CL.13641 |
| Tony Martin | 12/51 | HMV B.10167 |
| Doris Day | 12/51 | Columbia DB.2971 |
| Teddy Johnson | 12/51 | Columbia DB.2996 |
| Sidney Torch and his Orchestra | 12/51 | Parlophone R.3467 |
| Bing Crosby | 12/51 | Brunswick 04841 |
| Lester Ferguson | 2/52 | Parlophone R.3491 |
| Ethel Smith (organ) | 2/52 | Brunswick 04875 |
| The Melachrino Strings | 2/52 | HMV B.10207 |
| Victor Silvester and his Ballroom Orchestra | 2/52 | Columbia FB.3630 |
| Mary Small | 2/52 | Vogue V.9026 |

## 356 OODLES OF NOODLES

| | | |
|---|---|---|
| *Composers*: Dennis Breeze & Conrad Leonard | | *Date of Entry*: 19.1.52 |
| *Publishers*: Edward Cox Music Co. Ltd. | | *Highest Position*: 16<br>*Weeks on Chart*: 12 |

*Recordings*:

| | | |
|---|---|---|
| Johnny Brandon | 1/52 | Columbia DB.3012 |
| Billy Cotton and his Band (Alan Breeze and The Bandits) | 2/52 | Decca F.9865 |

## 357 | THE LITTLE WHITE CLOUD THAT CRIED

| | | |
|---|---|---|
| *Composer*: Johnnie Ray | | *Date of Entry*: 2.2.52 |
| *Publishers*: Larry Spier Ltd. | | *Highest Position*: 3 |
| | | *Weeks on Chart*: 19 |

*Recordings*:

| | | |
|---|---|---|
| Johnnie Ray and The Four Lads | 1/52 | Columbia DB.2995 |
| Joy Nichols with The Men of Song | 1/52 | Parlophone R.3489 |
| Dorothy Squires | 1/52 | Columbia DB.3005 |
| Jimmy Young | 2/52 | Polygon P.1035 |
| Roberta Lee | 2/52 | Brunswick 04876 |
| Vera Lynn | 2/52 | Decca F.9839 |
| Maurice Winnick and his Sweet Music for Dancing | 2/52 | HMV BD.6123 |
| Lou Dinning | 2/52 | Capitol CL.13664 |
| Mickey Katz and his Orchestra (Mickey Katz) [Parody titled 'Little White Knish . . .'] | 6/52 | Capitol CL.13751 |

## 358 | CHARMAINE

| | | |
|---|---|---|
| *Composers*: Erno Rapee & Lew Pollack | | *Date of Entry*: 9.2.52/ Pos: 21/Wks: 1 |
| *Publishers*: Keith Prowse Music Publishing Co. Ltd. | | *Re-entry*: 23.2.52/ Pos: 19/Wks: 6 |
| | | *2nd re-entry*: 26.4.52/ Pos: 23/Wks: 2 |

Note: Originally published in 1926, this song had a burst of popularity round 1939–40. The only version to survive in the catalogues from that era was the Jimmy Lunceford Orchestra recording on Brunswick 02983 which had a vocal by Dan Grissom.)

*Later recordings*:

| | | |
|---|---|---|
| Guy Lombardo and his Royal Canadians (Jimmy Brown) | 1/49 | Brunswick 04158 |
| Mantovani and his Orchestra | 6/51 | Decca F.9696 |
| The Four Knights | 1/52 | Capitol CL.13652 |
| The Melachrino Strings | 1/52 | HMV B.10197 |
| Ethel Smith (organ) | 2/52 | Brunswick 04875 |
| Billy May and his Orchestra | 2/52 | Capitol CL.13677 |
| Victor Silvester and his Ballroom Orchestra | 3/52 | Columbia FB.3635 |
| Billy Daniels | 4/52 | London L.1134 |
| Josef Locke | 7/52 | Columbia DB.3109★ |
| The Delta Rhythm Boys | 12/52 | Esquire 5–081★ |

## 359 | I WANNA SAY HELLO

| | | |
|---|---|---|
| *Composers*: Jimmy MacDonald & Jack Hoffman | | *Date of Entry*: 9.2.52/ Pos: 24/Wks: 1 |
| *Publishers*: Sterling Music Publishing Co. Ltd. | | *Re-entry*: 1.3.52/ Pos: 9/Wks: 14 |
| | | *2nd re-entry*: 28.6.52/ Pos: 23/Wks: 1 |

*Recordings*:

| | | |
|---|---|---|
| The Four Knights | 12/51 | Capitol CL.13649 |
| Sir Hubert Pimm (piano) with Ellen Sutton | 12/51 | London L.1130 |
| Billy Cotton and his Band (The Bandits) | 1/52 | Decca F.9827 |
| Sophie Tucker | 4/52 | Oriole CB.1088 |
| Dorothy Loudon with The Honky-Tonks | 4/52 | HMV B.10269 |
| Sophie Tucker | 6/54 | Mercury MB.2961★ |

## 360 | ROLLIN' STONE

| | | |
|---|---|---|
| *Composer*: Irving Gordon | | *Date of Entry*: 16.2.52 |
| *Publishers*: Edward Kassner Music Co. Ltd. | | *Highest Position*: 12 |
| | | *Weeks on Chart*: 9 |

*Recordings*:

| | | |
|---|---|---|
| Perry Como with The Fontane Sisters | 12/51 | HMV B.10188 |
| Terry Gilkyson | 12/51 | Brunswick 04853 |
| Joe Loss and his Orchestra | 1/52 | HMV BD.6121 |
| The Stargazers | 1/52 | Decca F.9836 |
| Roy Stevens | 2/52 | Vogue V.9023 |
| Teddy Johnson with the Peter Knight Singers | 3/52 | Columbia DB.3045 |

## 361 | SLOW COACH

| | | |
|---|---|---|
| *Composers*: Pee Wee King, Redd Stewart & Chilton Price | | *Date of Entry*: 16.2.52 |
| *Publishers*: Chappell & Co. Ltd. | | *Highest Position*: 3 |
| | | *Weeks on Chart*: 21 |

(Note: The original American title 'Slow poke' was changed to 'Slow coach' on recordings issued in the UK. Pee Wee King re-recorded his version for the UK market; the waxings by Helen O'Connell and Hawkshaw Hawkins had 'Slow coach' on the label, 'Slow poke' in the lyric.)

*Recordings*:

| | | |
|---|---|---|
| Pee Wee King and his Golden West Cowboys (Redd Stewart) | 1/52 | HMV B.10203 |
| Billy Thorburn's The Organ, the Dance Band and Me (The Bobolinks) | 1/52 | Parlophone F.2480 |
| Johnny Brandon | 1/52 | Columbia DB.3012 |
| Helen O'Connell | 1/52 | Capitol CL.13657 |
| Hawkshaw Hawkins | 2/52 | Vogue V.9027 |
| Ray Ellington and his Quartet (Ray Ellington) | 2/52 | Decca F.9863 |
| The Radio Revellers and Geraldo and his Orchestra | 3/52 | Columbia DB.3027 |
| The Squadronaires cond. Ronnie Aldrich (Roy Edwards) | 4/52 | Decca F.9896 |

## 362 UNFORGETTABLE

| | | | |
|---|---|---|---|
| *Composer:* Irving Gordon | | *Date of Entry:* 16.2.52 | |
| *Publishers:* Bourne Music Ltd. | | *Highest Position:* 1 | |
| | | *Weeks on Chart:* 23 | |

*Recordings:*

| | | |
|---|---|---|
| Dick James | 11/51 | Decca F.9784 |
| Luckie Robinson | 11/51 | Polygon P.1026 |
| Nat 'King' Cole | 12/51 | Capitol CL.13637 |
| Billy May and his Orchestra | 3/52 | Capitol CL.13696 |
| Dorothy Squires | 3/52 | Columbia DB.3046 |
| Ray Martin and his Concert Orchestra | 4/52 | Columbia DB.3051 |
| Victor Silvester and his Ballroom Orchestra | 4/52 | Columbia FB.3639 |
| Joe Loss and his Orchestra | 4/52 | HMV BD.6129 |

## 363 ONLY FOOLS

| | | |
|---|---|---|
| *Composers:* David Heneker & Tommy Duggan | *Date of Entry:* 16.2.52/ Pos: 24/Wks: 1 |
| *Publishers:* Sun Music Publishing Co. Ltd. | *Re-entry:* 1.3.52/ Pos: 12/Wks: 13 |

*Recordings:*

| | | |
|---|---|---|
| Jimmy Young | 10/51 | Polygon P.1017 |
| Victor Silvester and his Ballroom Orchestra | 1/52 | Columbia FB.3628 |
| Dennis Hale | 1/52 | Parlophone R.3476 |
| Lee Lawrence | 1/52 | Decca F.9833 |
| Roberto Inglez and his Orchestra | 2/52 | Parlophone R.3492 |
| Camarata and his Music (Pat Terry) | 2/52 | Brunswick 04873 |
| Eric Winstone and his Orchestra (Franklyn Boyd) | 2/52 | Nixa NY.7741 |
| David Hughes | 2/52 | HMV B.10208 |
| Norton Colville and his Band for Dancers | 2/52 | Decca F.9846 |

## 364 THEN I'LL BE THERE

| | | |
|---|---|---|
| *Composer:* Billy Merrin | *Date of Entry:* 23.2.52/ Pos: 24/Wks: 1 |
| *Publishers:* David Toff Music Publishing Ltd. | *Re-entry:* 15.3.52/ Pos: 24/Wks: 2 |

*Recordings:*

| | | |
|---|---|---|
| Bill Hurley with Billy Hill (piano) | 11/51 | Nixa NY.7701 |
| Joe Loss and his Orchestra (Rose Brennan and The Loss Chords) | 12/51 | HMV BD.1279 |
| Harry Dawson | 1/52 | Decca F.9843 |
| Bill Hurley with Billy Hill (piano) | 2/52 | Nixa NY.7711 |

## 365 CRY

| | | | |
|---|---|---|---|
| *Composer:* Churchill Kohlman | | *Date of Entry:* 8.3.52 | |
| *Publishers:* Francis Day & Hunter Ltd. | | *Highest Position:* 2 | |
| | | *Weeks on Chart:* 22 | |

*Recordings:*

| | | |
|---|---|---|
| Vera Lynn | 12/51 | Decca F.9817 |
| Jimmy Young | 1/52 | Polygon P.1033 |
| The Four Knights | 1/52 | Capitol CL.13652 |
| Johnnie Ray | 1/52 | Columbia DB.2995 |
| Paul Chapman | 1/52 | Brunswick 04864 |
| The Maple Leaf Four | 1/52 | Nixa NY.7722 |

## 366 SATURDAY RAG

| | | | |
|---|---|---|---|
| *Composers:* John Jerome & Hal Biddy | | *Date of Entry:* 8.3.52 | |
| *Publishers:* John Fields Music Co. Ltd. | | *Highest Position:* 7 | |
| | | *Weeks on Chart:* 17 | |

*Recordings:*

| | | |
|---|---|---|
| The Tanner Sisters | 2/52 | HMV B.10215 |
| Billy Thorburn's The Organ, the Dance Band and Me (The Bobolinks) | 3/52 | Parlophone F.2487 |
| Les Howard and The Stargazers | 3/52 | Decca F.9875 |
| Chris Hamalton (Hammond organ) | 4/52 | London L.1200 |
| The Five Smith Brothers | 5/52 | Parlophone R.3522 |

## 367 BECAUSE OF RAIN

| | |
|---|---|
| *Composers:* Ruth Poll, Nat Cole & Bill Harrington | *Date of Entry:* 8.3.52/ Pos: 24/Wks: 1 |
| *Publishers:* Magna Music Co. Ltd. | *Re-entry:* 12.4.52/ Pos: 24/Wks: 1 |
| | *2nd re-entry:* 24.5.52/ Pos: 24/Wks: 1 |

*Recordings:*

| | | |
|---|---|---|
| Nat 'King' Cole | 12/51 | Capitol CL.13637 |
| Ella Fitzgerald | 2/52 | Brunswick 04866 |
| Les Howard | 5/52 | Decca F.9888 |

## 368 WE WON'T LIVE IN A CASTLE

*Composer*: Bob Merrill

*Publishers*: Campbell Connelly & Co. Ltd.

*Date of Entry*: 15.3.52

*Highest Position*: 4
*Weeks on Chart*: 26

*Recordings*:

| | | |
|---|---|---|
| Eve Boswell | 3/52 | Parlophone R.3501 |
| Guy Mitchell | 3/52 | Columbia DB.3018 |
| Billy Thorburn's The Organ, the Dance Band and Me (The Bobolinks) | 3/52 | Parlophone F.2487 |
| Joe Loss and his Orchestra | 3/52 | HMV BD.6127 |
| Billy Cotton and his Band (Doreen Stephens, Alan Breeze and Chorus) | 3/52 | Decca F.9882 |
| Jimmy Young | 3/52 | Polygon P.1039 |
| Teddy Johnson with The Peter Knight Singers | 4/52 | Columbia DB.3038 |
| Victor Silvester and his Ballroom Orchestra | 4/52 | Columbia FB.3638 |
| Donald Peers | 4/52 | HMV B.10240 |

## 369 AND SO TO SLEEP AGAIN

*Composers*: Joe Marsala & Sunny Skylar

*Publishers*: Edward Kassner Music Co. Ltd.

*Date of Entry*: 15.3.52

*Highest Position*: 21
*Weeks on Chart*: 1

*Recordings*:

| | | |
|---|---|---|
| Larry Cross | 11/51 | Parlophone R.3459 |
| April Stevens | 11/51 | HMV B.10152 |
| Dorothy Squires | 11/51 | Columbia DB.2950 |
| Margaret Whiting | 11/51 | Capitol CL.13619 |
| Vera Lynn | 11/51 | Decca F.9804 |
| Jimmy Young | 11/51 | Polygon P.1024 |
| Dick Haymes with The Four Hits and a Miss | 11/51 | Brunswick 04815 |
| Victor Silvester and his Ballroom Orchestra | 12/51 | Columbia FB.3627 |
| Paul Weston and his Orchestra (The Norman Luboff Choir) | 12/51 | Columbia DB.2968 |
| Patti Page | 1/52 | Oriole CB.1061 |
| Patti Page | 6/54 | Mercury MB.2950★ |

## 370 TELL ME WHY

*Composers*: Martin Gold & Al Alberts

*Publishers*: Edwin H. Morris & Co. Ltd.

*Date of Entry*: 22.3.52

*Highest Position*: 3
*Weeks on Chart*: 24

*Recordings*:

| | | |
|---|---|---|
| Roberta Lee | 2/52 | Brunswick 04876 |
| The Four Aces featuring Al Alberts | 2/52 | Brunswick 04883 |
| Norman Kay | 2/52 | Capitol CL.13687 |
| Eddie Fisher | 3/52 | HMV B.10236 |
| Dennis Lotis | 4/52 | Melodisc P.211 |
| Franklyn Boyd | 4/52 | Columbia DB.3043 |
| Billy Cotton and his Band with Charles Smitton – organ (Alan Breeze and The Bandits) | 4/52 | Decca F.9891 |
| Victor Silvester and his Ballroom Orchestra | 5/52 | Columbia FB.3641 |

## 371 AT LAST! AT LAST! (L'âmes des Poètes) (Longtemps, Longtemps)

*Composers*: Charles Trenet & Florence Miles

*Publishers*: Pickwick Music Ltd.

*Date of Entry*: 22.3.52

*Highest Position*: 11
*Weeks on Chart*: 20

*Recordings*:

| | | |
|---|---|---|
| Bill Hurley (Titled 'Long, Long Ago') | 11/51 | Nixa NY.7701 |
| Evelyne Dorat (Titled 'L'Âmes des Poètes') | 1/52 | Polygon P.1034 |
| Norrie Paramor and his Orchestra | 2/52 | Columbia DB.3007 |
| Lee Lawrence | 2/52 | Decca F.9879 |
| Roberto Inglez and his Orchestra | 2/52 | Parlophone R.3499 |
| Tony Martin | 3/52 | HMV B.10219 |
| Ted Straeter and his Orchestra | 3/52 | MGM.486 |
| Bing Crosby | 3/52 | Brunswick 04900 |
| Guy Lombardo and his Royal Canadians (Buddy Brown and Fred Kreitzer – two pianos) | 4/52 | Brunswick 04908 |
| Ray Martin and his Concert Orchestra | 4/52 | Polygon P.1040 |
| David Hughes | 5/52 | Columbia DB.3071 |
| Kurt Burling and his Rococo Orchestra | 5/52 | HMV B.10264 |

(Note: The original recording by Charles Trenet, recorded in 1950, was available here as an import on Columbia DCF.92.)

## 372 BE MY LIFE'S COMPANION

| Composers: Bob Hilliard & Milton DeLugg | | Date of Entry: 29.3.52 |
| Publishers: Edwin H. Morris & Co. Ltd. | | Highest Position: 5 |
| | | Weeks on Chart: 16 |

Recordings:

| The Mills Brothers | 2/52 | Brunswick 04892 |
|---|---|---|
| The Johnston Brothers | 3/52 | Decca F.9872 |
| Rosemary Clooney | 4/52 | Columbia DB.3037 |
| Sid Phillips and his Band (Denny Dennis) | 4/52 | HMV BD.6128 |
| Joe Loss and his Orchestra | 4/52 | HMV BD.6129 |

## 373 PLEASE MR SUN

| Composers: Sid Frank & Ray Getzov | | Date of Entry: 5.4.52 |
| Publishers: Chappell & Co. Ltd. | | Highest Position: 13 |
| | | Weeks on Chart: 12 |

Recordings:

| Johnnie Ray and The Four Lads | 2/52 | Columbia DB.3006 |
|---|---|---|
| Perry Como | 3/52 | HMV B.10232 |
| Tommy Edwards | 3/52 | MGM.482 |
| Les Baxter and his Chorus and Orchestra | 3/52 | Capitol CL.13703 |
| Eve Boswell | 4/52 | Parlophone R.3517 |
| Dennis Lotis | 4/52 | Melodisc P.211 |
| Teddy Johnson and The Peter Knight Singers | 4/52 | Columbia DB.3038 |
| Bill Kenny | 4/52 | Brunswick 04905 |
| Vera Lynn | 4/52 | Decca F.9898 |
| Victor Silvester and his Ballroom Orchestra | 5/52 | Columbia FB.3641 |
| Harry Roy and his Orchestra | 5/52 | Nixa NY.7764 |

## 374 NEVER

| Composers: Lionel Newman & Eliot Daniel | | Date of Entry: 5.4.52/ Pos: 24/Wks: 1 |
| Publishers: Francis Day & Hunter Ltd. | | Re-entry: 19.4.52/ Pos: 2/Wks: 23 |

Recordings:

| Bill Hurley | 12/51 | Nixa NY.7702 |
|---|---|---|
| Toni Arden | 1/52 | Columbia DB.2998 |
| Lee Lawrence | 1/52 | Decca F.9833 |
| Camarata and his Music (Fred Darian) | 2/52 | Brunswick 04873 |
| Bill Hurley | 2/52 | Nixa NY.7711 |
| Bob Eberly | 2/52 | Capitol CL.13673 |
| Jan Garber and his Orchestra (Roy Cordell) | 3/52 | Capitol CL.13697 |
| Dickie Valentine | 3/52 | Melodisc P.210 |
| Lester Ferguson | 4/52 | Parlophone R.3508 |
| David Hughes | 4/52 | Columbia DB.3039 |
| Dennis Day | 4/52 | HMV B.10242 |

## 375 ANY TIME

| Composer: Herbert 'Happy' Lawson | | Date of Entry: 12.4.52 |
| Publishers: Victoria Music Co. Ltd. | | Highest Position: 17 |
| | | Weeks on Chart: 18 |

Recordings:

| Dick Haymes and The Troubadours | 11/48 | Brunswick 03996 |
|---|---|---|
| Eddie Fisher | 1/52 | HMV B.10190 |
| Helen O'Connell | 2/52 | Capitol CL.13699 |
| Les Howard | 2/52 | Decca F.9878 |
| Dennis Hale | 3/52 | Parlophone R.3506 |
| Dorothy Squires | 4/52 | Columbia DB.3042 |
| Victor Silvester and his Ballroom Orchestra | 4/52 | Columbia FB.3639 |

## 376 A-ROUND THE CORNER (Beneath the berry tree)

| Composer: Traditional, adapted by Josef Marais | | Date of Entry: 19.4.52 |
| Publishers: Dash Music Co. Ltd. | | Highest Position: 1 |
| | | Weeks on Chart: 20 |

Recordings:

| Jo Stafford with The Norman Luboff Choir | 3/52 | Columbia DB.3025 |
|---|---|---|
| The Weavers | 4/52 | Brunswick 04916 |
| The Stargazers | 5/52 | Decca F.9905 |
| Edmundo Ros and his Rumba Band (Edmundo Ros) | 5/52 | Decca F.9926 |
| The Tanner Sisters | 6/52 | HMV B.10286 |

## 377 WHEEL OF FORTUNE

| Composers: Bennie Benjamin & George Weiss | | Date of Entry: 19.4.52 |
| Publishers: Victoria Music Co. Ltd. | | Highest Position: 6 |
| | | Weeks on Chart: 19 |

Recordings:

| Eddie Wilcox and his Orchestra (Sunny Gale) | 4/52 | Parlophone R.3518 |
|---|---|---|
| Billy Williams Quartette | 4/52 | MGM.496 |
| The Bell Sisters | 4/52 | HMV B.10239 |
| Bill Johnson with Ted Heath and his Music | 4/52 | Decca F.9893 |
| Kay Starr | 4/52 | Capitol CL.13717 |
| Arthur Prysock | 4/52 | Brunswick 04911 |
| The Beverley Sisters | 5/52 | Columbia DB.3062 |
| Bobby Wayne | 5/52 | Oriole CB.1101 |
| Victor Silvester and his Ballroom Orchestra | 6/52 | Columbia FB.3645 |
| Mickey Katz and his Orchestra (Mickey Katz) [Titled: 'I'm a Schlemiel of Fortune'] | 7/52 | Capitol CL.13761 |
| Bobby Wayne | 6/54 | Mercury MB.2974★ |

## 378 THERE'S A PAWNSHOP ON A CORNER IN PITTSBURGH, PENNSYLVANIA

| | |
|---|---|
| *Composer*: Bob Merrill | *Date of Entry*: 3.5.52 |
| *Publishers*: Cinephonic Music Co. Ltd. | *Highest Position*: 6<br>*Weeks on Chart*: 20 |

*Recordings*:

| | | |
|---|---|---|
| Bill Johnson with Ted Heath and his Music | 4/52 | Decca F.9893 |
| Guy Mitchell (Titled '. . . on the corner . . .') | 4/52 | Columbia DB.3056 |
| Jerry Gray and his Orchestra (Tommy Traynor) | 5/52 | Brunswick 04935 |
| Mickey Katz and his Orchestra and Chorus (Titled 'Schvitzburg . . .') | 8/52 | Capitol CL.13771 |

## 379 THE BLACKSMITH BLUES

| | |
|---|---|
| *Composer*: Jack Holmes | *Date of Entry*: 3.5.52/<br>Pos: 2/Wks: 20 |
| *Publishers*: Chappell & Co. Ltd. | *Re-entry*: 27.9.52/<br>Pos: 23/Wks: 1 |

*Recordings*:

| | | |
|---|---|---|
| Sy Oliver and his Orchestra (Trudy Richards) | 3/52 | Brunswick 04906 |
| Bill Darnel | 4/52 | Brunswick 04912 |
| Ted Heath and his Music (Lita Roza) | 4/52 | Decca F.9911 |
| Ella Mae Morse | 4/52 | Capitol CL.13727 |
| Harry James and his Orchestra (Toni Harper) | 5/52 | Columbia DB.3053 |
| Art Mooney and his Orchestra (Shorty Long) | 5/52 | MGM.503 |
| Sid Phillips and his Band (Denny Dennis) | 5/52 | HMV BD.6132 |
| Ronald Chesney (harmonica) and George Elliott (guitar) | 7/52 | HMV B.10300 |
| Oscar Rabin and his Band (Patti Forbes) | 7/52 | Parlophone F.2497 |
| Bill Macey and his Orchestra | 7/52 | Columbia DB.3115 |

## 380 THE GANDY DANCERS' BALL

| | |
|---|---|
| *Composers*: Paul Weston & Paul Mason Howard | *Date of Entry*: 10.5.52 |
| *Publishers*: Walt Disney Music Co. Ltd. | *Highest Position*: 13<br>*Weeks on Chart*: 17 |

(The record companies seem to have had trouble deciding if it was one Gandy Dancer or two. The issues by the American artists listed below were labelled 'The Gandy Dancer's Ball' while the two releases on Decca saw the apostrophe moved to make it 'The Gandy Dancers' Ball'.)

*Recordings*:

| | | |
|---|---|---|
| Frankie Laine with The Norman Luboff Choir | 4/52 | Columbia DB.3057 |
| The Weavers | 4/52 | Brunswick 04920 |
| Tennessee Ernie | 5/52 | Capitol CL.13707 |
| Billy Cotton and his Band (Alan Breeze and The Bandits) | 5/52 | Decca F.9915 |
| Harry Farmer (Hammond organ) | 5/52 | Decca F.9929 |
| Frankie Laine with The Norman Luboff Choir | 1/53 | Columbia (45) SCM.5017★ |

## 381 A GUY IS A GUY

| | |
|---|---|
| *Composer*: Oscar Brand | *Date of Entry*: 10.5.52/<br>Pos: 24/Wks: 1 |
| *Publishers*: Leeds Music Ltd. | *Re-entry*: 31.5.52/<br>Pos: 15/Wks: 9 |

*Recordings*:

| | | |
|---|---|---|
| Doris Day | 4/52 | Columbia DB.3058 |
| Diana Coupland | 5/52 | Decca F.9918 |
| Ella Fitzgerald | 5/52 | Brunswick 04929 |
| Mickey Katz and his Orchestra (Mickey Katz) [Titled 'A Schmo is a Schmo'] | 9/52 | Capitol CL.13784★ |

## 382 MY CONCERTO

| | |
|---|---|
| *Composers*: Alex Alstone & Sid Tepper | *Date of Entry*: 17.5.52 |
| *Publishers*: Grosvenor Music Ltd. | *Highest Position*: 22<br>*Weeks on Chart*: 1 |

*Recordings*:

| | | |
|---|---|---|
| Tommy Edwards | 1/52 | MGM.466 |
| Ray Anthony and his Orchestra (Tommy Mercer) | 2/52 | Capitol CL.13671 |
| Anne Shelton | 2/52 | Decca F.9850 |

## 383 AUF WIEDERSEH'N SWEETHEART

| | | |
|---|---|---|
| **Composers:** Eberhard Storch, John Sexton & John Turner | | *Date of Entry:* 24.5.52 |
| **Publishers:** Peter Maurice Music Co. Ltd. | | *Highest Position:* 1 *Weeks on Chart:* 34 |

*Recordings:*

| | | |
|---|---|---|
| Vera Lynn with Soldiers and Airmen of HM Forces | 5/52 | Decca F.9927 |
| Teddy Johnson | 7/52 | Columbia DB.3083 |
| Billy Thorburn's The Organ, the Dance Band and Me (The Bobolinks) | 7/52 | Parlophone F.2496 |
| Victor Silvester and his Ballroom Orchestra | 7/52 | Columbia FB.3647 |
| Billy Cotton and his Band (Doreen Stephens and Chorus) | 7/52 | Decca F.9947 |
| Les Baxter and his Chorus and Orchestra | 8/52 | Capitol CL.13775 |
| Sharkey and his Band | 9/52 | Capitol CL.13789 |

## 384 BE ANYTHING (But be mine)

| | | |
|---|---|---|
| **Composer:** Irving Gordon | | *Date of Entry:* 24.5.52/ Pos: 8/Wks: 16 |
| **Publishers:** Cinephonic Music Co. Ltd. | | *Re-entry:* 20.9.52/ Pos: 24/Wks: 1 |

*Recordings:*

| | | |
|---|---|---|
| Alan Dean with Leroy Holmes and his Orchestra | 4/52 | MGM.495 |
| David Hughes | 5/52 | Columbia DB.3071 |
| Jimmy Young | 5/52 | Polygon P.1042 |
| Vera Lynn | 5/52 | Decca F.9912 |
| Helen O'Connell | 5/52 | Capitol CL.13745 |
| Roberto Inglez and his Orchestra | 6/52 | Parlophone R.3542 |
| Don Estes | 6/52 | HMV B.10274 |
| Joe Loss and his Orchestra (Howard Jones) | 6/52 | HMV B.10287 |
| Dorothy Squires | 6/52 | Columbia DB.3086 |
| Peggy Lee | 6/52 | Brunswick 04939 |
| Victor Silvester and his Ballroom Orchestra | 8/52 | Columbia FB.3650 |
| Eddy Howard and his Orchestra (Eddy Howard and The Jack Halloran Choir) | 10/52 | Oriole CB.1112★ |
| Eddy Howard and his Orchestra (Eddy Howard and The Jack Halloran Choir) | 6/54 | Mercury MB.2980★ |

## 385 KISS OF FIRE

| | | |
|---|---|---|
| **Composers:** Lester Allen & Robert Hill, adapted from A.G. Villoldo | | *Date of Entry:* 31.5.52/ Pos: 24/Wks: 1 |
| **Publishers:** Duchess Music Ltd. | | *Re-entry:* 14.6.52/ Pos: 2/Wks: 25 |

*Recordings:*

| | | |
|---|---|---|
| Jimmy Young | 5/52 | Polygon P.1041 |
| Anne Shelton | 5/52 | Decca F.9917 |
| Billy Eckstine | 6/52 | MGM.509 |
| Lester Ferguson | 6/52 | Parlophone R.3533 |
| Tony Martin | 6/52 | HMV B.10273 |
| David Hughes | 6/52 | Columbia DB.3091 |
| Dick Beavers | 6/52 | Capitol CL.13765 |
| Louis Armstrong and his Orchestra (Louis Armstrong) | 7/52 | Brunswick 04956 |
| Mickey Katz and his Orchestra (Mickey Katz) [Titled 'Kiss of Meyer'] | 8/52 | Capitol CL.13771 |
| Victor Silvester and his Silver Strings | 8/52 | Columbia DB.3130 |
| Georgia Gibbs | 10/52 | Oriole CB.1110 |
| Billy Eckstine | 1/53 | MGM. (45) SP.1011★ |
| Georgia Gibbs | 6/54 | Mercury MB.2978★ |

## 386 BLUE TANGO

| | | |
|---|---|---|
| **Composers:** Leroy Anderson with lyrics added by Mitchell Parish | | *Date of Entry:* 7.6.52 |
| **Publishers:** Mills Music Ltd. | | *Highest Position:* 2 *Weeks on Chart:* 35 |

*Recordings:*

| | | |
|---|---|---|
| Leroy Anderson and his 'Pops' Concert Orchestra | 2/52 | Brunswick 04870 |
| Les Baxter and his Chorus and Orchestra | 3/52 | Capitol CL.13703 |
| Ray Martin and his Concert Orchestra | 4/52 | Columbia DB.3051 |
| Edmundo Ros and his Rumba Band | 5/52 | Decca F.9926 |
| Hugo Winterhalter and his Orchestra | 6/52 | HMV B.10277 |
| Lee Lawrence | 8/52 | Decca F.9971 |
| Alma Cogan | 8/52 | HMV B.10338 |
| Reginald Dixon (organ) | 8/52 | Columbia FB.3654 |
| Ray Martin and his Concert Orchestra | 1/53 | Columbia (45) SCM.5001 |

## 387 DANCE ME LOOSE

| | | |
|---|---|---|
| **Composers:** Mel Howard & Lee Erwin | | *Date of Entry:* 7.6.52 |
| **Publishers:** Magna Music Co. Ltd. | | *Highest Position:* 20 *Weeks on Chart:* 4 |

*Recordings:*

| | | |
|---|---|---|
| Russ Morgan and his Orchestra (Russ Morgan and The Morganaires) | 2/52 | Brunswick 04886 |
| Arthur Godfrey with The Chordettes | 3/52 | Columbia DB.3019 |
| The Stargazers | 5/52 | Decca F.9905 |
| Eve Boswell and Derek Roy | 7/52 | Parlophone R.3549★ |

## 388 | THE HOMING WALTZ

| *Composers*: Tommie Connor & Johnny Reine | *Date of Entry*: 21.6.52 |
|---|---|
| *Publishers*: Michael Reine Music Co. Ltd. | *Highest Position*: 1<br>*Weeks on Chart*: 34 |

*Recordings*:

| | | |
|---|---|---|
| Alma Cogan and Larry Day | 7/52 | HMV B.10307 |
| Billy Cotton and his Band (Alan Breeze,<br>The Mill Girls and Chorus) | 7/52 | Decca F.9947 |
| Dickie Valentine | 7/52 | Decca F.9954 |
| Vera Lynn with Sailors, Soldiers and<br>Airmen of HM Forces | 7/52 | Decca F.9959 |
| Teddy Johnson | 7/52 | Columbia DB.3132 |
| Victor Silvester and his Ballroom<br>Orchestra | 8/52 | Columbia FB.3651 |
| Alma Cogan and Larry Day | 1/53 | HMV (45) 7M.107 |

## 389 | SINGING IN THE RAIN

| *Composers*: Arthur Freed & Nacio Herb Brown | *Date of Entry*: 28.6.52 |
|---|---|
| *Publishers*: Robbins Music Corporation Ltd. | *Highest Position*: 24<br>*Weeks on Chart*: 1 |

*Recordings*:

| | | |
|---|---|---|
| The Tuneful 20s Orchestra cond.<br>Tolchard Evans and Ray Terry (Dinah<br>Kaye) | 2/52 | Parlophone R.3497 |
| Gene Kelly | 4/52 | MGM.490 |
| Kathran Field with The Men about Town | 6/52 | Esquire 5−064 |
| Donald Peers with Don Phillips (piano) | 12/52 | HMV B.10393★ |
| Gene Kelly | 1/53 | MGM. (45) SP.1012★ |

## 390 | I'M YOURS

| *Composer*: Robert Mellin | *Date of Entry*: 5.7.52/<br>Pos: 5/Wks: 24 |
|---|---|
| *Publishers*: Robert Mellin Music Ltd. | *Re-entry*: 3.1.53/<br>Pos: 24/Wks: 1 |

*Recordings*:

| | | |
|---|---|---|
| The Four Aces featuring Al Alberts | 6/52 | Brunswick 04949 |
| Eddie Fisher | 6/52 | HMV B.10278 |
| David Hughes | 7/52 | Columbia DB.3112 |
| Dick Beavers | 8/52 | Capitol CL.13775 |
| Victor Silvester and his Ballroom<br>Orchestra | 8/52 | Columbia FB.3650 |
| Eve Boswell | 8/52 | Parlophone R.3561 |
| Eddie Fisher | 1/53 | HMV (45) 7M.101 |

## 391 | FROM THE TIME YOU SAY GOODBYE (The parting song)

| *Composer*: Leslie Sturdy | *Date of Entry*: 5.7.52 |
|---|---|
| *Publishers*: Pickwick Music Ltd. | *Highest Position*: 7<br>*Weeks on Chart*: 16 |

*Recordings*:

| | | |
|---|---|---|
| Vera Lynn with Soldiers and Airmen of<br>HM Forces | 5/52 | Decca F.9927 |
| Dinah Shore with The Peter King Singers | 7/52 | HMV B.10299 |
| Robert Wilson | 7/52 | HMV B.10306 |
| Billy Thorburn's The Organ, the Dance<br>Band and Me (The Bobolinks) | 7/52 | Parlophone F.2496 |
| Gary Miller | 7/52 | Columbia DB.3111 |
| Victor Silvester and his Ballroom<br>Orchestra | 7/52 | Columbia FB.3648 |
| Burl Ives | 7/52 | Brunswick 04957 |

## 392 | HIGH NOON (Do not forsake me)

| *Composers*: Ned Washington & Dimitri Tiomkin | *Date of Entry*: 5.7.52 |
|---|---|
| *Publishers*: Robbins Music Corporation Ltd. | *Highest Position*: 2<br>*Weeks on Chart*: 22 |

*Recordings*:

| | | |
|---|---|---|
| Wilfrid Thomas | 7/52 | Parlophone R.3555 |
| Lita Roza | 7/52 | Decca F.9938 |
| Tex Ritter with instrumental<br>accompaniment (Recorded in USA) | 7/52 | Capitol CL.13768 |
| Bill Hayes | 7/52 | MGM.525 |
| Tex Ritter with Wordless Chorus and<br>instr. acc. by Johnny Douglas<br>(Recorded in the UK) | 7/52 | Capitol CL.13778 |
| Frankie Laine | 8/52 | Columbia DB.3113 |
| Billy May and his Orchestra | 12/52 | Capitol CL.13848★ |

## 393 | STAR OF HOPE

| *Composers*: Phil Boutelje & Harry Tobias from a<br>theme of Emile Waldteufel | *Date of Entry*: 5.7.52 |
|---|---|
| *Publishers*: Ascherberg, Hopwood & Crew Ltd. | *Highest Position*: 23<br>*Weeks on Chart*: 2 |

*Recordings*:

| | | |
|---|---|---|
| Jo Stafford with The Lee Brothers | 3/52 | Columbia DB.3014 |
| Webster Booth | 4/52 | Decca F.9910 |
| Don Cherry and Eileen Wilson | 4/52 | Brunswick 04915 |
| Margaret Whiting and Jimmy Wakely | 4/52 | Capitol CL.13716 |
| Billy Cotton and his Band (Doreen<br>Stephens and Choir) | 6/52 | Decca F.9923 |
| Victor Silvester and his Ballroom<br>Orchestra | 9/52 | Columbia FB.3653★ |
| Jo Stafford with The Lee Brothers | 1/53 | Columbia (45)<br>SCM.5011★ |

## 394 TRUST IN ME

*Composers:* Milton Ager, Jean Schwartz & Ned Wever
*Publishers:* Lawrence Wright Music Co. Ltd.

*Date of Entry:* 12.7.52

*Highest Position:* 11
*Weeks on Chart:* 19

(Note: This song was first popular in 1937. Of the recordings issued then, only one was still available in 1952, that by Connee Boswell on Brunswick 02401.)

*Recordings:*

| | | |
|---|---|---|
| Eddie Fisher | 4/52 | HMV B.10247 |
| Lou Dinning with Quartet | 4/52 | Capitol CL.13713 |
| Teddy Johnson | 7/52 | Columbia DB.3083 |
| Wally Peterson and Joy Nichols | 7/52 | Parlophone R.3554 |
| Victor Silvester and his Ballroom Orchestra | 7/52 | Columbia FB.3648 |
| Billy Cotton and his Band (Alan Breeze and The Bandits) | 9/52 | Decca F.9965 |
| Eddie Fisher | 3/53 | HMV (45) 7M.116* |

## 395 FAITH

*Composers:* Tolchard Evans, Stanley Damerell & Floyd Huddleston
*Publishers:* Hit Songs Ltd.

*Date of Entry:* 19.7.52/
Pos: 22/Wks: 1
*Re-entry:* 9.8.52/
Pos: 21/Wks: 2
*2nd re-entry:* 6.9.52/
Pos: 13/Wks: 5
*3rd re-entry:* 18.10.52/
Pos: 18/Wks: 11

*Recordings:*

| | | |
|---|---|---|
| Mantovani and his Orchestra | 4/52 | Decca F.9892 |
| Bill Hurley | 4/52 | Nixa NY.7703 |
| Jimmy Young | 5/52 | Polygon P.1041 |
| Victor Silvester and his Ballroom Orchestra | 6/52 | Columbia FB.3644 |
| Victor Marchese | 7/52 | MGM.528 |
| Vaughn Monroe and his Orchestra (Vaughn Monroe) | 8/52 | HMV B.10320 |
| Roy Stuart Murray | 9/52 | Decca F.9967 |
| Dorothy Squires | 10/52 | Columbia DB.3163 |

## 396 WHEN YOU'RE IN LOVE

*Composers:* Carl Fischer & Frankie Laine

*Publishers:* Campbell Connelly & Co. Ltd.

*Date of Entry:* 19.7.52/
Pos: 24/Wks: 1
*Re-entry:* 2.8.52/
Pos: 14/Wks: 14

*Recordings:*

| | | |
|---|---|---|
| Dick Haymes | 3/52 | Brunswick 04897 |
| Frankie Laine with The Norman Luboff Choir and Carl Fischer (piano) | 4/52 | Columbia DB.3057 |
| Lee Lawrence | 8/52 | Decca F.9971 |
| Roberto Inglez and his Orchestra | 10/52 | Parlophone R.3581 |

## 397 HEART OF A CLOWN

*Composers:* Steve Nelson, Jack Rollins & Frances Kane
*Publishers:* Maddox Music Co. Ltd.

*Date of Entry:* 19.7.52/
Pos: 23/Wks: 2
*Re-entry:* 9.8.52/
Pos: 24/Wks: 2

*Recordings:*

| | | |
|---|---|---|
| Tommy Furtado | 4/52 | MGM.497 |
| Bobby Wayne (reverse side: Wheel of Fortune) | 5/52 | Oriole CB.1101 |
| Harry Secombe | 6/52 | HMV B.10288 |
| Norman Wisdom | 6/52 | Columbia DB.3084 |
| Reg Dixon | 7/52 | Decca F.9931 |
| Nellie Lutcher | 7/52 | Capitol CL.13770 |
| Bobby Wayne (reverse side: The Missouri Waltz) | 9/52 | Oriole CB.1108* |
| Bobby Wayne (reissue of CB.1101) | 6/54 | Mercury MB.2974* |
| Bobby Wayne (reissue of CB.1108) | 6/54 | Mercury MB.2977* |

## 398 THE DAY OF JUBILO (Tell it to the preacher)

*Composer:* Terry Gilkyson

*Publishers:* Campbell Connelly & Co. Ltd.

*Date of Entry:* 26.7.52

*Highest Position:* 7
*Weeks on Chart:* 16

*Recordings:*

| | | |
|---|---|---|
| Guy Mitchell | 7/52 | Columbia DB.3104 |
| The Stargazers | 7/52 | Decca F.9960 |

## 399 DIDJA EVER?

*Composers:* Vic Mizzy & Mann Curtis

*Publishers:* Edward Cox Music Co. Ltd.

*Date of Entry:* 26.7.52

*Highest Position:* 24
*Weeks on Chart:* 1

*Recordings:*

| | | |
|---|---|---|
| Mary Small | 7/52 | Vogue V.9039 |
| Sid Phillips and his Band (Denny Dennis) | 8/52 | HMV BD.6134* |
| Debbie Reynolds and Carleton Carpenter | 8/52 | MGM.538* |

## 400 I'M GONNA LIVE TILL I DIE

*Composers:* Al Hoffman, Mann Curtis & Walter Kent
*Publishers:* Campbell Connelly & Co. Ltd.

*Date of Entry:* 2.8.52/
Pos: 19/Wks: 3
*Re-entry:* 13.9.52/
Pos: 23/Wks: 2

*Recordings:*

| | | |
|---|---|---|
| Frankie Laine | 3/52 | Oriole CB.1086 |
| Teddy Johnson | 6/52 | Columbia DB.3085 |
| Frankie Laine | 6/54 | Mercury MB.2859* |
| Frank Sinatra with Ray Anthony and his Orchestra | 2/55 | Capitol CL.14238* |

## 401 WALKIN' MY BABY BACK HOME

*Composers*: Roy Turk, Fred Ahlert & Harry Richman     *Date of Entry*: 2.8.52

*Publishers*: Victoria Music Co. Ltd.     *Highest Position*: 6
*Weeks on Chart*: 26

*Recordings*:

| | | |
|---|---|---|
| Jo Stafford | 2/49 | Capitol CL.13048 |
| Johnnie Ray | 5/52 | Columbia DB.3060 |
| Nat 'King' Cole with Billy May and his Orchestra | 7/52 | Capitol CL.13774 |
| Mickey Katz and his Orchestra (Mickey Katz) [Titled 'Schleppin' my baby . . .'] | 11/52 | Capitol CL.13821 |
| Johnnie Ray | 1/53 | Columbia (45) SCM.5015 |

## 402 SOMEWHERE ALONG THE WAY

*Composers*: Sammy Gallop & Kurt Adams     *Date of Entry*: 16.8.52

*Publishers*: Magna Music Co. Ltd.     *Highest Position*: 7
*Weeks on Chart*: 22

*Recordings*:

| | | |
|---|---|---|
| Tony Bennett | 7/52 | Columbia DB.3101 |
| Nat 'King' Cole | 7/52 | Capitol CL.13774 |
| Greta Keller | 9/52 | Parlophone R.3569 |
| Joe Loss and his Orchestra (Rose Brennan) | 10/52 | HMV B.10359 |
| Victor Silvester and his Ballroom Orchestra | 12/52 | Columbia FB.3661 |

## 403 MEET MISTER CALLAGHAN

*Composer*: Eric Spear     *Date of Entry*: 16.8.52

*Publishers*: David Toff Music Publishing Co. Ltd.     *Highest Position*: 7
*Weeks on Chart*: 21

*Recordings*:

| | | |
|---|---|---|
| Frank Chacksfield's Tunesmiths | 8/52 | Oriole CB.1107 |
| Harry Grove and his Trio | 8/52 | Decca F.9969 |
| Sid Phillips and his Band | 8/52 | HMV BD.6135 |
| Ray Martin and his Orchestra | 8/52 | Columbia DB.3150 |
| The Melachrino Strings featuring William Hill-Bowen (harp) | 9/52 | HMV B.10330 |
| Billy Thorburn's The Organ, the Dance Band and Me | 9/52 | Parlophone F. 2500 |
| Victor Silvester and his Ballroom Orchestra | 9/52 | Columbia FB.3652 |
| Semprini (piano) | 9/52 | HMV B.10335 |
| Cyril Stapleton and his Orchestra | 9/52 | Decca F.9974 |
| Les Paul (guitar) | 9/52 | Capitol CL.13793 |
| Slim and the Boys | 9/52 | Polygon P.1046 |

## 404 SUGARBUSH

*Composer*: Josef Marais (Music derived from a Veldt song)     *Date of Entry*: 23.8.52 / Pos: 6 / Wks: 25
*Publishers*: Chappell & Co. Ltd.     *Re-entry*: 21.2.53 / Pos: 24 / Wks: 1

*Recordings*:

| | | |
|---|---|---|
| The Stargazers | 7/52 | Decca F.9960 |
| Doris Day and Frankie Laine with the Norman Luboff Choir | 8/52 | Columbia DB.3123 |
| Sid Phillips and his Band (Denny Dennis and Chorus) | 8/52 | HMV BD.6134 |
| Eve Boswell | 8/52 | Parlophone R.3561 |
| Eve Boswell | 1/53 | Parlophone (45) MSP.6006 |

## 405 I'LL WALK ALONE

*Composers*: Sammy Cahn & Jule Styne     *Date of Entry*: 23.8.52

*Publishers*: Edwin H. Morris & Co. Ltd     *Highest Position*: 23
*Weeks on Chart*: 2

*Recordings*:

| | | |
|---|---|---|
| Ambrose and his Orchestra (Anne Shelton) | 6/44 | Decca F.8430 |
| Mary Martin | 9/45 | Brunswick 03563 |
| Franklyn Boyd | 5/52 | Columbia DB.3069 |
| Larry Cross | 5/52 | Parlophone R.3528 |
| Patty Andrews | 5/52 | Brunswick 04923 |
| The Peter King Singers | 6/52 | HMV B.10272 |
| Jane Froman | 6/52 | Capitol CL.13755 |
| Burt Taylor | 7/52 | Columbia DB.3100 |
| Billy Cotton and his Band (Alan Breeze and The Bandits) | 10/52 | Decca F.9990★ |

## 406 DELICADO

*Composer*: Waldyr Azevedo     *Date of Entry*: 30.8.52 / Pos: 20 / Wks: 5
*Publishers*: Lafleur & Co. Ltd.     *Re-entry*: 11.10.52 / Pos: 23 / Wks: 2

*Recordings*:

| | | |
|---|---|---|
| Edmundo Ros and his Orchestra | 4/52 | Decca F.9884 |
| Stan Kenton and his Orchestra | 6/52 | Capitol CL.13749 |
| Ronald Chesney (harmonica) and George Elliott (guitar) | 7/52 | HMV B.10300 |
| Frank Cordell and his Orchestra | 7/52 | HMV B.10305 |
| Roberto Inglez and his Orchestra | 7/52 | Parlophone R.3550 |
| Percy Faith and his Orchestra | 7/52 | Columbia DB.3103 |
| Waldyr Azevedo and his Orchestra | 7/52 | Brunswick 04951 |
| Los Musicos | 7/52 | MGM.531 |
| Roberto Inglez and his Orchestra | 3/53 | Parlophone (45) MSP.6014★ |

## 407 | THE ROCK OF GIBRALTAR

*Composer*: Terry Gilkyson

*Publishers*: Dash Music Co. Ltd.

*Date of Entry*: 6.9.52

*Highest Position*: 9
*Weeks on Chart*: 11

*Recordings*:

| | | |
|---|---|---|
| Frankie Laine | 8/52 | Columbia DB.3113 |
| Billy Cotton and his Band (Alan Breeze and The Bandits) | 10/52 | Decca F.9990 |

## 408 | HERE IN MY HEART

*Composers*: Bill Borrelli, Pat Genaro & Lou Levinson

*Publishers*: Robert Mellin Ltd.

*Date of Entry*: 6.9.52

*Highest Position*: 1
*Weeks on Chart*: 28

*Recordings*:

| | | |
|---|---|---|
| Al Martino | 7/52 | Capitol CL.13779 |
| Issy Bonn with Eddie Calvert (trumpet) | 8/52 | Columbia DB.3126 |
| Larry Day | 8/52 | HMV B.10323 |
| Dennis Lotis | 9/52 | Polygon P.1045 |
| David Hughes | 9/52 | Columbia DB.3145 |
| Victor Silvester and his Ballroom Orchestra | 9/52 | Columbia FB.3652 |
| Lee Lawrence | 9/52 | Decca F.9970 |
| Dick Haymes and The Andrews Sisters | 9/52 | Brunswick 04979 |
| Eve Boswell | 10/52 | Parlophone R.3584 |
| Harry Secombe | 10/52 | HMV B.10345 |

## 409 | WHEN I TAKE MY SUGAR TO TEA

*Composers*: Irving Kahal, Sammy Fain & Pierre Norman

*Publishers*: Bradbury Wood Ltd

*Date of Entry*: 6.9.52

*Highest Position*: 23
*Weeks on Chart*: 2

*Recording*:

| | | |
|---|---|---|
| Billy May and his Orchestra (The Maytimers) | 2/52 | Capitol CL.13677 |

## 410 | THE ISLE OF INNISFREE

*Composer*: Richard Farrelly

*Publishers*: Peter Maurice Music Co. Ltd.

*Date of Entry*: 13.9.52

*Highest Position*: 2
*Weeks on Chart*: 28

*Recordings*:

| | | |
|---|---|---|
| Terry, the Irish Minstrel | 4/50 | HMV B.9896 |
| Victor Young and his Singing Strings | 4/51 | Brunswick 04687 |
| Bing Crosby | 3/52 | Brunswick 04900 |
| Norrie Paramor and his Orchestra | 8/52 | Columbia DB.3128 |
| Anne Shelton | 10/52 | Decca F.9994 |
| Josef Locke | 11/52 | Columbia DB.3182 |
| Paddy Kierney | 11/52 | Parlophone R.3597 |
| Joe Loss and his Orchestra (Rose Brennan) | 11/52 | HMV B.10378 |
| Jimmy Young | 12/52 | Decca F.10018 |
| Victor Silvester and his Ballroom Orchestra | 12/52 | Columbia FB.3660 |

## 411 | BOTCH-A-ME (Ba-Ba-Baciami Piccina)

*Composers*: R. Morbelli, L. Astore & Eddie Stanley

*Publishers*: Edward Kassner Music Co. Ltd.

*Date of Entry*: 20.9.52

*Highest Position*: 14
*Weeks on Chart*: 7

*Recordings*:

| | | |
|---|---|---|
| Rosemary Clooney | 8/52 | Columbia DB.3129 |
| Ted Heath and his Music (Lita Roza) | 9/52 | Decca F.9980 |
| Annette Klooger | 9/52 | Polygon P.1049 |
| Mickey Katz and his Orchestra (Mickey Katz) [Titled 'Patch-a Me'] | 11/52 | Capitol CL.13821 |
| Rosemary Clooney | 1/53 | Columbia (45) SCM.5019★ |

## 412 | HALF AS MUCH

*Composer*: Curley Williams

*Publishers*: Robbins Music Co.

*Date of Entry*: 20.9.52

*Highest Position*: 2
*Weeks on Chart*: 21

*Recordings*:

| | | |
|---|---|---|
| Hank Williams and his Drifting Cowboys | 7/52 | MGM.527 |
| Rosemary Clooney | 8/52 | Columbia DB.3129 |
| Alma Cogan | 8/52 | HMV B.10338 |
| Larry Cross | 10/52 | Parlophone R.3585 |
| Lita Roza | 10/52 | Decca F.9988 |
| Guy Lombardo and his Royal Canadians (Kenny Martin and The Lombardo Quartet) | 11/52 | Brunswick 05002 |
| Wally Fryer and his Perfect Tempo Dance Orchestra | 12/52 | Decca F.10022 |
| Rosemary Clooney | 1/53 | Columbia (45) SCM.5019 |

## 413 TAKE MY HEART

*Composers*: Bill Borrelli, Lou Levinson & Pat Genaro
*Publishers*: Dash Music Co. Ltd.

*Date of Entry*: 27.9.52 / Pos: 22 / Wks: 3
*Re-entry*: 25.10.52 / Pos: 24 / Wks: 1
*2nd re-entry*: 6.12.52 / Pos: 18 / Wks: 1

*Recordings*:
| | | |
|---|---|---|
| Al Martino | 7/52 | Capitol CL.13769 |
| Jimmy Young | 9/52 | Decca F.9972 |
| Dennis Lotis | 9/52 | Polygon P.1045 |
| Dennis Day | 9/52 | HMV B.10337 |
| Vic Damone | 10/52 | Oriole CB.1131 |
| Toni Arden | 11/52 | Columbia DB.3174 |
| Franklyn Boyd | 11/52 | HMV B.10380 |
| Vic Damone | 6/54 | Mercury MB.2994★ |

## 414 RAINDROPS

*Composers*: Vaughn Horton, Teddy Powell & Jack Little
*Publishers*: Box & Cox (Publications) Ltd

*Date of Entry*: 27.9.52

*Highest Position*: 24
*Weeks on Chart*: 1

*Recordings*:
| | | |
|---|---|---|
| Lily Ann Carol and The High Hatters | 6/52 | HMV B.10279 |
| The Johnston Brothers with Dickie Valentine | 6/52 | Decca F.9933 |
| The Four Sensations | 6/52 | Melodisc P.216 |
| The Radio Revellers | 7/52 | Columbia DB.3106 |

## 415 FEET UP!

*Composer*: Bob Merrill
*Publishers*: Cinephonic Music Co. Ltd.

*Date of Entry*: 4.10.52

*Highest Position*: 4
*Weeks on Chart*: 19

*Recordings*:
| | | |
|---|---|---|
| Guy Mitchell | 9/52 | Columbia DB.3151 |
| Ray Ellington and The Stargazers | 11/52 | Decca F.10023 |
| Mickey Katz and his Orchestra (Mickey Katz) [Titled 'Feet up, pat him on the pipick'] | 12/52 | Capitol CL.13841 |
| Guy Mitchell | 1/53 | Columbia (45) SCM.5018 |

## 416 BELLE OF THE BALL

*Composer*: Leroy Anderson
*Publishers*: Mills Music Ltd.

*Date of Entry*: 4.10.52 .

*Highest Position*: 23
*Weeks on Chart*: 1

*Recordings*:
| | | |
|---|---|---|
| Leroy Anderson and his 'Pops' Concert Orchestra | 2/52 | Brunswick 04870 |
| Kurt Burling and his Rococo Orchestra | 3/52 | HMV B.10224 |
| Ray Martin and his Concert Orchestra | 6/52 | Columbia DB.3072 |
| Johnny Dankworth (alto sax) with Strings | 6/52 | Esquire 5−066 |
| Mantovani and his Orchestra | 8/52 | Decca F.9956 |
| David Hughes with Chorus (Lyrics by Norman Newell) | 1/53 | Philips PB.101★ |
| Ray Martin and his Concert Orchestra | 1/53 | Columbia (45) SCM.5001★ |

## 417 ZING A LITTLE ZONG

*Composers*: Harry Warren & Leo Robin
*Publishers*: Maddox Music Co. Ltd.

*Date of Entry*: 4.10.52

*Highest Position*: 8
*Weeks on Chart*: 20

*Recordings*:
| | | |
|---|---|---|
| Dorothy Loudon | 9/52 | HMV B.10333 |
| Helen O'Connell | 9/52 | Capitol CL.13788 |
| Bing Crosby and Jane Wyman with Jud Conlon's Rhythmaires | 9/52 | Brunswick 04981 |
| Robert Q. Lewis with Robert's Quties | 9/52 | MGM.552 |

## 418 IF I HAD WINGS

*Composers*: John Klenner & Sam Fiedel
*Publishers*: Edward Kassner Music Co. Ltd.

*Date of Entry*: 11.10.52

*Highest Position*: 24
*Weeks on Chart*: 1

*Recordings*:
| | | |
|---|---|---|
| Jimmy Young | 9/52 | Decca F.9972 |
| David Hughes | 10/52 | Columbia DB.3162 |
| Tony Alamo | 11/52 | MGM.569★ |

## 419 FORGET-ME-NOT

*Composers*: Johnny Reine, Johnny May & Bill Sinclair
*Publishers*: Michael Reine Music Co. Ltd.

*Date of Entry*: 18.10.52

*Highest Position*: 5
*Weeks on Chart*: 20

*Recordings*:
| | | |
|---|---|---|
| Vera Lynn with The Johnston Singers | 10/52 | Decca F.9985 |
| Ronnie Ronalde | 11/52 | Columbia PB.3190 |
| The Five Smith Brothers | 11/52 | Parlophone R.3589 |
| Joe Loss and his Orchestra (Howard Jones) | 11/52 | HMV B.10378 |

## 420 WALKIN' TO MISSOURI

| | | |
|---|---|---|
| *Composer*: Bob Merrill | | *Date of Entry*: 25.10.52 |
| *Publishers*: Dash Music Co. Ltd. | | *Highest Position*: 2 |
| | | *Weeks on Chart*: 22 |

Recordings:

| | | |
|---|---|---|
| Tony Brent | 9/52 | Columbia DB.3147 |
| Sid Phillips and his Band (Denny Dennis) | 10/52 | HMV BD.6136 |
| Lita Roza with Vocal Group | 10/52 | Decca F.9988 |
| Russ Morgan and his Orchestra (Russ Morgan and the Morganaires) | 10/52 | Brunswick 04994 |
| Ken Griffin (organ) | 11/52 | Columbia DB.3171 |

## 421 YOU BELONG TO ME

| | | |
|---|---|---|
| *Composers*: Pee Wee King, Redd Stewart & Chilton Price | | *Date of Entry*: 1.11.52 |
| *Publishers*: Chappell & Co. Ltd. | | *Highest Position*: 1 |
| | | *Weeks on Chart*: 24 |

Recordings:

| | | |
|---|---|---|
| Jo Stafford | 10/52 | Columbia DB.3152 |
| Larry Cross | 10/52 | Parlophone R.3585 |
| Alma Cogan with Jimmy Watson (trumpet) | 10/52 | HMV B.10344 |
| Patti Page | 10/52 | Oriole CB.1129 |
| Grady Martin and his Slew Foot Five (Cecil Bayley) | 10/52 | Brunswick 04997 |
| Dean Martin | 10/52 | Capitol CL.13815 |
| Joni James | 10/52 | MGM.561 |
| Monty Norman | 10/52 | Polygon P.1051 |
| Dickie Valentine with Ted Heath and his Music | 11/52 | Decca F.10002 |
| Ken Griffin (organ) | 11/52 | Columbia DB.3171 |
| Victor Silvester and his Ballroom Orchestra | 11/52 | Columbia FB.3659 |
| Jan Garber and his Orchestra (Roy Cordell) | 11/52 | Capitol CL.13823 |
| Jimmy Young | 12/52 | Decca F.10018 |
| Wally Fryer and his Perfect Tempo Dance Orchestra | 12/52 | Decca F.10022 |
| Mickey Katz and his Orchestra | 12/52 | Capitol CL. 13841 |
| Jo Stafford | 1/53 | Columbia (45) SCM.5013 |
| Alma Cogan with Jimmy Watson (trumpet) | 1/53 | HMV (45) 7M.106 |
| Patti Page | 6/54 | Mercury MB.2992★ |

## 422 FAITH CAN MOVE MOUNTAINS

| | | |
|---|---|---|
| *Composers*: Guy Wood & Ben Raleigh | | *Date of Entry*: 8.11.52 |
| *Publishers*: Dash Music Co. Ltd. | | *Highest Position*: 7 |
| | | *Weeks on Chart*: 18 |

Recordings:

| | | |
|---|---|---|
| Johnnie Ray and The Four Lads | 10/52 | Columbia DB.3154 |
| Harry Secombe | 10/52 | HMV B.10345 |
| Jimmy Young | 10/52 | Decca F.9986 |
| Nat 'King' Cole | 10/52 | Capitol CL.13811 |

## 423 MY LOVE AND DEVOTION

| | | |
|---|---|---|
| *Composer*: Milton Carson | | *Date of Entry*: 8.11.52 |
| *Publishers*: John Fields Music Co. Ltd. | | *Highest Position*: 17 |
| | | *Weeks on Chart*: 11 |

Recordings:

| | | |
|---|---|---|
| Baxter Scott | 11/51 | Decca F.9805 |
| Jimmy Young | 11/51 | Polygon P.1025 |
| Larry Cross | 12/51 | Parlophone R.3465 |
| Doris Day | 9/52 | Columbia DB.3157 |
| Perry Como | 10/52 | HMV B.10357 |
| Gordon Jenkins and his Orchestra (Don Burke, Betty Mulliner and Elizabeth Rinker) | 10/52 | Brunswick 04992 |
| Teddy Johnson | 10/52 | Columbia DB.3183 |
| Perry Como | 1/53 | HMV (45) 7M.102 |
| Wally Fryer and his Perfect Tempo Dance Orchestra | 2/53 | Decca F.10063★ |

## 424 BECAUSE YOU'RE MINE

| | | |
|---|---|---|
| *Composers*: Nicholas Brodszky & Sammy Cahn | | *Date of Entry*: 15.11.52 |
| *Publishers*: Robbins Music Corporation Ltd. | | *Highest Position*: 5 |
| | | *Weeks on Chart*: 29 |

Recordings:

| | | |
|---|---|---|
| Mario Lanza with The Jeff Alexander Choir | 10/52 | HMV DA.2017 |
| Nat 'King' Cole | 10/52 | Capitol CL.13811 |
| Lee Lawrence | 10/52 | Decca F.9995 |
| John Raitt | 10/52 | Brunswick 04999 |
| Billy Eckstine | 10/52 | MGM.557 |
| Mario Lanza with The Jeff Alexander Choir | 12/52 | HMV (45) 7R.144 |

## 425 | WHEN I FALL IN LOVE

*Composers*: Victor Young & Edward Heyman    *Date of Entry*: 15.11.52

*Publishers*: Avenue Music    *Highest Position*: 21
    *Weeks on Chart*: 1

*Recordings*:
| | | |
|---|---|---|
| Doris Day with The Norman Luboff Choir | 9/52 | Columbia DB.3157 |
| Jeri Southern with Chorus | 9/52 | Brunswick 04978 |
| Ron Goodwin and his Concert Orchestra | 3/53 | Parlophone R.3649★ |
| Victor Silvester and his Ballroom Orchestra | 4/53 | Columbia FB.3671★ |

(Note: See also song No. 808 for the song's return to the Charts in May 1957.)

## 426 | MOON ABOVE MALAYA (China nights)

*Composers*: Jimmy Kennedy & John Turner    *Date of Entry*: 22.11.52/
    Pos: 22 / Wks: 1

*Publishers*: Macmelodies Ltd.    *Re-entry*: 6.12.52 /
    Pos: 23 / Wks: 1

*Recordings*:
| | | |
|---|---|---|
| Jimmy Young | 10/52 | Decca F.9986 |
| Joyce Frazer | 11/52 | Columbia DB.3191 |
| Eve Boswell | 11/52 | Parlophone R.3599 |
| Reggie Goff | 1/53 | Polygon P.1062★ |
| Eve Boswell | 1/53 | Parlophone (45) MSP.6006★ |

## 427 | ECSTASY

*Composer*: Jose Belmonte    *Date of Entry*: 22.11.52/
    Pos: 23/Wks: 1

*Publishers*: Sydney Bron Music Co.    *Re-entry*: 7.2.53/
    Pos: 22/Wks: 3
    *2nd re-entry*: 14.3.53 /
    Pos: 24 / Wks: 1

*Recordings*:
| | | |
|---|---|---|
| Sidney Torch and his Orchestra | 9/52 | Parlophone R.3578 |
| Edmundo Ros and his Orchestra | 10/52 | Decca F.9996 |
| Ray Martin and his Concert Orchestra | 11/52 | Columbia DB.3199 |
| The Melachrino Strings | 12/52 | HMV B.10382 |
| Robin Richmond (Hammond organ) | 12/52 | Polygon P.1059 |
| Geraldo and his New Concert Orchestra | 1/53 | Philips PB.105 |
| Ray Martin and his Concert Orchestra | 3/53 | Columbia (45) SCM.5020 |

## 428 | I WENT TO YOUR WEDDING

*Composer*: Jessie Mae Robinson    *Date of Entry*: 29.11.52

*Publishers*: Victoria Music Publishing Co. Ltd.    *Highest Position*: 7
    *Weeks on Chart*: 17

*Recordings*:
| | | |
|---|---|---|
| Alma Cogan | 10/52 | HMV B.10344 |
| Hank Snow | 10/52 | HMV B.10354 |
| Lita Roza | 10/52 | Decca F.9992 |
| Patti Page | 10/52 | Oriole CB.1129 |
| Grady Martin and his Slew Foot Five (Cecil Bayley) | 10/52 | Brunswick 04997 |
| Jimmy Wakely | 10/52 | Capitol CL.13813 |
| Swing and Sway with Sammy Kaye (Jeff Clay and Choir) | 11/52 | Columbia DB.3185 |
| Joyce Frazer | 11/52 | Columbia DB.3191 |
| Guy Lombardo and his Royal Canadians (Kenny Gardner) | 11/52 | Brunswick 05002 |
| Dick James | 11/52 | Parlophone R.3606 |
| Alma Cogan | 1/53 | HMV (45) 7M.106 |
| Spike Jones and his City Slickers (Sir Fredric Gas) | 5/53 | HMV B.10482★ |
| Patti Page | 6/54 | Mercury MB.2992★ |

## 429 | I'LL NEVER FORGET YOU

*Composers*: Peter Hart & Guy Leslie    *Date of Entry*: 29.11.52

*Publishers*: Cecil Lennox Music Co. Ltd.    *Highest Position*: 24
    *Weeks on Chart*: 1

*Recordings*:
| | | |
|---|---|---|
| Bill Hurley | 11/52 | HMV B.10365 |
| David Hughes | 1/53 | Philips PB.101★ |
| David Whitfield | 2/53 | Decca F.10062★ |

## 430 | SNOWFLAKES

*Composer*: Marjorie Kurtz    *Date of Entry*: 6.12.52

*Publishers*: Maddox Music Co. Ltd.    *Highest Position*: 24
    *Weeks on Chart*: 1

*Recordings*:
| | | |
|---|---|---|
| Dorothy Squires | 10/52 | Columbia DB.3163 |
| Evelyn Knight | 10/52 | Brunswick 04987 |
| Mandy Miller | 11/52 | Parlophone R.3595 |

## 431 | TAKES TWO TO TANGO

*Composers*: Al Hoffman & Dick Manning          *Date of Entry*: 13.12.52

*Publishers*: Francis Day & Hunter Ltd.          *Highest Position*: 14
                                                 *Weeks on Chart*: 14

*Recordings*:

| | | |
|---|---|---|
| Jeanne Gayle | 10/52 | Capitol CL.13814 |
| Louis Armstrong | 10/52 | Brunswick 04995 |
| Fran Warren | 10/52 | MGM.559 |
| Monty Norman | 10/52 | Polygon P.1053 |
| Harry Farmer (Hammond organ) | 1/53 | Decca F.10035 |
| Hermione Gingold and Gilbert Harding | 1/53 | Philips PB.104 |
| Wally Fryer and his Perfect Tempo Dance Orchestra | 2/53 | Decca F.10063 |

## 432 | OUTSIDE OF HEAVEN

*Composers*: Sammy Gallop & Chester Conn          *Date of Entry*: 13.12.52

*Publishers*: Bradbury Wood Ltd.          *Highest Position*: 2
                                          *Weeks on Chart*: 23

*Recordings*:

| | | |
|---|---|---|
| Eddie Fisher | 11/52 | HMV B.10362 |
| Vera Lynn | 11/5 | Decca F.10009 |
| Margaret Whiting | 11/52 | Capitol CL.13826 |
| David Carey | 11/52 | Columbia DB.3200 |
| Fred Waring and his Pennsylvanians (Joe Marine) | 12/52 | Brunswick 05027 |
| Gerry Brereton | 12/52 | Parlophone R.3609 |
| Eddie Fisher | 3/53 | HMV (45) 7M.117 |
| Victor Silvester and his Ballroom Orchestra | 4/53 | Columbia FB.3672 |

## 433 | COMES A-LONG A-LOVE

*Composer*: Al Sherman          *Date of Entry*: 20.12.52

*Publishers*: Edward Kassner Music Co. Ltd.          *Highest Position*: 6
                                                     *Weeks on Chart*: 15

*Recordings*:

| | | |
|---|---|---|
| Kay Starr | 10/52 | Capitol CL.13808 |
| The Tanner Sisters | 11/52 | HMV B.10390 |
| Harry Farmer (Hammond organ) | 1/53 | Decca F.10035 |

# 1953

This being Coronation year, it was a great opportunity for Tin Pan Alley to come out fighting and this it did to great effect with seven songs appearing in the charts which reflected that June event. The first of them, which became the only No. 1 of the seven, was *In a golden coach* and it is reputed to be one of the last million sellers of sheet music. Its predecessor at No. 1, *Doggie in the window*, has also been mentioned as a possible seven-figure sale and it could well be that these were the last to reach that magical figure – although we have seen *I'm walking behind you* listed in another publication of earlier days. It certainly appears that this year of 1953 saw the last of the big sellers as far as sheet music was concerned – but still those charts ruled. Indeed, Bob Merrill achieved an amazing hat-trick by again being top composer of the year, this time with six in the charts, including the aforementioned *Doggie*. The most recorded song of all these 14 years, *April in Portugal*, entered in June, but an event of quite unbelievable proportions began on the 27th of that same month when *Limelight* became No. 1, *Moulin Rouge* No 2 and *I Believe* No. 3 for these three songs were to stay in these same three positions for no less than 17 consecutive weeks – *Limelight* thereby becoming the second longest No.1 to *Galway Bay*. *I believe*, which had been No. 1 on 13 June, returned to that spot on 24 October – a gap of 19 weeks between the top spots. In the States, *Vaya con Dios* was the year's top sheet music seller but never rose higher than No. 5 here in Britain. The giant Philips company

| Pos | MOST WEEKS ON THE CHARTS TOP SIX | Wks |
|---|---|---|
| 1 | *I believe* | 38 |
| 2 | *Wonderful Copenhagen* | 37 |
| 3 | *The Moulin Rouge theme* | 33 |
| 4 | *The theme from Limelight* | 32 |
| 5 | *I'm walking behind you* | 31 |
| 6= | *Pretend* | 25 |
| 6= | *April in Portugal* | 25 |

produced its first PB series singles here in January, and what a list of artists it signed up. From America came the entire Columbia catalogue, thereby removing it from the EMI's Columbia label; also from the UK's Columbia company came singers Johnny Brandon, David Hughes and the

113

Beverley Sisters, while Wally Stott was signed to be the British Musical Director. There were, too, the four 'G's' – Geraldo, Gracie Fields, Gary Miller and Glen Mason. The first popular 45 rpm singles from the four EMI labels appeared in January but these early issues did not always match the month by month listing of their 78 rpm counterparts, with even the A and B sides being different on occasion. The US sheet music chart for the Christmas week featured no less than seven Christmas songs out of the fifteen listed.

# SONG CHARTS

## 434 THAT'S A-WHY

*Composer*: Bob Merrill

*Publishers*: Campbell Connelly & Co. Ltd.

*Date of Entry*: 3.1.53

*Highest Position*: 8
*Weeks on Chart*: 14

*Recordings*:

| | | |
|---|---|---|
| Ted Heath and his Music (Lita Roza and Dennis Lotis) | 11/52 | Decca F.10027 |
| Guy Mitchell and Mindy Carson | 12/52 | Columbia DB.3203 |
| Guy Mitchell and Mindy Carson | 3/53 | Columbia (45) SCM. 5022 |

## 435 BROKEN WINGS

*Composers*: John Jerome & Bernard Grun

*Publishers*: John Fields Music Co. Ltd

*Date of Entry* 10.1.53 /
Pos: 23 / Wks: 1
*Re-entry*: 24.1.53 /
Pos: 1 / Wks: 20

*Recordings*:

| | | |
|---|---|---|
| Dickie Valentine | 7/52 | Decca F.9954 |
| Art and Dottie Todd | 1/53 | HMV B10399 |
| The Stargazers | 2/53 | Decca F.10047 |
| Gerry Brereton | 2/53 | Parlophone R.3639 |
| David Carey | 2/53 | Columbia DB.3245 |
| Victor Silvester and his Ballroom Orchestra | 3/53 | Columbia FB.3669 |
| The Sam Browne Singers | 3/53 | Philips PB.112 |
| Beryl Templeman | 3/53 | Oriole CB.1163 |
| David Carey | 5/53 | Columbia (45) SCM.5030 |

## 436 SETTIN' THE WOODS ON FIRE

*Composers*: Edward G. Nelson & Fred Rose

*Publishers*: New World Publishers Ltd.

*Date of Entry*: 10.1.53 /
Pos: 24 / Wks: 2
*Re-entry*: 31.1.53 /
Pos: 19 / Wks: 4

*Recordings*:

| | | |
|---|---|---|
| Fran Warren | 10/52 | MGM.559 |
| Hank Williams and his Drifting Cowboys (Hank Williams) | 10/52 | MGM.566 |
| Jo Stafford and Frankie Laine | 11/52 | Columbia DB.3168 |
| Ted Heath and his Music (Lita Roza and Dennis Lotis) | 11/52 | Decca F.10027 |
| Marvin Shiner with Grady Martin and his Slew Foot Five | 12/52 | Brunswick 05021 |
| Billy Thorburn's The Organ, the Dance Band and Me (The Bobolinks) | 1/53 | Parlophone F.2507 |
| Jo Stafford and Frankie Laine | 1/53 | Columbia (45) SCM.5014 |

## 437 DON'T LET THE STARS GET IN YOUR EYES

*Composer*: Slim Willet

*Publishers*: Edwin H. Morris & Co Ltd

*Date of Entry*: 17.1.53

*Highest Position*: 1
*Weeks on Chart*: 16

*Recordings*:

| | | |
|---|---|---|
| Dennis Lotis | 12/52 | Decca F.10043 |
| Gisele MacKenzie | 1/53 | Capitol CL.13855 |
| Perry Como with The Ramblers | 1/53 | HMV B.10400 |
| Jack Gray | 1/53 | Parlophone R.3625 |
| Red Foley | 1/53 | Brunswick 05041 |
| Gracie Fields | 1/53 | Philips PB.106 |
| Troise and his Novelty Orchestra with The Four-in-A-Chord | 2/53 | Columbia DB.3244 |
| Perry Como with The Ramblers | 3/53 | HMV (45) 7M.118 |
| Lola Ameche | 3/53 | Oriole CB.1143 |
| Bobby Maxwell (harp) with The Windy City Symphony | 3/53 | Oriole CB.1158 |
| Mickey Katz and his Orchestra (Mickey Katz) [Titled 'Don't let the Schmaltz get in your eyes'] | 3/53 | Capitol CL.13889 |
| Lola Ameche | 6/54 | Mercury MB.3003★ |
| Bobby Maxwell (harp) with The Windy City Symphony | 6/54 | Mercury MB.3016★ |

## 438 | WONDERFUL COPENHAGEN

| | | |
|---|---|---|
| Composer: Frank Loesser | | Date of Entry: 17.1.53 / Pos: 2 / Wks 31 |
| Publishers: Edwin H. Morris & Co. Ltd. | | Re-entry: 29.8.53 / Pos: 18 / Wks: 6 |

Recordings:

| | | |
|---|---|---|
| Danny Kaye | 12/52 | Brunswick 05023 |
| Paul Weston and his Orchestra with The Norman Luboff Choir | 12/52 | Columbia DB.3195 |
| Hugo Winterhalter and his Orchestra and Chorus | 2/53 | HMV B.10438 |
| Josef Locke | 3/53 | Columbia DB.3253 |
| Hugo Winterhalter and his Orchestra and Chorus | 5/53 | HMV (45) 7M.131 |

## 439 | MAKE IT SOON

| | | |
|---|---|---|
| Composers: Henri Salvador, Maurice Pon & William Engvick | | Date of Entry: 17.1.53 / Pos: 23 / Wks: 1 |
| Publishers: Campbell Connelly & Co. Ltd. | | Re-entry: 31.1.53 / Pos: 11/ Wks: 11 |

Recordings:

| | | |
|---|---|---|
| Tony Brent | 10/52 | Columbia DB.3187 |
| The Tanner Sisters | 11/52 | HMV B.10364 |
| The Stargazers | 2/53 | Decca F.10047 |

## 440 | TAKE ME IN YOUR ARMS AND HOLD ME

| | | |
|---|---|---|
| Composer: Cindy Walker | | Date of Entry: 17.1.53 |
| Publishers: Campbell Connelly & Co. Ltd. | | Highest Position: 24 Weeks on Chart: 1 |

Recordings:

| | | |
|---|---|---|
| Les Paul and Mary Ford | 9/52 | Capitol CL.13793 |
| Alma Cogan | 11/52 | HMV B.10370 |
| Pearl Carr | 12/52 | Columbia DB.3205 |
| Bob Harvey (vocal and piano) | 12/52 | Parlophone R.3610 |

## 441 | HEART AND SOUL

| | | |
|---|---|---|
| Composers: Hoagy Carmichael & Frank Loesser | | Date of Entry: 24.1.53 / Pos: 23 / Wks: 1 |
| Publishers: Bradbury Wood Ltd. | | Re-entry: 14.2.53 / Pos: 22 / Wks: 1 |

(Note: From the ten records which were released following the song's first popularity in 1938 only one survived in the catalogue until the 1953 revival – the Connee Boswell version on Brunswick 02677.)

Later recordings:

| | | |
|---|---|---|
| The Ralph Sharon Sextet | 9/51 | Melodisc 1176 |
| The Four Aces featuring Al Alberts | 1/53 | Brunswick 05040 |
| Roberto Inglez and his Orchestra | 2/53 | Parlophone R.3640 |
| Carole Carr | 2/53 | HMV B.10420 |

## 442 | NOW

| | | |
|---|---|---|
| Composers: Joe Priolo, Pat Noto & Andy Perri | | Date of Entry: 24.1.53 |
| Publishers: Dash Music Co. Ltd | | Highest Position: 5 Weeks on Chart: 17 |

Recordings:

| | | |
|---|---|---|
| Al Martino | 12/52 | Capitol CL.13835 |
| Joe Loss and his Orchestra (Howard Jones) | 1/53 | HMV B.10405 |
| Julie Dawn | 1/53 | Columbia DB.3227 |
| Dick James | 1/53 | Parlophone R.3629 |

## 443 | THE GLOW WORM

| | | |
|---|---|---|
| Composers: Paul Lincke, Lilla Cayley Robinson & Johnny Mercer | | Date of Entry: 7.2.53 |
| Publishers: Lafleur & Co. Ltd | | Highest Position: 8 Weeks on Chart: 11 |

(Note: The only survivor of earlier recordings of this Paul Lincke piece still available when it reached the charts in 1953 via the Johnny Mercer lyrics was the version by The Royal Artillery Band, Woolwich on Decca F.7577 which was titled 'The Glow Worm Idyll'.)

Later recordings:

| | | |
|---|---|---|
| Johnny Mercer | 5/51 | Capitol CL.13520 |
| The Mills Brothers | 11/52 | Brunswick 05007 |
| The Kordites | 12/52 | HMV B.10395 |
| Cyril Stapleton and his Orchestra (The Clubmen) | 1/53 | Decca F.10039 |
| The Malcolm Mitchell Trio | 1/53 | Parlophone R.3626 |
| Johnny Brandon | 1/53 | Philips PB.100 |
| Max Geldray (harmonica) | 2/53 | Columbia DB.3232 |
| Victor Silvester and his Ballroom Orchestra | 2/53 | Columbia FB.3667 |
| Ken Mackintosh and his Orchestra | 2/53 | HMV BD.6142 |
| Sydney Thompson and his Old-Tyme Dance Orchestra | 10/53 | Parlophone R.3747* |

## 444 WHY DON'T YOU BELIEVE ME?

*Composers:* Lew Douglas, King Laney & Roy Rodde
*Publishers:* Francis Day & Hunter Ltd

*Date of Entry:* 14.2.53
*Highest Position:* 9
*Weeks on Chart:* 14

*Recordings:*

| | | |
|---|---|---|
| Jimmy Young | 1/53 | Decca F.10036 |
| Lita Roza | 1/53 | Decca F.10040 |
| Joni James | 1/53 | MGM.582 |
| Jill Allan | 1/53 | Columbia DB.3223 |
| Dennis Hale | 1/53 | Parlophone R.3630 |
| Guy Lombardo and his Royal Canadians (Kenny Gardner) | 1/53 | Brunswick 05047 |
| Patti Page | 1/53 | Oriole CB.1145 |
| Bill Hurley | 2/53 | HMV B.10417 |
| Joe Loss and his Orchestra (Rose Brennan) | 2/53 | HMV B.10427 |
| Sharkey and his Kings of Dixieland (Sharkey) | 2/53 | Capitol CL.13872 |
| Joni James | 3/53 | MGM. (45) SP.1013 |
| Mickey Katz and his Orchestra (Sue Allen and Mickey Katz) | 3/53 | Capitol CL.13889 |
| Patti Page | 6/54 | Mercury MB.3005★ |

## 445 HI-LILI, HI-LO

*Composers:* Helen Deutsch & Bronislaw Kaper
*Publishers:* Robbins Music Corporation Ltd.

*Date of Entry:* 14.2.53 / Pos: 23 / Wks: 2
*Re-entry:* 19.9.53 / Pos: 24 / Wks: 1

*Recordings:*

| | | |
|---|---|---|
| Leslie Caron and Mel Ferrer | 12/52 | MGM.578 |
| Dinah Shore | 12/52 | HMV B.10385 |
| Lita Roza | 1/53 | Decca F.10040 |
| Eve Boswell | 1/53 | Parlophone R.3628 |
| Vincent Roberto | 2/53 | Philips PB.108 |
| Ray Martin and his Concert Orchestra | 9/53 | Columbia DB.3346 |
| Lita Roza | 9/53 | Decca F.10162 |
| Victor Young and his Singing Strings | 9/53 | Brunswick 05159 |
| Ray Martin and his Concert Orchestra | 11/53 | Columbia (45) SCM.5063★ |

## 446 SHE WEARS RED FEATHERS

*Composer:* Bob Merrill
*Publishers:* Dash Music Co. Ltd.

*Date of Entry:* 21.2.53
*Highest Position:* 3
*Weeks on Chart:* 16

*Recordings:*

| | | |
|---|---|---|
| Guy Mitchell | 2/53 | Columbia DB.3238 |
| The Ray Ellington Quartet with The Peter Knight Singers | 2/53 | Decca F.10059 |
| Donald Peers with The Kordites | 2/53 | HMV B.10442 |
| Guy Mitchell | 5/53 | Columbia (45) SCM.5032 |

## 447 THE LOVE OF MY LIFE

*Composers:* Johnny Reine & Johnny May
*Publishers:* Michael Reine Music Co. Ltd.

*Date of Entry:* 21.2.53
*Highest Position:* 18
*Weeks on Chart:* 9

*Recordings:*

| | | |
|---|---|---|
| Billy Thorburn's The Organ, the Dance Band and Me (The Bobolinks) | 1/53 | Parlophone F.2507 |
| Vera Lynn with The Johnston Singers | 1/53 | Decca F.10044 |
| Bill Hurley | 2/53 | HMV B.10417 |
| Line Renaud | 3/53 | Columbia DB.3247 |
| Victor Silvester and his Ballroom Orchestra | 3/53 | Columbia FB.3668 |

## 448 (How much is) THAT DOGGIE IN THE WINDOW

*Composer:* Bob Merrill
*Publishers:* Campbell Connelly & Co. Ltd.

*Date of Entry:* 28.2.53
*Highest Position:* 1
*Weeks on Chart:* 19

*Recordings:*

| | | |
|---|---|---|
| Lita Roza | 3/53 | Decca F.10070 |
| Patti Page | 3/53 | Oriole CB.1156 |
| Carole Carr with Children's Choir and Rustler the Dog | 3/53 | HMV B.10436 |
| John Slater | 3/53 | Columbia DB.3252 |
| Mandy Miller | 4/53 | Parlophone R.3669 |
| Homer and Jethro (Titled 'That Hound Dog in the Window') | 11/53 | HMV B.10581★ |
| Patti Page | 6/54 | Mercury MB.3014★ |

## 449 IN A GOLDEN COACH (There's a heart of gold)

*Composer:* Ronald Jamieson
*Publishers:* Box & Cox Publications Ltd.

*Date of Entry:* 28.2.53
*Highest Position:* 1
*Weeks on Chart:* 22

*Recordings:*

| | | |
|---|---|---|
| Billy Cotton and his Band (Doreen Stephens with narration by Billy Cotton) | 2/53 | Decca F.10058 |
| Lily Strange and the People of Hoxton | 3/53 | Parlophone R.3648 |
| Teddy Johnson | 4/53 | Columbia DB.3268 |
| Donald Peers | 4/53 | HMV B.10487 |
| Dickie Valentine | 4/53 | Decca F.10098 |
| Bob and Alf Pearson | 5/53 | Parlophone F.2515 |
| Daphne and David | 5/53 | Columbia DB.3277 |
| Victor Silvester and his Ballroom Orchestra | 5/53 | Columbia FB.3676 |

## 450 KEEP IT A SECRET

*Composer*: Jessie Mae Robinson

*Publishers*: Cinephonic Music Co. Ltd.

*Date of Entry*: 28.2.53 / Pos: 23 / Wks: 1
*Re-entry*: 28.3.53 / Pos: 24 / Wks: 1

*Recordings*:

| | | |
|---|---|---|
| June Hutton and Axel Stordahl with The Boys Next Door | 12/52 | Capitol CL.13844 |
| Jimmy Young | 1/53 | Decca F.10036 |
| Bing Crosby with Jud Conlon's Rhythmaires | 1/53 | Brunswick 05037 |
| Dinah Shore | 1/53 | HMV B.10407 |
| Jo Stafford | 1/53 | Columbia DB.3211 |
| Gerry Brereton | 1/53 | Parlophone R.3620 |
| Sharkey and his Kings of Dixieland (Sharkey) | 2/53 | Capitol CL.13872 |
| Dinah Shore | 3/53 | HMV (45) 7M.119 |
| Jo Stafford | 3/53 | Columbia (45) SCM.5026 |

## 451 THE RUBY AND THE PEARL

*Composers*: Jay Livingston & Ray Evans

*Publishers*: New World Publishers Ltd.

*Date of Entry*: 7.3.53

*Highest Position*: 21
*Weeks on Chart*: 1

*Recordings*:

| | | |
|---|---|---|
| Jeri Southern | 11/52 | Brunswick 05012 |
| Leroy Holmes and his Orchestra and Chorus | 11/52 | MGM.574 |
| Frankie Laine | 11/52 | Columbia DB.3170 |
| Perry Como | 11/52 | HMV B.10375 |
| Nat 'King' Cole | 11/52 | Capitol CL.13816 |
| Frankie Laine | 1/53 | Columbia (45) SCM.5016 |
| Perry Como | 1/53 | HMV (45) 7M.102 |

## 452 GOT YOU ON MY MIND

*Composers*: Howard Biggs & Joe Thomas

*Publishers*: B. Feldman & Co. Ltd.

*Date of Entry*: 7.3.53 / Pos: 23 / Wks: 1
*Re-entry*: 28.3.53 / Pos: 23 / Wks: 1

*Recordings*:

| | | |
|---|---|---|
| Buddy Morrow and his Orchestra (Frank Lester and The Quartet) | 11/52 | HMV B.10371 |
| Joe Loss and his Orchestra (Rose Brennan and The Kordites) | 12/52 | HMV B.10391 |
| Tony Brent | 12/52 | Columbia DB.3226 |

## 453 LITTLE RED MONKEY

*Composer*: Jack Jordan (lyrics added by Stephen Gale)

*Publishers*: Robbins Music Corporation Ltd.

*Date of Entry*: 14.3.53

*Highest Position*: 6
*Weeks on Chart*: 18

*Recordings*:

| | | |
|---|---|---|
| Frank Chacksfield's Tunesmiths (Jack Jordan – clavioline) | 2/53 | Parlophone R.3658 |
| The Harry Grove Trio | 3/53 | Decca F.10079 |
| Ivor Mairants and his Guitar Group | 4/53 | Decca F.10095 |
| The Melachrino Strings | 4/53 | HMV B.10461 |
| Joy Nichols, Dick Bentley and Jimmy Edwards | 4/53 | Parlophone R.3684 |
| Ken Griffin (organ) | 4/53 | Philips PB.131 |
| Rosemary Clooney | 4/53 | Philips PB.141 |
| Rose Murphy | 5/53 | London L.1176 |
| Ray Ellington | 5/53 | Columbia DB.3287 |
| The Harmonicats | 5/53 | Oriole CB.1178 |
| Mel Blanc | 5/53 | Capitol CL.13922 |
| Roberto Inglez and his Orchestra | 6/53 | Parlophone R.3690 |
| Ray Ellington | 7/53 | Columbia (45) SCM.5050 |
| The Harmonicats | 6/54 | Mercury MB.3034★ |

## 454 OH, HAPPY DAY

*Composers*: Donald Howard Koplow & Nancy Binns Reed

*Publishers*: Chappell & Co. Ltd.

*Date of Entry*: 14.3.53

*Highest Position*: 4
*Weeks on Chart*: 19

*Recordings*:

| | | |
|---|---|---|
| David Carey | 2/53 | Columbia DB.3245 |
| Dick Todd | 3/53 | Brunswick 05061 |
| Don Cameron | 3/53 | HMV B.10434 |
| Don Howard | 3/53 | London L.1163 |
| The Pilgrim | 3/53 | Parlophone R.3656 |
| The Johnston Brothers | 3/53 | Decca F.10071 |
| The Four Knights | 3/53 | Capitol CL.13861 |
| David Carey | 5/53 | Columbia (45) SCM.5030 |

## 455 TILL I WALTZ AGAIN WITH YOU

*Composer*: Sidney Prosen

*Date of Entry*: 21.3.53

*Publishers*: Francis Day & Hunter Ltd.

*Highest Position*: 10
*Weeks on Chart*: 14

*Recordings*:

| | | |
|---|---|---|
| Jimmy Young | 2/53 | Decca F.10069 |
| Dick Todd | 3/53 | Brunswick 05061 |
| Joan Regan | 3/53 | Decca F.10068 |
| Alma Cogan | 3/53 | HMV B.10449 |
| Gary Miller | 3/53 | Philips PB.115 |
| Charlie Gore and Ruby Wright | 3/53 | Parlophone R.3663 |
| Eileen Draper | 4/53 | Columbia DB.3260 |
| Gisele MacKenzie | 4/53 | Capitol CL.13920 |
| Ken Griffin (organ) | 4/53 | Philips PB.131 |
| Russ Morgan and his Orchestra (Russ Morgan and The Morganaires) | 5/53 | Brunswick 05089 |
| Victor Silvester and his Ballroom Orchestra | 5/53 | Columbia FB.3677 |
| Jerry Murad's Harmonicats | 5/53 | Oriole CB.1169 |
| Charlie Gore and Ruby Wright | 5/53 | Parlophone (45) MSP.6025 |
| Jerry Murad's Harmonicats | 6/54 | Mercury MB.3025★ |

## 456 I TALK TO THE TREES

*Composers*: Alan Jay Lerner & Frederick Loewe

*Date of Entry*: 21.3.53 /
Pos: 10 / Wks: 8

*Publishers*: Chappell & Co. Ltd.

*Re-entry*: 23.5.53 /
Pos: 13 / Wks: 12

*Recordings*:

| | | |
|---|---|---|
| Greta Keller | 12/52 | Parlophone R.3600 |
| Murray Arnold | 1/53 | Vogue V.9046 |
| Edmundo Ros and his Orchestra (Edmundo Ros) | 2/53 | Decca F.10060 |
| Joy Nichols | 4/53 | Parlophone R.3666 |
| Anne Shelton | 5/53 | Decca F.10105 |
| David Hughes | 5/53 | Philips PB.134 |
| Allan Jones | 5/53 | HMV B.10490 |
| Allan Jones | 7/53 | HMV (45) 7M.135 |
| Leslie A. Hutchinson – 'Hutch' | 7/53 | Oriole CB.1185 |

## 457 THE DUMMY SONG

*Composers*: Lew Brown, Billy Rose & Ray Henderson

*Date of Entry*: 21.3.53

*Publishers*: Keith Prowse Music Publishing Co. Ltd.

*Highest Position*: 24
*Weeks on Chart*: 1

(Note: This song was first published in 1925.)

*Recordings*:

| | | |
|---|---|---|
| The Hoosier Hot Shots (VC) | 7/52 | Brunswick 04963 |
| Anne Shelton with Ted Heath and his Music | 11/52 | Decca F.10013 |
| Max Bygraves with Peter Brough and 'Archie Andrews' | 2/53 | HMV B.10444 |
| Louis Armstrong | 9/53 | Brunswick 05163★ |

## 458 I'D LOVE TO FALL ASLEEP (and wake up in your arms)

*Composers*: Louis Gasté & Sonny Miller

*Date of Entry*: 28.3.53 /
Pos: 20 / Wks: 2

*Publishers*: B. Feldman & Co. Ltd.

*Re-entry*: 18.4.53/
Pos: 23/Wks: 1
*2nd re-entry*: 2.5.53 /
Pos: 24 / Wks: 1

*Recordings*:

| | | |
|---|---|---|
| Line Renaud | 3/53 | Columbia DB.3247 |
| Billy Thorburn's The Organ, the Dance Band and Me (The Song Pedlars) | 3/53 | Parlophone F.2511 |
| Penny Nicholls | 3/53 | HMV B.10447 |
| Derrick Francis with The Coronets | 3/53 | Polygon P.1064 |
| Shirley Abicair | 3/53 | Decca F.10078 |
| Beryl Templeman with The Wondertones | 3/53 | Oriole CB.1162 & CB.1163 |
| Muriel Smith | 4/53 | Philips PB.122 |

## 459 I WILL NEVER CHANGE (I'll always love you)

*Composers*: Cy Coben & Camarata

*Date of Entry*: 28.3.53 /
Pos: 22 / Wks: 1

*Publishers*: Yale Music Corporation Ltd.

*Re-entry*: 18.4.53 /
Pos: 24 /Wks: 1
*2nd re-entry*: 23.5.53 /
Pos: 23 / Wks: 1

*Recordings*:

| | | |
|---|---|---|
| Anne Shelton with the George Mitchell Choir | 4/51 | Decca F.9664 |
| Johnny Desmond | 11/51 | MGM.450 |
| Dick James | 11/52 | Parlophone R.3606 |

## 460 I'M WALKING BEHIND YOU

| Composer: Billy Reid | | Date of Entry: 4.4.53 |
|---|---|---|
| Publishers: Peter Maurice Music Co. Ltd. | | Highest Position: 2 |
| | | Weeks on Chart: 31 |

Recordings:

| Gary Miller | 3/53 | Philips PB.115 |
|---|---|---|
| Dorothy Squires | 3/53 | Polygon P.1068 |
| Billy Cotton and his Band (Doreen Stephens) | 4/53 | Decca F.10096 |
| Jimmy Young | 4/53 | Decca F.10080 |
| Eddie Fisher with Sally Sweetland | 5/53 | HMV B.10489 |
| Frank Sinatra | 5/53 | Capitol CL.13924 |
| Donald O'Connor | 6/53 | Brunswick 05121 |
| Vic Damone | 7/53 | Oriole CB.1186 |
| Eddie Fisher with Sally Sweetland | 7/53 | HMV (45) 7M.133 |
| Ethel Smith (organ) | 8/53 | Brunswick 05147 |
| Vic Damone | 6/54 | Mercury MB. 3040★ |

## 461 PRETEND

| Composers: Lew Douglas, Cliff Parman & Frank Lavere | | Date of Entry: 4.4.53 |
|---|---|---|
| Publishers: Leeds Music Ltd. | | Highest Position: 3 |
| | | Weeks on Chart: 25 |

Recordings:

| Henri Rene and his Orchestra with Franz Dietchmann (zither) | 2/53 | HMV B.10425 |
|---|---|---|
| Nat 'King' Cole | 2/53 | Capitol CL.13878 |
| Ralph Marterie and his Orchestra | 3/53 | Oriole CB.1159 |
| Franklyn Boyd | 4/53 | HMV B.10481 |
| Julie Dawn | 6/53 | Columbia DB.3304 |
| Victor Silvester and his Ballroom Orchestra | 6/53 | Columbia FB.3679 |
| Guy Lombardo and his Royal Canadians (Kenny Gardner) | 6/53 | Brunswick 05117 |
| Ethel Smith (organ) | 8/53 | Brunswick 05146 |
| Ralph Marterie and his Orchestra | 6/54 | Mercury MB.3017★ |

## 462 ALL THE TIME AND EV'RYWHERE

| Composer: Bob Merrill | | Date of Entry: 4.4.53 / Pos: 21 / Wks: 1 |
|---|---|---|
| Publishers: Cinephonic Music Co. Ltd. | | Re-entry: 25.4.53 / Pos: 23 / Wks: 3 |

Recordings:

| Dickie Valentine | 1/53 | Decca F.10038 |
|---|---|---|
| Mindy Carson | 1/53 | Columbia DB.3212 |

## 463 PRETTY LITTLE BLACK-EYED SUSIE

| Composers: Kay Twomey, Fred Wise & Ben Weisman | | Date of Entry: 11.4.53 |
|---|---|---|
| Publishers: Cinephonic Music Co. Ltd. | | Highest Position: 6 |
| | | Weeks on Chart: 23 |

Recordings:

| Benny Lee | 4/53 | Decca F.10091 |
|---|---|---|
| Guy Mitchell | 4/53 | Columbia DB.3255 |
| Guy Mitchell | 6/53 | Columbia (45) SCM.5037 |

## 464 CELEBRATION RAG

| Composers: Rodd Arden & Jimmy Harper | | Date of Entry: 11.4.53 |
|---|---|---|
| Publishers: Bradbury Wood Ltd. | | Highest Position: 11 |
| | | Weeks on Chart: 15 |

Recordings:

| Donald Peers | 4/53 | HMV B.10487 |
|---|---|---|
| Bob and Alf Pearson | 5/53 | Parlophone F.2515 |
| Chris Hamalton (Hammond organ) | 6/53 | London L.1177 |
| The Stargazers | 6/53 | Decca F.10133 |

## 465 I BELIEVE

| Composers: Ervin Drake, Jimmy Shirl, Irvin Graham & Al Stillman | | Date of Entry: 11.4.53 |
|---|---|---|
| Publishers: Cinephonic Music Co. Ltd. | | Highest Position: 1 |
| | | Weeks on Chart: 40 |

Recordings:

| Frankie Laine | 2/53 | Philips PB.117 |
|---|---|---|
| Jane Froman | 4/53 | Capitol CL.13902 |
| Ronnie Ronalde | 4/53 | Columbia DB.3285 |
| David Whitfield | 4/53 | Decca F.10099 |
| Eve Boswell | 5/53 | Parlophone R.3689 |
| Allan Jones | 5/53 | HMV B.10490 |
| Allan Jones | 7/53 | HMV (45) 7M.135 |
| Victor Silvester and his Ballroom Orchestra | 7/53 | Columbia FB.3681 |
| Ethel Smith (organ) | 8/53 | Brunswick 05146 |

## 466 SIDE BY SIDE

| | | |
|---|---|---|
| *Composer*: Harry Woods | | *Date of Entry*: 11.4.53/<br>Pos: 24/Wks: 1 |
| *Publishers*: Lawrence Wright Music Co. Ltd. | | *Re-entry*: 9.5.53/<br>Pos: 23/Wks: 1 |

(Note: First published, and recorded, in 1927, this song was a 'natural' for a revival during World War Two. All recordings issued during these two eras had been deleted by the time the song reached the charts in 1953.)

*Later recordings*:

| | | |
|---|---|---|
| The Keynotes with Primo Scala and his Banjo and Accordion Band | 7/48 | Decca F.8925 |
| Betty Garrett and Larry Parks | 5/50 | MGM.285 |
| Kay Starr | 2/53 | Capitol CL.13871 |
| Frank Petty Trio (featuring Mike di Napoli – piano) | 3/53 | MGM.610 |
| Frank Petty Trio (featuring Mike di Napoli – piano) | 4/53 | MGM (45) SP.1033 |
| Grady Martin and his Slew Foot Five (Dottie Dillard and Jack Shook) | 4/53 | Brunswick 05080 |
| The Beverley Sisters | 4/53 | Philips PB.129 |
| Harry Davidson and his Orchestra | 12/53 | Columbia DX.1892★ |
| Harry Davidson and his Orchestra | 12/53 | Columbia (45) SCD.2028★ |

## 467 DOWNHEARTED

| | | |
|---|---|---|
| *Composers*: Bob Hilliard & Dave Mann | | *Date of Entry*: 18.4.53 |
| *Publishers*: New World Publishers Ltd. | | *Highest Position*: 6<br>*Weeks on Chart*: 20 |

*Recordings*:

| | | |
|---|---|---|
| Eddie Fisher | 3/53 | HMV B.10450 |
| The Johnston Brothers | 3/53 | Decca F.10071 |
| Victor Silvester and his Ballroom Orchestra | 4/53 | Columbia FB.3671 |
| Eddie Fisher | 5/53 | HMV (45) 7M.126 |
| Guy Lombardo and his Royal Canadians (Kenny Gardner) | 5/53 | Brunswick 05094 |

## 468 THE WINDSOR WALTZ

| | | |
|---|---|---|
| *Composers*: Johnny Reine & Johnny May | | *Date of Entry*: 25.4.53 |
| *Publishers*: Michael Reine Music Co. Ltd. | | *Highest Position*: 5<br>*Weeks on Chart*: 14 |

*Recordings*:

| | | |
|---|---|---|
| Gerry Brereton | 4/53 | Parlophone R.3671 |
| Vera Lynn with Chorus of members of HM Forces | 4/53 | Decca F.10092 |
| Les Howard | 4/53 | HMV B.10464 |
| Joan Dowling | 4/53 | Columbia DB.3265 |
| Dickie Valentine | 4/53 | Decca F.10098 |

## 469 WILD HORSES

| | | |
|---|---|---|
| *Composer*: K.C. Rogan, based on 'Wilder Reiter' by Robert Schumann | | *Date of Entry*: 25.4.53 /<br>Pos: 17 / Wks: 9 |
| *Publishers*: Edwin H. Morris & Co. Ltd. | | *Re-entry*: 11.7.53 /<br>Pos: 24 / Wks: 1 |

*Recordings*:

| | | |
|---|---|---|
| Perry Como | 4/53 | HMV B.10454 |
| Julie Dawn | 4/53 | Columbia DB.3261 |
| Jon Orvelle | 4/53 | Parlophone R.3664 |
| David Hughes with The Rita Williams Singers | 4/53 | Philips PB.120 |
| Dennis Lotis with Ted Heath and his Music | 4/53 | Decca F.10090 |
| Ray Anthony and his Orchestra (Jo Ann Greer) | 4/53 | Capitol CL.13906 |
| Perry Como | 5/53 | HMV (45) 7M.124 |
| Julie Dawn | 5/53 | Columbia (45) SCM.5035 |

## 470 EVEN NOW

| | | |
|---|---|---|
| *Composers*: Richard Adler, Jerry Ross & Dan Howell | | *Date of Entry*: 25.4.53 |
| *Publishers*: Pickwick Music Ltd. | | *Highest Position*: 24<br>*Weeks on Chart*: 1 |

*Recordings*:

| | | |
|---|---|---|
| Eddie Fisher | 2/53 | HMV B.10421 |
| Jimmy Young with The Clubmen | 2/53 | Decca F.10069 |
| Eddie Fisher | 5/53 | HMV (45) 7M.125★ |

## 471 HOLD ME, THRILL ME, KISS ME

| | | |
|---|---|---|
| *Composer*: Harry Noble | | *Date of Entry*: 9.5.53 |
| *Publishers*: Mills Music Ltd. | | *Highest Position*: 5<br>*Weeks on Chart*: 22 |

*Recordings*:

| | | |
|---|---|---|
| Noble and King (vocal) [Titled 'Hold me'] | 9/51 | Parlophone R.3432 |
| Elisabeth Welch [Titled 'Hold me'] | 1/52 | Decca F.9832 |
| Roberta Lee | 2/53 | Brunswick 05059 |
| Muriel Smith | 4/53 | Philips PB.122 |
| Gerry Brereton | 4/53 | Parlophone R.3671 |
| Jimmy Young | 4/53 | Decca F.10080 |
| Alma Cogan | 4/53 | HMV B.10460 |
| Joan Dowling | 4/53 | Columbia DB.3265 |
| The Orioles | 6/53 | London L.1180 |

## 472 THE MOULIN ROUGE THEME
### (The Song from the Moulin Rouge – Where is your heart?)

*Composers*: Georges Auric & Willian Engvick  
*Publishers*: Campbell Connelly & Co. Ltd.  

*Date of Entry*: 16.5.53  
*Highest Position*: 1  
*Weeks on Chart*: 38  

(Note: All the versions listed below are titled '(The) Song from (the) Moulin Rouge' – the word 'the' being optional. There is only one exception with the Ethel Smith recording being titled 'The Moulin Rouge Theme'.)

*Recordings*:

| | | |
|---|---|---|
| Mantovani and his Orchestra | 3/53 | Decca F.10094 |
| Percy Faith and his Orchestra (Felicia Sanders) | 4/53 | Philips PB.128 |
| June Hutton and Axel Stordahl with The Stordahl Orchestra | 5/53 | Capitol CL.13918 |
| Ron Goodwin and his Concert Orchestra | 5/53 | Parlophone R.3686 |
| Norrie Paramor and his Orchestra | 5/53 | Columbia DB.3281 |
| Henri Rene and his Orchestra (sax solo: Alvy West) | 5/53 | HMV B.10483 |
| Jean Sablon with The Melachrino Strings | 5/53 | HMV B.10496 |
| Buddy de Franco (clarinet) with orch. cond. by Richard Maltby | 5/53 | MGM.631 |
| Victor Young and his Singing Strings | 6/53 | Brunswick 05110 |
| Ron Goodwin and his Concert Orchestra | 7/53 | Parlophone (45) MSP.6035 |
| Norrie Paramor and his Orchestra | 7/53 | Columbia (45) SCM.5051 |
| Victor Silvester and his Ballroom Orchestra | 7/53 | Columbia FB.3682 |
| Leslie A. Hutchinson – 'Hutch' | 7/53 | Oriole CB.1189 |
| Ethel Smith (organ) | 7/53 | Brunswick 05145 |
| Line Renaud | 8/53 | Columbia DB.3328/ (45) SCM.5055 |
| Buddy de Franco (clarinet) with orch. cond. by Richard Maltby | 11/53 | MGM. (45) SP.1056 |

## 473 CORONATION WALTZ

*Composers*: Christine Hurst & George Warren  
*Publishers*: Northern Music Ltd.  

*Date of Entry*: 16.5.53 / Pos: 23 / Wks: 1  
*Re-entry*: 30.5.53 / Pos: 23 / Wks: 1  

*Recording*:

| | | |
|---|---|---|
| Harry Davidson and his Orchestra | 4/53 | Columbia DX.1871 |

## 474 CORONATION RAG

*Composer*: Winifred Atwell  
*Publishers*: Magna Music Co. Ltd.  

*Date of Entry*: 16.5.53  
*Highest Position*: 16  
*Weeks on Chart*: 7  

*Recording*:

| | | |
|---|---|---|
| Winifred Atwell (piano) | 5/53 | Decca F.10110 |

## 475 THE THEME FROM LIMELIGHT
### (Terry's Theme from Limelight, Eternally)

*Composers*: Charles Chaplin, with lyrics for 'Eternally' added by Geoffrey Parsons and John Turner  
*Publishers*: Bourne Music Ltd.  

*Date of Entry*: 23.5.53  
*Highest Position*: 1  
*Weeks on Chart*: 36  

(Note: Records titled 'The Theme from Limelight' except where stated.)

*Recordings*:

| | | |
|---|---|---|
| Frank Chacksfield and his Orchestra ('Terry's Theme from Limelight') | 5/53 | Decca F.10106 |
| The Melachrino Strings | 5/53 | HMV B.10497 |
| Ron Goodwin and his Concert Orchestra | 5/53 | Parlophone R.3686 |
| Wally Stott and his Orchestra | 6/53 | Philips PB.150 |
| Jean Campbell ('Eternally') | 6/53 | Parlophone R.3703 |
| Ray Burns ('Eternally') | 6/53 | Columbia DB.3306 |
| Jimmy Young ('Eternally') | 6/53 | Decca F.10130 |
| Ron Goodwin and his Concert Orchestra | 7/53 | Parlophone (45) MSP.6035 |
| Victor Young and his Singing Strings ('Terry's Theme from Limelight') | 7/53 | Brunswick 05130 |
| Bill McGuffie (piano) | 8/53 | Parlophone R.3721 |
| Victor Silvester and his Ballroom Orchestra | 8/53 | Columbia FB.3684 |
| Jackie Gleason and his Orchestra ('Terry's Theme from Limelight') | 8/53 | Capitol CL.13962 |
| Vic Damone ('Eternally') | 9/53 | Oriole CB.1212 |
| Vic Damone ('Eternally') | 6/54 | Mercury MB.3052★ |

## 476 A WALTZ FOR THE QUEEN

*Composers*: Harry S. Pepper & Kenneth Wright  
*Publishers*: Francis Day & Hunter Ltd.  

*Date of Entry*: 23.5.53 / Pos: 24 / Wks: 1  
*Re-entry*: 6.6.53 / Pos: 24 / Wks: 1  

*Recording*:

| | | |
|---|---|---|
| Sydney Thompson and his Olde-Tyme Dance Orchestra | 5/53 | Parlophone R.3683/ (45) MSP.6029 |

## 477 TELL ME YOU'RE MINE (Per un Bacio d'amor)

| | |
|---|---|
| *Composers*: U. Bertini, Ronald Fredianelli & Nino Ravasini | *Date of Entry*: 30.5.53 |
| *Publishers*: Chappell & Co. Ltd. | *Highest Position*: 8 |
| | *Weeks on Chart*: 18 |

(The sheet music is titled 'Oh, my Wonderful One' with 'Tell me you're mine' in slightly smaller print, but all the recordings listed below are titled 'Tell me you're mine'.)

*Recordings*:

| | | |
|---|---|---|
| The Stargazers | 4/53 | Decca F.10086 |
| Eileen Draper | 4/53 | Columbia DB.3260 |
| David Hughes with The Rita Williams Singers | 4/53 | Philips PB.120 |
| The Gaylords featuring Ronnie Vincent | 4/53 | Oriole CB.1164 |
| Don Cameron | 5/53 | HMV B.10471 |
| Russ Morgan and his Orchestra (Joan Elms) | 5/53 | Brunswick 05089 |
| Eve Boswell | 5/53 | Parlophone R.3689 |
| Lee Lawrence | 8/53 | Decca F.10151 |
| The Gaylords featuring Ronnie Vincent | 6/54 | Mercury MB.3020★ |

## 478 HAVE YOU HEARD

| | |
|---|---|
| *Composers*: Lew Douglas, Frank Lavere & Roy Rodde | *Date of Entry*: 6.6.53 |
| *Publishers*: Francis Day & Hunter Ltd. | *Highest Position*: 12 |
| | *Weeks on Chart*: 17 |

*Recordings*:

| | | |
|---|---|---|
| Joni James | 4/53 | MGM.619/(45) SP.1025 |
| Dick James | 4/53 | Parlophone R.3670 |
| Tony Brent | 4/53 | Columbia DB.3278 |
| Franklyn Boyd | 4/53 | HMV B.10481 |
| Russ Morgan and his Orchestra (Russ Morgan) | 4/53 | Brunswick 05082 |
| The Beverley Sisters | 4/53 | Philips PB.129 |
| Lita Roza | 5/53 | Decca F.10109 |
| Ronnie Scott and his Orchestra (Johnnie Grant) | 5/53 | Esquire 5–088 |
| Tony Brent | 6/53 | Columbia (45) SCM.5042 |
| Ken Griffin (organ) | 8/53 | Philips PB.171 |

## 479 APRIL IN PORTUGAL (Coimbra, The Whisp'ring Serenade)

| | |
|---|---|
| *Composers*: Raul Ferrâo with Spanish lyrics by Jose Galhardo and English lyrics by Jimmy Kennedy | *Date of Entry*: 13.6.53 |
| *Publishers*: Chappell & Co. Ltd. | *Highest Position*: 4 |
| | *Weeks on Chart*: 25 |

*Recordings*:

| | | |
|---|---|---|
| Edmundo Ros and his Orchestra (Titled 'Coimbra') | 10/50 | Decca F.9529 |
| Roberto Inglez and his Orchestra (Titled 'Coimbra') | 4/51 | Parlophone R.3376 |
| Renato and his Guitar (Titled 'Coimbra') | 6/51 | Nixa BY.1506 |
| Victor Silvester and his Ballroom Orchestra | 9/52 | Columbia FB.3653 |
| Blue Barron and his Orchestra (Betty Clark and The Blue Notes) [Titled 'The Whisp'ring Serenade'] | 11/52 | MGM.573 |
| Florian Zabach (violin) | 5/53 | Brunswick 05096 |
| Les Baxter and his Orchestra | 5/53 | Capitol CL.13921 |
| Norrie Paramor and his Orchestra | 5/53 | Columbia DB.3281 |
| Edmundo Ros and his Orchestra | 5/53 | Decca F.10120 |
| The Melachrino Strings | 5/53 | HMV B.10497 |
| The Fela Sowande Rhythm Group | 5/53 | Decca F.10111 |
| Tony Martin | 6/53 | HMV B.10500 |
| Jane Morgan | 6/53 | Parlophone R.3699 |
| Georgia Carr | 6/53 | Capitol CL.13950 |
| The Johnston Brothers with The Pianotones | 6/53 | Decca F.10124 |
| Geraldo and his New Concert Orchestra | 6/53 | Philips PB.149 |
| Louis Armstrong and his Orchestra (Louis Armstrong) | 6/53 | Brunswick 05122 |
| Norrie Paramor and his Orchestra | 7/53 | Columbia (45) SCM.5051 |
| Tony Martin | 7/53 | HMV (45) 7M.136 |
| Richard Hayman and his Orchestra | 7/53 | Oriole CB.1182 |
| Vic Damone | 7/53 | Oriole CB.1186 |
| Ken Griffin (organ) | 8/53 | Philips PB.171 |
| Ethel Smith (organ) | 8/53 | Brunswick 05147 |
| Line Renaud | 8/53 | Columbia DB.3328/ (45) SCM.5055 |
| Richard Hayman and his Orchestra | 6/54 | Mercury MB.3038★ |
| Vic Damone | 6/54 | Mercury MB.3040★ |

## 480 YOUR CHEATIN' HEART

*Composer*: Hank Williams

*Publishers*: Bradbury Wood Ltd.

*Date of Entry*: 13.6.53 /
Pos: 21 / Wks: 1
*Re-entry*: 27.6.53 /
Pos: 8 / Wks: 21

*Recordings*:

| | | |
|---|---|---|
| Frankie Laine with The Norman Luboff Choir | 2/53 | Philips PB.117 |
| Joni James | 3/53 | MGM.603 |
| Louis Armstrong | 4/53 | Brunswick 05088 |
| Jan Garber and his Orchestra (Bill St Claire) | 4/53 | Capitol CL.13907 |
| Joni James | 4/53 | MGM (45) SP.1026 |
| Benny Lee | 4/53 | Decca F.10091 |
| Don Cameron | 5/53 | HMV B.10471 |
| Donald Peers | 5/53 | HMV B.10488 |

## 481 HOT TODDY

*Composers*: Ralph Flanagan & Herb Hendler

*Publishers*: Aberbach (London) Ltd.

*Date of Entry*: 13.6.53

*Highest Position*: 7
*Weeks on Chart*: 19

*Recordings*:

| | | |
|---|---|---|
| Ted Heath and his Music | 4/53 | Decca F.10093 |
| Ralph Flanagan and his Orchestra | 4/53 | HMV B.10451 |
| Red Foley | 4/53 | Brunswick 05076 |

## 482 TELL ME A STORY

*Composer*: Terry Gilkyson

*Publishers*: Cinephonic Music Co. Ltd.

*Date of Entry*: 20.6.53 /
Pos: 23 / Wks: 2
*Re-entry*: 11.7.53/
Pos: 17/Wks: 4
*2nd Re-entry*: 15.8.53 /
Pos: 23 / Wks: 1

*Recordings*:

| | | |
|---|---|---|
| Frankie Laine and Jimmy Boyd with The Norman Luboff Choir | 3/53 | Philips PB.126 |
| Carroll Levis and Mickey Maguire with The Stargazers | 6/53 | Decca F.10114 |

## 483 THE QUEEN OF TONGA

*Composer*: Jack Fishman

*Publishers*: Campbell Connelly & Co. Ltd.

*Date of Entry*: 27.6.53

*Highest Position*: 13
*Weeks on Chart*: 8

*Recordings*:

| | | |
|---|---|---|
| Edmundo Ros and his Orchestra (Edmundo Ros and The Ros-Childs) | 7/53 | Decca F.10147 |
| John Paris with The Ebonaires | 7/53 | HMV B.10527 |

## 484 SEVEN LONELY DAYS

*Composers*: Alden Shuman, Earl Shuman & Marshall Brown

*Publishers*: Leo Feist Ltd.

*Date of Entry*: 4.7.53

*Highest Position*: 4
*Weeks on Chart*: 22

*Recordings*:

| | | |
|---|---|---|
| Gisele MacKenzie with vocal group | 4/53 | Capitol CL.13920 |
| Guy Lombardo and his Royal Canadians (Kenny Gardner) | 5/53 | Brunswick 05094 |
| Cyril Stapleton and his Orchestra (Jean Campbell and vocal group) | 5/53 | Decca F.10104 |
| Bonnie Lou | 5/53 | Parlophone R.3688 |
| Joe Loss and his Orchestra (Rose Brennan) | 5/53 | HMV B.10480 |
| June Whitfield with The Rita Williams Singers | 5/53 | Philips PB.137 |
| Georgia Gibbs with The Yale Brothers | 5/53 | Oriole CB.1173 |
| Lita Roza with The Johnston Brothers | 6/53 | Decca F.10128 |
| Bonnie Lou | 7/53 | Parlophone (45) MSP.6021 |
| Georgia Gibbs with The Yale Brothers | 6/54 | Mercury MB.3029★ |

## 485 THE BREEZE

*Composers*: Tony Sacco, Dick Smith & Al Lewis

*Publishers*: Campbell Connelly & Co. Ltd.

*Date of Entry*: 4.7.53

*Highest Position*: 24
*Weeks on Chart*: 1

*Recordings*:

| | | |
|---|---|---|
| Kay Starr | 4/53 | Capitol CL.13900 |
| Trudy Richards | 8/53 | London L.1192★ |
| Humphrey Lyttleton and his Band | 2/54 | Parlophone R.3819/ (45)MSP.6076★ |

## 486 I'VE NEVER BEEN IN LOVE BEFORE

*Composer*: Frank Loesser

*Date of Entry*: 18.7.53

*Publishers*: Edwin H. Morris & Co. Ltd.

*Highest Position*: 18
*Weeks on Chart*: 4

*Recordings*:

| | | |
|---|---|---|
| Edmund Hockridge | 5/53 | Parlophone R.3697 |
| Billy Eckstine | 5/53 | MGM.627 |
| Bing Crosby | 5/53 | Brunswick 05104 |
| Robert Alda and Isabel Bigley | 5/53 | Brunswick 05103 |
| Lizbeth Webb | 6/53 | HMV B.10508 |
| Jerry Wayne | 6/53 | Philips PB.146 |
| Margaret Whiting | 6/53 | Capitol CL.13952 |
| Doris Day | 7/53 | Columbia DB.3309 |
| Victor Silvester and his Ballroom Orchestra | 7/53 | Columbia FB.3681 |
| Edmund Hockridge | 7/53 | Parlophone (45) MSP.6028 |
| Lizbeth Webb | 7/53 | HMV (45) 7M.140 |
| Leslie A. Hutchinson – 'Hutch' | 9/53 | Oriole CB.1191★ |
| Billy Eckstine | 11/53 | MGM (45) SP.1055★ |

## 487 SAY YOU'RE MINE AGAIN

*Composers*: Charles Nathan & Dave Heisler

*Date of Entry*: 18.7.53

*Publishers*: Edwin H. Morris & Co. Ltd.

*Highest Position*: 7
*Weeks on Chart*: 16

*Recordings*:

| | | |
|---|---|---|
| June Hutton and Axel Stordahl with The Boys Next Door | 5/53 | Capitol CL.13918 |
| Dolores Gray | 6/53 | Brunswick 05111 |
| Jimmy Young with The Stargazers | 7/53 | Decca F.10132 |
| Joyce Frazer | 7/53 | Columbia DB.3318 |
| Perry Como with The Ramblers | 7/53 | HMV B.10511 |
| Jane Morgan | 7/53 | Parlophone R.3713 |
| Perry Como with The Ramblers | 8/53 | HMV (45) 7M.149 |

## 488 SAY 'SI SI' (Para vigo me voy)

*Composers*: Ernesto Lecuona, Francis Luban & Al Stillman

*Date of Entry*: 25.7.53 / Pos: 20 / Wks: 1

*Publishers*: Lawrence Wright Music Co. Ltd.

*Re-entry*: 29.8.53 / Pos: 24 / Wks: 1

(Note: Eight earlier versions, including those by Glenn Miller and Harry Roy, had been deleted by the Fifties. Only one early recording survived in the catalogues – by The Andrews Sisters.)

| | | |
|---|---|---|
| The Andrews Sisters | 6/40 | Brunswick 02996 |

*Later recordings*:

| | | |
|---|---|---|
| Edmundo Ros and his Rumba Band (Edmundo Ros) | 12/51 | Decca F.9810 |
| Art Mooney's Little Band (Alan Foster and The Cloverleafs) | 6/53 | MGM.646 |
| The Mills Brothers | 7/53 | Brunswick 05129 |
| Xavier Cugat and his Orchestra (Abbe Lane) | 8/53 | HMV B.10525 |
| Max Bygraves with Peter Brough and 'Archie Andrews' | 8/53 | HMV B.10546 |
| Jimmy Palmer and his Orchestra (Tiny McDaniel and Ensemble) | 9/53 | Oriole CB.1194★ |
| Max Bygraves with Peter Brough and 'Archie Andrews' | 11/53 | HMV (45) 7M.154★ |
| Jimmy Palmer and his Orchestra (Tiny McDaniel and Ensemble) | 6/54 | Mercury MB.3044★ |

## 489 CAN'T I?

*Composer*: Leroy Lovett

*Date of Entry*: 25.7.53

*Publishers*: Southern Music Publishing Co. Ltd.

*Highest Position*: 12
*Weeks on Chart*: 14

*Recordings*:

| | | |
|---|---|---|
| Richard Hayes with The Jack Halloran Singers | 5/53 | Oriole CB.1171 |
| Nat 'King' Cole with Billy May and his Orchestra | 6/53 | Capitol CL.13937 |
| Lee Lawrence | 8/53 | Decca F.10151 |
| Victor Silvester and his Ballroom Orchestra | 12/53 | Columbia FB.3696★ |
| Richard Hayes with The Jack Halloran Singers | 6/54 | Mercury MB.3027★ |

## 490 | KISS

*Composers:* Haven Gillespie & Lionel Newman

*Publishers:* Leo Feist Ltd.

*Date of Entry:* 25.7.53 /
Pos: 24 / Wks: 1
*Re-entry:* 8.8.53/
Pos: 9/Wks: 18

*Recordings:*

| | | |
|---|---|---|
| Ginny Gibson | 3/53 | MGM.605 |
| Dean Martin | 3/53 | Capitol CL.13893 |
| Toni Arden | 6/53 | Philips PB.148 |
| Victor Silvester and his Ballroom Orchestra | 1/54 | Columbia FB.3700★ |

## 491 | MOTHER NATURE AND FATHER TIME

*Composers:* Kay Twomey, Fred Wise & Ben Weisman

*Publishers:* Aberbach (London) Ltd.

*Date of Entry:* 1.8.53

*Highest Position:* 12
*Weeks on Chart:* 14

*Recordings:*

| | | |
|---|---|---|
| Nat 'King' Cole | 5/53 | Capitol CL.13912 |
| Ray Burns | 6/53 | Columbia DB.3306 |
| Victor Silvester and his Ballroom Orchestra | 7/53 | Columbia FB.3682 |
| Dick James | 7/53 | Parlophone R.3706 |
| Dick James | 8/53 | Parlophone (45) MSP.6039 |
| Ted Heath and his Music (Dickie Valentine) | 10/53 | Decca F.10178 |

## 492 | THE BRIDGE OF SIGHS

*Composer:* Billy Reid

*Publishers:* Peter Maurice Music Co. Ltd.

*Date of Entry:* 1.8.53

*Highest Position:* 4
*Weeks on Chart:* 21

*Recordings:*

| | | |
|---|---|---|
| David Whitfield | 6/53 | Decca F.10129 |
| Reggie Goff | 6/53 | Polygon P.1074 |
| Eve Boswell | 7/53 | Parlophone R.3715 |
| Eddie MacDonald | 8/53 | HMV B.10520 |
| David Hughes | 8/53 | Philips PB.177 |
| Victor Silvester and his Ballroom Orchestra | 9/53 | Columbia FB.3687 |
| Teddy Johnson | 10/53 | Columbia DB.3372 |
| Anne Shelton | 10/53 | HMV B.10596 |
| Guy Lombardo and his Royal Canadians | 12/53 | Brunswick 05219 |
| Georgia Gibbs | 12/53 | Oriole CB.1234 |
| Anne Shelton | 12/53 | HMV (45) 7M.164 |
| Georgia Gibbs | 6/54 | Mercury MB.3071★ |

## 493 | LET'S WALK THAT-A-WAY

*Composers:* Kay Twomey, Fred Wise & Ben Weisman

*Publishers:* Aberbach (London) Ltd.

*Date of Entry:* 1.8.53

*Highest Position:* 9
*Weeks on Chart:* 16

*Recordings:*

| | | |
|---|---|---|
| Doris Day and Johnnie Ray | 6/53 | Philips PB.157 |
| The Malcolm Mitchell Trio | 7/53 | Parlophone R.3711 |
| Dennis Lotis and The Stargazers | 8/53 | Decca F.10153 |

## 494 | IS IT ANY WONDER?

*Composers:* Bob Hayes & Roy Rodde

*Publishers:* Leeds Music Ltd.

*Date of Entry:* 15.8.53

*Highest Position:* 14
*Weeks on Chart:* 12

*Recordings:*

| | | |
|---|---|---|
| Joan Dowling | 6/53 | Columbia DB.3307 |
| Jimmy Young | 6/53 | Decca F.10130 |
| Ella Mae Morse | 6/53 | Capitol CL.13930 |
| Joni James | 6/53 | MGM.642/ (45) SP.1041 |
| Billy Thorburn's The Organ, the Dance Band and Me (Doreen Harris) | 7/53 | Parlophone F.2518 |
| Donald Peers | 7/53 | HMV B.10506 |
| Ethel Smith (organ) | 7/53 | Brunswick 05135 |
| Victor Silvester and his Ballroom Orchestra | 8/53 | Columbia FB.3685 |
| David Hughes | 8/53 | Philips PB.177 |

## 495 | RUBY

*Composers:* Heinz Roemheld & Mitchell Parish

*Publishers:* Leo Feist Ltd.

*Date of Entry:* 22.8.53 /
Pos: 22 / Wks: 1
*Re-entry:* 5.9.53/
Pos: 19/Wks: 3

*Recordings:*

| | | |
|---|---|---|
| Lew Douglas and his Orchestra (The Jack Halloran Choir) | 4/53 | MGM.626 |
| Max Geldray (harmonica) | 5/53 | Columbia DB.3301 |
| Victor Young and his Singing Strings with George Fields (harmonica) | 6/53 | Brunswick 05110 |
| Les Baxter and his Orchestra featuring Danny Welton (harmonica) | 6/53 | Capitol CL.13933 |
| Vaughn Monroe and his Orchestra (Vaughn Monroe and Chorus) | 7/53 | HMV B.10510/(45) 7M.144 |
| Philip Green and his Orchestra | 7/53 | Parlophone R.3712 |
| Richard Hayman and his Orchestra | 7/53 | Oriole CB.1188 |
| Ethel Smith (organ) | 7/53 | Brunswick 05145 |
| Harry James and his Orchestra with Tony Gumina (accordion) | 7/53 | Philips PB.165 |
| Bill McGuffie (piano) | 8/53 | Parlophone R.3721 |
| Richard Hayman and his Orchestra | 6/54 | Mercury MB.3041★ |

## 496 NUMBER ONE
## (That's my darling, darling Caroline)

| | |
|---|---|
| Composer: James Willet-Robertson | Date of Entry: 22.8.53 |
| Publishers: New World Publishers Ltd. | Highest Position: 23 |
| | Weeks on Chart: 1 |

Recordings:

| | | |
|---|---|---|
| The Singers and Central Band of the RAF cond. Wing Comdr. A.E. Sims, OBE | 5/53 | Columbia DB.3279 |
| Ken Mackintosh, his saxophone, and his Orchestral (Vocal Group) | 9/53 | HMV BD.1294★ |

## 497 LOOK AT THAT GIRL

| | |
|---|---|
| Composer: Bob Merrill | Date of Entry: 22.8.53 / Pos: 6 / Wks: 16 |
| Publishers: Cinephonic Music Co. Ltd. | Re-entry: 26.12.53/ Pos: 23/Wks: 1 |

Recordings:

| | | |
|---|---|---|
| Frankie Vaughan with Ken Mackintosh and his Orchestra | 7/53 | HMV B.10529 |
| Guy Mitchell | 7/53 | Philips PB.162 |
| Dennis Lotis and The Stargazers | 8/53 | Decca F.10153 |
| Victor Silvester and his Ballroom Orchestra | 10/53 | Columbia FB.3691 |

## 498 POPPA PICCOLINO
## (Papaveri e Papere)

| | |
|---|---|
| Composers: Music by Vittorio Mascheroni, Italian lyrics by Nino Rastelli & Mario Panzeri. English lyrics by Bob Musel | Date of Entry: 5.9.53 |
| Publishers: Chappell & Co. Ltd. | Highest Position: 1 |
| | Weeks on Chart: 26 |

Recordings:

| | | |
|---|---|---|
| Beniamino Gigli (tenor) with Chorus [Titled 'Papaveri e Papere'] | 6/53 | HMV DA.2038 |
| Lys Assia [Titled 'Ba-Loom Ba-La'] | 8/53 | Decca F.10149 |
| Diana Decker | 8/53 | Columbia DB.3325 |
| Billy Cotton and his Band (Alan Breeze and The Bandits) | 10/53 | Decca F.10179 |
| The Beverley Sisters | 10/53 | Philips PB.166 |
| Petula Clark and The Children of Dr Barnardo's Homes | 10/53 | Polygon P.1082 |
| Allan Jones | 11/53 | HMV B.10588 |
| Allan Jones | 12/53 | HMV (45) 7M.161 |

## 499 BIG HEAD
## (pronounced as 'Big 'ead')

| | |
|---|---|
| Composer: Jack Meadows | Date of Entry: 19.9.53 / Pos: 24 / Wks: 2 |
| Publishers: Lawrence Wright Music Co. Ltd. | Re-entry: 7.11.53 / Pos: 18 / Wks: 9 |

Recordings:

| | | |
|---|---|---|
| Max Bygraves with The Song Pedlars [Titled 'Big 'ead'] | 8/53 | HMV B.10546 |
| Max Bygraves with The Song Pedlars [Titled 'Big 'ead'] | 11/53 | HMV (45) 7M.154 |
| Billy Cotton and his Band (Billy Cotton and Alan Breeze) | 12/53 | Decca F.10217 |

## 500 WHERE THE WINDS BLOW

| | |
|---|---|
| Composer: Terry Gilkyson | Date of Entry: 26.9.53 / Pos: 20 / Wks: 3 |
| Publishers: Dash Music Co. Ltd. | Re-entry: 24.10.53 / Pos: 24 / Wks: 1 |

Recordings:

| | | |
|---|---|---|
| Frankie Laine | 7/53 | Philips PB.167 |
| Wilfrid Thomas with Ivor Mairants (guitar) | 9/53 | Parlophone R.3739 |

## 501 VAYA CON DIOS
## (May God be with you)

| | |
|---|---|
| Composers: Larry Russell, Inez James & Buddy Pepper | Date of Entry: 26.9.53 |
| Publishers: Maddox Music Ltd. | Highest Position: 5 |
| | Weeks on Chart: 19 |

Recordings:

| | | |
|---|---|---|
| Les Paul and Mary Ford | 7/53 | Capitol CL.13943 |
| Jean Campbell | 9/53 | Parlophone R.3737 |
| David Carey | 9/53 | Columbia DB.3338 |
| Carole Carr | 9/53 | HMV B.10570 |
| The Stargazers | 9/53 | Decca F.10170 |
| Guy Lombardo and his Royal Canadians (Kenny Gardner and Bill Flanagan) | 9/53 | Brunswick 05140 |
| The Beverley Sisters | 10/53 | Philips PB.166 |
| Joe Loss and his Orchestra | 11/53 | HMV BD.6150 |
| Victor Silvester and his Ballroom Orchestra | 12/53 | Columbia FB.3696 |
| Earl Cadillac, his alto sax, and his Orchestra | 4/54 | Vogue V.2221★ |

## 502 FLIRTATION WALTZ

*Composers*: R. Heywood

*Publishers*: Bourne Music Ltd.

*Date of Entry*: 3.10.53 /
Pos:12 / Wks: 16
*Re-entry*; 30.1.54 /
Pos: 24 / Wks: 1

*Recordings*:

| | | |
|---|---|---|
| Frank Chacksfield and his Orchestra with Roy Plummer (guitar) | 12/51 | Polygon P.1027 |
| Felix King, his Piano and Strings | 2/52 | Decca F.9848 |
| Charles Smart (Compton organ) and Harold Smart (Hammond organ) | 3/52 | Parlophone R.3505 |
| Harry Roy and his Orchestra | 3/52 | Nixa NY.7761 |
| The Melachrino Strings | 8/52 | HMV B.10314 |
| Charles Smart (Compton organ) and Harold Smart (Hammond organ) | 3/53 | Parlophone (45) MSP.6016 |
| Winifred Atwell (piano) | 9/53 | Decca F.10161 |
| Art Mooney and his Orchestra (The Cloverleafs) | 1/54 | MGM.700 |
| Les Baxter and his Orchestra and Chorus | 2/54 | Capitol CL.14062★ |

## 503 THE MELBA WALTZ (Dreamtime)

*Composers*: Mischa Spoliansky & Norman Newell

*Publishers*: Chappell & Co. Ltd.

*Date of Entry*: 3.10.53 /
Pos: 23 / Wks: 1
*Re-entry*: 7.11.53 /
Pos: 24 / Wks: 3

*Recordings*:

| | | |
|---|---|---|
| Ron Goodwin and his Concert Orchestra | 9/53 | Parlophone R. 3736 |
| Norrie Paramor and his Orchestra | 9/53 | Columbia DB.3336 |
| Victor Young and his Singing Strings | 9/53 | Brunswick 05157 |
| Patrice Munsel | 9/53 | HMV B.10532 |
| Jeff Morley and his Orchestra | 9/53 | Philips PB.168 |
| Mantovani and his Orchestra | 9/53 | Decca F.10174 |
| The Melachrino Strings | 10/53 | HMV B.10552 |
| Josef Locke | 10/53 | Columbia DB.3363 |
| Ron Goodwin and his Concert Orchestra | 11/53 | Parlophone (45) MSP.6044 |
| Norrie Paramor and his Orchestra | 11/53 | Columbia (45) SCM.5065 |
| Patrice Munsel | 11/53 | HMV (45) 7M.152 |

## 504 HEY JOE

*Composer*: Boudleaux Bryant

*Publishers*: Robbins Music Corporation Ltd.

*Date of Entry*: 3.10.53

*Highest Position*: 14
*Weeks on Chart*: 9

*Recordings*:

| | | |
|---|---|---|
| Frankie Laine with The Norman Luboff Choir | 8/53 | Philips PB.172 |
| Ronnie Meede | 9/53 | Decca F.10167 |
| Frankie Vaughan | 10/53 | HMV B.10560 |

## 505 SWEDISH RHAPSODY (Midsummer vigil)

*Composer*: Hugo Alfven, adaptation by Percy Faith

*Publishers*: Campbell Connelly & Co. Ltd.

*Date of Entry*: 10.10.53

*Highest Position*: 2
*Weeks on Chart*: 34

*Recordings*:

| | | |
|---|---|---|
| Percy Faith and his Orchestra | 4/53 | Philips PB.128 |
| Ethel Smith (organ) | 5/53 | Brunswick 05120 |
| Mantovani and his Orchestra | 8/53 | Decca F.10168 |
| Ray Martin and his Concert Orchestra | 9/53 | Columbia DB.3346 |
| Harold Smart (Hammond organ) and his Quartet | 10/53 | Parlophone R.3753 |
| Joe Loss and his Orchestra | 11/53 | HMV BD.6150 |
| Ray Martin and his Concert Orchestra | 11/53 | Columbia (45) SCM.5063 |
| Harold Smart (Hammond organ) and his Quartet | 11/53 | Parlophone (45) MSP.6050 |
| Earl Cadillac, his alto sax, and his Orchestra | 3/54 | Vogue V.2217 |
| Malcolm Lockyer and his Strict Tempo Music for Dancing | 6/54 | Decca F.10320★ |
| Mantovani and his Orchestra | 10/54 | Decca 45-F.10168★ |

## 506 YOU'RE JUST IN LOVE

*Composer*: Irving Berlin

*Publishers*: Irving Berlin Ltd.

*Date of Entry*: 10.10.53

*Highest Position*: 23
*Weeks on Chart*: 1

*Recordings*:

| | | |
|---|---|---|
| Ethel Merman and Dick Haymes | 3/52 | Brunswick 04877 |
| Guy Mitchell and Rosemary Clooney | 3/52 | Columbia DB.3018 |
| Joe Loss and his Orchestra | 3/52 | HMV BD.6126 |
| Perry Como with The Fontane Sisters | 3/52 | HMV B.10221 |
| Billie Worth and Jeff Warren | 5/52 | Columbia DB.3068 |
| Roberto Inglez and his Orchestra | 5/52 | Parlophone R.3521 |
| Victor Silvester and his Ballroom Orchestra | 5/52 | Columbia FB.3640 |

## 507 WHEN YOU HEAR BIG BEN (You're home again)

*Composers*: Harry Leon, Mark Malloy & Jack Scott

*Publishers*: Box & Cox (Publications) Ltd.

*Date of Entry*: 10.10.53

*Highest Position*: 5
*Weeks on Chart*: 19

*Recordings*:

| | | |
|---|---|---|
| Josef Locke with Reginald Dixon (organ) | 6/53 | Columbia DB.3320 |
| Vera Lynn | 8/53 | Decca F.10150 |
| Eddie MacDonald | 8/53 | HMV B.10520 |
| Billy Cotton and his Band (Doreen Stephens and Choir) | 10/53 | Decca F.10179 |

## 508 BE MINE

| | | |
|---|---|---|
| *Composers:* Tolchard Evans & Johnny May | | *Date of Entry:* 10.10.53/ Pos: 23/Wks: 2 |
| *Publishers:* Sydney Bron Music Co. | | *Re-entry:* 5.12.53 / Pos: 23 / Wks: 1 |

*Recordings:*

| | | |
|---|---|---|
| Gerry Brereton | 9/53 | Parlophone R.3729 |
| Al Martino | 9/53 | Capitol CL.13973 |
| Victor Silvester and his Ballroom Orchestra | 10/53 | Columbia FB.3690 |
| Billy Cotton and his Band (Doreen Stephens) | 10/53 | Decca F.10186 |
| Norman Grant and his Orchestra for Dancers | 10/54 | Esquire 5–098★ |

## 509 ANSWER ME (Mütterlein)

| | |
|---|---|
| *Composers:* Gerhard Winkler, Fred Rauch & Carl Sigman | *Date of Entry:* 17.10.53 |
| *Publishers:* Bourne Music Ltd. | *Highest Position:* 1 |
| | *Weeks on Chart:* 27 |

*Recordings:*

| | | |
|---|---|---|
| David Whitfield | 10/53 | Decca F.10192 |
| Frankie Laine with The Norman Luboff Choir | 10/53 | Philips PB.196 |
| Anne Shelton with The George Mitchell Choir | 10/53 | HMV B.10596 |
| Jean Campbell | 10/53 | Parlophone R.3769 |
| Monty Norman | 11/53 | Columbia DB.3398 |
| Harry Farmer (organ) | 12/53 | Decca F.10216 |
| Reggie Goff | 12/53 | Polygon P.1087 |
| Anne Shelton with The George Mitchell Choir | 12/53 | HMV (45) 7M.164 |
| Victor Silvester and his Ballroom Orchestra | 1/54 | Columbia FB. 3699 |
| Nat 'King' Cole | 2/54 | Capitol CL.14055 |

## 510 WISH YOU WERE HERE

| | |
|---|---|
| *Composer:* Harold Rome | *Date of Entry:* 24.10.53 |
| *Publishers:* Chappell & Co. Ltd. | *Highest Position:* 7 |
| | *Weeks on Chart:* 16 |

*Recordings:*

| | | |
|---|---|---|
| Gerry Brereton | 10/53 | Parlophone R.3752 |
| Eddie Fisher | 10/53 | HMV B.10564 |
| Jimmy Young | 10/53 | Decca F.10187 |
| Fran Warren | 10/53 | MGM.683 |
| Roberto Inglez and his Orchestra | 11/53 | Parlophone R.3765 |
| Eddie Fisher | 11/53 | HMV (45) 7M.159 |
| Jackie Brown (Hammond organ) | 11/53 | Columbia DB.3382 |
| Bruce Trent | 11/53 | Philips PB.200 |
| Victor Silvester and his Ballroom Orchestra | 12/53 | Columbia FB.3697 |

## 511 I SAW MOMMY KISSING SANTA CLAUS

| | |
|---|---|
| *Composer:* Tommie Connor | *Date of Entry:* 31.10.53 |
| *Publishers:* Edwin H. Morris & Co. Ltd. | *Highest Position:* 1 |
| | *Weeks on Chart:* 11 |

*Recordings:*

| | | |
|---|---|---|
| The Beverley Sisters | 10/53 | Philips PB.188 |
| Mickey Maguire with The Keynotes | 11/53 | Decca F.10203 |
| Molly Bee | 11/53 | Capitol CL.14017 |
| Billy Cotton and his Band (The Mill Girls and The Bandits) | 11/53 | Decca F.10206 |
| Jimmy Boyd accompanied by Norman Luboff | 11/53 | Columbia DB.3365 |
| Spike Jones and his City Slickers (George Rock and The Mitchell Boys' Choir) | 11/53 | HMV B.10580 |
| Peter Brough and 'Archie Andrews' | 12/53 | HMV BD.1306 |
| Jimmy Boyd accompanied by Norman Luboff | 12/53 | Columbia (45) SCM.5072 |
| Spike Jones and his City Slickers (George Rock and The Mitchell Boys' Choir) | 12/53 | HMV (45) 7M.160 |
| The Beverley Sisters | 11/54 | Philips PB.378★ |

## 512 CRYING IN THE CHAPEL

| | |
|---|---|
| *Composer:* Artie Glenn | *Date of Entry:* 31.10.53 |
| *Publishers:* Edwin H. Morris & Co. Ltd. | *Highest Position:* 12 |
| | *Weeks on Chart:* 12 |

*Recordings:*

| | | |
|---|---|---|
| The Orioles | 9/53 | London L.1201 |
| Rex Allen | 9/53 | Brunswick 05162 |
| Wesley Tuttle | 9/53 | Capitol CL.13975 |
| Ella Fitzgerald with The Ray Charles Singers | 9/53 | Brunswick 05149 |
| June Valli | 10/53 | HMV B.10568 |
| Lee Lawrence | 10/53 | Decca F.10177 |
| Robert Earl with The Rita Williams Singers | 10/53 | Philips PB.185 |
| Ken Griffin (organ) | 10/53 | Philips PB.198 |
| Darrell Glenn | 11/53 | Oriole CB.1235 |
| Katie Stevens | 1/54 | Columbia DB.3410 |

## 513 CHICKA BOOM

| | |
|---|---|
| *Composer:* Bob Merrill | *Date of Entry:* 7.11.53 |
| *Publishers:* Dash Music Co. Ltd. | *Highest Position:* 9 |
| | *Weeks on Chart:* 15 |

*Recordings:*

| | | |
|---|---|---|
| The Keynotes | 10/53 | Decca F.10185 |
| Guy Mitchell | 10/53 | Philips PB.178 |
| Sonny Player with The Batsmen | 10/53 | Parlophone R.3763 |

## 514 YOU, YOU, YOU

| | | |
|---|---|---|
| *Composers:* Robert Mellin & Lotar Olias | *Date of Entry:* 7.11.53 / Pos: 21 /Wks: 1 | |
| *Publishers:* Robert Mellin Ltd. | *Re-entry:* 21.11.53 / Pos: 11 / Wks: 12 | |

*Recordings:*

| | | |
|---|---|---|
| The Ames Brothers | 9/53 | HMV B.10543 |
| The Stargazers | 9/53 | Decca F.10170 |
| Teddy Johnson | 10/53 | Columbia DB.3372 |
| Ken Remo | 10/53 | MGM.677 |
| The Ames Brothers | 11/53 | HMV (45) 7M.153 |
| Ken Remo | 11/53 | MGM (45) SP.1063 |
| Billy Thorburn and his Strict Tempo Music | 12/53 | Parlophone F.2524 |

## 515 GOLDEN TANGO

| | | |
|---|---|---|
| *Composers:* Victor Silvester & Ernest Wilson | *Date of Entry:* 14.11.53/ Pos: 23/Wks: 1 | |
| *Publishers:* Lawrence Wright Music Co. Ltd. | *Re-entry:* 28.11.53 / Pos: 11 / Wks: 18 | |
| | *2nd re-entry:* 17.4.54 / Pos: 20 / Wks: 1 | |

(Note: The original title of this song was 'Gold of the Incas' and it was recorded by Victor Silvester under this title and released in February 1953. When the recording by Winifred Atwell under the title 'Golden Tango' was released seven months later and became a hit, the Silvester release was retitled 'Golden Tango'.)

*Recordings:*

| | | |
|---|---|---|
| Victor Silvester and his Silver Strings | 2/53 | Columbia DB.3235 |
| Winifred Atwell (piano) | 9/53 | Decca F.10161 |
| Frank Chacksfield and his Orchestra | 10/53 | Decca F.10181 |
| Charles Williams and his Concert Orchestra | 11/53 | Columbia DB.3370 |

## 516 RICOCHET

| | | |
|---|---|---|
| *Composers:* Larry Coleman, Joe Darion & Norman Gimbel | *Date of Entry:* 21.11.53 | |
| *Publishers:* Victoria Music Publishing Co. Ltd. | *Highest Position:* 5 Weeks on Chart: 16 | |

*Recordings:*

| | | |
|---|---|---|
| Joan Regan and The Squadronaires dir. Ronnie Aldrich | 10/53 | Decca F.10193 |
| Vicki Young | 10/53 | Capitol CL.13996 |
| Billie Anthony | 12/53 | Columbia DB.3400 |
| Alma Cogan with Ken Mackintosh and his Orchestra | 12/53 | HMV B.10615/ (45) 7M.173 |
| Guy Lombardo and his Royal Canadians | 12/53 | Brunswick 05219 |
| Billy Thorburn and his Strict Tempo Music | 1/54 | Parlophone F.2527 |

## 517 IF YOU LOVE ME – I won't care (Hyme à l'amour)

| | | |
|---|---|---|
| *Composers:* Marguerite Monnot & Edith Piaf. English lyrics by Geoffrey Parsons | *Date of Entry:* 21.11.53 | |
| *Publishers:* World Wide Music Co. Ltd. | *Highest Position:* 5 Weeks on Chart: 20 | |

*Recordings:*

| | | |
|---|---|---|
| Maurice Winnick and his Sweet Music (Doreen Lundy) [Titled 'While we love'] | 12/51 | HMV BD.6115 |
| Dorothy Squires | 9/53 | Polygon P.1077 |
| Rose Brennan with Joe Loss and his Orchestra | 10/53 | HMV B.10572 |
| Robert Earl | 10/53 | Philips PB.185 |
| Ray Burns | 10/53 | Columbia DB.3352 |
| Vera Lynn with Charles Smart (organ) | 11/53 | Decca F.10196 |
| Eve Boswell | 11/53 | Parlophone R.3759 |
| Kay Starr | 4/54 | Capitol CL.14111 |
| Bing Crosby | 7/54 | Brunswick 05313★ |

(Notes: The Maurice Winnick recording was deleted by HMV on 31 January 1954. The Edith Piaf version was available to special order on Columbia DCF.58 and DCF.67. For the return of the song to the charts in 1959, see Song No. 1083.)

## 518 RAGS TO RICHES

| | | |
|---|---|---|
| *Composers:* Richard Adler & Jerry Ross | *Date of Entry:* 5.12.53 | |
| *Publishers:* Chappell & Co. Ltd. | *Highest Position:* 3 Weeks on Chart: 17 | |

*Recordings:*

| | | |
|---|---|---|
| David Hughes | 11/53 | Philips PB.208 |
| David Whitfield and Stanley Black and his Orchestra | 11/53 | Decca F.10207 |
| Georgie Shaw | 11/53 | Brunswick 05191 |
| Billy Ward and his Dominoes | 12/53 | Parlophone R.3789 |
| Harry Farmer (Hammond organ) | 12/53 | Decca F.10216 |
| Reggie Goff | 12/53 | Polygon P.1087 |
| Ray Burns | 12/53 | Columbia DB.3393/ (45) SCM.5077 |
| Les Howard | 12/53 | HMV B.10610/ (45) 7M.171 |
| Billy Thorburn and his Strict Tempo Music | 1/54 | Parlophone F.2527 |
| Tony Bennett | 1/54 | Philips PB.216 |

## 519 WHERE DID MY SNOWMAN GO?

*Composers*: Freddie Poser & Geoffrey Venis    *Date of Entry*: 5.12.53

*Publishers*: Polyphone Music Co.    *Highest Position*: 22
*Weeks on Chart*: 3

*Recordings*:

| | | |
|---|---|---|
| Petula Clark with Children of Dr Barnardo's Homes | 11/52 | Polygon P.1056 |
| Billy Cotton and his Band (The Mill Girls and The Bandits) | 11/53 | Decca F.10201 |
| Molly Bee | 11/53 | Capitol CL.14017 |
| Rex Allen with Children's Chorus | 12/53 | Brunswick 05223 |
| Patti Page | 1/54 | Oriole CB.1251 |
| Patti Page | 6/54 | Mercury MB.3086★ |

## 520 WHEN SANTA GOT STUCK UP THE CHIMNEY

*Composer*: Jimmy Grafton    *Date of Entry*: 12.12.53

*Publishers*: Michael Reine Music Co. Ltd.    *Highest Position*: 13
*Weeks on Chart*: 4

*Recordings*:

| | | |
|---|---|---|
| Billy Cotton and his Band (Billy Cotton and The Bandits) | 12/53 | Decca F.10217 |
| Billy Cotton and his Band (Billy Cotton and The Bandits) | 12/54 | Decca F.10405 (&45-) |

## 521 OH! MY PA-PA (O Mein Papa)

*Composers*: Paul Burkhard, Geoffrey Parsons & John Turner    *Date of Entry*: 12.12.53

*Publishers*: Peter Maurice Music Co. Ltd.    *Highest Position*: 1
*Weeks on Chart*: 26

*Recordings*:

(a) Titled 'Oh! My Pa-Pa'

| | | |
|---|---|---|
| Lys Assia with Frank Weir and his Orchestra | 12/53 | Decca F.10227 |
| The Radio Revellers | 12/53 | Polygon P.1092 |
| Annette Klooger | 1/54 | Parlophone R.3793 |

| | | |
|---|---|---|
| Diana Decker | 1/54 | Columbia DB.3407/ (45)SCM.5083 |
| Billy Cotton and his Band (Alan Breeze and The Bandits) | 1/54 | Decca F.10226 |
| Muriel Smith | 1/54 | Philips PB.218 |
| Ray Anthony and his Orchestra (Ray Anthony – trumpet) [The Anthony Choir] | 1/54 | Capitol CL.14045 |
| The Beverley Sisters | 2/54 | Philips PB.231 |
| Russ Morgan and his Orchestra (Phil Capicotto – trumpet) [The Morganaires] | 2/54 | Brunswick 05245 |

(b) Titled 'O Mein Papa'

| | | |
|---|---|---|
| Lys Assia with orchestra conducted by Paul Burkhard (In German) | 5/53 | Decca F.10097 |
| Eddie Calvert – the Man with the Golden Trumpet | 9/53 | Columbia DB.3337 |
| The Brasshats conducted by Reg Owen | 12/53 | Decca F.10218 |
| Lys Assia with orchestra conducted by Paul Burkhard [In German] | 10/54 | Decca 45-F.10097★ |

(c) Titled 'O my Papa'

| | | |
|---|---|---|
| Eddie Fisher | 12/53 | HMV B.10614/ (45) 7M.172 |
| Ken Mackintosh and his Orchestra (The Peter Knight Singers) | 1/54 | HMV BD.1307 |

## 522 ISTANBUL (Not Constantinople)

*Composers*: Jimmy Kennedy & Nat Simon    *Date of Entry*: 12.12.53

*Publishers*: Aberbach (London) Ltd.    *Highest Position*: 9
*Weeks on Chart*: 11

*Recordings*:

| | | |
|---|---|---|
| Frankie Vaughan with The Peter Knight Singers | 11/53 | HMV B.10599/ (45) 7M.167 |
| Ken Mackintosh, his Saxophone, and his Orchestra | 12/53 | HMV BD.1302 |
| The Malcolm Mitchell Trio | 12/53 | Parlophone R.3783 |
| The Four Lads | 12/53 | Philips PB.176 |
| Edmundo Ros and his Orchestra (Edmundo Ros and The Johnston Brothers) | 12/53 | Decca F.10214 |
| The Radio Revellers | 12/53 | Polygon P.1090 |
| Joe 'Fingers' Carr and his Ragtime Band | 1/54 | Capitol CL.14049 |
| Edmundo Ros and his Orchestra (Edmundo Ros and The Johnston Brothers) | 10/54 | Decca 45-F.10214★ |

# 1954

For the first time a song stayed in the charts for more than a year – this was *The happy wanderer*. Published by Bosworth's, it was their only hit of the year and they advertised it as 'a best-selling record (The Obernkirchen Children's Choir) in January and a best-selling song in February'. The two most popular sheet music successes of the year in America were *Wanted* and *Changing partners*. The latter, published by Robert Mellin Limited, was the subject of a strange agreement between the publishers and the record companies – Mellin's insisted that all recordings of the song should be issued here on the same day, and therefore a glance at Song No. 534 will show that eleven recordings of the song went on sale on that day in February. Jack Jackson broadcast his final 'Round-up' show on 3 April but some of the big song successes here came from Doris Day's musical 'Calamity Jane' with no less than three of them getting into the sheet music charts and *Secret love* staying at the top for seven weeks. *Ebb tide,* which had been a big hit for Frank Chacksfield in the States (No. 2) and a No. 1 sheet music seller for three weeks at the end of 1953, surprisingly reached only 9th place in both British charts. The first Decca group popular 45 rpm issues were released in October, with quite a few earlier issues being 'honoured' in this way with a microgroove pressing including 1949's *Harry Lime theme*. Woolworth's produced its Embassy label as the year drew to a close and Larry Cross's *Three coins in the fountain* was the first issue on WB.101. The magic seemed to have deserted Bob

| | MOST WEEKS ON THE CHARTS TOP SIX | |
|---|---|---|
| Pos | | Wks |
| 1 | *The happy wanderer* | 45 |
| 2 | *Heart of my heart* | 32 |
| 3= | *Don't laugh at me* | 30 |
| 3= | *The book* | 30 |
| 3= | *Secret love* | 30 |
| 3= | *Little things mean a lot* | 30 |

Merrill in 1954 – only two songs of his reached the charts, with the highest placed at No. 22. In June much of the Oriole/Mercury catalogue was split so that the American Mercury titles now appeared on their own label with MB series numbering. It is reputed that only a handful were actually pressed, due to considerable stocks still being available of the Oriole-labelled records, but all are included in this volume as they were listed in a Mercury numerical catalogue of the time. However, the few that did have the new Mercury number and were available were still pressed by Oriole Records. The long awaited Coral recordings became available from August via Decca and labelled as Vogue Coral.

# SONG CHARTS

## 523   CLOUD LUCKY SEVEN

| | |
|---|---|
| *Composers*: Charles Tobias & Peter De Rose | *Date of Entry*: 2.1.54 |
| *Publishers*: Robbins Music Corporation Ltd. | *Highest Position*: 6 <br> *Weeks on Chart*: 16 |

*Recordings*:

| | | |
|---|---|---|
| Frankie Vaughan with The Peter Knight Singers | 11/53 | HMV B.10599/ (45) 7M.167 |
| Guy Mitchell | 11/53 | Philips PB.210 |

## 524   HELLO YOUNG LOVERS

| | |
|---|---|
| *Composers*: Richard Rodgers & Oscar Hammerstein II | *Date of Entry*: 2.1.54 |
| *Publishers*: Williamson Music Ltd. | *Highest Position*: 24 <br> *Weeks on Chart*: 1 |

*Recordings*:

| | | |
|---|---|---|
| Gertrude Lawrence | 10/53 | Brunswick 05169 |
| Frank Sinatra | 10/53 | Columbia DB.3347 |
| Perry Como | 10/53 | HMV B.10541 |
| Margaret Whiting | 10/53 | Capitol CL.13990 |
| Bing Crosby | 10/53 | Brunswick 05172 |
| Jane Powell | 10/53 | MGM.675 |
| Perry Como | 11/53 | HMV (45) 7M.155 |
| Jane Powell | 11/53 | MGM (45) SP.1062 |
| Valerie Hobson | 11/53 | Philips PB.192 |
| Eddy Howard and his Orchestra (Eddy Howard) | 11/53 | Oriole CB.1233 |
| Eddy Howard and his Orchestra (Eddy Howard) | 6/54 | Mercury MB.3070★ |

## 525   EBB TIDE

| | |
|---|---|
| *Composers*: Robert Maxwell & Carl Sigman | *Date of Entry*: 9.1.54 |
| *Publishers*: Robbins Music Corporation Ltd. | *Highest Position*: 9 <br> *Weeks on Chart*: 18 |

*Recordings*:

| | | |
|---|---|---|
| Frank Chacksfield and his Orchestra | 6/53 | Decca F.10122 |
| Bill McGuffie Quartet with Marie Korchinska (harp) | 9/53 | Parlophone R.3741 |
| Jimmy Young | 10/53 | Decca F.10187 |
| Vic Damone | 10/53 | Oriole CB.1226 |
| David Hughes | 11/53 | Philips PB.208 |
| Charlie Applewhite | 12/53 | Brunswick 05214 |
| Bobby Maxwell (harp) | 12/53 | Oriole CB.1237 |
| Lita Roza with Ted Heath and his Music | 1/54 | Decca F.10239 |
| The Ink Spots | 2/54 | Parlophone R.3817/ (45) MSP.6074 |
| Jerry Colonna | 2/54 | Brunswick 05243 |
| Victor Silvester and his Ballroom Orchestra | 3/54 | Columbia FB.3705 |
| Vic Damone | 6/54 | Mercury MB.3064★ |
| Bobby Maxwell (harp) | 6/54 | Mercury MB.3073★ |
| Jerry Colonna | 10/54 | Brunswick 45–05243★ |

## 526   BLOWING WILD (The Ballad of Black Gold)

| | |
|---|---|
| *Composers*: Dimitri Tiomkin & Paul Francis Webster | *Date of Entry*: 9.1.54 |
| *Publishers*: Harms-Connelly Ltd. | *Highest Position*: 10 <br> *Weeks on Chart*: 12 |

*Recordings*:

| | | |
|---|---|---|
| Frankie Laine | 11/53 | Philips PB.207 |
| Edmundo Ros and his Orchestra (Edmundo Ros and The Johnston Brothers) | 12/53 | Decca F.10214 |
| Jack Parnell and his Orchestra (Dennis Hale) | 4/54 | Parlophone R.3852/ (45) MSP.6094 |
| Edmundo Ros and his Orchestra (Edmundo Ros and The Johnston Brothers) | 10/54 | Decca 45-F.10214★ |

## 527 THE CREEP

| | | |
|---|---|---|
| *Composers*: Andy Burton & Carl Sigman | | *Date of Entry*: 9.1.54 |
| *Publishers*: Robbins Music Corporation Ltd. | | *Highest Position*: 15 *Weeks on Chart*: 9 |

*Recordings*:
| | | |
|---|---|---|
| Ken Mackintosh, his Saxophone, and his Orchestra | 10/53 | HMV BD.1295 |
| Ted Heath and his Music | 12/53 | Decca F.10222 |
| Robin Richmond (organ and clavioline) | 12/53 | Polygon P.1091 |
| Jack Parnell and his Music Makers (The Sapphires) | 1/54 | Parlophone R.3802/ (45) MSP.6066 |
| The Tanner Sisters | 1/54 | HMV B.10629 |
| Stan Kenton and his Orchestra | 1/54 | Capitol CL.14054 |
| Art Mooney and his Orchestra | 1/54 | MGM.700 |
| The Johnston Brothers | 1/54 | Decca F.10234 |
| Lee Roy and his Band | 2/54 | Philips PB.226 |
| Jerry Gray and his Orchestra (Linda Lee) | 2/54 | Brunswick 05247 |
| Ralph Marterie and his Orchestra | 2/54 | Oriole CB.1259 |
| Ralph Marterie and his Orchestra | 6/54 | Mercury MB.3094★ |
| Ted Heath and his Music | 10/54 | Decca 45-F.10222★ |
| The Johnston Brothers | 10/54 | Decca 45-F.10234★ |

## 528 TENNESSEE WIG WALK

| | | |
|---|---|---|
| *Composers*: Larry Coleman & Norman Gimbel | | *Date of Entry*: 16.1.54 |
| *Publishers*: Francis Day & Hunter Ltd. | | *Highest Position*: 3 *Weeks on Chart*: 21 |

*Recordings*:
| | | |
|---|---|---|
| Bonnie Lou | 9/53 | Parlophone R.3730 |
| Bonnie Lou | 11/53 | Parlophone (45) MSP.6048 |
| Russ Morgan and his Orchestra (Betsy Gay) | 11/53 | Brunswick 05202 |
| Suzi Miller and The Johnston Brothers | 2/54 | Decca F.10264 |

## 529 THAT'S AMORE

| | | |
|---|---|---|
| *Composers*: Harry Warren & Jack Brooks | | *Date of Entry*: 16.1.54 |
| *Publishers*: Victoria Music Publishing Co. Ltd. | | *Highest Position*: 5 *Weeks on Chart*: 14 |

*Recordings*:
| | | |
|---|---|---|
| Dean Martin | 11/53 | Capitol CL.14008 |
| Dennis Lotis | 2/54 | Decca F.10243 |
| Blue Barron and his Orchestra (The Blue Notes) | 2/54 | MGM.717 |

## 530 FROM HERE TO ETERNITY

| | | |
|---|---|---|
| *Composers*: Fred Karger & Robert Wells | | *Date of Entry*: 23.1.54/ Pos: 13/Wks: 10 |
| *Publishers*: Dash Music Co. Ltd. | | *Re-entry*: 10.4.54/ Pos: 23/Wks: 1 |

*Recordings*:
| | | |
|---|---|---|
| Monty Norman | 11/53 | Columbia DB.3398 |
| Les Howard | 12/53 | HMV B.10610/ (45) 7M.171 |
| Joe Loss and his Orchestra | 12/53 | HMV BD.6154 |
| Gerry Brereton | 12/53 | Parlophone R.3777/ (45) MSP.6056 |
| Stanley Black and his Orchestra | 12/53 | Decca F.10209 |
| Frank Sinatra | 12/53 | Capitol CL.14023 |
| Gary Miller | 1/54 | Philips PB.217 |
| Roy Hamilton | 6/55 | Philips PB.448★ |

## 531 DON'T EVER LEAVE ME

| | | |
|---|---|---|
| *Composers*: Max & Harry Nesbitt & Rodd Arden | | *Date of Entry*: 23.1.54/ Pos: 24/Wks: 1 |
| *Publishers*: Bluebird Music Co. | | *Re-entry*: 13.2.54/ Pos: 23/Wks: 1 |

*Recordings*:
| | | |
|---|---|---|
| Eve Boswell | 12/53 | Parlophone R.3784 |
| The Radio Revellers | 12/53 | Polygon P.1092 |

## 532 MY HEART BELONGS TO ONLY YOU

| | | |
|---|---|---|
| *Composers*: Frank & Dorothy Daniels | | *Date of Entry*: 30.1.54 |
| *Publishers*: Edward Kassner Music Co. Ltd. | | *Highest Position*: 16 *Weeks on Chart*: 7 |

*Recordings*:
| | | |
|---|---|---|
| June Christy | 2/53 | Capitol CL.13867 |
| Peter Morton | 6/53 | Columbia DB.3298 |
| Suzi Miller | 12/53 | Decca F.10205 |
| Annette Klooger | 1/54 | Parlophone R.3793 |
| Rose Brennan with Joe Loss and his Orchestra | 1/54 | HMV B.10630 |

## 533 | I SEE THE MOON

| Composer: Meredith Willson | | Date of Entry: 6.2.54 |
|---|---|---|
| Publishers: B. Feldman & Co. Ltd. | | Highest Position: 1 |
| | | Weeks on Chart: 22 |

Recordings:

| The Stargazers with Syd Dean and his Orchestra | 12/53 | Decca F.10213 |
|---|---|---|
| Dick Todd | 3/54 | Brunswick 05259 |
| Lou Preager and his Orchestra (The Ragpickers) | 3/54 | Polygon P.1106 |
| Don Cameron with Morton Fraser's Harmonica Band | 3/54 | HMV B.10675 |
| The Stargazers with Syd Dean and his Orchestra | 10/54 | Decca 45-F.10213★ |

## 534 | CHANGING PARTNERS

| Composers: Larry Coleman & Joe Darion | | Date of Entry: 6.2.54 |
|---|---|---|
| Publishers: Robert Mellin Ltd. | | Highest Position: 2 |
| | | Weeks on Chart: 27 |

Recordings:

| Patti Page | 2/54 | Oriole CB.1254 |
|---|---|---|
| Dorothy Squires | 2/54 | Polygon P.1096 |
| The Beverley Sisters | 2/54 | Philips PB.231 |
| Lita Roza | 2/54 | Decca F.10240 |
| Kay Starr | 2/54 | Capitol CL.14050 |
| Bing Crosby with Jud Conlon's Rhythmaires | 2/54 | Brunswick 05244 |
| Ray Burns | 2/54 | Columbia DB.3427 |
| Dinah Shore | 2/54 | HMV B.10636/ (45) 7M.183 |
| Donald Peers | 2/54 | HMV B.10640 |
| Joe Loss and his Orchestra | 2/54 | HMV BD.6160 |
| Vivian Blaine | 2/54 | Parlophone R.3807 |
| Vivian Blaine | 3/54 | Parlophone (45) MSP.6070 |
| Victor Silvester and his Ballroom Orchestra | 3/54 | Columbia FB.3704 |
| Billy Thorburn and his Strict Tempo Music | 3/54 | Parlophone F.2531 |
| Malcolm Lockyer and his Strict Tempo Music for Dancing | 4/54 | Decca F.10304 |
| Homer and Jethro [Titled 'Swappin' Partners'] | 5/54 | HMV B.10687/ (45) 7M.211 |
| Patti Page | 6/54 | Mercury MB.3089 |
| Bing Crosby with Jud Conlon's Rhythmaires | 10/54 | Brunswick 45-05244★ |
| Lita Roza | 10/54 | Decca 45-F.10240★ |

## 535 | TENDERLY

| Composers: Jack Lawrence & Walter Gross | | Date of Entry: 6.2.54/ Pos: 24/Wks: 1 |
|---|---|---|
| Publishers: Edwin H. Morris & Co. Ltd. | | Re-entry: 27.2.54/ Pos: 22/Wks: 2 |
| | | 2nd re-entry: 3.4.54/ Pos: 23/Wks: 1 |

Recordings:

| Randy Brooks and his Orchestra | 6/48 | Brunswick 03900 |
|---|---|---|
| Clark Dennis with The Walter Gross Trio | 2/49 | Capitol CL.13043 |
| Woody Herman and his Orchestra | 4/50 | Capitol CL.13184 |
| Sarah Vaughan | 10/50 | MGM.331 |
| Ray Anthony and his Orchestra | 11/50 | Capitol CL.13397 |
| George Shearing (piano) | 1/51 | MGM.353 |
| The Melachrino Strings | 3/52 | HMV B.10230 |
| Rosemary Clooney | 7/52 | Columbia DB.3099 |
| David Rose and his Orchestra | 9/52 | MGM.554 |
| Billy May and his Orchestra | 11/52 | Capitol CL.13817 |
| The Jud Conlon Singers | 12/53 | Brunswick 05215 |
| Eddie Calvert – The Man with the Golden Trumpet | 1/54 | Columbia DB.3409/ (45) SCM.5084 |
| Dick James | 1/54 | Parlophone R.3791 |
| Joe Loss and his Orchestra | 1/54 | HMV BD.6157 |
| Philip Green and his Orchestra | 2/54 | Parlophone R.3808 |
| Semprini (piano) | 2/54 | HMV B.10634 |
| Walter Gross (piano) | 2/54 | MGM.712/(45) (45) SP.1070 |
| Nat 'King' Cole | 3/54 | Capitol CL.14061 |
| Philip Green and his Orchestra | 3/54 | Parlophone (45) MSP.6071 |
| Billy Eckstine | 3/54 | MGM.724/ (45) SP.1082 |
| Stan Kenton and his Orchestra | 4/54 | Capitol CL.14092 |

## 536 | DON'T LEAVE ME NOW

| Composer: Edward Lisbona | Date of Entry: 6.2.54 |
|---|---|
| Publishers: Victoria Music Publishing Co. Ltd. | Highest Position: 24 |
| | Weeks on Chart: 1 |

Recordings:

| Don Cherry | 6/52 | Brunswick 04926 |
|---|---|---|
| Dickie Valentine | 7/53 | Decca F.10134 |
| Vera Lynn | 12/53 | Decca F.10230 |
| Anne Shelton | 1/54 | HMV B.10628 |

## 537 | DON'T LAUGH AT ME ('cause I'm a fool)

| Composers: Norman Wisdom & June Tremayne | Date of Entry: 13.2.54 |
|---|---|
| Publishers: David Toff Music Publishing Co. Ltd. | Highest Position: 3 |
| | Weeks on Chart: 30 |

Recordings:

| Norman Wisdom | 9/52 | Columbia DB.3133 |
|---|---|---|
| Dick James | 2/54 | Parlophone R.3826 |
| Judy Wayne | 6/54 | Capitol CL.14127 |

## 538 | THE BOOK

| | | |
|---|---|---|
| Composers: Hans Gottwald & Paddy Roberts | | Date of Entry: 13.2.54/ Pos: 8/Wks: 29 |
| Publishers: Edward Kassner Music Co. Ltd. | | Re-entry: 11.9.54/ Pos: 23/Wks: 1 |

Recordings:

| | | |
|---|---|---|
| David Whitfield | 2/54 | Decca F.10242 |
| Anne Shelton with The George Mitchell Choir | 2/54 | HMV B.10641/ (45) 7M.186 |
| Dick Lee with Choir | 2/54 | Columbia DB.3433 |
| Robert Earl | 2/54 | Philips PB.238 |
| Gerry Brereton | 2/54 | Parlophone R.3825/ (45) MSP.6081 |
| Dick Lee with Choir | 3/54 | Columbia (45) SCM.5094 |
| Victor Silvester and his Ballroom Orchestra | 3/54 | Columbia FB.3704 |
| David Whitfield | 10/54 | Decca 45-F.10242★ |

## 539 | THE HAPPY WANDERER – Val de ri, Val de ra (Der Fröhliche Wanderer)

| | | |
|---|---|---|
| Composers: Friedrich Wilhelm Möller with German lyrics by Florenz Siegesmund & Edith Möller and English lyrics by Antonia Ridge | | Date of Entry: 20.2.54 |
| Publishers: Bosworth & Co. Ltd. | | Highest Position: 1 Weeks on Chart: 54 |

Recordings:

| | | |
|---|---|---|
| The Obernkirchen Children's Choir [In German] | 1/54 | Parlophone R.3799 |
| Diana Decker | 2/54 | Columbia DB.3434/ (45) SCM.5096 |
| Vivian Blaine | 2/54 | Parlophone R.3822 |
| The Beverley Sisters | 2/54 | Philips PB.239 |
| The Stargazers | 2/54 | Decca F.10259 |
| Frank Weir, his Saxophone, and his Chorus and Orchestra | 2/54 | Decca F.10271 |
| Tommy Leonetti | 5/54 | Capitol CL.14112 |
| Louis Prima and his Orchestra (Louis Prima) | 7/54 | Brunswick 05314 |
| The Stargazers | 10/54 | Decca 45-F.10259 |
| Frank Weir, his Saxophone, and his Chorus and Orchestra | 10/54 | Decca 45-F.10271 |
| The Skyliners (reverse side: Silent Night) | 12/54 | Embassy WB.112 |
| The Skyliners (reverse side: The Donkey Serenade) | 2/55 | Embassy WB.118 |

## 540 | THE LUXEMBOURG POLKA

| | | |
|---|---|---|
| Composer: Emile Reisdorff | | Date of Entry: 20.2.54 |
| Publishers: Dash Music Co. Ltd. | | Highest Position: 15 Weeks on Chart: 12 |

Recordings:

| | | |
|---|---|---|
| Mantovani and his Orchestra | 1/54 | Decca F.10233 |
| Joe Loss and his Orchestra | 2/54 | HMV BD.6161 |
| Wally Stott and his Orchestra | 2/54 | Philips PB.222 |
| Norrie Paramor and his Orchestra | 2/54 | Columbia DB.3443 |
| Billy Thorburn and his Strict Tempo Music | 3/54 | Parlophone F.2531 |
| Mantovani and his Orchestra | 10/54 | Decca 45-F.10233★ |

## 541 | THE CUFF OF MY SHIRT

| | | |
|---|---|---|
| Composer: Bob Merrill | | Date of Entry: 20.2.54/ Pos: 24/Wks: 1 |
| Publishers: Campbell Connelly & Co. Ltd. | | Re-entry: 6.3.54/ Pos: 22/Wks: 3 |
| | | 2nd re-entry: 3.4.54/ Pos: 24/Wks: 1 |

Recordings:

| | | |
|---|---|---|
| Guy Mitchell | 2/54 | Philips PB.225 |
| Frankie Vaughan with The Kordites and Ken Mackintosh and his Orchestra | 2/54 | HMV B.10635/ (45) 7M.182 |
| Micky Andrews | 2/54 | Columbia DB.3425 |
| Dennis Lotis and The Stargazers | 2/54 | Decca F.10268 |

## 542 | BELL BOTTOM BLUES

| | | |
|---|---|---|
| Composers: Hal David & Leon Carr | | Date of Entry: 27.2.54 |
| Publishers: Michael Reine Music Co. Ltd. | | Highest Position: 3 Weeks on Chart: 19 |

Recordings:

| | | |
|---|---|---|
| Alma Cogan | 2/54 | HMV B.10653/ (45) 7M.188 |
| Billie Anthony | 2/54 | Columbia DB.3446 |
| Ted Heath and his Music (Lita Roza) | 2/54 | Decca F.10269 |
| Shani Wallis | 3/54 | Philips PB.241 |
| The Radio Revellers | 3/54 | Polygon P.1107 |
| Billy Thorburn and his Strict Tempo Music | 5/54 | Parlophone F.2535 |
| Ted Heath and his Music (Lita Roza) | 10/54 | Decca 45-F.10269★ |

## 543 THE JONES BOY

| Composers: Mann Curtis & Vic Mizzy | Date of Entry: 13.3.54 |
|---|---|
| Publishers: Bradbury Wood Ltd. | Highest Position: 14<br>Weeks on Chart: 8 |

Recordings:

| | | |
|---|---|---|
| Max Bygraves | 2/54 | HMV B.10643/<br>(45) 7M.180 |
| The Mills Brothers | 2/54 | Brunswick 05240 |
| Billy Cotton and his Band (The Bandits) | 2/54 | Decca F.10266 |
| The Coronets | 2/54 | Columbia DB.3442 |
| The Malcolm Mitchell Trio | 3/54 | Parlophone R.3830/<br>(45) MSP.6084 |

## 544 BIMBO

| Composer: Rodney Morris | Date of Entry: 13.3.54/<br>Pos: 7/Wks: 18 |
|---|---|
| Publishers: Macmelodies Ltd. | Re-entry: 24.7.54/<br>Pos: 24/Wks: 1 |

Recordings:

| | | |
|---|---|---|
| Ruby Wright | 2/54 | Parlophone R.3816/<br>(45) MSP.6073 |
| Jim Reeves | 2/54 | London HL.8014 |
| Suzi Miller and The Johnston Brothers | 2/54 | Decca F.10264 |
| Gene Autry | 4/54 | Philips PB.273 |
| Guy Lombardo and his Royal Canadians (Kenny Gardner and The Lombardo Trio) | 4/54 | Brunswick 05283 |
| Malcolm Lockyer and his Strict Tempo Music for Dancing | 4/54 | Decca F.10305 |
| Eddy Howard and his Orchestra (Eddy Howard) | 5/54 | Oriole CB.1289 |
| Billy Thorburn and his Strict Tempo Music | 5/54 | Parlophone F.2535 |
| Eddy Howard and his Orchestra (Eddy Howard) | 6/54 | Mercury MB.3118 |
| Jim Reeves | 10/54 | London 45-HL.8014* |

## 545 (The gang that sang) HEART OF MY HEART

| Composer: Ben Ryan | Date of Entry: 13.3.54 |
|---|---|
| Publishers: Francis Day & Hunter Ltd. | Highest Position: 4<br>Weeks on Chart: 32 |

Recordings:

| | | |
|---|---|---|
| Frankie Laine | 5/52 | Oriole CB.1097 |
| Jerry Shard and his Music | 2/54 | Capitol CL.14058 |
| The Four Aces featuring Al Alberts | 2/54 | Brunswick 05256 |
| Max Bygraves with Vocal Quartet | 2/54 | HMV B.10654/<br>(45) 7M.194 |
| Billy Cotton and his Band (Alan Breeze, Billy Cotton and The Gang) | 2/54 | Decca F.10266 |
| The Coronets | 2/54 | Columbia DB.3442 |
| Shani Wallis | 3/54 | Philips PB.241 |
| Joe Loss and his Orchestra | 3/54 | HMV BD.6163 |
| Benny Lee, Avril Angers, Janet Brown and Peter Butterworth | 5/54 | Parlophone R.3869 |
| Frankie Laine | 6/54 | Mercury MB.2970 |
| The Four Aces featuring Al Alberts | 10/54 | Brunswick 45-05256 |

## 546 HEARTLESS

| Composer: Ken Morris | Date of Entry: 20.3.54/<br>Pos: 21/Wks: 4 |
|---|---|
| Publishers: Bluebird Music Co. | Re-entry: 24.4.54/<br>Pos: 24/Wks: 2 |

Recordings:

| | | |
|---|---|---|
| Frankie Vaughan with The Kordites and Ken Mackintosh and his Orchestra | 2/54 | HMV B.10635/<br>(45) 7M.182 |
| Johnny Brandon with The Phantoms | 3/54 | Polygon P.1103 |

## 547 | SECRET LOVE

| | | |
|---|---|---|
| Composers: Sammy Fain & Paul Francis Webster | | Date of Entry: 27.3.54 |
| Publishers: Harms–Connelly Ltd. | | Highest Position: 1 |
| | | Weeks on Chart: 30 |

Recordings:

| | | |
|---|---|---|
| Doris Day | 2/54 | Philips PB.230 |
| Monty Norman | 2/54 | Columbia DB.3435 |
| Joe Loss and his Orchestra | 3/54 | HMV BD.6163 |
| Bing Crosby | 3/54 | Brunswick 05269 |
| Lita Roza | 3/54 | Decca F.10277 |
| Ray Anthony and his Orchestra (Tommy Mercer and The Anthony Choir) | 3/54 | Capitol CL.14083 |
| Slim Whitman | 3/54 | London HL.8039 |
| Victor Silvester and his Ballroom Orchestra | 4/54 | Columbia FB.3708 |
| Gordon Jenkins and his Chorus and Orchestra (Stuart Foster) | 4/54 | Brunswick 05285 |
| Malcolm Lockyer and his Strict Tempo Music for Dancing | 4/54 | Decca F.10305 |
| Billy Thorburn and his Strict Tempo Music | 7/54 | Parlophone F.2537 |
| Slim Whitman | 10/54 | London 45-HL.8039 |
| Bing Crosby | 10/54 | Brunswick 45–05269 |
| Lita Roza | 10/54 | Decca 45-F.10277 |
| Spike Jones and his City Slickers (Tony Martinez) | 10/55 | HMV POP.110/ (45) 7M.324★ |

## 548 | TWO EASTER SUNDAY SWEETHEARTS

| | | |
|---|---|---|
| Composers: Tommie Connor & Kay Anderson | | Date of Entry: 3.4.54 |
| Publishers: Edwin H. Morris & Co. Ltd. | | Highest Position: 14 |
| | | Weeks on Chart: 5 |

Recordings:

| | | |
|---|---|---|
| Vera Lynn | 2/54 | Decca F.10253 |
| Jimmy Boyd with The Norman Luboff Choir | 3/54 | Philips PB.253 |
| Les Howard | 4/54 | HMV B.10679 |
| Vera Lynn | 10/54 | Decca 45-F.10253★ |

## 549 | FROM THE VINE CAME THE GRAPE (from the grape came the wine)

| | | |
|---|---|---|
| Composers: Leonard Whitcup & Paul Cunningham | | Date of Entry: 3.4.54 |
| Publishers: Chappell & Co. Ltd. | | Highest Position: 22 |
| | | Weeks on Chart: 3 |

Recordings:

| | | |
|---|---|---|
| Frankie Vaughan | 3/54 | HMV B.10655 |
| Micky Andrews | 3/54 | Columbia DB.3445 |
| Harry Dawson | 3/54 | Philips PB.245 |
| Suzi Miller with The Squadronaires dir. by Ronnie Aldrich | 3/54 | Decca F.10275 |
| Roy Edwards | 3/54 | Polygon P.1104 |
| The Gaylords | 3/54 | Oriole CB.1267 |
| The Hilltoppers featuring Jimmy Sacca | 3/54 | London HL.8026 |
| Bill McGuffie (piano) | 4/54 | Parlophone R.3848 |
| The Gaylords | 6/54 | Mercury MB.3101★ |
| The Hilltoppers featuring Jimmy Sacca | 10/54 | London 45-HL.8026★ |

## 550 | SOMEONE ELSE'S ROSES

| | | |
|---|---|---|
| Composer: Milton Carson | | Date of Entry: 10.4.54 |
| Publishers: John Fields Music Co. Ltd. | | Highest Position: 5 |
| | | Weeks on Chart: 21 |

Recordings:

| | | |
|---|---|---|
| Vivian Blaine | 2/54 | Parlophone R.3822 |
| Joan Regan | 2/54 | Decca F.10257 |
| Victor Silvester and his Ballroom Orchestra | 6/54 | Columbia FB.3712 |
| Joe Loss and his Orchestra | 6/54 | HMV BD.6171 |
| Doris Day | 6/54 | Philips PB.302 |
| The Regent Ballroom Orchestra | 7/54 | Decca F.10352 |

## 551 | MAKE LOVE TO ME

| | | |
|---|---|---|
| Composers: Alan Copeland & Bill Norvas (Based on 'Tin Roof Blues' by Leon Roppolo, Paul Mares, Ben Pollack, George Brunies, Mel Stitzel & Walter Melrose) | | Date of Entry: 10.4.54/ Pos: 10/Wks: 15 |
| Publishers: Edwin H. Morris & Co. Ltd. | | Re-entry: 31.7.54/ Pos: 22/Wks: 1 |

Recordings:

| | | |
|---|---|---|
| Billie Anthony | 2/54 | Columbia DB.3446 |
| Lita Roza with Ted Heath and his Music | 2/54 | Decca F.10269 |
| Jo Stafford | 3/54 | Philips PB.233 |
| Alma Cogan with Ken Mackintosh and his Orchestra | 4/54 | HMV B.10677/ (45) 7M.196 |
| The Commanders | 4/54 | Brunswick 05279 |
| Sid Phillips and his Band | 6/54 | HMV BD.6173 |
| Malcolm Lockyer and his Strict Tempo Music for Dancing | 6/54 | Decca F.10319 |
| Geraldine Farrar | 6/54 | Melodisc 1297 |
| Lita Roza with Ted Heath and his Music | 10/54 | Decca 45-F.10269★ |

## 552 | FRIENDS AND NEIGHBOURS

| | | |
|---|---|---|
| *Composers*: Marvin Scott & Malcolm Lockyer | *Date of Entry*: 17.4.54/ Pos: 2/Wks: 23 | |
| *Publishers*: Michael Reine Music Co. Ltd. | *Re-entry*: 23.10.54/ Pos: 21/Wks: 1 | |

*Recordings*:

| | | |
|---|---|---|
| Billy Cotton and his Band (The Bandits) | 4/54 | Decca F.10299 |
| Max Bygraves with The Tanner Sisters | 4/54 | HMV B.10703/ (45) 7M.220 |
| Benny Lee, Avril Angers, Janet Brown and Peter Butterworth | 5/54 | Parlophone R.3869 |
| Malcolm Lockyer and his Strict Tempo Music for Dancing | 6/54 | Decca F.10320 |
| Max Miller | 6/54 | Philips PB.296 |
| John Slater | 6/54 | Columbia DB.3488 |
| Billy Cotton and his Band (The Bandits) | 10/54 | Decca 45-F.10299 |

## 553 | SUCH A NIGHT

| | | |
|---|---|---|
| *Composer*: Lincoln Chase | *Date of Entry*: 24.4.54 | |
| *Publishers*: Sterling Music Publishing Co. Ltd. | *Highest Position*: 10 *Weeks on Chart*: 16 | |

*Recordings*:

| | | |
|---|---|---|
| Johnnie Ray | 3/54 | Philips PB.244 |
| Dennis Lotis with The Johnston Brothers and Ted Heath and his Music | 4/54 | Decca F.10287 |
| Jane Turzy | 4/54 | Brunswick 05284 |
| Bunny Paul | 4/54 | Columbia DB.3469/ (45) SCM.5112 |
| Dennis Lotis with The Johnston Brothers and Ted Heath and his Music | 10/54 | Decca 45-F.10287★ |

## 554 | CROSS OVER THE BRIDGE

| | | |
|---|---|---|
| *Composers*: Bennie Benjamin & George Weiss | *Date of Entry*: 24.4.54 | |
| *Publishers*: New World Publishers Ltd. | *Highest Position*: 8 *Weeks on Chart*: 17 | |

*Recordings*:

| | | |
|---|---|---|
| Patti Page | 3/54 | Oriole CB.1269 |
| The Beverley Sisters | 3/54 | Philips PB.257 |
| Anne Shelton with The Kordites | 4/54 | HMV B.10680/ (45) 7M.197 |
| Billie Anthony and Tony Brent | 4/54 | Columbia DB.3450 |
| Virginia Somers | 4/54 | Decca F.10301 |
| Bobby Limb and his Orchestra (Bobby Limb) | 5/54 | Decca F.10306 |
| Patti Page | 6/54 | Mercury MB.3103 |
| Virginia Somers | 10/54 | Decca 45-F.10301★ |

## 555 | SHADOW WALTZ

| | | |
|---|---|---|
| *Composer*: Paul Dubois | *Date of Entry*: 24.4.54/ Pos: 19/Wks: 2 | |
| *Publishers*: Sterling Music Publishing Co. Ltd. | *Re-entry*: 15.5.54/ Pos: 19/Wks: 4 *2nd re-entry*: 19.6.54/ Pos: 21/Wks: 3 | |

*Recordings*:

| | | |
|---|---|---|
| Wally Stott and his Orchestra | 2/54 | Philips PB.222 |
| Mantovani and his Orchestra | 2/54 | Decca F.10250 |
| The Telecast Orchestra cond. Elliott Mayes | 2/54 | Oriole CB.1261 |
| Larry Adler (harmonica) | 4/54 | HMV B.10672 |
| Joan Turner | 5/54 | Philips PB.277 |
| The Regent Ballroom Orchestra | 7/54 | Decca F.10352 |
| Nelson Riddle and his Orchestra | 7/54 | Capitol CL.14073 |
| Mantovani and his Orchestra | 10/54 | Decca 45-F.10250★ |

## 556 | (Oh baby mine) I GET SO LONELY

| | | |
|---|---|---|
| *Composer*: Pat Ballard | *Date of Entry*: 24.4.54 | |
| *Publishers*: Edwin H. Morris & Co. Ltd. | *Highest Position*: 7 *Weeks on Chart*: 22 | |

*Recordings*:

| | | |
|---|---|---|
| Bing Crosby with Guy Lombardo and his Royal Canadians | 3/54 | Brunswick 05277 |
| Geraldo and his Orchestra (Jill Day, Larry Cross and The Tophatters) | 3/54 | Philips PB.262 |
| The Four Knights | 3/54 | Capitol CL.14076 |
| Anne Shelton | 4/54 | HMV B.10680/ (45) 7M.197 |
| Tony Brent and Billie Anthony | 4/54 | Columbia DB.3450 |
| The Johnston Brothers | 4/54 | Decca F.10286 |
| Joe Loss and his Orchestra | 6/54 | HMV BD.6172 |
| Malcolm Lockyer and his Strict Tempo Music for Dancing | 6/54 | Decca F.10319 |
| Arthur 'Guitar Boogie' Smith | 7/54 | MGM.755/ (45) SP.1096 |
| The Four Knights | 10/54 | Capitol 45-CL.14076★ |
| Bing Crosby with Guy Lombardo and his Royal Canadians | 10/54 | Brunswick 45-05277★ |
| The Johnston Brothers | 10/54 | Decca 45-F.10286★ |

## 557 THE DEADWOOD STAGE

*Composers*: Sammy Fain & Paul Francis Webster

*Publishers*: Harms–Connelly Ltd.

*Date of Entry*: 1.5.54/
Pos: 18/Wks: 13
*Re-entry*: 14.8.54/
Pos: 24/Wks: 1
*2nd re-entry*: 28.8.54/
Pos: 23/Wks: 1

*Recording*:

| | | |
|---|---|---|
| Doris Day | 2/54 | Philips PB.230 |

## 558 THE LITTLE SHOEMAKER
## (Le petit Cordonnier)

*Composers*: Rudi Revil, Francis Lemarque, John Turner & Geoffrey Parsons

*Publishers*: Bourne Music Ltd.

*Date of Entry*: 8.5.54

*Highest Position*: 2
*Weeks on Chart*: 28

*Recordings*:

| | | |
|---|---|---|
| Petula Clark | 4/54 | Polygon P.1117 |
| Alma Cogan | 5/54 | HMV B.10698/ (45) 7M.219 |
| Frank Weir, his saxophone, and his Orchestra (The Michael Twins) | 5/54 | Decca F.10324 |
| Annie Cordy | 5/54 | Columbia DB.3479 |
| Eve Boswell | 5/54 | Parlophone R.3877 |
| The Regent Ballroom Orchestra | 7/54 | Decca F.10353 |
| The Gaylords | 7/54 | Mercury MB.3141 |
| Petula Clark | 1/56 | Pye Nixa N.15024★ |

## 559 LOVE ME

*Composers*: Alan Ferguson & Stephen Mervyn

*Publishers*: The B.F. Wood Music Co. Inc.

*Date of Entry*: 8.5.54/
Pos: 21/Wks: 1
*Re-entry*: 22.5.54/
Pos: 23/Wks: 1

*Recordings*:

| | | |
|---|---|---|
| Rose Brennan | 3/54 | HMV B.10649 |
| Annette Klooger | 3/54 | Parlophone R.3828 |
| Teddy Johnson | 3/54 | Columbia DB.3441/ (45) SCM.5098 |
| Cyril Shane | 3/54 | Planet E.1004 |
| Reggie Goff with The Velvetones and his Sextet | 3/54 | Polygon P.1109 |
| Victor Silvester and his Ballroom Orchestra | 4/54 | Columbia FB.3709 |

## 560 YOUNG AT HEART

*Composers*: Carolyn Leigh & Johnny Richards

*Publishers*: Victoria Music Publishing Co. Ltd.

*Date of Entry*: 8.5.54/
Pos: 10/Wks: 21
*Re-entry*: 9.10.54/
Pos: 23/Wks: 1

*Recordings*:

| | | |
|---|---|---|
| Frank Sinatra | 2/54 | Capitol CL.14064 |
| Lita Roza | 3/54 | Decca F.10277 |
| Norman Wisdom | 3/54 | Philips PB.259 |
| Evelyn Lynne | 3/54 | London HL.8038 |
| Bing Crosby with Guy Lombardo and his Royal Canadians | 3/54 | Brunswick 05277 |
| Joe Loss and his Orchestra | 4/54 | HMV BD.6166 |
| Alma Warren | 4/54 | Parlophone R.3842 |
| Billy May and his Orchestra | 7/54 | Capitol CL.14135 |
| Ray Anthony and his Orchestra (Tommy Mercer) | 9/54 | Capitol CL.14143 |
| Frank Sinatra | 10/54 | Capitol 45-CL.14064 |
| Lita Roza | 10/54 | Decca 45-F.10277 |
| Bing Crosby with Guy Lombardo and his Royal Canadians | 10/54 | Brunswick 45–05277 |

## 561 THE HOMECOMING WALTZ

*Composers*: Johnny Reine & Johnny May

*Publishers*: Michael Reine Music Co. Ltd.

*Date of Entry*: 15.5.54

*Highest Position*: 23
*Weeks on Chart*: 1

*Recordings*:

| | | |
|---|---|---|
| Vera Lynn with Chorus of Men and Women of HM Forces | 4/54 | Decca F.10290 |
| Joe Loss and his Orchestra | 5/54 | HMV BD.6170 |
| Joan Turner | 5/54 | Philips PB.277 |
| The Five Smith Brothers | 5/54 | Parlophone R.3859 |
| Vera Lynn with Chorus of Men and Women of HM Forces | 10/54 | Decca 45-F.10290★ |

## 562 A DIME AND A DOLLAR

*Composers*: Jay Livingston & Ray Evans

*Publishers*: Maddox Music Co. Ltd.

*Date of Entry*: 15.5.54

*Highest Position*: 24
*Weeks on Chart*: 2

*Recordings*:

| | | |
|---|---|---|
| Guy Mitchell | 3/54 | Philips PB.248 |
| The Keynotes | 4/54 | Decca F.10302 |
| Joe Loss and his Orchestra | 5/54 | HMV BD.6169 |
| The Keynotes | 10/54 | Decca 45-F.10302★ |

## 563 | IDLE GOSSIP

| | | |
|---|---|---|
| *Composers*: Joseph Meyer & Floyd Huddleston | | *Date of Entry*: 29.5.54/ Pos: 8/Wks: 19 |
| *Publishers*: Sydney Bron Music Co. | | *Re-entry*: 30.10.54/ Pos: 23/Wks: 1 |

*Recordings*:

| | | |
|---|---|---|
| Russ Morgan and his Orchestra (Juanita Crowley) | 12/53 | Brunswick 05213 |
| Perry Como | 4/54 | HMV B.10667/ (45) 7M.200 |
| Joe Loss and his Orchestra | 5/54 | HMV BD.6170 |
| Jean Campbell | 5/54 | Parlophone R.3867 |
| Lita Roza | 6/54 | Decca F.10335 |

## 564 | WANTED

| | | |
|---|---|---|
| *Composers*: Jack Fulton & Lois Steele | | *Date of Entry*: 29.5.54 |
| *Publishers*: Harms-Connelly Ltd. | | *Highest Position*: 4 Weeks on Chart: 19 |

*Recordings*:

| | | |
|---|---|---|
| Bobbie Britton with The Keynotes | 4/54 | Decca F.10288 |
| Perry Como | 4/54 | HMV B.10691/ (45) 7M.215 |
| Tony Brent | 4/54 | Columbia DB.3468 |
| Gary Miller | 5/54 | Philips PB.278 |
| Bobby Limb and his Orchestra (Johnny O'Connor) | 5/54 | Decca F.10306 |
| Al Martino | 5/54 | Capitol CL.14128 |
| Joe Loss and his Orchestra | 6/54 | HMV BD.6171 |
| Victor Silvester and his Ballroom Orchestra | 7/54 | Columbia FB.3715 |
| The Kenny Baker Quartet | 7/54 | Parlophone R.3887/ (45) MSP.6114 |
| The Regent Ballroom Orchestra | 7/54 | Decca F.10353 |
| Ray Anthony and his Orchestra (Tommy Mercer) | 7/54 | Capitol CL.14142 |
| Bobbie Britton with The Keynotes | 10/54 | Decca 45-F.10288 |
| Al Martino | 10/54 | Capitol 45-CL.14128 |
| Bob Dale | 11/54 | Embassy WB.106★ |

## 565 | LITTLE THINGS MEAN A LOT

| | | |
|---|---|---|
| *Composers*: Carl Stutz & Edith Lindeman | | *Date of Entry*: 5.6.54 |
| *Publishers*: Robbins Music Corporation Ltd. | | *Highest Position*: 1 Weeks on Chart: 33 |

*Recordings*:

| | | |
|---|---|---|
| Kitty Kallen | 5/54 | Brunswick 05287 |
| Jimmy Young | 5/54 | Decca F.10317 |
| Alma Cogan | 6/54 | HMV B.10717/ (45) 7M.228 |
| Joe Loss and his Orchestra | 7/54 | HMV BD.6175 |
| One Beverley Sister – Joy | 7/54 | Philips PB.309 |
| Teddy Johnson | 7/54 | Columbia DB.3502 |
| Ray Anthony and his Orchestra (Marcie Miller) | 7/54 | Capitol CL.14142 |
| Kitty Kallen | 10/54 | Brunswick 45-05287 |
| Rita Williams | 11/54 | Embassy WB.107 |

## 566 | BOB'S YER UNCLE! (an' Fanny's yer aunt)

| | | |
|---|---|---|
| *Composers*: Tommie Connor & Eddie Lisbona | | *Date of Entry*: 12.6.54 |
| *Publishers*: Campbell Connelly & Co. Ltd. | | *Highest Position*: 22 Weeks on Chart: 1 |

*Recordings*:

| | | |
|---|---|---|
| Guy Mitchell | 5/54 | Philips PB.293 |
| John Slater | 6/54 | Columbia DB.3488 |
| Billy Cotton and his Band (Alan Breeze and The Bandits) | 6/54 | Decca F.10325 |

## 567 | NEVER NEVER LAND (ooh-la)

| | | |
|---|---|---|
| *Composers*: Gerhard Froboess, Ralph Butler, Sy Cromwell & S.A. Beecher | | *Date of Entry*: 12.6.54/ Pos: 23/Wks: 1 |
| *Publishers*: Keith Prowse Music Publishing Co. Ltd. | | *Re-entry*: 26.6.54/ Pos: 7/Wks: 20 |

*Recordings*:

| | | |
|---|---|---|
| Helen van Capellen with The Parakeets | 5/54 | Decca F.10312 |
| Frank Weir, his saxophone, and his Orchestra (Maureen Childs and The Little Tinkers) | 5/54 | Decca F.10324 |
| Diana Decker | 6/54 | Columbia DB.3489/ (45) SCM.5123 |
| Peter Sellers | 6/54 | HMV B.10724 |
| Joe Loss and his Orchestra | 7/54 | HMV BD.6175 |
| Two Beverley Sisters – Babs and Teddie | 7/54 | Philips PB.309 |

## 568 CLEO AND ME-O

| | | |
|---|---|---|
| *Composer*: Bob Merrill | | *Date of Entry*: 12.6.54 |
| *Publishers*: Campbell Connelly & Co. Ltd. | | *Highest Position*: 24<br>*Weeks on Chart*: 1 |

Recordings:

| | | |
|---|---|---|
| Dickie Valentine and Joan Regan with<br>   The Keynotes | 4/54 | Decca F.10300 |
| The Four Lads and Jill Corey | 5/54 | Philips PB.272 |
| The Malcolm Mitchell Trio | 5/54 | Parlophone R.3866 |

## 569 CARA MIA

| | | |
|---|---|---|
| *Composers*: Tulio Trapani & Lee Lange | | *Date of Entry*: 19.6.54/<br>Pos: 1/Wks: 22 |
| *Publishers*: Robbins Music Corporation Ltd. | | *Re-entry*: 27.11.54/<br>Pos: 21/Wks: 1 |

Recordings:

| | | |
|---|---|---|
| David Whitfield with Mantovani and his<br>   Orchestra | 6/54 | Decca F.10327 |
| Josef Locke | 7/54 | Columbia DB.3503 |
| Ron Goodwin and his Concert Orchestra | 7/54 | Parlophone R.3889 |
| Ron Goodwin and his Concert Orchestra | 9/54 | Parlophone (45)<br>   MSP.6115 |
| The Regent Ballroom Orchestra | 9/54 | Decca F.10365 |
| David Whitfield with Mantovani and his<br>   Orchestra | 10/54 | Decca 45-F.10327 |

## 570 THE MAN WITH THE BANJO

| | | |
|---|---|---|
| *Composers*: Robert Mellin & Fritz Schulz Reichel | | *Date of Entry*: 19.6.54/<br>Pos: 23/Wks: 1 |
| *Publishers*: Robert Mellin Ltd. | | *Re-entry*: 17.7.54/<br>Pos: 23/Wks: 1 |

Recordings:

| | | |
|---|---|---|
| The Ames Brothers | 5/54 | HMV B.10685/<br>   (45) 7M.209 |
| Joe Loss and his Orchestra | 5/54 | HMV BD.6169 |
| Glen Mason | 5/54 | Philips PB.284 |
| The Stargazers | 5/54 | Decca F.10310 |
| Diana Decker | 5/54 | Columbia DB.3480/<br>   (45) SCM.5120 |
| The Hedley Ward Trio | 6/54 | Melodisc 1294 |
| Dick Todd | 7/54 | Brunswick 05301 |
| The Melody Three with Primo Scala and<br>   his Band | 7/54 | Polygon P.1120 |

## 571 THREE COINS IN THE FOUNTAIN

| | | |
|---|---|---|
| *Composers*: Sammy Cahn & Jule Styne | | *Date of Entry*: 10.7.54 |
| *Publishers*: Leo Feist Ltd. | | *Highest Position*: 2<br>*Weeks on Chart*: 21 |

Recordings:

| | | |
|---|---|---|
| The Four Aces featuring Al Alberts | 7/54 | Brunswick 05308 |
| Marti Stevens | 7/54 | MGM.758 |
| Dinah Shore | 7/54 | HMV B.10730/<br>   (45) 7M.236 |
| Frank Sinatra | 7/54 | Capitol CL.14120 |
| Billy Ward and his Dominoes | 7/54 | Parlophone R.3882/<br>   (45) MSP.6112 |
| Toni Arden | 7/54 | Philips PB.307 |
| Tony Brent | 7/54 | Columbia DB.3496 |
| Julius La Rosa | 7/54 | London HL.8057 |
| Ron Goodwin and his Concert Orchestra | 7/54 | Parlophone R.3889 |
| Ron Goodwin and his Concert Orchestra | 9/54 | Parlophone (45)<br>   MSP.6115 |
| Ray Anthony and his Orchestra (Tommy<br>   Mercer and The Anthony Choir) | 9/54 | Capitol CL.14143 |
| The Lumberjacks | 9/54 | Decca F.10371 |
| Victor Silvester and his Ballroom<br>   Orchestra | 9/54 | Columbia FB.3716 |
| Harry James and his Orchestra | 9/54 | Philips PB.326 |
| The Four Aces featuring Al Alberts | 10/54 | Brunswick 45-05308 |
| Frank Sinatra | 10/54 | Capitol 45-CL.14120 |
| Larry Cross | 11/54 | Embassy WB.101 |

## 572 DREAM, DREAM, DREAM

| | | |
|---|---|---|
| *Composer*: Jimmy McHugh | | *Date of Entry*: 10.7.54 |
| *Publishers*: Leo Feist Ltd. | | *Highest Position*: 22<br>*Weeks on Chart*: 1 |

Recordings:

| | | |
|---|---|---|
| Axel Stordahl and his Orchestra | 2/54 | Capitol CL.14060 |
| Percy Faith and his Orchestra | 3/54 | Philips PB.260 |
| Mantovani and his Orchestra | 4/54 | Decca F.10292 |
| Mantovani and his Orchestra | 10/54 | Decca 45-F.10292★ |

## 573 THE STORY OF TINA (Dia Prasina Matia)

| | | |
|---|---|---|
| *Composer:* D. Katrivanou with English lyrics by Christopher Hassall | *Date of Entry:* 10.7.54 | |
| *Publishers:* Macmelodies Ltd. | *Highest Position:* 3 | |
| | *Weeks on Chart:* 27 | |

*Recordings:*

| | | |
|---|---|---|
| Ronnie Harris | 7/54 | Columbia DB.3499 |
| Jan Rosol | 7/54 | Polygon P.1126 |
| Gerry Brereton | 7/54 | Parlophone R.3891 |
| The Regent Ballroom Orchestra | 9/54 | Decca F.10365 |
| Lee Lawrence | 9/54 | Decca F.10367 |
| Charlie Applewhite | 9/54 | Brunswick 05331 |
| Victor Silvester and his Ballroom Orchestra | 9/54 | Columbia FB.3717 |
| Al Martino | 9/54 | Capitol CL.14163 |
| Al Martino | 10/54 | Capitol 45-CL.14163 |
| Lee Lawrence | 10/54 | Decca 45-F.10367 |
| Bob Dale | 11/54 | Embassy WB.106 |

## 574 JILTED

| | | |
|---|---|---|
| *Composers:* Robert Colby & Dick Manning | *Date of Entry:* 17.7.54 | |
| *Publishers:* Sterling Music Publishing Co. Ltd. | *Highest Position:* 22 | |
| | *Weeks on Chart:* 1 | |

*Recordings:*

| | | |
|---|---|---|
| Joan Regan | 5/54 | Decca F.10311 |
| Frankie Vaughan and Alma Cogan | 5/54 | HMV B.10712 |
| Diana Decker | 5/54 | Columbia DB.3480/ (45) SCM.5120 |
| Red Foley | 5/54 | Brunswick 05307 |
| Frankie Vaughan and Alma Cogan | 6/54 | HMV (45) 7M.226 |
| Billy Thorburn and his Strict Tempo Music | 7/54 | Parlophone F.2537 |
| Teresa Brewer | 8/54 | Vogue Coral Q.2001* |

## 575 MY FRIEND

| | | |
|---|---|---|
| *Composers:* Ervin Drake & Jimmy Shirl | *Date of Entry:* 24.7.54 | |
| *Publishers:* Chappell & Co. Ltd. | *Highest Position:* 1 | |
| | *Weeks on Chart:* 27 | |

*Recordings:*

| | | |
|---|---|---|
| Eddie Fisher | 7/54 | HMV B.10729/ (45) 7M.235 |
| Edmund Hockridge | 7/54 | Parlophone R.3884 |
| Vera Lynn | 7/54 | Decca F.10339 |
| Issy Bonn | 7/54 | Columbia DB.3504 |
| Frankie Laine | 7/54 | Philips PB.316 |
| Joe Marine | 7/54 | Brunswick 05233 |
| Ray Anthony and his Orchestra (Tommy Mercer and The Anthony Choir) | 7/54 | Capitol CL.14146 |
| Bill Hurley | 12/54 | Embassy WB.105 |

## 576 WEST OF ZANZIBAR (Jambo)

| | | |
|---|---|---|
| *Composer:* Georges Sigara | *Date of Entry:* 24.7.54 | |
| *Publishers:* Bluebird Music Co. | *Highest Position:* 13 | |
| | *Weeks on Chart:* 15 | |

*Recordings:*

| | | |
|---|---|---|
| Anthony Steel and The Radio Revellers | 4/54 | Polygon P.1114 |
| The Johnston Brothers | 5/54 | Decca F.10326 |
| Ray Anthony and his Orchestra (The Skyliners) | 10/54 | Capitol CL.14182 |
| Anthony Steel and The Radio Revellers | 1/56 | Pye Nixa N.15023* |

## 577 GILLY GILLY OSSENFEFFER KATZENELLEN BOGEN BY THE SEA

| | | |
|---|---|---|
| *Composers:* Al Hoffman & Dick Manning | *Date of Entry:* 31.7.54 | |
| *Publishers:* Larry Spier Ltd. | *Highest Position:* 4 | |
| | *Weeks on Chart:* 17 | |

*Recordings:*

| | | |
|---|---|---|
| The Four Lads | 7/54 | Philips PB.304 |
| Max Bygraves | 7/54 | HMV B.10734/ (45) 7M.237 |
| George Elrick and The Lumberjacks | 9/54 | Decca F.10371 |
| The Four-in-A-Chord | 11/54 | Embassy WB.108 |

## 578 SMILE (Theme from 'Modern Times')

| | | |
|---|---|---|
| *Composers:* Charles Chaplin, John Turner & Geoffrey Parsons | *Date of Entry:* 7.8.54 | |
| *Publishers:* Bourne Music Ltd. | *Highest Position:* 4 | |
| | *Weeks on Chart:* 27 | |

*Recordings:*

| | | |
|---|---|---|
| Petula Clark | 7/54 | Polygon P.1128 |
| Frank Chacksfield and his Orchestra | 7/54 | Decca F.10354 |
| David Whitfield | 7/54 | Decca F.10355 |
| The Melachrino Orchestra | 7/54 | HMV B.10738 |
| Ron Goodwin and his Concert Orchestra | 7/54 | Parlophone R.3890 |
| Gerry Brereton | 7/54 | Parlophone R.3891 |
| Joe 'Mr Piano' Henderson | 7/54 | Polygon P.1129 |
| Billy Daniels with Benny Payne at the piano | 7/54 | Mercury MB.3142 |
| Ray Burns | 7/54 | Columbia DB.3506 |
| Lita Roza | 8/54 | Decca F.10356 |
| Nat 'King' Cole | 8/54 | Capitol CL.14149 |
| Ron Goodwin and his Concert Orchestra | 9/54 | Parlophone (45) MSP.6116 |
| Frank Chacksfield and his Orchestra | 10/54 | Decca 45-F.10354 |
| David Whitfield | 10/54 | Decca 45-F.10355 |
| Nat 'King' Cole | 10/54 | Capitol 45-CL.14149 |
| Victor Young and his Singing Strings (piano solo: Ray Turner) | 10/54 | Brunswick 05337 (& 45-) |
| Duke Ellington and his Famous Orchestra | 10/54 | Capitol CL.14186 (& 45-) |
| Bill McGuffie and his Music | 10/54 | Philips PB.356 |
| Rita Williams | 11/54 | Embassy WB.107 |

## 579 | MIDNIGHT

| | | |
|---|---|---|
| *Composer*: Teddy Peters | | *Date of Entry*: 14.8.54 |
| *Publishers*: The B.F. Wood Music Co. Inc. | | *Highest Position*: 23 |
| | | *Weeks on Chart*: 2 |

*Recordings*:

| | | |
|---|---|---|
| Eddie Calvert – The Man with the Golden Trumpet | 3/54 | Columbia DB.3444/ (45) SCM.5097 |
| Roy Edwards | 11/54 | Polygon P.1140★ |

## 580 | THE BLACK HILLS OF DAKOTA

| | | |
|---|---|---|
| *Composers*: Sammy Fain & Paul Francis Webster | | *Date of Entry*: 21.8.54 |
| *Publishers*: Harms-Connelly Ltd. | | *Highest Position*: 19 |
| | | *Weeks on Chart*: 4 |

*Recording*:

| | | |
|---|---|---|
| Doris Day with Vocal Quartet | 6/54 | Philips PB.287 |

## 581 | A SKY-BLUE SHIRT AND A RAINBOW TIE

| | | |
|---|---|---|
| *Composers*: Jack Birch & John Redmond | | *Date of Entry*: 21.8.54 |
| *Publishers*: Lawrence Wright Music Co. Ltd. | | *Highest Position*: 9 |
| | | *Weeks on Chart*: 25 |

*Recordings*:

| | | |
|---|---|---|
| Norman Brooks | 1/54 | London L.1228 |
| The Ray Ellington Quartet | 7/54 | Columbia DB.3500 |
| The Hedley Ward Trio | 7/54 | Melodisc 1298 |
| The Jerry Allen Trio (The Allentones) | 10/54 | Decca F.10381 |
| Norman Brooks | 10/54 | London 45-L.1228 |
| Jack Parnell and his Orchestra (Jack Parnell) | 11/54 | Parlophone R.3944/ (45) MSP.6138 |
| Ian Stewart and his Music | 11/54 | Parlophone F.2542 |
| The Regent Ballroom Orchestra | 11/54 | Decca F.10409 (&45-) |

## 582 | WAIT FOR ME, DARLING

| | | |
|---|---|---|
| *Composers*: Albert Hague & Bill Barr | | *Date of Entry*: 4.9.54 |
| *Publishers*: Lafleur & Co. Ltd. | | *Highest Position*: 15 |
| | | *Weeks on Chart*: 17 |

*Recordings*:

| | | |
|---|---|---|
| Georgia Gibbs | 7/54 | Mercury MB.3130 |
| Joan Regan with The Johnston Brothers | 7/54 | Decca F.10362 |
| Les Howard | 9/54 | HMV B.10741 |
| Bonnie Lou | 9/54 | Parlophone R.3895/ (45) MSP.6117 |
| David Hughes | 9/54 | Philips PB.320 |
| Joan Regan with The Johnston Brothers | 10/54 | Decca 45-F.10362 |

## 583 | SWAY (Quien Sera)

| | | |
|---|---|---|
| *Composers*: Pablo Beltran Ruiz & Norman Gimbel | | *Date of Entry*: 4.9.54 |
| *Publishers*: Latin-American Music Publishing Co. Ltd. | | *Highest Position*: 9 |
| | | *Weeks on Chart*: 14 |

*Recordings*:

| | | |
|---|---|---|
| Roberto Inglez and his Mambo Orchestra [Titled 'Quien Sera'] | 6/54 | Parlophone R.3876 |
| Dean Martin | 7/54 | Capitol CL.14138 |
| Tony Brent | 7/54 | Columbia DB.3496 |
| Ray Anthony and his Orchestra (Ray Anthony and The Quartet) | 7/54 | Capitol CL.14146 |
| Buddy Pipp's Highlifers | 7/54 | Lyragon J.728 |
| Norman Grant and his Orchestra for Dancers | 7/54 | Esquire 5−095 |
| Bob Carroll | 7/54 | London HL.8058 |
| Eileen Barton | 8/54 | Vogue Coral Q.2009 |
| Dean Martin | 10/54 | Capitol 45-CL.14138 |
| The Four-in-A-Chord | 12/54 | Embassy WB.115 |

## 584 | SH-BOOM (Life could be a dream)

| | | |
|---|---|---|
| *Composers*: James Keyes, Claude & Carl Feaster, Floyd F. McRae & James Edwards | | *Date of Entry*: 4.9.54/ Pos: 24/Wks: 1 |
| *Publishers*: Aberbach (London) Ltd. | | *Re-entry*: 18.9.54/ Pos: 16/Wks: 11 |

*Recordings*:

| | | |
|---|---|---|
| The Crew-Cuts | 7/54 | Mercury MB.3140 |
| The Johnston Brothers | 8/54 | Decca F.10364 |
| Ken Mackintosh and his Orchestra (The Mackpies) | 9/54 | HMV BD.1327 |
| The Billy Williams Quartet | 9/54 | Vogue Coral Q.2012 |
| The Chords | 9/54 | Columbia DB.3512/ (45) SCM.5133 |
| Stan Freberg with The Toads | 10/54 | Capitol CL.14187 (& 45-) |
| Svend Asmussen and his Orchestra and Chorus | 10/54 | Philips PB.343 |
| The Johnston Brothers | 10/54 | Decca 45-F.10364 |
| The Four-in-A-Chord | 11/54 | Embassy WB.108 |

## 585 | THERE MUST BE A REASON

| | | |
|---|---|---|
| *Composers*: Benny Davis & Ted Murray | | *Date of Entry*: 11.9.54 |
| *Publishers*: Campbell Connelly & Co. Ltd. | | *Highest Position*: 5 |
| | | *Weeks on Chart*: 21 |

*Recordings*:

| | | |
|---|---|---|
| Frankie Laine | 7/54 | Philips PB.306 |
| Vera Lynn | 7/54 | Decca F.10339 |

## 586 HOLD MY HAND

| Composers: Jack Lawrence & Richard Myers | | Date of Entry: 18.9.54 |
| --- | --- | --- |
| Publishers: Bradbury Wood Ltd. | | Highest Position: 1 |
| | | Weeks on Chart: 24 |

Recordings:

| Don Cornell | 8/54 | Vogue Coral Q.2013 |
| --- | --- | --- |
| Lorrae Desmond | 9/54 | Decca F.10375 |
| Ronnie Harris | 9/54 | Columbia DB.3520/ |
| | | (45) SCM.5138 |
| Gary Miller | 9/54 | Philips PB.335 |
| Don Cornell | 10/54 | Vogue Coral |
| | | 45-Q.2013 |
| Tony Mansell | 10/54 | Parlophone R.3919/ |
| | | (45) MSP.6130 |
| Lorrae Desmond | 10/54 | Decca 45-F.10375 |
| Archie Lewis | 10/54 | Melodisc P.220 |
| Ian Stewart and his Music | 11/54 | Parlophone F.2542 |
| Nat 'King' Cole | 12/54 | Capitol CL.14203 |
| | | (& 45-) |
| Larry Cross | 12/54 | Embassy WB.102 |

## 587 IF I GIVE MY HEART TO YOU

| Composers: Jimmy Brewster, Jimmy Crane & Al Jacobs | | Date of Entry: 25.9.54 |
| --- | --- | --- |
| Publishers: Robbins Music Corporation Ltd. | | Highest Position: 2 |
| | | Weeks on Chart: 26 |

Recordings:

| Anne Shelton with Ken Mackintosh and his Orchestra | 9/54 | HMV B.10745/(45) 7M.240 |
| --- | --- | --- |
| Joan Regan | 9/54 | Decca F.10373 |
| Dinah Shore | 9/54 | HMV B.10756/ |
| | | (45) 7M.250 |
| The Wright Brothers | 9/54 | MGM.764 |
| Denise Lor | 9/54 | Parlophone R.3893/ |
| | | (45) MSP.6120 |
| Doris Day with The Mellomen | 9/54 | Philips PB.325 |
| Connee Boswell | 9/54 | Brunswick 05319 |
| Joan Regan | 10/54 | Decca 45-F.10373 |
| Connee Boswell | 10/54 | Brunswick 45-05319 |
| Billy Thorburn and his Strict Tempo Music | 10/54 | Parlophone F.2539 |
| Monica Lewis | 10/54 | Capitol CL.14179 |
| Duke Ellington and his Famous Orchestra | 10/54 | Capitol CL.14186 |
| | | (& 45-) |
| Buddy Greco | 11/54 | Vogue Coral Q.2021 |
| The Regent Ballroom Orchestra | 11/54 | Decca F.10409 |
| | | (& 45-) |
| Beryl Templeman | 11/54 | Embassy WB.104 |
| Nat 'King' Cole | 12/54 | Capitol CL.14203 |
| | | (& 45-) |

## 588 MAKE HER MINE

| Composers: Chester Conn & Sammy Gallop | | Date of Entry: 25.9.54 |
| --- | --- | --- |
| Publishers: Bradbury Wood Ltd. | | Highest Position: 16 |
| | | Weeks on Chart: 7 |

Recordings:

| Archie Lewis | 3/54 | Melodisc 1282 |
| --- | --- | --- |
| Leslie A. Hutchinson – 'Hutch' | 7/54 | Oriole CB.1292 |
| Nat 'King' Cole | 8/54 | Capitol CL.14149 |
| Nat 'King' Cole | 10/54 | Capitol 45-CL.14149 |

## 589 THIS OLE HOUSE

| Composer: Stuart Hamblen | | Date of Entry: 2.10.54 |
| --- | --- | --- |
| Publishers: Duchess Music Ltd. | | Highest Position: 3 |
| | | Weeks on Chart: 23 |

Recordings:

| Billie Anthony | 9/54 | Columbia DB.3519/ |
| --- | --- | --- |
| | | (45) SCM.5143 |
| Rosemary Clooney | 9/54 | Philips PB.336 |
| Billy Cotton and his Band (Doreen Stephens and The Bandits) | 9/54 | Decca F.10377 |
| Billy Cotton and his Band (Doreen Stephens and The Bandits) | 10/54 | Decca 45-F.10377 |
| Herb and Kay | 10/54 | Parlophone R.3916/ |
| | | (45) MSP.6127 |
| Alma Cogan with Vocal Group | 10/54 | HMV B.10761/ |
| | | (45) 7M.269 |
| Joan Regan with The Keynotes | 10/54 | Decca F.10397 (&45-) |
| Rex Allen and Tex Williams | 11/54 | Brunswick 05341 |
| | | (& 45-) |
| Penny Nicholls | 12/54 | Embassy WB.111 |

(Note: The recording by the composer, Stuart Hamblen, was available to special order on HMV JO.413 and (45) 7MC.20.)

## 590 MY SON, MY SON

| Composers: Eddie Calvert, Melville Farley & Bob Howard | | Date of Entry: 9.10.54 |
| --- | --- | --- |
| Publishers: Edward Kassner Music Co. Ltd. | | Highest Position: 3 |
| | | Weeks on Chart: 16 |

Recordings:

| Eddie Calvert – The Man with the Golden Trumpet | 9/54 | Columbia DB.3507/ |
| --- | --- | --- |
| | | (45) SCM.5129 |
| Vera Lynn with Frank Weir, his saxophone, and his Orchestra and Chorus | 9/54 | Decca F.10372 |
| Frankie Vaughan | 9/54 | HMV B.10766/ |
| | | (45) 7M.252 |
| Robert Earl | 9/54 | Philips PB.331 |
| Vera Lynn with Frank Weir, his saxophone, and his Orchestra and Chorus | 10/54 | Decca 45-F.10372 |
| Beryl Templeman | 12/54 | Embassy WB.114 |

## 591 THE HIGH AND THE MIGHTY

*Composers*: Dimitri Tiomkin & Ned Washington    *Date of Entry*: 16.10.54

*Publishers*: Harms–Connelly Ltd.    *Highest Position*: 15
*Weeks on Chart*: 11

*Recordings*:
| | | |
|---|---|---|
| Norrie Paramor and his Orchestra | 9/54 | Columbia DB.3515/ (45) SCM.5136 |
| Les Baxter and his Orchestra and Chorus | 9/54 | Capitol CL.14147 |
| Victor Young and his Singing Strings (Whistling: Muzzy Marcellino) | 9/54 | Brunswick 05320 |
| Leroy Holmes and his Orchestra (Whistling: Fred Lowery) | 9/54 | MGM.765 |
| Harry James and his Orchestra | 9/54 | Philips PB.326 |
| Gary Miller | 9/54 | Philips PB.335 |
| Victor Young and his Singing Strings (Whistling: Muzzy Marcellino) | 10/54 | Brunswick 45–05320 |
| Dimitri Tiomkin and his Orchestra | 10/54 | Vogue Coral Q.2016 (& 45-) |
| Jimmy Young | 10/54 | Decca F.10370 |
| Tony Mansell | 10/54 | Parlophone R.3919/ (45) MSP.6130 |
| Tommy Reilly (harmonica) | 10/54 | Parlophone R.3924 |
| Perez 'Prez' Prado and his Orchestra | 10/54 | HMV B.10760/ (45) 7M.255 |
| Ronald Chesney (harmonica) | 10/54 | HMV B.10767 |
| Johnny Desmond | 10/54 | Vogue Coral Q.2019 (& 45-) |
| Richard Hayman and his Orchestra | 10/54 | Mercury MB.3155 |
| Victor Silvester and his Ballroom Orchestra | 11/54 | Columbia FB.3724 |
| The Roland Shaw Orchestra (Whistling: Johnny Johnston) | 11/54 | Decca F.10407 (&45-) |
| The Embassy Orchestra directed by Jack Coles | 12/54 | Embassy WB.109 |

## 592 THEY WERE DOIN' THE MAMBO

*Composers*: Sonny Burke & Don Raye    *Date of Entry*: 23.10.54

*Publishers*: Edwin H. Morris & Co. Ltd.    *Highest Position*: 24
*Weeks on Chart*: 1

*Recordings*:
| | | |
|---|---|---|
| Bobby Wayne | 9/54 | Mercury MB.3151 |
| Vaughn Monroe | 9/54 | HMV B.10751/ (45) 7M.247 |
| Dennis Lotis with Ted Heath and his Music | 9/54 | Decca F.10374 |
| Eric Jupp and his Orchestra (The Coronets) | 10/54 | Columbia DB.3522/ (45) SCM.5140 |
| Les Brown and his Band of Renown (Butch Stone and Ensemble) | 10/54 | Vogue Coral Q.2018 |
| Tex Williams | 11/54 | Brunswick 05341 (& 45-)★ |

## 593 I LOVE PARIS

*Composer*: Cole Porter    *Date of Entry*: 30.10.54

*Publishers*: Chappell & Co. Ltd.    *Highest Position*: 14
*Weeks on Chart*: 13

*Recordings*:
| | | |
|---|---|---|
| Ronnie Harris | 10/54 | Columbia DB.3529/ (45) SCM.5139 |
| Tony Martin | 10/54 | HMV B.10771/ (45) 7M.258 |
| Les Baxter and his Chorus and Orchestra | 10/54 | Capitol CL.14166 (& 45-) |
| Charlie Applewhite | 10/54 | Brunswick 05336 |
| Jan Rosol and Gwen Campbell | 10/54 | Polygon P.1136 |
| Georgia Gibbs | 10/54 | Mercury MB.3152 |
| Irene Hilda | 10/54 | Parlophone R.3945 |
| Leslie A. Hutchinson – 'Hutch' | 10/54 | Decca F.10388 (&45-) |
| Joe Loss and his Orchestra | 11/54 | HMV BD.6180 |
| Victor Silvester and his Ballroom Orchestra | 11/54 | Columbia FB.3723 |
| Beryl Templeman | 11/54 | Embassy WB.104 |
| Patti Lewis | 11/54 | Philips PB.367 |
| The Regent Ballroom Orchestra | 1/55 | Decca F.10446 (&45-) |
| Bing Crosby | 1/55 | Brunswick 05377 (& 45-) |
| Luis Mariano | 3/55 | HMV B.10843 |
| Humphrey Lyttleton and his Band | 3/55 | Parlophone R.3996 |

## 594 SANTO NATALE (Merry Christmas)

*Composers*: Belle Nardone, Al Hoffman & Dick Manning    *Date of Entry*: 6.11.54

*Publishers*: Larry Spier Ltd.    *Highest Position*: 2
*Weeks on Chart*: 11

*Recordings*:
| | | |
|---|---|---|
| David Hughes | 10/54 | Philips PB.350 |
| David Whitfield | 10/54 | Decca F.10399 (&45-) |
| Josef Locke | 11/54 | Columbia DB.3544/ (45) SCM.5152 |
| Victor Silvester and his Ballroom Orchestra | 12/54 | Columbia FB.3727 |
| Billy Thorburn and his Strict Tempo Music | 12/54 | Parlophone F.2544 |
| Ronnie Gaylord | 12/54 | Mercury MB.3178 |

## 595 YOUR HEART, MY HEART

| | | |
|---|---|---|
| *Composers*: Olias, Weiss & Rothenburg, with English lyrics added by Carl Sigman | | *Date of Entry*: 6.11.54 |
| *Publishers*: Bourne Music Ltd. | | *Highest Position*: 24 *Weeks on Chart*: 1 |

*Recordings*:

| | | |
|---|---|---|
| Frankie Laine with The Norman Luboff Choir | 9/54 | Philips PB.311 |
| Dick James | 11/54 | Parlophone R.3940 |
| Woolf Phillips and his Orchestra (Dennis Morley) | 12/54 | Decca F.10416 (& 45-)★ |

## 596 NO ONE BUT YOU

| | | |
|---|---|---|
| *Composers*: Nicholas Brodszky & Jack Lawrence | | *Date of Entry*: 13.11.54 |
| *Publishers*: Robbins Music Corporation Ltd. | | *Highest Position*: 7 *Weeks on Chart*: 23 |

*Recordings*:

| | | |
|---|---|---|
| Billy Eckstine | 9/54 | MGM.763/ (45) SP.1101 |
| Carlos Thompson | 9/54 | MGM.759/ (45) SP.1097 |
| Connie Russell | 10/54 | Capitol CL.14171 (& 45-) |
| Lorrae Desmond | 10/54 | Decca F.10398 (& 45-) |
| Al Martino | 11/54 | Capitol CL.14202 (& 45-) |
| The Roland Shaw Orchestra (Kim Bennett) | 11/54 | Decca F.10407 (&45-) |
| Charlie Applewhite | 1/55 | Brunswick 05358 (& 45-) |
| The Regent Ballroom Orchestra | 1/55 | Decca F.10445 (&45-) |
| Victor Silvester and his Ballroom Orchestra | 3/55 | Columbia FB.3735 |

## 597 VENI-VIDI-VICI

| | | |
|---|---|---|
| *Composers*: Paul Francis Webster & Jerry Livingston | | *Date of Entry*: 13.11.54 |
| *Publishers*: Dash Music Co. Ltd. | | *Highest Position*: 5 *Weeks on Chart*: 14 |

*Recordings*:

| | | |
|---|---|---|
| Ronnie Hilton | 11/54 | HMV B.10785 |
| Ray Martin and his Concert Orchestra | 11/54 | Columbia DB.3539/ (45) SCM.5150 |
| Dick James | 11/54 | Parlophone R.3940 |
| The Five Smith Brothers | 11/54 | Decca F.10403 (&45-) |
| The Gaylords | 11/54 | Mercury MB.3163 |
| Joe Loss and his Orchestra | 12/54 | HMV BD.6183 |
| The-Four-in-A-Chord | 2/55 | Embassy WB.120 |

## 598 AM I A TOY OR TREASURE?

| | | |
|---|---|---|
| *Composers*: Arthur Altman, Louis C. Singer & Irving Taylor | | *Date of Entry*: 13.11.54 |
| *Publishers*: Cinephonic Music Co. Ltd. | | *Highest Position*: 24 *Weeks on Chart*: 1 |

*Recording*:

| | | |
|---|---|---|
| Kay Starr | 9/54 | Capitol CL.14151 |
| Kay Starr | 10/54 | Capitol 45-CL.14151 |

## 599 I CAN'T TELL A WALTZ FROM A TANGO

| | | |
|---|---|---|
| *Composers*: Al Hoffman & Dick Manning | | *Date of Entry*: 20.11.54 |
| *Publishers*: Michael Reine Music Co. Ltd. | | *Highest Position*: 2 *Weeks on Chart*: 17 |

*Recordings*:

| | | |
|---|---|---|
| Patti Page | 10/54 | Mercury MB.3161 |
| Alma Cogan | 11/54 | HMV B.10786/ (45) 7M.271 |
| Ray Burns | 11/54 | Columbia DB.3545/ (45) SCM.5153 |
| Lorrae Desmond and The Johnston Brothers | 11/54 | Decca F.10404 (&45-) |
| Patti Lewis | 11/54 | Philips PB.367 |
| Benny Hill | 1/55 | Decca F.10442 (&45-) |
| Rita Williams | 2/55 | Embassy WB.119 |

## 600 I NEED YOU NOW

| | | |
|---|---|---|
| *Composers*: Jimmie Crane & Al Jacobs | | *Date of Entry*: 20.11.54 |
| *Publishers*: B. Feldman & Co. Ltd. | | *Highest Position*: 20 *Weeks on Chart*: 2 |

*Recordings*:

| | | |
|---|---|---|
| Eddie Fisher | 9/54 | HMV B.10755/ (45) 7M.251 |
| The Stargazers | 9/54 | Decca F.10379 |
| The Stargazers | 10/54 | Decca 45-F.10379 |

## 601 | COUNT YOUR BLESSINGS INSTEAD OF SHEEP

*Composer*: Irving Berlin

*Publishers*: Irving Berlin Ltd.

*Date of Entry*: 20.11.54/
Pos: 21/Wks: 1

*Re-entry*: 4.12.54/
Pos: 6/Wks: 17

*Recordings*:

| | | |
|---|---|---|
| Eddie Fisher | 11/54 | HMV B.10779/ (45) 7M.266 |
| Jean Campbell | 11/54 | Parlophone R.3938 |
| Bing Crosby | 11/54 | Brunswick 05339 (& 45-) |
| Rosemary Clooney with The Mellomen | 11/54 | Philips PB.375 |
| Woolf Phillips and his Orchestra (Jean, Jo, Joy & Penny) | 12/54 | Decca F.10416 (&45-) |
| Gordon MacRae | 12/54 | Capitol CL.14193 (& 45-) |
| Larry Cross | 12/54 | Embassy WB.113 |
| Ian Stewart and his Music | 1/55 | Parlophone F.2547 |

## 602 | THE MAMA DOLL SONG

*Composers*: Nat Simon & Charles Tobias

*Publishers*: Leeds Music Ltd.

*Date of Entry*: 27.11.54

*Highest Position*: 19
*Weeks on Chart*: 8

*Recordings*:

| | | |
|---|---|---|
| Patti Page | 10/54 | Mercury MB.3161 |
| The Beverley Sisters | 11/54 | Philips PB.370 |
| The Coronets | 11/54 | Columbia DB.3533 |
| Jean Campbell | 11/54 | Parlophone R.3938 |
| Lita Roza | 11/54 | Decca F.10393 (&45-) |
| The Regent Ballroom Orchestra | 1/55 | Decca F.10445 (&45-) |

## 603 | I STILL BELIEVE

*Composer*: Billy Reid

*Publishers*: Macmelodies Ltd.

*Date of Entry*: 4.12.54/
Pos: 11/Wks: 17

*Re-entry*: 16.4.55/
Pos: 23/Wks: 3

*Recordings*:

| | | |
|---|---|---|
| Ronnie Harris | 10/54 | Columbia DB.3529/ (45) SCM.5139 |
| Johnny Francis | 10/54 | Decca F.10380 |
| Archie Lewis | 10/54 | Melodisc P.220 |
| Ronnie Hilton | 11/54 | HMV B.10785 |
| Al Martino | 11/54 | Capitol CL.14192 (& 45-) |
| Victor Silvester and his Ballroom Orchestra | 12/54 | Columbia FB.3726 |
| Beryl Templeman | 12/54 | Embassy WB.114 |

## 604 | HEARTBEAT

*Composer*: Jerry Stevens

*Publishers*: Edward Kassner Music Co. Ltd.

*Date of Entry*: 4.12.54/
Pos: 21/Wks: 6

*Re-entry*: 22.1.55/
Pos: 12/Wks: 11

*Recordings*:

| | | |
|---|---|---|
| Ruby Murray | 11/54 | Columbia DB.3542 |
| Karen Chandler | 12/54 | Vogue Coral Q.2030 |
| Lita Roza | 12/54 | Decca F.10427 (&45-) |
| Victor Silvester and his Ballroom Orchestra | 1/55 | Columbia FB.3729 |
| Penny Nicholls and The Four-in-A-Chord | 2/55 | Embassy WB.123 |

## 605 | NOT AS A STRANGER

*Composers*: John Schroeder & Abner Silver
*Publishers*: Pickwick Music Ltd.

*Date of Entry*: 4.12.54
*Highest Position*: 24
*Weeks on Chart*: 1

*Recordings*:

| | | |
|---|---|---|
| David Hughes | 10/54 | Philips PB.350 |
| Tony Bennett | 11/54 | Philips PB.357 |
| Al Martino | 11/54 | Capitol CL.14202 (& 45-) |
| The Four Guys | 11/54 | Mercury MB.3169 |
| Johnny Stevens | 12/54 | Decca F.10413 (&45-) |

## 606 | MISTER SANDMAN

*Composer*: Pat Ballard
*Publishers*: Edwin H. Morris & Co. Ltd.

*Date of Entry*: 11.12.54
*Highest Position*: 1
*Weeks on Chart*: 20

*Recordings*:

| | | |
|---|---|---|
| Vaughn Monroe | 9/54 | HMV B.10751/ (45) 7M.247 |
| Max Bygraves | 11/54 | HMV B.10801 |
| The Chordettes | 11/54 | Columbia DB.3553/ (45) SCM.5158 |
| Dickie Valentine | 11/54 | Decca F.10415 (&45-) |
| Joe Loss and his Orchestra | 12/54 | HMV BD.6184 |
| The Four Aces featuring Al Alberts | 12/54 | Brunswick 05355 (& 45-) |
| Buddy Morrow and his Orchestra (vocal Quartet) | 12/54 | Mercury MB.3170 |
| Les Paul and Mary Ford | 12/54 | Capitol CL.14212 (& 45-) |
| The Lancers | 12/54 | Vogue Coral Q.2038 (& 45-) |
| The Four-in-A-Chord | 12/54 | Embassy WB.115 |
| Les Elgart and his Orchestra and Chorus | 12/54 | Philips PB.385 |
| Victor Silvester and his Ballroom Orchestra | 1/55 | Columbia FB.3728 |
| Max Bygraves | 1/55 | HMV B.10821 |
| The Regent Ballroom Orchestra | 1/55 | Decca F.10446 (&45-) |

## 607 | THE FINGER OF SUSPICION

| | |
|---|---|
| *Composers*: Paul Mann & Al Lewis | *Date of Entry*: 11.12.54 |
| *Publishers*: Pickwick Music Ltd. | *Highest Position*: 2 |
| | *Weeks on Chart*: 19 |

*Recordings*:

| | | |
|---|---|---|
| The Coronets | 11/54 | Columbia DB.3533 |
| Dickie Valentine with The Stargazers | 11/54 | Decca F.10394 (&45-) |
| Jane Froman | 12/54 | Capitol CL.14209 (& 45-) |
| Bonnie Lou | 2/55 | Parlophone R.3989/ (45) MSP.6157 |
| Bob Dale | 2/55 | Embassy WB.121 |
| The Regent Ballroom Orchestra | 3/55 | Decca F.10482 (&45-) |
| The Naturals | 3/55 | MGM.807/ (45) SP.1123 |

# 1955

One might say with confidence that by the time the year was through, the record chart was dominant. Certainly, some who perhaps should know better have stated that 'pop' music began in 1955. Surely pop, or popular, music goes back as far as the human race, but in order to try to keep all things in perspective it is necessary here to cut off some years on either side. Those who would say there was nothing before 1955 obviously have rock 'n' roll in mind, while those who say there was nothing after 1955 stopped listening at that point because they, too, have rock 'n' roll in mind. However, as far as we are concerned here, the sheet music and record charts still continued and provided much interest to the popular music devotee. But it was true that while the sales of the sheet music were slowly falling, the sales of records were growing steadily and signs of the differences between the charts were growing more marked year by year. Take, for example, *The dam busters march*, which was popularised by the film. This created a new record with its 57-week run in the sheet music charts, but the recording by the RAF Central Band stayed just one week in the record charts! In contrast, the seven Ruby Murray hits in the record listings were all listed at some time in the sheet music charts. The BBC Light Programme broadcast three concerts in its Festival of Dance Music series from the Royal Albert Hall in February and March, featuring top bands and singers such as Ted Heath, Geraldo, the Show Band, Ken Mackintosh and the Squadronaires with Alma Cogan, Frankie Vaughan, Joan Regan, Max

| | MOST WEEKS ON THE CHARTS TOP SIX | |
|---|---|---|
| Pos | | Wks |
| 1 | *Softly, softly* | 43 |
| 2= | *Stranger in paradise* | 29 |
| 2= | *I wonder* | 29 |
| 4 | *Unchained melody* | 28 |
| 5= | *Under the bridges of Paris* | 27 |
| 5= | *Cherry pink and apple blossom white* | 27 |
| 5= | *Ev'rywhere* | 27 |

Bygraves and the Stargazers. Mambos had a brief spell of popularity with both *Mambo Italiano*, another Merrill song, and *Cherry pink and apple blossom white* topping the chart. Big changes were afoot in the record world though, particularly in the EMI stable with the cheaper 78s, the Columbia FB, the

Parlophone F and HMV BD series all disappearing. HMV took its popular music away from the B series and started the POP label, the first issues appearing in October and thereby compounding the 'pop' theory. At the same time, the Columbia and Parlophone companies adopted brighter record labels in line with HMV. EMI also discontinued its numbering styles for 45s, going over to the Decca style of prefixing the 78 number with 45-. The first Pye Nixa issues with the N prefix arrived in September, while in November Capitol issued its last records under the Decca banner – from January 1956 they would be released by EMI. As far as television was concerned, the day to note was Thursday, 22 September, for that was the day on which Commercial Television came to Britain. The first 'Sunday Night at the London Palladium' was shown on 25 September with special guest stars Guy Mitchell and Gracie Fields. Other ITV notables in this first year included 'Music Shop' and the arrival of Jack Jackson 'on the box'. A 'Disc Festival' was organised by the *Daily Mirror* in November and housed at the Palladium. Continental sheet music sales were in sharp decline at this time, much more so than here, and sales of 10,000 were considered good, with 20,000 almost unheard of. August saw Slim Whitman's *Rose Marie* at the top of the best selling record charts – but the song never appeared at all in the sheet music charts.

# SONG CHARTS

## 608 HAPPY DAYS AND LONELY NIGHTS

*Composers*: Fred Fisher & Billy Rose
*Publishers*: Lawrence Wright Music Co. Ltd.

*Date of Entry*: 1.1.55
*Highest Position*: 4
*Weeks on Chart*: 19

*Recordings*:

| | | |
|---|---|---|
| Frankie Vaughan | 11/54 | HMV B.10783 (45) 7M.270 |
| Suzi Miller and The Johnston Brothers | 11/54 | Decca F.10389 (&45-) |
| The Fontane Sisters | 11/54 | London HL.8099 (& 45-) |
| Billy Thorburn and his Strict Tempo Music | 12/54 | Parlophone F.2544 |
| Ruby Murray | 1/55 | Columbia DB.3577 |
| Bob Dale | 2/55 | Embassy WB.121 |
| Joe Loss and his Orchestra | 3/55 | HMV BD.6192 |

## 609 WHITE CHRISTMAS

*Composer*: Irving Berlin
*Publishers*: Irving Berlin Ltd.

*Date of Entry*: 1.1.55
*Highest Position*: 24
*Weeks on Chart*: 1

*Recordings*:

| | | |
|---|---|---|
| Bing Crosby with The Ken Darby Singers | 10/42 | Brunswick 03384 |
| Vera Lynn | 10/42 | Decca F.8201 |
| The Ink Spots | 10/47 | Brunswick 03811 |
| Gracie Fields | 10/48 | Decca F.8985 |
| Guy Lombardo and his Royal Canadians (Tony Craig) | 10/48 | Brunswick 03948 |
| Carmen Cavallaro (piano) | 10/48 | Brunswick 03949 |
| Ethel Smith (organ) | 10/48 | Brunswick 03950 |
| Jo Stafford | 11/51 | Capitol CL.13632 |
| Perry Como | 11/52 | HMV B.10374 |
| Mantovani and his Orchestra | 11/52 | Decca F.10017 |
| Louis Armstrong | 12/52 | Brunswick 05032 |
| Ray Martin and his Concert Orchestra | 11/53 | Columbia DB.3376 |
| Les Paul and Mary Ford | 11/53 | Capitol CL.14018 |
| Ray Martin and his Concert Orchestra | 12/53 | Columbia (45) SCM.5071 |
| Eddie Fisher | 11/54 | HMV B.10779/ (45) 7M.266 |
| Rosemary Clooney with The Mellomen | 11/54 | Philips PB.376 |
| Bing Crosby with The Ken Darby Singers | 12/54 | Brunswick 45-03384 |
| Frank Sinatra | 12/54 | Capitol CL.14174 (& 45-) |
| Bing Crosby, Danny Kaye, Peggy Lee and Trudy Stevens | 12/54 | Brunswick 05354 (& 45-) |
| Bob Dale | 11/55 | Embassy WB.159★ |

## 610 MAMBO ITALIANO

*Composer*: Bob Merrill

*Publishers*: Campbell Connelly & Co. Ltd.

*Date of Entry*: 8.1.55

*Highest Position*: 1
*Weeks on Chart*: 16

*Recordings*:

| | | |
|---|---|---|
| Rosemary Clooney with The Mellomen | 12/54 | Philips PB.382 |
| Dean Martin | 1/55 | Capitol CL.14227 (& 45-) |
| Marie Benson | 1/55 | Decca F.10452 (&45-) |
| Alma Cogan with vocal group | 2/55 | HMV B.10832 |
| The Ray Ellington Quartet | 2/55 | Columbia DB.3578 |
| The Four-in-A-Chord | 2/55 | Embassy WB.122 |

## 611 THE NAUGHTY LADY OF SHADY LANE

*Composers*: Sid Tepper & Roy C. Bennett

*Publishers*: Sterling Music Publishing Co. Ltd.

*Date of Entry*: 15.1.55

*Highest Position*: 3
*Weeks on Chart*: 17

*Recordings*:

| | | |
|---|---|---|
| The Ames Brothers | 12/54 | HMV B.10800 |
| Archie Bleyer and his Chorus and Orchestra | 12/54 | London HL.8111 (& 45-) |
| The Ames Brothers | 1/55 | HMV (45) 7M.281 |
| Dean Martin | 1/55 | Capitol CL.14226 (& 45-) |
| The Beverley Sisters | 1/55 | Philips PB.395 |
| Alma Cogan with vocal group | 2/55 | HMV B.10832 |
| The Ray Ellington Quartet | 2/55 | Columbia DB.3578 |
| Billy Cotton and his Band (The Bandits) | 2/55 | Decca F.10459 (&45-) |
| The Four-in-A-Chord | 2/55 | Embassy WB.120 |
| Aimable, his Accordion and Electric Organ | 11/55 | Vogue V.9057★ |

## 612 | PAPA LOVES MAMBO

| | | |
|---|---|---|
| *Composers*: Al Hoffman, Dick Manning & Bix Reichner | | *Date of Entry*: 15.1.55 |
| *Publishers*: Macmelodies Ltd. | | *Highest Position*: 21<br>*Weeks on Chart*: 1 |

*Recordings*:

| | | |
|---|---|---|
| Perry Como and The Ray Charles Singers | 10/54 | HMV B.10776/<br>(45) 7M.263 |
| Johnnie Ray | 10/54 | Philips PB.346 |
| Ted Heath and his Music (The Johnston Brothers and Duncan Campbell) | 11/54 | Decca F.10401 (&45-) |
| Nat 'King' Cole | 12/54 | Capitol CL.14207<br>(& 45-) |

## 613 | SOFTLY, SOFTLY

| | | |
|---|---|---|
| *Composers*: Pierre Dudan, Paddy Roberts & Mark Paul | | *Date of Entry*: 15.1.55 |
| *Publishers*: Cavendish Music Co. Ltd. | | *Highest Position*: 1<br>*Weeks on Chart*: 43 |

*Recordings*:

| | | |
|---|---|---|
| Ruby Murray | 1/55 | Columbia DB.3558/<br>(45) SCM.5162 |
| Alma Cogan with Choir and Organ | 1/55 | HMV B.10828/<br>(45) 7M.286 |
| Kim Bennett | 1/55 | Decca F.10449 (&45-) |
| Joe Loss and his Orchestra | 2/55 | HMV BD.6189 |
| Mantovani and his Orchestra and Chorus (Solo voice: Kim Bennett) | 3/55 | Decca F.10468 (&45-) |
| Victor Silvester and his Ballroom Orchestra | 3/55 | Columbia FB.3735 |
| The Regent Ballroom Orchestra | 3/55 | Decca F.10487 (&45-) |
| Guy Lombardo and his Royal Canadians (The Lombardo Quartet) | 3/55 | Brunswick 05412<br>(& 45-) |
| Doreen Harris | 5/55 | Embassy WB.127 |
| Aimable, his Accordion and Electric Organ (Titled 'La Tamise et mon jardin') | 10/55 | Vogue V.9056 |

## 614 | SOMEBODY

| | | |
|---|---|---|
| *Composer*: Joe Henderson | | *Date of Entry*: 22.1.55 |
| *Publishers*: Bourne Music Ltd. | | *Highest Position*: 13<br>*Weeks on Chart*: 10 |

*Recordings*:

| | | |
|---|---|---|
| Petula Clark | 7/54 | Polygon P.1128 |
| The Stargazers with Sonny Farrar and his Banjo Band | 12/54 | Decca F.10437 (&45-) |
| Joe Loss and his Orchestra | 3/55 | HMV BD.6192 |
| Petula Clark | 1/56 | Pye Nixa N.15024★ |

## 615 | A BLOSSOM FELL

| | | |
|---|---|---|
| *Composers*: Howard Barnes, Harold Cornelius & Dominic John | | *Date of Entry*: 22.1.55 /<br>Pos: 3 / Wks: 18 |
| *Publishers*: John Fields Music Co. Ltd. | | *Re-entry*: 4.6.55/<br>Pos: 24/Wks: 1 |

*Recordings*:

| | | |
|---|---|---|
| Ronnie Hilton | 1/55 | HMV B.10808/<br>(45) 7M.285 |
| Johnny O'Connor | 1/55 | Polygon P.1151 |
| Dickie Valentine | 1/55 | Decca F.10430 (&45-) |
| Nat 'King' Cole | 1/55 | Capitol CL.14235<br>(& 45-) |
| The Regent Ballroom Orchestra | 3/55 | Decca F.10482 (&45-) |
| Victor Silvester and his Ballroom Orchestra | 4/55 | Columbia FB.3736 |
| Wally Carr | 4/55 | Embassy WB.131 |

## 616 | MAJORCA (Midinette)

| | | |
|---|---|---|
| *Composers*: Louis Gasté, Johnny Lehmann & George Bunnet | | *Date of Entry*: 29.1.55 |
| *Publishers*: Mills Music Ltd. | | *Highest Position*: 7<br>*Weeks on Chart*: 15 |

*Recordings*:

| | | |
|---|---|---|
| Norrie Paramor and his Orchestra | 12/54 | Columbia DB.3552/<br>(45) SCM.5157 |
| Petula Clark | 12/54 | Polygon P.1146 |
| Ronald Chesney (harmonica) | 1/55 | HMV B.10815 |
| Joe Loss and his Orchestra | 1/55 | HMV BD.6185 |
| Sidney Torch and his Orchestra | 1/55 | Parlophone R.3965 |
| Monty Kelly and his Orchestra | 1/55 | Polygon P.1147 |
| The Johnston Brothers | 1/55 | Decca F.10451 (&45-) |
| Bob Manning | 3/55 | Capitol CL.14256<br>(& 45-) |
| Petula Clark | 1/56 | Pye Nixa N.15026★ |

## 617 | SHAKE, RATTLE AND ROLL

| | | |
|---|---|---|
| *Composer*: Charles Calhoun | | *Date of Entry*: 29.1.55 /<br>Pos: 22 / Wks: 4 |
| *Publishers*: Campbell Connelly & Co. Ltd. | | *Re-entry*: 5.3.55/<br>Pos: 24/Wks: 1 |

*Recordings*:

| | | |
|---|---|---|
| Bill Haley and his Comets | 11/54 | Brunswick 05338<br>(& 45-) |
| The Deep River Boys | 12/54 | HMV B.10790/<br>(45) 7M.280 |
| Jack Parnell and his Orchestra (Jack Parnell and The Crackerjacks) | 2/55 | Parlophone R.3986 |
| The Four-in-A-Chord | 2/55 | Embassy WB.122 |
| Johnny Franks and his Rhythm | 6/55 | Melodisc P.230★ |

## 618 GIVE ME YOUR WORD

*Composers*: George Wyle & Irving Taylor

*Publishers*: Campbell Connelly & Co. Ltd.

*Date of Entry*: 29.1.55 / Pos: 24 / Wks: 1

*Re-entry*: 12.2.55 / Pos: 2 / Wks: 23

*Recordings*:
| | | |
|---|---|---|
| Tennessee Ernie Ford | 7/54 | Capitol CL.14005 |
| Jimmy Young | 11/54 | Decca F.10406 (& 45-) |
| Lee Lawrence | 3/55 | Columbia DB.3593/ (45) SCM.5175 |
| Larry Cross | 4/55 | Embassy WB.128 |
| Billy Thorburn and his Strict Tempo Music | 5/55 | Parlophone F.2552 |

## 619 LET ME GO LOVER

*Composers*: Jenny Lou Carson & Al Hill
*Publishers*: Aberbach (London) Ltd

*Date of entry*: 5.2.55
*Highest position*: 2
*Weeks on chart*: 18

*Recordings*:
| | | |
|---|---|---|
| Patti Page | 1/55 | Mercury MB.3182 |
| Rose Brennan | 1/55 | HMV B.10812 |
| Joan Weber | 1/55 | Philips PB.389 |
| Lita Roza | 1/55 | Decca F.10431 (& 45-) |
| Peggy Lee | 1/55 | Brunswick 05360 (& 45-) |
| Dean Martin | 1/55 | Capitol CL.14226 (& 45-) |
| Teresa Brewer with The Lancers | 1/55 | Vogue Coral Q.72043 (& 45-) |
| Ruby Murray | 1/55 | Columbia DB.3577 |
| Penny Nicholls and The Four-in-A-Chord | 2/55 | Embassy WB.123 |
| The Regent Ballroom Orchestra | 3/55 | Decca F.10487 (& 45-) |
| Jerry Colonna with The Three Lovers | 4/55 | Parlophone R.4007/ (45) MSP.6165 |

## 620 MOBILE

*Composers*: Bob Wells & David Holt

*Publishers*: Leeds Music Ltd.

*Date of Entry*: 5.2.55

*Highest Position*: 6
*Weeks on Chart*: 19

*Recordings*:
| | | |
|---|---|---|
| Ray Burns | 1/55 | Columbia DB.3563 |
| Marie Benson | 1/55 | Decca F.10452 (& 45-) |
| The Sauter-Finegan Orchestra (Andy Roberts, Anita Darian and The Doodlers) | 4/55 | HMV B.10856 |
| Julius La Rosa | 7/55 | London HL.8154 (& 45-)★ |

## 621 TOMORROW

*Composers*: Peter Hart & Bob Geraldson
*Publishers*: Cavendish Music Co. Ltd.

*Date of Entry*: 12.2.55
*Highest Position*: 6
*Weeks on Chart*: 26

*Recordings*:
| | | |
|---|---|---|
| Johnny Brandon and The Phantoms | 9/54 | Polygon P.1131 |
| Max Bygraves | 3/55 | HMV B.10842 |
| Lita Roza | 3/55 | Decca F.10479 (& 45-) |
| Danny Purches | 4/55 | Columbia DB.3604 |
| The Ken-Tones | 4/55 | Parlophone R.4013 |
| Johnny Brandon and The Phantoms | 1/56 | Pye Nixa N.15025★ |

## 622 TEACH ME TONIGHT

*Composers*: Sammy Cahn & Gene De Paul

*Publishers*: Leeds Music Ltd.

*Date of Entry*: 19.2.55 / Pos: 24 / Wks: 1

*Re-entry*: 5.3.55/ Pos: 21/Wks: 2

*Recordings*:
| | | |
|---|---|---|
| Janet Brace | 4/54 | Brunswick 05272 |
| Anne Shelton | 11/54 | HMV B.10789/ (45) 7M.279 |
| Billie Anthony | 12/54 | Columbia DB.3550/ (45) SCM.5155 |
| Nat 'King' Cole with Billy May and his Orchestra | 12/54 | Capitol CL.14207 (& 45-) |
| The De Castro Sisters | 12/54 | London HL.8104 (& 45-) |
| Jo Stafford | 12/54 | Philips PB.383 |
| Kathy Lloyd | 12/54 | Decca F.10418 (&45-) |
| The Modernaires with Paula Kelly and Georgie Auld (tenor sax) | 12/54 | Vogue Coral Q.2024 |
| Janet Brace | 1/55 | Brunswick 45–05272 |
| Dinah Washington | 1/55 | Mercury MB.3188 |
| Benny Hill | 1/55 | Decca F.10442 (& 45-) |

## 623 PRIZE OF GOLD

*Composers*: Ned Washington & Lester Lee
*Publishers*: Victoria Music Publishing Co. Ltd.

*Date of Entry*: 26.2.55
*Highest Position*: 5
*Weeks on Chart*: 19

*Recordings*:
| | | |
|---|---|---|
| Ronnie Hilton | 1/55 | HMV B.10808/ (45) 7M.285 |
| Joan Regan | 1/55 | Decca F.10432 (& 45-) |
| The Melachrino Strings | 1/55 | HMV B.10822 |
| Rita Williams | 2/55 | Embassy WB.119 |
| Charlie Applewhite | 4/55 | Brunswick 05411 (& 45-) |
| Micki Marlo | 4/55 | Capitol CL.14271 (& 45-) |

## 624 GIVE ME THE RIGHT

| | | |
|---|---|---|
| *Composers*: Marty Gold & Tom Glazer | | *Date of Entry*: 26.2.55 |
| *Publishers*: Keith Prowse & Co. Ltd. | | *Highest Position*: 21 |
| | | *Weeks on Chart*: 4 |

Recordings:
| | | |
|---|---|---|
| Georgie Shaw | 12/54 | Brunswick 05356 |
| | | (& 45-) |
| Johnny O'Connor | 1/55 | Polygon P.1151 |
| David Hughes | 1/55 | Philips PB.396 |
| Johnny Francis | 1/55 | Decca F.10440 (& 45-) |
| Monty Norman | 2/55 | Columbia DB.3571 |
| Victor Silvester and his Ballroom Orchestra | 2/55 | Columbia FB.3730 |

## 625 UNDER THE BRIDGES OF PARIS

| | | |
|---|---|---|
| *Composers*: Vincent Scotto, Jean Rodor & Dorcas Cochran | | *Date of Entry*: 12.3.55 |
| *Publishers*: Southern Music Publishing Co. Ltd. | | *Highest Position*: 4 |
| | | *Weeks on Chart*: 27 |

Recordings:
| | | |
|---|---|---|
| Eartha Kitt | 3/54 | HMV B.10647/ |
| | | (45) 7M.191 |
| Dean Martin | 3/55 | Capitol CL.14255 |
| | | (& 45-) |
| Percy Faith and his Orchestra | 3/55 | Philips PB.415 |
| Victor Silvester and his Ballroom Orchestra | 5/55 | Columbia FB.3742 |

## 626 PAPER KISSES

| | | |
|---|---|---|
| *Composer*: John Jerome | | *Date of Entry*: 12.3.55 / Pos: 23 / Wks: 1 |
| *Publishers*: John Fields Music Co. Ltd. | | *Re-entry*: 26.3.55 / Pos: 21 / Wks: 4 |

Recordings:
| | | |
|---|---|---|
| Alma Cogan | 1/55 | HMV B.10828/ |
| | | (45) 7M.286 |
| Victor Silvester and his Ballroom Orchestra | 2/55 | Columbia FB.3731 |
| Washboard Joe and his Scrubbers | 2/55 | Parlophone R.3984 |

## 627 IF ANYONE FINDS THIS, I LOVE YOU

| | | |
|---|---|---|
| *Composers*: Sidney Lippman & Sylvia Dee | | *Date of Entry*: 19.3.55 |
| *Publishers*: Michael Reine Music Co. Ltd. | | *Highest Position*: 6 |
| | | *Weeks on Chart*: 16 |

Recordings:
| | | |
|---|---|---|
| Kay Starr | 3/55 | HMV B.10837/ |
| | | (45) 7M.300 |
| Ruby Murray with Anne Warren | 3/55 | Columbia DB.3580/ |
| | | (45) SCM.5169 |
| Jimmy Young | 3/55 | Decca F.10483 |
| | | (& 45-) |
| The Beverley Sisters | 3/55 | Philips PB.426 |
| Billy Thorburn and his Strict Tempo Music | 5/55 | Parlophone F.2552 |

## 628 READY, WILLING AND ABLE

| | | |
|---|---|---|
| *Composers*: Al Rinker, Floyd Huddleston & Dick Gleason | | *Date of Entry*: 19.3.55 |
| *Publishers*: Berry Music Co. Ltd. | | *Highest Position*: 9 |
| | | *Weeks on Chart*: 20 |

Recordings:
| | | |
|---|---|---|
| Doris Day | 2/55 | Philips PB.402 |
| Eve Boswell | 2/55 | Parlophone R.3994 |
| | | (45) MSP.6158 |
| Gary Crosby and The Cheerleaders | 2/55 | Brunswick 05378 |
| | | (& 45-) |
| The Coronets with The Big Ben Banjo Band | 3/55 | Columbia DB.3583 |
| Billy Cotton and his Band (The Mill Girls) | 3/55 | Decca F.10491 |
| | | (& 45-) |

## 629 OPEN UP YOUR HEART

| | | |
|---|---|---|
| *Composer*: Stuart Hamblen | | *Date of Entry*: 19.3.55 |
| *Publishers*: Duchess Music Ltd. | | *Highest Position*: 12 |
| | | *Weeks on Chart*: 14 |

Recordings:
| | | |
|---|---|---|
| The Cowboy Church Sunday School | 1/55 | Brunswick 05371 |
| | | (& 45-) |
| Tony Brent and Anne Warren | 2/55 | Columbia DB.3579/ |
| | | (45) SCM.5170 |
| Little Sister Gail and Big Sister Rosemary Clooney | 2/55 | Philips PB.409 |
| Joan and Rusty Regan | 2/55 | Decca F.10474 |
| | | (& 45-) |
| The McGuire Sisters | 2/55 | Vogue Coral |
| | | Q.72052 (& 45-) |
| Washboard Joe and his Scrubbers | 4/55 | Parlophone R.4008 |

## 630 CHERRY PINK AND APPLE BLOSSOM WHITE

*Composers*: Louiguy, Jacques Larue & Mack David          *Date of Entry*: 26.3.55

*Publishers*: Maddox Music Co. Ltd.          *Highest Position*: 2
*Weeks on Chart*: 27

*Recordings*:

| | | |
|---|---|---|
| Perez 'Prez' Prado and his Orchestra (Trumpet solo: Billy Regis) | 2/55 | HMV B.10833/ (45) 7M.295 |
| Xavier Cugat and his Orchestra | 3/55 | Philips PB.413 |
| Edmundo Ros and his Orchestra | 3/55 | Decca F.10480 (& 45-) |
| Eddie Calvert – The Man with the Golden Trumpet | 3/55 | Columbia DB.3581/ (45) SCM.5168 |
| Alan Dale | 4/55 | Vogue Coral Q.72072 (& 45-) |
| Georgia Gibbs | 5/55 | Mercury MB.3217 |
| Les Baxter and his Orchestra and Chorus | 5/55 | Capitol CL.14237 (& 45-) |
| Guy Lombardo and his Royal Canadians (Bill Flanagan) | 6/55 | Brunswick 05443 (& 45-) |
| Rita Williams with The Four-in-A-Chord | 6/55 | Embassy WB.132 |
| Victor Young and his Singing Strings | 7/55 | Brunswick 05448 (& 45-) |

## 631 TWEEDLE-DEE

*Composer*: Winfield Scott          *Date of Entry*: 2.4.55 / Pos: 14 / Wks: 11

*Publishers*: Robbins Music Corporation Ltd.          *Re-entry*: 2.7.55/ Pos: 23/Wks: 3

*Recordings*:

| | | |
|---|---|---|
| Vicki Young and Vocal Group | 1/55 | Capitol CL.14228 (& 45-) |
| Georgia Gibbs | 2/55 | Mercury MB.3196 |
| Bonnie Lou and her Gang | 2/55 | Parlophone R.3989/ (45) MSP.6157 |
| LaVern Baker with The Gliders | 2/55 | Columbia DB.3591 |
| Suzi Miller with The Johnston Brothers and The Tony Kinsey Trio | 2/55 | Decca F.10475 (& 45-) |
| LaVern Baker with The Gliders | 3/55 | Columbia (45) SCM.5172 |
| Billie Anthony | 3/55 | Columbia DB.3592/ (45) SCM.5174 |
| Alma Cogan | 3/55 | HMV B.10848/ (45) 7M.301 |
| Frankie Vaughan | 3/55 | Philips PB.423 |
| The Kirchin Band – Ivor & Basil | 4/55 | Parlophone R.4010 |
| The Four-in-A-Chord | 4/55 | Embassy WB.130 |
| Teresa Brewer | 4/55 | Vogue Coral Q.72066 (& 45-) |
| Johnny Franks and his Rhythm | 6/55 | Melodisc P.230 |

## 632 UNSUSPECTING HEART

*Composers*: Joe Beal, Bob Singer, Freddy James & Joe Shank          *Date of Entry*: 2.4.55

*Publishers*: Berry Music Co. Ltd.          *Highest Position*: 10
*Weeks on Chart*: 19

*Recordings*:

| | | |
|---|---|---|
| Georgie Shaw | 1/55 | Brunswick 05362 (& 45-) |
| Terri Stevens | 2/55 | Parlophone R.3983 |
| Anita Ellis | 2/55 | Philips PB.398 |
| Kathy Lloyd | 2/55 | Decca F.10464 (& 45-) |
| Frankie Vaughan with Vocal Group | 3/55 | HMV B.10845/ (45) 7M.298 |
| Fay Brown | 3/55 | Columbia DB.3582 |
| Billy McCormack | 3/55 | Polygon P.1156 |
| Wally Carr | 4/55 | Embassy WB.131 |

## 633 STRANGER IN PARADISE

*Composers*: Robert Wright & George Forrest (based on themes of A. Borodin)          *Date of Entry*: 2.4.55

*Publishers*: Frank Music Co. Ltd.          *Highest Position*: 1
*Weeks on Chart*: 29

*Recordings*:

| | | |
|---|---|---|
| Edmund Hockridge | 4/55 | Parlophone R.4011 |
| Winifred Atwell (piano) | 4/55 | Decca F.10496 (&45-) |
| Bing Crosby | 4/55 | Brunswick 05410 (& 45-) |
| Gordon MacRae | 4/55 | Capitol CL.14276 (&45-) |
| Mantovani and his Orchestra | 4/55 | Decca F.10495 (&45-) |
| John Sebastian (harmonica) | 4/55 | London HL.8131 (& 45-) |
| Vic Damone | 4/55 | Mercury MB.3208 |
| Doretta Morrow and Richard Kiley | 4/55 | Philips PB.435 |
| Don Cornell | 4/55 | Vogue Coral Q.72073 (& 45-) |
| Eddie Calvert – The Man with the Golden Trumpet | 4/55 | Columbia DB.3594 |
| Ronnie Harris | 4/55 | Columbia DB.3595/ (45) SCM.5176 |
| Tony Martin | 4/55 | HMV B.10849/ (45) 7M.302 |
| Tony Bennett | 4/55 | Philips PB.420 |
| George Shearing and his Quintet | 4/55 | MGM.817 |
| Tony Osborne and his Orchestra (Reg Gray) | 4/55 | Polygon P.1158 |
| The Four Aces | 4/55 | Brunswick 05418 (& 45-) |
| Keith Warwick | 4/55 | Embassy WB.126 |
| Joe Loss and his Orchestra | 5/55 | HMV BD.6196 |
| Victor Silvester and his Ballroom Orchestra | 5/55 | Columbia FB.3743 |

## 634 (I'm always hearing) WEDDING BELLS

| | | |
|---|---|---|
| *Composers*: Robert Mellin & Herbert Jarczyk | *Date of Entry*: 9.4.55 / | Pos: 22 / Wks: 1 |
| *Publishers*: Robert Mellin Ltd. | *Re-entry*: 23.4.55 / | Pos: 19 / Wks: 4 |

*Recordings*:

| | | |
|---|---|---|
| Eddie Fisher | 2/55 | HMV B.10839/ (45) 7M.294 |
| Guy Lombardo and his Royal Canadians (Kenny Gardner) | 3/55 | Brunswick 05412 (& 45-) |

## 635 I WONDER

| | | |
|---|---|---|
| *Composers*: Sam M. Lewis, George W. Meyer & Pete Wendling | *Date of Entry*: 23.4.55 | |
| *Publishers*: Macmelodies Ltd. | *Highest Position*: 2 | *Weeks on Chart*: 29 |

*Recordings*:

| | | |
|---|---|---|
| Jane Froman | 2/55 | Capitol CL.14254 (& 45-) |
| Robert Earl | 4/55 | Philips PB.433 |
| Ronnie Harris | 4/55 | Columbia DB.3595/ (45) SCM.5176 |
| Dickie Valentine | 4/55 | Decca F.10493 (&45-) |
| Keith Warwick | 4/55 | Embassy WB.126 |
| The Deep River Boys | 7/55 | HMV B.10902 |

## 636 YOU, MY LOVE

| | | |
|---|---|---|
| *Composers*: Mack Gordon & Jimmy Van Heusen | *Date of Entry*: 23.4.55 | |
| *Publishers*: Dash Music Co. Ltd. | *Highest Position*: 11 | *Weeks on Chart*: 25 |

*Recordings*:

| | | |
|---|---|---|
| Ron Goodwin and his Concert Orchestra | 2/55 | Parlophone R.3982/ (45) MSP.6154 |
| Doris Day | 2/55 | Philips PB.402 |
| Frank Sinatra | 2/55 | Capitol CL.14240 (& 45-) |
| Victor Young and his Singing Strings | 2/55 | Brunswick 05386 (& 45-) |
| Shirley Wilson | 3/55 | Columbia DB.3585 |
| Victor Silvester and his Ballroom Orchestra | 11/55 | Columbia DB.3685/ (45) SCM.5203★ |

## 637 UNCHAINED MELODY

| | | |
|---|---|---|
| *Composers*: Alex North & Hy Zaret | *Date of Entry*: 30.4.55 | |
| *Publishers*: Frank Music Co. Ltd. | *Highest Position*: 1 | *Weeks on Chart*: 28 |

*Recordings*:

| | | |
|---|---|---|
| Jimmy Young | 4/55 | Decca F.10502 (&45-) |
| Al Hibbler | 4/55 | Brunswick 05420 (& 45-) |
| Les Baxter and his Chorus and Orchestra | 4/55 | Capitol CL.14257 (& 45-) |
| Liberace (piano) | 4/55 | Philips PB.430 |
| Ken Mackintosh, his alto sax, and his Orchestra | 5/55 | HMV BD.1338 |
| Jean Carson | 5/55 | HMV B.10871 |
| The Crew Cuts | 5/55 | Mercury MB.3222 |
| Dick James | 5/55 | Parlophone R.4027/ (45) MSP.6170 |
| Fay Brown | 6/55 | Columbia DB.3623/ (45) SCM.5185 |
| Cliff Townsend (alto sax) | 6/55 | Columbia DB.3630 |
| Leroy Holmes and his Orchestra (Whistling by Fred Lowery) | 6/55 | MGM.831/ (45) SP.1133 |
| Roy Hamilton | 6/55 | Philips PB.448 |
| Don Cornell | 6/55 | Vogue Coral Q.72080 (&45-) |
| The Kingtones | 6/55 | Embassy WB.133 |

## 638 WHERE WILL THE DIMPLE BE?

| | | |
|---|---|---|
| *Composers*: Bob Merrill & Al Hoffman | *Date of Entry*: 30.4.55 | |
| *Publishers*: Cinephonic Music Co. Ltd. | *Highest Position*: 4 | *Weeks on Chart*: 24 |

*Recordings*:

| | | |
|---|---|---|
| Rosemary Clooney with The Mellomen and Thurl Ravenscroft (bass) | 4/55 | Philips PB.428 |
| Lorrae Desmond with The Melodaires | 4/55 | Decca F.10510 (&45-) |
| Alma Cogan | 6/55 | HMV B.10887 |
| Pearl Carr | 7/55 | Embassy WB.135 |

## 639 CHEE-CHEE-OO-CHEE

**Composers:** Saverio Saracini, John Turner & Geoffrey Parsons

**Publishers:** Peter Maurice Music Co. Ltd.

**Date of Entry:** 7.5.55

**Highest Position:** 17
**Weeks on Chart:** 11

Recordings:

| | | |
|---|---|---|
| The Johnston Brothers | 4/55 | Decca F.10513 (&45-) |
| Petula Clark | 4/55 | Polygon P.1164 |
| Alma Cogan with Vocal Group | 4/55 | HMV B.10862/ (45) 7M.293 |
| Jill Day | 5/55 | Parlophone R.4021/ (45) MSP.6169 |
| Dean Martin | 6/55 | Capitol CL.14311 (& 45-) |
| The Mariners | 6/55 | Philips PB.467 |
| The Kingtones | 6/55 | Embassy WB.133 |
| Joe Loss and his Orchestra | 7/55 | HMV BD.6203 |

## 640 EARTH ANGEL

**Composer:** Curtis Williams

**Publishers:** Chappell & Co. Ltd.

**Date of Entry:** 14.5.55 / Pos: 19 / Wks: 1
**Re-entry:** 28.5.55 / Pos: 10 / Wks: 14

Recordings:

| | | |
|---|---|---|
| Les Baxter and The Bombers | 1/55 | Capitol CL.14239 (& 45-) |
| The Penguins | 1/55 | London HL.8114 (& 45-) |
| The Crew Cuts | 3/55 | Mercury MB.3202 |
| The Southlanders | 5/55 | Parlophone R.4025 |
| The Ray Ellington Quartet | 5/55 | Columbia DB.3606 |
| Pat O'Day | 5/55 | MGM.823/ (45) SP.1129 |
| Larry Cross | 7/55 | Embassy WB.137 |

## 641 DON'T WORRY
## (and ev'rything will be alright)

**Composer:** Ed Franks

**Publishers:** Vocable Music Co. Ltd.

**Date of Entry:** 14.5.55

**Highest Position:** 9
**Weeks on Chart:** 19

Recordings:

| | | |
|---|---|---|
| Johnny Brandon | 4/55 | Polygon P.1163 |
| Lee Lawrence | 5/55 | Columbia DB.3615/ (45) SCM.5181 |
| The Five Smith Brothers | 5/55 | Decca F.10527 (&45-) |
| Joy Nichols | 5/55 | Mercury MB.3232 |
| The Maple Leaf Four | 7/55 | Embassy WB.142 |
| Johnny Brandon | 1/56 | Pye Nixa N.15025* |

## 642 MELODY OF LOVE

**Composers:** Harry Engelman & Tom Glazer (based on a poem by Mary Carolyn Davies)

**Publishers:** Campbell Connelly & Co. Ltd.

**Date of Entry:** 14.5.55 / Pos: 23 / Wks: 2
**Re-entry:** 18.6.55 / Pos: 16 / Wks: 10

Recordings:

| | | |
|---|---|---|
| The Four Aces | 1/55 | Brunswick 05379 (& 45-) |
| Tony Martin and Dinah Shore | 2/55 | HMV B.10831 |
| The Ink Spots | 2/55 | Parlophone R.3977/ (45) MSP.6152 |
| Franklyn MacCormack (Narrator) with Herbert Foote at the Organ | 2/55 | MGM.802 |
| Frank Sinatra with Ray Anthony and his Orchestra | 2/55 | Capitol CL.14238 (& 45-) |
| Kim Bennett | 2/55 | Decca F.10460 (&45-) |
| Stanley Black and his Romantic Music | 2/55 | Decca F.10462 (&45-) |
| Billy Vaughn and his Orchestra | 2/55 | London HL.8112 (& 45-) |
| David Carroll and his Orchestra | 2/55 | Mercury MB.3194 |
| The McGuire Sisters | 2/55 | Vogue Coral Q.72052 (& 45-) |
| Joe Loss and his Orchestra | 3/55 | HMV BD.6191 |
| Shirley Wilson | 3/55 | Columbia DB.3585 |
| David Carroll and his Orchestra (poem read by Paul Tremaine) | 3/55 | Mercury MB.3204 |
| The Beverley Sisters | 3/55 | Philips PB.426 |
| Earl Bostic and his Alto Sax and his Orchestra | 4/55 | Parlophone R.4003/ (45)MSP.6162 |

## 643 DREAMBOAT

**Composer:** Jack Hoffman

**Publishers:** Leeds Music Ltd.

**Date of Entry:** 21.5.55

**Highest Position:** 2
**Weeks on Chart:** 21

Recordings:

| | | |
|---|---|---|
| The Sunshine Band | 4/55 | Columbia DB.3616 |
| The Five de Marco Sisters | 4/55 | Brunswick 05425 (& 45-) |
| The Paulette Sisters | 4/55 | Capitol CL.14294 (& 45-) |
| The Johnston Brothers | 5/55 | Decca F.10526 (&45-) |
| Alma Cogan | 5/55 | HMV B.10872 |
| The Tanner Sisters | 5/55 | Mercury MB.3233 |
| Victor Silvester and his Ballroom Orchestra | 6/55 | Columbia FB.3745 |
| Joe Loss and his Orchestra | 7/55 | HMV BD.6202 |
| The Maple Leaf Four | 7/55 | Embassy WB.142 |

## 644 SINCERELY

| Composers: Harvey Fuqua & Alan Freed | Date of Entry: 21.5.55 / Pos: 24 / Wks: 1 |
| Publishers: Dash Music Co. Ltd. | Re-entry: 11.6.55 / Pos: 13 / Wks: 12 |

Recordings:

| The McGuire Sisters | 2/55 | Vogue Coral Q.72050 (&45-) |
| Rose Brennan with Joe Loss and his Orchestra | 3/55 | HMV B.10846/ (45) 7M.299 |
| Muriel Smith | 3/55 | Philips PB.422 |
| Billy Fields and The Naturals | 4/55 | MGM.818/ (45) SP.1126 |
| Eddie Calvert – The Man with the Golden Trumpet | 4/55 | Columbia DB.3594 |
| Louis Armstrong | 4/55 | Brunswick 05415 (& 45-) |
| Jill Day | 5/55 | Parlophone R.4021/ (45) MSP.6169 |

## 645 STOWAWAY

| Composers: Jerry Livingston & Carolyn Leigh | Date of Entry: 28.5.55 |
| Publishers: Edwin H. Morris & Co. Ltd. | Highest Position: 7 Weeks on Chart: 17 |

Recordings:

| Barbara Lyon | 5/55 | Columbia DB.3619 |
| Margaret Whiting | 5/55 | Capitol CL. 14307 (& 45-) |
| Lorrae Desmond | 5/55 | Decca F.10533 (&45-) |
| Dinah Shore with The Skylarks | 6/55 | HMV B.10886 |
| Alma Warren | 6/55 | Parlophone R.4035 |
| Rita Williams with The Four-in-A-Chord | 6/55 | Embassy WB.132 |
| Victor Silvester and his Ballroom Orchestra | 7/55 | Columbia FB.3749 |
| Billy Thorburn and his Strict Tempo Music | 7/55 | Parlophone F.2553 |

## 646 THE PENDULUM SONG

| Composers: Al Hoffman & John Murray | Date of Entry: 28.5.55 / Pos: 24 / Wks: 1 |
| Publishers: Edward Kassner Music Co. Ltd. | Re-entry: 18.6.55 / Pos: 24 / Wks: 1 |

Recordings:

| Nelson Riddle and his Orchestra and Chorus | 3/55 | Capitol CL.14262 (& 45-) |
| Petula Clark and The Radio Revellers | 5/55 | Polygon P.1169 |
| Barbara Lyon | 5/55 | Columbia DB.3619 |
| Max Bygraves | 5/55 | HMV B.10876 |

## 647 EVERMORE

| Composers: Gerry Levine & Paddy Roberts | Date of Entry: 11.6.55 |
| Publishers: Edward Kassner Music Co. Ltd. | Highest Position: 2 Weeks on Chart: 25 |

Recordings:

| Edna Savage | 5/55 | Parlophone R.4017 |
| Ruby Murray | 5/55 | Columbia DB.3617/ (45) SCM.5180 |
| Jean Carson | 5/55 | HMV B.10871 |
| Joe Loss and his Orchestra | 6/55 | HMV BD.6199 |
| Jackie Bond (sax) and his Orchestra | 6/55 | Polygon P.1170 |

## 648 THE CRAZY OTTO RAG

| Composers: Mack Wolfson, Emile Trent, Edward White & Fred Lawrence | Date of Entry: 25.6.55 / Pos: 22 / Wks: 2 |
| Publishers: Edward Kassner Music Co. Ltd. | Re-entry: 23.7.55 / Pos: 21 / Wks: 4 |

Recordings:

| Will Glahé and his Sunshine Sextet | 4/55 | Decca F.10520 (&45-) |
| Petula Clark and The Radio Revellers | 5/55 | Polygon P.1169 |
| The Southlanders | 5/55 | Parlophone R.4025 |
| The Big Ben Banjo Band with The Coronets | 5/55 | Columbia DB.3620 |
| The Stargazers | 5/55 | Decca F.10523 (&45-) |
| Hugo and Luigi (vocal & piano) with The Hefferan Singers | 5/55 | Mercury MB.3221 |
| Hoagy Carmichael | 5/55 | Vogue Coral Q.72078 (&45-) |
| Joe Loss and his Orchestra | 6/55 | HMV BD.6200 |
| Penny Nicholls | 7/55 | Embassy WB.134 |

## 649 EV'RYWHERE

| Composers: Larry Kahn & Tolchard Evans | Date of Entry: 25.6.55 / Pos: 24 / Wks: 1 |
| Publishers: Sydney Bron Music Co. | Re-entry: 9.7.55/ Pos: 1/Wks: 27 |

Recordings:

| David Whitfield | 4/55 | Decca F.10515 (&45-) |
| David Hughes | 6/55 | Philips PB.457 |
| Billy Thorburn and his Strict Tempo Music | 10/55 | Parlophone R.4075 |
| Victor Silvester and his Ballroom Orchestra | 11/55 | Columbia DB.3685/ (45) SCM.5203 |

## 650 EVERY DAY OF MY LIFE

| | | |
|---|---|---|
| *Composers*: Jimmy Crane & Al Jacobs | | *Date of Entry*: 9.7.55 |
| *Publishers*: Robbins Music Corporation Ltd. | | *Highest Position*: 5 |
| | | *Weeks on Chart*: 23 |

*Recordings*:

| | | |
|---|---|---|
| Denise Lor | 1/55 | Parlophone R.3969/ |
| | | (45) MSP.6148 |
| Malcolm Vaughan | 6/55 | HMV B.10874 |
| David Hughes | 6/55 | Philips PB.457 |
| Vera Lynn (Titled 'Ev'ry day of my life') | 6/55 | Decca F.10566 (&45-) |

## 651 MAMA

| | | |
|---|---|---|
| *Composers*: C.A. Bixio, B. Cherubini, Geoffrey Parsons & John Turner | | *Date of Entry*: 9.7.55 |
| *Publishers*: Macmelodies Ltd. | | *Highest Position*: 15 |
| | | *Weeks on Chart*: 11 |

Notes: The original Italian version of this song was recorded in November 1940 by Beniamino Gigli and released on HMV DA.5397 under the title 'Mamma' – it was still available on special order in 1955. The Vic Damone recording listed below on both Oriole and Mercury has different lyrics by Harold Barlow and Phil Brito.)

*Recordings*:

| | | |
|---|---|---|
| Vic Damone | 8/53 | Oriole CB.1196 |
| Vic Damone | 6/54 | Mercury MB.3046 |
| Lenny Baker (flugelhorn) | 4/55 | Polygon P.1159 |
| David Whitfield | 4/55 | Decca F.10515 (&45-) |
| Malcolm Vaughan | 6/55 | HMV B.10874 |
| Gino Caroli | 6/55 | Parlophone R.4031 |
| Danny Purches | 6/55 | Columbia DB.3626/ |
| | | (45) SCM.5183 |
| Victor Silvester and his Ballroom Orchestra | 7/55 | Columbia FB.3748 |
| Keith Warwick | 7/55 | Embassy WB.139 |

## 652 HEY, MR BANJO

| | | |
|---|---|---|
| *Composers*: Freddy Morgan & Norman Malkin | | *Date of Entry*: 16.7.55 |
| *Publishers*: B.F. Wood Music Co. Inc. | | *Highest Position*: 24 |
| | | *Weeks on Chart*: 1 |

*Recordings*:

| | | |
|---|---|---|
| The Sunnysiders (vocal & inst) | 4/55 | London HLA.8135 |
| | | (& 45-) |
| The Big Ben Banjo Band with The Coronets | 5/55 | Columbia DB.3620 |
| The Stargazers | 5/55 | Decca F.10523 (&45-) |
| The Banjo Boys | 5/55 | Capitol CL.14298 |
| | | (& 45-) |
| Guy Lombardo and his Royal Canadians (The Lombardo Trio) | 5/55 | Brunswick 05413 |
| | | (& 45-) |
| Gene Sheldon (banjo) with The Encores | 6/55 | MGM.835 |

## 653 THAT'S HOW A LOVE SONG WAS BORN

| | | |
|---|---|---|
| *Composers*: Norman Newell & Philip Green | | *Date of Entry*: 23.7.55 |
| *Publishers*: Chappell & Co. Ltd. | | *Highest Position*: 16 |
| | | *Weeks on Chart*: 10 |

*Recordings*:

| | | |
|---|---|---|
| Frankie Vaughan | 5/55 | Philips PB.438 |
| Ray Burns with The Coronets | 7/55 | Columbia DB.3640 |

## 654 TAKE ME BACK AGAIN

| | | |
|---|---|---|
| *Composers*: Redd Evans, Martin Kahn & Arthur Berman | | *Date of Entry*: 23.7.55 |
| *Publishers*: Francis Day & Hunter Ltd. | | *Highest Position*: 24 |
| | | *Weeks on Chart*: 1 |

*Recordings*:

| | | |
|---|---|---|
| Tony Bennett | 4/55 | Philips PB.420 |
| Malcolm Vaughan | 9/55 | HMV B.10923★ |
| Malcolm Vaughan | 10/55 | HMV (45) 7M.317★ |

## 655 JOHN AND JULIE

| | | |
|---|---|---|
| *Composer*: Philip Green | | *Date of Entry*: 30.7.55 |
| *Publishers*: David Toff Music Publishing Co. Ltd. | | *Highest Position*: 7 |
| | | *Weeks on Chart*: 14 |

*Recordings*:

| | | |
|---|---|---|
| Eddie Calvert – the Man with the Golden Trumpet | 6/55 | Columbia DB.3624 |
| Bill McGuffie (piano) | 7/55 | Philips PB.483 |
| Reginald Conway and his Orchestra with The Rita Williams Singers | 7/55 | Embassy WB.145 |
| Victor Silvester and his Ballroom Orchestra | 9/55 | Columbia FB.3751 |
| Billy Thorburn and his Strict Tempo Music | 10/55 | Parlophone R.4075 |
| Joe Loss and his Orchestra | 10/55 | HMV POP.114 |

## 656 | STARS SHINE IN YOUR EYES

**Composers:** Nino Rota, Geoffrey Parsons & John Turner

*Date of Entry:* 6.8.55

**Publishers:** Peter Maurice Music Co. Ltd.

*Highest Position:* 8
*Weeks on Chart:* 15

Recordings:

| | | |
|---|---|---|
| Ronnie Hilton | 7/55 | HMV B.10901 |
| Edna Savage | 7/55 | Parlophone R.4043/ (45) MSP.6175 |
| Billy McCormack | 7/55 | Polygon P.1176 |
| Dickie Bennett | 8/55 | Decca F.10595 (&45-) |
| Raymond Siozade and his 'Atomic' Accordion | 8/55 | Vogue V.9051 |
| Len Mercer and his Magic Strings | 8/55 | Vogue V.9052 |
| David Rose and his Orchestra | 9/55 | MGM.848 |
| Joe Loss and his Orchestra | 10/55 | HMV POP.107 |
| Benny Lee | 10/55 | Embassy WB.152 |
| Lou Kennedy (organ) | 10/55 | Columbia DB.3668 |
| Lou Kennedy (organ) | 11/55 | Columbia (45) SCM.5198 |

## 657 | LEARNIN' THE BLUES

**Composer:** Dolores Vicki Silvers

*Date of Entry:* 13.8.55

**Publishers:** Campbell Connelly & Co. Ltd.

*Highest Position:* 4
*Weeks on Chart:* 15

Recordings:

| | | |
|---|---|---|
| Frank Sinatra | 5/55 | Capitol CL.14296 (& 45-) |
| Ray Anthony and his Orchestra | 7/55 | Capitol CL.14321 (& 45-) |
| Benny Lee with The Embassy Rhythm Group | 7/55 | Embassy WB.136 |
| Bobbie Britton with Ted Heath and his Music | 7/55 | Decca F.10563 (&45) |
| Rosemary Clooney | 7/55 | Philips PB.493 |
| Tommy Rogers and his Ballroom Orchestra dir. Harry Gold | 12/55 | Parlophone R.4101/ (45) MSP.6191 |
| Illinois Jacquet and his Orchestra | 4/56 | Columbia Clef LB.10023★ |

## 658 | COOL WATER

**Composer:** Bob Nolan

*Date of Entry:* 13.8.55

**Publishers:** B. Feldman & Co. Ltd.

*Highest Position:* 13
*Weeks on Chart:* 12

(Note: From the original 1948 recordings only one had been deleted before this revival – that by Vaughn Monroe and his Orchestra with The Sons of the Pioneers on HMV BD.1224 – release date 12/48.)

Recordings:

| | | |
|---|---|---|
| Sam Browne with The Quads and The Squadronaires | 11/48 | Decca F.9033 |
| The Sons of the Pioneers with Bob Nolan | 12/48 | Brunswick 04001 |
| Nellie Lutcher (vocal) with her Rhythm | 12/48 | Capitol CL.13018 |
| Bing Crosby and The Andrews Sisters | 2/53 | Brunswick 05019 |
| Sir Hubert Pimm (piano) (Titled 'Cool Water Blues') | 2/53 | London L.1162 |
| Billy May and his Orchestra ('Water' by Bob Morse) | 1/54 | Capitol CL.14038 |
| Frankie Laine with The Mellomen | 6/55 | Philips PB.465 |

## 659 | BLUE STAR (The Medic Theme)

**Composers:** Victor Young & Edward Heyman

*Date of Entry:* 20.8.55

**Publishers:** Chappell & Co. Ltd.

*Highest Position:* 1
*Weeks on Chart:* 25

Recordings:

| | | |
|---|---|---|
| Les Baxter and his Orchestra and Chorus (Titled 'The Medic Theme') | 4/55 | Capitol CL.14257 (& 45-) |
| Cyril Stapleton and his Orchestra featuring Julie Dawn | 7/55 | Decca F.10559 (&45-) |
| Charlie Applewhite | 7/55 | Brunswick 05416 (& 45-) |
| Reginald Conway and his Orchestra with The Rita Williams Singers | 7/55 | Embassy WB.144 |
| Felicia Sanders | 8/55 | Philips PB.492 |
| Les Howard | 9/55 | HMV B.10928 |
| Ray Burns | 9/55 | Columbia DB.3670 |
| Ron Goodwin and his Concert Orchestra | 9/55 | Parlophone R.4074 |
| Joe Loss and his Orchestra | 10/55 | HMV POP.114 |
| Eve Boswell | 10/55 | Parlophone R.4082 |
| Victor Silvester and his Ballroom Orchestra | 11/55 | Columbia DB.3686/ (45) SCM.5204 |

## 660 CLOSE THE DOOR

*Composers:* Fred Ebb & Paul Klein          *Date of Entry:* 27.8.55

*Publishers:* Duchess Music Ltd.          *Highest Position:* 8
          *Weeks on Chart:* 16

*Recordings:*

| | | |
|---|---|---|
| The Stargazers | 8/55 | Decca F.10594 (&45-) |
| Jim Lowe | 8/55 | London HLD.8171 (& 45-) |
| The Four-in-A-Chord | 9/55 | Embassy WB.149 |
| Benny Lee with Children's Chorus | 11/55 | Parlophone R.4099 |

Note: The last recording listed above was released for the purpose of playing Musical Chairs, being one of a series titled Benny Lee's Children's Party.)

## 661 THREE GALLEONS (Les tres carabelas)

*Composers:* Augusto Alguero, G Moreu & Paddy Roberts          *Date of Entry:* 3.9.55

*Publishers:* B. Feldman & Co. Ltd.          *Highest Position:* 23
          *Weeks on Chart:* 1

*Recordings:*

| | | |
|---|---|---|
| Ron Goodwin and his Concert Orchestra | 7/55 | Parlophone R.4041 |
| Robert Earl | 7/55 | Philips PB.481 |
| Reginald Conway and his Orchestra | 7/55 | Embassy WB.145 |
| Les Howard | 9/55 | HMV B.10928 |
| Johnny Douglas and his Orchestra and Chorus | 9/55 | Decca F.10615 |

## 662 CLOSE YOUR EYES

*Composer:* Bernice Petkere          *Date of Entry:* 3.9.55

*Publishers:* Keith Prowse Music Publishing Co. Ltd.          *Highest Position:* 24
          *Weeks on Chart:* 1

*Recordings:*

| | | |
|---|---|---|
| Ronnie Scott (tenor sax) with The Ronnie Ball Trio | 12/51 | Esquire 10–185 |
| Tony Bennett | 5/55 | Philips PB.445 |
| Harry Belafonte | 6/55 | Capitol CL.14312 (& 45-) |
| The Lancers | 6/55 | Vogue Coral Q.72081 (& 45-) |
| The Tony Kinsey Quartet | 9/55 | Decca F.10606 (&45-) |
| Jean Carson | 11/55 | HMV POP.124★ |
| The Roy Eldridge and Benny Carter Orchestra | 11/55 | Columbia Clef LB.10008★ |

## 663 LOVE ME OR LEAVE ME

*Composers:* Gus Kahn & Walter Donaldson          *Date of Entry:* 10.9.55
*Publishers:* Keith Prowse Music Publishing Co. Ltd.          *Highest Position:* 14
          *Weeks on Chart:* 10

*Recordings:*

| | | |
|---|---|---|
| Benny Goodman and his Orchestra | 12/36 | HMV.B8504 |
| Danny Kaye | 5/50 | Brunswick 04505 |
| Bing Crosby | 2/52 | Brunswick 04867 |
| Ella Mae Morse | 4/52 | Capitol CL.13727 |
| The Gerry Mulligan Quartet featuring Chet Baker | 10/54 | Vogue V.2259 |
| Lena Horne | 5/55 | HMV B.10869/ (45) 7M.309 |
| Sammy Davis Jnr | 6/55 | Brunswick 05428 (& 45-) |
| Billy Eckstine | 7/55 | MGM.841/ (45) SP.1136 |
| Doris Day | 7/55 | Philips PB.479 |

## 664 THE MAN FROM LARAMIE

*Composers:* Ned Washington & Lester Lee          *Date of Entry:* 10.9.55
*Publishers:* Chappell & Co. Ltd.          *Highest Position:* 2
          *Weeks on Chart:* 20

*Recordings:*

| | | |
|---|---|---|
| Al Martino | 8/55 | Capitol CL.14343 (& 45-) |
| Jimmy Young | 8/55 | Decca F.10597 (&45-) |
| Ralph Young | 8/55 | Brunswick 05466 (& 45-) |
| The Voices of Walter Schumann | 9/55 | HMV B.10919/ (45) 7M.323 |
| Ben Bowers | 9/55 | Columbia DB.3650/ (45) SCM.5192 |
| Edmund Hockridge | 9/55 | Parlophone R.4051 |
| James Brown and The Trail Winders | 9/55 | MGM.851 |
| Gary Miller | 9/55 | Pye Nixa N.15004 |
| The Maple Leaf Four | 9/55 | Oriole CB.1310 |
| Bob Dale | 9/55 | Embassy WB.150 |
| The Regent Ballroom Orchestra | 12/55 | Decca F.10657 (&45-) |

## 665 I'LL COME WHEN YOU CALL

*Composers:* Josephine & David Caryll          *Date of Entry:* 17.9.55

*Publishers:* Michael Reine Music Co. Ltd.          *Highest Position:* 7
          *Weeks on Chart:* 16

*Recordings:*

| | | |
|---|---|---|
| Ruby Murray | 9/55 | Columbia DB.3643 |
| Janie Marden with Frank Weir, his saxophone, Chorus and Orchestra | 9/55 | Decca F.10605 (&45-) |
| Victor Silvester and his Ballroom Orchestra | 10/55 | Columbia DB.3666 |
| Joe Loss and his Orchestra | 12/55 | HMV POP.136/ (45) 7M.341 |

## 666 THE YELLOW ROSE OF TEXAS

*Composer*: Don George      *Date of entry*: 24.9.55

*Publishers*: Maddox Music Co. Ltd.    *Highest Position*: 2
                                   *Weeks on Chart*: 22

*Recordings*:

| | | |
|---|---|---|
| Billy Cotton and his Band (The Bandits) | 8/55 | Decca F.10602 (&45–) |
| Ronnie Hilton | 9/55 | HMV B.10924 |
| Gary Miller with The Beryl Stott Chorus | 9/55 | Pye Nixa N.15004 |
| Mitch Miller and his Orchestra and Chorus | 9/55 | Philips PB.505 |
| Michael Holliday | 9/55 | Columbia DB.3657 |
| Johnny Desmond | 9/55 | Vogue Coral Q.72099 (& 45–) |
| 'Texas' Bill Strength | 9/55 | Capitol CL.14357 (& 45–) |
| Bob Dale | 9/55 | Embassy WB.150 |
| The Regent Ballroom Orchestra | 12/55 | Decca F.10657 (&45–) |
| Stan Freberg with Jud Conlon's Rhythmaires and Alvin Stoller (drums) | 1/56 | Capitol CL.14509 (& 45–) |

## 667 HAVE YOU EVER BEEN LONELY?

*Composers*: George Brown, Peter De Rose   *Date of Entry*: 24.9.55/
     & William J. Hill                       Pos: 23/Wks: 2
*Publishers*: Lawrence Wright            *Re-entry*: 15.10.55/
     Music Co. Ltd.                    Pos: 23/Wks: 2
                                    *2nd re-entry*: 26.11.55/
                                    Pos: 22/Wks: 2

*Recordings*:

| | | |
|---|---|---|
| The Beverley Sisters | 8/55 | Decca F.10603 (&45–) |
| The Three Deuces | 9/55 | Columbia DB.3642 |
| Ronnie Hilton | 9/55 | HMV B.10924 |
| Victor Silvester and his Ballroom Orchestra | 9/55 | Columbia FB.3751 |
| Pauline Shepherd | 9/55 | Pye Nixa N.15000 |
| The Southlanders | 10/55 | Parlophone R.4069/ (45) MSP.6182 |
| Tommy Rogers and his Ballroom Orchestra dir. Harry Gold | 10/55 | Parlophone R.4070 |
| Beryl Templeman | 10/55 | Embassy WB.151 |
| Joe Loss and his Orchestra | 11/55 | HMV POP.117/ (45) 7M.329 |
| Jaye P. Morgan | 1/56 | Brunswick 05519★ |

## 668 THE DAM BUSTERS MARCH

*Composer*: Eric Coates         *Date of Entry*: 24.9.55 /
                                     Pos: 24 / Wks: 1
*Publishers*: Chappell & Co. Ltd.     *Re-entry*: 8.10.55 /
                                     Pos: 10 / Wks: 40
                                     *2nd re-entry*: 21.7.56 /
                                     Pos: 16 / Wks: 16

*Recordings*:

| | | |
|---|---|---|
| Sidney Torch and his Orchestra | 5/55 | Parlophone R.4024 |
| The Central Band of the RAF cond. Wing Comdr. A.E. Sims OBE | 6/55 | HMV B.10877 |
| Concert Orchestra cond. Eric Coates | 10/55 | Pye Nixa N.15003 |
| Billy Cotton and his Band (Narration by Billy Cotton) | 10/55 | Decca F.10630 (&45–) |

## 669 HERNANDO'S HIDEAWAY

*Composers*: Richard Adler & Jerry Ross   *Date of Entry*: 1.10.55

*Publishers*: Frank Music Co. Ltd.     *Highest Position*: 5
                                   *Weeks on Chart*: 15

*Recordings*:

| | | |
|---|---|---|
| Ray Martin and his Concert Orchestra | 9/55 | Columbia DB.3658 |
| The Johnston Brothers | 9/55 | Decca F.10608 (&45–) |
| Lita Roza | 9/55 | Decca F.10611 (&45–) |
| Archie Bleyer and his Orchestra and Chorus | 9/55 | London HLA.8176 (& 45–) |
| Johnnie Ray | 9/55 | Philips PB.495 |
| Bill McGuffie (piano) | 9/55 | Philips PB.496 |
| Ethel Smith (organ) | 9/55 | Brunswick 05470 (& 45–) |
| Billy May and his Orchestra | 9/55 | Capitol CL.14353 (& 45–) |
| Ray Anthony and his Orchestra (Ray Anthony) | 9/55 | Capitol CL.14354 (& 45–) |
| Alma Cogan | 9/55 | HMV B.10929 |
| Benny Lee with The Three Oscars | 10/55 | Embassy WB.152 |
| George Browne and his Calypso Band | 10/55 | Melodisc 1337 |
| Victor Silvester and his Ballroom Orchestra | 11/55 | Columbia DB.3686/ (45) SCM.5204 |
| Aimable with accordion and electric organ | 11/55 | Vogue V.9057 |
| Tommy Rogers and his Ballroom Orchestra dir. Harry Gold | 12/55 | Parlophone R.4101/ (45) MSP.6191 |

## 670 | HEY THERE

*Composers*: Richard Adler & Jerry Ross

*Publishers*: Frank Music Co. Ltd.

*Date of Entry*: 1.10.55

*Highest Position*: 3
*Weeks on Chart*: 18

*Recordings*:
| | | |
|---|---|---|
| Ronnie Hilton | 9/55 | HMV B.10930 |
| Rita Williams | 9/55 | Embassy WB.147 |
| Barbara Lyon | 9/55 | Columbia DB.3649 |
| The Johnston Brothers | 9/55 | Decca F.10608 (&45-) |
| Lita Roza | 9/55 | Decca F.10611 (&45-) |
| Rosemary Clooney | 9/55 | Philips PB.494 |
| Johnnie Ray | 9/55 | Philips PB.495 |
| Bill McGuffie (piano) | 9/55 | Philips PB.496 |
| Sammy Davis Jnr | 9/55 | Brunswick 05469 (& 45-) |
| Victor Silvester and his Ballroom Orchestra | 10/55 | Columbia DB.3667 |
| The Tony Kinsey Quartet | 11/55 | Decca F.10648 (&45-) |
| Edmund Hockridge | 11/55 | HMV POP.131 |

## 671 | GO ON BY

*Composer*: Stuart Hamblen

*Publishers*: Bluebird Music Co.

*Date of Entry*: 1.10.55

*Highest Position*: 12
*Weeks on Chart*: 13

*Recordings*:
| | | |
|---|---|---|
| Suzi Miller | 8/55 | Decca F.10593 (&45-) |
| The Cowboy Church Sunday School | 8/55 | Brunswick 05455 (& 45-) |
| Alma Cogan | 8/55 | HMV B.10917 |
| Rosemary Clooney | 9/55 | Philips PB.499 |
| The Canadians | 9/55 | Embassy WB.148 |

Note: The version by the composer, Stuart Hamblen, was available to special order on HMV JO.445 and [45] 7MC.30 [9/55].)

## 672 | I'LL NEVER STOP LOVING YOU

*Composers*: Sammy Cahn & Nicholas Brodszky

*Publishers*: Robbins Music Corporation Ltd.

*Date of Entry*: 15.10.55/
Pos: 10/Wks: 12
*Re-entry*: 14.1.56 /
Pos: 24 / Wks: 2

*Recordings*:
| | | |
|---|---|---|
| David Whitfield | 8/55 | Decca F.10596 (&45-) |
| Les Baxter and his Orchestra and Chorus | 8/55 | Capitol CL.14344 (& 45-) |
| Slim Whitman | 8/55 | London HLU.8167 (& 45-) |
| Doris Day | 9/55 | Philips PB.497 |
| Pearl Carr | 11/55 | Embassy WB.154 |

## 673 | TWENTY TINY FINGERS

*Composers*: Sid Tepper & Roy C. Bennett

*Publishers*: Francis Day & Hunter Ltd.

*Date of Entry*: 15.10.55/
Pos: 1/Wks: 17
*Re-entry*: 18.2.56 /
Pos: 24 / Wks: 1

*Recordings*:
| | | |
|---|---|---|
| The Stargazers with Syd Dean and his Band | 10/55 | Decca F.10626 (&45-) |
| Marie Benson | 10/55 | Philips PB.512 |
| The Coronets | 10/55 | Columbia DB.3671 |
| Art Mooney and his Orchestra (The Cloverleafs) | 10/55 | MGM.855/ (45) SP.1141 |
| The Four-in-A-Chord | 11/55 | Embassy WB.158 |
| Alma Cogan | 11/55 | HMV POP.129/ (45) 7M.337 |

## 674 | THE BANJO'S BACK IN TOWN

*Composers*: Earl Shuman, Alden Shuman & Marshall Brown

*Publishers*: Leeds Music Ltd.

*Date of Entry*: 22.10.55

*Highest Position*: 18
*Weeks on Chart*: 7

*Recordings*:
| | | |
|---|---|---|
| Suzi Miller | 8/55 | Decca F.10593 (&45-) |
| Alma Cogan | 8/55 | HMV B.10917 |
| Billie Anthony | 8/55 | Columbia DB.3648/ (45) SCM.5191 |
| Teresa Brewer | 8/55 | Vogue Coral Q.72098 (& 45-) |
| Penny Nicholls | 11/55 | Embassy WB.156 |

## 675 | LOVE IS A MANY-SPLENDOURED THING

*Composers*: Sammy Fain & Paul Francis Webster

*Publishers*: Robbins Music Corporation Ltd.

*Date of Entry*: 29.10.55/ Pos: 1/Wks: 21

*Re-entry*: 31.3.56 / Pos: 22 / Wks: 2

*Recordings*:

| | | |
|---|---|---|
| The Four Aces featuring Al Alberts | 9/55 | Brunswick 05480 (& 45-) |
| Don Costa and his Orchestra and Chorus | 10/55 | London HLF.8186 (& 45-) |
| Eddie Calvert – The Man with the Golden Trumpet | 10/55 | Columbia DB.3659/ (45) SCM.5194 |
| David Rose and his Orchestra | 10/55 | MGM.860/(45) SP.1143 |
| Nat 'King' Cole | 10/55 | Capitol CL.14364 (& 45-) |
| David Hughes | 10/55 | Philips PB.508 |
| Woody Herman and his Orchestra | 10/55 | Capitol CL.14366 (& 45-) |
| Don Cornell | 10/55 | Vogue Coral Q.72104 (& 45-) |
| Sidney Simone and his Orchestra ftg Cecil Pressling (alto sax) | 10/55 | Oriole CB.1311 |
| Frank Chacksfield and his Orchestra and Chorus | 10/55 | Decca F.10639 (&45-) |
| Joe Loss and his Orchestra | 12/55 | HMV POP.136/ (45) 7M.341 |
| Victor Silvester and his Ballroom Orchestra | 1/56 | Columbia DB.3713/ (45) SCM.5220 |
| Keith Warwick | 1/56 | Embassy WB.163 |

## 676 | SUDDENLY THERE'S A VALLEY

*Composers*: Chuck Meyer & Biff Jones
*Publishers*: Aberbach (London) Ltd.

*Date of Entry*: 5.11.55
*Highest Position*: 3
*Weeks on Chart*: 18

*Recordings*:

| | | |
|---|---|---|
| Petula Clark | 10/55 | Pye Nixa N.15013 |
| Lee Lawrence | 10/55 | Columbia DB.3681/ (45) SCM.5201 |
| Jo Stafford and The Norman Luboff Choir | 10/55 | Philips PB.509 |
| The Mills Brothers | 10/55 | Brunswick 05488 (& 45-) |
| Patty Andrews | 10/55 | Capitol CL.14374 (& 45-) |
| Gogi Grant | 10/55 | London HLB.8192 (& 45-) |
| Julius La Rosa | 10/55 | London HLA.8193 (& 45-) |
| Kathie Kay | 11/55 | HMV POP.126/ (45) 7M.335 |
| Kay Armen | 11/55 | MGM.865/ (45) SP.1146 |
| Joe Loss and his Orchestra | 1/56 | HMV POP.152/ (45) 7M.356 |
| Keith Warwick | 1/56 | Embassy WB.163 |

## 677 | SEVENTEEN

*Composers*: John F. Young Jnr., Chuck Gorman & Boyd Bennett
*Publishers*: World Wide Music Co. Ltd.

*Date of Entry*: 5.11.55
Pos: 13 / Wks: 15
*Re-entry*: 25.2.56 /
Pos: 22 / Wks: 1

*Recordings*:

| | | |
|---|---|---|
| The Fontane Sisters | 9/55 | London HLD.8177 (& 45-) |
| Confrey Phillips | 10/55 | Columbia DB.3664 |
| Boyd Bennett and his Rockets (Big Moe) | 10/55 | Parlophone R.4063/ (45) MSP.6180 |
| Ella Mae Morse | 10/55 | Capitol CL.14362 (& 45-) |
| Frankie Vaughan | 10/55 | Philips PB.511 |
| Don Lang | 10/55 | HMV POP.115 |

## 678 | CHRISTMAS ALPHABET

*Composers*: Buddy Kaye & Jules Loman

*Publishers*: Pickwick Music Ltd.

*Date of Entry*: 12.11.55

*Highest Position*: 1
*Weeks on Chart*: 9

*Recordings*:

| | | |
|---|---|---|
| Dickie Valentine | 10/55 | Decca F.10628 (&45-) |
| The McGuire Sisters | 10/55 | Vogue Coral Q.72108 (& 45-) |
| Shirley Abicair | 12/55 | Parlophone R.4111 |

## 679 | MEET ME ON THE CORNER

*Composers*: Peter Hart & Paddy Roberts

*Publishers*: Berry Music Co. Ltd.

*Date of Entry*: 12.11.55
Pos: 7/Wks: 13

*Re-entry*: 25.2.56 /
Pos: 24 / Wks: 1

*Recordings*:

| | | |
|---|---|---|
| Frankie Vaughan | 10/55 | Philips PB.511 |
| The Coronets | 10/55 | Columbia DB.3671 |
| Max Bygraves | 10/55 | HMV POP.116 |

## 680 ROCK AROUND THE CLOCK

| | | |
|---|---|---|
| *Composers*: Jimmy De Knight & Max C. Freedman | | *Date of Entry*: 12.11.55/ Pos: 7/Wks: 15 |
| *Publishers*: Edward Kassner Music Co. Ltd. | | *Re-entry*: 29.9.56 Pos: 7/Wks: 11 |
| | | *2nd re-entry*: 29.12.56 / Pos: 22 / Wks: 3 |

*Recordings*:

| | | |
|---|---|---|
| Bill Haley and his Comets | 9/54 | Brunswick 05317 |
| Bill Haley and his Comets | 1/55 | Brunswick 45–05317 |
| The Deep River Boys with Sid Phillips and his Band | 10/55 | HMV POP.113 |
| The MGM Studio Orchestra cond. Charles Wolcott | 10/55 | MGM.861/ (45) SP.1144 |
| The Hedley Ward Trio | 12/55 | Melodisc 1344 |
| The Canadians | 12/55 | Embassy WB.161 |
| The Parlophone Pops Orchestra cond. Ron Goodwin | 12/56 | Parlophone R.4250 |

(Note: The recording by the Parlophone Pops Orchestra was No. 2 in a series 'Sing it yourself'. The record was accompanied by a leaflet containing the words of the two songs on the record.)

## 681 RELAX-AY-VOO

| | | |
|---|---|---|
| *Composers*: Arthur Schwartz & Sammy Cahn | | *Date of Entry*: 19.11.55 |
| *Publishers*: Pickwick Music Ltd. | | *Highest Position*: 21 *Weeks on Chart*: 4 |

*Recordings*:

| | | |
|---|---|---|
| Dean Martin and Line Renaud | 9/55 | Capitol CL.14356 (& 45-) |
| The Keynotes | 11/55 | Decca F.10643 (&45-) |
| Victor Silvester and his Ballroom Orchestra | 1/56 | Columbia DB.3713/ (45) SCM.5220★ |
| Rita Williams and Bob Dale | 1/56 | Embassy WB.165★ |

## 682 THE VERY FIRST CHRISTMAS OF ALL

| | | |
|---|---|---|
| *Composers*: Paddy Roberts & Peter Hart | | *Date of Entry*: 19.11.55 |
| *Publishers*: Dash Music Co. Ltd. | | *Highest Position*: 13 *Weeks on Chart*: 7 |

*Recording*:

| | | |
|---|---|---|
| Ruby Murray | 11/55 | Columbia DB.3680 |

## 683 NEVER DO A TANGO WITH AN ESKIMO

| | | |
|---|---|---|
| *Composer*: Tommie Connor | | *Date of Entry*: 3.12.55 |
| *Publishers*: Michael Reine Music Co. Ltd. | | *Highest Position*: 15 *Weeks on Chart*: 7 |

*Recordings*:

| | | |
|---|---|---|
| Alma Cogan | 11/55 | HMV POP.129/ (45) 7M.337 |
| The Four-in-A-Chord | 12/55 | Embassy WB.162 |

## 684 HE

| | | |
|---|---|---|
| *Composers*: Richard Mullan & Jack Richards | | *Date of Entry*: 10.12.55 |
| *Publishers*: B. Feldman & Co. Ltd. | | *Highest Position*: 22 *Weeks on Chart*: 3 |

*Recordings*:

| | | |
|---|---|---|
| Robert Earl | 10/55 | Philips PB.517 |
| Al Hibbler | 10/55 | Brunswick 05492 (& 45-) |
| The McGuire Sisters | 10/55 | Vogue Coral Q.72108 (& 45-) |
| Dick James | 11/55 | Parlophone R.4098/ (45) MSP. 6190 |
| Kay Armen | 11/55 | MGM.865/ (45) SP.1146 |
| Ronnie Hilton | 11/55 | HMV POP.128 |
| Roy Smith | 11/55 | Decca F.10644 (&45-) |
| Ronnie Hilton | 12/55 | HMV (45) 7M.336 |

## 685 THE SHIFTING, WHISPERING SANDS

| | | |
|---|---|---|
| *Composers*: V.C. Gilbert & Mary M. Hadler | | *Date of Entry*: 10.12.55 |
| *Publishers*: Peter Maurice Music Co. Ltd. | | *Highest Position*: 8 *Weeks on Chart*: 14 |

*Recordings*:

| | | |
|---|---|---|
| Billy Vaughn and his Orchestra and Chorus (Narrator: Ken Nordene)– 2 parts | 11/55 | London HLD.8205 (& 45-) |
| Monty Norman and Chorus | 11/55 | HMV POP.145/ (45) 7M.349 |
| Eamonn Andrews (Narrator) with Ron Goodwin and his Orchestra and Chorus – 2 parts | 11/55 | Parlophone R.4106 |
| Frank Chacksfield and his Orchestra and Chorus | 11/55 | Decca F.10653 (&45-) |
| Geraldo and his Orchestra and Chorus | 1/56 | Philips PB.543 |
| Mark Pasquin with The Rita Williams Singers | 1/56 | Embassy WB.166 |
| Jerry Colonna with Vocal Group | 2/56 | HMV POP.165/ (45) 7M.369 |

## 686 ARRIVEDERCI DARLING (Arrivederci Roma)

*Composers*: Renato Rascel, S.Giovannini, P. Garinei & Jack Fishman

*Date of Entry*: 17.12.55

*Publishers*: Berry Music Co. Ltd.

*Highest Position*: 16
*Weeks on Chart*: 8

*Recordings*:

| | | |
|---|---|---|
| Rino Salviati and his Guitar (Arrivederci Roma) [In Italian] | 10/55 | Durium DC.16578 |
| Lys Assia and The Johnston Brothers | 10/55 | Decca F.10635 (&45-) |
| Edna Savage with Chorus of Servicemen from The Nuffield Centre | 11/55 | Parlophone R.4097/ (45) MSP.6189 |
| The Radio Revellers | 11/55 | Pye Nixa N.15011 |
| Jo Stafford | 11/55 | Philips PB.527 |
| The Three Suns (inst.) with The Satellites (vocal) | 12/55 | HMV POP.142/(45) 7M.346 |
| Anne Shelton | 12/55 | HMV POP.146 |
| Pearl Carr | 12/55 | Embassy WB.155 |
| Francisco Cavez and his Orchestra | 1/56 | Parlophone R.4123/ (45) MSP.6205 |
| Eddie Barclay and his Orchestra | 2/56 | Felsted SD.80032 |

## 687 WHEN YOU LOSE THE ONE YOU LOVE

*Composers*: Don Pelosi, Rod Arden & Jimmy Harper

*Date of Entry*: 17.12.55

*Publishers*: Bradbury Wood Ltd.

*Highest Position*: 6
*Weeks on Chart*: 20

*Recordings*:

| | | |
|---|---|---|
| Shelley Moore | 10/55 | Columbia DB.3663 |
| David Whitfield with Mantovani and his Orchestra | 10/55 | Decca F.10627 (&45-) |
| Dorothy Squires | 10/55 | Pye Nixa N.15010 |
| Issy Bonn | 11/55 | Columbia DB.3683 |
| Shelley Moore | 11/55 | Columbia (45) SCM.5197 |
| Don Rennie | 11/55 | Parlophone R.4085 |
| Keith Warwick | 11/55 | Embassy WB.153 |

## 688 WITH YOUR LOVE (Mes Mains)

*Composers*: Gilbert Becaud, Pierre Delanoe, John Turner & Geoffrey Parsons

*Date of Entry*:17.12.55

*Publishers*: Macmelodies Ltd.

*Highest Position*: 3
*Weeks on Chart*: 18

*Recordings*:

| | | |
|---|---|---|
| Robert Earl | 10/55 | Philips PB.517 |
| Vera Lynn | 10/55 | Decca F.10622 (&45- |
| Petula Clark | 10/55 | Pye Nixa N.15013 |
| Tony Brent | 10/55 | Columbia DB.3675/ (45) SCM.5200 |
| Malcolm Vaughan with The Peter Knight Singers | 11/55 | HMV POP.130/ (45) 7M.338 |

## 689 OLD PI-ANNA RAG

*Composers*: Elizabeth Bryce & Donald Phillips

*Date of Entry*: 31.12.5!

*Publishers*: Lawrence Wright Music Co. Ltd.

*Highest Position*: 21
*Weeks on Chart*: 11

*Recordings*:

| | | |
|---|---|---|
| Dickie Valentine | 11/55 | Decca F.10645 (&45- |
| Billie Anthony | 12/55 | Columbia DB.3698/ (45) SCM.5210 |
| Billy Thorburn and his Strict Tempo Music (vocal group) | 1/56 | Parlophone R.4125/ (45) MSP.6207 |
| Victor Silvester and his Ballroom Orchestra | 2/56 | Columbia DB.3726/ (45) SCM.5233 |

## 690 THE LITTLE LAPLANDER (Hey Reindeer)

*Composers*: Juan Delgado & Alex Masters

*Date of Entry*: 31.12.55

*Publishers*: Good Music Ltd.

*Highest Position*: 24
*Weeks on Chart*: 1

*Recordings*:

| | | |
|---|---|---|
| Max Bygraves with Children's Chorus | 10/55 | HMV POP.116 |
| Harry Roy and his Orchestra | 11/55 | Oriole CB.1313 |
| Ron Goodwin and his Concert Orchestra | 11/55 | Parlophone R. 4094 |

# 1956

It was often true that a song which never reached No. 1 in the music charts stayed in the charts longer than one that did – and we can see the evidence of that here with the year's longest-staying tune, *The dam busters march,* beating four No. 1 songs. A good example of publishers' sales technique is shown in a story about *Whatever will be, will be.* The song was sold to dealers at 1/- (5p) per copy for the first four weeks at what was termed a 'novelty rate'. They were told that the price would be increased to 1/2d (6p) on the Monday of the fifth week. The publishers sold nearly 70,000 on the last Friday before the price increases alone. David Jacobs, who had done a series of six half-hour record shows for the BBC in 1954, was asked to take over the year-old 'Pick of the Pops' and so began a run of five years with the programme. Yet another example of the increasing differences between the sheet music and record charts came with *Autumn concerto.* Record sales of this were low, but the music sales kept it in the charts for seven months – with a run of four weeks at No. 3. *I'll be home,* as recorded by Pat Boone, seemed to be heard every Sunday on 'Family Favourites' but could only rate No. 7 in the charts – despite a No. 1 in the record listings. There were quite a few changes among the record companies, with HMV ceasing to produce its B series after September. We had the first Polydor BM issues and Pye's Mercury MTs. In

December, a new label appeared with but a seven-month lifespan – Conquest. Some of its 12 singles you will find listed here. Artists included the King Brothers, Les Howard, Bryan Johnson, Geoff Love and his Orchestra – and Sabrina.

| | MOST WEEKS ON THE CHARTS TOP SIX | |
|---|---|---|
| Pos | | Wks |
| 1 | The dam busters march | 43 |
| 2 | My September love | 33 |
| 3 | It's almost tomorrow | 31 |
| 4 | Whatever will be, will be | 28 |
| 5 | Walk hand in hand | 26 |
| 6 | Serenade | 25 |

# SONG CHARTS

## 691 THE BALLAD OF DAVY CROCKETT

| | | |
|---|---|---|
| *Composers:* George Bruns & Tom Blackburn | | *Date of Entry:* 7.1.56 |
| *Publishers:* Walt Disney Music Co. Ltd. | | *Highest Position:* 1 |
| | | *Weeks on Chart:* 24 |

*Recordings:*

| | | |
|---|---|---|
| Gary Miller | 12/55 | Pye Nixa N.15020 |
| Billy Cotton and his Band (Billy Cotton) | 1/56 | Decca F.10664 (&45-) |
| Bill Hayes | 1/56 | London HLA.8220 (& 45-) |
| Burl Ives | 1/56 | Brunswick 05510 (& 45-) |
| The Arizona Boys' Choir | 1/56 | Columbia DB.3707/ (45) SCM.5215 |
| Dick James | 1/56 | Parlophone R.4117/ (45) MSP.6199 |
| Tennessee Ernie Ford | 1/56 | Capitol CL.14506 (& 45-) |
| Larry Cross | 1/56 | Embassy WB.160 |
| Steve Allen | 1/56 | Vogue Coral Q.72118 (& 45-) |
| Fess Parker | 1/56 | Philips PB.534 |
| Max Bygraves | 1/56 | HMV POP.153/ (45) 7M.357 |
| Ronnie Ronalde | 1/56 | Columbia DB.3705/ (45) SCM.5214 |
| George Browne and his Calypso Band | 5/56 | Melodisc 1347 |
| Mickey Katz and his Orchestra [Titled 'Duvid Crockett'] | 5/56 | Capitol CL.14579 (& 45-) |

## 692 LOVE AND MARRIAGE

| | | |
|---|---|---|
| *Composers:* Sammy Cahn & Jimmy Van Heusen | | *Date of Entry:* 7.1.56 |
| *Publishers:* Barton Music Co. Ltd. | | *Highest Position:* 2 |
| | | *Weeks on Chart:* 13 |

*Recordings:*

| | | |
|---|---|---|
| Joan Regan | 12/55 | Decca F.10659 (&45-) |
| Frank Sinatra | 1/56 | Capitol CL.14503 (& 45-) |
| Confrey Phillips | 1/56 | Columbia DB.3716/ (45) SCM.5223 |
| Alma Cogan | 1/56 | HMV POP.163/ (45) 7M.367 |
| Rita Williams and Bob Dale | 1/56 | Embassy WB.165 |
| Dorothy Collins | 1/56 | Vogue Coral Q.72116 (& 45-) |
| Dinah Shore | 1/56 | HMV POP.148/ (45) 7M.352 |
| Jack Parnell and his Orchestra | 2/56 | Parlophone R.4134 |

## 693 SIXTEEN TONS

| | | |
|---|---|---|
| *Composer:* Merle Travis | | *Date of Entry:* 7.1.56 |
| *Publishers:* Campbell Connelly & Co. Ltd. | | *Highest Position:* 4 |
| | | *Weeks on Chart:* 12 |

*Recordings:*

| | | |
|---|---|---|
| Frankie Laine with The Mellomen | 1/56 | Philips PB.539 |
| Red Sovine | 1/56 | Brunswick 05513 (& 45-) |
| Tennessee Ernie Ford | 1/56 | Capitol CL.14500 (& 45-) |
| Johnny Desmond | 1/56 | Vogue Coral Q.72115 (& 45-) |
| Edmundo Ros and his Orchestra (Edmundo Ros) | 1/56 | Decca F.10669 (&45-) |
| Larry Cross | 1/56 | Embassy WB.160 |
| Michael Holliday | 1/56 | Columbia DB.3714/ (45) SCM.5221 |
| Edmund Hockridge with The Beryl Stott Chorus | 1/56 | Pye Nixa N.15039 |
| Jack Parnell and his Orchestra (Jack Parnell) | 2/56 | Parlophone R.4134 |
| Max Bygraves [Parody titled 'Seventeen Tons' – new lyrics by Shore] | 5/56 | HMV POP.208* |
| Max Bygraves [Parody titled 'Seventeen Tons' – new lyrics by Shore] | 6/56 | HMV (45) 7M.400* |

## 694 PICKIN' A CHICKEN

| | | |
|---|---|---|
| *Composers:* Garfield de Mortimer, Derek Bernfield & Paddy Roberts | | *Date of Entry:* 7.1.56/ Pos: 7/Wks: 19 |
| *Publishers:* Berry Music Ltd. | | *Re-entry:* 26.5.56/ Pos: 24/Wks: 1 |

*Recording:*

| | | |
|---|---|---|
| Eve Boswell | 10/55 | Parlophone R.4082 |

## 695 | (Love is) THE TENDER TRAP

*Composers*: Sammy Cahn & Jimmy Van Heusen

*Publishers*: Campbell Connelly & Co. Ltd.

*Date of Entry*: 7.1.56/
Pos: 7/Wks: 19
*Re-entry*: 26.5.56/
Pos: 24/Wks: 1

*Recordings*:

| | | |
|---|---|---|
| Ella Fitzgerald | 1/56 | Brunswick 05514 (& 45–) |
| Debbie Reynolds | 1/56 | MGM.881/ (45) SP.1155 |
| Patti Lewis | 1/56 | Philips PB.541 |
| The Stargazers | 1/56 | Decca F.10668 (&45–) |
| Frank Sinatra | 1/56 | Capitol CL.14511 (& 45–) |
| Joe Loss and his Orchestra | 2/56 | HMV POP.175/ (45) 7M.378 |
| Tommy Watt and his Orchestra | 2/56 | Parlophone R.4135/ (45) MSP.6213 |
| Denny Dennis | 2/56 | Embassy WB.167 |
| Victor Silvester and his Ballroom Orchestra | 3/56 | Columbia DB.3741/ (45) SCM.5248 |

## 696 | YOUNG AND FOOLISH

*Composers*: Arnold Horwitt & Albert Hague

*Publishers*: Chappell & Co. Ltd.

*Date of Entry*: 14.1.56/
Pos: 2/Wks: 20
*Re-entry*: 9.6.56/
Pos: 24/Wks: 1

*Recordings*:

| | | |
|---|---|---|
| Jo Stafford | 1/56 | Philips PB.538 |
| Eve Boswell | 1/56 | Parlophone R.4126/ (45) MSP.6208 |
| Ronnie Hilton | 1/56 | HMV POP.154/ (45) 7M.358 |
| Edmund Hockridge | 1/56 | Pye Nixa N.15039 |
| The McGuire Sisters | 1/56 | Vogue Coral Q.72117 (& 45–) |
| Dean Martin | 1/56 | Capitol CL.14519 (& 45–) |
| Joe Loss and his Orchestra | 2/56 | HMV POP.174/(45) 7M.377 |
| Lee Lawrence | 2/56 | Columbia DB.3721/ (45) SCM.5228 |
| Pearl Carr | 2/56 | Embassy WB.164 |
| Victor Silvester and his Ballroom Orchestra | 3/56 | Columbia DB.3742/ (45) SCM.5249 |
| The Regent Ballroom Orchestra | 3/56 | Decca F.10718 (&45–) |

## 697 | ROBIN HOOD

*Composer*: Carl Sigman

*Publishers*: New World Publications Ltd.

*Date of Entry*: 21.1.56

*Highest Position*: 9
*Weeks on Chart*: 19

*Recordings*:

| | | |
|---|---|---|
| Gary Miller with The Beryl Stott Chorus | 12/55 | Pye Nixa N.15020 |
| Joe Reisman and his Orchestra and Chorus | 1/56 | HMV POP.160/ (45) 7M.364 |
| Dick James with Stephen James and his Chums | 1/56 | Parlophone R.4117/ (45) MSP.6199 |
| Edmundo Ros and his Orchestra (Edmundo Ros) | 1/56 | Decca F.10669 (&45–) |
| Nelson Riddle and his Orchestra with vocal group | 1/56 | Capitol CL.14510 (& 45–) |
| Billy Cotton and his Band (Doreen Stephens, Alan Breeze and The Bandits) | 1/56 | Decca F.10682 (&45–) |
| Alan Dale | 1/56 | Vogue Coral Q.72121 (& 45–) |
| Ronnie Ronalde | 2/56 | Columbia DB.3734/ (45) SCM.5241 |
| Bob Dale and The Rita Williams Singers | 2/56 | Embassy WB.171 |

## 698 | STEALIN'

*Composers*: Al Lewis & Larry Stock

*Publishers*: Leeds Music Ltd.

*Date of Entry*: 28.1.56

*Highest Position*: 18
*Weeks on Chart*: 8

*Recordings*:

| | | |
|---|---|---|
| Alma Warren | 1/56 | Parlophone R.4118/ (45) MSP.6200 |
| Frankie Vaughan | 1/56 | Philips PB.544 |
| Dennis Hale | 1/56 | Decca F.10674 (&45–) |
| Ray Burns | 1/56 | Columbia DB.3717/ (45) SCM.5224 |
| Victor Silvester and his Ballroom Orchestra | 2/56 | Columbia DB.3726/ (45) SCM.5233 |

## 699 | DREAMS CAN TELL A LIE

*Composers*: Howard Barnes, Harold Cornelius & Dominic John

*Publishers*: John Fields Music Co. Ltd.

*Date of Entry*: 28.1.56/
Pos: 17/Wks: 9
*Re-entry*: 7.4.56/
Pos: 24/Wks: 1

*Recordings*:

| | | |
|---|---|---|
| Dickie Valentine with The Keynotes | 1/56 | Decca F.10667 (&45–) |
| Kathie Kay | 1/56 | HMV POP.159/ (45) 7M.363 |
| Steve Arlen | 1/56 | Philips PB.545 |
| Nat 'King' Cole | 1/56 | Capitol CL.14513 (& 45–) |

## 700 MEMORIES ARE MADE OF THIS

| | | | |
|---|---|---|---|
| *Composers*: Richard Dehr, Frank Miller & Terry Gilkyson | | *Date of Entry*: 4.2.56 | |
| *Publishers*: Montclare Music Co. Ltd. | | *Highest Position*: 1 *Weeks on Chart*: 24 | |

*Recordings*:

| | | |
|---|---|---|
| Dave King and The Keynotes | 1/56 | Decca F.10684 (&45-) |
| Gale Storm | 1/56 | London HLD.8232 (& 45-) |
| Petula Clark | 2/56 | Pye Nixa N.15040 |
| Mindy Carson and The Columbians | 2/56 | Philips PB.548 |
| Denny Dennis and The Canadians | 2/56 | Embassy WB.167 |
| Benny Hill with The Coronets | 2/56 | Columbia DB.3731/ (45) SCM.5238 |
| Dean Martin | 2/56 | Capitol CL.14523 (& 45-) |
| Joe Loss and his Orchestra | 3/56 | HMV POP.184/ (45) 7M.387 |
| The Regent Ballroom Orchestra | 3/56 | Decca F.10718 (&45-) |

## 701 IT'S ALMOST TOMORROW

| | | | |
|---|---|---|---|
| *Composers*: Gene Adkinson & Wade Buff | | *Date of Entry*: 11.2.56 | |
| *Publishers*: Macmelodies Ltd. | | *Highest Position*: 1 *Weeks on Chart*: 31 | |

*Recordings*:

| | | |
|---|---|---|
| The Dream Weavers | 1/56 | Brunswick 05515 (& 45-) |
| Snooky Lanson | 1/56 | London HLD.8223 (& 45-) |
| Dennis Hale | 1/56 | Decca F.10674 (&45-) |
| Eve Boswell | 2/56 | Parlophone R.4143 |
| Jo Stafford | 2/56 | Philips PB.557 |
| Lawrence Welk and his Champagne Music (Alice Lon and The Sparklers) | 2/56 | Vogue Coral Q.72134 (& 45-) |
| Eve Boswell | 3/56 | Parlophone (45) MSP.6220 |
| Ken Kirkham | 3/56 | Columbia DB.3737/ (45) SCM.5244 |
| The Four-in-A-Chord | 3/56 | Embassy WB.173 |
| The Regent Ballroom Orchestra | 3/56 | Decca F.10719 (&45-) |
| Joe Loss and his Orchestra | 4/56 | HMV POP.195 |

## 702 ZAMBEZI (Sweet African)

| | | | |
|---|---|---|---|
| *Composers*: Nico Carstens, Anton De Waal & Bob Hilliard | | *Date of Entry*: 11.2.56 | |
| *Publishers*: John Fields Music Co. Ltd. | | *Highest Position*: 3 *Weeks on Chart*: 18 | |

*Recordings*:

| | | |
|---|---|---|
| Lou Busch and his Orchestra and Chorus | 1/56 | Capitol CL.14504 (& 45-) |
| The Stargazers | 2/56 | Decca F.10696 (&45-) |
| Eddie Calvert – The Man with the Golden Trumpet | 2/56 | Columbia DB.3747 |
| Joe Loss and his Orchestra with Frank Gillespie (sax) | 3/56 | HMV POP.183/ (45) 7M.386 |
| Tony Mansell | 3/56 | Parlophone R.4145/ (45) MSP.6222 |
| The Canadians | 3/56 | Embassy WB.175 |

## 703 BAND OF GOLD

| | | | |
|---|---|---|---|
| *Composers*: Bob Musel & Jack Taylor | | *Date of Entry*: 11.2.56 | |
| *Publishers*: Essex Music Ltd. | | *Highest Position*: 6 *Weeks on Chart*: 13 | |

*Recordings*:

| | | |
|---|---|---|
| Rosemary Squires | 1/56 | Decca F.10685 (&45-) |
| Don Cherry | 2/56 | Philips PB.549 |
| Barbara Lyon | 2/56 | Columbia DB.3725/ (45) SCM.5232 |
| Petula Clark | 2/56 | Pye Nixa N.15040 |
| The Hi Fi Four | 2/56 | Parlophone R.4130/ (45) MSP.6210 |
| Kit Carson | 2/56 | Capitol CL.14524 (& 45-) |
| Rose Brennan | 2/56 | HMV POP.180/ (45) 7M.383 |
| Rita Williams | 2/56 | Embassy WB.169 |

## 704 JIMMY UNKNOWN

| | | | |
|---|---|---|---|
| *Composers*: Ruth Roberts & Bill Katz | | *Date of Entry*: 11.2.56 | |
| *Publishers*: Sydney Bron Music Co. | | *Highest Position*: 7 *Weeks on Chart*: 15 | |

*Recordings*:

| | | |
|---|---|---|
| Mary Morgan | 1/56 | Parlophone R.4122/ (45) MSP.6204 |
| Kathie Kay | 1/56 | HMV POP.159/ (45) 7M.363 |
| Doris Day | 1/56 | Philips PB.542 |
| Lita Roza | 1/56 | Decca F.10679 (&45-) |
| Billy Thorburn and his Strict Tempo Music | 3/56 | Parlophone R.4153/ (45) MSP.6227 |
| The Regent Ballroom Orchestra | 3/56 | Decca F.10719 (&45-) |

## 705 ONLY YOU

*Composers*: Buck Ram & Ande Rand

*Publishers*: Sherwin Music Co. Ltd.

*Date of Entry*: 25.2.56/
Pos: 12/Wks: 19
*Re-entry*: 14.7.56/
Pos: 24/Wks: 2
*2nd re-entry*: 25.8.56/
Pos: 21/Wks: 2
*3rd re-entry*: 27.10.56/
Pos: 22/Wks: 1

*Recordings*:

| | | |
|---|---|---|
| Billy Eckstine | 6/55 | MGM.830 |
| The Rhythmettes | 6/55 | HMV B.10880 |
| Louis Armstrong and The All-Stars (Louis Armstrong) | 1/56 | Brunswick 05512 (& 45-) |
| The Hilltoppers | 1/56 | London HLD.8221 (& 45-) |
| Steve Martin | 1/56 | Columbia DB.3703/ (45) SCM.5212 |
| Victor Silvester and his Ballroom Orchestra | 1/56 | Columbia DB.3712/ (45) SCM.5219 |
| Annie Ross | 1/56 | Decca F.10680 (&45-) |
| Malcolm Vaughan | 3/56 | HMV POP.186/ (45) 7M.389 |
| The Canadians | 3/56 | Embassy WB.175 |
| The Platters | 8/56 | Mercury MT.117 |

## 706 MEMORIES OF YOU

*Composers*: Eubie Blake & Andy Razaf

*Publishers*: Lawrence Wright Music Co. Ltd.

*Date of Entry*: 3.3.56

*Highest Position*: 22
*Weeks on Chart*: 2

*Recordings*:

| | | |
|---|---|---|
| The Pud Brown Trio | 1/54 | Capitol CL.14043 |
| Steve Allen and his Chorus and Orchestra | 1/56 | Vogue Coral Q.72126 (& 45-) |
| Joe 'Fingers' Carr and the Carr-Hops | 1/56 | Capitol CL.14520 (& 45-) |
| The Benny Goodman Trio with Rosemary Clooney | 2/56 | Philips PB.547 |
| Sid Phillips and his Band | 2/56 | HMV POP.169/ (45) 7M.372 |
| Eddie Calvert – The Man with the Golden Trumpet | 2/56 | Columbia DB.3730/ (45) SCM.5237 |
| Frank Chacksfield and his Orchestra | 2/56 | Decca F.10689 (&45-) |
| Benny Goodman and his Sextet (recorded 1939) | 2/56 | Columbia DB.3732/ (45) SCM.5239 |
| Johnny Dankworth and his Orchestra | 3/56 | Parlophone R.4148 |
| Art Mooney and his Orchestra (The Cloverleafs) | 3/56 | MGM.892/(45) SP.1166 |

## 707 MY SEPTEMBER LOVE

*Composers*: Tolchard Evans & Richard Mullan

*Publishers*: Sydney Bron Music Co.

*Date of Entry*: 3.3.56/
Pos: 24/Wks: 1
*Re-entry*: 17.3.56/
Pos: 1/Wks: 32

*Recordings*:

| | | |
|---|---|---|
| Robert Earl | 2/56 | Philips PB.552 |
| David Whitfield | 2/56 | Decca F.10690 (&45-) |
| Victor Silvester and his Ballroom Orchestra | 4/56 | Columbia DB.3753 |
| Tommy Rogers and his Ballroom Orchestra dir. Harry Gold | 5/56 | Parlophone R.4166/ (45) MSP.6232 |
| Billy McCormack | 6/56 | Embassy WB.189 |
| The Famous ECCLES and Miss Freda Thing | 12/56 | Parlophone R.4251 (& 45-)* |

## 708 THE ROCK AND ROLL WALTZ

*Composers*: Shorty Allen & Dick Ware

*Publishers*: Maddox Music Co. Ltd.

*Date of Entry*: 10.3.56

*Highest Position*: 4
*Weeks on Chart*: 21

*Recordings*:

| | | |
|---|---|---|
| Kay Starr | 2/56 | HMV POP.168/ (45) 7M.371 |
| Ted Heath and his Music (Annette Klooger) | 2/56 | Decca F.10701 (&45-) |
| Lawrence Welk and his Champagne Music | 3/56 | Vogue Coral Q.72141 (& 45-) |
| Penny Nicholls and The Canadians | 3/56 | Embassy WB.176 |

## 709 CHAIN GANG

*Composers*: Sol Quasha & Herb Yakus

*Publishers*: Bluebird Music Co.

*Date of Entry*: 10.3.56/
Pos: 24/Wks: 1
*Re-entry*: 24.3.56/
Pos: 21/Wks: 4

*Recordings*:

| | | |
|---|---|---|
| Jimmy Young | 2/56 | Decca F.10694 (&45-) |
| Johnny Oliver | 3/56 | MGM.891/ (45) SP.1165 |
| Lawrence Welk and his Champagne Music (Larry Hooper and The Sparklers) | 3/56 | Vogue Coral Q.72140 (& 45-) |
| Bobby Scott | 3/56 | London HL.8254 (& 45-) |
| Larry Cross with The Rita Williams Singers | 3/56 | Embassy WB.178 |

## 710 THE POOR PEOPLE OF PARIS (Poor John – La Goulante du pauvre Jean)

*Composers*: Marguerite Monnot, Rene Rouzaud & Jack Lawrence
*Publishers*: Berry Music Ltd.

*Date of Entry*: 17.3.56

*Highest Position*: 2
*Weeks on Chart*: 22

*Recordings*:

| | | |
|---|---|---|
| Eddie Barclay and his Orchestra [Titled 'La Goulante du Pauvre Jean'] | 11/54 | Felsted SD.80022 |
| Winifred Atwell (piano) | 1/56 | Decca F.10681 (&45-) |
| Les Baxter and his Orchestra and Chorus | 2/56 | Capitol CL.14533 (& 45-) |
| Norrie Paramor and his Orchestra | 3/56 | Columbia DB.3745/ (45) SCM.5251 |
| Russ Morgan and his Orchestra | 3/56 | Brunswick 05537 (& 45-) |
| Lawrence Welk and his Champagne Music | 3/56 | Vogue Coral Q.72140 (& 45-) |
| Geraldo and his Orchestra | 3/56 | Oriole CB.1322 |
| Joe Loss and his Orchestra | 4/56 | HMV POP.194 |
| Primo Scala and his Accordion Band | 4/56 | Embassy WB.179 |
| Victor Silvester and his Ballroom Orchestra | 5/56 | Columbia DB.3762/ (45) SCM.5257 |
| Claude Luter and his Orchestra | 6/56 | Vogue V.2395 |

## 711 THE THEME FROM 'THE THREEPENNY OPERA' (Moritat)

*Composers*: Kurt Weill, Berthold Brecht & Marc Blitzstein
*Publishers*: Arcadia Music Publishing Co. Ltd.

*Date of Entry*: 17.3.56

*Highest Position*: 8
*Weeks on Chart*: 15

*Recordings*:

| | | |
|---|---|---|
| Owen Bradley and his Orchestra | 2/56 | Brunswick 05528 (& 45-) |
| The Eric Rogers Trio | 2/56 | Decca F.10692 (&45-) |
| Billy Vaughn and his Orchestra | 2/56 | London HLD.8238 (& 45-) |
| Les Paul (guitar) [Titled 'Moritat – Theme from Threepenny Opera'] | 2/56 | Capitol CL.14534 (& 45-) |
| Louis Armstrong and his All-Stars | 3/56 | Philips PB.574 |
| Joe 'Mr Piano' Henderson and his Music | 3/56 | Pye Nixa N.15044 |
| Turk Murphy and his Band | 3/56 | Philips PB.564 |
| Frank Cordell and his Orchestra | 3/56 | HMV POP.188 |
| Ernie Englund (trumpet) | 3/56 | Pye Nixa N.15035 |
| Lawrence Welk and his Sparkling Sextet | 3/56 | Vogue Coral Q.72141 (& 45-) |
| Richard Hayman (harmonica) and Jan August (piano) | 3/56 | Mercury MT.103 |
| Norrie Paramor and his Orchestra | 3/56 | Columbia DB.3745/ (45) SCM.5251 |
| The Dick Hyman Trio | 3/56 | MGM.890/(45) SP.1164 |
| Primo Scala and his Accordion Band | 4/56 | Embassy WB.179 |
| Victor Silvester and his Ballroom Orchestra | 5/56 | Columbia DB.3761/ (45) SCM.5256 |
| Maria Remusat | 5/56 | Felsted SD.80042 |
| Sidney Bechet (soprano saxophone) | 6/56 | Vogue V.2394 (&45-) |

## 712 THE GREAT PRETENDER

*Composer*: Buck Ram

*Publishers*: Southern Music Publishing Co. Ltd.

*Date of Entry*: 17.3.56

*Highest Position*: 14
*Weeks on Chart*: 11

*Recordings*:

| | | |
|---|---|---|
| Jimmy Parkinson | 2/56 | Columbia DB.3729/ (45) SCM.5236 |
| Jackie Riggs | 3/56 | London HLF.8244 (& 45-) |
| Anne Shelton | 3/56 | Philips PB.567 |
| Sam Browne and The Rita Williams Singers | 3/56 | Embassy WB.177 |
| Stan Freberg with The Toads | 4/56 | Capitol CL.14571 (& 45-) |
| Joe Loss and his Orchestra | 5/56 | HMV POP.207/ (45) 7M.399 |
| The Platters | 8/56 | Mercury MT.117★ |

## 713 LIPSTICK AND CANDY AND RUBBER SOLE SHOES

*Composer*: Bob Haymes

*Publishers*: Leeds Music Ltd.

*Date of Entry*: 24.3.56

*Highest Position*: 21
*Weeks on Chart*: 3

*Recording*:

| | | |
|---|---|---|
| Julius La Rosa | 3/56 | HMV POP.181/ (45) 7M.384 |

## 714 WILLIE CAN

*Composers*: Felice & Boudleaux Bryant

*Publishers*: Frank Music Co. Ltd.

*Date of Entry*: 31.3.56

*Highest Position*: 5
*Weeks on Chart*: 15

*Recordings*:

| | | |
|---|---|---|
| Alma Cogan with Desmond Lane (penny whistle) | 3/56 | HMV POP.187 |
| Mitch Miller and his Orchestra and Chorus | 3/56 | Philips PB.562 |
| The Beverley Sisters | 3/56 | Decca F.10705 (&45-) |
| Diana Decker | 3/56 | Columbia DB.3739/ (45) SCM.5246 |
| Pauline Shepherd with The Beryl Stott Chorus | 3/56 | Pye Nixa N.15043 |
| Shirley Abicair | 3/56 | Parlophone R.4150/ (45) MSP.6224 |
| Rita Williams and The Rita Williams Singers | 4/56 | Embassy WB.182 |

## 715 COOKIE

*Composers*: Garfield de Mortimer, Paddy Roberts & William Young

*Date of Entry*: 31.3.56/ Pos: 24/Wks: 1

*Publishers*: Berry Music Co. Ltd.

*Re-entry*: 12.5.56/ Pos: 24/Wks: 1

*Recordings*:
| | | |
|---|---|---|
| Eve Boswell | 2/56 | Parlophone R.4143 |
| Eve Boswell | 3/56 | Parlophone (45) MSP.6220 |
| Tommy Rogers and his Ballroom Orchestra dir. Harry Gold | 5/56 | Parlophone R.4166/ (45) MSP.6232 |

## 716 COME NEXT SPRING

*Composers*: Max Steiner & Lenny Adelson

*Date of Entry*: 7.4.56/ Pos: 19/Wks: 7

*Publishers*: Frank Music Co. Ltd.

*Re-entry*: 2.6.56/ Pos: 23/Wks: 1

*Recordings*:
| | | |
|---|---|---|
| Tony Bennett | 1/56 | Philips PB.537 |
| Ken Mackintosh (sax) with Kenny Bardell and The Peter Knight Singers with Rhythm acc. | 2/56 | HMV POP.176/ (45) 7M.379 |
| Joan Small | 2/56 | Parlophone R.4142/ (45) MSP.6219 |
| Cyril Stapleton and his Orchestra | 3/56 | Decca F.10703 (&45-) |
| Keith Warwick | 3/56 | Embassy WB.174 |
| Victor Silvester and his Ballroom Orchestra | 6/56 | Columbia DB.3777/ (45) SCM.5269 |

## 717 NO OTHER LOVE

*Composers*: Richard Rodgers & Oscar Hammerstein II

*Date of Entry*: 14.4.56

*Publishers*: Chappell & Co. Ltd.

*Highest Position*: 1
*Weeks on Chart*: 22

*Recordings*:
| | | |
|---|---|---|
| The Johnston Brothers | 4/56 | Decca F.10721 (&45-) |
| Ronnie Hilton | 4/56 | HMV POP.198 |
| David Rose and his Orchestra featuring Danny Welton – harmonica | 4/56 | MGM.898 |
| Edmund Hockridge | 4/56 | Pye Nixa N.15048 |
| Bill McGuffie and his Music | 4/56 | Philips PB.584 |
| Rita Williams | 4/56 | Embassy WB.182 |
| Ron Goodwin and his Concert Orchestra | 4/56 | Parlophone R.4162 |
| Gordon Jenkins and his Orchestra | 4/56 | Brunswick 05556 (& 45-) |
| Julius La Rosa | 4/56 | London HLA.8272 (& 45-) |
| Bing Crosby | 4/56 | Brunswick 05558 (& 45-) |

| | | |
|---|---|---|
| Ronnie Hilton | 5/56 | HMV (45) 7M.390 |
| Victor Silvester and his Ballroom Orchestra | 5/56 | Columbia DB.3762/ (45) SCM.5257 |
| Joe Loss and his Orchestra | 6/56 | HMV POP.216/ (45) 7M.408 |

## 718 DON'T RINGA DA BELL

*Composers*: Johnny Reine & Sonny Miller

*Date of Entry*: 14.4.56

*Publishers*: Michael Reine Music Co. Ltd.

*Highest Position*: 16
*Weeks on Chart*: 9

*Recordings*:
| | | |
|---|---|---|
| Edmundo Ros and his Orchestra (Edmundo Ros) | 3/56 | Decca F.10716 (&45-) |
| Alma Cogan | 4/56 | HMV POP.189 |
| Barbara Lyon and Ronnie Harris | 4/56 | Columbia DB.3749 |
| Shani Wallis with The Beryl Stott Chorus and Joe Henderson (harpsichord) | 4/56 | Pye Nixa N.15049 |
| Penny Nicholls | 6/56 | Embassy WB.188 |

## 719 YOU CAN'T BE TRUE TO TWO

*Composers*: Al Hoffman & Dick Manning

*Date of Entry*: 21.4.56

*Publishers*: Dash Music Co. Ltd.

*Highest Position*: 4
*Weeks on Chart*: 19

*Recordings*:
| | | |
|---|---|---|
| Dave King and The Keynotes | 4/56 | Decca F.10720 (&45-) |
| Mindy Carson | 4/56 | Philips PB.579 |
| Denny Dennis with The Rita Williams Singers | 4/56 | Embassy WB.181 |
| Jimmy Parkinson with The Coronets | 4/56 | Columbia DB.3755 |

## 720 A TEAR FELL

*Composers*: Eugene Randolph & Dorian Burton

*Date of Entry*: 21.4.56

*Publishers*: Robbins Music Corporation Ltd.

*Highest Position*: 6
*Weeks on Chart*: 19

*Recordings*:
| | | |
|---|---|---|
| Teresa Brewer | 3/56 | Vogue CoraL Q.72146 (& 45-) |
| Edna Savage | 4/56 | Parlophone R.4159 |
| Ivory Joe Hunter | 4/56 | London HLE.8261 (& 45-) |
| Jill Day | 4/56 | HMV POP.199/(45) 7M.391 |
| Beryl Templeman | 5/56 | Embassy WB.184 |
| Joe Loss and his Orchestra | 6/56 | HMV POP.217/(45) 7M.409 |

## 721 OUT OF TOWN

| | | |
|---|---|---|
| *Composers*: Leslie Bricusse & Robin Beaumont | *Date of Entry*: 21.4.56 | |
| *Publishers*: Edward Kassner Music Co. Ltd. | *Highest Position*: 3 | |
| | *Weeks on Chart*: 23 | |

*Recordings*:

| Max Bygraves | 2/56 | HMV POP.164/ |
|---|---|---|
| | | (45) 7M.368 |
| Victor Silvester and his Ballroom Orchestra | 7/56 | Columbia DB.3790/ (45) SCM.5279 |

## 722 I'LL BE HOME

| | | |
|---|---|---|
| *Composers*: Ferdinand Washington & Stan Lewis | *Date of Entry*: 5.5.56 | |
| *Publishers*: Box & Cox Publications Ltd. | *Highest Position*: 7 | |
| | *Weeks on Chart*: 19 | |

*Recordings*:

| Pat Boone | 3/56 | London HLD.8253 (& 45-) |
|---|---|---|
| Billy McCormack | 6/56 | Embassy WB.189 |

## 723 THE ITALIAN THEME

| | | |
|---|---|---|
| *Composers*: Angel Giacomazzi & Clyde Hamilton | *Date of Entry*: 19.5.56 | |
| *Publishers*: World Wide Music Co. Ltd. | *Highest Position*: 23 | |
| | *Weeks on Chart*: 1 | |

*Recordings*:

| Cyril Stapleton and his Orchestra | 3/56 | Decca F.10703 (&45-) |
|---|---|---|
| Dorothy Collins | 10/56 | Vogue Coral Q.72198 (& 45-)★ |
| The Barry Sisters | 11/56 | Columbia DB.3843 (& 45-)★ |

## 724 MISTER CUCKOO (Sing your song)

| | | |
|---|---|---|
| *Composers*: Willy Mattes, Geoffrey Parsons & John Turner | *Date of Entry*: 19.5.56 | |
| *Publishers*: Macmelodies Ltd. | *Highest Position*: 9 | |
| | *Weeks on Chart*: 14 | |

*Recordings*:

| Edmundo Ros and his Orchestra (Edmundo Ros) | 3/56 | Decca F.10716 (&45-) |
|---|---|---|
| Frank Weir, his soprano sax, and his Orchestra and Chorus | 4/56 | Parlophone R.4157 |
| Frank Weir, his soprano sax, and his Orchestra and Chorus | 5/56 | Parlophone (45) MSP.6228 |
| The Three Kayes | 5/56 | HMV POP.209/ (45) 7M.401 |

## 725 HOT DIGGITY

| | | |
|---|---|---|
| *Composers*: Al Hoffman & Dick Manning | *Date of Entry*: 26.5.56 | |
| *Publishers*: Peter Maurice Music Co. Ltd. | *Highest Position*: 1 | |
| | *Weeks on Chart*: 21 | |

*Recordings*:

| The Stargazers | 5/56 | Decca F.10731 (&45-) |
|---|---|---|
| Perry Como | 5/56 | HMV POP.221/ (45) 7M.404 |
| Glen Mason | 5/56 | Parlophone R.4176/ (45) MSP.6240 |
| Michael Holliday with The Four Shepherd Boys | 5/56 | Columbia DB.3783/ (45) SCM.5273 |
| Marion Ryan | 6/56 | Pye Nixa N.15058 |
| Penny Nicholls | 6/56 | Embassy WB.190 |

## 726 THE HAPPY WHISTLER

| | | |
|---|---|---|
| *Composer*: Don Robertson | *Date of Entry*: 26.5.56 | |
| *Publishers*: Sydney Bron Music Co. | *Highest Position*: 11 | |
| | *Weeks on Chart*: 9 | |

*Recordings*:

| Don Robertson | 5/56 | Capitol CL.14575 (& 45-) |
|---|---|---|
| Cyril Stapleton and his Orchestra (ftg Desmond Lane – penny whistle) | 5/56 | Decca F.10735 (&45-) |
| Ronnie Ronalde | 5/56 | Columbia DB.3785/ (45) SCM.5275 |
| Billy Thorburn and his Strict Tempo Music | 7/56 | Parlophone R.4190/ (45) MSP.6251 |
| 'Winnie the Whistler' | 7/56 | Embassy WB.192 |

## 727 WHO ARE WE?

| | | |
|---|---|---|
| *Composers*: Jerry Livingston & Paul Francis Webster | *Date of Entry*: 2.6.56 | |
| *Publishers*: Bourne Music Ltd. | *Highest Position*: 2 | |
| | *Weeks on Chart*: 24 | |

*Recordings*:

| Vera Lynn | 3/56 | Decca F.10715 (&45-) |
|---|---|---|
| Gogi Grant | 3/56 | London HLB.8257 (& 45-) |
| Betty Miller with The Beryl Stott Chorus | 4/56 | Pye Nixa N.15047 |
| Don Rennie | 5/56 | Parlophone R.4172/ (45) MSP.6237 |
| Gordon MacRae | 5/56 | Capitol CL.14576 (& 45-) |
| Ronnie Hilton | 6/56 | HMV POP.221/ (45) 7M.413 |

## 728 TOO YOUNG TO GO STEADY

*Composers*: Harold Adamson & Jimmy McHugh        *Date of Entry*: 2.6.56

*Publishers*: Robbins Music Corporation Ltd.        *Highest Position*: 7
                                                    *Weeks on Chart*: 13

*Recordings*:
| | | |
|---|---|---|
| Lita Roza | 4/56 | Decca F.10728 (&45-) |
| Patti Page | 5/56 | Mercury MT.104 |
| Nicky Kidd | 5/56 | Beltona BL.2645 |
| Anne Shelton | 5/56 | Philips PB.437 |
| Larry Cross | 5/56 | Embassy WB.183 |
| Nat 'King' Cole | 5/56 | Capitol CL.14573 (& 45-) |

## 729 IVORY TOWER

*Composers*: Jack Fulton & Lois Steele        *Date of Entry*: 2.6.56

*Publishers*: Edwin H. Morris & Co. Ltd.        *Highest Position*: 14
                                                *Weeks on Chart*: 17

*Recordings*:
| | | |
|---|---|---|
| Cathy Carr | 4/56 | London HLH.8274 (& 45-) |
| Rita Williams | 5/56 | Embassy WB.185 |
| Otis Williams and The Charms | 5/56 | Parlophone R.4175/ (45) MSP.6239 |
| The Three Kayes | 5/56 | HMV POP.209/ (45) 7M.401 |
| Gale Storm | 5/56 | London HLD.8283 (& 45-) |
| Jean Campbell | 6/56 | Polydor BM.6027 |
| Joe Loss and his Orchestra | 7/56 | HMV POP.237/ (45) 7M.426 |

## 730 TRY ANOTHER CHERRY TREE

*Composers*: Earl Shuman, Alden Shuman &        *Date of Entry*: 16.6.56
Marshall Brown

*Publishers*: Duchess Music Ltd.        *Highest Position*: 20
                                        *Weeks on Chart*: 5

*Recording*:
| | | |
|---|---|---|
| Max Bygraves with Children's Chorus | 5/56 | HMV POP.208 (45) 7M.400 |

## 731 SERENADE

*Composers*: Sammy Cahn & Nicholas Brodszky        *Date of Entry*: 16.6.56

*Publishers*: Blossom Music Ltd.        *Highest Position*: 9
                                        *Weeks on Chart*: 25

*Recordings*:
| | | |
|---|---|---|
| Mario Lanza | 6/56 | HMV DA.2085 |
| Slim Whitman | 6/56 | London HLU.8287 (& 45-) |
| Eddie Calvert – The Man with the Golden Trumpet | 6/56 | Columbia DB.3779 |
| David Rose and his Orchestra | 6/56 | MGM.906/ (45) SP.1174 |
| Ray Heindorf and his Orchestra | 6/56 | Philips PB.588 |

## 732 BLUE SUEDE SHOES

*Composer*: Carl Perkins        *Date of Entry*: 16.6.56

*Publishers*: Aberbach (London) Ltd.        *Highest Position*: 24
                                            *Weeks on Chart*: 1

*Recordings*:
| | | |
|---|---|---|
| Carl Perkins | 4/56 | London HLU.8271 (& 45-) |
| Roy Hall | 4/56 | Brunswick 05555 (& 45-) |
| Jim Lowe | 4/56 | London HLD.8276 (& 45-) |
| Boyd Bennett and his Rockets | 5/56 | Parlophone R.4167/ (45) MSP.6233 |
| Elvis Presley | 5/56 | HMV POP.213/ (45) 7M.405 |
| The Canadians | 6/56 | Embassy WB.187 |

## 733 THE WAYWARD WIND

*Composers*: Stan Lebowsky & Herb Newman        *Date of Entry*: 23.6.56

*Publishers*: J.R. Lafleur & Sons Ltd.        *Highest Position*: 6
                                              *Weeks on Chart*: 18

*Recordings*:
| | | |
|---|---|---|
| Tex Ritter | 5/56 | Capitol CL.14581 (& 45-) |
| Jimmy Young | 6/56 | Decca F.10736 (&45-) |
| Gogi Grant | 6/56 | London HLB.8282 (& 45-) |
| Shirley Bassey | 6/56 | Philips PB.598 |
| Denny Dennis | 7/56 | Embassy WB.194 |

## 734 WHATEVER WILL BE, WILL BE (Que Sera, Sera)

| | |
|---|---|
| *Composers*: Jay Livingston & Ray Evans | *Date of Entry*: 23.6.56 |
| *Publishers*: Melcher–Toff Music Ltd. | *Highest Position*: 1<br>*Weeks on Chart*: 34 |

*Recordings*:

| | | |
|---|---|---|
| Doris Day | 5/56 | Philips PB.586 |
| Eve Lombard | 7/56 | Embassy WB.193 |
| George Cates and his Orchestra and Chorus | 7/56 | Vogue Coral Q.72179 (& 45-) |
| Billy Cotton and his Band (Billy Cotton) | 7/56 | Decca F.10767 (&45-) |
| The Parlophone Pops Orchestra and Chorus cond. Ron Goodwin | 10/56 | Parlophone R.4229 |

(Note: The recording by the Parlophone Pops Orchestra was No. 1 in a series 'Sing it Yourself'. The record was accompanied by a leaflet containing words of the two songs on the record.)

## 735 WALK HAND IN HAND

| | |
|---|---|
| *Composer*: Johnny Cowell | *Date of Entry*: 30.6.56 |
| *Publishers*: Duchess Music Ltd. | *Highest Position*: 1<br>*Weeks on Chart*: 26 |

*Recordings*:

| | | |
|---|---|---|
| Vera Lynn | 5/56 | Decca F.10737 (&45-) |
| Andy Williams | 5/56 | London HLA.8284 (& 45-) |
| Jimmy Parkinson with The Bill Shepherd Chorus | 6/56 | Columbia DB.3775/ (45) SCM.5267 |
| Tony Martin | 6/56 | HMV POP.222/ (45) 7M.414 |
| Denny Vaughan | 6/56 | Oriole CB.1330 |
| Ronnie Carroll | 7/56 | Philips PB.605 |

## 736 WHY DO FOOLS FALL IN LOVE?

| | |
|---|---|
| *Composers*: Frankie Lymon & George Goldner | *Date of Entry*: 7.7.56 |
| *Publishers*: Chappell & Co. Ltd. | *Highest Position*: 4<br>*Weeks on Chart*: 18 |

*Recordings*:

| | | |
|---|---|---|
| Gloria Mann | 5/56 | Brunswick 05569 (& 45-) |
| Gale Storm | 5/56 | London HLD.8286 (& 45-) |
| Annette Klooger and The Four Jones Boys | 5/56 | Decca F.10738 (&45-) |
| The Teenagers featuring Frankie Lymon | 6/56 | Columbia DB.3772/ (45) SCM.5265 |
| Marion Ryan | 6/56 | Pye Nixa N.15058 |
| Alma Cogan with Vocal Group | 6/56 | HMV POP.223 |
| Alma Cogan with Vocal Group | 7/56 | HMV (45) 7M.415 |

## 737 THE BIRDS AND THE BEES

| | |
|---|---|
| *Composers*: Mack David & Harry Warren | *Date of Entry*: 14.7.56 |
| *Publishers*: Maddox Music Co. Ltd. | *Highest Position*: 6<br>*Weeks on Chart*: 19 |

*Recordings*:

| | | |
|---|---|---|
| Alan Dale | 5/56 | Vogue Coral Q.72166 (& 45-) |
| Rush Adams with vocal assists by Loulie Jean Normon | 6/56 | MGM.908/(45) SP.1176 |
| Alma Cogan with vocal group | 6/56 | HMV POP.223 |
| Barbara Lyon | 6/56 | Columbia DB.3786 |
| Dave King with The Keynotes | 6/56 | Decca F.10741 (&45-) |
| Dick Noel | 6/56 | London HLH.8295 (& 45-) |
| Alma Cogan with vocal group | 7/56 | HMV (45) 7M.415 |
| Barbara Lyon | 7/56 | Columbia (45) SCM.5276 |
| Billy Thorburn and his Strict Tempo Music | 7/56 | Parlophone R.4190/ (45) MSP.6251 |
| Eve Lombard | 7/56 | Embassy WB.193 |

## 738 MOUNTAIN GREENERY

| | |
|---|---|
| *Composers*: Richard Rodgers & Lorenz Hart | *Date of Entry*: 21.7.56 |
| *Publishers*: New World Publications Ltd. | *Highest Position*: 3<br>*Weeks on Chart*: 20 |

*Recordings*:

| | | |
|---|---|---|
| Mel Torme | 2/56 | Vogue Coral Q.72150 (& 45-) |
| Joe Loss and his Orchestra | 9/56 | HMV POP.246 (& 45-) |
| Victor Silvester and his Ballroom Orchestra | 10/56 | Columbia DB.3828 (& 45-) |
| Larry Cross | 10/56 | Embassy WB.208 |

## 739 BY THE FOUNTAINS OF ROME

| | |
|---|---|
| *Composers*: Matyas Seiber & Norman Newell | *Date of Entry*: 28.7.56 |
| *Publishers*: Sterling Music Publishing Co. Ltd. | *Highest Position*: 7<br>*Weeks on Chart*: 16 |

*Recordings*:

| | | |
|---|---|---|
| Maxine Daniels | 6/56 | Oriole CB.1332 |
| David Hughes | 7/56 | Philips PB.606 |
| Edmund Hockridge with The Beryl Stott Chorus | 7/56 | Pye Nixa N.15063 |
| Johnny Douglas and his Orchestra | 7/56 | Decca F.10764 (&45-) |
| Victor Silvester and his Ballroom Orchestra | 10/56 | Columbia DB.3829 (& 45-) |

## 740 | WATCHING THE WORLD GO BY

*Composers*: Jean Senn & Sunny Skylar          *Date of Entry*: 28.7.56

*Publishers*: Bourne Music Ltd.          *Highest Position*: 23
*Weeks on Chart*: 1

*Recording*:
| | | |
|---|---|---|
| Dean Martin | 6/56 | Capitol CL.14586 (& 45-) |

## 741 | YOU'LL NEVER WALK ALONE

*Composers*: Richard Rodgers &          *Date of Entry*: 4.8.56/
    Oscar Hammerstein II          Pos: 22/Wks: 1
*Publishers*: Williamson Music Ltd.          *Re-entry*: 8.9.56/
Pos: 23/Wks: 2
*2nd re-entry*: 29.9.56/
Pos: 21/Wks: 4

*Recordings*:
| | | |
|---|---|---|
| Frank Sinatra with The Ken Lane Singers | 6/50 | Columbia DB.2705 |
| Judy Garland | 6/50 | Brunswick 04530 |
| Fred Waring and his Pennsylvanians (The Glee Club) | 7/50 | Brunswick 04536 |
| The Melachrino Strings | 1/55 | HMV B.10811 |
| Roy Hamilton | 2/55 | Philips PB.368 |
| Ray Bloch and his Orchestra and Chorus | 5/56 | Vogue Coral Q.72165 (& 45-) |
| Jane Froman | 11/56 | Capitol CL.14658 (& 45-)★ |

## 742 | THE GAL WITH THE YALLER SHOES

*Composers*: Sammy Cahn & Nicholas Brodszky          *Date of Entry*: 4.8.56/
Pos: 23/Wks: 3
*Publishers*: Robbins Music Corporation Ltd.          *Re-entry*: 1.9.56/
Pos: 19/Wks: 5

*Recordings*:
| | | |
|---|---|---|
| Michael Holliday | 5/56 | Columbia DB.3783/ (45) SCM.5273 |
| The Four Aces featuring Al Alberts | 5/56 | Brunswick 05566 (& 45-) |
| The Bob Bissetto Quartet (vocal and instrumental) | 7/56 | Embassy WB.191 |

## 743 | A SWEET OLD-FASHIONED GIRL

*Composer*: Bob Merrill          *Date of Entry*: 11.8.56

*Publishers*: Campbell Connelly & Co. Ltd.          *Highest Position*: 6
*Weeks on Chart*: 18

*Recordings*:
| | | |
|---|---|---|
| Teresa Brewer | 6/56 | Vogue Coral Q.72172 (& 45-) |
| Billie Anthony | 7/56 | Columbia DB.3798 (45) SCM.5286 |
| Rita Williams | 10/56 | Embassy WB.204 |

## 744 | YOU ARE MY FIRST LOVE

*Composers*: Lester Powell & Paddy Roberts          *Date of Entry*: 18.8.56

*Publishers*: Grosvenor Music Ltd.          *Highest Position*: 10
*Weeks on Chart*: 14

*Recordings*:
| | | |
|---|---|---|
| Ruby Murray | 5/56 | Columbia DB.3770 |
| Victor Silvester and his Ballroom Orchestra | 7/56 | Columbia DB.3789 (45) SCM.5278 |
| Nat 'King' Cole | 2/57 | Capitol CL.14688 (& 45-)★ |

## 745 | BELIEVE IN ME (Sur ma vie)

*Composers*: Charles Aznavour, Geoffrey Parsons          *Date of Entry*: 25.8.56
    & John Turner

*Publishers*: Macmelodies Ltd.          *Highest Position*: 16
*Weeks on Chart*: 7

*Recordings*:
| | | |
|---|---|---|
| Robert Earl | 6/56 | Philips PB.593 |
| Alan Kent | 6/56 | Polydor BM.6028 |
| Dawn Lake | 10/56 | Decca F.10794 (&45-) |

## 746 | LAY DOWN YOUR ARMS

*Composers*: Ake Gerhard, Leon Land & Paddy Roberts

*Date of Entry*: 1.9.56

*Publishers*: Francis Day & Hunter Ltd.

*Highest Position*: 1
*Weeks on Chart*: 21

*Recordings*:
| | | |
|---|---|---|
| Anne Shelton | 8/56 | Philips PB.616 |
| The Three Kaye Sisters | 9/56 | HMV POP.251 (& 45-) |
| Billie Anthony | 9/56 | Columbia DB.3818 (& 45-) |
| Russ Morgan and his Orchestra (Susy Goday and The Morganaires) | 10/56 | Brunswick 05602 (& 45-) |
| The Chordettes | 10/56 | London HLA.8323 (& 45-) |
| The Parlophone Pops Orchestra and Chorus cond. Ron Goodwin | 10/56 | Parlophone R.4229 |
| Beryl Templeman | 10/56 | Embassy WB.210 |
| R.S.M. Terry-Thomas and The Band of the WRECS with Chorus | 10/56 | Decca F.10804 (&45-) |

(Note: The recording by the Parlophone Pops Orchestra was No. 1 in a series 'Sing it Yourself'. The record was accompanied by a leaflet containing words of the two songs on the record.)

## 747 | BORN TO BE WITH YOU

*Composer*: Don Robertson

*Date of Entry*: 1.9.56

*Publishers*: Edwin H. Morris & Co. Ltd.

*Highest Position*: 15
*Weeks on Chart*: 9

*Recordings*:
| | | |
|---|---|---|
| The Chordettes | 8/56 | London HLA.8302 (& 45-) |
| The Beverley Sisters | 8/56 | Decca F.10770 (&45-) |
| Patti Page | 8/56 | Mercury MT.116 |
| The Four Lads | 9/56 | Philips PB.619 |
| Rita Williams | 10/56 | Embassy WB.204 |

## 748 | AUTUMN CONCERTO

*Composers*: C. Bargoni, Paul Siegel, Geoffrey Parsons & John Turner

*Date of Entry*: 15.9.56

*Publishers*: Macmelodies Ltd.

*Highest Position*: 3
*Weeks on Chart*: 30

*Recordings*:
| | | |
|---|---|---|
| The Melachrino Orchestra | 9/56 | HMV B.10958 (& 45-) |
| Norrie Paramor and his Orchestra | 9/56 | Columbia DB.3815 (& 45-) |
| Joan Small | 9/56 | Parlophone R.4211 (& 45-) |
| Ted Heath and his Music (Bobbie Britton) | 9/56 | Decca F.10777 (&45-) |
| Billy Vaughn and his Orchestra | 9/56 | London HLD.8319 (& 45-) |
| Victor Silvester and his Ballroom Orchestra | 10/56 | Columbia DB.3828 (& 45-) |
| Billy Thorburn and his Strict Tempo Music | 10/56 | Parlophone R.4221 (& 45-) |
| Primo Scala and his Accordion Band | 10/56 | Embassy WB.203 |
| Carmen Cavallaro (piano) | 10/56 | Brunswick 05609 (& 45-) |
| Cyril Ornadel and his Orchestra | 11/56 | Oriole CB.1344 |
| Georges Blanes | 2/57 | Polydor BM.6057 |

## 749 | MORE

*Composers*: Alex Alstone & Tom Glazer

*Date of Entry*: 15.9.56

*Publishers*: Berry Music Co. Ltd.

*Highest Position*: 1
*Weeks on Chart*: 24

*Recordings*:
| | | |
|---|---|---|
| Perry Como with The Ray Charles Singers | 9/56 | HMV POP.240 (& 45-) |
| Robert Earl | 9/56 | Philips PB.622 |
| Jimmy Young | 9/56 | Decca F.10774 (&45-) |
| David Ross | 9/56 | Embassy WB.201 |
| Alan Kent | 10/56 | Polydor BM.6031 |
| Victor Silvester and his Ballroom Orchestra | 11/56 | Columbia DB.3847 (& 45-) |

## 750 | A WOMAN IN LOVE

*Composer*: Frank Loesser

*Date of Entry*: 15.9.56

*Publishers*: Edwin H. Morris & Co. Ltd.

*Highest Position*: 2
*Weeks on Chart*: 22

*Recordings*:
| | | |
|---|---|---|
| The Four Aces featuring Al Alberts | 8/56 | Brunswick 05589 (& 45-) |
| Frankie Laine | 9/56 | Philips PB.617 |
| The Melachrino Orchestra | 9/56 | HMV B.10958 (& 45-) |
| Ronnie Hilton | 9/56 | HMV POP.248 (& 45-) |
| Billy McCormack | 9/56 | Embassy WB.197 |
| Edmund Hockridge | 9/56 | Pye Nixa N.15067 |
| Gordon MacRae | 9/56 | Capitol CL.14622 (& 45-) |
| Billy Thorburn and his Strict Tempo Music | 10/56 | Parlophone R.4221 (& 45-) |
| Johnny Green | 10/56 | Oriole CB.1339 |
| Victor Silvester and his Ballroom Orchestra | 11/56 | Columbia DB.3846 (& 45-) |

## 751 | MY UNFINISHED SYMPHONY

| | | |
|---|---|---|
| *Composer:* Milton Carson | *Date of Entry:* 22.9.56 | |
| *Publishers:* John Fields Music Co. Ltd. | *Highest Position:* 23 *Weeks on Chart:* 3 | |

*Recordings:*

| | | |
|---|---|---|
| David Whitfield | 8/56 | Decca F.10769 (&45-) |
| Joe Loss and his Orchestra | 11/56 | HMV POP.275 (& 45-)★ |

## 752 | ROCKIN' THROUGH THE RYE

| | | |
|---|---|---|
| *Composers:* Bill Haley & Arrett 'Rusty' Keefer | *Date of Entry:* 6.10.56 | |
| *Publishers:* Sterling Music Publishing Co. Ltd. | *Highest Position:* 8 *Weeks on Chart:* 17 | |

*Recordings:*

| | | |
|---|---|---|
| Sid Phillips and his Band [Titled 'Rockin' thru' the Rye'] | 5/56 | HMV POP.204 (45) 7M.396 |
| Bill Haley and his Comets | 8/56 | Brunswick 05582 (& 45-) |
| The Canadians | 10/56 | Embassy WB.205 |

## 753 | GLENDORA

| | | |
|---|---|---|
| *Composer:* Ray Stanley | *Date of Entry:* 13.10.56 | |
| *Publishers:* Campbell Connelly & Co. Ltd. | *Highest Position:* 22 *Weeks on Chart:* 5 | |

*Recordings:*

| | | |
|---|---|---|
| Perry Como | 9/56 | HMV POP.240 (& 45-) |
| Johnny Webb | 9/56 | Columbia DB.3805 (& 45-) |
| Glen Mason | 9/56 | Parlophone R.4203 (& 45-) |
| Johnny Brandon | 9/56 | Decca F.10778 (&45-) |
| David Ross | 9/56 | Embassy WB.201 |
| Steve Race and the Tic-Tac Men | 9/56 | Polydor BM.6034 |

## 754 | WHEN MEXICO GAVE UP THE RHUMBA

| | | |
|---|---|---|
| *Composer:* Gale Jones | *Date of Entry:* 20.10.56 | |
| *Publishers:* Leo Feist Ltd. | *Highest Position:* 10 *Weeks on Chart:* 17 | |

*Recording:*

| | | |
|---|---|---|
| Mitchell Torok | 8/56 | Brunswick 05586 (& 45-) |

## 755 | LOVE ME AS THOUGH THERE WERE NO TOMORROW

| | | |
|---|---|---|
| *Composers:* Harold Adamson & Jimmy McHugh | *Date of Entry:* 20.10.56 | |
| *Publishers:* Robbins Music Corporation Ltd. | *Highest Position:* 16 *Weeks on Chart:* 12 | |

*Recordings:*

| | | |
|---|---|---|
| Nat 'King' Cole | 8/56 | Capitol CL.14621 (& 45-) |
| Ronnie Carroll | 9/56 | Philips PB.623 |
| Eddie Parker | 9/56 | Columbia DB.3804 (& 45-) |
| Denny Dennis | 9/56 | Embassy WB.198 |
| Malcolm Vaughan | 9/56 | HMV POP.250 (& 45-) |
| Jackie Lee | 9/56 | Polydor BM.6030 |
| Dorothy Collins | 9/56 | Vogue Coral Q.72193 (& 45-) |
| Dick Kallman | 10/56 | Brunswick 05608 (& 45-) |

## 756 | JUST WALKING IN THE RAIN

| | | |
|---|---|---|
| *Composers:* Johnny Bragg & Robert S. Riley | *Date of Entry:* 27.10.56 | |
| *Publishers:* Frank Music Co. Ltd. | *Highest Position:* 1 *Weeks on Chart:* 23 | |

*Recordings:*

| | | |
|---|---|---|
| Johnnie Ray | 9/56 | Philips PB.624 |
| Judy Kileen | 10/56 | London HLU.8328 (& 45-) |
| Billy Cotton and his Band (Billy Cotton and Chorus) | 10/56 | Decca F.10805 (&45-) |
| The Tanner Sisters | 11/56 | Oriole CB.1345 |
| Billy McCormack | 12/56 | Embassy WB.216 |

## 757 | IN THE MIDDLE OF THE HOUSE

| | | |
|---|---|---|
| *Composer:* Bob Hilliard | *Date of Entry:* 27.10.56 | |
| *Publishers:* John Fields Music Co. Ltd. | *Highest Position:* 7 *Weeks on Chart:* 13 | |

*Recordings:*

| | | |
|---|---|---|
| The Johnston Brothers with The Keynotes | 10/56 | Decca F.10781 (&45-) |
| Jimmy Parkinson | 10/56 | Columbia DB.3833 (& 45-) |
| Milton Berle | 10/56 | Vogue Coral Q.72197 (& 45-) |
| Alma Cogan | 10/56 | HMV POP.261 (& 45-) |
| Larry Cross | 12/56 | Embassy WB.211 |

## 758 THE GREEN DOOR

*Composers*: Marvin Moore & Bob Davie        *Date of Entry*: 3.11.56

*Publishers*: Francis Day & Hunter Ltd.        *Highest Position*: 2
*Weeks on Chart*: 20

*Recordings*:
| | | |
|---|---|---|
| Jim Lowe | 9/56 | London HLD.8317 (& 45-) |
| Ray Ellington and his Quartet (Ray Ellington) | 10/56 | Columbia DB.3838 (& 45-) |
| Frankie Vaughan | 10/56 | Philips PB.640 |
| The Maple Leaf Four | 10/56 | Oriole CB.1337 |
| David Ross | 10/56 | Embassy WB.209 |
| Glen Mason | 11/56 | Parlophone R.4244 (& 45-) |
| The Tanner Sisters | 11/56 | Oriole CB.1345 |

## 759 A HOUSE WITH LOVE IN IT

*Composers*: Sidney Lippman & Sylvia Dee        *Date of Entry*: 3.11.56

*Publishers*: Lawrence Wright Music Co. Ltd.        *Highest Position*: 7
*Weeks on Chart*: 17

*Recordings*:
| | | |
|---|---|---|
| The Four Lads | 10/56 | Philips PB.629 |
| Vera Lynn | 10/56 | Decca F.10799 (& 45-) |
| Ronnie Harris | 10/56 | Columbia DB.3836 (& 45-) |
| Kathie Kay | 10/56 | HMV POP.265 (& 45-) |
| Lorrae Desmond | 10/56 | Parlophone R.4239 (& 45-) |
| Dickie Henderson | 11/56 | Oriole CB.1346 |
| Billy McCormack | 12/56 | Embassy WB.216 |

## 760 TWO DIFFERENT WORLDS

*Composers*: Sid Wayne & Al Frisch        *Date of Entry*: 10.11.56

*Publishers*: Larry Spier Ltd.        *Highest Position*: 4
*Weeks on Chart*: 18

*Recordings*:
| | | |
|---|---|---|
| Dick Kallman | 10/56 | Brunswick 05608 (& 45-) |
| Ronnie Hilton | 10/56 | HMV POP.274 (& 45-) |
| Steve Clayton | 10/56 | Vogue Coral Q.72200 (& 45-) |
| Don Rondo | 10/56 | Columbia DB.3854 (& 45-) |
| David Hughes | 11/56 | Philips PB.642 |
| Roger Williams (piano) and Jane Morgan (vocal) | 11/56 | London HLU.8341 (& 45-) |

| | | |
|---|---|---|
| Dick Haymes | 11/56 | Capitol CL.14659 (& 45-) |
| Julie Dawn with Vocal Group | 12/56 | Oriole CB.1347 |
| Victor Silvester and his Ballroom Orchestra | 1/57 | Columbia DB.3869 (& 45-) |
| Jane Forrest | 1/57 | Embassy WB.218 |

## 761 CHRISTMAS ISLAND

*Composer*: Lyle Moraine        *Date of Entry*: 10.11.56

*Publishers*: Macmelodies Ltd.        *Highest Position*: 7
*Weeks on Chart*: 9

(Note: Of the two versions of this song issued earlier, the one by the Andrews Sisters on Brunswick 03947 issued in 10/48 was deleted some time before the chart success. The other, recorded by Bob Atcher and the Dinning Sisters on Capitol CL.13418 and released in December, 1950, was still in the catalogue shortly before the revival.)

*Later recording*:
| | | |
|---|---|---|
| Dickie Valentine | 10/56 | Decca F.10798 (&45-) |

## 762 TRUE LOVE

*Composer*: Cole Porter        *Date of Entry*: 17.11.56

*Publishers*: Chappell & Co. Ltd.        *Highest Position*: 2
*Weeks on Chart*: 35

*Recordings*:
| | | |
|---|---|---|
| Kitty Kallen | 10/56 | Brunswick 05612 (& 45-) |
| Ted Heath and his Music (Bobbie Britton) | 10/56 | Decca F.10807 (&45-) |
| David Hughes | 11/56 | Philips PB.642 |
| Jane Powell | 11/56 | HMV POP.267 (& 45-) |
| Ruby Murray with The Bill Shepherd Chorus | 11/56 | Columbia DB.3849 (& 45-) |
| Eve Boswell (vocal and piano) | 11/56 | Parlophone R.4230 (& 45-) |
| Bing Crosby and Grace Kelly | 11/56 | Capitol CL.14645 (& 45-) |
| Margaret Whiting | 11/56 | Capitol CL.14647 (& 45-) |
| The Four Grads | 11/56 | Oriole CB.1341 |
| Jean Campbell | 12/56 | Polydor BM.6042 |
| Joe Loss and his Orchestra | 1/57 | HMV POP.293 (& 45-) |
| Rita Williams | 1/57 | Embassy WB.217 |
| Billy Thorburn and his Strict Tempo Music | 2/57 | Parlophone R.4276 (& 45-) |
| Victor Silvester and his Ballroom Orchestra | 2/57 | Columbia DB.3890 (& 45-) |

## 763 | ST THERESE OF THE ROSES

*Composers*: Art Strauss & Remus Harris

*Publishers*: Dash Music Co. Ltd.

*Date of Entry*: 17.11.56

*Highest Position*: 7
*Weeks on Chart*: 23

*Recordings*:
| | | |
|---|---|---|
| Malcolm Vaughan | 9/56 | HMV POP.250 (& 45-) |
| Billy Ward and The Dominoes | 9/56 | Brunswick 05599 (& 45-) |
| Victor Silvester and his Ballroom Orchestra | 1/57 | Columbia DB.3868 (& 45-) |
| Eve Lombard | 3/57 | Embassy WB.222 |

## 764 | MY PRAYER

*Composers*: Georges Boulanger & Jimmy Kennedy

*Publishers*: World Wide Music Co. Ltd.

*Date of Entry*: 17.11.56/
Pos: 14/Wks: 16
*Re-entry*: 16.3.57/
Pos: 22/Wks: 1

*Recordings*:
| | | |
|---|---|---|
| Jeff Chandler | 4/55 | Brunswick 05417 (& 45-) |
| Edna Savage | 10/56 | Parlophone R.4226 (& 45-) |
| The Platters | 10/56 | Mercury MT.120 |
| Victor Silvester and his Ballroom Orchestra | 12/56 | Columbia DB.3862 (& 45-) |

## 765 | CHRISTMAS AND YOU

*Composers*: Russell Faith & Clarence Kehner

*Publishers*: Duchess Music Ltd.

*Date of Entry*: 24.11.56

*Highest Position*: 15
*Weeks on Chart*: 5

(Note: A version of the song by Joni James on MGM.696 was issued in December 1953 but was due for deletion in December 1956 – ironically at the time of the song's popularity.)

*Later recording*:
| | | |
|---|---|---|
| Dave King | 10/56 | Decca F.10791 (&45-) |

## 766 | CINDY, OH CINDY

*Composers*: Bob Barron & Burt Long

*Publishers*: Dash Music Co. Ltd.

*Date of Entry*: 24.11.56

*Highest Position*: 7
*Weeks on Chart*: 19

*Recordings*:
| | | |
|---|---|---|
| Eddie Fisher | 11/56 | HMV POP.273 (& 45-) |
| Tony Brent | 11/56 | Columbia DB.3844 (& 45-) |
| Vince Martin with The Tarriers | 11/56 | London HLN.8340 (& 45-) |
| Denny Dennis | 12/56 | Embassy WB.213 |
| Bryan Johnson | 12/56 | Conquest CP.101 |
| Eric Batty's Jazz Aces | 10/57 | Esquire 10–506★ |

## 767 | THAT DEAR OLD GENTLEMAN

*Composer*: Paddy Roberts

*Publishers*: Berry Music Co. Ltd.

*Date of Entry*: 8.12.56

*Highest Position*: 21
*Weeks on Chart*: 3

*Recording*:
| | | |
|---|---|---|
| Max Bygraves | 11/56 | HMV POP.262 (& 45-) |

## 768 | HAPPINESS STREET

*Composers*: Mack Wolfson & Edward White

*Publishers*: Sydney Bron Music Co.

*Date of Entry*: 8.12.56/
Pos: 22/Wks: 4
*Re-entry*: 12.1.57/
Pos: 22/Wks: 1

*Recordings*:
| | | |
|---|---|---|
| The Four Jones Boys | 10/56 | Decca F.10789 (&45-) |
| Patti Lewis | 10/56 | Columbia DB.3825 (& 45-) |
| Jill Day | 10/56 | HMV POP.254 (& 45-) |
| Tony Bennett | 10/56 | Philips PB.628 |
| Georgia Gibbs | 10/56 | Mercury MT.118 |
| David Ross | 10/56 | Embassy WB.209 |

## 769 | DAVY CROCKETT IS HELPING SANTA CLAUS

*Composers*: Tommie Connor & Frank Stanton

*Publishers*: Unit Music Publishing Co.

*Date of Entry*: 15.12.56

*Highest Position*: 18
*Weeks on Chart*: 3

*Recording*:
| | | |
|---|---|---|
| Joe Lynch | 11/56 | Beltona BE.2668 |

## 770 COME HOME TO MY ARMS

| | | |
|---|---|---|
| *Composers*: Leslie Baguley & Emily Jane | *Date of Entry*: 15.12.56 | |
| *Publishers*: Chappell & Co. Ltd. | *Highest Position*: 17 | |
| | *Weeks on Chart*: 8 | |

*Recordings*:

| | | |
|---|---|---|
| The Beverley Sisters | 11/56 | Decca F.10813 (&45-) |
| Dorothy Squires with The Beryl Stott Chorus | 11/56 | Pye Nixa N.15075 |
| The Tanner Sisters | 12/56 | Oriole CB.1350 |
| Rita Williams | 1/57 | Embassy WB.217 |

## 771 SINGING THE BLUES

| | | |
|---|---|---|
| *Composer*: Melvin Endsley | *Date of Entry*: 29.12.56 | |
| *Publishers*: Frank Music Co. Ltd. | *Highest Position*: 1 | |
| | *Weeks on Chart*: 28 | |

*Recordings*:

| | | |
|---|---|---|
| Tommy Steele and The Steelmen | 11/56 | Decca F.10819 (&45-) |
| Guy Mitchell | 12/56 | Philips PB.650 |
| David Ross | 1/57 | Embassy WB.219 |
| Les Howard | 1/57 | Conquest CP.103 |
| Billy Thorburn and his Strict Tempo Music | 2/57 | Parlophone R.4276 (& 45-) |
| The Happy Wanderers Street Band | 4/57 | Esquire 10–498 |

## 772 A LETTER TO A SOLDIER

| | | |
|---|---|---|
| *Composer*: Gee Langdon | *Date of Entry*: 29.12.56 | |
| *Publishers*: David Toff Music Publishing Co. Ltd. | *Highest Position*: 16 | |
| | *Weeks on Chart*: 8 | |

*Recordings*:

| | | |
|---|---|---|
| Barbara Lyon | 12/56 | Columbia DB.3865 (& 45-) |
| Terry Burton | 12/56 | Philips PB.653 |
| Gracie Fields | 12/56 | Decca F.10824 (&45-) |
| Jane Forrest | 1/57 | Embassy WB.218 |
| Annita Ray | 6/57 | Conquest CP.113★ |

# 1957

The steady march of rock 'n' roll was interrupted, for a few months at least, by a new craze, skiffle. Groups abounded everywhere and every label had its very own skiffle group, turning some memorable (and not so memorable) traditional tunes into vast hits. Slightly overshadowed, calypso had a mini boom, too, with Harry Belafonte at the forefront. Saturday, 16 February saw the launching of BBC TV's 'Six-Five Special' with a theme owing much to the skiffle influence. It was introduced by Josephine Douglas and Pete Murray, now back from his long spell in Luxembourg. Exactly one month later, on the Light Programme at 6 p.m., David Jacobs celebrated six months with 'Pick of the Pops' by playing no less than ten – yes, ten – versions of *Heart* in his three-quarter hour show. In the final broadcast on 16 September 1961, David recalled the occasion in these words: 'I rather disgraced myself by getting carried away with a certain song. The phones rang with irate listeners.' Perhaps it should be mentioned that David played no complete version, the usual length being around one minute and between each recording of *Heart* he played other things such as *I'll find you* by David Whitfield and *Mangos* by the Stargazers. *Forgotten dreams*, which spent just a handful of weeks in the lower reaches of the record charts, was the year's second longest running song in the sheet music charts and reached No. 2. Oriole released their first 45 rpm discs, and we saw the first appearance in this country of RCA records. For the first time in the history of the Radio Luxembourg Top

| Pos | MOST WEEKS ON THE CHARTS TOP SIX | Wks |
|-----|------------------|-----|
| 1 | *Around the world* | 33 |
| 2= | *Forgotten dreams* | 31 |
| 2= | *True love* | 31 |
| 4 | *Puttin' on the style* | 28 |
| 5 | *Singing the blues* | 27 |
| 6 | *Island in the sun* | 26 |

Twenty show they were unable to play one of the songs. When *All* reached the chart, it was announced on that Sunday night of 31 March that they had no record of it yet. The song was at No. 20 so they played No. 21 – *By you, by you, by you* – instead. Jack Jackson refused to play *The Garden of Eden* on his Sunday ITV show as he regarded it as unsuitable for Sunday viewing. Nearly five years of the BBC Show Band came to an end with a Gala Farewell broadcast in June.

# SONG CHARTS

## 773 THE GARDEN OF EDEN

| | | |
|---|---|---|
| *Composer*: Dennise Haas Norwood | | *Date of Entry*: 5.1.57 |
| *Publishers*: Duchess Music Ltd. | | *Highest Position*: 2<br>*Weeks on Chart*: 16 |

*Recordings*:

| | | |
|---|---|---|
| Winifred Atwell (piano) | 12/56 | Decca F.10825 (&45–) |
| Joe Valino | 1/57 | HMV POP.283<br>(& 45–) |
| Dick James | 1/57 | Parlophone R.4255<br>(& 45–) |
| Gary Miller with The Beryl Stott Chorus | 1/57 | Pye Nixa N.15070 |
| Monty Norman | 1/57 | HMV POP.281<br>(& 45–) |
| Billy Cotton and his Band (Alan Breeze<br>and The Bandits) | 1/57 | Decca F.10841 (&45–) |
| Frankie Vaughan | 1/57 | Philips PB.660 |
| Matt Monro | 1/57 | Decca F.10845 (&45–) |
| David Ross | 1/57 | Embassy WB.219 |

## 774 FRIENDLY PERSUASION

| | | |
|---|---|---|
| *Composers*: Dimitri Tiomkin &<br>Paul Francis Webster | | *Date of Entry*: 5.1.57 |
| *Publishers*: Robbins Music Corporation Ltd. | | *Highest Position*: 4<br>*Weeks on Chart*: 18 |

*Recordings*:

| | | |
|---|---|---|
| The Four Aces featuring Al Alberts | 11/56 | Brunswick 05623<br>(& 45–) |
| Pat Boone | 11/56 | London HLD.8346<br>(& 45–) |
| George Cates and his Orchestra and<br>Chorus | 11/56 | Vogue Coral<br>Q.72210 (& 45–) |
| Dimitri Tiomkin and his Chorus and<br>Orchestra | 11/56 | Vogue Coral<br>Q.72211 (& 45–) |
| Lou Busch and his Orchestra with vocal<br>group | 11/56 | Capitol CL.14667<br>(& 45–) |
| Fred Lucas | 12/56 | Columbia DB.3861<br>(& 45–) |
| Terry Burton | 12/56 | Philips PB.653 |
| David Rose and his Orchestra | 12/56 | MGM.938 (& 45–) |
| Joe Loss and his Orchestra | 2/57 | HMV POP.298<br>(& 45–) |
| Gerry Grant | 2/57 | Embassy WB.221 |

## 775 RAZZLE DAZZLE

| | | |
|---|---|---|
| *Composer*: Charles Calhoun | | *Date of Entry*: 12.1.57 |
| *Publishers*: Robert Mellin Ltd. | | *Highest Position*: 24<br>*Weeks on Chart*: 1 |

*Recordings*:

| | | |
|---|---|---|
| Bill Haley and his Comets | 7/55 | Brunswick 05453<br>(& 45–) |
| Ella Mae Morse | 8/55 | Capitol CL.14341<br>(& 45–) |

## 776 I DREAMED

| | | |
|---|---|---|
| *Composers*: Charles Grean & Marvin Moore | | *Date of Entry*: 12.1.57 |
| *Publishers*: Duchess Music Ltd. | | *Highest Position*: 6<br>*Weeks on Chart*: 17 |

*Recordings*:

| | | |
|---|---|---|
| The Beverley Sisters | 1/57 | Decca F.10832 (&45–) |
| Billie Anthony | 1/57 | Columbia DB.3874<br>(& 45–) |
| Jill Day | 1/57 | HMV POP.288<br>(& 45–) |
| Betty Johnson | 1/57 | London HLU.8365<br>(& 45–) |
| Penny Nicholls | 2/57 | Embassy WB.224 |
| Victor Silvester and his Ballroom<br>Orchestra | 5/57 | Columbia DB.3944<br>(& 45–) |

## 777 YOU, ME AND US

| | | |
|---|---|---|
| *Composers*: Traditional, based on 'Cielito Lindo'.<br>Lyrics: John Jerome | | *Date of Entry*: 19.1.57 |
| *Publishers*: John Fields Music Co. Ltd. | | *Highest Position*: 5<br>*Weeks on Chart*: 15 |

*Recordings*:

| | | |
|---|---|---|
| Alma Cogan | 1/57 | HMV POP.284<br>(& 45–) |
| Eve Lombard | 3/57 | Embassy WB.222 |

## 778 MOONLIGHT GAMBLER

*Composers*: Bob Hilliard & Philip Springer
*Publishers*: Edwin H. Morris & Co. Ltd.

*Date of Entry*: 19.1.57
*Highest Position*: 18
*Weeks on Chart*: 9

*Recordings*:
| | | |
|---|---|---|
| Frankie Laine | 12/56 | Philips PB.638 |
| Winifred Atwell (piano) | 12/56 | Decca F.10825 (&45-) |
| Gerry Grant | 2/57 | Embassy WB.221 |

## 779 ADORATION WALTZ

*Composers*: Al Lewis & Larry Stock

*Publishers*: Sydney Bron Music Co.

*Date of Entry*: 26.1.57/
Pos: 7/Wks: 18
*Re-entry*: 15.6.57/
Pos: 24/Wks: 1

*Recordings*:
| | | |
|---|---|---|
| David Whitfield | 1/57 | Decca F.10833 (&45-) |
| Billy McCormack | 4/57 | Embassy WB.227 |
| Victor Silvester and his Ballroom Orchestra | 4/57 | Columbia DB.3924 (& 45-) |

## 780 GIVE HER MY LOVE (when you meet her)

*Composers*: Leslie Baguley, Tommie Connor & Johnny Reine
*Publishers*: Michael Reine Music Co. Ltd.

*Date of Entry*: 26.1.57
*Highest Position*: 15
*Weeks on Chart*: 12

*Recordings*:
| | | |
|---|---|---|
| The Johnston Brothers | 12/56 | Decca F.10828 (&45-) |
| Jill Day | 1/57 | HMV POP.288 (& 45-) |
| Anne Shelton | 1/57 | Philips PB.661 |

## 781 DON'T YOU ROCK ME, DADDY-O

*Composers*: Adapted from the Traditional Sea Shanty 'Sail Away, Lady' by Wally Whyton & Bill Varley
*Publishers*: Essex Music Ltd.

*Date of Entry*: 2.2.57
*Highest Position*: 13
*Weeks on Chart*: 14

*Recordings*:
| | | |
|---|---|---|
| The Lonnie Donegan Skiffle Group | 1/57 | Pye Nixa N.15080 |
| The Bob Cort Skiffle Group | 1/57 | Decca FJ.10831 (&45-) |
| The Vipers Skiffle Group | 1/57 | Parlophone R.4261 (& 45-) |
| The Cranes Skiffle Group | 2/57 | Embassy WB.223 |
| The Station Skiffle Group with Jim Miller | 8/57 | Esquire 10–503★ |
| Morris and Mitch (vocal and narrator) [Parody titled 'What is a Skiffler?'] | 9/57 | Decca F.10929 (& 45-)★ |

## 782 YOUNG LOVE

*Composers*: Carole Joyner & Ric Cartey

*Publishers*: Cromwell Music Ltd.

*Date of Entry*: 9.2.57

*Highest Position*: 1
*Weeks on Chart*: 21

*Recordings*:
| | | |
|---|---|---|
| Tab Hunter | 1/57 | London HLD.8380 (& 45-) |
| Sonny James | 1/57 | Capitol CL.14683 (& 45-) |
| The Crew Cuts | 3/57 | Mercury MT.140 |
| David Ross | 3/57 | Embassy WB.230 |

## 783 KNEE DEEP IN THE BLUES

*Composer*: Melvin Endsley

*Publishers*: Leeds Music Ltd.

*Date of Entry*: 16.2.57

*Highest Position*: 5
*Weeks on Chart*: 14

*Recordings*:
| | | |
|---|---|---|
| Tommy Steele and The Steelmen | 2/57 | Decca F.10849 (&45-) |
| Guy Mitchell | 2/57 | Philips PB.669 |
| Ricky James | 2/57 | HMV POP.306 (& 45-) |
| Joe Loss and his Orchestra | 3/57 | HMV POP.313 (& 45-) |
| Penny Nicholls | 3/57 | Embassy WB.228 |

## 784 DON'T FORBID ME

*Composer*: Charles Singleton

*Publishers*: Campbell Connelly & Co. Ltd.

*Date of Entry*: 16.2.57

*Highest Position*: 2
*Weeks on Chart*: 15

*Recordings*:
| | | |
|---|---|---|
| Pat Boone | 1/57 | London HLD.8370 (& 45-) |
| Glen Mason | 2/57 | Parlophone R.4271 (& 45-) |
| Freddy | 3/57 | Polydor BM.6063 |
| David Ross | 3/57 | Embassy WB.230 |

## 785 THE BANANA BOAT SONG

| | | |
|---|---|---|
| Composers: West Indian Traditional, arrangers as listed | Date of Entry: 16.2.57 | |
| Publishers: Edwin H. Morris & Co. Ltd. | Highest Position: 2 Weeks on Chart: 20 | |

Recordings:
(a) Adapted by Alan Arkin, Bob Carey & Eric Darling:

| | | |
|---|---|---|
| Steve Lawrence | 1/57 | Vogue Coral Q.72228 (& 45-) |
| The Fontane Sisters | 1/57 | London HLD.8378 (& 45-) |
| Shirley Bassey | 2/57 | Philips PB.668 |
| The Tarriers | 2/57 | Columbia DB.3891 (& 45-) |
| Dorothy Squires with The Beryl Stott Group | 2/57 | Pye Nixa N.15082 |
| Inia te Wiata | 2/57 | HMV POP.301 (& 45-) |
| Peter Lowe | 2/57 | Parlophone R.4270 (& 45-) |
| Sarah Vaughan | 2/57 | Mercury MT.139 |
| Freddy (the Arkin, Carey & Darling arrangement further adapted by Horst Wende) | 3/57 | Polydor BM.6063 |
| Joe Loss and his Orchestra [Titled 'Mambo – The Banana Boat Song'] | 3/57 | HMV POP.312 (& 45-) |

(b) Adapted by Harry Belafonte, 'Lord' Burgess & William Attaway:

| | | |
|---|---|---|
| Harry Belafonte with Millard Thomas (guitar) [Titled 'Banana Boat (Day-O)'] | 2/57 | HMV POP.308 (& 45-) |
| Belafonte with Millard Thomas (guitar) [Titled 'Banana Boat Song (Day-O)'] | 11/58 | RCA.1089 (& 45-)★ |

(c) Adapted by Harry Belafonte, 'Lord' Burgess & William Attaway and arranged by Stan Freberg:

| | | |
|---|---|---|
| Stan Freberg with interruptions by Peter Leeds [Titled 'Banana Boat'] | 4/57 | Capitol CL.14712 (& 45-) |

(d) Arranged by Mel:

| | | |
|---|---|---|
| George Browne and his Jamaican Calypso Band [Titled 'Day-O (Banana Boat Song)'] | 4/57 | Melodisc 1404 |

## 786 BLUEBERRY HILL

| | | |
|---|---|---|
| Composers: Al Lewis, Larry Stock & Vincent Rose | Date of Entry: 23.2.57 | |
| Publishers: Victoria Music Publishing Co. Ltd. | Highest Position: 23 Weeks on Chart: 5 | |

Recordings:

| | | |
|---|---|---|
| Louis Armstrong | 11/49 | Brunswick 04372 |
| Teddy Foster (vocal) with his Orchestra and the Peter Knight Singers | 9/54 | Parlophone R.3897 |
| Fats Domino | 10/56 | London HLU.8330 (& 45-) |

## 787 THE WISDOM OF A FOOL

| | | |
|---|---|---|
| Composers: Abner Silver & Roy Alfred | Date of Entry: 2.3.57 | |
| Publishers: Leeds Music Ltd. | Highest Position: 8 Weeks on Chart: 11 | |

Recordings:

| | | |
|---|---|---|
| Annette Klooger with Ted Heath and his Music | 1/57 | Decca F.10844 (&45-) |
| Ronnie Hilton | 2/57 | HMV POP.291 (& 45-) |
| Peter Lowe | 2/57 | Parlophone R.4270 (& 45-) |
| The Five Keys | 2/57 | Capitol CL.14686 (& 45-) |
| Ronnie Carroll | 2/57 | Philips PB.667 |
| Pauline Shepherd with The Beryl Stott Chorus | 2/57 | Pye Nixa N.15084 |
| Norman Wisdom | 2/57 | Columbia DB.3903 (& 45-) |

## 788 IF I LOST YOU

| | | |
|---|---|---|
| Composers: Tolchard Evans & Richard Mullan | Date of Entry: 2.3.57 | |
| Publishers: Robbins Music Corporation Ltd. | Highest Position: 22 Weeks on Chart: 2 | |

Recording:

| | | |
|---|---|---|
| David Whitfield | 1/57 | Decca F.10833 (&45-) |

## 789 ALL OF YOU

| | | |
|---|---|---|
| Composer: Cole Porter | Date of Entry: 9.3.57/ Pos: 20/Wks: 1 | |
| Publishers: Chappell & Co. Ltd. | Re-entry: 23.3.57/ Pos: 19/Wks: 3 | |

Recordings:

| | | |
|---|---|---|
| Mel Torme | 10/56 | Vogue Coral Q.72202 (& 45-) |
| Don Cornell | 10/56 | Vogue Coral Q.72203 (& 45-) |
| Sammy Davis Jr | 12/56 | Brunswick 05629 (& 45-) |
| Bryan Johnson | 12/56 | Conquest CP.101 |
| Tony Martin | 1/57 | HMV POP.282 (& 45-) |
| Connie Russell | 1/57 | Capitol CL.14676 (& 45-) |
| Victor Silvester and his Ballroom Orchestra | 2/57 | Columbia DB.3889 (& 45-) |
| Michael Holliday | 8/57 | Columbia DB.3973 (& 45-)★ |
| Fred Astaire and Cyd Charisse | 8/57 | MGM.963 (& 45-)★ |

## 790 BY YOU, BY YOU, BY YOU

*Composers*: Bob Davie and Marvin Moore          *Date of Entry*: 16.3.57

*Publishers*: Cinephonic Music Co. Ltd.          *Highest Position*: 17
                                                 *Weeks on Chart*: 9

*Recordings*:
Jim Lowe with Bob Davie (piano)          1/57     London HLD.8368
                                                  (& 45-)
Lee Lawrence with The Coronets           2/57     Columbia DB.3885
                                                  (& 45-)
Pauline Shepherd                         2/57     Pye Nixa N.15084

## 791 ALL

*Composers*: Alan Stranks & Reynell Wreford          *Date of Entry*: 16.3.57

*Publishers*: Anglo-Continental Music Co. Ltd.          *Highest Position*: 14
                                                        *Weeks on Chart*: 10

*Recordings*:
Robert Earl                              4/57     Philips PB.684
Victor Silvester and his Ballroom        5/57     Columbia DB.3939
   Orchestra                                      (& 45-)

## 792 HEART

*Composers*: Richard Adler & Jerry Ross          *Date of Entry*: 23.3.57

*Publishers*: Frank Music Co. Ltd.          *Highest Position*: 1
                                            *Weeks on Chart*: 18

*Recordings*:
The Johnston Brothers                    3/57     Decca F.10860 (&45-)
Max Bygraves                             3/57     Decca F.10862 (&45-)
The McGuire Sisters                      3/57     Vogue Coral
                                                  Q.72238 (& 45-)
Ronnie Hilton                            3/57     HMV POP.318
                                                  (& 45-)
Ruby Murray with The Bill Shepherd       3/57     Columbia DB.3911
   Chorus                                         (& 45-)
Tony Bennett                             3/57     Philips PB.672
The Four Aces featuring Al Alberts       3/57     Brunswick 05651
                                                  (& 45-)
Dennis Lotis with The Beryl Stott Chorus 3/57     Pye Nixa N. 15042
The Tunettes                             3/57     Embassy WB.231
Joe Loss and his Orchestra               4/57     HMV POP.326/
                                                  (& 45-)
Victor Silvester and his Ballroom        4/57     Columbia DB.3930
   Orchestra                                      (& 45-)
The King Brothers                        4/57     Conquest CP.109

## 793 LOOK HOMEWARD, ANGEL

*Composer*: Wally Gold          *Date of Entry*: 23.3.57

*Publishers*: Unit Music Publishing Co.          *Highest Position*: 7
                                                 *Weeks on Chart*: 15

*Recordings*:
Johnnie Ray                              1/57     Philips PB.655
Paul Rich                                5/57     Embassy WB.239

## 794 MARIANNE

*Composers*: Terry Gilkyson, Frank Miller &          *Date of Entry*: 30.3.57
   Richard Dehr

*Publishers*: Montclare Music Co. Ltd.          *Highest Position*: 7
                                                *Weeks on Chart*: 13

*Recordings*:
The Hilltoppers                          2/57     London HLD.8381
                                                  (& 45-)
Terry Gilkyson and The Easy Riders with  3/57     Philips PB.670
   vocal by Rich Dehr
Ray Ellington and his Quartet (Ray       3/57     Columbia DB.3905
   Ellington)                                     (& 45-)
The King Brothers                        3/57     Parlophone R.4288
                                                  (& 45-)
The Tunettes                             4/57     Embassy WB.234
Sir Lancelot                             6/57     Polydor BM.6076

## 795 THE GOOD COMPANIONS

*Composers*: C.A. Rossi, Paddy Roberts &          *Date of Entry*: 6.4.57
   Geoffrey Parsons

*Publishers*: Peter Maurice Music Co. Ltd.          *Highest Position*: 9
                                                    *Weeks on Chart*: 20

*Recordings*:
Billy Cotton and his Band (Billy Cotton  3/57     Decca F.10857 (&45-)
   and The Bandits)
Janette Scott and John Fraser with The   3/57     Pye Nixa N. 15085
   Beryl Stott Chorus (part of 2-song side
   as follows: Where there's you [1 min.
   35 secs] & The Good Companions
   [1.50])

## 796 MANGOS

| *Composers*: Sid Wayne & Dee Libbey | | *Date of Entry*: 6.4.57 |
| *Publishers*: Sydney Bron Music Co. | | *Highest Position*: 8 |
| | | *Weeks on Chart*: 10 |

*Recordings*:

| Rosemary Clooney | 3/57 | Philips PB.671 |
|---|---|---|
| Lucille Mapp | 3/57 | Columbia DB.3916 (& 45-) |
| The Stargazers | 3/57 | Decca F.10867 (&45-) |
| Jill Day with Vocal Group | 3/57 | HMV POP.320 (& 45-) |
| Beryl Templeman | 5/57 | Embassy WB.235 |
| Roger King Mozian (trumpet) and his Orchestra | 7/57 | Brunswick 05689 (& 45-)★ |
| Marion Ryan | 4/60 | Columbia 45-DB.4448★ |

## 797 CUMBERLAND GAP

| *Composers*: Traditional, new lyrics and music by Lonnie Donegan | | *Date of Entry*: 13.4.57 |
| *Publishers*: Essex Music Ltd. | | *Highest Position*: 12 |
| | | *Weeks on Chart*: 8 |

*Recordings*:

| The Vipers Skiffle Group (arr. Whyton) | 3/57 | Parlophone R.4289 (& 45-) |
|---|---|---|
| Dickie Bishop with The Sidekicks | 3/57 | Decca F.10869 (&45-) |
| Lonnie Donegan and his Skiffle Group (arr. Donegan) | 3/57 | Pye Nixa N.15087 |
| Morris and Mitch | 5/57 | Decca F.10900 (&45-) |
| The Cranes Skiffle Group | 5/57 | Embassy WB.238 |

## 798 I'LL FIND YOU

| *Composers*: Tolchard Evans & Richard Mullan | | *Date of Entry*: 13.4.57/ Pos: 22/Wks: 1 |
| *Publishers*: Robbins Music Corporation Ltd. | | *Re-entry*: 27.4.57/ Pos: 12/Wks: 14 |

*Recordings*:

| David Whitfield | 3/57 | Decca F.10864 (&45-) |
|---|---|---|
| Bill McGuffie and his Music | 4/57 | Philips PB.680 |
| Ron Goodwin and his Concert Orchestra | 4/57 | Parlophone R.4297 (& 45-) |

## 799 LOVE IS A GOLDEN RING

| *Composers*: Richard Dehr, Frank Miller & Terry Gilkyson | | *Date of Entry*: 20.4.57 |
| *Publishers*: Montclare Music Co. Ltd. | | *Highest Position*: 21 |
| | | *Weeks on Chart*: 1 |

*Recordings*:

| Dave King | 3/57 | Decca F.10865 (&45-) |
|---|---|---|
| Frankie Laine with The Easy Riders | 3/57 | Philips PB.676 |

## 800 CHAPEL OF THE ROSES

| *Composers*: Abel Baer & Remus Harris | | *Date of Entry*: 20.4.57 |
| *Publishers*: Victoria Music Publishing Co. Ltd. | | *Highest Position*: 5 |
| | | *Weeks on Chart*: 19 |

*Recordings*:

| Don Cherry | 5/51 | Brunswick 04709 |
|---|---|---|
| Malcolm Vaughan | 4/57 | HMV POP.325 (& 45-) |
| Dickie Valentine | 4/57 | Decca F.10874 (&45-) |
| Lee Lawrence with The Bill Shepherd Chorus | 4/57 | Columbia DB.3922 (& 45-) |
| Patti Forbes | 6/57 | Embassy WB.242 |

## 801 BUTTERFLY

| *Composers*: Bernie Lowe & Kal Mann (see note below) | | *Date of Entry*: 27.4.57 |
| *Publishers*: Aberbach (London) Ltd. | | *Highest Position*: 1 |
| | | *Weeks on Chart*: 18 |

*Recordings*:

| Charlie Gracie | 3/57 | Parlophone R.4290 (& 45-) |
|---|---|---|
| Tony Brent | 3/57 | Columbia DB.3918 (& 45-) |
| Andy Williams | 4/57 | London HLA.8399 (& 45-) |
| Billy Williams | 4/57 | Vogue Coral Q.72241 (& 45-) |
| David Ross | 5/57 | Embassy WB.236 |

(Note: This song is credited on some records to 'Anthony September' which is actually a pseudonym for Lowe and Mann.)

## 802 ROUND AND ROUND

| | | |
|---|---|---|
| *Composers*: Lou Stallman & Joe Shapiro | | *Date of Entry*: 27.4.57/<br>Pos: 21/Wks: 1 |
| *Publishers*: Rush Music Ltd. | | *Re-entry*: 11.5.57/<br>Pos: 18/Wks: 9 |

*Recordings*:

| | | |
|---|---|---|
| Jimmy Parkinson | 3/57 | Columbia DB.3912<br>(& 45-) |
| Perry Como with The Ray Charles<br>Singers | 4/57 | HMV POP.328<br>(& 45-) |
| Jimmy Young with The Michael Sammes<br>Singers | 4/57 | Decca F.10875 (&45-) |
| Glen Mason | 4/57 | Parlophone R.4291<br>(& 45-) |
| The Four Lads | 5/57 | Philips PB.693 |
| Denny Dennis | 5/57 | Embassy WB.237 |

## 803 NINETY NINE WAYS

| | | |
|---|---|---|
| *Composer*: Anthony September (see note under<br>Song No. 801) | | *Date of Entry*: 4.5.57 |
| *Publishers*: Good Music Ltd. | | *Highest Position*: 3<br>*Weeks on Chart*: 14 |

*Recordings*:

| | | |
|---|---|---|
| Charlie Gracie | 3/57 | Parlophone R.4290<br>(& 45-) |
| Tab Hunter | 4/57 | London HLD.8410<br>(& 45-) |
| Ricky James | 4/57 | HMV POP.334<br>(& 45-) |
| David Ross | 6/57 | Embassy WB.241 |

## 804 ROCK-A-BILLY

| | | |
|---|---|---|
| *Composers*: Woody Harris & Eddie Deane | | *Date of Entry*: 4.5.57 |
| *Publishers*: Joy Music Ltd. | | *Highest Position*: 4<br>*Weeks on Chart*: 13 |

*Recordings*:

| | | |
|---|---|---|
| Vic Chester | 4/57 | Decca F.10882 (&45-) |
| Guy Mitchell | 4/57 | Philips PB.685 |
| Don Lang and his Frantic Five | 4/57 | HMV POP.335<br>(& 45-) |
| Billie Anthony | 4/57 | Columbia DB.3935<br>(& 45-) |

## 805 FREIGHT TRAIN

| | | |
|---|---|---|
| *Composers*: Traditional, adaptation and new<br>lyrics by Paul James & Fred Williams | | *Date of Entry*: 11.5.57 |
| *Publishers*: Pan-Musik Ltd. | | *Highest Position*: 11<br>*Weeks on Chart*: 14 |

*Recordings*:

| | | |
|---|---|---|
| The Chas McDevitt Skiffle Group with<br>Nancy Whiskey | 1/57 | Oriole CB.1352<br>(& 45-) |
| Liz Winters with The Bob Cort Skiffle<br>Group | 4/57 | Decca F.10878 (&45-) |
| The Cranes Skiffle Group | 5/57 | Embassy WB.238 |
| The 2.19 Skiffle Group with Mik Lauder<br>and Mike Wallace (Titled 'Freight Train<br>Blues') | 5/57 | Esquire 10-497 |
| Rusty Draper with The Dick Noel<br>Singers | 7/57 | Mercury MT.155 |

## 806 AROUND THE WORLD

| | | |
|---|---|---|
| *Composers*: Victor Young & Harold Adamson | | *Date of Entry*: 11.5.57/<br>Pos: 1/Wks: 31 |
| *Publishers*: Chappell & Co. Ltd. | | *Re-entry*: 21.12.57/<br>Pos: 21/Wks: 4 |

*Recordings*:

| | | |
|---|---|---|
| Mantovani and his Orchestra | 4/57 | Decca F.10888 (&45-) |
| Ronnie Hilton | 5/57 | HMV POP.338<br>(& 45-) |
| Bing Crosby | 5/57 | Brunswick 05674<br>(& 45-) |
| Victor Young and his Orchestra | 5/57 | Brunswick 05674<br>(& 45-) |
| Lawrence Welk and his Champagne<br>Music | 5/57 | Vogue Coral<br>Q.72256 (& 45-) |
| Jack Haskell | 5/57 | London HL.8426<br>(& 45-) |
| Ronnie Carroll | 5/57 | Philips PB.695 |
| Gracie Fields | 5/57 | Columbia DB.3953<br>(& 45-) |
| Joe Loss and his Orchestra | 6/57 | HMV POP.356<br>(& 45-) |
| Victor Silvester and his Ballroom<br>Orchestra | 6/57 | Columbia DB.3958<br>(& 45-) |
| Jane Morgan | 7/57 | London HLR.8436<br>(& 45-) |

## 807 | MR WONDERFUL

| | | |
|---|---|---|
| *Composers:* Jerry Bock, Larry Holofcener & George Weiss | | *Date of Entry:* 18.5.57 |
| *Publishers:* Valando Music Co. Ltd. | | *Highest Position:* 2 |
| | | *Weeks on Chart:* 22 |

*Recordings:*

| | | |
|---|---|---|
| Peggy Lee | 4/57 | Brunswick 05671 (& 45-) |
| Ruby Murray | 4/57 | Columbia DB.3933 (& 45-) |
| Dorothy Collins | 4/57 | Vogue Coral Q.72252 (& 45-) |
| Yana | 5/57 | HMV POP.340 (& 45-) |
| Marion Ryan with The Beryl Stott Chorus | 5/57 | Pye Nixa N. 15091 |
| The Beverley Sisters | 5/57 | Decca F.10893 (&45-) |
| Patti Forbes | 6/57 | Embassy WB.242 |
| Victor Silvester and his Ballroom Orchestra | 6/57 | Columbia DB.3964 (& 45-) |

## 808 | WHEN I FALL IN LOVE

| | | |
|---|---|---|
| *Composers:* Victor Young & Edward Heyman | | *Date of Entry:* 18.5.57 |
| *Publishers:* New World Publishers Ltd. | | *Highest Position:* 3 |
| | | *Weeks on Chart:* 23 |

(Note: This song first appeared in the Charts in November 1952 [see Song No. 425] with four recordings available. Of these four, three survived to the 1957 entry – the exception being the Victor Silvester version. The recording by Silvester listed below was a new recording of the song.)

*Later recordings:*

| | | |
|---|---|---|
| Nat 'King' Cole | 4/57 | Capitol CL.14709 (& 45-) |
| The Hal McKusick Quintet with The Key Men | 5/57 | Vogue Coral Q.72258 (& 45-) |
| Joe Loss and his Orchestra | 6/57 | HMV POP.356 (& 45-) |
| Victor Silvester and his Ballroom Orchestra | 8/57 | Columbia DB.3982 (& 45-) |

## 809 | I'D GIVE YOU THE WORLD

| | | |
|---|---|---|
| *Composers:* Harold Spina & Heino Gaze | | *Date of Entry:* 25.5.57/ Pos: 12/Wks: 24 |
| *Publishers:* Macmelodies Ltd. | | *Re-entry:* 23.11.57/ Pos: 23/Wks: 1 |

*Recordings:*

| | | |
|---|---|---|
| Eddie Ames | 3/57 | HMV POP.311 (& 45-) |
| David Whitfield (Some 78s labelled 'I'd give the World') | 3/57 | Decca F.10864 (&45-) |
| Teddy Johnson and Pearl Carr | 4/57 | Polydor BM.6068 |
| Ronnie Hilton | 5/57 | HMV POP.338 (& 45-) |

## 810 | YES TONIGHT, JOSEPHINE

| | | |
|---|---|---|
| *Composers:* Winfield Scott & Dorothy Goodman | | *Date of Entry:* 25.5.57 |
| *Publishers:* Berry Music Co. Ltd. | | *Highest Position:* 7 |
| | | *Weeks on Chart:* 13 |

*Recordings:*

| | | |
|---|---|---|
| Johnnie Ray | 5/57 | Philips PB.686 |
| The Tunettes | 7/57 | Embassy WB.245 |

## 811 | A WHITE SPORT COAT (and a pink carnation)

| | | |
|---|---|---|
| *Composer:* Marty Robbins | | *Date of Entry:* 1.6.57 |
| *Publishers:* Frank Music Ltd. | | *Highest Position:* 3 |
| | | *Weeks on Chart:* 18 |

*Recordings:*

| | | |
|---|---|---|
| Terry Dene | 5/57 | Decca F.10895 (&45-) |
| The King Brothers | 5/57 | Parlophone R.4310 (& 45-) |
| Marty Robbins | 5/57 | Philips PB.696 |
| Johnny Desmond with Dick Jacobs and his Skiffle Band | 6/57 | Vogue Coral Q.72261 (& 45-) |
| Victor Silvester and his Ballroom Orchestra | 7/57 | Columbia DB.3963 (& 45-) |
| Paul Rich | 7/57 | Embassy WB.244 |

## 812 | FORGOTTEN DREAMS

| | | |
|---|---|---|
| *Composer:* Leroy Anderson | | *Date of Entry:* 1.6.57 |
| *Publishers:* Mills Music Ltd. | | *Highest Position:* 2 |
| | | *Weeks on Chart:* 49 |

*Recordings:*

| | | |
|---|---|---|
| Leroy Anderson and his 'Pops' Concert Orchestra | 11/55 | Brunswick 05485 (& 45-) |
| Cyril Stapleton and his Orchestra | 6/57 | Decca F.10912 (&45-) |
| Phil Tate and his Orchestra | 7/57 | Oriole CB.1382 (& 45-) |
| Victor Silvester and his Ballroom Orchestra | 7/57 | Columbia DB.3976 (& 45-) |
| Eddie Calvart (trumpet) | 7/57 | Columbia DB.3975 (& 45-) |
| Semprini (piano) | 7/57 | HMV POP.372 (& 45-) |
| Joe 'Mr Piano' Henderson | 8/57 | Pye Nixa N.15099 |

## 813 | WE WILL MAKE LOVE

| | | |
|---|---|---|
| *Composer:* Ron Hulme | | *Date of Entry:* 8.6.57 |
| *Publishers:* Melcher-Toff Music Co. Ltd. | | *Highest Position:* 3<br>*Weeks on Chart:* 23 |

*Recordings:*

| | | |
|---|---|---|
| Russ Hamilton | 3/57 | Oriole CB.1359<br>(& 45-) |
| Jean Campbell | 5/57 | Polydor BM.6069 |
| Kathie Kay | 5/57 | HMV POP.352<br>(& 45-) |
| Johnny Southern with The Western<br>   Rhythm Kings | 5/57 | Melodisc 1413 |

## 814 | PUTTIN' ON THE STYLE

| | | |
|---|---|---|
| *Composers:* Traditional, with new lyric and<br>   arrangement by Norman Cazden | | *Date of Entry:* 22.6.57 |
| *Publishers:* Essex Music Ltd. | | *Highest Position:* 7<br>*Weeks on Chart:* 31 |

*Recordings:*

| | | |
|---|---|---|
| Lonnie Donegan and his Skiffle Group | 5/57 | Pye Nixa N.15093 |
| Dickie Valentine | 6/57 | Decca F.10906 (&45-) |

## 815 | TRAVELLIN' HOME<br>(based on 'Westering Home')

| | | |
|---|---|---|
| *Composers:* Alex Masters & Richard Dix | | *Date of Entry:* 29.6.57 |
| *Publishers:* Virginia Music Co. | | *Highest Position:* 19<br>*Weeks on Chart:* 5 |

*Recording:*

| | | |
|---|---|---|
| Vera Lynn | 6/57 | Decca F.10903 (&45-) |
| Vera Lynn | 6/60 | Decca 45-F.11249* |

## 816 | ISLAND IN THE SUN

| | | |
|---|---|---|
| *Composers:* Harry Belafonte & Irving Burgess | | *Date of Entry:* 6.7.57 |
| *Publishers:* B. Feldman & Co. Ltd. | | *Highest Position:* 3<br>*Weeks on Chart:* 27 |

*Recordings:*

| | | |
|---|---|---|
| Harry Belafonte | 6/57 | RCA.1007 (& 45-) |
| Gerry Grant | 10/57 | Embassy WB.253 |

## 817 | DARK MOON

| | | |
|---|---|---|
| *Composer:* Ned Miller | | *Date of Entry:* 6.7.57 |
| *Publishers:* Francis Day & Hunter Ltd. | | *Highest Position:* 12<br>*Weeks on Chart:* 14 |

*Recordings:*

| | | |
|---|---|---|
| Gale Storm | 5/57 | London HLD.8424<br>(& 45-) |
| Tony Brent | 6/57 | Columbia DB.3950<br>(& 45-) |
| The Kaye Sisters | 6/57 | Philips PB.705 |
| Joe Loss and his Orchestra | 7/57 | HMV POP.368 (&<br>45-) |
| Eve Lombard | 9/57 | Embassy WB.246 |

## 818 | ALL SHOOK UP

| | | |
|---|---|---|
| *Composers:* Otis Blackwell & Elvis Presley | | *Date of Entry:* 6.7.57 |
| *Publishers:* Belinda (London) Ltd. | | *Highest Position:* 10<br>*Weeks on Chart:* 17 |

*Recordings:*

| | | |
|---|---|---|
| Elvis Presley with The Jordanaires | 6/57 | HMV POP.359<br>(& 45-) |
| David Hill | 8/57 | Vogue V.9076<br>(& 45-) |
| Shorty Mitchell | 9/57 | Embassy WB.249 |

## 819 | LOVE LETTERS IN THE SAND

| | | |
|---|---|---|
| *Composers:* J. Fred Coots, Nick & Charles Kenny | | *Date of Entry:* 13.7.57 |
| *Publishers:* Francis Day & Hunter Ltd. | | *Highest Position:* 1<br>*Weeks on Chart:* 26 |

*Recordings:*

| | | |
|---|---|---|
| Joan Savage | 6/57 | Columbia DB.3968<br>(& 45-) |
| Pat Boone | 6/57 | London HLD.8445<br>(& 45-) |
| Gary Miller with the Beryl Stott Chorus | 7/57 | Pye Nixa N. 15094 |
| Joe Loss and his Orchestra | 7/57 | HMV POP.368<br>(& 45-) |
| Victor Silvester and his Ballroom<br>   Orchestra | 9/57 | Columbia DB.3991<br>(& 45-) |
| David Ross | 9/57 | Embassy WB.247 |

## 820 WONDERFUL, WONDERFUL

*Composers*: Ben Raleigh & Sherman Edwards | *Date of Entry*: 13.7.57

*Publishers*: Leeds Music Ltd. | *Highest Position*: 8
*Weeks on Chart*: 13

*Recordings*:
| | | |
|---|---|---|
| Ray Burns | 6/57 | Columbia DB.3966 (& 45-) |
| Joan Regan | 6/57 | Decca F.10911 (&45-) |
| Ronnie Hilton | 6/57 | HMV POP.364 (& 45-) |
| Gary Miller with The Beryl Stott Chorus | 7/57 | Pye Nixa N.15094 |
| Johnny Mathis | 7/57 | Philips PB.713 |
| Jan Peerce | 7/57 | RCA.1012 (& 45-) |
| Victor Silvester and his Ballroom Orchestra | 10/57 | Columbia DB.4008 (& 45-) |

## 821 WITH ALL MY HEART

*Composers*: Peter de Angelis & Robert Marcucci | *Date of Entry*: 20.7.57

*Publishers*: Sydney Bron Music Co. | *Highest Position*: 3
*Weeks on Chart*: 22

*Recordings*:
| | | |
|---|---|---|
| Joan Savage | 6/57 | Columbia DB.3968 (& 45-) |
| Dave King | 6/57 | Decca F.10910 (&45-) |
| Judy Scott | 6/57 | Brunswick 05687 (& 45-) |
| Eve Boswell | 7/57 | Parlophone R.4328 (& 45-) |
| Buddy Greco (vocal) and his Skiffle Gang | 7/57 | London HLR.8452 (& 45-) |
| Petula Clark | 7/57 | Pye Nixa. N.15096 |
| Jodi Sands | 7/57 | London HL.8456 (& 45-) |
| Victor Silvester and his Ballroom Orchestra | 9/57 | Columbia DB.3990 (& 45-) |
| Julie James | 9/57 | Embassy WB.251 |
| Petula Clark | 2/58 | Pye Nixa (45) 7N.15096★ |
| Marino Marini and his Quartet (English vocal by Ruggero Cori) | 3/58 | Durium DC.16629 (& 45-)★ |

## 822 BYE BYE LOVE

*Composers*: Felice & Boudleaux Bryant | *Date of Entry*: 27.7.57
*Publishers*: Acuff-Rose Publications Ltd. | *Highest Position*: 12
*Weeks on Chart*: 15

*Recordings*:
| | | |
|---|---|---|
| The Everly Brothers | 6/57 | London HLA.8440 (& 45-) |

| | | |
|---|---|---|
| Webb Pierce | 6/57 | Brunswick 05682 (& 45-) |
| The Beverley Sisters | 6/57 | Decca F.10909 (&45-) |
| Rory Blackwell and his Blackjacks (Rory Blackwell) | 6/57 | Parlophone R.4326 (& 45-) |
| Chuck Miller | 7/57 | Mercury MT.157 |
| John Fraser with The Beryl Stott Group | 7/57 | Pye Nixa N.15098 |
| The Dene Boys | 7/57 | HMV POP.374 (& 45-) |
| Denny Dennis | 9/57 | Embassy WB.248 |

## 823 LITTLE DARLIN'

*Composers*: Maurice Williams | *Date of Entry*: 27.7.57

*Publishers*: Campbell Connelly & Co. Ltd. | *Highest Position*: 22
*Weeks on Chart*: 4

*Recordings*:
| | | |
|---|---|---|
| The Diamonds | 5/57 | Mercury MT.148 |
| The Gladiolas | 6/57 | London HL.8435 (& 45-) |
| Roberto Del Gado and his Orchestra (Titled 'Little darling') | 6/57 | Polydor BM.6077 |
| The Tunettes | 7/57 | Embassy WB.245 |

## 824 START MOVIN' (in my direction)

*Composers*: David Hill & Bobby Stevenson | *Date of Entry*: 3.8.57

*Publishers*: Bradbury Wood Ltd. | *Highest Position*: 15
*Weeks on Chart*: 8

*Recordings*:
| | | |
|---|---|---|
| Larry Page | 6/57 | Columbia DB.3965 (& 45-) |
| Sal Mineo | 6/57 | Philips PB.707 |
| Terry Dene | 7/57 | Decca F.10914 (&45-) |
| Donald Peers | 7/57 | Oriole CB.1385 |

## 825 FIRE DOWN BELOW

*Composers*: Ned Washington & Lester Lee | *Date of Entry*: 3.8.57
*Publishers*: Dash Music Co. Ltd. | *Highest Position*: 16
*Weeks on Chart*: 7

*Recordings*:
| | | |
|---|---|---|
| Barbara Lyon | 4/57 | Columbia DB.3931 (& 45-) |
| Jeri Southern | 5/57 | Brunswick 05665 (& 45-) |

| Edric Connor | 6/57 | Oriole CB.1377 |
| Victor Silvester and his Ballroom Orchestra | 6/57 | Columbia DB.3960 (& 45-) |
| Gordon Jenkins and his Orchestra | 6/57 | Capitol CL.14749 (& 45-) |
| Roger King Mozian, his trumpet, and his Orchestra | 7/57 | Brunswick 05690 (& 45-) |
| Shirley Bassey | 8/57 | Philips PB.723 |
| Edo Martin and his Latin Band (Beryl Wayne) | 11/57 | Melodisc Mel.1432 (& 45-)★ |

## 826 SCARLET RIBBONS (for her hair)

*Composers*: Jack Segal & Evelyn Danzig

*Publishers*: Mills Music Ltd.

*Date of Entry*: 10.8.57/ Pos: 15/Wks: 12

*Re-entry*: 12.12.59/ Pos: 27/Wks: 3

*Recordings*:

| Dick Haymes | 3/50 | Brunswick 04458 |
| Ruby Murray | 6/57 | Columbia DB.3955 (& 45-) |
| Harry Belafonte with Millard Thomas (guitar) | 6/57 | HMV POP.360 (& 45-) |
| Teri Southern | 9/57 | Brunswick 05709 (& 45-) |
| Eddy Arnold | 9/57 | RCA.1017 (& 45-) |
| Gracie Fields with The Rita Williams Singers | 11/57 | Columbia DB.4047 (& 45-) |
| The Kingston Trio | 9/58 | Capitol 45-CL.14918 |
| The Browns | 11/59 | RCA.1157 (& 45-) |
| Enoch Light and his Vibrant Strings | 11/59 | Top Rank 45- JAR.234 |
| Belafonte (Harry) with Millard Thomas (guitar) | 11/62 | RCA. 45- RCA.1315★ |

## 827 LAST TRAIN TO SAN FERNANDO

*Composers*: Randolph Padmore & Sylvester Devere

*Publishers*: Essex Music Ltd.

*Date of Entry*: 17.8.57

*Highest Position*: 8
*Weeks on Chart*: 15

*Recordings*:

| Johnny Duncan and his Blue Grass Boys | 6/57 | Columbia DB.3959 (& 45-) |
| David Ross | 9/57 | Embassy WB.252 |

## 828 DIANA

*Composer*: Paul Anka

*Publishers*: Robert Mellin Ltd.

*Date of Entry*: 24.8.57
*Highest Position*: 2
*Weeks on Chart*: 25

*Recordings*:

| Paul Anka | 7/57 | Columbia DB.3980 (& 45-) |
| David Ross | 9/57 | Embassy WB.252 |

## 829 IN THE MIDDLE OF AN ISLAND

*Composers*: Nick Acquaviva & Ted Varnick

*Publishers*: Edwin H. Morris & Co. Ltd.

*Date of Entry*: 24.8.57
*Highest Position*: 8
*Weeks on Chart*: 14

*Recordings*:

| Marion Keene | 7/57 | HMV POP.375 (& 45-) |
| The King Brothers with The Rita Williams Singers | 7/57 | Parlophone R.4338 (& 45-) |
| Tony Bennett | 8/57 | Philips PB.724 |
| Bob Sharples and his Chorus and Orchestra | 8/57 | Decca F.10922 (&45-) |
| Tennessee Ernie Ford with Quartet | 8/57 | Capitol CL.14759 (& 45-) |
| Denny Dennis | 9/57 | Embassy WB.248 |

## 830 SHIRALEE

*Composer*: Tommy Steele

*Publishers*: Robbins Music Corporation Ltd.

*Date of Entry*: 24.8.57
*Highest Position*: 22
*Weeks on Chart*: 2

*Recording*:

| Tommy Steele and The Steelmen | 5/57 | Decca F.10896 (&45-) |

## 831 TAMMY

*Composers*: Jay Livingston & Ray Evans

*Publishers*: Macmelodies Ltd.

*Date of Entry*: 31.8.57
*Highest Position*: 1
*Weeks on Chart*: 29

*Recordings*:

| The Ames Brothers | 8/57 | RCA.1015 (& 45-) |
| Debbie Reynolds | 8/57 | Vogue Coral Q.72274 (& 45-) |
| Pat Kirby | 9/57 | Brunswick 05697 (& 45-) |
| Dennis Lotis | 9/57 | Columbia DB.3993 (& 45-) |
| Kathie Kay | 9/57 | HMV POP.385 (& 45-) |
| Joe Loss and his Orchestra | 9/57 | HMV POP.387 (& 45-) |
| Richard Hayman and his Orchestra | 9/57 | Mercury MT.168 |
| Julie James | 9/57 | Embassy WB.251 |
| Victor Silvester and his Ballroom Orchestra | 10/57 | Columbia DB.4008 (& 45-) |

## 832 IN THE MIDDLE OF A DARK, DARK NIGHT

*Composer*: Bob Merrill
*Publishers*: Joy Music Ltd.

*Date of Entry*: 31.8.57
*Highest Position*: 23
*Weeks on Chart*: 2

*Recording*:
Guy Mitchell                    7/57    Philips PB.712

## 833 A HANDFUL OF SONGS

*Composers*: Tommy Steele, Lionel Bart & Michael Pratt
*Publishers*: Peter Maurice Music Co. Ltd.

*Date of Entry*: 7.9.57
*Highest Position*: 8
*Weeks on Chart*: 14

*Recording*:
Tommy Steele and The Steelmen    8/57    Decca F.10923 (&45-)

## 834 WANDERIN' EYES

*Composers*: Kal Mann, Bernie Lowe & Hal Norton
*Publishers*: Sydney Bron Music Co.

*Date of Entry*: 14.9.57
*Highest Position*: 5
*Weeks on Chart*: 16

*Recordings*:
Charlie Gracie          8/57    London HL.8467 (& 45-)
Frankie Vaughan         9/57    Philips PB.729
David Ross             11/57    Embassy WB.257

## 835 MANDOLIN SERENADE

*Composers*: Charles Chaplin, John Turner & Geoffrey Parsons
*Publishers*: Bourne Music Ltd.

*Date of Entry*: 14.9.57/
Pos: 24/Wks: 1
*Re-entry*: 28.9.57/
Pos: 24/Wks: 1
*2nd re-entry*: 12.10.57/
Pos: 21/Wks: 2

*Recordings*:
Norrie Paramor and his Orchestra    7/57    Columbia DB.3974 (& 45-)
Orchestra conducted by Charles Chaplin    7/57    HMV POP.370 (& 45-)
Mantovani and his Orchestra    7/57    Decca F.10918 (&45-)
Kenneth McKellar    7/57    Decca F.10920 (&45-)
Joe Loss and his Orchestra    8/57    HMV POP.388 (& 45-)
Murray Campbell (trumpet) with Wally Stott and his Orchestra    8/57    Philips PB.718
Teddy Johnson    11/57    Pye Nixa N.15110/ (45) 7N.15110★

## 836 I'M GONNA SIT RIGHT DOWN AND WRITE MYSELF A LETTER

*Composers*: Fred Ahlert & Joe Young
*Publishers*: Maddox Music Co. Ltd.

*Date of Entry*: 21.9.57
*Highest Position*: 17
*Weeks on Chart*: 9

*Recordings*:
Thomas 'Fats' Waller and his Rhythm    7/50    HMV B.9935
Billy Williams    6/57    Vogue Coral Q.72266 (& 45-)
Victor Silvester and his Ballroom Orchestra    9/57    Columbia DB.3991 (& 45-)
The Tunettes    9/57    Embassy WB.250

## 837 MAN ON FIRE

*Composers*: Sammy Fain & Paul Francis Webster
*Publishers*: Robbins Music Corporation Ltd.

*Date of Entry*: 5.10.57
*Highest Position*: 5
*Weeks on Chart*: 15

*Recordings*:
George Cates and his Orchestra    8/57    Vogue Coral Q.72275 (& 45-)
Jimmy Young    8/57    Decca F.10925 (&45-)
Bing Crosby    8/57    Capitol CL.14761 (& 45-)
Frankie Vaughan    9/57    Philips PB.729
Gerry Grant    11/57    Embassy WB.258
Victor Silvester and his Ballroom Orchestra    1/58    Columbia DB.4053 (& 45-)

## 838 WHITE SILVER SANDS

*Composer*: Charles G. Matthews
*Publishers*: Southern Music Publishing Co. Ltd.

*Date of Entry*: 5.10.57
*Highest Position*: 12
*Weeks on Chart*: 7

*Recordings*:
Don Lang and his Frantic Five with The Norman Quartet    8/57    HMV POP.382 (& 45-)
Jimmy Jackson    8/57    Columbia DB.3988 (& 45-)
The Owen Bradley Quintet with The Anita Kerr Quartet    8/57    Brunswick 05700 (& 45-)
The Basil Kirchin Band (The Moonbeams)    9/57    Parlophone R.4344 (& 45-)
Don Rondo    9/57    London HLJ.8466 (& 45-)
Joe Loss and his Orchestra    9/57    HMV POP.387 (& 45-)
Gerry Grant    10/57    Embassy WB.253

## 839 | REMEMBER YOU'RE MINE

*Composers*: Bernie Lowe & Kal Mann    *Date of Entry*: 12.10.57

*Publishers*: Belinda (London) Ltd.    *Highest Position*: 9
  *Weeks on Chart*: 17

*Recordings*:
Pat Boone                9/57    London HLD.8479
                                 (& 45-)
Gerry Grant              11/57   Embassy WB.258

## 840 | THAT'LL BE THE DAY

*Composers*: Norman Petty, Buddy Holly &    *Date of Entry*: 19.10.57
  Jerry Allison

*Publishers*: Southern Music Publishing Co. Ltd.    *Highest Position*: 6
  *Weeks on Chart*: 13

*Recordings*:
Buddy Holly and The Crickets    9/57    Vogue Coral
                                        Q.72279 (& 45-)
Larry Page               10/57   Columbia DB.4012
                                 (& 45-)
The Tunettes             11/57   Embassy WB.259

## 841 | WEDDING RING

*Composer*: Ron Hulme    *Date of Entry*: 19.10.57

*Publishers*: David Toff Music Publishing Co. Ltd.    *Highest Position*: 24
  *Weeks on Chart*: 1

*Recording*:
Russ Hamilton with The Tonettes    9/57    Oriole CB.1388
                                           (& 45-)

## 842 | LET ME BE LOVED

*Composers*: Jay Livingston & Ray Evans    *Date of Entry*: 26.10.57

*Publishers*: Frank Music Ltd.    *Highest Position*: 7
  *Weeks on Chart*: 18

*Recordings*:
Mantovani and his Orchestra featuring    9/57    Decca F.10935 (&45-)
  Stan Newsome (trumpet)
Ronnie Harris with The Rita Williams    9/57    Columbia DB.4007
  Singers                                       (& 45-)
Tommy Sands              9/57    Capitol CL.14781
                                 (& 45-)
Joe Loss and his Orchestra    10/57    HMV POP.398
                                       (& 45-)

John Richards            10/57   HMV POP.401
                                 (& 45-)
Steve Martin             10/57   Philips PB.746
Edna Savage              10/57   Parlophone R.4360
                                 (& 45-)
Victor Silvester and his Ballroom    11/57    Columbia DB.4024
  Orchestra                                   (& 45-)
Denny Dennis             11/57   Embassy WB.255

## 843 | AN AFFAIR TO REMEMBER

*Composers*: Harry Warren, Harold Adamson &    *Date of Entry*: 26.10.57
  Leo McCarey

*Publishers*: Leo Feist Ltd.    *Highest Position*: 11
  *Weeks on Chart*: 20

*Recordings*:
Carmen Cavallaro and his Orchestra    9/57    Brunswick 05708
  (Miriam Workman)                            (& 45-)
Vic Damone               10/57   Philips PB.745
Victor Silvester and his Ballroom    11/57    Columbia DB.4023
  Orchestra                                   (& 45-)

## 844 | BE MY GIRL

*Composer*: Arthur Singer    *Date of Entry*: 2.11.57

*Publishers*: Sheldon Music Ltd.    *Highest Position*: 5
  *Weeks on Chart*: 12

*Recordings*:
Don Fox                  8/57    Decca F.10927 (&45-)
Johnny Madara with vocal group    9/57    HMV POP.389
                                          (& 45-)
Jim Dale                 9/57    Parlophone R.4343
                                 (& 45-)
Frankie Brent with The Beryl Stott    9/57    Pye Nixa N.15103
  Group
David Ross               12/57   Embassy WB.261

## 845 | MY DIXIE DARLING

*Composer*: A.P. Carter    *Date of Entry*: 2.11.57/
                            *Pos*: 19/Wks: 8

*Publishers*: Southern Music Publishing Co. Ltd.    *Re-entry*: 4.1.58/Pos:
                                                    23/Wks: 1

*Recording*:
Lonnie Donegan and his Skiffle Group    9/57    Pye Nixa N.15108

197

## 846 MARY'S BOY CHILD (Mary's little boy chile)

*Composer*: Jester Hairston

*Publishers*: Bourne Music Ltd.

*1957 Date of Entry*: 9.11.57/Pos: 1/ Wks: 13
*1958 Date of Entry*: 25.10.58/Pos: 2/ Wks: 12
*1959 Date of Entry*: 7.11.59/Pos: 5/ Wks: 9

*Recordings*:
| | | |
|---|---|---|
| Harry Belafonte | 10/57 | RCA.1022 (& 45-) |
| Gracie Fields with The Rita Williams Singers | 11/57 | Columbia DB.4047 (& 45-) |
| Bob Dale | 12/57 | Embassy WB.263 |
| George Browne (vocal) and his Band with The Humming Birds | 1/58 | Melodisc Mel.1443 (& 45-) |
| Bob Dale | 11/58 | Embassy 45-WB.263 |
| Nina and Frederik | 11/59 | Columbia DB.4375 (& 45-) |
| Roger Williams (piano) | 11/59 | London HLR.8986 (& 45-) |

## 847 GOT-TA HAVE SOMETHING IN THE BANK, FRANK

*Composers*: Bob Hilliard & Mort Garson

*Publishers*: Campbell Connelly & Co. Ltd.

*Date of Entry*: 9.11.57/ Pos: 15/Wks: 9
*Re-entry*: 18.1.58/ Pos: 24/Wks: 1

*Recordings*:
| | | |
|---|---|---|
| Bob Jaxon (Titled 'Gotta . . .') | 10/57 | RCA.1019 (& 45-) |
| Frankie Vaughan and The Kaye Sisters | 10/57 | Philips PB.751 |

## 848 ALONE

*Composers*: Morton & Selma Craft

*Publishers*: Duchess Music Ltd.

*Date of Entry*: 16.11.57

*Highest Position*: 1
*Weeks on Chart*: 16

*Recordings*:
| | | |
|---|---|---|
| Petula Clark with The Beryl Stott Group | 11/57 | Pye Nixa N.15112/ (45) 7N.15112 |
| The Southlanders | 11/57 | Decca F.10946 (&45-) |
| The Brother Sisters | 11/57 | Mercury MT.186 |
| The Kaye Sisters | 11/57 | Philips PB.752 |
| The Shepherd Sisters | 11/57 | HMV POP.411 (& 45-) |
| Eve Lombard | 12/57 | Embassy WB.264 |
| Victor Silvester and his Ballroom Orchestra | 1/58 | Columbia DB.4054 (& 45-) |

## 849 WAKE UP LITTLE SUSIE

*Composers*: Felice & Boudleaux Bryant
*Publishers*: Acuff-Rose Publishing Co. Ltd.

*Date of Entry*: 23.11.57
*Highest Position*: 4
*Weeks on Chart*: 15

*Recordings*:
| | | |
|---|---|---|
| The Everly Brothers | 10/57 | London HLA.8498 (& 45-) |
| The King Brothers | 11/57 | Parlophone R.4367 (& 45-) |
| David Ross | 12/57 | Embassy WB.261 |

## 850 MY SPECIAL ANGEL

*Composer*: Jimmy Duncan
*Publishers*: Yale Music Corporation Ltd.

*Date of Entry*: 30.11.57
*Highest Position*: 1
*Weeks on Chart*: 19

*Recordings*:
| | | |
|---|---|---|
| Bobby Helms with The Anita Kerr Singers | 11/57 | Brunswick 05721 (& 45-) |
| Malcolm Vaughan | 11/57 | HMV POP.419 (& 45-) |
| Robert Earl | 11/57 | Philips PB.767 |
| Frank d'Rone | 12/57 | Mercury MT.183 |
| Paul Rich | 12/57 | Embassy WB.266 (& 45-) |
| Victor Silvester and his Ballroom Orchestra | 2/58 | Columbia DB.4068 (& 45-) |

## 851 HE'S GOT THE WHOLE WORLD IN HIS HANDS

*Composers*: Traditional, arranged as shown
*Publishers*: Sterling Music Publishing Co. Ltd.

*Date of Entry*: 30.11.57
*Highest Position*: 12
*Weeks on Chart*: 9

*Recordings*:
| | | |
|---|---|---|
| George Beverly Shea (arr. Shea) [Titled 'Got the whole world in His hands'] | 3/55 | HMV B.10838 |
| Laurie London (arr. Geoff Love) | 10/57 | Parlophone R.4359 (& 45-) |
| David Ross | 12/57 | Embassy WB.265 |

## 852 I LOVE YOU, BABY

*Composer*: Paul Anka
*Publishers*: Sherwin Music Co. Ltd.

*Date of Entry*: 30.11.57
*Highest Position*: 7
*Weeks on Chart*: 14

*Recordings*:
| | | |
|---|---|---|
| Paul Anka | 11/57 | Columbia DB.4022 (& 45-) |
| David Ross | 12/57 | Embassy WB.265 |

## 853 MA (he's making eyes at me)

| | | |
|---|---|---|
| *Composers*: Sidney Clare & Con Conrad | | *Date of Entry*: 14.12.57 |
| *Publishers*: B. Feldman & Co. Ltd. | | *Highest Position*: 3<br>*Weeks on Chart*: 14 |

*Recordings*:

| | | |
|---|---|---|
| Eddie Cantor | 5/48 | Brunswick 03880 |
| The Ferko String Band with Vocal<br>Chorus | 10/55 | London HLF.8183<br>(& 45-) |
| The Johnny Otis Show (Marie Adams<br>and The Three Tons of Joy) | 10/57 | Capitol CL.14794<br>(& 45-) |
| Chris Howland and The Boys | 4/58 | Columbia DB.4114<br>(& 45-)★ |
| The Bentley Brothers (Titled 'Ma, she's<br>making eyes at me') | 10/59 | Top Rank<br>45-JAR.208★ |

## 854 APRIL LOVE

| | | |
|---|---|---|
| *Composers*: Sammy Fain & Paul Francis Webster | | *Date of Entry*: 14.12.57 |
| *Publishers*: Robbins Music Corporation Ltd. | | *Highest Position*: 2<br>*Weeks on Chart*: 28 |

*Recordings*:

| | | |
|---|---|---|
| Pat Boone | 11/57 | London HLD.8512<br>(& 45-) |
| Joe Loss and his Orchestra | 11/57 | HMV POP.421<br>(& 45-) |
| Ronnie Carroll | 11/57 | Philips PB.768 |
| Bob Dale | 12/57 | Embassy WB.267 |
| Victor Silvester and his Ballroom<br>Orchestra | 2/58 | Columbia DB.4069<br>(& 45-) |

## 855 KISSES SWEETER THAN WINE

| | | |
|---|---|---|
| *Composers*: Paul Campbell & Joel Newman | | *Date of Entry*: 28.12.57 |
| *Publishers*: Francis Day & Hunter Ltd. | | *Highest Position*: 2<br>*Weeks on Chart*: 12 |

*Recordings*:

| | | |
|---|---|---|
| The Weavers | 10/51 | Brunswick 04774 |
| Jimmie Rodgers | 12/57 | Columbia DB.4052<br>(& 45-) |
| Frankie Vaughan | 12/57 | Philips PB.775 |
| Bob Dale | 12/57 | Embassy WB.267 |

# 1958

What can you say about Joe Henderson's *Trudie*? It was the longest running entry in the sheet music charts with but just one week in top spot. We had the hula hoop craze in '58 but *The hula hoop song* lasted one week only in the charts. Harry Belafonte added *Son of Mary* and *I heard the bells on Christmas Day* to his 1957 revival, *Mary's boy child*, at Christmas. The long-awaited 'My Fair Lady' produced three songs to the charts, the most successful being *On the street where you live*, while Max Bygraves's double hit of *Tulips from Amsterdam* and *You need hands* reached No. 3 in the record charts and a top placing for *Tulips* in the sheet music lists. On to the scene came Cliff Richard. The beginnings of an Italian song boom was seen with *Volare* and *More than ever* while ITV's Bernard Bresslaw of 'Army Game' fame recorded *Mad passionate love* and his own version of *You need hands* – *You need feet*. Pete Murray began his long-running show, 'Pete's Party' on 17 August and although originally scheduled for just 20 weeks, it ran well into the Sixties. Less than two months later, on 4 October, the BBC introduced the 'Saturday Club' presented by Brian Matthew. The first programme featured Terry Dene and Gary Miller and occupied the 10 a.m. to 12 noon slot on the Light. TV's 'Six-Five Special' reached its terminus on 22 November, after a journey of a year and three-quarters. Philips, perhaps surprisingly, became one of the last of the major record companies to begin pressing 45s, with the first one appearing in January. At the same time it introduced its Fontana label. Mercury, having moved from Pye to EMI, began its AMT series in October and a month later came the first Pye International releases. And, of course, 1958 was the first year to watch 'Oh, Boy' – ITV's classic series featured rock stars like Cliff Richard, Marty Wilde, the Dallas Boys and Lord Rockingham's XI. Also in 1958, the number of songs on the Sheet Music chart was increased from 24 to 30 from 16 August.

| | MOST WEEKS ON THE CHARTS TOP SIX | |
|---|---|---|
| Pos | | Wks |
| 1 | *Tulips from Amsterdam* | 36 |
| 2= | *You need hands* | 34 |
| 2= | *On the street where you live* | 34 |
| 4 | *I may never pass this way again* | 29 |
| 5 | *I could have danced all night* | 28 |
| 6 | *Trudie* | 26 |

# SONG CHARTS

## 856 ALL THE WAY

*Composers*: Sammy Cahn & Jimmy Van Heusen    *Date of Entry*: 11.1.58

*Publishers*: Barton Music Co. Ltd.    *Highest Position*: 4
   *Weeks on Chart*: 20

*Recordings*:

| | | |
|---|---|---|
| Frank Sinatra | 11/57 | Capitol CL.14800 (& 45-) |
| The Five Dallas Boys | 11/57 | Columbia DB.4041 (& 45-) |
| Victor Silvester and his Ballroom Orchestra | 1/58 | Columbia DB.4054 (& 45-) |
| Gerry Grant | 3/58 | Embassy WB.271 |

## 857 LONG BEFORE I KNEW YOU

*Composers*: Jule Styne, Betty Comden & Adolph Green    *Date of Entry*: 11.1.58

*Publishers*: Chappell & Co. Ltd.    *Highest Position*: 18
   *Weeks on Chart*: 4

*Recordings*:

| | | |
|---|---|---|
| Petula Clark | 11/57 | Pye Nixa N.15112/ (45) 7N.15112 |
| Steve Lawrence | 11/57 | Vogue Coral Q.72286 (& 45-) |
| Dickie Valentine | 11/57 | Decca F.10949 (& 45-) |
| Vic Damone | 11/57 | Philips PB.765 |
| Victor Silvester and his Ballroom Orchestra | 11/57 | Columbia DB.4037 (& 45-) |
| Sammy Davis Jr. | 11/57 | Brunswick 05724 (& 45-) |

## 858 PEGGY SUE

*Composers*: Jerry Allison & Norman Petty    *Date of Entry*: 11.1.58

*Publishers*: Southern Music Publishing Co. Ltd.    *Highest Position*: 14
   *Weeks on Chart*: 10

*Recordings*:

| | | |
|---|---|---|
| Buddy Holly | 11/57 | Vogue Coral Q.72293 (& 45-) |
| Paul Rich | 2/58 | Embassy WB.270 |

## 859 OH BOY!

*Composers*: Sunny West, Norman Petty & Bill Tilghman    *Date of Entry*: 11.1.58

*Publishers*: Southern Music Publishing Co. Ltd.    *Highest Position*: 11
   *Weeks on Chart*: 12

*Recordings*:

| | | |
|---|---|---|
| Buddy Holly and The Crickets | 12/57 | Coral Q.72298 (& 45-) |
| Paul Rich | 2/58 | Embassy WB.270 |

## 860 THE STORY OF MY LIFE

*Composers*: Burt Bacharach & Hal David    *Date of Entry*: 18.1.58
*Publishers*: Sterling Music Publishing Co. Ltd.    *Highest Position*: 1
   *Weeks on Chart*: 19

*Recordings*:

| | | |
|---|---|---|
| Marty Robbins | 1/58 | Fontana H.102 |
| Alma Cogan | 1/58 | HMV POP.433 (& 45-) |
| Michael Holliday | 1/58 | Columbia DB.4058 (& 45-) |
| Dave King | 1/58 | Decca F.10973 (&45-) |
| Gary Miller with The Beryl Stott Group | 1/58 | Pye Nixa N.15120/ (45) 7N.15120 |
| Gerry Grant | 3/58 | Embassy WB.271 |
| Victor Silvester and his Ballroom Orchestra | 3/58 | Columbia DB.4088 (& 45-) |

## 861 LOVE ME FOREVER

*Composers*: Gary Lynes & Beverly Guthrie    *Date of Entry*: 18.1.58
*Publishers*: Unit Music Publishing Co. Ltd.    *Highest Position*: 3
   *Weeks on Chart*: 15

*Recordings*:

| | | |
|---|---|---|
| The Kaye Sisters | 1/58 | Philips PB.778 |
| Eydie Gorme with Bernie Glow (trumpet) | 1/58 | HMV POP.432 (& 45-) |
| Marion Ryan with The Beryl Stott Chorus | 1/58 | Pye Nixa N.15121/ (45) 7N.15121 |
| The Four Esquires | 1/58 | London HLO.8533 (& 45-) |
| Rita Williams | 1/58 | Oriole CB.1417 (& 45-) |
| Victor Silvester and his Ballroom Orchestra | 3/58 | Columbia DB.4089 (& 45-) |
| Denny Dennis | 3/58 | Embassy WB.273 |

## 862 | JAILHOUSE ROCK

| | | |
|---|---|---|
| *Composers*: Jerry Leiber & Mike Stoller | *Date of Entry*: 25.1.58 | |
| *Publishers*: Belinda (London) Ltd. | *Highest Position*: 6 | |
| | *Weeks on Chart*: 12 | |

*Recordings*:

| | | |
|---|---|---|
| Elvis Presley | 1/58 | RCA.1028 (& 45-) |
| Hal Munro | 2/58 | Embassy WB.269 |

## 863 | PUT A LIGHT IN THE WINDOW

| | | |
|---|---|---|
| *Composers*: Rhoda Roberts & Kenny Jacobson | *Date of Entry*: 25.1.58 | |
| *Publishers*: Dominion Music Ltd. | *Highest Position*: 9 | |
| | *Weeks on Chart*: 10 | |

*Recordings*:

| | | |
|---|---|---|
| The King Brothers | 1/58 | Parlophone R.4389 (& 45-) |
| The Four Lads | 1/58 | Philips PB.776 |
| Gary Miller with The Beryl Stott Group | 1/58 | Pye Nixa N.15120/ (45) 7N.15120 |
| The Southlanders | 1/58 | Decca F.10982 (& 45-) |
| Rikki Henderson | 3/58 | Embassy WB.275 |

## 864 | CHICAGO

| | | |
|---|---|---|
| *Composer*: Fred Fisher | *Date of Entry*: 25.1.58 | |
| *Publishers*: B. Feldman & Co. Ltd. | *Highest Position*: 14 | |
| | *Weeks on Chart*: 9 | |

(Note: Twelve earlier recordings of this 1922 song had been deleted before it was revived in 1958.)

*Later recordings*:

| | | |
|---|---|---|
| The Earl Hines Quartet | 5/50 | Esquire 10–055 |
| The Joe Daniels Jazz Group | 5/56 | Parlophone R.4173 |
| Bob Scobey's Band | 10/56 | Good Time Jazz GV.2403 |
| Joe Loss and his Orchestra | 5/57 | HMV POP.344 (& 45-) |
| Frank Sinatra | 11/57 | Capitol CL.14800 (& 45-) |
| Bing Crosby | 12/57 | Brunswick 05726 (& 45-) |
| Victor Silvester and his Ballroom Orchestra | 3/58 | Columbia DB.4089 (& 45-) |
| The Clark Sisters | 1/59 | London HLD.8791 (& 45-)★ |

## 865 | GREAT BALLS OF FIRE

| | | |
|---|---|---|
| *Composers*: Jack Hammer & Otis Blackwell | *Date of Entry*: 1.2.58 | |
| *Publishers*: Aberbach (London) Ltd. | *Highest Position*: 24 | |
| | *Weeks on Chart*: 1 | |

*Recordings*:

| | | |
|---|---|---|
| Georgia Gibbs | 11/57 | RCA.1029 (& 45-) |
| Jerry Lee Lewis | 12/57 | London HLS.8529 (& 45-) |

## 866 | MAGIC MOMENTS

| | | |
|---|---|---|
| *Composers*: Burt Bacharach & Hal David | *Date of Entry*: 8.2.58 | |
| *Publishers*: Chappell & Co. Ltd. | *Highest Position*: 1 | |
| | *Weeks on Chart*: 21 | |

*Recordings*:

| | | |
|---|---|---|
| Perry Como with The Ray Charles | 1/58 | RCA.1036 (& 45-) |
| Ronnie Hilton | 1/58 | HMV POP.446 (& 45-) |
| Denny Dennis | 3/58 | Embassy WB.273 |
| Victor Silvester and his Ballroom Orchestra | 4/58 | Columbia DB.4103 (& 45-) |

## 867 | AT THE HOP

| | | |
|---|---|---|
| *Composers*: Artie Singer, Johnny Medora & Dave White | *Date of Entry*: 8.2.58 | |
| *Publishers*: Yale Music Corporation Ltd. | *Highest Position*: 8 | |
| | *Weeks on Chart*: 11 | |

*Recordings*:

| | | |
|---|---|---|
| Danny and The Juniors | 1/58 | HMV POP.436 (& 45-) |
| Nick Todd | 1/58 | London HLD.8537 (& 45-) |
| Paul Rich | 3/58 | Embassy WB.272 |

## 868 | SUGARTIME (Sugar in the morning)

| | | |
|---|---|---|
| *Composers*: Charlie Phillips & Odis Echols | *Date of Entry*: 8.2.58 | |
| *Publishers*: Southern Music Publishing Co. Ltd. | *Highest Position*: 3 | |
| | *Weeks on Chart*: 19 | |

*Recordings*:

| | | |
|---|---|---|
| Jim Dale | 2/58 | Parlophone R.4402 (& 45-) |
| Alma Cogan with The Michael Sammes Singers | 2/58 | HMV POP.450 (& 45-) |
| The McGuire Sisters | 2/58 | Coral Q.72305 (& 45-) |
| Joe Loss and his Orchestra | 3/58 | HMV POP.457 (& 45-) |
| Rikki Henderson | 3/58 | Embassy WB.275 |

## 869 LIECHTENSTEINER POLKA

*Composers*: Edmund Koetscher & Rudi Lindt, English Lyrics by Joseph Seener
*Publishers*: Aberbach (London) Ltd.

*Date of Entry*: 8.2.58/ Pos: 24/Wks: 1
*Re-entry*: 22.3.58/ Pos: 23/Wks: 1

*Recordings*:

| | | |
|---|---|---|
| The Big Ben Banjo Band | 10/57 | Columbia DB.4049 (& 45–) |
| Will Glahé and his Musik | 11/57 | Decca F.10961 (& 45–) |
| Derek Roy | 12/57 | Oriole CB.1410 |

## 870 CATCH A FALLING STAR

*Composers*: Lee Pockriss & Paul Vance
*Publishers*: B. Feldman & Co. Ltd.

*Date of Entry*: 15.2.58
*Highest Position*: 2
*Weeks on Chart*: 17

*Recordings*:

| | | |
|---|---|---|
| Perry Como with The Ray Charles Singers | 1/58 | RCA.1036 (& 45–) |
| Jeremy Lubbock (vocal and piano) | 1/58 | Parlophone R.4399 (& 45–) |
| Wally Stott and his Chorus and Orchestra | 3/58 | Philips PB.796 |
| Rikki Henderson | 4/58 | Embassy WB.277 |

## 871 YOU ARE MY DESTINY

*Composer*: Paul Anka
*Publishers*: Robert Mellin Ltd.

*Date of Entry*: 15.2.58
*Highest Position*: 12
*Weeks on Chart*: 10

*Recordings*:

| | | |
|---|---|---|
| Paul Anka | 1/58 | Columbia DB.4063 (& 45–) |
| Paul Rich | 3/58 | Embassy WB.274 |
| Victor Silvester and his Ballroom Orchestra | 4/58 | Columbia DB.4104 (& 45–) |

## 872 MANDY (The Pansy) (La Panse)

*Composers*: Furio Rendine, Gigi Pisano, with English Lyrics by Jack Elliott
*Publishers*: Peter Maurice Music Co. Ltd.

*Date of Entry*: 1.3.58
*Highest Position*: 8
*Weeks on Chart*: 15

*Recordings*:

| | | |
|---|---|---|
| Marino Marini and his Quartet (Ruggero Cori) [Titled 'La Panse': in Italian] | 10/56 | Durium DC.16594 |
| Eddie Calvert – The Man with the Golden Trumpet [Titled 'Mandy (La Panse)'] | 6/57 | Columbia DB.3956 (& 45–) |
| Les Baxter and his Chorus and Orchestra [Titled 'La Panse – The Little Flower'] | 11/57 | Capitol CL.14796 (& 45–) |
| Edmundo Ros and his Orchestra [Titled 'The Pansy'] | 11/57 | Decca F.10954 (& 45–) |
| Marino Marini and his Quartet [Titled 'The Pansy (Mandy)': in English] | 3/58 | Durium DC.16629 (& 45–) |
| The Kaye Sisters [Titled 'The Pansy'] | 3/58 | Philips PB.806(&45–) |
| Victor Silvester and his Ballroom Orchestra [Titled 'Mandy – The Pansy'] | 4/58 | Columbia DB.4104 (& 45–) |

## 873 RAUNCHY

*Composers*: Bill Justis & Sidney Manker
*Publishers*: Aberbach (London) Ltd.

*Date of Entry*: 8.3.58
*Highest Position*: 11
*Weeks on Chart*: 9

*Recordings*:

| | | |
|---|---|---|
| Bill Justis (alto sax) | 12/57 | London HLS.8517 (& 45–) |
| Billy Vaughn and his Orchestra | 12/57 | London HLD.8522 (& 45–) |
| Ernie Freeman (tenor sax) | 12/57 | London HLP.8523 (& 45–) |
| Ken Mackintosh and his Orchestra | 12/57 | HMV POP.426 (& 45–) |
| Winifred Atwell (piano) | 2/58 | Decca F.10987 (& 45–) |
| Ted Heath and his Music | 3/58 | Decca F.11000 (& 45–) |

## 874 NAIROBI

*Composer*: Bob Merrill
*Publishers*: Leeds Music Ltd.

*Date of Entry*: 8.3.58
*Highest Position*: 7
*Weeks on Chart*: 10

*Recordings*:

| | | |
|---|---|---|
| Tommy Steele and The Steelmen | 2/58 | Decca F.10991 (& 45–) |
| Bob Merrill | 2/58 | Columbia DB.4086 (& 45–) |
| Dave Grant | 3/58 | Embassy WB.276 |

## 875 WHY DON'T THEY UNDERSTAND?

*Composers*: Jack Fishman & Joe Henderson
*Publishers*: Henderson Music Ltd.

*Date of Entry*: 8.3.58
*Highest Position*: 17
*Weeks on Chart*: 10

*Recordings*:

| | | |
|---|---|---|
| The Zodiacs | 7/57 | Oriole CB.1383 |
| Glen Mason | 7/57 | Parlophone R.4334 (& 45–) |
| John Fraser with The Beryl Stott Group | 7/57 | Pye Nixa N.15098 |
| George Hamilton IV | 12/57 | HMV POP.429 (& 45–) |
| Victor Silvester and his Ballroom Orchestra | 3/58 | Columbia DB.4088 (& 45–) |

| 876 | BABY LOVER | | |
|---|---|---|---|

*Composer*: Wandra Merrell

*Date of Entry*: 15.3.58

*Publishers*: Cromwell Music Ltd.

*Highest Position*: 19
*Weeks on Chart*: 4

*Recordings*:
| | | | |
|---|---|---|---|
| Petula Clark with The Beryl Stott Group | 2/58 | Pye Nixa N.15126/ (45) 7N.15126 | |
| Little Johnny with The Three Teenagers | 2/58 | Decca F.10990 (& 45–) | |
| The Twin Tunes Quintet (vocal) | 2/58 | RCA.1046 (& 45–) | |

| 877 | THE SWINGIN' SHEPHERD BLUES | | |
|---|---|---|---|

*Composers*: Moe Koffman, Rhoda Roberts & Kenny Jacobson

*Date of Entry*: 22.3.58

*Publishers*: Sherwin Music Co.

*Highest Position*: 1
*Weeks on Chart*: 19

*Recordings*:
| | | | |
|---|---|---|---|
| Ken Mackintosh and his Orchestra with vocal group | 1/58 | HMV POP.441 (& 45–) | |
| The Johnny Pate Quintet featuring Lennie Druss (flute) | 2/58 | Parlophone R.4404 (& 45–) | |
| The Moe Koffman Quartet | 2/58 | London HLJ.8549 (& 45–) | |
| Ted Heath and his Music | 3/58 | Decca F.11000 (& 45–) | |
| The Johnny Gregory Sextet | 4/58 | Embassy WB.280 (& 45–) | |
| Ella Fitzgerald (vcl) with her Shepherds (inst) | 5/58 | HMV POP.486 (& 45–) | |

| 878 | TO BE LOVED | | |
|---|---|---|---|

*Composers*: Tyran Carlo, Berry Gordy Jr & Gwen Gordy

*Date of Entry*: 22.3.58

*Publishers*: Duchess Music Ltd.

*Highest Position*: 6
*Weeks on Chart*: 16

*Recordings*:
| | | | |
|---|---|---|---|
| Malcolm Vaughan with The Michael Sammes Singers | 2/58 | HMV POP.459 (& 45–) | |
| Jackie Wilson | 2/58 | Coral Q.72306 (& 45–) | |
| Ronnie Carroll | 3/58 | Philips PB.801 | |
| Victor Silvester and his Ballroom Orchestra | 5/58 | Columbia DB.4124 (& 45–) | |

| 879 | DON'T | | |
|---|---|---|---|

*Composers*: Jerry Leiber & Mike Stoller

*Date of Entry*: 22.3.58

*Publishers*: Belinda (London) Ltd.

*Highest Position*: 22
*Weeks on Chart*: 4

*Recordings*:
| | | | |
|---|---|---|---|
| Elvis Presley with The Jordanaires | 2/58 | RCA.1043 (& 45–) | |
| Hal Munro | 4/58 | Embassy WB.278 | |

| 880 | I MAY NEVER PASS THIS WAY AGAIN | | |
|---|---|---|---|

*Composers*: Murray Wizell & Irving Melsher

*Date of Entry*: 29.3.58

*Publishers*: Chappell & Co. Ltd.

*Highest Position*: 1
*Weeks on Chart*: 29

*Recordings*:
| | | | |
|---|---|---|---|
| Robert Earl | 3/58 | Philips PB.805 | |
| Dennis Lotis with The Rita Williams Singers | 3/58 | Columbia DB.4090 (& 45–) | |
| Ronnie Hilton with the Michael Sammes Singers | 3/58 | HMV POP.468 (& 45–) | |
| Glen Mason | 3/58 | Parlophone R.4415 (& 45–) | |
| Joan Regan | 4/58 | Decca F.11009 (& 45–) | |
| Perry Como with The Ray Charles Singers | 5/58 | RCA.1062 (& 45–) | |
| Victor Silvester and his Ballroom Orchestra | 6/58 | Columbia DB.4143 (& 45–) | |

| 881 | OH-OH, I'M FALLING IN LOVE AGAIN | | |
|---|---|---|---|

*Composers*: Al Hoffman, Dick Manning & Mark Markwell

*Date of Entry*: 29.3.58

*Publishers*: Chappell & Co. Ltd.

*Highest Position*: 10
*Weeks on Chart*: 9

*Recordings*:
| | | | |
|---|---|---|---|
| Marion Ryan with The Beryl Stott Group | 2/58 | Pye Nixa N.15130/ (45) 7N.15130 | |
| Jimmie Rodgers | 2/58 | Columbia DB.4078 (& 45–) | |
| Donald Peers | 3/58 | Oriole CB.1431 (& 45–) | |
| Marty Wilde and The Wildcats | 3/58 | Philips PB.804 (& 45–) | |
| Bill Kent | 3/58 | Decca F.10997 | |

## 882 | TEQUILA

| | | |
|---|---|---|
| *Composer*: Chuck Rio | | *Date of Entry*: 5.4.58 |
| *Publishers*: Challenge Music Ltd. | | *Highest Position*: 12 |
| | | *Weeks on Chart*: 7 |

*Recordings*:

| | | |
|---|---|---|
| Stan Kenton and his Orchestra | 3/58 | Capitol CL.14847 (& 45-) |
| The Champs | 3/58 | London HLU.8580 (& 45-) |
| Don Lang and his Frantic Five | 3/58 | HMV POP.465 (& 45-) |
| Eddie Platt and his Orchestra | 3/58 | Columbia DB.4101 (& 45-) |
| Ted Heath and his Music | 3/58 | Decca F.11003 |
| Johnny Gray (tenor sax) with the Ken Jones Orchestra | 4/58 | Fontana H.123 (& 45-) |
| Ralph Marterie and his Orchestra | 4/58 | Mercury MT.204/ (45) 7MT.204 |
| The Bill Shepherd Orchestra with The Beryl Stott Group | 4/58 | Pye Nixa N.15137/ (45) 7N.15137 |
| The Johnny Gregory Sextet | 4/58 | Embassy WB.280 (& 45-) |

## 883 | WHOLE LOTTA WOMAN

| | | |
|---|---|---|
| *Composer*: Marvin Rainwater | | *Date of Entry*: 5.4.58 |
| *Publishers*: Sheldon Music Ltd. | | *Highest Position*: 7 |
| | | *Weeks on Chart*: 12 |

*Recordings*:

| | | |
|---|---|---|
| Marvin Rainwater | 1/58 | MGM.974 (& 45-) |
| The Most Brothers | 2/58 | Decca F.10998 (& 45-) |
| Paul Rich | 4/58 | Embassy WB.281 (& 45-) |

## 884 | MAYBE BABY

| | | |
|---|---|---|
| *Composers*: Norman Petty & Charles Hardin | | *Date of Entry*: 12.4.58 |
| *Publishers*: Southern Music Publishing Co. Ltd. | | *Highest Position*: 19 |
| | | *Weeks on Chart*: 4 |

*Recordings*:

| | | |
|---|---|---|
| Buddy Holly and The Crickets | 2/58 | Coral Q.72307 (& 45-) |
| Paul Rich | 5/58 | Embassy WB.283 (& 45-) |

## 885 | LA DEE DAH

| | | |
|---|---|---|
| *Composers*: Frank C. Slay Jr & Bob Crewe | | *Date of Entry*: 12.4.58 |
| *Publishers*: Cromwell Music Ltd. | | *Highest Position*: 21 |
| | | *Weeks on Chart*: 2 |

*Recordings*:

| | | |
|---|---|---|
| Colin Hicks with The Beryl Stott Group | 2/58 | Pye Nixa N.15125/ (45) 7N.15125 |
| Jackie Dennis | 2/58 | Decca F.10992 (& 45-) |
| Bonnie Lou and Rusty York | 2/58 | Parlophone R.4409 (& 45-) |
| Billie and Lillie with Billy Ford's Thunderbirds | 3/58 | London HLU.8564 (& 45-) |
| Paul Rich | 4/58 | Embassy WB.281 (& 45-) |

## 886 | LOLLIPOP

| | | |
|---|---|---|
| *Composers*: Beverly Ross & Julius Dixon | | *Date of Entry*: 19.4.58 |
| *Publishers*: Anglo-Pic Music Co. Ltd. | | *Highest Position*: 2 |
| | | *Weeks on Chart*: 15 |

*Recordings*:

| | | |
|---|---|---|
| The Chordettes | 3/58 | London HLD.8584 (& 45-) |
| Ronald and Ruby | 3/58 | RCA.1053 (& 45-) |
| The Mudlarks | 3/58 | Columbia DB.4099 (& 45-) |
| Gary Miller with The Beryl Stott Group | 4/58 | Pye Nixa N.15136/ (45) 7N.15136 |
| Mal Perry | 4/58 | Fontana H.125 |

## 887 | A WONDERFUL TIME UP THERE

| | | |
|---|---|---|
| *Composer*: Lee Roy Abernathy | | *Date of Entry*: 19.4.58/ Pos: 7/Wks: 16 |
| *Publishers*: Edwin H. Morris & Co. Ltd. | | *Re-entry*: 16.8.58/ Pos: 30/Wks: 1 |
| | | *2nd re-entry*: 6.9.58/ Pos: 26/Wks: 1 |

*Recordings*:

| | | |
|---|---|---|
| Pat Boone | 3/58 | London HLD.8574 (& 45-) |
| Rikki Henderson | 5/58 | Embassy WB.282 (& 45-) |

## 888 | TULIPS FROM AMSTERDAM

*Composers*: Ralf Arnie & Gene Martyn

*Publishers*: Hans Sikorski Ltd

*Date of Entry*: 26.4.58/
Pos: 1/Wks: 37
*Re-entry*: 17.1.59/
Pos: 30/Wks: 1

*Recordings*:

| | | |
|---|---|---|
| Max Bygraves | 3/58 | Decca F.11004 (& 45-) |
| Rikki Henderson | 6/58 | Embassy WB.286 (& 45-) |

## 889 | YOU NEED HANDS

*Composer*: Roy Irwin

*Publishers*: Lakeview Music Publishing Co.

*Date of Entry*: 26.4.58/
Pos: 22/Wks: 2
*Re-entry*: 24.5.58/
Pos: 6/Wks: 36

*Recordings*:

| | | |
|---|---|---|
| Max Bygraves with The Clarke Brothers | 3/58 | Decca F.11004 (& 45-) |
| Eydie Gorme | 5/58 | HMV POP.493 (& 45-) |
| Rikki Henderson | 8/58 | Embassy WB.289 (& 45-) |
| Bernard Bresslaw (Parody titled 'You need feet' – adapted by Sid Colin) | 8/58 | HMV POP.522 (& 45-) |

## 890 | IT'S TOO SOON TO KNOW

*Composer*: Deborah Chessler

*Publishers*: Edwin H. Morris & Co. Ltd.

*Date of Entry*: 26.4.58/
Pos: 24/Wks: 1
*Re-entry*: 17.5.58/
Pos: 24/Wks: 1

*Recordings*:

| | | |
|---|---|---|
| Pat Boone | 3/58 | London HLD.8574 (& 45-) |
| Rikki Henderson | 5/58 | Embassy WB.282 (& 45-) |
| Victor Silvester and his Ballroom Orchestra | 6/58 | Columbia DB.4161 (& 45-)★ |

## 891 | WHO'S SORRY NOW?

*Composers*: Bert Kalmar, Harry Ruby & Ted Snyder

*Publishers*: B. Feldman & Co. Ltd.

*Date of Entry*: 3.5.58

*Highest Position*: 1
*Weeks on Chart*: 23

(Note: Only one recording from the many released in the Twenties. Thirties and Forties remained in the catalogues of 1958 and that was the one by Bob Crosby and the Bobcats on Decca F.6790.)

*Later recordings*:

| | | |
|---|---|---|
| Sidney Bechet (soprana sax) with Humphrey Lyttleton and his Band | 1/50 | Melodisc 1104 |
| Carlo Krahmer's Chicagoans | 1/51 | Esquire 10–081 |
| The Frank Petty Trio featuring Mike di Napoli (piano) | 3/53 | MGM.610 |
| The Castle Jazz Band, Kid Ory's Creole Band, Charlie Le Vere's Chicago Loopers and Pete Daily's Chicagoans | 5/53 | Brunswick 05090 |
| Bobby Mickleburgh's Bob Cats | 4/54 | Esquire 10–360 |
| Tommy Rogers and his Ballroom Orchestra directed by Harry Gold | 11/54 | Parlophone F.2541 |
| Sid Phillips and his Band | 7/55 | HMV BD.6201 |
| Johnnie Ray | 2/56 | Philips PB.546 |
| Joe Loss and his Orchestra | 3/56 | HMV POP.184/ (45) 7M.387 |
| Victor Silvester and his Ballroom Orchestra | 3/56 | Columbia DB.3742/ (45) SCM.5249 |
| The Hedley Ward Trio | 3/56 | Melodisc 1352 |
| Connie Francis | 2/58 | MGM.975 (& 45-) |
| Lisa Noble | 4/58 | Decca F.11006 (& 45-) |
| Beryl Templeman | 6/58 | Embassy WB.285 (& 45-) |

## 892 | GRAND COOLIE DAM

*Composers*: Woody Guthrie & Lonnie Donegan

*Publishers*: Essex Music Ltd.

*Date of Entry*: 3.5.58

*Highest Position*: 11
*Weeks on Chart*: 11

*Recording*:

| | | |
|---|---|---|
| Lonnie Donegan and his Skiffle Group | 4/58 | Pye Nixa N.15129/ (45) 7N.15129 |

## 893 A VERY PRECIOUS LOVE

| Composers: Sammy Fain & Paul Francis Webster | Date of Entry: 3.5.58 |
| Publishers: Blossom Music Ltd. | Highest Position: 11 |
| | Weeks on Chart: 21 |

Recordings:

| The Johnston Brothers | 2/58 | Decca F.10996 (& 45-) |
| The Ames Brothers | 2/58 | RCA.1049 (& 45-) |
| Doris Day | 3/58 | Philips PB.799 (& 45-) |
| Jimmy Young | 3/58 | Columbia DB.4100 (& 45-) |
| Slim Whitman | 3/58 | London HLP.8590 (& 45-) |
| Bonnie Guitar | 3/58 | London HLD.8591 (& 45-) |
| Jack Jones | 5/58 | Capitol 45-CL.14871 |
| Gene Kelly | 6/58 | RCA.1068 (& 45-) |
| Victor Silvester and his Ballroom Orchestra | 7/58 | Columbia DB.4162 (& 45-) |
| Terri Lorraine | 9/58 | Embassy WB.292 (& 45-) |

## 894 ON THE STREET WHERE YOU LIVE

| Composers: Alan Jay Lerner & Frederick Loewe | Date of Entry: 10.5.58 |
| Publishers: Chappell & Co. Ltd. | Highest Position: 1 |
| | Weeks on Chart: 38 |

Recordings:

| Buddy Greco and his Quartet | 5/58 | London HLR.8613 (& 45-) |
| Lawrence Welk and his Champagne Music (Larry Deane) | 5/58 | Coral Q.72317 (& 45-) |
| Vic Damone | 5/58 | Philips PB.819 (& 45-) |
| Joe Loss and his Orchestra | 5/58 | HMV POP.477 (& 45-) |
| Ronnie Hilton with The Michael Sammes Singers | 5/58 | HMV POP.479 (& 45-) |
| Mario Lanza with The Jeff Alexander Chorus | 5/58 | RCA.1059 (& 45-) |
| Victor Silvester and his Ballroom Orchestra | 5/58 | Columbia DB.4123 (& 45-) |
| David Whitfield | 5/58 | Decca F.11018 (& 45-) |
| Gary Miller with The Beryl Stott Chorus | 5/58 | Pye Nixa N.15140/ (45) 7N.15140 |
| Paul Rich | 9/58 | Embassy WB.295 (& 45-) |

## 895 I COULD HAVE DANCED ALL NIGHT

| Composers: Alan Jay Lerner & Frederick Loewe | Date of Entry: 10.5.58/ Pos: 6/Wks: 24 |
| Publishers: Chappell & Co. Ltd. | Re-entry: 1.11.58/ Pos: 22/Wks: 3 |
| | 2nd re-entry: 13.12.58/ Pos: 27/Wks: 1 |
| | 3rd re-entry: 10.1.59/ Pos: 27/Wks: 3 |

Recordings:

| Rosemary Clooney | 5/58 | Philips PB.800 (& 45-) |
| Joe Loss and his Orchestra | 5/58 | HMV POP.478 (& 45-) |
| Norrie Paramor and his Concert Orchestra (vocal chorus) | 5/58 | Columbia DB.4119 (& 45-) |
| Victor Silvester and his Ballroom Orchestra | 5/58 | Columbia DB.4123 (& 45-) |
| Jeannie Carson with The Rita Williams Singers | 5/58 | Columbia DB.4125 (& 45-) |
| Lawrence Welk and his Champagne Music (Alice Lon and The Sparklers) | 5/58 | Coral Q.72317 (& 45-) |
| Mantovani and his Orchestra | 5/58 | Decca F.11017 (& 45-) |
| Sylvia Syms | 5/58 | Brunswick 05744 (& 45-) |
| Lita Roza | 5/58 | Pye Nixa N.15139/ (45) 7N.15139 |
| Julie Andrews | 7/58 | Philips PB.846 (& 45-) |
| Marino Marini and his Quartet | 10/58 | Durium DC.16634 (& 45-) |

## 896 STAIRWAY OF LOVE

| Composers: Sid Tepper & Roy C. Bennett | Date of Entry: 10.5.58 |
| Publishers: Leeds Music Ltd. | Highest Position: 1 |
| | Weeks on Chart: 21 |

Recordings:

| Terry Dene | 4/58 | Decca F.11016 (& 45-) |
| Marion Ryan with The Beryl Stott Group | 5/58 | Pye Nixa N.15138/ (45) 7N.15138 |
| Michael Holliday | 5/58 | Columbia DB.4121 (& 45-) |
| Alma Cogan with The Michael Sammes Singers | 5/58 | HMV POP.482 (& 45-) |
| Steve Martin | 5/58 | Philips PB.820 (& 45-) |
| Marty Robbins | 5/58 | Fontana H.128 (& 45-) |
| Joe Loss and his Orchestra | 6/58 | HMV POP.494 (& 45-) |
| Victor Silvester and his Ballroom Orchestra | 6/58 | Columbia DB.4161 (& 45-) |
| Beryl Templeman | 6/58 | Embassy WB.285 (& 45-) |

| 897 | TOM HARK | | |
|---|---|---|---|

*Composer*: Rupert Bopape
*Publishers*: Southern Music Publishing Co. Ltd.

*Date of Entry*: 17.5.58
*Highest Position*: 7
*Weeks on Chart*: 11

Recordings:
| | | |
|---|---|---|
| Elias and his Zig-Zag Jive Flutes | 3/58 | Columbia DB.4109 (& 45-) |
| Ted Heath and his Music | 5/58 | Decca F.11025 (&45-) |

| 898 | KEWPIE DOLL | | |
|---|---|---|---|

*Composers*: Sid Tepper & Roy C. Bennett
*Publishers*: Leeds Music Ltd.

*Date of Entry*: 24.5.58
*Highest Position*: 10
*Weeks on Chart*: 13

Recordings:
| | | |
|---|---|---|
| Frankie Vaughan | 4/58 | Philips PB.825 (& 45-) |
| Perry Como with The Ray Charles Singers | 5/58 | RCA.1055 (&45-) |
| Rikki Henderson | 6/58 | Embassy WB.286 (& 45-) |

| 899 | WEAR MY RING | | |
|---|---|---|---|

*Composers*: Bert Carroll & Russell Moody
*Publishers*: Belinda (London) Ltd.

*Date of Entry*: 31.5.58
*Highest Position*: 22
*Weeks on Chart*: 2

Recordings:
| | | |
|---|---|---|
| Elvis Presley and The Jordanaires (Titled 'Wear my ring around your neck') | 4/58 | RCA.1058 (& 45-) |
| Hal Munro | 6/58 | Embassy WB.284 (& 45-) |

| 900 | LITTLE SERENADE (Piccolissima Serenata) | | |
|---|---|---|---|

*Composers*: Gianni Ferrio, Antonio Amurri, Geoffrey Parsons & John Turner
*Publishers*: Macmelodies Ltd.

*Date of Entry*: 31.5.58/ Pos: 23/Wks: 1
*Re-entry*: 14.6.58/Pos: 21/Wks: 1
*2nd re-entry*: 12.7.58/ Pos: 17/Wks: 9
*3rd re-entry*: 20.9.58/ Pos: 24/Wks: 4

Recordings:
| | | |
|---|---|---|
| Ted Heath and his Music | 3/58 | Decca F.11003 (& 45-) |
| Eddie Calvert – The Man with the Golden Trumpet | 3/58 | Columbia DB.4105 (& 45-) |
| Frank Cordell and his Orchestra with The Michael Sammes Singers | 4/58 | HMV POP.473 (& 45-) |
| Tony Brent | 5/58 | Columbia DB.4128 (& 45-) |
| The Johnston Brothers | 5/58 | Decca F.11021 (&45-) |
| Les Baxter and his Orchestra [Titled 'Piccolissima Serenata'] | 6/59 | Capitol 45-CL.15034★ |

| 901 | THE SECRET OF HAPPINESS (The Impala Theme) | | |
|---|---|---|---|

*Composers*: Hoyt Curtin & Carl Sigmund
*Publishers*: Essex Music Ltd.

*Date of Entry*:31.5.58
*Highest Position*: 24
*Weeks on Chart*: 1

Recordings:
| | | |
|---|---|---|
| Tony Osborne and his Orchestra | 5/58 | HMV POP.483 (& 45-) |
| Lorrae Desmond | 5/58 | Parlophone R.4430 (& 45-) |
| Kathie Kay with The Michael Sammes Singers | 5/58 | HMV POP.485 |
| Dinah Shore | 5/58 | RCA.1060 (& 45-) |
| Valerie Masters | 5/58 | Fontana H.132 (& 45-) |

| 902 | WITCH DOCTOR | | |
|---|---|---|---|

*Composer*: Ross Bagdasarin
*Publishers*: Bourne Music Ltd.

*Date of Entry*: 7.6.58
*Highest Position*: 8
*Weeks on Chart*: 10

Recordings:
| | | |
|---|---|---|
| David Seville with orchestra and vocal accompaniment effects by The Chipmunks | 5/58 | London HLU.8619 (& 45-) |
| Don Lang and his Frantic Five | 5/58 | HMV POP.488 (& 45-) |
| Jimmy Lloyd | 5/58 | Philips PB.827 (& 45-) |
| Paul Rich | 6/58 | Embassy WB.287 (& 45-) |
| Mickey Katz and his Orchestra (Titled 'Knish Doctor') | 9/58 | Capitol 45-CL.14926★ |

| 903 | TWILIGHT TIME | | |
|---|---|---|---|

*Composers*: Buck Ram, Morty Nevins, Al Nevins & Artie Dunn
*Publishers*: Victoria Music Publishing Co. Ltd.

*Date of Entry*: 7.6.58/ Pos: 7 / Wks: 17
*Re-entry*: 11.10.58/ Pos: 22 / Wks: 1:

Recordings:
| | | |
|---|---|---|
| The Platters | 5/58 | Mercury MT.214/ (45) 7MT.214 |
| Joe Loss and his Orchestra | 7/58 | HMV POP.508 (& 45-) |
| Earl Bostic and his Orchestra | 7/58 | Parlophone R.4460 (& 45-) |
| Rikki Henderson | 8/58 | Embassy WB.289 (& 45-) |

## 904 | THE BOOK OF LOVE

*Composers*: Warren Davies, George Malone
& Charles Patrick

*Publishers*: Francis Day & Hunter Ltd.

*Date of Entry*: 14.6.58

*Highest Position*: 7
*Weeks on Chart*: 11

*Recordings*:

| | | |
|---|---|---|
| The Monotones | 5/58 | London HLM.8625 (& 45-) |
| The Mudlarks | 5/58 | Columbia DB.4133 (& 45-) |
| Barry Barnett | 5/58 | HMV POP.487 (& 45-) |
| Paul Rich | 8/58 | Embassy WB.288 (& 45-) |

## 905 | ALL I HAVE TO DO IS DREAM

*Composer*: Boudleaux Bryant

*Publishers*: Acuff-Rose Publishing Co. Ltd.

*Date of Entry*: 14.6.58/
Pos: 2/Wks: 22

*Re-entry*: 22.11.58 /
Pos: 30 / Wks: 1

*Recordings*:

| | | |
|---|---|---|
| Barry Barnett | 5/58 | HMV POP.487 (& 45-) |
| The Everly Brothers | 5/58 | London HLA.8618 (& 45-) |
| Paul Rich | 6/58 | Embassy WB.287 (& 45-) |

## 906 | RETURN TO ME

*Composers*: Danny Di Minno &
Carmen Lombardo

*Publishers*: Southern Music Publishing Co. Ltd.

*Date of Entry*: 21.6.58

*Highest Position*: 4
*Weeks on Chart*: 23

*Recordings*:

| | | |
|---|---|---|
| Dean Martin | 3/58 | Capitol CL.14844 (& 45-) |
| Denny Dennis | 8/58 | Embassy WB.291 (& 45-) |
| Victor Silverster and his Ballroom Orchestra | 10/58 | Columbia DB.4198 (& 45-) |

## 907 | I NEED YOU

*Composer*: Joe Henderson
*Publishers*: Henderson Music Ltd.

*Date of Entry*: 21.6.58
*Highest Position*: 23
*Weeks on Chart*: 2

*Recordings*:

| | | |
|---|---|---|
| Marion Ryan with The Beryl Stott Group | 5/58 | Pye Nixa N.15138/ (45) 7N.15138 |
| Yana | 5/58 | HMV POP.481 (& 45-) |

## 908 | BIG MAN

*Composers*: Bruce Belland & Glenn Larson

*Publishers*: Grosvenor Music Ltd.

*Date of Entry*: 28.6.58
Pos: 5 / Wks: 14

*Re-entry*: 25.10.58 /
Pos: 30 / Wks: 1

*Recordings*:

| | | |
|---|---|---|
| The Four Preps | 5/58 | Capitol CL.14873 (& 45-) |
| The Stargazers | 6/58 | Decca F.11034 (& 45-) |
| The Five Dallas Boys | 6/58 | Columbia DB.4154 (& 45-) |
| Hal Burton | 8/58 | Embassy WB.290 (& 45-) |

## 909 | PURPLE PEOPLE EATER

*Composer*: Sheb Wooley
*Publishers*: Peter Maurice Music Co. Ltd.

*Date of Entry*: 28.6.58
*Highest Position*: 21
*Weeks on Chart*: 4

*Recordings*:

| | | |
|---|---|---|
| Jackie Dennis | 5/58 | Decca F.11033 (& 45-) |
| Sheb Wooley | 6/58 | MGM.981 (& 45-) |
| Barry Cryer | 6/58 | Fontana H.139 (& 45-) |
| Paul Rich | 8/58 | Embassy WB.288 (& 45-)★ |
| Mickey Katz and his Orchestra (Mickey Katz) [Titled 'The Poiple Kishke Eater'] | 9/58 | Capitol 45- CL.14926★ |

## 910 | TRUDIE

*Composer*: Joe Henderson
*Publishers*: Henderson Music Ltd.

*Date of Entry*: 5.7.58 /
Pos: 1 / Wks: 76

*Re-entry*: 9.1.60/
Pos: 25/Wks: 5

*Recordings*:

| | | |
|---|---|---|
| Joe 'Mr Piano' Henderson with The Beryl Stott Chorus | 5/58 | Pye Nixa N.15147/ (45) 7N.15147 |
| Harry Grove and his Music | 8/58 | Decca F.11050 (& 45-) |

## 911 SUGAR MOON

| | |
|---|---|
| *Composer*: Danny Wolfe | *Date of Entry*: 5.7.58 |
| *Publishers*: Frank Music Co. Ltd. | *Highest Position*: 12 |
| | *Weeks on Chart*: 13 |

*Recordings*:

| | | |
|---|---|---|
| Pat Boone | 6/58 | London HLD.8640 (& 45-) |
| Denny Dennis | 8/58 | Embassy WB.291 (& 45-) |

## 912 THE ONLY MAN ON THE ISLAND

| | |
|---|---|
| *Composers*: Bob Hilliard & Dave Mann | *Date of Entry*: 19.7.58 |
| *Publishers*: Sydney Bron Music Co. | *Highest Position*: 8 |
| | *Weeks on Chart*: 14 |

*Recordings*:

| | | |
|---|---|---|
| Tommy Steele and The Steelmen | 6/58 | Decca F.11041 (& 45-) |
| Vic Damone | 7/58 | Philips PB.837 (& 45-) |
| Dennis Lois | 7/58 | Columbia DB.4158 (& 45-) |
| Victor Silvester and his Ballroom Orchestra | 9/58 | Columbia DB.4186 (& 45-) |
| Paul Rich | 9/58 | Embassy WB.293 (& 45-) |

## 913 EV'RY HOUR, EV'RY DAY OF MY LIFE

| | |
|---|---|
| *Composer*: Clint Ballard Jr. | *Date of Entry*: 19.7.58 |
| *Publishers*: George Wiener Music Ltd. | *Highest Position*: 24 |
| | *Weeks on Chart*: 1 |

*Recordings*:

| | | |
|---|---|---|
| Vera Lynn (Titled 'Every hour, every day of my life') | 6/58 | Decca F.11038 (& 45-) |
| Malcolm Vaughan with The Michael Sammes Singers | 6/58 | HMV POP.502 (& 45-) |

## 914 ENDLESS SLEEP

| | |
|---|---|
| *Composers*: Jody Reynolds & Dolores Nance | *Date of Entry*: 26.7.58 |
| *Publishers*: Hill & Range Songs (London) Ltd. | *Highest Position*: 17 |
| | *Weeks on Chart*: 14 |

*Recordings*:

| | | |
|---|---|---|
| Gene Ross | 5/58 | Parlophone R.4434 (& 45-) |
| Marty Wilde and The Wildcats | 6/58 | Philips PB.835 (&45-) |
| Jody Reynolds | 6/58 | London HL.8651 (& 45-) |
| Paul Rich | 9/58 | Embassy WB.297 (& 45-) |

## 915 WHEN

| | |
|---|---|
| *Composers*: Jack Reardon & Paul Evans | *Date of Entry*: 2.8.58 |
| *Publishers*: Southern Music Publishing Co. Ltd. | *Highest Position*: 3 |
| | *Weeks on Chart*: 22 |

*Recordings*:

| | | |
|---|---|---|
| The Kalin Twins | 7/58 | Brunswick 05751 (& 45-) |
| Barry Barnett with The Michael Sammes Singers | 7/58 | HMV POP.511 (& 45-) |
| Johnny Worth | 9/58 | Embassy WB.299 (& 45-) |

## 916 HARD HEADED WOMAN

| | |
|---|---|
| *Composer*: Claude de Metruis | *Date of Entry*: 2.8.58 / Pos: 22 / Wks: 1 |
| *Publishers*: Belinda (London) Ltd. | *Re-entry*: 23.8.58 / Pos: 30 / Wks: 1 |

*Recordings*:

| | | |
|---|---|---|
| Elvis Presley with The Jordanaires | 7/58 | RCA.1070 (& 45-) |
| Paul Rich | 9/58 | Embassy WB.297 (& 45-) |

## 917 RAVE ON

| | |
|---|---|
| *Composers*: Norman Petty, Bill Tilghman & Sunny West | *Date of Entry*: 2.8.58 |
| *Publishers*: Southern Music Publishing Co. Ltd. | *Highest Position*: 22 |
| | *Weeks on Chart*: 4 |

*Recordings*:

| | | |
|---|---|---|
| Buddy Holly | 6/58 | Coral Q.72325 (& 45-) |
| Hal Burton | 8/58 | Embassy WB.290 (& 45-) |

## 918 PATRICIA

| | |
|---|---|
| *Composer*: Perez Prado | *Date of Entry*: 9.8.58 |
| *Publishers*: Latin-American Music Publishing Co. Ltd. | *Highest Position*: 13 |
| | *Weeks on Chart*: 13 |

*Recordings*:

| | | |
|---|---|---|
| Perez Prado and his Orchestra | 6/58 | RCA.1067 (& 45-) |
| Geoff Love and his Latin-American Rhythm | 7/58 | Columbia DB.4169 (& 45-) |
| Gordon Franks and his Orchestra | 9/58 | Embassy WB.294 (& 45-) |

## 919 WHEN THE BOYS TALK ABOUT THE GIRLS

| | | |
|---|---|---|
| *Composer:* Bob Merrill | | *Date of Entry:* 9.8.58 / Pos: 21 / Wks: 3 |
| *Publishers:* Lawrence Wright Music Co. Ltd. | | *Re-entry:* 6.9.58/ Pos: 25/Wks: 2 |

*Recordings:*

| | | |
|---|---|---|
| Valerie Carr | 5/58 | Columbia DB.4131 (& 45-) |
| Valerie Shane | 6/58 | Philips PB.833 (& 45-) |
| Victor Silvester and his Ballroom Orchestra | 10/58 | Columbia DB.4198 (& 45-)★ |

## 920 LITTLE BERNADETTE

| | |
|---|---|
| *Composers:* Peter Hart & Christopher Richardson | *Date of Entry:* 16.8.58 |
| *Publishers:* Berry Music Co. Ltd. | *Highest Position:* 10 *Weeks on Chart:* 13 |

*Recording:*

| | | |
|---|---|---|
| Harry Belafonte | 8/58 | RCA.1072 (& 45-) |

## 921 DEVOTION

| | |
|---|---|
| *Composer:* O. Cesana | *Date of Entry:* 16.8.58 |
| *Publishers:* Grosvenor Music Ltd. | *Highest Position:* 17 *Weeks on Chart:* 10 |

*Recordings:*

| | | |
|---|---|---|
| Petula Clark with The Beryl Stott Chorus | 7/58 | Pye Nixa N.15152/ (45) 7N.15152 |
| Peter Elliott | 7/58 | Parlophone R.4457 (& 45-) |
| Janice Harper | 7/58 | Capitol CL.14899 (& 45-) |
| Rikki Henderson | 9/58 | Embassy WB.298 (& 45-) |
| Victor Silvester and his Ballroom Orchestra | 11/58 | Columbia DB.4209 (& 45-)★ |

## 922 GOTTA HAVE RAIN

| | | |
|---|---|---|
| *Composer:* Max Bygraves | | *Date of Entry:* 16.8.58 / Pos: 25 / Wks: 1 |
| *Publishers:* Lakeview Music Publishing Co. | | *Re-entry:* 30.8.58 / Pos: 24 / Wks: 2 |

*Recordings:*

| | | |
|---|---|---|
| Max Bygraves | 7/58 | Decca F.11046 (& 45-) |
| Eydie Gorme | 7/58 | HMV POP.513 (& 45-) |

## 923 LITTLE TRAIN (Die Kleine Bimmelbahn)

| | |
|---|---|
| *Composers:* Charles Andre & Erich Storz | *Date of Entry:* 16.8.58 |
| *Publishers:* B.F. Wood Music Co. Inc. | *Highest Position:* 25 *Weeks on Chart:* 2 |

*Recording:*

| | | |
|---|---|---|
| Max Bygraves | 7/58 | Decca F.11046 (&45-) |

## 924 WOULDN'T IT BE LOVERLY?

| | |
|---|---|
| *Composers:* Alan Jay Lerner & Frederick Loewe | *Date of Entry:* 16.8.58 |
| *Publishers:* Chappell & Co. Ltd. | *Highest Position:* 27 *Weeks on Chart:* 1 |

*Recordings:*

| | | |
|---|---|---|
| Jo Stafford | 5/58 | Philips PB.818 (& 45-) |
| Joe Loss and his Orchestra | 5/58 | HMV POP.478 (& 45-) |
| Jeannie Carson with The Rita Williams Singers | 5/58 | Columbia DB.4125 (& 45-) |

## 925 FLY AWAY LOVERS

| | |
|---|---|
| *Composers:* Frank Stanton & Tommie Connor | *Date of Entry:* 16.8.58 |
| *Publishers:* David Toff Music Publishing Co. Ltd. | *Highest Position:* 22 *Weeks on Chart:* 3 |

*Recording:*

| | | |
|---|---|---|
| Alma Cogan with The Michael Sammes Singers | 7/58 | HMV POP.500 (& 45-) |

## 926 LEFT RIGHT OUT OF MY (YOUR) HEART

| | | |
|---|---|---|
| *Composers:* Earl Shuman & Mort Garson | | *Date of Entry:* 23.8.58 / Pos: 24 / Wks: 2 |
| *Publishers:* Sterling Music Publishing Co. Ltd. | | *Re-entry:* 13.9.58 / Pos: 29 / Wks: 1 |

*Recordings:*
(a) Titled 'Left right out of my heart'

| | | |
|---|---|---|
| The Beverley Sisters | 6/58 | Decca F.11042 (& 45-) |
| Eve Boswell | 7/58 | Parlophone R.4455 (& 45-) |
| Joan Savage | 7/58 | Columbia DB.4159 (& 45-) |

(b) Titled 'Left right out of your heart'

| | | |
|---|---|---|
| Patti Page | 7/58 | Mercury MT.223 (& 45-) |

## 927 | HILLSIDE IN SCOTLAND

| | | |
|---|---|---|
| *Composers*: Stanley Clayton, Ruth Roberts & William Katz | | *Date of Entry*: 23.8.58 |
| *Publishers*: Carrie Music Ltd. | | *Highest Position*: 26<br>*Weeks on Chart*: 3 |

*Recordings*:

| | | |
|---|---|---|
| Debbie Reynolds | 5/58 | Coral Q.72324<br>(& 45-) |
| Kathie Kay | 6/58 | HMV POP.498<br>(& 45-) |
| Lita Roza | 6/58 | Pye Nixa N.15149/<br>(45) 7N.15149 |
| Nancy Whiskey | 7/58 | Oriole CB.1452<br>(& 45-) |
| Bridie Gallagher | 7/58 | Beltona BE.2705 |

## 928 | I KNOW WHERE I'M GOING

| | | |
|---|---|---|
| *Composers*: Traditional | | *Date of Entry*: 23.8.58 /<br>Pos: 28 / Wks: 2 |
| *Publishers*: Cavendish Music Co. Ltd. | | *Re-entry*: 20.9.58 /<br>Pos: 28 / Wks: 2 |

*Recordings*:

| | | |
|---|---|---|
| Kathleen Ferrier (contralto) | 10/52 | Decca M.681 |
| The Tarriers | 6/58 | Columbia DB.4148<br>(& 45-) |
| George Hamilton IV | 6/58 | HMV POP.505<br>(& 45-) |
| Glen Mason | 6/58 | Parlophone R.4451<br>(& 45-) |
| Nancy Whiskey | 7/58 | Oriole CB.1452<br>(& 45-) |

## 929 | VOLARE<br>(Nel blu dipinto di blu)

| | | |
|---|---|---|
| *Composers*: Domenico Modugno, Franco Migliacci & Mitchell Parish | | *Date of Entry*: 30.8.58 |
| *Publishers*: Robbins Music Corporation Ltd. | | *Highest Position*: 1<br>*Weeks on Chart*: 21 |

*Recordings*:

| | | |
|---|---|---|
| Marino Marini and his Quartet | 8/58 | Durium DC.16632<br>(& 45-) |
| The McGuire Sisters | 8/58 | Coral Q.72334 (& 45-) |
| Alan Dale | 8/58 | MGM.986 (& 45-) |
| Dean Martin | 8/58 | Capitol CL.14910<br>(& 45-) |
| Domenico Modugno | 8/58 | Oriole ICB.5000<br>(& 45-) |
| Lita Roza with The Beryl Stott Chorus<br>(Titled 'Nel blu dipinto di blu') | 8/58 | Pye Nixa N.15155/<br>(45) 7N.15155 |

| | | |
|---|---|---|
| Anne Shelton | 8/58 | Philips PB.852<br>(& 45-) |
| The Music of Nelson Riddle (tenor sax:<br>Plas Johnson) | 8/58 | Capitol 45-CL.14911 |
| Ronald Chesney (harmonica) | 8/58 | HMV POP.519<br>(& 45-) |
| Cyril Stapleton and his Orchestra | 8/58 | Decca F.11049<br>(& 45-) |
| Jimmy Young | 8/58 | Columbia DB.4176<br>(& 45-) |
| Joe Loss and his Orchestra (played as a<br>cha cha) | 9/58 | HMV POP.523<br>(& 45-) |
| Rikki Henderson | 9/58 | Embassy WB.298<br>(& 45-) |
| Charlie Drake | 10/58 | Parlophone R.4478<br>(& 45-) |
| Ted Heath and his Music | 10/58 | Decca F.11063<br>(& 45-) |
| Victor Silvester and his Ballroom<br>Orchestra | 10/58 | Columbia DB.4197<br>(& 45-) |

## 930 | TORERO

| | | |
|---|---|---|
| *Composers*: Renato Carosone, D. Nisa,<br>Al Hoffman & Dick Manning | | *Date of Entry*: 30.8.58 |
| *Publishers*: Leeds Music Ltd. | | *Highest Position*: 25<br>*Weeks on Chart*: 3 |

*Recordings*:

| | | |
|---|---|---|
| The Andrews Sisters | 5/58 | Capitol 45-CL.14878 |
| The Kaye Sisters | 5/58 | Philips PB.832 (& 45-) |
| The King Brothers with The Rita<br>Williams Singers | 5/58 | Parlophone R.4438<br>(& 45-) |
| Julius La Rosa | 6/58 | RCA.1063 (& 45-) |
| The Southlanders | 6/58 | Decca F.11032<br>(& 45-) |
| Renato Carosone (vocal) and his Sextet | 6/58 | Parlophone R.4433<br>(& 45-) |
| Ralph Marterie and his Orchestra | 8/58 | Mercury MT.232/<br>(45) 7MT.232 |
| Rikki Henderson | 9/58 | Embassy WB.294<br>(& 45-) |

## 931 | EVERYBODY LOVES A LOVER

| | | |
|---|---|---|
| *Composers*: Richard Adler & Robert Allen | | *Date of Entry*: 30.8.58 /<br>Pos: 27 / Wks: 1 |
| *Publishers*: Larry Spier Ltd. | | *Re-entry*: 4.10.58 /<br>Pos: 26 / Wks: 1<br>*2nd re-entry*: 18.10.58 /<br>Pos: 25 / Wks: 5 |

*Recordings*:

| | | |
|---|---|---|
| Doris Day | 8/58 | Philips PB.843 (& 45-) |
| Joe Loss and his Orchestra | 9/58 | HMV POP.524<br>(& 45-) |

## 932 | CAROLINA MOON

*Composers*: Joe Burke & Benny Davis    *Date of Entry*: 30.8.58

*Publishers*: Lawrence Wright Music Co. Ltd.    *Highest Position*: 3
*Weeks on Chart*: 23

*Recordings*:
| | | |
|---|---|---|
| Connie Francis | 8/58 | MGM.985 (& 45-) |
| Joe Loss and his Orchestra | 9/58 | HMV POP 524 (& 45-) |
| Maureen Evans | 10/58 | Embassy WB.300 |

## 933 | MOON TALK

*Composers*: Al Hoffman & Dick Manning    *Date of Entry*: 6.9.58

*Publishers*: Leeds Music Ltd.    *Highest Position*: 11
*Weeks on Chart*: 15

*Recordings*:
| | | |
|---|---|---|
| Perry Como with The Ray Charles Singers | 8/58 | RCA.1071 (& 45-) |
| Rikki Henderson | 10/58 | Embassy WB.302 (& 45-) |
| Victor Silvester and his Ballroom Orchestra | 11/58 | Columbia DB.4209 (& 45-) |

## 934 | STUPID CUPID

*Composers*: Howard Greenfield & Neil Sedaka    *Date of Entry*: 6.9.58

*Publishers*: Aldon Music Ltd.    *Highest Position*: 7
*Weeks on Chart*: 17

*Recordings*:
| | | |
|---|---|---|
| Connie Francis | 8/58 | MGM.985 (& 45-) |
| Maureen Evans | 10/58 | Embassy WB.300 (& 45-) |

## 935 | IF DREAMS CAME TRUE

*Composers*: Robert Allen & Al Stillman    *Date of Entry*: 13.9.58

*Publishers*: Grosvenor Music Ltd.    *Highest Position*: 17
*Weeks on Chart*: 13

*Recordings*:
| | | |
|---|---|---|
| Pat Boone | 8/58 | London HLD.8675 (& 45-) |
| Rikki Henderson | 10/58 | Embassy WB.302 (& 45-) |

## 936 | THINK IT OVER

*Composers*: Buddy Holly, Norman Petty & Jerry Allison    *Date of Entry*: 13.9.58

*Publishers*: Southern Music Publishing Co. Ltd.    *Highest Position*: 27
*Weeks on Chart*: 1

*Recording*:
| | | |
|---|---|---|
| Buddy Holly and The Crickets | 7/58 | Coral Q.72329 (& 45-) |

## 937 | GOT A MATCH?

*Composers*: Billy Mure & Dick Wolf    *Date of Entry*: 13.9.58

*Publishers*: Cromwell Music Ltd.    *Highest Position*: 28
*Weeks on Chart*: 1

*Recordings*:
| | | |
|---|---|---|
| Lou Stein and his Orchestra | 7/58 | Mercury (45) 7MT.226 |
| Russ Conway (piano) | 7/58 | Columbia DB.4166 (& 45-) |
| Frank Gallup | 7/58 | HMV POP.509 (& 45-) |
| The Daddy-O's | 7/58 | Oriole CB.1454 (& 45-) |
| Wee Willie Harris | 7/58 | Decca F.11044 (& 45-) |

## 938 | MAD PASSIONATE LOVE

*Composers*: Dick Sherman & David E. Coleman    *Date of Entry*: 13.9.58

*Publishers*: Duchess Music Ltd.    *Highest Position*: 6
*Weeks on Chart*: 17

*Recording*:
| | | |
|---|---|---|
| Bernard Bresslaw | 8/58 | HMV POP.522 (& 45-) |

## 939 | POOR LITTLE FOOL

*Composer*: Shari Sheeley    *Date of Entry*: 20.9.58

*Publishers*: Commodore-Imperial Music Ltd.    *Highest Position*: 14
*Weeks on Chart*: 11

*Recordings*:
| | | |
|---|---|---|
| Ricky Nelson | 8/58 | London HLP.8670 (& 45-) |
| Paul Rich | 10/58 | Embassy WB.301 (& 45-) |

## 940 BORN TOO LATE

| | | |
|---|---|---|
| *Composers*: Fred Tobias & Charles Strouse | *Date of Entry*: 20.9.58 | |
| *Publishers*: Anglo-Pic Music Co. Ltd. | *Highest Position*: 6 *Weeks on Chart*: 13 | |

*Recordings*:

| | | |
|---|---|---|
| The Poni-Tails (some records labelled 'Pony-Tails') | 8/58 | HMV POP.516 (& 45-) |
| Maureen Evans | 10/58 | Embassy WB.303 (& 45-) |

## 941 GIRL OF MY DREAMS

| | | |
|---|---|---|
| *Composer*: Sonny Clapp | *Date of Entry*: 27.9.58 | |
| *Publishers*: Lawrence Wright Music Co. Ltd. | *Highest Position*: 22 *Weeks on Chart*: 6 | |

(Note: Many earlier recordings of the song had been deleted before its revival here, including versions by Layton and Johnstone, Bing Crosby and Perry Como.)

*Later recordings*:

| | | |
|---|---|---|
| Bobby Mickleburgh's Bob Cats | 4/55 | Esquire 10–440 |
| Amos Milburn and his Band | 5/57 | Vogue V.9064 (& 45-) |
| Gerry Granahan | 8/58 | London HL.8668 (& 45-) |
| Tony Brent | 8/58 | Columbia DB.4177 (& 45-) |
| Joe Loss and his Orchestra | 10/58 | HMV POP.535 (& 45-) |

## 942 MORE THAN EVER (Come Prima)

| | | |
|---|---|---|
| *Composers*: M. Panzeri, S. Taccani & Y. Di Piola – English words by Mary Bond | *Date of Entry*: 4.10.58 | |
| *Publishers*: Chappell & Co. Ltd. | *Highest Position*: 1 *Weeks on Chart*: 20 | |

*Recordings*:
(a) Titled 'Come Prima':

| | | |
|---|---|---|
| Marino Marini and his Quartet | 8/58 | Durium DC.16632 (& 45-) |
| Norrie Paramor and his Orchestra | 10/58 | Columbia DB.4196 (& 45-) |
| Les Baxter and his Orchestra | 12/58 | Capitol CL.14964 (& 45-) |
| Domenico Modugno | 12/58 | Oriole CB.1475 (& 45-) |

(b) Titled 'More than ever':

| | | |
|---|---|---|
| Edmund Hockridge | 9/58 | Pye Nixa N.15160/ (45) 7N.15160 |
| Tony Dalli | 9/58 | Columbia DB.4195 (& 45-) |

| | | |
|---|---|---|
| Jackie Dennis | 10/58 | Decca F.11060 (& 45-) |
| Malcolm Vaughan with The Michael Sammes Singers | 10/58 | HMV POP.538 (& 45-) |
| Joe Loss and his Orchestra | 10/58 | HMV POP.535 (& 45-) |
| Robert Earl | 10/58 | Philips PB.867 (& 45-) |
| Jackie Rae | 10/58 | Fontana H.155 (& 45-) |
| Ted Heath and his Music | 10/58 | Decca F.11063 (& 45-) |
| Eve Boswell | 10/58 | Parlophone R.4479 (& 45-) |
| Barry Kendall | 10/58 | Embassy WB.304 (& 45-) |
| Victor Silvester and his Ballroom Orchestra | 11/58 | Columbia DB.4208 (& 45-) |

## 943 A CERTAIN SMILE

| | | |
|---|---|---|
| *Composers*: Sammy Fain & Paul Francis Webster | *Date of Entry*: 4.10.58 | |
| *Publishers*: Robbins Music Corporation Ltd. | *Highest Position*: 2 *Weeks on Chart*: 26 | |

*Recordings*:

| | | |
|---|---|---|
| Johnny Mathis | 8/58 | Fontana H.142 (& 45-) |
| The Jones Boys | 8/58 | Columbia DB.4170 (& 45-) |
| Sandy Stewart | 9/58 | London HLE.8683 (& 45-) |
| Sunny Gale | 9/58 | Brunswick 05753 (& 45-) |
| Paul Rich | 9/58 | Embassy WB.295 (& 45-) |
| Andy Russell | 9/58 | RCA.1076 (& 45-) |
| Victor Silvester and his Ballroom Orchestra | 10/58 | Columbia DB.4197 (& 45-) |
| Mantovani and his Orchestra | 11/58 | Decca F.11078 (& 45-) |

## 944 BIRD DOG

| | | |
|---|---|---|
| *Composer*: Boudleaux Bryant | *Date of Entry*: 4.10.58 | |
| *Publishers*: Acuff-Rose Publishing Co. Ltd. | *Highest Position*: 8 *Weeks on Chart*: 14 | |

*Recordings*:

| | | |
|---|---|---|
| The Everly Brothers | 8/58 | London HLA.8685 (& 45-) |
| Paul Rich | 10/58 | Embassy WB.301 (& 45-) |
| Morris and Mitch | 12/58 | Decca F.11086 (& 45-) |

## 945 | SPLISH SPLASH

| | | |
|---|---|---|
| *Composers:* Bobby Darin & Jean Murray | *Date of Entry:* 4.10.58 | |
| *Publishers:* Good Music Ltd. | *Highest Position:* 28 | |
| | *Weeks on Chart:* 1 | |

*Recordings:*

| | | |
|---|---|---|
| Bobby Darin | 7/58 | London HLE.8666 (& 45-) |
| Charlie Drake | 7/58 | Parlophone R.4461(& 45-) |
| Johnny Worth | 9/58 | Embassy WB.299 (& 45-) |

## 946 | KING CREOLE

| | | |
|---|---|---|
| *Composers:* Jerry Leiber & Mike Stoller | *Date of Entry:* 11.10.58 | |
| *Publishers:* Seventeen Savile Row Ltd. | *Highest Position:* 21 | |
| | *Weeks on Chart:* 6 | |

*Recordings:*

| | | |
|---|---|---|
| Elvis Presley with The Jordanaires | 9/58 | RCA.1081 (& 45-) |
| Johnny Worth | 10/58 | Embassy WB.305 (& 45-) |

## 947 | THE WORLD GOES AROUND AND AROUND

| | | |
|---|---|---|
| *Composers:* Tolchard Evans & Canwell Charles | *Date of Entry:* 11.10.58 | |
| *Publishers:* Sydney Bron Music Co. | *Highest Position:* 24 | |
| | *Weeks on Chart:* 3 | |

*Recordings:*

| | | |
|---|---|---|
| Marion Ryan | 8/58 | Pye Nixa N.15157/ (45) 7N.15157 |
| Victor Silvester and his Ballroom Orchestra | 11/58 | Columbia DB.4208 (& 45-)★ |

## 948 | IT'S ALL IN THE GAME

| | | |
|---|---|---|
| *Composer:* General Charles Gates Dawes – adaptation and lyrics by Carl Sigman | *Date of Entry:* 18.10.58 | |
| *Publishers:* Blossom Music Ltd. | *Highest Position:* 4 | |
| | *Weeks on Chart:* 17 | |

(Note: All but one of the recordings issued at the beginning of 1952 had been deleted by the time this song went into the charts in 1958.)

*Recordings:*

| | | |
|---|---|---|
| Louis Armstrong with Gordon Jenkins and his Orchestra | 1/52 | Brunswick 04858 |
| Nat 'King' Cole | 5/57 | Capitol CL.14733 (& 45-) |
| Tommy Edwards | 9/58 | MGM.989 (& 45-) |
| Barry Kendall | 10/58 | Embassy WB.304 (& 45-) |
| Victor Silvester and his Ballroom Orchestra | 12/58 | Columbia DB.4227 (& 45-) |

## 949 | MOVE IT

| | | |
|---|---|---|
| *Composer:* Ian Samwell | *Date of Entry:* 18.10.58 | |
| *Publishers:* B.F. Wood Music Co. Inc. | *Highest Position:* 14 | |
| | *Weeks on Chart:* 8 | |

*Recordings:*

| | | |
|---|---|---|
| Cliff Richard with The Drifters | 8/58 | Columbia DB.4178 (& 45-) |
| Hal Burton | 11/58 | Embassy WB.308 (& 45-) |

## 950 | THERE'S NEVER BEEN A NIGHT

| | | |
|---|---|---|
| *Composers:* Irwin Schuster & Bob Davie | *Date of Entry:* 25.10.58/ Pos: 28/Wks: 1 | |
| *Publishers:* Leeds Music Ltd. | *Re-entry:* 8.11.58 / Pos: 26 / Wks: 3 | |
| | *2nd re-entry:* 13.12.58 / Pos: 29 / Wks: 3 | |

*Recordings:*

| | | |
|---|---|---|
| Alma Cogan with The Michael Sammes Singers | 9/58 | HMV POP.531 (& 45-) |
| The Mudlarks | 9/58 | Columbia DB.4190 (& 45-) |
| Betty Johnson | 9/58 | London HLE.8701 (& 45-) |
| Shirley Bassey | 10/58 | Philips PB.860 (& 45-) |

## 951 | LITTLE ONE

| | | |
|---|---|---|
| *Composer:* Ronald Hulme | *Date of Entry:* 25.10.58/ Pos: 29/Wks: 1 | |
| *Publishers:* David Toff Music Publishing Co. Ltd. | *Re-entry:* 15.11.58 / Pos: 29 / Wks: 1 | |

*Recordings:*

| | | |
|---|---|---|
| Russ Hamilton | 2/58 | Oriole CB.1404 (& 45-) |
| Ruby Murray | 9/58 | Columbia DB.4192 (& 45-) |

## 952 | HOOTS MON

| | | |
|---|---|---|
| *Composer:* Harry Robertson | *Date of Entry:* 1.11.58 / Pos: 5 / Wks: 16 | |
| *Publishers:* Southern Music Publishing Co. Ltd. | *Re-entry:* 14.3.59 / Pos: 29 / Wks: 1 | |

*Recordings:*

| | | |
|---|---|---|
| Lord Rockingham's XI | 9/58 | Decca F.11059 (& 45-) |
| Gordon Franks and his Orchestra | 1/59 | Embassy WB.312 (& 45-) |

## 953 THE HULA HOOP SONG

| | | |
|---|---|---|
| *Composers*: Carl Maduri & Donna Kohler | | *Date of Entry*: 1.11.58 |
| *Publishers*: Leeds Music Ltd. | | *Highest Position*: 27 |
| | | *Weeks on Chart*: 1 |

*Recordings*:

| | | |
|---|---|---|
| Georgia Gibbs | 10/58 | Columbia DB.4201 (& 45-) |
| Teresa Brewer | 10/58 | Coral Q.72340 (& 45-) |
| Maureen Evans | 11/58 | Embassy WB.309 (& 45-) |

## 954 SOMEDAY

| | | |
|---|---|---|
| *Composer*: Jimmie Hodges | | *Date of Entry*: 1.11.58 |
| *Publishers*: Duchess Music Ltd. | | *Highest Position*: 6 |
| | | *Weeks on Chart*: 21 |

(Note: This is a revival of the song titled 'Someday you'll want me to want you' – see Song No. 32. None of the recordings listed for 1946 were still available.)

*Later recordings*:

| | | |
|---|---|---|
| Billy Farrell (Titled 'Someday you'll want me to want you') | 5/58 | Philips PB.828 (& 45-) |
| Jodie Sands | 9/58 | HMV POP.533 (& 45-) |
| Ricky Nelson | 10/58 | London HLP.8732 (& 45-) |

## 955 SUSIE DARLIN'

| | | |
|---|---|---|
| *Composer*: Robin Luke | | *Date of Entry*: 8.11.58 |
| *Publishers*: B.F. Wood Music Co. Inc. | | *Highest Position*: 24 |
| | | *Weeks on Chart*: 5 |

*Recordings*:

| | | |
|---|---|---|
| Robin Luke | 8/58 | London HLD.8676 (& 45-) |
| Barry Barnett | 9/58 | HMV POP.532 (& 45-) |
| Chris Howland | 9/58 | Columbia DB.4194 (& 45-) |
| Hal Burton | 11/58 | Embassy WB.308 (& 45-) |

## 956 BLUE, BLUE DAY

| | | |
|---|---|---|
| *Composer*: Don Gibson | | *Date of Entry*: 8.11.58 |
| *Publishers*: Acuff-Rose Publishing Co. Ltd. | | *Highest Position*: 30 |
| | | *Weeks on Chart*: 1 |

*Recordings*:

| | | |
|---|---|---|
| Lorrae Desmond | 8/58 | Parlophone R.4463 (& 45-) |
| Don Gibson | 8/58 | RCA.1073 (& 45-) |

## 957 IT'S ONLY MAKE BELIEVE

| | | |
|---|---|---|
| *Composers*: Conway Twitty & Jack Nance | | *Date of Entry*: 15.11.58 |
| *Publishers*: Francis Day & Hunter Ltd. | | *Highest Position*: 2 |
| | | *Weeks on Chart*: 16 |

*Recordings*:

| | | |
|---|---|---|
| Conway Twitty with The Jordanaires | 10/58 | MGM.992 (& 45-) |
| Jimmy Starr | 10/58 | London HL.8731 (& 45-) |
| Johnny Worth | 1/59 | Embassy WB.315 (& 45-) |

## 958 LOVE MAKES THE WORLD GO ROUND

| | | |
|---|---|---|
| *Composer*: Ollie Jones | | *Date of Entry*: 15.11.58 |
| *Publishers*: Chappell & Co. Ltd. | | *Highest Position*: 13 |
| | | *Weeks on Chart*: 13 |

*Recordings*:

| | | |
|---|---|---|
| Tennessee Ernie Ford | 7/58 | Capitol 45-CL.14896 |
| Perry Como with The Ray Charles Singers | 10/58 | RCA.1086 (& 45-) |
| Rikki Henderson | 2/59 | Embassy WB.314 (& 45-) |

## 959/ 960 TOM DOOLEY

For the first time in the history of the British Sheet Music Charts, two arrangements of the same song appeared at the same time. It has proved difficult to tie up exactly the recordings with the two sheet music versions, and what we have managed to establish is as follows:
Song No. 959 – The version as recorded by The Kingston Trio
Song No. 960 – The version as recorded by Lonnie Donegan and his Skiffle Group
Each of the versions was published by a different publisher and details as shown below will specify which recording applies to which publisher, although there are some recordings which do not exactly tie-in with either publisher. Record labels, examined in each case, are no help at all in these latter cases. Examination of the play-list on Radio Luxembourg's Top Twenty Show at the time shows that on the first week of entry, the Lonnie Donegan recording was played. However, the sales of both versions of the sheet music had been combined to produce that first week's placing. On each of the subsequent weeks the correct versions of either Donegan or the Kingston Trio was played to match the sheet music publisher as listed by the Music Publisher's Association, which of course meant that for nine weeks both versions appeared in the same Top Twenty.

We have listed each version in the normal way below, with recordings shown under each as usual, but we have had to add another section to include those versions which, as stated above, do not attach themselves particularly to either publisher.

## 959 TOM DOOLEY

*Composers*: Traditional arranged by Dave Guard
*Publishers*: Ardmore & Beechwood Ltd.

*Date of Entry*: 22.11.58
*Highest Position*: 14
*Weeks on Chart*: 11

(Note: The Sheet Music for this version contains a spoken verse introduction and is arranged in the key of F. There is also a variance in one line of the lyric as opposed to Song No. 960, the Lonnie Donegan recording – the Kingston Trio sing 'Down in the lonesome valley' while Lonnie Donegan's has 'In some lonesome valley'.)

*Recordings*:

| | | |
|---|---|---|
| The Kingston Trio | 11/58 | Capitol CL.14951 (& 45-) |
| Johnny Worth | 1/59 | Embassy WB.312 (& 45-) |

## 960 TOM DOOLEY

*Composers*: Traditional, arranged by Frank Warner, Alan Lomax & John A. Lomax
*Publishers*: Essex Music Ltd.

*Date of Entry*: 22.11.58
*Highest Position*: 7
*Weeks on Chart*: 15

(Note: The Sheet Music for this version is arranged in the key of G.)

*Recordings*:

| | | |
|---|---|---|
| Lonnie Donegan and his Skiffle Group | 11/58 | Pye Nixa N.15172/ (45) 7N.15172 |
| Pinky and Perky | 12/58 | Decca F.11095 (& 45-) |

## 959/960 TOM DOOLEY

*Other recorded versions are as follows:*

| | | |
|---|---|---|
| The Tarriers (arr. Alan Arkin, Bob Carey & Eric Darling) | 6/57 | Columbia DB.3961 (& 45-) |
| The City Ramblers Skiffle Group with Jimmie MacGregor | 8/57 | Tempo A.161 (& 45-) |
| The 2.19 Skiffle Group with Mik Lauder and Mike Wallace | 10/57 | Esquire 10–509 |
| Rikki Price (arr. Richards) | 11/58 | Fontana H.162 (& 45-) |
| The Nigerian Union Rhythm Group (sub-titled 'Oko Iyawo Atiale') [trad. lyrics arr. B. Hughes] | 2/59 | Melodisc 1503 |

## 961 MANDOLINS IN THE MOONLIGHT

*Composers*: George Weiss & Aaron Schroeder
*Publishers*: Yale Music Corporation Ltd.

*Date of Entry*: 22.11.58
*Highest Position*: 6
*Weeks on Chart*: 16

*Recording*:

| | | |
|---|---|---|
| Perry Como with The Ray Charles Singers | 10/58 | RCA.1086 (& 45-) |

## 962 I HEARD THE BELLS ON CHRISTMAS DAY

*Composer*: John Marks, who wrote the music and adapted words originally written by Henry Wadsworth Longfellow
*Publishers*: Chappell & Co. Ltd.

*Date of Entry*: 22.11.58
*Highest Position*: 14
*Weeks on Chart*: 6

*Recordings*:

| | | |
|---|---|---|
| Fred Waring and his Pennsylvanians with organ and bells | 10/58 | Capitol 45-CL.14946 |
| Belafonte | 10/58 | RCA.1084 (& 45-) |
| Bing Crosby with The Ken Darby Singers | 11/58 | Brunswick 05764 (& 45-) |
| Barry Kendall | 12/58 | Embassy WB.311 (& 45-) |

## 963 SON OF MARY

*Composers*: Adapted from the traditional melody 'Greensleeves' by M. Okun, R. Corman & C. Carter
*Publishers*: Chappell & Co. Ltd.

*Date of Entry*: 29.11.58
*Highest Position*: 12
*Weeks on Chart*: 6

*Recording*:

| | | |
|---|---|---|
| Belafonte | 10/58 | RCA.1084 (& 45-) |

## 964 THE END

*Composers*: Sid Jacobson & Jimmy Krondes
*Publishers*: Sydney Bron Music Co.

*Date of Entry*: 29.11.58/ Pos: 26/Wks: 1
*Re-entry*: 3.1.59/ Pos: 24/Wks: 1

*Recordings*:

| | | |
|---|---|---|
| Earl Grant | 10/58 | Brunswick 05762 (& 45-) |
| Glen Mason | 10/58 | Parlophone R.4485 (& 45-) |
| Jimmy Lloyd | 11/58 | Philips PB.871 (& 45-) |

## 965 REAL LOVE

*Composers*: Bobby Darin & Woody Harris
*Publishers*: Progressive Music Ltd.

*Date of Entry*: 6.12.58/ Pos: 14/Wks: 9
*Re-entry*: 14.2.59 / Pos: 26 / Wks: 1

*Recordings*:

| | | |
|---|---|---|
| Ruby Murray | 9/58 | Columbia DB.4192 (& 45-) |
| The Chas McDevitt Group (Shirley Douglas) | 9/58 | Oriole CB.1457 (& 45-) |

## 966 | TEA FOR TWO CHA CHA

| | | |
|---|---|---|
| *Composer*: Vincent Youmans | | *Date of Entry*: 6.12.58 / Pos: 14 / Wks: 12 |
| *Publishers*: Chappell & Co. Ltd. | | *Re-entry*: 28.3.59 / Pos: 30 / Wks: 1 |

(Note: This was a cha cha arrangement of the Vincent Youmans and Irving Caesar song 'Tea for Two'. Therefore it is not relevant to list here any recorded versions of the song set in any other style but in the cha cha rhythms.)

*Recordings*:

| | | |
|---|---|---|
| The Tommy Dorsey Orchestra featuring Warren Covington (trombone) | 9/58 | Brunswick 05757 (& 45-) |
| Gordon Franks and his Orchestra | 1/59 | Embassy WB.310 (& 45-) |

## 967 | THE DAY THE RAINS CAME
### (Le Jour ou la pluie viendra)

| | | |
|---|---|---|
| *Composers*: Gilbert Becaud, Pierre Delanoe & Carl Sigman | | *Date of Entry*: 13.12.58 |
| *Publishers*: John Fields Music Co. Ltd. | | *Highest Position*: 1 *Weeks on Chart*: 18 |

*Recordings*:

| | | |
|---|---|---|
| Raymonde Le Fevre and his Orchestra | 11/58 | Felsted 45-SD.80057 |
| Jane Morgan ('A' side – Titled 'The Day the rains came') | 11/58 | London HLR.8751 (& 45-) |
| Jane Morgan ('B' side – Titled 'Le Jour ou la pluie viendra') | 11/58 | London HLR.8751 (& 45-) |
| Al Saxon | 11/58 | Fontana H.164 (& 45-) |
| The Jones Boys | 11/58 | Columbia DB.4217 (& 45-) |
| Ronnie Hilton with The Michael Sammes Singers | 11/58 | HMV POP.556 (& 45-) |
| Georges Jouvin (trumpet) and his Ensemble | 12/58 | HMV POP.565 (& 45-) |
| Gilbert Becaud | 12/58 | HMV POP.574 (& 45-) |
| Claude Luter and his Orchestra | 2/59 | Vogue V.9132 (& 45-) |
| Maureen Evans | 2/59 | Embassy WB.316 (& 45-) |

## 968 | AS I LOVE YOU
### (more and more and more)

| | | |
|---|---|---|
| *Composers*: Jay Livingston & Ray Evans | | *Date of Entry*: 20.12.58/ Pos: 1/Wks: 23 |
| *Publishers*: Macmelodies Ltd. | | *Re-entry*: 13.6.59 / Pos: 26/ Wks: 1 |

*Recordings*:

| | | |
|---|---|---|
| Carmen McRae | 3/58 | Brunswick 05738 (& 45-) |
| Shirley Bassey | 8/58 | Philips PB.845 (& 45-) |
| Ronnie Hilton with The Michael Sammes Singers | 12/58 | HMV POP.559 (& 45-) |
| Victor Silvester and his Ballroom Orchestra | 2/59 | Columbia DB.4258 (& 45-) |
| Jean Scott | 3/59 | Embassy WB.323 (& 45-) |

## 969 | WINTER WONDERLAND

| | | |
|---|---|---|
| *Composers*: Felix Bernard & Dick Smith | | *Date of Entry*: 20.12.58 |
| *Publishers*: Francis Day & Hunter Ltd. | | *Highest Position*: 27 *Weeks on Chart*: 3 |

(Note: The recording by Perry Como with The Satisfyers, first released in 12/47 on HMV BD.1187, was deleted from the catalogue on 30 September 1958, less than three months before the song's chart entry.)

*Later recordings*:

| | | |
|---|---|---|
| The Chet Baker Quartet | 5/54 | Vogue V.2232 |
| Rosemary Clooney | 11/55 | Philips PB.530 |
| Terry Lightfoot and his Jazzmen | 11/57 | Columbia DB.4032 (& 45-) |
| The King Brothers | 11/57 | Parlophone R.4367 (& 45-) |
| Johnny Mathis | 11/58 | Fontana H.165 (& 45-) |

## 970 | TO KNOW HIM IS TO LOVE HIM

| | | |
|---|---|---|
| *Composer*: Philip Spector | | *Date of Entry*: 20.12.58 |
| *Publishers*: Bourne Music Ltd. | | *Highest Position*: 3 *Weeks on Chart*: 18 |

*Recordings*:

| | | |
|---|---|---|
| The Teddy Bears | 10/58 | London HLN.8733 (& 45-) |
| Evelyn Kingsley with The Towers (inst) | 10/58 | Capitol 45-CL.14944 |
| Maureen Evans | 2/59 | Embassy WB.319 (& 45-) |

# 1959

What a year this was for pianist Russ Conway. As well as having the longest running song in the sheet music charts, he also had two No. 1s on the record charts. Russ, real name Trevor Stanford, had started as a song plugger with Chappell's and had impressed the music company's boss, Teddy Holmes, with his salesmanship. When Trevor began to think about playing piano for a living it was Holmes who dreamed up his new name 'Russ' – the Conway came from the late Steve Conway. He enjoyed his biggest success in September when three of his tunes were in the top four. On 6 September Luxembourg played Nos 1 and 4 by Russ, but played Tony Hatch's version of *Side saddle* at No 3. The interloper at No. 2 was Cliff's *Living doll*. And, by the way, *Trampolina* was at No. 16 that week. Amidst all the rock and Conways, there were still several 'old-fashioned' ballads around. One of these, written by Eula Parker, once of the Stargazers, was her inspiration following a visit to Lourdes. *The village of St Bernadette* was the song and Eula performed it on her return on ATV's 'Lunch Box' show. She was subsequently contacted by several publishers and eventually she signed up with Francis Day & Hunter who then offered the song to Anne Shelton. 'Juke Box Jury' was born on 1 June and the original guest panel consisted of Pete Murray – billed as 'Britain's No. 1 dee-jay' – Alma Cogan, Gary Miller and Susan Stranks, with David Jacobs as presenter. The BBC's reply to ITV's 'Oh Boy' was 'Drumbeat' and this first appeared on 4 August. Top Rank

| | MOST WEEKS ON THE CHARTS TOP SIX | |
|---|---|---|
| Pos | | Wks |
| 1 | *Side saddle* | 51 |
| 2 | *Trudie* | 50 |
| 3 | *Gigi* | 36 |
| 4 | *Roulette* | 34 |
| 5 | *May you always* | 33 |
| 6 | *Petite fleur* | 27 |

219

produced its first records in January with the JAR prefix – the initials, of course, of boss J. Arthur Rank. The last Radio Luxembourg 'Top Twenty' based on sheet music sales went out on Sunday 27 December. Representing the UK in the Eurovision Song Contest were Pearl Carr and Teddy Johnson. The morning after they sang *Sing, little birdie* in the home qualifying competition, the publishers were faced with a queue of customers for sheet music copies of the song. In the actual event, Teddy and Pearl came second to the entry from the Netherlands. Buddy Holly, Ritchie Valens and the Big Bopper were killed in a plane crash in the States, and this sad event prompted the song tribute titled *The Three stars*. The Cliff Adams Singers began their long-running radio series, 'Sing Something Simple', on 3 July. Cliff Richard's backing group, The Drifters, changed its name to The Shadows in September to avoid a clash with the American group, The Drifters. Almost exactly ten years after 'The Harry Lime Theme' entered the sheet music charts, the TV series first appeared on British screens.

# SONG CHARTS

## 971 | THE WORLD OUTSIDE

*Composers*: Richard Addinsell & Carl Sigman (based on a theme from Addinsell's 'Warsaw Concerto')

*Date of Entry*: 3.1.59

*Publishers*: Keith Prowse Music Publishing Co. Ltd.

*Highest Position*: 2
*Weeks on Chart*: 16

*Recordings*:

| | | |
|---|---|---|
| Roger Williams (piano) | 11/58 | London HLR.8758 (& 45–) |
| The Four Coins | 11/58 | Fontana H.168 (& 45–) |
| The Four Aces (backed by 'The Christmas Tree') | 12/58 | Brunswick 05767 (& 45–) |
| The Four Aces (backed by 'The Inn of the Sixth Happiness') | 12/58 | Brunswick 05773 (& 45–) |
| Ronnie Hilton with The Michael Sammes Singers | 12/58 | HMV POP.559 (& 45–) |
| Victor Silvester and his Ballroom Orchestra | 12/58 | Columbia DB.4228 (& 45–) |
| Russ Conway (piano) with The Rita Williams Singers | 12/58 | Columbia DB.4234 |

## 972 | KISS ME, HONEY HONEY, KISS ME

*Composers*: Al Timothy & Michael Julien
*Publishers*: Lakeview Music Publishing Co. Ltd.

*Date of Entry*: 3.1.59
*Highest Position*: 3
*Weeks on Chart*: 17

*Recordings*:

| | | |
|---|---|---|
| Shirley Bassey | 10/58 | Philips PB.860 (& 45–) |
| Gogi Grant | 2/59 | RCA.1105 (& 45–) |
| Maureen Evans | 2/59 | Embassy WB.319 (& 45–) |

## 973 | HIGH CLASS BABY

*Composer*: Ian Samwell
*Publishers*: Kalith Music Ltd.

*Date of Entry*: 3.1.59
*Highest Position*: 25
*Weeks on Chart*: 2

*Recordings*:

| | | |
|---|---|---|
| Cliff Richard with The Drifters | 11/58 | Columbia DB.4203 (& 45–) |
| Rikki Henderson | 2/59 | Embassy WB.318 (& 45–)* |

## 974 | (I love to play) MY UKELELE

*Composer*: Roy Irwin

*Date of Entry*: 10.1.59

*Publishers*: Lakeview Music Publishing Co.

*Highest Position*: 17
*Weeks on Chart*: 7

*Recording*:

| | | |
|---|---|---|
| Max Bygraves | 11/58 | Decca F.11077 (& 45–) |

## 975 | SIDE SADDLE

*Composer*: Trevor H. Stanford

*Date of Entry*: 10.1.59/ Pos: 1/Wks: 61

*Publishers*: Mills Music Ltd.

*Re-entry*: 19.3.60/ Pos: 21/Wks: 7
*2nd re-entry*: 14.5.60/ Pos: 24/Wks: 1

*Recordings*:

| | | |
|---|---|---|
| Russ Conway (piano) | 2/59 | Columbia DB.4256 (& 45–) |
| Tony Hatch (piano) | 4/59 | Top Rank JAR.107 (& 45–) |
| Joe Julian and his Piano | 4/59 | Embassy WB.331 (& 45–) |

## 976 | YOU ALWAYS HURT THE ONE YOU LOVE

*Composers*: Allan Roberts & Doris Fisher

*Date of Entry*: 10.1.59

*Publishers*: Pickwick Music Ltd.

*Highest Position*: 13
*Weeks on Chart*: 7

(Note: This song first appeared in the Sheet Music Charts in 1946 – see Song No. 21. All the recordings listed under the song in 1946 had been deleted by the time the song regained popularity here.)

*Later recordings*:

| | | |
|---|---|---|
| Bunk Johnson (trumpet) and his New Orleans Band | 3/54 | Vocalion V.1036 |
| The Fontane Sisters | 6/56 | London HLD.8289 (& 45–) |
| Connie Francis | 12/58 | MGM.998 (& 45–) |
| Maureen Evans | 2/59 | Embassy WB.316 (& 45–) |

## 977 | CHANTILLY LACE

*Composer*: J.P. Richardson
*Publishers*: Southern Music Publishing Co. Ltd.

*Date of Entry*: 10.1.59
*Highest Position*: 27
*Weeks on Chart*: 1

*Recordings*:
| | | |
|---|---|---|
| The Big Bopper – J.P. Richardson | 10/58 | Mercury AMT.1002 (& 45-) |
| Johnny Worth | 1/59 | Embassy WB.315 (& 45-) |

## 978 | COME ON, LET'S GO

*Composer*: Ritchie Valens
*Publishers*: Essex Music Ltd.

*Date of Entry*: 10.1.59
*Highest Position*: 29
*Weeks on Chart*: 1

*Recordings*:
| | | |
|---|---|---|
| Tommy Steele | 10/58 | Decca F.11072 (& 45-) |
| Ritchie Valens | 11/58 | Pye Int. N.25000/ (45) 7N.25000 |

## 979 | TONIGHT

*Composers*: Leonard Bernstein & Stephen Sondheim
*Publishers*: Chappell & Co. Ltd.

*Date of Entry*: 10.1.59
*Highest Position*: 23
*Weeks on Chart*: 3

*Recordings*:
| | | |
|---|---|---|
| Edmund Hockridge with The Beryl Stott Chorus | 11/58 | Pye Nixa N.15167/ (45) 7N.15167 |
| David Galbraith | 12/58 | Columbia DB.4226 (& 45-) |
| Victor Silvester and his Ballroom Orchestra | 1/59 | Columbia DB.4239 (& 45-) |
| Rosemary Clooney | 1/59 | Philips PB.900 (& 45-) |
| Barry Kendall | 3/59 | Embassy WB.321 (& 45-)★ |

## 980 | TOM THUMB'S TUNE

*Composer*: Peggy Lee
*Publishers*: Robbins Music Corporation Ltd.

*Date of Entry*: 17.1.59
*Highest Position*: 27
*Weeks on Chart*: 1

*Recordings*:
| | | |
|---|---|---|
| Eric Rogers and his Music | 11/58 | Decca F.11080 (& 45-) |
| Charlie Drake | 11/58 | Parlophone R.4496 (& 45-) |
| Patience and Prudence | 1/59 | London HLU.8773 (& 45-) |

## 981 | I GOT STUNG

*Composers*: Aaron Schroeder & David Hill
*Publishers*: Hill & Range Songs (London) Ltd.

*Date of Entry*: 17.1.59
*Highest Position*: 13
*Weeks on Chart*: 8

*Recordings*:
| | | |
|---|---|---|
| Elvis Presley | 1/59 | RCA.1100 (& 45-) |
| Johnny Worth | 2/59 | Embassy WB.317 (& 45-) |

## 982 | BABY FACE

*Composers*: Harry Akst & Benny Davis
*Publishers*: Francis Day & Hunter Ltd.

*Date of Entry*: 24.1.59
*Highest Position*: 17
*Weeks on Chart*: 10

*Recordings*:
| | | |
|---|---|---|
| Al Jolson (this version also includes the song 'I'm looking over a four-leaf clover') | 11/49 | Brunswick 04376 |
| Little Richard and his Band | 12/58 | London HLU.8770 (& 45-) |
| Johnny Worth | 2/59 | Embassy WB.317 (& 45-) |
| Joe Loss and his Orchestra | 12/59 | HMV POP.680 (& 45-)★ |

## 983 | THIS OLD MAN (Knick Knack Paddy Whack)

*Composer*: Trad. Nursery Rhyme, adapted and arranged by Malcolm Arnold
*Publishers*: B. Feldman & Co. Ltd.

*Date of Entry*: 24.1.59
*Highest Position*: 28
*Weeks on Chart*: 1

*Recordings*:
| | | |
|---|---|---|
| Cyril Stapleton and his Orchestra with Children's Chorus [Titled 'Nick Nack Paddy Whack'] | 12/58 | Decca F.11094 (& 45-) |
| Dr Barnardo's Children | 12/58 | Pye Nixa N.15180/ (45) 7N.15180 |
| Mitch Miller and his Orchestra and Chorus [Titled 'The Children's Marching Song'] | 1/59 | Philips PB.893 (& 45-) |
| The Spinners | 1/59 | Columbia DB.4243 (& 45-) |

## 984 A PUB WITH NO BEER

*Composer*: Gordon Parsons
*Publishers*: Good Music Ltd.

*Date of Entry*: 24.1.59
*Highest Position*: 2
*Weeks on Chart*: 18

*Recordings*:

| | | |
|---|---|---|
| Slim Dusty with Dick Carr and his Bushlanders | 11/58 | Columbia DB.4212 (& 45-) |
| Johnny Ashcroft | 2/59 | Felsted AF.118 (& 45-) |
| Johnny Worth | 4/59 | Embassy WB.329 (& 45-) |

## 985 I'LL BE WITH YOU IN APPLE BLOSSOM TIME

*Composers*: Albert Von Tilzer & Neville Fleeson
*Publishers*: Francis Day & Hunter Ltd.

*Date of Entry*: 31.1.59/
Pos: 7/Wks: 14
*Re-entry*: 6.6.59/
Pos: 26/Wks: 1

*Recordings*:

| | | |
|---|---|---|
| Richard Hayman (harmonica) and Jan August (piano) | 3/56 | Mercury MT.103 |
| Harry Grove and his Music [Titled 'Apple Blossom Time'] | 8/58 | Decca F.11050 (& 45-) |
| Rosemary June | 1/59 | Pye Int. N.25005/ (45) 7N.25005 |
| The Andrews Sisters (reissue of Brns.03174 released 7/41) | 2/59 | Brunswick 05782 (& 45-) |
| The Rhythmettes | 2/59 | Coral Q.72358 (& 45-) |
| Victor Silvester and his Ballroom Orchestra | 3/59 | Columbia DB.4271 (& 45-) |

## 986 ONE NIGHT

*Composers*: Dave Bartholomew & Pearl King
*Publishers*: Commodore-Imperial Music Ltd.

*Date of Entry*: 31.1.59/
Pos: 21/Wks: 2
*Re-entry*: 21.2.59/
Pos: 22/Wks: 2

*Recordings*:

| | | |
|---|---|---|
| Smiley Lewis | 8/56 | London HLU.8312 (& 45-) |
| Elvis Presley | 1/59 | RCA.1100 (& 45-) |
| Rikki Henderson | 2/59 | Embassy WB.318 (& 45-) |

## 987 I'LL REMEMBER TONIGHT

*Composers*: Sammy Fain & Paul Francis Webster
*Publishers*: Robbins Music Corporation Ltd.

*Date of Entry*: 31.1.59/
Pos: 26/Wks: 1
*Re-entry*: 7.3.59/
Pos: 23/Wks: 2

*Recordings*:

| | | |
|---|---|---|
| Pat Boone | 1/59 | London HLD.8775 (& 45-) |
| Victor Silvester and his Ballroom Orchestra | 3/59 | Columbia DB.4271 (& 45-) |

## 988 LAST NIGHT ON THE BACK PORCH

*Composers*: Lew Brown & Carl Schraubstader
*Publisher*: Keith Prowse Music Publishing Co. Ltd.

*Date of Entry*: 31.1.59/
Pos: 13/Wks: 13
*Re-entry*: 9.5.59/
Pos: 26/Wks: 1

*Recordings*:

| | | |
|---|---|---|
| Alma Cogan with The Michael Sammes Singers | 1/59 | HMV POP.573 (& 45-) |
| Joe Loss and his Orchestra | 2/59 | HMV POP.588 (& 45-) |

## 989 THE WONDERFUL SECRET OF LOVE

*Composer*: Irving Gordon
*Publishers*: Leeds Music Ltd.

*Date of Entry*: 31.1.59
*Highest Position*: 10
*Weeks on Chart*: 14

*Recordings*:

| | | |
|---|---|---|
| Robert Earl | 1/59 | Philips PB.891 (& 45-) |
| Paul Rich | 4/59 | Embassy WB.330 (& 45-) |

## 990 SMOKE GETS IN YOUR EYES

*Composers*: Jerome Kern & Otto Harbach
*Publishers*: Sterling Music Publishing Co. Ltd.

*Date of Entry*: 7.2.59
Pos: 3/Wks: 21
*Re-entry*: 18.7.59/
Pos: 26/Wks: 1
*2nd re-entry*: 8.8.59/
Pos: 30/Wks: 1

*Recordings*:

| | | |
|---|---|---|
| The Ronnie Scott Quartet | 12/52 | Esquire 10-265 |
| The Red Rodney New Stars | 7/54 | Esquire 10-379 |
| Jeri Southern | 5/57 | Brunswick 05665 (& 45-) |
| Dickie Barrett | 3/58 | MGM.976 (& 45-) |
| The Platters | 1/59 | Mercury AMT.1016 (& 45-) |
| Tab Smith (alto sax) | 2/59 | London HLM.8801 (& 45-) |
| Joe Loss and his Orchestra | 3/59 | HMV POP.602 (& 45-) |
| Paul Rich | 3/59 | Embassy WB.322 (& 45-) |

## 991 PROBLEMS

| Composers: Felice & Boudleaux Bryant | | Date of Entry: 7.2.59 |
|---|---|---|
| Publishers: Acuff-Rose Publishing Co. Ltd. | | Highest Position: 17 |
| | | Weeks on Chart: 7 |

Recordings:

| The Everly Brothers | 1/59 | London HLA.8781 (& 45-) |
|---|---|---|
| Paul Rich | 3/59 | Embassy WB.322 (& 45-) |

## 992 GIGI

| Composers: Alan Jay Lerner & Frederick Loewe | | Date of Entry: 7.2.59/ Pos: 5/Wks: 35 |
|---|---|---|
| Publishers: Chappell & Co. Ltd. | | Re-entry: 17.10.59/ Pos: 30/Wks: 1 |

Recordings:

| Bing Crosby | 1/59 | Brunswick 05770 (& 45-) |
|---|---|---|
| The Five Dallas Boys | 1/59 | Columbia DB.4244 (& 45-) |
| Charles Margulis (trumpet) | 1/59 | London HLL.8774 (& 45-) |
| Ronnie Hilton with The Michael Sammes Singers | 1/59 | HMV POP.560 (& 45-) |
| Joe Loss and his Orchestra | 1/59 | HMV POP.570 (& 45-) |
| Billy Eckstine | 1/59 | Mercury AMT.1018 (& 45-) |
| Vic Damone | 1/59 | Philips PB.889 (& 45-) |
| Victor Silvester and his Ballroom Orchestra | 2/59 | Columbia DB.4257 (& 45-) |
| Robert Merrill | 3/59 | RCA.1109 (& 45-) |
| The Embassy Singers and Players cond. Gordon Franks | 3/59 | Embassy WB.320 (& 45-) |
| Liberace (piano) | 6/59 | Coral Q.72371 (& 45-) |

## 993 MY HEART SINGS (En écoutant mon coeur chanter)

| Composers: Georges Herpin, 'Jamblan' & Harold Rome | | Date of Entry: 7.2.59/ Pos: 29/Wks: 1 |
|---|---|---|
| Publishers: Peter Maurice Music Co. Ltd. | | Re-entry: 21.2.59/ Pos: 23/Wks: 5 |

Recordings:

| Kathryn Grayson | 6/48 | MGM.130 |
|---|---|---|
| Paul Anka | 1/59 | Columbia DB.4241 (& 45-) |
| Johnny Worth | 3/59 | Embassy WB.325 (& 45-) |

(Note: The Kathryn Grayson recording listed above was deleted from the MGM catalogue exactly one week prior to the song entering the charts. It earns its inclusion above by virtue of such a 'near miss'.)

## 994 WILLINGLY (Melodie perdue)

| Composers: Hubert Giraud, Jean Broussolle & Carl Sigman | | Date of Entry: 7.2.59/ Pos: 23/Wks: 4 |
|---|---|---|
| Publishers: Macmelodies Ltd. | | Re-entry: 28.3.59/ Pos: 24/Wks: 3 |
| | | 2nd re-entry: 2.5.59/ Pos: 25/Wks: 1 |

Recordings:

| Monte Kelly and his Orchestra | 1/59 | London HLL.8777 (& 45-) |
|---|---|---|
| Johnny Desmond | 1/59 | Philips PB.890 (& 45-) |
| Al Alberts | 1/59 | Coral Q.72352 (& 45-) |
| Mal Perry | 1/59 | Fontana H.172 (& 45-) |
| David Whitfield | 1/59 | Decca F.11101 (& 45-) |
| Joe Loss and his Orchestra | 2/59 | HMV POP.589 (& 45-) |
| Malcolm Vaughan | 2/59 | HMV POP.590 (& 45-) |

## 995 DOES YOUR CHEWING GUM LOSE ITS FLAVOUR (On the bedpost overnight?)

| Composers: Billy Rose, Matty Bloom & Ernest Breuer | | Date of Entry: 14.2.59 |
|---|---|---|
| Publishers: B. Feldman & Co. Ltd. | | Highest Position: 7 |
| | | Weeks on Chart: 11 |

Recordings:

| Lonnie Donegan and his Skiffle Group | 1/59 | Pye Nixa N.15181 (45) 7N.15181 |
|---|---|---|
| Pinky and Perky | 3/59 | Decca F.11116 (& 45-) |
| Paul Rich | 4/59 | Embassy WB.327 (& 45-) |

CAMPBELL CONNELLY
PUBLICATIONS

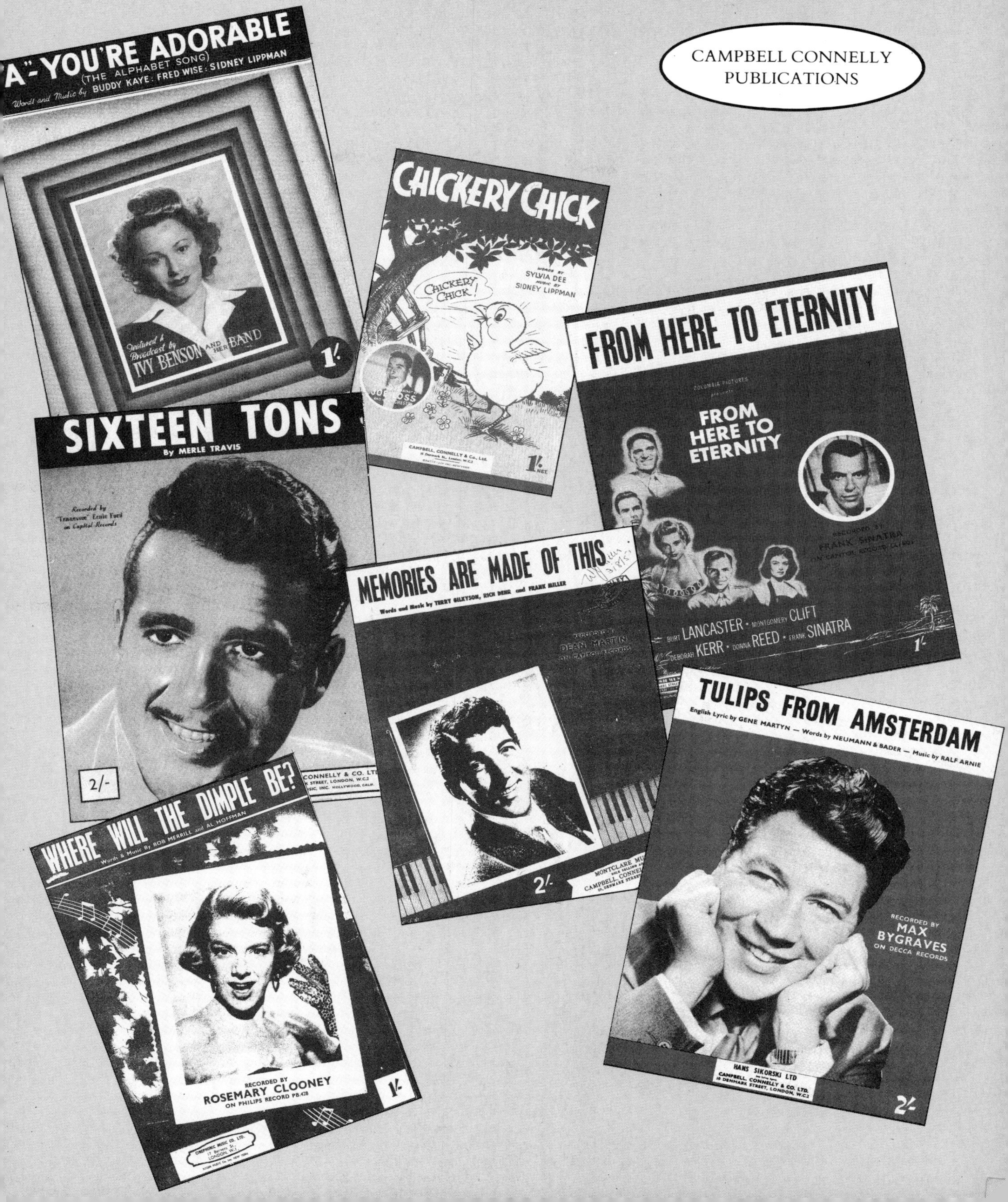

# IF ANYONE FINDS THIS, I LOVE YOU

By SID LIPPMAN and SYLVIA DEE

FEATURED & RECORDED BY
RUBY MURRAY

MICHAEL REINE MUSIC CO.LTD.22 DENMARK ST.LONDON

Sole Selling Agents: SOUTHERN MUSIC PUBLISHING CO.LTD.,8,DENMARK ST.,LONDON.

# It's all Over Now

by Sunny Skylar & Don Marcotte

Featured & Broadcast by
HARRY EVANS

1/-

CAMPBELL, CONNELLY & CO., LTD.
10 DENMARK STREET, LONDON, W.C.2
BROADCAST MUSIC INC., NEW YORK

# LITTLE DARLIN

Words and Music by MAURICE WILLIAMS

RECORDED BY
THE DIAMONDS
ON MERCURY RECORD

CAMPBELL CONNELLY & CO. LTD.
10, DENMARK ST., LONDON, W.C.2
EXCELLOREC MUSIC CO. NASHVILLE TENN.

# THE LITTLE OLD MILL
## (WENT ROUND AND ROUND)

Featured and Broadcast by
JOE LOSS
AND HIS BAND.

Words & Music by
DON PELOSI, LEWIS ILDA & LEO TOWERS.

1/-

IRWIN DASH MUSIC

# MONDAY,
# TUESDAY,
# WEDNESDAY,
I LOVE YOU

Words & Music by
ROSS PARKER

Featured and Broadcast by
THE SQUADRONAIRES
DIRECTED BY
JIMMY MILLER

IRWIN DASH MUSIC CO LTD
PUT DASH in your programmes

# NOW

Words and Music
JOE PRIOLO
PAT NOTO
and
ANDY PE

Broadcast and Recorded by
Dick James
on Parlophone Record

1/-

# Make-Believe World

Featured & Broadcast
DENNY DENNIS

Words & Music by
BOX, COX & LEWIS ILDA

(WRITERS OF "I'M IN LOVE WITH TWO SWEETHEARTS"
& "JUST A LITTLE FOND AFFECTION)

1/- NET

IRWIN DASH MUSIC Co LTD

# My FIRST LOVE
# My LAST LOVE
# FOR ALWAYS

By
BILLY REID

DOROTHY SQUIRES

IRWIN DASH MUSIC Co Ltd

THEY CALL ME
## THE ROCK OF GIBRALTAR
WORDS AND MUSIC BY TERRY GILKYSON

Recorded by
FRANKIE LAINE
ON COLUMBIA RECORD DB 3113

DASH MUSIC Co Ltd

MONTCLARE MUSIC CORP, HOLLYWOOD USA

1/-

Once upon a
Winter-Time

WORDS BY
JOHNNY BRANDON
MUSIC BY
R·S·MARTIN

1/-

FEATURED AND BROADCAST BY
JACK LEON

CINEPHONIC MUSIC CO·LTD · 100 CHARING CROSS RD · LONDON WC2

# OH! MY ACHIN' HEART

Featured & Broadcast by
BILLY TERNENT

BY
FREDDY JAMES
LITTLE JACK LITTLE
AND
JACK PALMER

CAMPBELL CONNELLY & Co. Ltd.
10 DENMARK STREET, LONDON, W.C.2.

1/-

## ST. THÉRÈSE OF THE ROSES
Words by REMUS HARRIS    Music by ARTHUR STRAUSS

RECORDED By
MALCOLM VAUGHAN
ON H.M.V. RECORDS

DASH MUSIC Co Ltd

2/-

## SEÑORA
BY RAMEY IDRISS & GEORGE TIBBLES

BROADCAST & RECORDED BY
THE RAY ELLINGTON QUARTET
On DECCA F.9496.

DASH Music Co. Ltd.,
17 Berners St.,
LONDON W.1

1/-

**AM I A**
## TOY OR A TREASURE
By IRVING TAYLOR
ARTHUR ALTMAN
AND
LOU SINGER

FEATURED & BROADCAST BY
**HARRY LEADER**
AND HIS BAND

CINEPHONIC MUSIC CO. LTD.
17 Berners St.,
LONDON W.1

## ANNIVERSARY SONG

COLUMBIA PICTURES
**TECHNICOLOR** PRODUCTION

The
**JOLSON STORY**

BY SAUL CHAPLIN
AND
AL JOLSON
BASED ON A THEME BY
IVANOVICI

WITH
LARRY PARKS · EVELYN KEYES
WILLIAM DEMAREST · BILL GOODWIN
Screenplay by Stephen Longstreet
Directed by ALFRED E. GREEN
Produced by SIDNEY SKOLSKY

1/-

CAMPBELL CONNELLY & CO. LTD.
10 DENMARK STREET, LONDON, W.C.2
MOOD MUSIC Co., New York.

## BECAUSE OF YO
By ARTHUR HAMMERSTEIN & DUDLEY WILKINSON

Featured & Broadcast by
**LEE LAWRENCE**

DASH MUSIC Co. LTD.
PUT DASH IN YOUR PROGRAMMES
BROADCAST MUSIC PIE NEW YORK

PRICE 1/- NETT

## BEST OF ALL
Words by
Ray Sonin
Music by
Wally Dewar

Featured & Broadcast by
**KEN LYON & GEORGE MURRELL**

CAMPBELL, CONNELLY & CO. LTD.
10 DENMARK STREET,
LONDON, W.C.2
1/-
MADE IN ENGLAND
CAMPBELL-CONNELL
16 FIFTH AVENUE, NEW
NEW YORK, U

## BLUE RIBBON GAL
WORDS BY
Ross Parker
MUSIC BY
IRWIN DASH

HARRY GOLD
"PIECES OF EIGHT"

IRWIN DASH MUSIC Co. LTD.
PUT DASH IN YOUR PROGRAMMES
1/-

## CHRISTOPHER COLUMBUS
(THE WORLD AIN'T BIG ENOUGH FOR ME)
By
TERR
GILKYS

RECORDED
GUY MITCH
ON
COLUMBIA R
DB 28

FEATURED AND BROADCAST BY
**AVRIL ANGERS**

CAMPBELL, CONNELLY & CO. LTD.

HE DAY OF JUBILO
(TELL IT TO THE PREACHER)
Recorded by
GUY MITCHELL
With Chorus and Orchestra
Under the direction of
MITCH MILLER
On COLUMBIA DB 3104
CAMPBELL CONN

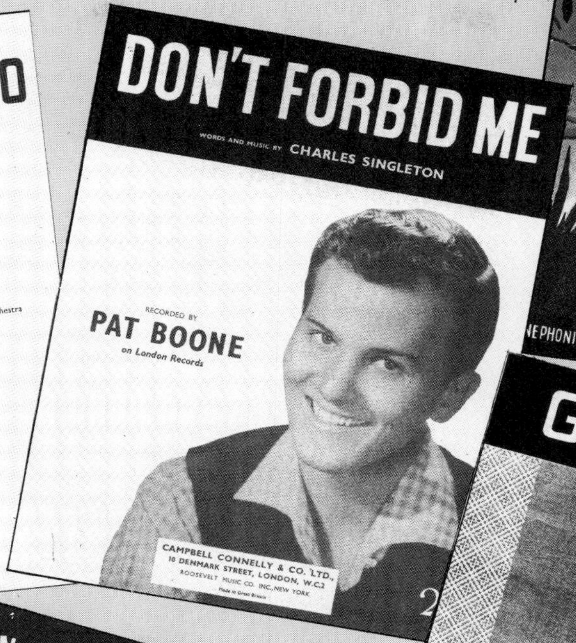
DON'T FORBID ME
WORDS AND MUSIC BY CHARLES SINGLETON
RECORDED BY
PAT BOONE
on London Records
CAMPBELL CONNELLY & CO. LTD.,
10 DENMARK STREET, LONDON, W.C.2
ROOSEVELT MUSIC CO. INC., NEW YORK
Made in Great Britain

The GREEN COCKATOO
by
Don Relleuro
NEPHONIC MUSIC CO·LTD·100 CHARING CROSS RD·LONDON·W.C.2
2/6

GLENDORA
Words & Music by
RAY STANLEY
Broadcast and Recorded by
GLEN MASON
ON PARLOPHONE RECORDS
CONNELLY & CO. LTD.,
STREET, LONDON, W.C.2
INC., HOLLYWOOD, CALIF.
2/-

THE FRENCH CAN-CAN POLKA
From Music by J. OFFENBACH
Words and Adaptation of Music by JIMMY KENNEDY
Broadcast & Recorded by
BILLY COTTON
ON DECCA F 9360
CAMPBELL, CONNELLY & CO. LTD.
10 DENMARK STREET,
LONDON, W.C.2
1/-
Made in England

GOT-TA HAVE
SOMETHING IN THE BANK, FRANK!
Words by BOB HILLIARD
Music by MORT GARSON
RECORDED BY
FRANKIE VAUGHAN
WITH THE
KAYE SISTERS
ON PHILIPS RECORD
PB 751
CAMPBELL CONNELLY & CO. LTD.,
10 DENMARK STREET, LONDON, W.C.2
REIS PUBLICATIONS INC., NEW YORK
Made in Great Britain
2/-

## 996 THE LITTLE DRUMMER BOY

Composers: Harry Simeone, Henry Onorati & Katherine Davis based on a traditional Czech carol 'Do the drum'
Publishers: Bregman, Vocco & Conn Ltd.

Date of Entry: 14.2.59/ Pos: 5/Wks: 17
Re-entry: 21.11.59/ Pos: 29/Wks: 1
2nd re-entry: 19.12.59/ Pos: 28/Wks: 2

Recordings:

| | | |
|---|---|---|
| The Harry Simeone Chorale | 1/59 | Top Rank JAR.101 (& 45-) |
| Michael Flanders with The Michael Sammes Singers | 1/59 | Parlophone R.4528 (& 45-) |
| The Beverley Sisters | 2/59 | Decca F.11107 (& 45-) |
| The Embassy Singers directed by Jacques Leroy | 3/59 | Embassy WB.324 (& 45-) |
| The Michael Sammes Singers | 11/59 | Fontana H.232 (& 45-) |
| The Harry Simeone Chorale | 11/59 | Top Rank 45-JAR.222 |
| Johnny Cash | 11/59 | Philips PB.979 (& 45-) |
| Eric Kay | 12/59 | London HL.9004 (& 45-) |

## 997 MY HAPPINESS

Composers: Betty Peterson & Borney Bergantine
Publishers: Sterling Music Publishing Co. Ltd.

Date of Entry: 21.2.59
Highest Position: 6
Weeks on Chart: 18

Note: This song first appeared in the Sheet Music Charts in 1948 – see Song No. 124. Only one version from that year remained in the catalogues of 1959 – that by Ella Fitzgerald and The Song Spinners. It was issued again on Brunswick 05783 with a 45 rpm pressing.)

Recordings:

| | | |
|---|---|---|
| Ella Fitzgerald with The Song Spinners | 7/48 | Brunswick 03934 |
| Connie Francis | 1/59 | MGM.1001 (& 45-) |
| Tab Smith (alto sax) [Titled 'My Happiness cha cha'] | 2/59 | London HLM.8801 (& 45-) |
| Joe Loss and his Orchestra | 3/59 | HMV POP.602 (& 45-) |
| Ella Fitzgerald with The Song Spinners | 3/59 | Brunswick 05783 (& 45-) |
| Jean Scott | 3/59 | Embassy WB.323 (& 45-) |
| Bert Weedon and his Music for Dancing | 5/59 | Top Rank JAR.122 (& 45-) |

## 998 PETITE FLEUR

Composer: Sidney Bechet
Publishers: Essex Music Ltd.

Date of Entry: 28.2.59
Highest Position: 2
Weeks on Chart: 27

Recordings:

| | | |
|---|---|---|
| The Wally Fawkes and Sandy Brown Quintet | 2/57 | Decca F-J.10855 (& 45-) |
| Sidney Bechet (soprano sax) and his All Stars | 1/59 | Vogue V.9141 (& 45-) |
| Chris Barber and his Jazz Band with Monty Sunshine (clarinet) | 1/59 | Pye Nixa NJ.2026/ (45) 7NJ.2026 |
| Wilbur de Paris and his New Orleans Band | 2/59 | London HLE.8816 (& 45-) |
| Teddy Johnson and Pearl Carr | 2/59 | Columbia DB.4260 (& 45-) |
| The Scamps | 3/59 | London HLW.8827 (& 45-) |
| Bob Crosby and his Bobcats | 3/59 | London HLD.8828 (& 45-) |
| Jacques Leroy and his Orchestra | 4/59 | Embassy WB.326 (& 45-) |
| The Gene Krupa Quartet | 5/59 | Columbia LB.10108 |
| Bert Weedon and his Music for Dancing | 5/59 | Top Rank JAR.122 |
| Victor Silvester and his Ballroom Orchestra | 6/59 | Columbia DB.4315 (& 45-) |

## 999 SING, LITTLE BIRDIE

Composers: Stan Butcher & Syd Cordell
Publishers: Good Music Ltd.

Date of Entry: 28.2.59
Highest Position: 2
Weeks on Chart: 19

Recordings:

| | | |
|---|---|---|
| Teddy Johnson and Pearl Carr | 3/59 | Columbia DB.4275 (& 45-) |
| Barry Kendall and June Lowe | 4/59 | Embassy WB.333 (& 45-) |
| Bert Weedon and his Music for Dancing | 5/59 | Top Rank JAR.121 (& 45-) |

## 1000 THERE GOES MY HEART

Composers: Benny Davis & Abner Silver
Publishers: Francis Day & Hunter Ltd.

Date of Entry: 28.2.59/ Pos: 29/Wks: 1
Re-entry: 9.5.59/ Pos: 28/Wks: 1
2nd re-entry: 23.5.59/ Pos: 29/Wks: 1
3rd re-entry: 29.8.59/ Pos: 30/Wks: 1

Recordings:

| | | |
|---|---|---|
| The Four Aces featuring Al Alberts | 3/55 | Brunswick 05401 (& 45-) |
| Roy Hamilton | 4/56 | Philips PB.583 |
| Joni James | 10/58 | MGM.991 (& 45-) |

## 1001 WAIT FOR ME (Ti Diro)

| Composers: Giovanni D'Anzi & Alfredo Bracchi | Date of Entry: 7.3.59 |
|---|---|
| Publishers: Sterling Music Publishing Co. Ltd. | Highest Position: 13 Weeks on Chart: 18 |

Recordings:

| Tony Dallara [Titled 'Ti Diro'] | 1/59 | Columbia DB.4254 (& 45-) |
|---|---|---|
| Kevin Scott with The Rita Williams Singers | 1/59 | Parlophone R.4520 (& 45-) |
| Marion Ryan with The Beryl Stott Chorus | 2/59 | Pye Nixa N.15184/ (45) 7N.15184 |
| Malcolm Vaughan | 2/59 | HMV POP.590 (& 45-) |
| Joe Loss and his Orchestra | 3/59 | HMV POP.601 (& 45-) |
| Victor Silvester and his Ballroom Orchestra | 4/59 | Columbia DB.4285 (& 45-) |

## 1002 THANK HEAVEN FOR LITTLE GIRLS

| Composers: Alan Jay Lerner & Frederick Loewe | Date of Entry: 7.3.59/ Pos: 23/Wks: 9 |
|---|---|
| Publishers: Chappell & Co. Ltd. | Re-entry: 25.7.59/ Pos: 26/Wks: 3 2nd re-entry: 29.8.59/ Pos: 28/Wks: 1 |

Recordings:

| The King Brothers with The Rita Williams Singers | 1/59 | Parlophone R.4513 (& 45-) |
|---|---|---|
| Victor Silvester and his Ballroom Orchestra | 2/59 | Columbia DB.4257 (& 45-) |
| The Embassy Singers and Players dir. Gordon Franks | 3/59 | Embassy WB.320 (& 45-) |

## 1003 ANGELINA (Dalla Strada Alle Stelle)

| Composers: Panzuti & Pinchi – translated by Peter Hart & Gabriel Diamond | Date of Entry: 7.3.59 |
|---|---|
| Publishers: Gabriel Music Ltd. | Highest Position: 27 Weeks on Chart: 7 |

Recordings:

| Eddie Calvert – The Man with the Golden Trumpet | 1/59 | Columbia DB.4252 (& 45-) |
|---|---|---|
| Barry Cryer | 1/59 | Fontana H.177 (& 45-) |
| Steve Lawrence (see note below) | 4/59 | HMV 45-POP.604 |

(Note: The Steve Lawrence recording has different lyrics [by Curtis] and is titled '[I don't care] Only Love Me' with 'Angelina' in brackets after the title on the disc.)

## 1004 KISS ME AND KISS ME AND KISS ME (Tre Volte Baciami)

| Composers: Arturo Casadei, Luciano Beretta. Al Hoffman & Dick Manning | Date of Entry: 7.3.59/ Pos: 22/Wks: 7 |
|---|---|
| Publishers: Leeds Music Ltd. | Re-entry: 16.5.59/ Pos: 30/Wks: 1 |

Recording:

| Perry Como with The Ray Charles Singers | 2/59 | RCA.1111 (& 45-) |
|---|---|---|

## 1005 CHICK

| Composer: Joe Henderson | Date of Entry: 14.3.59/ Pos: 6/Wks: 23 |
|---|---|
| Publishers: Henderson Music Ltd. | Re-entry: 12.9.59/ Pos: 29/Wks: 1 |

Recordings:

| Joe 'Mr Piano' Henderson with The Beryl Stott Chorus | 3/59 | Pye Nixa N.15187/ (45) 7N.15187 |
|---|---|---|
| Tony Hatch (piano) | 4/59 | Top Rank JAR.107 (& 45-) |

## 1006 MAY YOU ALWAYS

| Composers: Larry Markes & Dick Charles | Date of Entry: 21.3.59 |
|---|---|
| Publishers: Essex Music Ltd. | Highest Position: 2 Weeks on Chart: 33 |

Recordings:

| The McGuire Sisters | 2/59 | Coral Q.72356 (& 45-) |
|---|---|---|
| Joan Regan | 2/59 | HMV POP.593 (& 45-) |
| The Jean-ettes | 2/59 | Pye Nixa N.15185/ (45) 7N.15185 |
| Maureen Evans | 6/59 | Embassy WB.344 (& 45-) |
| John Warren's Strictempo Orchestra cond. Bill Shepherd | 1/60 | Pye N.15246/ (45) 7N.15246★ |

## 1007 TOMBOY

| Composers: Joe Farrell & Jim Conway | Date of Entry: 21.3.59 |
|---|---|
| Publishers: John Fields Music Co. Ltd. | Highest Position: 14 Weeks on Chart: 10 |

Recordings:

| Perry Como with The Ray Charles Singers | 2/59 | RCA.1111 (& 45-) |
|---|---|---|
| Rikki Henderson | 4/59 | Embassy WB.328 (& 45-) |
| Victor Silvester and his Ballroom Orchestra | 5/59 | Columbia 45-DB.4301 |

## 1008 IF ONLY I COULD LIVE MY LIFE AGAIN

*Composers*: Gilbert Becaud, Pierre Delanoe, L. Amade & Elly Leighton
*Publishers*: Peter Maurice Music Co. Ltd.

*Date of Entry*: 28.3.59
*Highest Position*: 13
*Weeks on Chart*: 12

*Recordings*:

| | | |
|---|---|---|
| Jane Morgan | 2/59 | London HLR.8810 (& 45-) |
| Teddy Johnson and Pearl Carr | 3/59 | Columbia DB.4275 (& 45-) |
| Victor Silvester and his Ballroom Orchestra | 6/59 | Columbia DB.4314 (& 45-) |

## 1009 IT DOESN'T MATTER ANY MORE

*Composer*: Paul Anka
*Publishers*: Monarch Music Ltd.

*Date of Entry*: 4.4.59
*Highest Position*: 2
*Weeks on Chart*: 21

*Recordings*:

| | | |
|---|---|---|
| Buddy Holly | 2/59 | Coral Q.72360 (& 45-) |
| Johnny Worth | 4/59 | Embassy WB.332 (& 45-) |

## 1010 VENUS

*Composer*: Ed Marshall
*Publishers*: Essex Music Ltd.

*Date of Entry*: 4.4.59
*Highest Position*: 7
*Weeks on Chart*: 17

*Recordings*:

| | | |
|---|---|---|
| Dickie Valentine | 2/59 | Pye Nixa N.15192/ (45) 7N.15192 |
| Frankie Avalon | 2/59 | HMV POP.603 (& 45-) |
| Joe Loss and his Orchestra | 4/59 | HMV 45-POP.605 |
| Paul Rich | 4/59 | Embassy WB.330 (& 45-) |

## 1011 DONNA

*Composer*: Ritchie Valens
*Publishers*: Aberbach (London) Ltd.

*Date of Entry*: 4.4.59
*Highest Position*: 6
*Weeks on Chart*: 17

*Recordings*:

| | | |
|---|---|---|
| Marty Wilde | 2/59 | Philips PB.902 (& 45-) |
| Ritchie Valens | 2/59 | London HL.8803 (& 45-) |
| Johnny Worth | 4/59 | Embassy WB.329 (& 45-) |

## 1012 CHARLIE BROWN

*Composers*: Jerry Leiber & Mike Stoller
*Publishers*: Progressive Music Ltd.

*Date of Entry*: 18.4.59
*Highest Position*: 8
*Weeks on Chart*: 11

*Recordings*:

| | | |
|---|---|---|
| The Coasters | 3/59 | London HLE.8819 (& 45-) |
| Bernard Bresslaw | 3/59 | HMV POP.599 (& 45-) |
| Ray Ellington with The Beryl Stott Group | 3/59 | Pye Nixa N.15189/ (45) 7N.15189 |
| The Saville Brothers | 4/59 | Embassy WB.331 (& 45-) |

## 1013 C'MON EVERYBODY

*Composers*: Eddie Cochran & Jerry Capehart
*Publishers*: Burlington Music Co. Ltd.

*Date of Entry*: 18.4.59
*Highest Position*: 24
*Weeks on Chart*: 7

*Recordings*:

| | | |
|---|---|---|
| Eddie Cochran | 1/59 | London HLU.8792 (& 45-) |
| Hal Munro | 5/59 | Embassy WB.336 (& 45-) |

## 1014 COME SOFTLY TO ME

*Composers*: Gary Troxel, Barbara Ellis & Gretchen Christopher (The Fleetwoods)
*Publishers*: Edwin H. Morris & Co. Ltd.

*Date of Entry*: 25.4.59
*Highest Position*: 4
*Weeks on Chart*: 14

*Recordings*:

| | | |
|---|---|---|
| The Fleetwoods (arr. Bonnie Guitar) | 4/59 | London HLU.8841 (& 45-) |
| Richard Barrett and The Chantels | 4/59 | HMV 45-POP.609 |
| Frankie Vaughan and The Kaye Sisters | 4/59 | Philips PB.913 (& 45-) |
| Ronnie Height | 4/59 | Decca F.11126 (& 45-) |
| Craig Douglas | 4/59 | Top Rank JAR.110 (& 45-) |
| Barry Kendall | 4/59 | Embassy WB.333 (& 45-) |

## 1015 (Now and then, there's) A FOOL SUCH AS I

*Composer*: Bill Trader

*Publishers*: Leeds Music Ltd.

*Date of Entry*: 25.4.59/
Pos: 7/Wks: 16
*Re-entry*: 22.8.59/
Pos: 23/Wks: 3

*Recordings*:

| | | |
|---|---|---|
| Grady Martin and his Slew Foot Five (Dottie Dillard and Jack Shook) | 4/53 | Brunswick 05080 |
| Elvis Presley with The Jordanaires | 4/59 | RCA.1113 (& 45–) |
| Johnny Worth | 5/59 | Embassy WB.335 (& 45–) |

## 1016 CIAO CIAO BAMBINA (Piove)

*Composers*: Domenico Modugno, 'Verde' & Mitchell Parish

*Publishers*: Robbins Music Corporation Ltd.

*Date of Entry*: 25.4.59/
Pos: 28/Wks: 2
*Re-entry*: 15.8.59/
Pos: 28/Wks: 3
*2nd re-entry*: 19.9.59/
Pos: 24/Wks: 3

*Recordings*:

| | | |
|---|---|---|
| Domenico Modugno | 2/59 | Oriole CB.1489 (& 45–) |
| Marino Marini and his Quartet | 2/59 | Durium DC.16636 (& 45–) |
| Tony Dallara with The Continentals [Titled 'Piove'] | 3/59 | Columbia DB.4273 (& 45–) |
| Teddy Reno | 3/59 | RCA.1108 (& 45–) |
| Vico Torriani | 3/59 | Decca F.11121 (& 45–) |
| Kevin Scott with The Rita Williams Singers | 4/59 | Parlophone 45–R.4540 |
| Peppino of Capri Quintet | 4/59 | Pye Int. (45) 7N.25017 |
| Rikki Henderson | 4/59 | Embassy WB.328 (& 45–) |
| Victor Silvester and his Ballroom Orchestra | 5/59 | Columbia 45–DB.4300 |
| Jacky Noguez | 8/59 | Pye Int. N.25031/ (45) 7N.25031 |
| Johnny's Boys | 9/59 | Decca F.11156 (& 45–) |
| Roberto Cardinali with The Rita Williams Singers | 10/59 | HMV 45-POP.662 |

## 1017 STAGGER LEE

*Composers*: Lloyd Price & Harold Logan

*Publishers*: Sheldon Music Ltd.

*Date of Entry*: 25.4.59

*Highest Position*: 29
*Weeks on Chart*: 1

*Recordings*:

| | | |
|---|---|---|
| Lloyd Price | 1/59 | HMV POP.580 (& 45–) |
| Paul Rich | 4/59 | Embassy WB.327 (& 45–) |

## 1018 I NEED YOUR LOVE TONIGHT

*Composers*: Sid Wayne & Bix Reichner

*Publishers*: Hill & Range Songs (London) Ltd.

*Date of Entry*: 2.5.59

*Highest Position*: 12
*Weeks on Chart*: 12

*Recordings*:

| | | |
|---|---|---|
| Elvis Presley with The Jordanaires | 4/59 | RCA.1113 (& 45–) |
| Rikki Henderson | 5/59 | Embassy WB.334 (& 45–) |

## 1019 MANHATTAN SPIRITUAL

*Composer*: Billy Maxted

*Publishers*: Good Music Ltd.

*Date of Entry*: 2.5.59

*Highest Position*: 26
*Weeks on Chart*: 1

*Recordings*:

| | | |
|---|---|---|
| Francis Bay and his Orchestra | 1/59 | Philips PB.899 (& 45–) |
| Reg Owen and his Orchestra | 1/59 | Pye Int. N.25009/ (45) 7N.25009 |

## 1020 FRENCH FOREIGN LEGION

*Composers*: Aaron Schroeder & Guy Wood

*Publishers*: Barton Music Ltd.

*Date of Entry*: 2.5.59

*Highest Position*: 28
*Weeks on Chart*: 1

*Recording*:

| | | |
|---|---|---|
| Frank Sinatra | 3/59 | Capitol CL.14997 (& 45–) |

## 1021 I KNEEL AT YOUR THRONE

| | | |
|---|---|---|
| *Composers*: Marvin Scott & Addy Baron | | *Date of Entry*: 2.5.59 |
| *Publishers*: Bourne Music Ltd. | | *Highest Position*: 28<br>*Weeks on Chart*: 2 |

*Recordings*:

| | | |
|---|---|---|
| Jimmy Lloyd | 3/59 | Philips PB.909<br>(& 45-) |
| Joe Medlin | 3/59 | Mercury AMT.1032<br>(& 45-) |

## 1022 ROULETTE

| | | |
|---|---|---|
| *Composer*: Trevor H. Stanford | | *Date of Entry*: 9.5.59 |
| *Publishers*: Mills Music Ltd. | | *Highest Position*: 1<br>*Weeks on Chart*: 38 |

*Recordings*:

| | | |
|---|---|---|
| Russ Conway (piano) | 5/59 | Columbia DB.4298<br>(& 45-) |
| Victor Silvester and his Ballroom<br>  Orchestra | 6/59 | Columbia DB.4329<br>(& 45-) |
| Joe Julian and his Piano | 6/59 | Embassy WB.341<br>(& 45-) |

## 1023 NEVER BE ANYONE ELSE BUT YOU

| | | |
|---|---|---|
| *Composer*: Baker Knight | | *Date of Entry*: 9.5.59 |
| *Publishers*: Commodore-Imperial Music Ltd. | | *Highest Position*: 9<br>*Weeks on Chart*: 18 |

*Recordings*:

| | | |
|---|---|---|
| Ricky Nelson | 2/59 | London HLP.8817<br>(& 45-) |
| Nikki Henderson | 5/59 | Embassy WB.334<br>(& 45-) |

## 1024 I MISS YOU SO

| | | |
|---|---|---|
| *Composers*: Jimmy Henderson, Bertha Scott &<br>  Sid Robin | | *Date of Entry*: 9.5.59 |
| *Publishers*: Blossom Music Co. Ltd. | | *Highest Position*: 24<br>*Weeks on Chart*: 4 |

*Recordings*:

| | | |
|---|---|---|
| Johnnie Ray | 4/57 | Philips PB.683 |
| Paul Anka | 4/59 | Columbia DB.4286<br>(& 45-) |

## 1025 SUDDENLY

| | | |
|---|---|---|
| *Composer*: Mike Pratt | | *Date of Entry*: 9.5.59 |
| *Publishers*: Peter Maurice Music Co. Ltd. | | *Highest Position*: 28<br>*Weeks on Chart*: 1 |

*Recording*:

| | | |
|---|---|---|
| Petula Clark with The Beryl Stott Group | 3/59 | Pye Nixa N.15191/<br>(45) 7N.15191 |

## 1026 IT'S LATE

| | | |
|---|---|---|
| *Composer*: Dorsey Burnette | | *Date of Entry*: 16.5.59/<br>Pos: 23/Wks: 9 |
| *Publishers*: Commodore-Imperial Music Ltd. | | *Re-entry*: 1.8.59<br>Pos: 26/Wks: 1<br>*2nd re-entry*: 15.8.59/<br>Pos: 25/Wks: 1 |

*Recordings*:

| | | |
|---|---|---|
| Ricky Nelson | 2/59 | London HLP.8817<br>(& 45-) |
| Hal Munro | 5/59 | Embassy WB.336<br>(& 45-) |

## 1027 I'VE WAITED SO LONG

| | | |
|---|---|---|
| *Composer*: Jerry Lordan | | *Date of Entry*: 16.5.59 |
| *Publishers*: Pan-Musik Ltd. | | *Highest Position*: 7<br>*Weeks on Chart*: 14 |

*Recordings*:

| | | |
|---|---|---|
| Anthony Newley | 4/59 | Decca F.11127<br>(& 45-) |
| Paul Rich | 5/59 | Embassy WB.337<br>(& 45-) |

## 1028 PINK SHOELACES

| | | |
|---|---|---|
| *Composer*: Mickie Grant | | *Date of Entry*: 16.5.59/<br>Pos: 28/Wks: 1 |
| *Publishers*: Ardmore & Beechwood Ltd. | | *Re-entry*: 13.6.59/<br>Pos: 30/Wks: 1 |

*Recordings*:

| | | |
|---|---|---|
| Dodie Stevens | 3/59 | London HLD.8834<br>(& 45-) |
| Alma Cogan | 3/59 | HMV 45-POP.608 |

## 1029 GOODBYE JIMMY, GOODBYE

| | | |
|---|---|---|
| *Composer*: Jack Vaughn | | *Date of Entry*: 23.5.59 |
| *Publishers*: Sydney Bron Music Co. | | *Highest Position*: 4 |
| | | *Weeks on Chart*: 24 |

*Recordings*:

| | | |
|---|---|---|
| Kathy Linden | 5/59 | Felsted AF.122 (& 45-) |
| The Kaye Sisters | 5/59 | Philips PB.925 (& 45-) |
| Ruby Murray | 5/59 | Columbia DB.4305 (& 45-) |
| Kathie Kay | 5/59 | HMV POP.625 (& 45-) |
| Maureen Evans | 6/59 | Embassy WB.344 (& 45-) |

## 1030 GUITAR BOOGIE SHUFFLE

| | | |
|---|---|---|
| *Composer*: Arthur 'Guitar Boogie' Smith | | *Date of Entry*: 30.5.59/ Pos: 24/Wks: 2 |
| *Publishers*: Southern Music Publishing Co. Ltd. | | *Re-entry*: 20.6.59/ Pos: 30/Wks: 1 |

*Recordings*:

| | | |
|---|---|---|
| Bert Weedon (guitar) | 5/59 | Top Rank JAR.117 (& 45-) |
| The Virtues | 5/59 | HMV 45-POP.621 |
| Bud Ashton (guitar) | 6/59 | Embassy WB.341 (& 45-) |

## 1031 MEAN STREAK

| | | |
|---|---|---|
| *Composer*: Ian Samwell | | *Date of Entry*: 30.5.59 |
| *Publishers*: Kalith Music Ltd. | | *Highest Position*: 26 |
| | | *Weeks on Chart*: 3 |

*Recordings*:

| | | |
|---|---|---|
| Cliff Richard and The Drifters | 4/59 | Columbia DB.4290 (& 45-) |
| Johnny Worth | 6/59 | Embassy WB.338 (& 45-) |

## 1032 I GO APE

| | | |
|---|---|---|
| *Composers*: Neil Sedaka & Howard Greenfield | | *Date of Entry*: 30.5.59/ Pos: 28/Wks: 2 |
| *Publishers*: Aldon Music Ltd. | | *Re-entry*: 27.6.59/ Pos: 24/Wks: 2 |

*Recordings*:

| | | |
|---|---|---|
| Neil Sedaka | 3/59 | RCA.1115 (& 45-) |
| Paul Rich | 5/59 | Embassy WB.337 (& 45-) |

## 1033 WHERE WERE YOU (on our Wedding Day)?

| | | |
|---|---|---|
| *Composers*: Harold Logan, Lloyd Price & John Patton | | *Date of Entry*: 30.5.59 Pos: 30/Wks: 1 |
| *Publishers*: Monarch Music Ltd. | | *Re-entry*: 27.6.59/ Pos: 28/Wks: 2 |

*Recordings*:

| | | |
|---|---|---|
| Lloyd Price | 4/59 | HMV 45-POP.598 |
| Hal Munro | 6/59 | Embassy WB.340 (& 45-) |

## 1034 DREAM LOVER

| | | |
|---|---|---|
| *Composer*: Bobby Darin | | *Date of Entry*: 6.6.59 |
| *Publishers*: Aldon Music Ltd. | | *Highest Position*: 4 |
| | | *Weeks on Chart*: 17 |

*Recordings*:

| | | |
|---|---|---|
| Tommy Leonetti | 2/59 | RCA.1107 (& 45-) |
| Joe Loss and his Orchestra | 4/59 | HMV 45-POP.606 |
| Lorie Mann | 4/59 | Top Rank JAR.116 (& 45-) |
| Bobby Darin | 5/59 | London HLE & HLK.8867 (& 45-) |
| Duffy Power | 5/59 | Fontana H.194 (& 45-) |
| Joe Gordon | 6/59 | HMV POP.634 (& 45-) |
| Hal Munro | 6/59 | Embassy WB.340 (& 45-) |

## 1035 PERSONALITY (You've got Personality)

| | | |
|---|---|---|
| *Composers*: Lloyd Price & Harold Logan | | *Date of Entry*: 13.6.59 |
| *Publishers*: Leeds Music Ltd. | | *Highest Position*: 7 |
| | | *Weeks on Chart*: 17 |

*Recordings*:

| | | |
|---|---|---|
| Anthony Newley | 5/59 | Decca F.11142 (& 45-) |
| Lloyd Price | 6/59 | HMV POP.626 (& 45-) |
| Joyce Shock | 6/59 | Philips PB.934 (& 45-) |
| Rikki Henderson | 6/59 | Embassy WB.343 (& 45-) |

## 1036   A TEENAGER IN LOVE

*Composers*: Jerome 'Doc' Pomus & Mort Shuman    *Date of Entry*: 13.6.59

*Publishers*: West One Music Ltd.    *Highest Position*: 3
         *Weeks on Chart*: 18

*Recordings*:

| | | |
|---|---|---|
| Dion and The Belmonts | 5/59 | London HLU.8874 (& 45-) |
| Marty Wilde | 5/59 | Philips PB.926 (& 45-) |
| Craig Douglas | 5/59 | Top Rank JAR.133 (& 45-) |
| Dickie Valentine | 5/59 | Pye Nixa N.15202/ (45) 7N.15202 |
| Rikki Henderson | 6/59 | Embassy WB.343 (& 45-) |

## 1037   KANSAS CITY

*Composers*: Jerry Leiber & Mike Stoller    *Date of Entry*: 13.6.59/
         Pos: 26/Wks: 1

*Publishers*: Macmelodies Ltd.    *Re-entry*: 4.7.59/
         Pos: 25/Wks: 5

*Recordings*:

| | | |
|---|---|---|
| Little Richard | 5/59 | London HLU.8868 (& 45-) |
| Jack Parnell (vocal and drums) | 5/59 | HMV 45-POP.630 |
| Johnny Duncan and the Blue Grass Boys | 5/59 | Columbia DB.4311 (& 45-) |
| Hank Ballard and The Midnighters | 5/59 | Parlophone 45-R.4558 |
| Wilbert Harrison (vocal and guitar) | 6/59 | Top Rank JAR.132 (& 45-) |
| Rikki Henderson | 6/59 | Embassy WB.339 (& 45-) |

## 1038   FORT WORTH JAIL

*Composer*: Dick Reinhart    *Date of Entry*: 13.6.59

*Publishers*: Peter Maurice Music Co. Ltd.    *Highest Position*: 29
         *Weeks on Chart*: 1

*Recordings*:

| | | |
|---|---|---|
| Lonnie Donegan and his Skiffle Group | 4/59 | Pye Nixa N.15198/ (45) 7N.15198 |
| Johnny Worth | 6/59 | Embassy WB.338 (& 45-) |

## 1039   POOR JENNY

*Composers*: Felice & Boudleaux Bryant    *Date of Entry*: 20.6.59/
         Pos: 23/Wks: 4

*Publishers*: Acuff-Rose Publishing Co. Ltd.    *Re-entry*: 8.8.59/
         Pos: 29/Wks: 1

*Recordings*:

| | | |
|---|---|---|
| The Everly Brothers | 5/59 | London HLA.8863 (& 45-) |
| Paul Rich | 7/59 | Embassy WB.346 (& 45-) |

## 1040   TAKE A MESSAGE TO MARY

*Composers*: Felice & Boudleaux Bryant    *Date of Entry*: 20.6.59/
         Pos: 22/Wks: 3

*Publishers*: Acuff-Rose Publishing Co. Ltd.    *Re-entry*: 8.8.59/
         Pos: 28/Wks: 2

*Recordings*:

| | | |
|---|---|---|
| The Everly Brothers | 5/59 | London HLA.8863 (& 45-) |
| Paul Rich | 6/59 | Embassy WB.342 (& 45-) |

## 1041   PIXILATED PENGUIN

*Composer*: Michael Carr    *Date of Entry*: 20.6.59/
         Pos: 22/Wks: 3

*Publishers*: Ardmore & Beechwood Ltd.    *Re-entry*: 8.8.59/
         Pos: 28/Wks: 2
         *2nd re-entry*: 1.8.59/
         Pos: 29/Wks: 1

*Recording*:

| | | |
|---|---|---|
| Russ Conway (piano) | 2/59 | Columbia DB.4256 (& 45-) |

## 1042   WHY SHOULD I BE LONELY?

*Composers*: Jimmie Rodgers & Estelle Lovell    *Date of Entry*: 20.6.59/
         Pos: 29/Wks: 1

*Publishers*: Southern Music Publishing Co. Ltd.    *Re-entry*: 22.8.59/
         Pos: 29/Wks: 1
         *2nd re-entry*: 12.9.59/
         Pos: 27/Wks: 2

*Recording*:

| | | |
|---|---|---|
| Tony Brent | 5/59 | Columbia 45-DB.4304 |

## 1043 THE BATTLE OF NEW ORLEANS

| | | |
|---|---|---|
| *Composers:* Traditional, arranged by Jimmie Driftwood | *Date of Entry:* 27.6.59/ Pos: 7/Wks: 15 | |
| *Publishers:* Acuff-Rose Publishing Co. Ltd. | *Re-entry:* 17.10.59/ Pos: 29/Wks: 1 | |
| | *2nd re-entry:* 7.11.59/ Pos: 29/Wks: 1 | |

*Recordings:*

| | | |
|---|---|---|
| Lonnie Donegan and his Skiffle Group | 6/59 | Pye N.15206/ (45) 7N.15206 |
| Johnny Horton | 6/59 | Philips PB.932 (& 45-) |
| Glen Mason | 6/59 | Parlophone R.4562 (& 45-) |
| Vaughn Monroe | 6/59 | RCA.1124 (& 45-) |
| Bob Cort | 6/59 | Decca F.11145 (& 45-) |
| Paul Rich | 7/59 | Embassy WB.345 (& 45-) |
| Homer and Jethro [Parody titled 'The Battle of Kookamonga' with revised lyrics by Reynolds] | 9/59 | RCA.1148 (& 45-) |

## 1044 TRAMPOLINA

| | | |
|---|---|---|
| *Composer:* Geoff Love | *Date of Entry:* 27.6.59 | |
| *Publishers:* Harvard Music Ltd. | *Highest Position:* 11 *Weeks on Chart:* 16 | |

*Recording:*

| | | |
|---|---|---|
| Russ Conway (piano) | 5/59 | Columbia DB.4298 (& 45-) |

## 1045 I KNOW

| | | |
|---|---|---|
| *Composers:* Carl Stutz & Edith Lindeman | *Date of Entry:* 4.7.59 | |
| *Publishers:* B. Feldman & Co. Ltd. | *Highest Position:* 11 *Weeks on Chart:* 18 | |

*Recordings:*

| | | |
|---|---|---|
| Perry Como with The Ray Charles Singers | 6/59 | RCA.1126 (& 45-) |
| Rikki Henderson | 9/59 | Embassy WB.349 (& 45-) |

## 1046 LIPSTICK ON YOUR COLLAR

| | | |
|---|---|---|
| *Composers:* Edna Lewis & George Goehring | *Date of Entry:* 4.7.59 | |
| *Publishers:* Joy Music Ltd. | *Highest Position:* 5 *Weeks on Chart:* 20 | |

*Recordings:*

| | | |
|---|---|---|
| Connie Francis | 6/59 | MGM.1018 (& 45-) |
| Maureen Evans | 9/59 | Embassy WB.348 (& 45-) |

## 1047 THE SUMMER OF THE SEVENTEENTH DOLL

| | | |
|---|---|---|
| *Composer:* Norman O'Brien | *Date of Entry:* 11.7.59 | |
| *Publishers:* Francis Day & Hunter Ltd. | *Highest Position:* 21 *Weeks on Chart:* 3 | |

*Recording:*

| | | |
|---|---|---|
| Winifred Atwell (piano) | 6/59 | Decca F.11143 (& 45-) |

## 1048 LIVING DOLL

| | | |
|---|---|---|
| *Composer:* Lionel Bart | *Date of Entry:* 11.7.59 | |
| *Publishers:* Peter Maurice Music Co. Ltd. | *Highest Position:* 2 *Weeks on Chart:* 29 | |

*Recordings:*

| | | |
|---|---|---|
| Cliff Richard and The Drifters | 5/59 | Columbia DB.4306 (& 45-) |
| Johnny Worth | 6/59 | Embassy WB.347 (& 45-) |

## 1049 THE HEART OF A MAN

| | | |
|---|---|---|
| *Composers:* Peggy Cochrane & Paddy Roberts | *Date of Entry:* 11.7.59 | |
| *Publishers:* David Toff Music Publishing Co. Ltd. | *Highest Position:* 4 *Weeks on Chart:* 20 | |

*Recordings:*

| | | |
|---|---|---|
| Frankie Vaughan | 5/59 | Philips PB.930 (& 45-) |
| Rikki Henderson | 6/59 | Embassy WB.339 (& 45-) |

## 1050 THE WONDER OF YOU

| | | |
|---|---|---|
| *Composer*: Baker Knight | | *Date of Entry*: 18.7.59/<br>Pos: 11/Wks: 14 |
| *Publishers*: Leeds Music Ltd. | | *Re-entry*: 31.10.59/<br>Pos: 27/Wks: 1 |

*Recordings*:
| | | |
|---|---|---|
| Ronnie Carroll | 7/59 | Philips PB.944<br>(& 45-) |
| Ronnie Hilton and The Riddelle Singers | 7/59 | HMV POP.638<br>(& 45-) |
| Kay Peterson | 7/59 | RCA.1131<br>(& 45-) |
| Sheila Buxton | 7/59 | Top Rank JAR.144<br>(& 45-) |

## 1051 WATERLOO

| | |
|---|---|
| *Composers*: John D. Loudermilk &<br>Marijohn Wilkin | *Date of Entry*: 18.7.59 |
| *Publishers*: Cedarwood Music Ltd. | *Highest Position*: 15<br>*Weeks on Chart*: 10 |

*Recordings*:
| | | |
|---|---|---|
| The Mudlarks | 6/59 | Columbia DB.4331<br>(& 45-) |
| Bob Cort | 6/59 | Decca F.11145<br>(& 45-) |
| Stonewall Jackson | 6/59 | Philips PB.941<br>(& 45-) |
| Homer and Jethro | 9/59 | RCA.1148<br>(& 45-) |
| Nikki Henderson | 9/59 | Embassy WB.349<br>(& 45-) |

## 1052 A BIG HUNK O' LOVE

| | |
|---|---|
| *Composers*: Aaron Schroeder & Sid Wyche | *Date of Entry*: 25.7.59/<br>Pos: 24/Wks: 3 |
| *Publishers*: Hill & Range Songs Ltd. | *Re-entry*: 22.8.59/<br>Pos: 24/Wks: 1<br>*2nd re-entry*: 5.9.59/<br>Pos: 25/Wks: 1 |

*Recordings*:
| | | |
|---|---|---|
| Elvis Presley with The Jordanaires | 7/59 | RCA.1136 (& 45-) |
| Paul Rich | 7/59 | Embassy WB.346<br>(& 45-) |

## 1053 THREE STARS

| | | |
|---|---|---|
| *Composer*: Tommy Dee | | *Date of Entry*: 1.8.59 |
| *Publishers*: Campbell Connelly & Co. Ltd. | | *Highest Position*: 28<br>*Weeks on Chart*: 1 |

(Note: This song was written as a tribute to Ritchie Valens, Buddy Holly and The Big Bopper – J.P. Richardson – who were all killed in an air crash on 23 February, 1959.)

*Recordings*:
| | | |
|---|---|---|
| Ruby Wright with narration by Dick Pike | 5/59 | Parlophone<br>45-R.4556 |
| Carol Kay with Tommy Dee (narrator)<br>and Teen Jones (inst) | 5/59 | Melodisc 1516<br>(& 45-) |

## 1054 THE WINDOWS OF PARIS

| | |
|---|---|
| *Composer*: Tony Osborne | *Date of Entry*: 1.8.59/<br>Pos: 27/Wks: 3 |
| *Publishers*: Mason Music Ltd. | *Re-entry*: 29.8.59/<br>Pos: 19/Wks: 9 |

*Recordings*:
| | | |
|---|---|---|
| Tony Osborne and his Orchestra | 6/59 | HMV 45-POP.633 |
| The Knightsbridge Strings | 8/59 | Top Rank JAR.170<br>(& 45-) |
| Victor Silvester and his Ballroom<br>Orchestra | 11/59 | Columbia DB.4372<br>(& 45-)★ |

## 1055 LONELY BOY

| | |
|---|---|
| *Composer*: Paul Anka | *Date of Entry*: 8.8.59/<br>Pos: 9/Wks: 13 |
| *Publishers*: Sydney Bron Music Co. | *Re-entry*: 21.11.59/<br>Pos: 25/Wks: 1 |

*Recordings*:
| | | |
|---|---|---|
| Paul Anka | 6/59 | Columbia DB.4324<br>(& 45-) |
| Johnny Worth | 6/59 | Embassy WB.347<br>(& 45-) |

## 1056 TWIXT TWELVE AND TWENTY

| | |
|---|---|
| *Composers*: Aaron Schroeder & Fredda Gold | *Date of Entry*: 8.8.59 |
| *Publishers*: Spoone Music Ltd. | *Highest Position*: 17<br>*Weeks on Chart*: 8 |

*Recording*:
| | | |
|---|---|---|
| Pat Boone | 7/59 | London HLD.8910<br>(& 45-) |

## 1057 ONLY SIXTEEN

| | | |
|---|---|---|
| Composer: Barbara Campbell | | Date of Entry: 15.8.59 |
| Publishers: Ardmore & Beechwood Ltd. | | Highest Position: 1 |
| | | Weeks on Chart: 17 |

Recordings:

| | | |
|---|---|---|
| Sam Cooke | 7/59 | HMV POP.642 |
| | | (& 45-) |
| Craig Douglas | 7/59 | Top Rank JAR.159 |
| | | (& 45-) |
| Al Saxon | 7/59 | Fontana H.205 |
| | | (& 45-) |
| Rikki Henderson | 9/59 | Embassy WB.351 |
| | | (& 45-) |

## 1058 CHINA TEA

| | | |
|---|---|---|
| Composer: Trevor H. Stanford | | Date of Entry: 15.8.59 |
| Publishers: Mills Music Ltd. | | Highest Position: 1 |
| | | Weeks on Chart: 25 |

Recordings:

| | | |
|---|---|---|
| Russ Conway (piano) | 8/59 | Columbia DB.4337 |
| | | (& 45-) |
| Joe Julian (piano) | 9/59 | Embassy WB.350 |
| | | (& 45-) |
| Victor Silvester and his Ballroom Orchestra | 10/59 | Columbia DB.4353 |
| | | (& 45-) |

## 1059 MY WISH CAME TRUE

| | | |
|---|---|---|
| Composer: Ivory Joe Hunter | | Date of Entry: 22.8.59 |
| Publishers: Southern Music Publishing Co. Ltd. | | Highest Position: 27 |
| | | Weeks on Chart: 1 |

Recording:

| | | |
|---|---|---|
| Elvis Presley with The Jordanaires | 7/59 | RCA.1136 (& 45-) |

## 1060 FOR A PENNY

| | | |
|---|---|---|
| Composer: Charles Singleton | | Date of Entry: 22.8.59 |
| Publishers: Roosevelt Music Ltd. | | Highest Position: 28 |
| | | Weeks on Chart: 1 |

Recording:

| | | |
|---|---|---|
| Pat Boone | 5/59 | London HLD.8855 |
| | | (& 45-) |

## 1061 HERE COMES SUMMER

| | | |
|---|---|---|
| Composer: Jerry Keller | | Date of Entry: 29.8.59 |
| Publishers: Mills Music Ltd. | | Highest Position: 5 |
| | | Weeks on Chart: 14 |

Recording:

| | | |
|---|---|---|
| Jerry Keller | 6/59 | London HLR.8890 |
| | | (& 45-) |

## 1062 SOMEONE

| | | |
|---|---|---|
| Composer: Bill Tennyson | | Date of Entry: 29.8.59 |
| Publishers: Johnny Mathis Music Ltd. | | Highest Position: 9 |
| | | Weeks on Chart: 12 |

Recordings:

| | | |
|---|---|---|
| Johnny Mathis | 7/59 | Fontana H.199 |
| | | (& 45-) |
| Victor Silvester and his Ballroom Orchestra | 11/59 | Columbia DB.4371 |
| | | (& 45-) |

## 1063 HIGH HOPES

| | | |
|---|---|---|
| Composers: Jimmy Van Heusen & Sammy Cahn | | Date of Entry: 5.9.59 |
| Publishers: Barton Music Ltd. | | Highest Position: 5 |
| | | Weeks on Chart: 24 |

Recordings:

| | | |
|---|---|---|
| Dave King | 8/59 | Pye Int. N.25032/ |
| | | (45) 7N.25032 |
| Frank Sinatra with 'A Bunch of Kids' | 8/59 | Capitol CL.15052 |
| | | (& 45-) |
| The Jonah Jones Quartet | 8/59 | Capitol 45-CL.1506C |
| Gerry Grant | 9/59 | Embassy WB.350 |
| | | (& 45-) |

## 1064 FORTY MILES OF BAD ROAD

| | | |
|---|---|---|
| Composers: Duane Eddy & Al Casey | | Date of Entry: 5.9.59 |
| | | Pos: 26/Wks: 2 |
| Publishers: Burlington Music Co. Ltd. | | Re-entry: 26.9.59 |
| | | Pos: 27/Wks: 1 |
| | | 2nd re-entry: 10.10.59/ |
| | | Pos: 27/Wks: 1 |
| | | 3rd re-entry: 7.11.59/ |
| | | Pos: 27/Wks: 1 |

Recordings:

| | | |
|---|---|---|
| Duane Eddy and his Twangy Guitar | 8/59 | London HLW.8929 |
| | | (& 45-) |
| Bud Ashton (guitar) | 10/59 | Embassy WB.355 |
| | | (& 45-) |

## 1065 PEGGY SUE GOT MARRIED

*Composer*: Buddy Holly

*Publishers*: Southern Music Publishing Co. Ltd.

*Date of Entry*: 5.9.59/
Pos: 28/Wks: 1
*Re-entry*: 26.9.59/
Pos: 23/Wks: 3

*Recordings*:
| | | |
|---|---|---|
| Buddy Holly with The Jack Hansen Combo | 9/59 | Coral Q.72376 (& 45-) |
| Rikki Henderson | 10/59 | Embassy WB.357 (& 45-) |
| The Crickets (inst) with David Box (vocal & guitar) | 1/61 | Coral 45-Q.72417★ |

## 1066 MONA LISA

*Composers*: Jay Livingston & Ray Evans

*Publishers*: Famous Chappell

*Date of Entry*: 12.9.59/
Pos: 25/Wks: 1
*Re-entry*: 26.9.59/
Pos: 14/Wks: 9

(Note: This song first appeared in the Sheet Music Charts in 1950 – see Song No. 243. Of the versions released then, only the Nat 'King' Cole recording was still available in 1959.)

*Later recordings*:
| | | |
|---|---|---|
| Conway Twitty | 7/59 | MGM.1029 (& 45-) |
| Carl Mann | 9/59 | London HLS.8935 (& 45-) |
| Paul Rich | 9/59 | Embassy WB.353 (& 45-) |
| Victor Silvester and his Ballroom Orchestra | 11/59 | Columbia DB.4372 (& 45-) |

## 1067 SOMETIME, SOMEWHERE

*Composers*: Frankie Vaughan & Lionel Bart
*Publishers*: Filmusic Ltd.

*Date of Entry*: 12.9.59/
*Highest Position*: 30
*Weeks on Chart*: 1

*Recording*:
| | | |
|---|---|---|
| Frankie Vaughan | 5/59 | Philips PB.930 (& 45-) |

## 1068 TALLAHASSEE LASSIE

*Composers*: Frank C. Slay, Bob Crewe & Frederick A. Picariello
*Publishers*: Francis Day & Hunter Ltd.

*Date of Entry*: 12.9.59
*Highest Position*: 30
*Weeks on Chart*: 1

*Recordings*:
| | | |
|---|---|---|
| Freddy Cannon | 6/59 | Top Rank JAR.135 (& 45-) |
| Tommy Steele | 7/59 | Decca F.11152 (& 45-) |

| | | |
|---|---|---|
| Rikki Henderson | 9/59 | Embassy WB.351 (& 45-) |

## 1069 THE THREE BELLS (Les Trois Cloches) (The Jimmy Brown Song)

*Composers*: Jean Villard (Gilles) & Bert Reisfeld

*Publishers*: Southern Music Publishing Co. Ltd.

*Date of Entry*: 19.9.59

*Highest Position*: 4
*Weeks on Chart*: 17

(Note: For the earlier popularity of this song under the title 'While the Angelus was ringing' see Song No. 165 in 1949.)

*Recordings*:
| | | |
|---|---|---|
| The Browns | 8/59 | RCA.1140 (& 45-) |
| Dick Flood | 8/59 | Felsted AF.125 (& 45-) |
| Shane Rimmer with The Spinners | 9/59 | Columbia 45-DB.4343 |
| Les Compagnons de la Chanson | 9/59 | Columbia 45-DB.4358 |
| Rikki Henderson | 10/59 | Embassy WB.357 (& 45-) |

## 1070 'TIL I KISSED YOU

*Composer*: Don Everly

*Publishers*: Acuff-Rose Publishing Co. Ltd.

*Date of Entry*: 19.9.59/
Pos: 27/Wks: 2
*Re-entry*: 10.10.59/
Pos: 20/Wks: 8
*2nd re-entry*: 12.12.59/
Pos: 29/Wks: 1

*Recordings*:
| | | |
|---|---|---|
| The Everly Brothers | 9/59 | London HLA.8934 (& 45-) |
| Paul Rich | 10/59 | Embassy WB.355 (& 45-) |

## 1071 BROKEN-HEARTED MELODY

*Composers*: Sherman Edwards & Hal David

*Publishers*: Peter Maurice Music Co. Ltd.

*Date of Entry*: 19.9.59/
Pos: 29/Wks: 2
*Re-entry*: 10.10.59/
Pos: 10/Wks: 12

*Recordings*:
| | | |
|---|---|---|
| Sarah Vaughan | 7/59 | Mercury 45-AMT.1057 |
| Tony Raymond | 8/59 | Fontana H.213 (& 45-) |
| Maureen Evans | 10/59 | Embassy WB.356 (& 45-) |

## 1072 ONE MORE SUNRISE (Morgen)

*Composers*: Peter Mosser with English lyrics by
    Noel Sherman

*Date of Entry*: 3.10.59

*Publishers*: Dominion Music Co. Ltd.

*Highest Position*: 3
*Weeks on Chart*: 15

*Recordings*:
| | | |
|---|---|---|
| (a) Titled 'One More Sunrise' | | |
|     Leslie Uggams | 9/59 | Philips PB.954 |
| Rex Allen | | (& 45-) |
| | 9/59 | Top Rank |
| Dickie Valentine | | 45-JAR.188 |
| | 9/59 | Pye N.15221/ |
| Barry Kendall | | (45) 7N.15221 |
| | 12/59 | Embassy WB.366 |
| (b) Titled 'Morgen' | | (& 45-) |
|     Eddie Calvert – The Man with the | 9/59 | Columbia DB.4342 |
|     Golden Trumpet | | (& 45-) |
| Vera Lynn | 9/59 | Decca F.11157 |
| | | (& 45-) |
| Ken Mackintosh (soprano sax) with | 9/59 | HMV 45-POP.656 |
|     rhythm | | |
| The Adams Singers directed by Cliff | 9/59 | Pye Int. N.25033/ |
|     Adams | | (45) 7N.25033 |
| Billy Vaughn and his Orchestra | 9/59 | London HLD.8952 |
| | | (& 45-) |
| Richard Maltby and his Orchestra and | 9/59 | Philips PB.955 |
|     Chorus | | (& 45-) |
| Ivo Robic | 10/59 | Polydor 45- |
| | | NH.23923 |
| Victor Silvester and his Ballroom | 12/59 | Columbia DB.4384 |
|     Orchestra | | (& 45-) |

## 1073 MACK THE KNIFE

*Composers*: Kurt Weill, Berthold Brecht &
    Mark Blitzstein

*Date of Entry*: 3.10.59

*Publishers*: Arcadia Music Publishing Co. Ltd.

*Highest Position*: 1
*Weeks on Chart*: 20

*Recordings*:
| | | |
|---|---|---|
| Bobby Darin | 9/59 | London HLK.8939 |
| | | (& 45-) |
| Louis Armstrong and his All-Stars (Louis | 10/59 | Philips PB.967 |
|     Armstrong) | | (& 45-) |
| Dick Jordan | 11/59 | Embassy WB.358 |
| | | (& 45-) |
| Ella Fitzgerald with The Paul Smith | 4/60 | HMV 45-POP.736★ |
|     Quartet | | |

(Note: The Louis Armstrong version is a reissue of Philips PB.574 which
was titled 'The Theme from the Threepenny Opera' - see Song No.
711.)

## 1074 SEA OF LOVE

*Composers*: George Khoury & Phil Baptiste

*Date of Entry*: 3.10.59

*Publishers*: Southern Music Publishing Co. Ltd.

*Highest Position*: 13
*Weeks on Chart*: 10

*Recordings*:
| | | |
|---|---|---|
| Phil Phillips with The Twilights | 8/59 | Mercury 45- |
| | | AMT.1059 |
| Marty Wilde | 9/59 | Philips PB.959 |
| | | (& 45-) |
| Johnny Worth | 11/59 | Embassy WB.359 |
| | | (& 45-) |

## 1075 LONESOME (Si tu vois ma mère)

*Composer*: Sidney Bechet

*Date of Entry*: 3.10.59

*Publishers*: Essex Music Ltd.

*Highest Position*: 30
*Weeks on Chart*: 1

*Recordings*:
| | | |
|---|---|---|
| Chris Barber and his Jazz Band (featuring | 6/59 | Columbia DB.4333 |
|     Monty Sunshine – clarinet) | | (& 45-) |
| Sidney Bechet (soprano sax) with Claude | 11/59 | Vogue 45-V.9157★ |
|     Luter and his Orchestra [Titled 'Si tu | | |
|     vois ma mère'] | | |

## 1076 TREBLE CHANCE

*Composer*: Joe Henderson

*Date of Entry*: 10.10.59

*Publishers*: Henderson Music Ltd.

*Highest Position*: 10
*Weeks on Chart*: 15

*Recording*:
| | | |
|---|---|---|
| Joe 'Mr Piano' Henderson | 9/59 | Pye N.15224/ |
| | | (45) 7N.15224 |

## 1077 DYNAMITE

*Composer*: Ian Samwell

*Date of Entry*: 10.10.59

*Publishers*: Kalith Music Ltd.

*Highest Position*: 30
*Weeks on Chart*: 1

*Recordings*:
| | | |
|---|---|---|
| Cliff Richard with The Shadows | 10/59 | Columbia DB.4351 |
| | | (& 45-) |
| Rikki Henderson | 11/59 | Embassy WB.361 |
| | | (& 45-)★ |

## 1078 | TRAVELLIN' LIGHT

Composers: Sid Tepper & Roy C. Bennett
Publishers: Kalith Music Ltd./Aberbach (London) Ltd.

*Date of Entry:* 17.10.59
*Highest Position:* 2
*Weeks on Chart:* 18

Recordings:

| Cliff Richard with The Shadows | 10/59 | Columbia DB.4351 (& 45-) |
| Dick Jordan | 11/59 | Embassy WB.360 (& 45-) |

## 1079 | LITTLE DONKEY

Composer: Eric Boswell
Publishers: Chappell & Co. Ltd.

*Date of Entry:* 17.10.59
*Highest Position:* 1
*Weeks on Chart:* 16

Recordings:

| Gracie Fields with The Rita Williams Singers | 10/59 | Columbia DB.4360 (& 45-) |
| The Beverley Sisters | 10/59 | Decca F.11172 (& 45-) |
| The Junior Chorale cond. Harold Habberjam | 10/59 | Top Rank 45-JAR.212 |
| Nina and Frederik | 11/60 | Columbia 45-DB.4536★ |

(Note: This returned to the Charts in November, 1960 – and made No. 1 for four weeks over Christmas – the only occasion among the songs listed that a song became No. 1 for a second time with such a gap between.)

## 1080 | PLENTY GOOD LOVIN'

Composer: Connie Francis
Publishers: Leeds Music Ltd.

*Date of Entry:* 17.10.59
*Highest Position:* 28
*Weeks on Chart:* 1

Recordings:

| Connie Francis | 8/59 | MGM.1036 (& 45-) |
| Maureen Evans | 10/59 | Embassy WB.356 (& 45-) |

## 1081 | MR BLUE

Composer: Dewayne Blackwell
Publishers: Edwin H. Morris & Co. Ltd.

*Date of Entry:* 24.10.59
*Highest Position:* 6
*Weeks on Chart:* 13

Recordings:

| Mike Preston | 10/59 | Decca F.11167 (& 45-) |
| The Fleetwoods | 10/59 | Top Rank 45-JAR.202 |
| David Macbeth with The Beryl Stott Group | 10/59 | Pye N.15231/ (45) 7N.15231 |
| Nikki Price | 10/59 | Fontana H.217 (& 45-) |

---

| Dick Jordan | 11/59 | Embassy WB.360 (& 45-) |

## 1082 | MAKIN' LOVE

Composer: Floyd Robinson

*Date of Entry:* 24.10.59

Publishers: Chappell & Co. Ltd.

*Highest Position:* 23
*Weeks on Chart:* 7

Recordings:

| Vince Eager | 9/59 | Top Rank 45-JAR.191 |
| The King Brothers | 9/59 | Parlophone 45- R.4577 |
| Floyd Robinson | 9/59 | RCA.1146 (& 45-) |
| Hylda Baker | 11/59 | Decca F.11186 (& 45-) |
| Paul Rich | 11/59 | Embassy WB.363 (& 45-) |

## 1083 | IF YOU LOVE ME – I won't care (Hymne à l'amour)

Composers: Marguerite Monnot & Edith Piaf. English lyrics by Geoffrey Parsons

*Date of Entry:* 24.10.59

Publishers: Peter Maurice Music Co. Ltd.

*Highest Position:* 28
*Weeks on Chart:* 2

(Note: This song first appeared in the Sheet Music Charts in 1953 – see Song No. 517.)

Recordings:

| Rose Brennan with Joe Loss and his Orchestra | 10/53 | HMV B.10572 |
| Shirley Bassey with The Rita Williams Singers | 9/59 | Columbia DB.4344 (& 45-) |
| LaVern Baker | 9/59 | London HLE.8945 (& 45-) |
| Kay Starr (reissue of CL.14111 but with 'Wheel of fortune' (Song No. 377) on the reverse side) | 6/60 | Capitol 45-CL.15137★ |

## 1084 | JUST A LITTLE TOO MUCH

Composer: Johnny Burnette

*Date of Entry:* 24.10.59

Publishers: Sterling Music Publishing Co. Ltd.

*Highest Position:* 30
*Weeks on Chart:* 1

Recordings:

| Ricky Nelson | 8/59 | London HLP.8927 (& 45-) |
| Johnny Worth | 10/59 | Embassy WB.354 (& 45-) |

## 1085 SNOW COACH

| | | |
|---|---|---|
| *Composer*: Trevor H. Stanford | | *Date of Entry*: 31.10.59 |
| *Publishers*: B. Feldman & Co. Ltd. | | *Highest Position*: 3 |
| | | *Weeks on Chart*: 17 |

*Recordings*:

| | | |
|---|---|---|
| Russ Conway (piano) | 10/59 | Columbia DB.4368 (& 45-) |
| Victor Silvester and his Ballroom Orchestra | 12/59 | Columbia DB.4384 (& 45-) |
| Joe Julian (piano) | 12/59 | Embassy WB.366 |

## 1086 RED RIVER ROCK

| | | |
|---|---|---|
| *Composers*: Traditional, arranged by Tom King, Ira Mack & Fred Mendelsohn | | *Date of Entry*: 7.11.59/ Pos: 25/Wks: 1 |
| *Publishers*: Burlington Music Co. Ltd. | | *Re-entry*: 28.11.59/ Pos: 25/Wks: 6 |
| | | *2nd re-entry*: 16.1.60/ Pos: 26/Wks: 1 |

*Recordings*:

| | | |
|---|---|---|
| Johnny and The Hurricanes | 9/59 | London HL.8948 (& 45-) |
| Gene Redd and The Globetrotters [Titled 'Red River Valley Rock'] | 10/59 | Parlophone 45-R.4584 |
| The Gordon Franks Sextet | 11/59 | Embassy WB.363 (& 45-) |

## 1087 COUNT ON ME

| | | |
|---|---|---|
| *Composers*: John Wolf & Ben Raleigh | | *Date of Entry*: 7.11.59 |
| *Publishers*: Sheldon Music Ltd. | | *Highest Position*: 28 |
| | | *Weeks on Chart*: 2 |

*Recording*:

| | | |
|---|---|---|
| Shirley Bassey with The Rita Williams Singers | 9/59 | Columbia DB.4344 (& 45-) |

## 1088 PUT YOUR HEAD ON MY SHOULDER

| | | |
|---|---|---|
| *Composer*: Paul Anka | | *Date of Entry*: 7.11.59 |
| *Publishers*: Spanka Music Co. | | *Highest Position*: 11 |
| | | *Weeks on Chart*: 12 |

*Recordings*:

| | | |
|---|---|---|
| Paul Anka | 10/59 | Columbia DB.4355 (& 45-) |
| Dick Jordan | 11/59 | Embassy WB.358 (& 45-) |
| Victor Silvester and his Ballroom Orchestra | 1/60 | Columbia 45-DB.4396 |

## 1089 WHAT DO YOU WANT TO MAKE THOSE EYES AT ME FOR?

| | | |
|---|---|---|
| *Composers*: Joseph McCarthy, Howard Johnson & Jimmy Monaco | | *Date of Entry*: 14.11.59 |
| *Publishers*: Francis Day & Hunter Ltd. | | *Highest Position*: 1 |
| | | *Weeks on Chart*: 22 |

*Recordings*:

| | | |
|---|---|---|
| Marie Adams with Johnny Otis and his Orchestra | 1/59 | Capitol 45-CL.149( |
| Emile Ford and The Checkmates | 10/59 | Pye N.15225 (45) 7N.15225 |
| Johnny Worth | 11/59 | Embassy WB.364 (& 45-) |
| Victor Silvester and his Ballroom Orchestra | 1/60 | Columbia 45-DB.4395 |

## 1090 SEVEN LITTLE GIRLS SITTING IN THE BACK SEAT

| | | |
|---|---|---|
| *Composers*: Lee Pockriss & Bob Hilliard | | *Date of Entry*: 14.11. |
| *Publishers*: Sheldon Music Ltd. | | *Highest Position*: 2 |
| | | *Weeks on Chart*: 19 |

*Recordings*:

| | | |
|---|---|---|
| The Avons | 10/59 | Columbia 45-DB.4363 |
| Paul Evans and The Curls | 10/59 | London HLL.8968 (& 45-) |
| The Lana Sisters and Al Saxon | 10/59 | Fontana H.221 (& 45-) |
| Gary Mills | 10/59 | Top Rank 45-JAR.219 |
| Barry Kendall | 11/59 | Embassy WB.364 (& 45-) |

## 1091 THE VILLAGE OF ST BERNADETTE

| | | |
|---|---|---|
| *Composer*: Eula Parker | | *Date of Entry*: 14.11.59/Pos: 8/ Wks: 11 |
| *Publishers*: Francis Day & Hunter Ltd. | | *Re-entry*: 13.2.60/ Pos: 29/Wks: 1 |

*Recordings*:

| | | |
|---|---|---|
| Anne Shelton | 10/59 | Philips PB.969 (& 45-) |
| Rosemary June | 12/59 | London HLT.9014 (& 45-) |
| Andy Williams | 12/59 | London HLA.9018 (& 45-) |
| Bobbie Britton | 12/59 | Embassy WB.367 (& 45-) |

## 1092 THE KEY

*Composers*: Murray Campbell & Jack Fishman

*Publishers*: Leeds Music Ltd.

*Date of Entry*: 21.11.59

*Highest Position*: 22
*Weeks on Chart*: 6

*Recording*:
Robert Earl                    9/59    Philips PB.960
                                       (& 45-)

## 1093 HEARTACHES BY THE NUMBER

*Composer*: Harland Howard

*Publishers*: Joy Music Ltd.

*Date of Entry*: 28.11.59

*Highest Position*: 3
*Weeks on Chart*: 19

*Recordings*:
Guy Mitchell                   10/59   Philips PB.964
                                       (& 45-)
Paul Rich                      1/60    Embassy WB.374
                                       (& 45-)

## 1094 WHAT DO YOU WANT?

*Composer*: Les Vandyke

*Publishers*: Mills Music Ltd.

*Date of Entry*: 28.11.59

*Highest Position*: 3
*Weeks on Chart*: 16

*Recordings*:
Adam Faith                     10/59   Parlophone R.4591
                                       (& 45-)
Johnny Worth                   12/59   Embassy WB.369
                                       (& 45-)

## 1095 OH, CAROL

*Composers*: Howard Greenfield & Neil Sedaka

*Publishers*: Nevins-Kirshner Music Ltd.

*Date of Entry*: 28.11.59

*Highest Position*: 25
*Weeks on Chart*: 3

*Recordings*:
Neil Sedaka                    10/59   RCA.1152 (& 45-)
Johnny Worth                   12/59   Embassy WB.369
                                       (& 45-)

## 1096 JINGLE BELL ROCK

*Composers*: Joe Beal & Jim Boothe

*Publishers*: Cromwell Music Ltd.

*Date of Entry*: 5.12.59

*Highest Position*: 6
*Weeks on Chart*: 8

*Recordings*:
Bobby Helms                    11/58   Brunswick 05765
                                       (& 45-)
Teresa Brewer                  12/58   Coral Q.72349
                                       (& 45-)
Max Bygraves                   11/59   Decca F.11176
                                       (& 45-)

## 1097 THE LITTLE WHITE BULL

*Composers*: Lionel Bart, Michael Pratt &
Jimmy Bennett

*Publishers*: Peter Maurice Music Co. Ltd.

*Date of Entry*: 5.12.59

*Highest Position*: 4
*Weeks on Chart*: 18

*Recordings*:
Tommy Steele                   11/59   Decca F.11177
                                       (& 45-)
Paul Rich                      2/60    Embassy 45-WB.378

## 1098 PIANO PARTY – MEDLEY

*Publishers*: Francis Day & Hunter Ltd.

*Date of Entry*: 12.12.59
*Highest Position*: 22
*Weeks on Chart*: 4

(Note: This is the only Sheet Music Album to appear in the Sheet Music Charts between 1946 and 1959 – and, therefore, the only medley to appear in this book.)

*Recording*:
Winifred Atwell (piano)        11/59   Decca F.11183
                                       (& 45-)

(Titles of songs on both record and album as follows: Baby Face/Comin' through the Rye/Annie Laurie/Little Brown Jug/Let him go, let him tarry/Put your arms around me, honey/I'll be with you in Apple Blossom Time/Shine on Harvest Moon/Blue Skies/I'll never say 'never again' again/I'll see you in my dreams).

239

## 1099 IVY WILL CLING

| | |
|---|---|
| *Composers*: Earl Shuman & Mort Garson | *Date of Entry*: 19.12.59 |
| *Publishers*: John Fields Music Co. Ltd. | *Highest Position*: 15<br>*Weeks on Chart*: 7 |

*Recordings*:

| | | |
|---|---|---|
| Arnold Stang with The Sunshine Kids | 11/59 | Fontana H.226<br>(& 45-) |
| Bernard Bresslaw with Children's Chorus | 11/59 | HMV POP.669<br>(& 45-) |
| The Knightsbridge Chorale | 1/60 | Top Rank<br>45-JAR.266 |

## 1100 18TH CENTURY ROCK

| | |
|---|---|
| *Composers*: Jimmy Leach, Alan Roper &<br>John Ross | *Date of Entry*: 19.12.59 |
| *Publishers*: Harvard Music Ltd. | *Highest Position*: 29<br>*Weeks on Chart*: 2 |

*Recording*:

| | | |
|---|---|---|
| Alyn Ainsworth with The Rock-a-fellas | 10/59 | Parlophone 45-<br>R.4594 |

# OUTSTANDING FEATS

## The No.1 hits
The first numbered chart did not appear until
w.e. 29th May, 1947

| First week at No. 1 | Title | Weeks |
|---|---|---|
| 29 May 47 | Among my souvenirs | 4 |
| 26 Jun 47 | Tell me, Marianne | 1 |
| 3 Jul 47 | Among my souvenirs | 4 |
| 31 Jul 47 | A gal in calico | 3 |
| 21 Aug 47 | People will say we're in love | 1 |
| 28 Aug 47 | Now is the hour | 14 |
| 4 Dec 47 | Apple blossom wedding | 1 |
| 11 Dec 47 | Now is the hour | 1 |
| 18 Dec 47 | Apple blossom wedding | 6 (1 =) |
| 22 Jan 48 | Peg o' my heart | 1 (=) |
| 29 Jan 48 | Tree in the meadow | 3 |
| 19 Feb 48 | Near you | 1 |
| 26 Feb 48 | Tree in the meadow | 8 |
| 22 Apr 48 | Near you | 1 |
| 29 Apr 48 | Galway Bay | 22 |
| 30 Sep 48 | So tired | 7 |
| 18 Nov 48 | Buttons and bows | 11 |
| 3 Feb 49 | On a slow boat to China | 7 |
| 24 Mar 49 | Far away places | 2 |
| 7 Apr 49 | Twelfth Street Rag | 6 |
| 19 May 49 | Lavender blue | 5 |
| 25 Jun 49 | The wedding of Lilli Marlene | 7 |
| 13 Aug 49 | Riders in the sky | 9 |
| 15 Oct 49 | I don't see me in your eyes any more | 3 (1 =) |
| 29 Oct 49 | Forever and ever | 1 (=) |
| 5 Nov 49 | You're breaking my heart | 8 |
| 31 Dec 49 | The Harry Lime Theme | 1 |
| 7 Jan 50 | You're breaking my heart | 2 |
| 21 Jan 50 | The hop scotch polka | 1 |
| 28 Jan 50 | The Harry Lime Theme | 1 |
| 4 Feb 50 | Dear hearts and gentle people | 1 |
| 11 Feb 50 | The Harry Lime Theme | 3 (1 =) |
| 25 Feb 50 | Dear hearts and gentle people | 2 (1 =) |
| 11 Mar 50 | Music! Music! Music! | 6 |
| 22 Apr 50 | I'd've baked a cake | 1 |
| 29 Apr 50 | My foolish heart | 10 |
| 8 Jul 50 | Bewitched | 1 |
| 15 Jul 50 | My foolish heart | 1 |
| 22 Jul 50 | Bewitched | 7 |
| 9 Sep 50 | Silver dollar | 7 |
| 28 Oct 50 | Goodnight Irene | 4 |
| 25 Nov 50 | Rudolph the red–nosed reindeer | 6 |
| 6 Jan 51 | I taut I taw a puddy tat | 3 |
| 27 Jan 51 | Beloved, be faithful | 1 |
| 3 Feb 51 | The petite waltz | 2 |
| 17 Feb 51 | The Tennessee waltz | 9 |
| 21 Apr 51 | Mockin' bird hill | 10 |
| 30 Jun 51 | With these hands | 3 |
| 21 Jul 51 | My resistance is low | 4 |
| 18 Aug 51 | Too young | 12 |
| 10 Nov 51 | Longing for you | 9 |
| 12 Jan 52 | The loveliest night of the year | 1 |
| 19 Jan 52 | Longing for you | 2 |
| 2 Feb 52 | The loveliest night of the year | 3 |
| 23 Feb 52 | There's always room at our house | 4 |
| 22 Mar 52 | Unforgettable | 10 (1 =) |
| 24 May 52 | A-round the corner | 3 (1 =) |
| 14 Jun 52 | Auf wiederseh'n sweetheart | 10 |
| 23 Aug 52 | The homing waltz | 9 |
| 25 Oct 52 | Here in my heart | 8 |
| 27 Dec 52 | You belong to me | 7 |
| 7 Feb 53 | Don't let the stars get in your eyes | 1 |
| 14 Feb 53 | Broken wings | 6 |
| 28 Mar 53 | (How much is) That doggie in the window | 6 |
| 9 May 53 | In a golden coach | 5 |
| 13 Jun 53 | I believe | 1 |
| 20 Jun 53 | The Moulin Rouge Theme | 1 |
| 27 Jun 53 | Theme from Limelight (Eternally) | 17 |
| 24 Oct 53 | I believe | 1 |
| 31 Oct 53 | Poppa Piccolino | 1 |
| 7 Nov 53 | Answer me | 10 (1 =) |
| 26 Dec 53 | I saw mommy kissing Santa Claus | 1 (=) |

| | | |
|---|---|--:|
| 16 Jan 54 | Oh my pa-pa | 8 |
| 13 Mar 54 | I see the Moon | 4 |
| 10 Apr 54 | The Happy Wanderer | 2 |
| 24 Apr 54 | I see the Moon | 1 |
| 1 May 54 | The Happy Wanderer | 3 |
| 22 May 54 | Secret love | 7 |
| 10 Jul 54 | Cara mia | 2 |
| 24 Jul 54 | Little things mean a lot | 12 |
| 16 Oct 54 | My friend | 1 |
| 23 Oct 54 | Hold my hand | 10 |
| 1 Jan 55 | Mister Sandman | 6 (1 =) |
| 5 Feb 55 | Mambo Italiano | 3 (1 =) |
| 26 Feb 55 | Softly, softly | 8 |
| 23 Apr 55 | Stranger in paradise | 7 |
| 11 Jun 55 | Unchained Melody | 12 |
| 3 Sep 55 | Ev'rywhere | 5 |
| 8 Oct 55 | Blue star | 8 |
| 3 Dec 55 | Christmas alphabet | 5 (1 =) |
| 31 Dec 55 | Twenty tiny fingers | 1 (=) |
| 7 Jan 56 | Love is a many-splendoured thing | 1 |
| 14 Jan 56 | The ballad of Davy Crockett | 7 |
| 3 Mar 56 | Memories are made of this | 3 |
| 24 Mar 56 | It's almost tomorrow | 6 |
| 5 May 56 | No other love | 6 |
| 16 Jun 56 | My September love | 2 |
| 30 Jun 56 | Hot diggity | 3 |
| 21 Jul 56 | Walk hand in hand | 6 |
| 1 Sep 56 | Whatever will be, will be | 5 |
| 6 Oct 56 | Lay down your arms | 4 |
| 3 Nov 56 | More | 5 |
| 8 Dec 56 | Just walking in the rain | 4 |
| 5 Jan 57 | Singing the blues | 11 |
| 23 Mar 57 | Young love | 4 |
| 20 Apr 57 | Heart | 4 |
| 18 May 57 | Butterfly | 1 |
| 25 May 57 | Around the World | 14 |
| 31 Aug 57 | Love letters in the sand | 4 |
| 28 Sep 57 | Tammy | 9 |
| 30 Nov 57 | Mary's Boy Child | 5 |
| 4 Jan 58 | Alone | 1 |
| 11 Jan 58 | My special angel | 3 |
| 1 Feb 58 | The story of my life | 4 |
| 1 Mar 58 | Magic moments | 8 |
| 26 Apr 58 | Swingin' Shepherd Blues | 1 |
| 3 May 58 | Magic moments | 1 |
| 10 May 58 | I may never pass this way again | 3 |

| | | |
|---|---|--:|
| 31 May 58 | Who's sorry now | 1 |
| 7 Jun 58 | Stairway of love | 1 |
| 14 Jun 58 | On the street where you live | 6 |
| 26 Jul 58 | Tulips from Amsterdam | 6 |
| 6 Sep 58 | Trudie | 1 |
| 13 Sep 58 | Volare | 6 |
| 25 Oct 58 | More than ever (Come Prima) | 12 |
| 17 Jan 59 | The day the rains came | 2 |
| 31 Jan 59 | As I love you | 6 |
| 14 Mar 59 | Side saddle | 12 |
| 6 Jun 59 | Roulette | 13 |
| 5 Sep 59 | Only sixteen | 5 |
| 10 Oct 59 | China tea | 1 |
| 17 Oct 59 | Only sixteen | 1 |
| 24 Oct 59 | China tea | 1 |
| 31 Oct 59 | Mack the Knife | 2 |
| 14 Nov 59 | Little donkey | 7 |

## *Most weeks at No. 1*
### (A) In total

| | |
|--:|---|
| 22 | Galway Bay 1948 |
| 17 | The Theme from 'Limelight' (Eternally) 1953 |
| 15 | Now is the hour 1947 |
| 14 | Around the world 1957 |
| 13 | Roulette 1959 |
| 12 | Too young 1951 |
| 12 | Little things mean a lot 1954 |
| 12 | Unchained Melody 1955 |
| 12 | More than ever (Come Prima) 1958 |
| 12 | Side saddle 1959 |
| 11 | Tree in the meadow 1948 |
| 11 | Buttons and bows 1948 |
| 11 | My foolish heart 1950 |
| 11 | Singing the blues 1957 |
| 10 | You're breaking my heart 1949 |
| 10 | Mockin' bird hill 1951 |
| 10 | Unforgettable 1952 (One week at No. 1 shared with another song) |
| 10 | Auf wiederseh'n sweetheart 1952 |
| 10 | Answer me 1953 (One week at No. 1 shared with another song) |
| 10 | Hold my hand 1954 |

### (B) Consecutive Weeks

| | |
|--:|---|
| 22 | Galway Bay 1948 |
| 17 | The Theme from 'Limelight' (Eternally) 1953 |

4 Now is the hour 1947
4 Around the world 1957
3 Roulette 1959
2 Too young 1951
2 Little things mean a lot 1954
2 Unchained Melody 1955
2 More than ever (Come Prima) 1958
2 Side saddle 1959
1 Buttons and bows 1948
1 Singing the blues 1957
0 My foolish heart 1950
0 Mockin' bird hill 1951
0 Unforgettable 1952 (One week at No. 1 shared with another song)
0 Auf wiederseh'n sweetheart 1952
0 Answer me 1953 (One week at No. 1 shared with another song)
0 Hold my hand 1954

## Highest number of weeks on chart for a song reaching No. 1
### (Since May, 1947)

| Wks | Title | Year/s |
| --- | --- | --- |
| 31 | Trudie (1 week at No. 1) | 1958–60 |
| 9 | Side saddle (12 weeks at No. 1) | 1959–60 |
| 4 | The happy wanderer (5 weeks at No. 1) | 1954–55 |
| 6 | The loveliest night of the year (4 weeks at No. 1) | 1951–52 |
| 3 | Softly softly (8 weeks at No. 1) | 1955 |
| 2 | Forever and ever (1 week equal at No. 1) | 1949–50 |
| 0 | I believe (2 weeks at No. 1) | 1953–54 |
| 9 | Galway Bay (22 weeks at No. 1) | 1948–49 |
| 8 | The Moulin Rouge Theme (1 week at No. 1) | 1953–54 |
| | On the street where you live (6 weeks at No. 1) | 1958–59 |
| | Tulips from Amsterdam (6 weeks at No. 1) | 1958–59 |
| | Roulette (13 weeks at No. 1) | 1959–60 |

## Lowest number of weeks on chart for a song reaching No. 1
### (Since May, 1949)

9 Christmas Alphabet (5 weeks at No. 1 including 1 equal) 1955–56

---

11 I saw Mommy kissing Santa Claus (1 week equal at No. 1) 1953–54
12 I'd've baked a cake (1 week at No. 1) 1950
13 Music! Music! Music! (6 weeks at No. 1) 1950
   Mary's Boy Child (5 weeks at No. 1) 1957–58
14 I taut I taw a puddy tat (3 weeks at No. 1) 1950–51

## Songs reaching No. 1 after most weeks on chart

32 The loveliest night of the year (1951–52)
23 Forever and ever (1949–50)

## Most number of weeks at No. 2 without ever reaching No. 1

| Wks at No. 2 | | |
| --- | --- | --- |
| 13 | Come back to Sorrento | 1947 |
| 9 | Forgotten dreams | 1957 |
| 8 | Golden earrings | 1948 |
| 8 | Mr Wonderful | 1957 |
| 7 | When you're in love | 1948–9 |
| 7 | Cry | 1952 |

(Note: Mention must be made of 'The Moulin Rouge Theme' which, while only one week at No. 1, was at No. 2 for 18 weeks, 17 of these consecutive.)

## Most weeks on charts
### (Year shown in brackets is the year of first appearance on the Charts)

81 Tudie (1958)
69 Side saddle (1959)
57 The dam busters march (1955)
54 The happy wanderer (1954)
49 Forgotten dreams (1957)
46 Be my love (1951)
   The loveliest night of the year (1951)
43 Softly softly (1955)
42 Forever and ever (1949)
40 I believe (1953)
39 Galway Bay (1948)
38 The dream of Olwen (1948)
   The Moulin Rouge Theme (1953)
   Tulips from Amsterdam (1958)
   You need hands (1958)
   On the street where you live (1958)
   Roulette (1959)

37 Wonderful Copenhagen (1953)
36 How can you buy Killarney? (1949)
   Good luck, good health, God bless you (1951)
   The Theme from Limelight (Eternally) (1953)
   Gigi (1959)
35 A rose in a garden of weeds (1949)
   Blue tango (1952)
   True love (1956)
   Around the world (1957)
34 Auf wiederseh'n sweetheart (1952)
   The homing waltz (1952)
   Swedish rhapsody (1953)
   Whatever will be, will be (1956)
   Mary's Boy Child (1957)
33 Jealous Heart (1950)
   Little things mean a lot (1954)
   My September love (1956)
   May you always (1959)
32 September Song (1951)
   Heart of my heart (1954)
31 The cuckoo waltz (1948)
   The petite waltz (1950)
   I'm walking behind you (1953)
   It's almost tomorrow (1956)
   Puttin' on the style (1957)
   I could have danced all night (1958)
30 To each his own (1946)
   Twelfth Street rag (1949)
   My foolish heart (1950)
   At the end of the day (1951)
   Don't laugh at me (1954)
   The Book (1954)
   Secret love (1954)
   Autumn concerto (1956)

(Note: 'My happiness' spent a total of 46 weeks in the Charts – 28 in 1948 and a further 18 when the song returned to the Charts in 1959.)

32 I believe (1953)
31 The loveliest night of the year (1951)
29 When you're in love (1948)
28 Near you (1948)
   My happiness (1948)★★
27 Come back to Sorrento (1947)
   Jealous heart (1950)
   True love (1956)
26 Now is the hour (1947)
   Buttons and bows (1948)
   Forever and ever (1949)
   The Theme from Limelight (Eternally) (1953)
   The Moulin Rouge Theme (1953)
   Softly softly (1955)
25 The little old mill (1947)
   How can you buy Killarney? (1949)
   I'm walking behind you (1953)
   Tulips from Amsterdam (1958)
24 Golden earrings (1948)
   My foolish heart (1950)
   Around the world (1957)
23 Bewitched (1950)
   Be my love (1951)
   Because of you (1951)
   Little things mean a lot (1954)
22 The cuckoo waltz (1948)
   Twelfth Street rag (1949)
   The Harry Lime Theme (1949)
   Too young (1951)
   Auf wiederseh'n sweetheart (1952)
   The homing waltz (1952)
   Unchained melody (1955)
   Whatever will be, will be (1956)
   Roulette (1959)

(★★This song returned to the charts in 1959 and spent another eight weeks in the Top Ten.)

## Most weeks in the Top Ten
(Year shown in brackets is the year of first appearance on the Charts)

39 Galway Bay (1948)
38 The dream of Olwen (1948)
37 Trudie (1958)
35 Forgotten dreams (1957)
   Side saddle (1959)
34 The happy wanderer (1954)

## Songs with the most recordings available

*78 and 45 rpm versions count as 1 throughout this listing. The recordings marked with an ★ in the general chronological listing do not count towards the overall total as they were obviously not available when the song was in the charts.*

22 April in Portugal (1953)
20 Tenderly (1954)
19 Stranger in Paradise (1955)
17 The High and the Mighty (1954), White Christmas (1955), The Theme from 'The Threepenny Opera' (1956)

16  The Tennessee Waltz (1951), Some Enchanted Evening (1951), I love
    Paris (1954), Volare (1958)
15  The Petite Waltz (1950), September Song (1951), My heart cries for
    you (1951), Too Young (1951), You belong to me (1952), Changing
    Partners (1954), Smile (1954), Melody of Love (1955), Hernando's
    Hideaway (1955), Who's sorry now? (1958), More than ever (1958)
14  You're breaking my heart (1949), Rudolph, the red-nosed reindeer
    (1950–53), Domino (1952), Oh! My Pa–Pa (1953), Three Coins in
    the Fountain (1954), If I give my heart to you (1954), Mister
    Sandman (1954), Unchained Melody (1955), The Ballad of Davy
    Crockett (1956)

## Least recorded songs

A total of 58 songs out of the 1100 featured only had one
recording to their credit. Of these, there were just 17 in the
first ten years, 1946–1955, but there were a further 18 in
the last year (1959) alone.

## Songs spending just one week in the charts

No less than 94 of the songs spent just one week on the
charts, but 48 of these scraped in by occupying last place in
the table.

# ARTIST INDEX

Each recording listed in the main portion of this book is listed here, analysed under each main artist, singing group or orchestra in alphabetical order. Where singers have recorded in pairs, i.e. Jo Stafford and Frankie Laine or Anne Ziegler and Webster Booth, reference should be made to the first named artist. Vocalists with orchestras are listed in brackets under the orchestra leader's name.

**Shirley Abicair**
458    I'd love to fall asleep
678    Christmas Alphabet
714    Willie Can

**Accordeon Serenaders, The**
2    Cruising down the River

**Paul Adam and His Mayfair Music**
147    Red Roses for a Blue Lady (Frank Holmes and Vocal Quartette)
149    Put your shoes on, Lucy (Bette Roberts)
162    The Echo told me a lie (Bette Roberts)
201    Some day my heart will awake (Rita Williams)
212    I'd've baked a cake (Paul Adam)

**Marie Adams**
1089    What do you want to make those eyes at me for? (with Johnny Otis and his Orchestra)

**Rush Adams**
737    The Birds and the Bees (with vocal assists by Loulie Jean Normon)

**Adams Singers, The, directed by Cliff Adams**
1072    Morgen

**Larry Adler**
555    The Shadow Waltz

**Aimable**
611    The Naughty Lady of Shady Lane
613    La Tamise et Mon Jardin
669    Hernando's Hideaway

**Alyn Ainsworth and the Rock-a-Fellas**
1100    18th Century Rock

**Tony Alamo**
418    If I had Wings

**Al Alberts**
994    Willingly
(see also The Four Aces featuring Al Alberts)

**Robert Alda and Isabel Bigley**
486    I've never been in love before

**Jeff Alexander Choir, The**
(see Mario Lanza; Frank Sinatra)

**Jeff Alexander Chorus, The**
(see Dick Haymes; Mario Lanza; Bing Crosby)

**Jill Allan**
444    Why don't you believe me?

**Chesney Allen**
(see Bud Flanagan and Chesney Allen)

**Jerry Allen Trio, The**
581    A sky-blue shirt and a rainbow tie (The Allentones)

**Rex Allen**
512    Crying in the Chapel
519    Where did my snowman go? (with Children's Chorus)
1072    One more sunrise
(see also Rex Allen and Tex Williams)

**Rex Allen and Tex Williams**
589    This Ole House

**Steve Allen**
691    The Ballad of Davy Crockett

**Steve Allen and his Orchestra and Chorus**
706    Memories of You

**Sue Allen**
(see Les Baxter and his Orchestra; Mickey Katz and his Orchestra)

**Allentones, The**
(see The Jerry Allen Trio)

**Ambrose and his Orchestra**
3    Chickery Chick (Alan Dean)
4    Homesick – that's all (Rita Marlowe)
6    In the Land of Beginning Again (Rita Marlowe)
9    Laughing on the Outside (Jane Lee)
13    Oh, what it seemed to be (Alan Dean)
67    A Gal in Calico (Alan Dean)
70    People will say we're in love (Alan Dean)
80    Oh, what a beautiful morning (Alan Dean)
150    It's Magic (Ray Burns)
155    It happened in Adano (Ray Burns)
156    Clopin Clopant (Ray Burns and Nadia Doré)
201    Some day my heart will awake (Ray Burns)
405    I'll walk alone (Anne Shelton)

**Lola Ameche**
437    Don't let the stars get in your eyes

**Eddie Ames**
809    I'd give you the world

**Ames Brothers, The**
514    You You You
570    The Man with the Banjo
611    The Naughty Lady of Shady Lane
831    Tammy
893    A very precious love
(see also Russ Morgan and his Orchestra)

**Lale Andersen**
37    Lilli Marlene

**Leroy Anderson and his 'Pops' Concert Orchestra**
267    Sleigh Ride
386    Blue Tango
416    Belle of the Ball
812    Forgotten dreams

**Eamonn Andrews**
685    The shifting, whispering sands (with Ron Goodwin and his Orchestra and Chorus)

**Julie Andrews**
895    I could have danced all night

**Micky Andrews**
541    The Cuff of my Shirt
549    From the vine came the grape

**Patty Andrews**
320    Too young
405    I'll walk alone
676    Suddenly there's a valley
(see also Danny Kaye and Patty Andrews)

**Andrews Sisters, The**
12    Money is the root of all evil
17    Down in the valley
23    Johnny Fedora
54    How lucky you are
73    A rainy night in Rio
92    The coffee song
96    Near you
104    Too fat polka
116    Heartbreaker
119    Toolie oolie doolie
148    The wedding of Lilli Marlene
177    The windmill song
220    Oh, you sweet one (w. Russ Morgan [vcl] and his Orchestra)
224    Choo'n gum
267    Sleigh ride
289    A penny a kiss – a penny a hug
296    A rainy day refrain
338    Lullaby of Broadway
488    Say 'si si'
761    Christmas Island
930    Torero
985    I'll be with you in apple blossom time
(see also Bing Crosby and The Andrews Sisters, Dan Dailey and The Andrews Sisters, Dick Haymes and The Andrews Sisters, Al Jolson and The Andrews Sisters, Danny Kaye and The Andrews Sisters, Carmen Miranda and The Andrews Sisters)

**Avril Angers**
(see Benny Lee, Avril Angers, Janet Brown and Peter Butterworth)

**Paul Anka**
828    Diana
852    I love you, baby
871    You are my destiny
993    My heart sings
1024    I miss you so
1055    Lonely boy
1088    Put your head on my shoulder

**Billie Anthony**
516    Ricochet
542    Bell bottom blues
551    Make love to me
589    This ole house
622    Teach me tonight
631    Tweedle-dee
674    The banjo's back in town
689    The old pi-anna rag
743    A sweet old-fashioned girl

746    Lay down your arms
776    I dreamed
804    Rock-a-Billy

**Billie Anthony and Tony Brent**
554    Cross over the bridge
556    I get so lonely

**Ray Anthony and his Orchestra**
77    They say it's wonderful (Ronnie Deauville)
93    The girl that I marry (Ronnie Deauville)
236    Candy and cake (Betty Holliday)
239    Sentimental me (Ronnie Deauville)
249    Count every star (Dick Noel)
256    Autumn leaves (Ronnie Deauville and The Skyliners)
269    Marshmallow world (Ronnie Deauville)
272    Nevertheless (Ronnie Deauville and The Skyliners)
286    Be my love (Ronnie Deauville)
316    My truly, truly fair (Tommy Mercer and Ensemble)
382    My concerto (Tommy Mercer)
469    Wild horses (Jo Ann Greer)
521    Oh! My papa (The Anthony Choir with Ray Anthony (trumpet)
535    Tenderly
547    Secret love (Tommy Mercer and The Anthony Choir)
560    Young at heart (Tommy Mercer)
564    Wanted (Tommy Mercer)
565    Little things mean a lot (Marcie Miller)
571    Three coins in the fountain (Tommy Mercer and The Anthony Choir)
575    My friend (Tommy Mercer and The Anthony Choir)
576    West of Zanzibar – Jambo (The Skyliners)
583    Sway (Ray Anthony and The Quartet)
657    Learnin' the blues
669    Hernando's hideaway (Ray Anthony)
     *(see also Frank Sinatra)*

**Anthony Choir, The**
*(see Ray Anthony and his Orchestra)*

**Charlie Applewhite**
525    Ebb tide
573    The story of Tina
593    I love Paris
596    No one but you
623    Prize of gold
659    Blue star

**Firth Archer**
*(see The Squadronaires directed by Jimmy Miller)*

**Toni Arden**
313    Too late now
320    Too young
374    Never
413    Take my heart
490    Kiss
571    Three coins in the fountain

**Aristokats, The**
*(see Sy Oliver and his Orchestra)*

**Arizona Boys' Choir, The**
691    The ballad of Davy Crockett

**Steve Arlen**
699    Dreams can tell a lie

**Kay Armen**
676    Suddenly there's a valley
684    He

**Louis Armstrong**
329    Because of you

431    Takes two to tango
457    The dummy song
480    Your cheatin' heart
609    White Christmas
644    Sincerely
786    Blueberry Hill
948    It's all in the game (with Gordon Jenkins Orch)
     *(see also Louis Armstrong and his Orchestra, Louis Armstrong and his All-Stars)*

**Louis Armstrong and his All-Stars**
705    Only you (Louis Armstrong)
711    The Theme from 'The Threepenny Opera' (Louis Armstrong)
1073    Mack the knife (Louis Armstrong)

**Louis Armstrong and his Orchestra**
215    C'est si bon (Louis Armstrong)
241    Once in a while
270    If (Louis Armstrong)
317    Unless (Louis Armstrong)
385    Kiss of fire (Louis Armstrong)
479    April in Portugal (Louis Armstrong)

**Eddy Arnold**
826    Scarlet ribbons

**Murray Arnold**
456    I talk to the trees

**Johnny Ashcroft**
984    The pub with no beer

**Bud Ashton**
1030    Guitar boogie shuffle
1064    Forty miles of bad road

**Svend Asmussen and his Orchestra**
584    Sh-boom

**Lys Assia**
324    Mademoiselle de Paris
498    Ba-loom ba-la
521    O mein papa (with orch. cond. Paul Burkhard)
521    Oh! My papa (with Frank Weir Orch)

**Lys Assia and The Johnston Brothers**
686    Arrivederci darling

**Fred Astaire and Cyd Charisse**
789    All of you

**Fred Astaire, Red Skelton and Anita Ellis**
272    Nevertheless

**Bob Atcher and The Dinning Sisters**
761    Christmas Island
     *(see also The Dinning Sisters)*

**Winifred Atwell**
312    Jezebel
346    The black and white rag
474    Coronation rag
502    Flirtation waltz
515    Golden tango
633    Stranger in paradise
710    The poor people of Paris
773    The Garden of Eden
778    Moonlight gambler
873    Raunchy
1047    The Summer of the Seventeenth Doll
1098    Piano Party – medley

**Jan August**
*(see Richard Hayman and Jan August)*

**Georgie Auld**
*(see The Modernaires)*

**Gene Autry**
32    Someday
127    Buttons and bows
240    Have I told you lately that I love you?

252    Rudolph, the red-nosed reindeer (with The Pinafores)
544    Bimbo

**Gene Autry and Jo Stafford**
277    My heart cries for you

**Frankie Avalon**
1010    Venus

**Avons, The**
1090    Seven little girls sitting in the back seat

**Waldyr Azevedo and his Orchestra**
406    Delicado

**Harry Babbitt**
*(see Kay Kyser and his Orchestra)*

**Pearl Bailey and 'Hot-Lips' Page**
182    Baby, it's cold outside

**Chet Baker**
*(see Gerry Mulligan Quartet)*

**Chet Baker Quartet, The**
969    Winter wonderland

**Hylda Baker**
1082    Makin' love

**Kenny Baker**
42    The old lamp-lighter (with Russ Morgan and his Orchestra)
87    Apple blossom wedding (with Russ Morgan and his Orchestra)

**Kenny Baker**
651    Mama

**Kenny Baker and his Band**
338    Lullaby of Broadway

**Kenny Baker and his Quartet**
564    Wanted

**LaVern Baker**
631    Tweedle-dee (with The Gliders)
1083    If you love me

**Ronnie Ball Trio, The**
*(see Ronnie Scott – tenor sax)*

**Hank Ballard and The Midnighters**
1037    Kansas City

**Bandits, The**
*(see Billy Cotton and his Band)*

**Banjo Boys, The**
652    Hey, Mr Banjo

**Chris Barber and his Jazz Band**
998    Petite fleur (w. Monty Sunshine – clarinet)
1075    Lonesome (w. Monty Sunshine – clarinet)

**Eddie Barclay and his Orchestra**
686    Arrivederci darling
710    La goulante du pauvre Jean

**George Barclay**
*(see Felix Mendelssohn and his Hawaiian Serenaders)*

**Kenny Bardell**
*(see Ken Mackintosh – sax)*

**Blue Lu Barker**
136    A little bird told me

**Charlie Barnet and his Orchestra**
7    Into each life some rain must fall (Kay Starr)
21    You always hurt the one you love (Kay Starr)

**Barry Barnet**
904    The book of love
905    All I have to do is dream
915    When (w. The Michael Sammes Singers)
955    Susie darlin'

**Frank Baron and his Orchestra**
*(see The Cherokeys)*

**Dickie Barrett**
990    Smoke gets in your eyes

**Richard Barrett and The Chantels**
1014    Come softly to me

**Carl Barriteau and his Orchestra**
7    Into each life some rain must fall (Mae Cooper)
14    Primrose Hill (Mae Cooper)
**Blue Barron and his Orchestra**
2    Cruising down the river (ensemble)
83    Chi-baba chi-baba (vocal ensemble)
113    Oh! My achin' heart (Charles Fisher and Quartet)
141    Powder your face with sunshine (Ensemble)
146    A strawberry Moon (Clyde Burke and Dolores Hawkins)
479    The whisp'ring serenade (Betty Clark and The Blue Notes)
529    That's amore (The Blue Notes)
**Barry Sisters, The**
723    The Italian Theme
**Eileen Barton**
583    Sway
**Hal Barton**
*(see Henry Jerome and his Orchestra)*
**Shirley Bassey**
733    The wayward wind
785    The banana boat song
825    Fire down below
950    There's never been a night
968    As I love you
972    Kiss me, honey honey, kiss me
1083    If you love me (w. The Rita Williams Singers)
1087    Count on me (w. The Rita Williams Singers)
**Elizabeth Batey**
*(see Joe Loss and his Orchestra)*
**Batsmen, The**
*(see Sonny Player)*
**Eric Batty's Jazz Aces**
766    Cindy, oh Cindy
**Les Baxter – vocal**
*(see Dick Beavers and Les Baxter)*
**Les Baxter and his Orchestra**
479    April in Portugal
495    Ruby (w. Danny Welton – harmonica)
900    Little serenade
942    More than ever
**Les Baxter and his Orchestra and Chorus**
285    The roving kind (Lindy Doherty)
288    So long (Lindy Doherty)
295    Sparrow in the tree top (Lindy Doherty)
317    Unless (Dick Beavers)
329    Because of you
333    Vanity (Sue Allen)
336    Longing for you (Sue Allen)
373    Please Mr Sun
383    Auf wiederseh'n sweetheart
386    Blue tango
502    Flirtation waltz
591    The high and the mighty
593    I love Paris
630    Cherry pink and apple blossom white
637    Unchained melody
659    The Medic Theme
672    I'll never stop loving you
710    The poor people of Paris
872    La Panse – the little flower
**Les Baxter and The Bombers**
640    Earth angel
**Les Baxter Chorus, The**
*(see Les Baxter and his Orchestra and Chorus, Jimmy Wakely)*

**Francis Bay and his Orchestra**
1019    Manhatten Spiritual
**Cecil Bayley**
*(see Grady Martin and his Slew Foot Five)*
**Beaux and the Belles, The**
*(see Phil Morrow's Music, Philip Green and his Orchestra)*
**Dick Beavers**
385    Kiss of fire
390    I'm yours
**Dick Beavers and Les Baxter**
347    Shrimp boats
**Gilbert Becaud**
967    The day the rains came
**Sidney Bechet**
711    The Theme from 'The Threepenny Opera'
891    Who's sorry now? (with Humphrey Lyttleton Band)
998    Petite fleur (with his All-Stars)
1075    Si tu vois ma mère (with Claude Luter Orch)
**Sidney Bechet Circle Seven, The**
275    September song
**Molly Bee**
511    I saw mommy kissing Santa Claus
519    Where did my snowman go?
**Harry Belafonte**
662    Close your eyes
785    Banana boat – day-o (with Millard Thomas – guitar)
816    Island in the Sun
826    Scarlet ribbons (with Millard Thomas – guitar)
846    Mary's boy child
920    Little Bernadette
**Belafonte, (Harry Belafonte)**
785    Banana boat song – day-o (with Millard Thomas – guitar)
962    I heard the bells on Christmas Day
963    Son of Mary
**Graeme Bell and his Ragtime Four**
346    The black and white rag
**Bell Sisters, The**
377    Wheel of fortune
**Boyd Bennett and his Rockets**
677    Seventeen (Big Moe)
732    Blue suede shoes
**Dickie Bennett**
656    Stars shine in your eyes
**Kim Bennett**
613    Softly, softly
642    Melody of love
     *(see also Roland Shaw and his Orchestra, Mantovani and his Orchestra and Chorus)*
**Tony Bennett**
329    Because of you
402    Somewhere along the way
518    Rags to riches
605    Not as a stranger
633    Stranger in paradise
654    Take me back again
662    Close your eyes
716    Come next Spring
768    Happiness Street
792    Heart
829    In the middle of an island
**Ivy Benson and her Girls' Band**
95    Tree in the meadow (Rita Williams)
**Marie Benson**
212    I'd've baked a cake (with Norrie's Novelties)
221    Let's do it again

274    Me and my imagination
610    Mambo Italiano
620    Mobile
673    Twenty tiny fingers
**Marie Benson and The Stargazers**
235    Silver dollar
**Dick Bentley**
*(see Joy Nichols, Dick Bentley and Jimmy Edwards)*
**Bentley Brothers, The**
853    Ma, she's making eyes at me
**Jack Berch and The Mullan Sisters**
251    Bibbidi bobbidi boo
**Milton Berle**
757    In the middle of the house
**Sara Berner**
*(see Spike Jones and his City Slickers)*
**Beverley Sisters, The**
263    Ferry Boat Inn
277    My heart cries for you
283    Teasin'
343    I wish I wuz
348    Sweetheart of yesterday
353    Sin
377    Wheel of fortune
466    Side by side
478    Have you heard
498    Poppa Piccolino
501    Vaya con Dios
511    I saw mommy kissing Santa Claus
521    Oh! My Papa
534    Changing partners
539    The happy wanderer
554    Cross over the bridge
602    The Mama Doll song
611    The naughty lady of shady lane
627    If anyone finds this, I love you
642    Melody of love
667    Have you ever been lonely?
714    Willie can
747    Born to be with you
770    Come home to my arms
776    I dreamed
807    Mr Wonderful
822    Bye bye love
926    Left right out of my heart
996    Little drummer boy
1079    Little donkey
**Babs & Teddie Beverley**
567    The never never land
**Joy Beverley**
565    Little things mean a lot
**Eve Beynon – also known as Eva Beynon**
*(see Billy Ternent and his Orchestra)*
**Harry Bidgood and his Orchestra**
*(see Billy Whitlock)*
**Big Ben Banjo Band, The, and The Coronets**
628    Ready, willing and able
648    The Crazy Otto rag
652    Hey, Mr Banjo
869    The Liechtensteiner polka
     *(see also The Coronets)*
**Big Bopper, The (J.P. Richardson)**
977    Chantilly lace
**Isabel Bigley**
*(see Robert Alda and Isabel Bigley)*
**Big Moe**
*(see Boyd Bennett and his Rockets)*
**Billie and Lillie**
885    La dee dah (with Billy Ford's Thunderbirds)

**Dickie Bishop and The Sidekicks**
797   Cumberland Gap
**Bob Bissetto Quartet, The**
742   The gal with the yaller shoes
**Stanley Black and his Orchestra**
61   Tell me, Marianne
137   Far away places
238   If I were a blackbird (Dick James, The
     Stargazers, and The George Mitchell Choir)
291   So in love
294   Mary Rose (Dick James, The Stargazers and
     The George Mitchell Choir)
345   Some enchanted evening
530   From here to eternity
     *(see also David Whitfield and Stanley Black and his*
     *Orchestra)*
**Stanley Black and his Romantic Music**
642   Melody of love
**Rory Blackwell and his Blackjacks**
822   Bye bye love
**Vivian Blaine**
534   Changing partners
539   The happy wanderer
550   Someone else's roses
**Mel Blanc**
120   Woody Woodpecker (with The Sportsmen)
259   I taut I taw a puddy tat
453   Little red monkey
**Georges Blanes**
748   Autumn concerto
**Archie Bleyer and his Chorus and Orchestra**
611   The naughty lady of shady lane
669   Hernando's hideaway
**Ray Bloch and his Orchestra and Chorus**
741   You'll never walk alone
**Blue Notes, The**
*(see Blue Barron and his Orchestra)*
**Kitty Bluett**
*(see Ted Ray and Kitty Bluett)*
**Ann Blyth**
310   The loveliest night of the year
**Bob and Jeanne**
164   Careless hands
**Bobolinks, The**
*(see Billy Thorburn's The Organ, the Dance Band and Me)*
**Bobolinks, The**
*(see Bob Crosby and his Orchestra)*
**Ray Bolger**
*(see Ethel Merman and Ray Bolger)*
**Harry Bolton**
*(see Syd Dean and his Band)*
**Jackie Bond (sax) and his Orchestra**
647   Evermore
**Johnny Bond and his Orchestra**
205   Music! Music! Music! (Rosemary Calvin and
     Ensemble)
**Issy Bonn**
1   Bless you
9   Laughing on the outside
10   Let bygones be bygones
28   Sweetheart, we'll never grow old
32   Someday
39   Till then
47   May I call you sweetheart?
51   The whole world is singing my song
75   Down the old Spanish trail
90   Peg o' my heart
*281   Good luck, good health, God bless you*
     *(w. The Keynotes & Charles Smart - organ)*

408   Here in my heart (with Eddie Calvert –
     trumpet)
575   My friend
687   When you lose the one you love
**Pat Boone**
722   I'll be home
774   Friendly persuasion
784   Don't forbid me
819   Love letters in the sand
839   Remember you're mine
854   April love
887   A wonderful time up there
890   It's too soon to know
911   Sugar Moon
935   If dreams came true
987   I'll remember tonight
1056   Twixt twelve and twenty
1060   For a penny
**Webster Booth**
262   I leave my heart in an English garden
344   At the end of the day
393   Star of Hope
     *(see also Anne Ziegler and Webster Booth)*
**Earl Bostic, his alto sax, and his Orchestra**
642   Melody of love
903   Twilight time
**Boston Promenade Orchestra, The, conducted**
**by Arthur Fiedler**
267   Sleigh ride
**Connee Boswell**
394   Trust in me
441   Heart and soul
587   If I give my heart to you
**Eve Boswell**
225   I remember the cornfields
228   Bewitched (with Geraldo and his Orchestra)
233   Your heart and my heart
234   If I loved you
261   Beloved, be faithful
277   My heart cries for you
368   We won't live in a castle
373   Please Mr Sun
390   I'm yours
404   Sugarbush
408   Here in my heart
426   Moon above Malaya
445   Hi-Lili, Hi-Lo
465   I believe
477   Tell me you're mine
492   The Bridge of Sighs
517   If you love me
531   Don't ever leave me
558   The little shoemaker
628   Ready, willing and able
659   Blue star
694   Pickin' a chicken
696   Young and foolish
701   It's almost tomorrow
715   Cookie
762   True love
821   With all my heart
926   Left right out of my heart
942   More than ever
     *(see also Geraldo and his Orchestra, Eve Boswell*
     *and Derek Roy)*
**Eve Boswell and Derek Roy**
387   Dance me loose
**Boswell Sisters, The**
338   Lullaby of Broadway

**Ben Bowers**
664   The man from Laramie
**David Box**
*(see The Crickets)*
**Franklyn Boyd**
370   Tell me why
405   I'll walk alone
413   Take my heart
461   Pretend
478   Have you heard
     *(see also Eric Winstone and his Orchestra)*
**Jimmy Boyd**
252   Rudolph, the red-nosed reindeer
511   I saw mommy kissing Santa Claus (with
     The Norman Luboff Choir)
548   Two Easter Sunday sweethearts (with The
     Norman Luboff Choir)
     *(see also Frankie Laine and Jimmy Boyd)*
**Boys Next Door, The**
*(see June Hutton and Axel Stordahl)*
**Janet Brace**
622   Teach me tonight
**Josephine Bradley and her Ballroom Orchestra**
8   It's a pity to say goodnight
16   Day by day
22   And then it's heaven
25   The 'Ampstead way
36   Five minutes more
46   April showers
48   For sentimental reasons
53   Don't fall in love
54   How lucky you are
123   So tired
131   The cuckoo waltz
145   How can you buy Killarney?
153   A – you're adorable
191   Is it too late?
195   Why is it?
202   We all have a song in our hearts
212   I'd've baked a cake
223   Me and my shadow
275   September song
**Owen Bradley and his Orchestra**
711   The Theme from 'The Threepenny Opera'
**Owen Bradley Quintet, The**
838   White silver sands (with The Anita Kerr
     Quartet)
**Johnny Brandon**
356   Oodles of noodles
361   Slow coach
443   The glow worm
546   Heartless (with The Phantoms)
621   Tomorrow (with The Phantoms)
641   Don't worry
753   Glendora
**Brass Hats, The, with Kenny Baker**
338   Lullaby of Broadway
**Brasshats, The, directed by Reg Owen**
521   O mein papa
**Bobby Breen**
320   Too young
331   White wedding
     *(see also Billy Ternent and his Orchestra)*
**Alan Breeze**
*(see Billy Cotton and his Band)*
**Rose Brennan**
517   If you love me (w. Joe Loss and his Orchestra)
532   My heart belongs to only you (with Joe Loss
     and his Orchestra)

559 Love me
619 Let me go, lover
644 Sincerely (with Joe Loss and his Orchestra)
703 Band of gold
1083 If you love me (with Joe Loss and his Orchestra)
*(see also Joe Loss and his Orchestra)*

**Buddy Brennen**
*(see Guy Lombardo and his Royal Canadians)*

**Frankie Brent**
844 Be my girl (with The Beryl Stott Group)

**Tony Brent**
420 Walkin' to Missouri
439 Make it soon
452 Got you on my mind
478 Have you heard
564 Wanted
571 Three coins in the fountain
583 Sway
629 Open up your heart (with Anne Warren)
688 With your love
766 Cindy, oh Cindy
801 Butterfly
817 Dark Moon
900 Little serenade
941 Girl of my dreams
1042 Why should I be lonely?
*(see also Billie Anthony and Tony Brent)*

**Gerry Brereton**
432 Outside of heaven
435 Broken wings
450 Keep it a secret
468 The Windsor waltz
471 Hold me, thrill me, kiss me
508 Be mine
510 Wish you were here
530 From here to eternity
538 The Book
573 The story of Tina
578 Smile

**Bernard Bresslaw**
889 You need feet
938 Mad passionate love
1012 Charlie Brown
1099 Ivy will cling (with Children's Chorus)

**Betty Brewer**
274 Me and my imagination

**Teresa Brewer**
205 Music! Music! Music! (with The Dixieland All-Stars)
224 Choo'n gum
265 The thing
336 Longing for you
343 I wish I wuz
574 Jilted
619 Let me go, lover (with The Lancers)
631 Tweedle-dee
674 The banjo's back in town
720 A tear fell
743 A sweet old-fashioned girl
953 The hula hoop song
1096 Jingle bell rock

**Teresa Brewer and Snooky Lanson**
289 A penny a kiss – a penny a hug

**Bobbie Britton**
564 Wanted (with The Keynotes)
657 Learnin' the blues (with Ted Heath and his Music)

1091 The village of St Bernadette
*(see also Ted Heath and his Music)*

**Hadda Brooks**
333 Vanity

**Norman Brooks**
581 A sky-blue shirt and a rainbow tie

**Randy Brooks and his Orchestra**
535 Tenderly

**Brother Sisters, The**
848 Alone

**Peter Brough and 'Archie Andrews'**
511 I saw mommy kissing Santa Claus
*(see also Max Bygraves)*

**Buddy Brown and Fred Kreitzer**
*(see Guy Lombardo and his Royal Canadians)*

**Don Brown**
*(see Tommy Tucker and his Orchestra)*

**Fay Brown**
632 Unsuspecting heart
637 Unchained melody

**Jackie Brown**
510 Wish you were here
*(see also Clive Wayne)*

**James Brown and The Trail Winders**
664 The man from Laramie

**Janet Brown**
*(see Benny Lee, Avril Angers, Janet Brown and Peter Butterworth)*

**Jimmy Brown**
*(see Guy Lombardo and his Royal Canadians)*

**Les Brown and his Band of Renown**
592 They were doin' the mambo (Butch Stone and Ensemble)

**Pud Brown Trio, The**
706 Memories of you

**George Browne and his (Jamaican) Calypso Band**
669 Hernando's hideaway
691 The ballad of Davy Crockett
785 Day-O (Banana boat song)
846 Mary's boy child (with The Humming Birds)

**Sam Browne**
95 Tree in the meadow
103 The old postman
116 Heartbreaker (with The Keynotes and Primo Scala and his Accordion Band)
658 Cool Water (with The Quads and The Squadronaires)
712 The great pretender (with The Rita Williams Singers)
*see also Peter Yorke and his Concert Orchestra; The New Mayfair Dance Orchestra; Maurice Winnick and his Orchestra; Vera Lynn and Sam Browne)*

**Sam Browne and his All-Star Singers, The**
288 So long
331 White wedding

**Sam Browne and The Squadronaires directed by Jimmy Miller**
110 Wishing waltz
112 Reflections on the water

**Sam Browne Singers, The**
435 Broken wings

**Browns, The**
826 Scarlet ribbons
1069 The three bells

**Dave Brubeck Trio, The**
275 September song

**Clyde Burke**
*(see Blue Barron and his Orchestra)*

**Don Burke**
*(see Gordon Jenkins and his Orchestra)*

**Kurt Burling and his Rococo Orchestra**
371 At last! At last!
416 Belle of the ball

**Smiley Burnette**
252 Rudolph, the red-nosed reindeer

**Mary Burns and her Boy Friends**
260 My Christmas wish

**Ray Burns**
475 Eternally
491 Mother Nature and Father Time
517 If you love me
518 Rags to riches
534 Changing partners
578 Smile
599 I can't tell a waltz from a tango
620 Mobile
653 That's how a love song was born (with The Coronets)
659 Blue star
698 Stealin'
820 Wonderful, wonderful
*(see also Ambrose and his Orchestra)*

**Hal Burton**
908 Big man
917 Rave on
949 Move it!
955 Susie darlin'

**Terry Burton**
772 A letter to a soldier
774 Friendly persuasion

**Lou Busch and his Orchestra and Chorus**
702 Zambezi
774 Friendly persuasion (with vocal group)

**Champ Butler**
311 I apologise
352 Down yonder

**Billy Butterfield and his Orchestra**
130 Maybe you'll be there (Pat O'Connor)

**Buttermilk Tussie**
*(see Red Ingle and his Natural Seven)*

**Peter Butterworth**
*(see Benny Lee, Avril Angers, Janet Brown and Peter Butterworth)*

**Sheila Buxton**
1050 The wonder of you

**Max Bygraves**
243 Mona Lisa
457 Dummy song (with Peter Brough and 'Archie Andrews')
488 Say 'si si' (with Peter Brough and 'Archie Andrews')
499 Big 'ead (with The Song Pedlars)
543 The Jones boy
545 Heart of my heart (with vocal quartet)
552 Friends and neighbours (with The Tanner Sisters)
577 Gilly Gilly Ossenfeffer Katzenellen Bogen by the Sea (with Children's Chorus)
606 Mister Sandman
621 Tomorrow
646 The pendulum song
679 Meet me on the corner
690 The little Laplander (with Children's Chorus)
691 The ballad of Davy Crockett (with Children's Chorus)
693 Seventeen tons

721 Out of town
730 Try another cherry tree (w. Children's
767 That dear old gentleman (with vocal group)
792 Heart
888 Tulips from Amsterdam
889 You need hands (with The Clarke Brothers)
922 Gotta have rain
923 Little train
974 My ukelele
1096 Jingle bell rock

**Cactus Kids, The**
(see 'Sheriff' Johnny Denis and his Ranchers)

**Earl Cadillac, his alto sax, and his Orchestra**
501 Vaya con Dios
505 Swedish rhapsody

**Cafe Vienna Quartet, The**
187 The Harry Lime Theme

**Calico Kids, The**
(see Bing Crosby)

**Eddie Calvert – The Man with the Golden Trumpet**
521 O mein papa
535 Tenderly
579 Midnight
590 My son, my son
630 Cherry pink and apple blossom white
633 Stranger in paradise
644 Sincerely
655 John and Julie
675 Love is a many-splendoured thing
702 Zambezi
706 Memories of you
731 Serenade
812 Forgotten dreams
872 Mandy
900 Little serenade
1003 Angelina
1072 Morgen
      (see also Issy Bonn)

**Eddie Calvert, trumpet, and his Orchestra**
345 Some enchanted evening

**Rosemary Calvin**
(see Johnny Bond and his Orchestra)

**Camarata and his Music**
363 Only fools (Pat Terry)
374 Never (Fred Darian)

**Len Camber**
5 I can't begin to tell you

**Don Cameron**
454 Oh, happy day
477 Tell me you're mine
480 Your cheatin' heart
533 I see the Moon (with Morton Fraser's Harmonica Band)

**John Cameron**
339 Love's roundabout

**Billie Campbell**
(see Johnny Denis and his Novelty Swing Sextet; Primo Scala and his Accordion Band)

**Duncan Campbell**
(see Ted Heath and his Music)

**Gwen Campbell**
(see Jan Rosol and Gwen Campbell)

**Jean Campbell**
475 Eternally
501 Vaya con Dios
509 Answer me
563 Idle gossip
601 Count your blessings instead of sheep

602 The Mama Doll song
729 Ivory Tower
762 True love
813 We will make love
      (see also Cyril Stapleton and his Orchestra)

**Murray Campbell**
835 Mandolin serenade (with Wally Stott Orch)

**Canadians, The**
671 Go on by
680 Rock around the clock
702 Zambezi
705 Only you
732 Blue suede shoes
752 Rockin' through the Rye
      (see also Denny Dennis; Penny Nicholls and The Canadians)

**Candy Candido**
315 Little white duck

**Freddy Cannon**
1068 Tallahassee Lassie

**Eddie Cantor**
853 Ma, he's making eyes at me

**Phil Capicotto**
(see Rus Morgan and his Orchestra)

**Capitol Symphonic Band, The, conducted by Louis Castellucci**
267 Sleigh ride

**Roberto Cardinali**
1016 Ciao ciao bambina (with The Rita Williams Singers)

**David Carey**
432 Outside of heaven
435 Broken wings
454 Oh, happy day
501 Vaya con Dios
      (see also Cyril Stapleton and his Orchestra)

**Hoagy Carmichael**
309 My resistance is low
648 The Crazy Otto rag

**Hoagy Carmichael and Cass Daley**
218 The old piano roll blues

**Edwina Carol**
(see Charlie Chester; Charlie Chester and Edwina Carol)

**Lily Ann Carol**
414 Raindrops (with The High Hatters)

**Gino Caroli**
651 Mama

**Leslie Caron and Mel Ferrer**
445 Hi-Lili, hi-lo

**Renato Carosone and his Sextet**
930 Torero

**Carleton Carpenter**
(see Debbie Reynolds and Carleton Carpenter)

**Paul Carpenter**
71 Time after time
130 Maybe you'll be there
      (see also Ted Heath and his Music)

**Carole Carr**
441 Heart and soul
448 That doggie in the window (with Children's Choir and Rustler the Dog)
501 Vaya con Dios
      (see also Geraldo and his Orchestra)

**Cathy Carr**
729 Ivory Tower

**Dick Carr and his Bushlanders**
(see Slim Dusty)

**Georgia Carr**
479 April in Portugal

**Joe 'Fingers' Carr and The Carr Hops**
242 Sam's song
308 Ivory rag
352 Down yonder
706 Memories of you
      (see also Margaret Whiting)

**Joe 'Fingers' Carr and his Ragtime Band**
522 Istanbul

**Pearl Carr**
440 Take me in your arms and hold me
638 Where will the dimple be?
672 I'll never stop loving you
686 Arrivederci darling
696 Young and foolish
      (see also Pearl Carr and The Keynotes; Teddy Johnson and Pearl Carr)

**Pearl Carr and The Keynotes**
18 There's a harvest moon tonight
326 There's no boat like a rowboat

**Rita Carr**
(see Lou Preager and his Orchestra)

**Valerie Carr**
919 When the boys talk about the girls

**Wally Carr**
615 A blossom fell
632 Unsuspecting heart

**Bob Carroll**
583 Sway
      (see also Jimmy Dorsey and his Orchestra)

**David Carroll and his Orchestra**
642 Melody of love
642 Melody of love (poem read by Paul Tremaine)

**Ronnie Carroll**
735 Walk hand in hand
755 Love me as though there were no tomorrow
787 Wisdom of a fool
806 Around the world
854 April love
878 To be loved
1050 The wonder of you

**Jean (Jeannie) Carson**
637 Unchained melody
647 Evermore
662 Close your eyes
895 I could have danced all night (with Rita Williams Singers)
924 Wouldn't it be loverly? (with Rita Williams Singers)

**Kit Carson**
703 Band of gold

**Mindy Carson**
236 Candy and cake
296 A rainy day refrain
462 All the time and ev'rywhere
700 Memories are made of this (with The Columbians)
719 You can't be true to two
      (see also Guy Mitchell and Mindy Carson)

**Russ Case and his Orchestra**
181 You're breaking my heart (The Quintones)

**Johnny Cash**
996 The little drummer boy

**Ray Castle**
24 So would I

**Castle Jazz Band, The**
891 Who's sorry now? (with Kid Ory's Creole Band, Charlie Le Vere's Chicago Loopers and Pete Daily's Chicagoans)

252

**George Cates and his Orchestra and Chorus**
734    Whatever will be will be
774    Friendly persuasion
837    Man on fire
**Cavaliers, The**
(see Carmen Cavallaro and his Orchestra)
**Jean Cavall**
24    So would I
39    Till then
52    Accordion
76    Mam'selle
99    Serenade of the bells
107    Teresa
126    La vie en rose
156    Clopin clopant
**Carmen Cavallaro and his Muted Strings**
291    So in love
**Carmen Cavallaro and his Orchestra**
111    The dream of Olwen
205    Music! Music! Music! (Bob Lido, The
        Cavaliers and Ensemble)
843    An affair to remember (Miriam Workman)
**Carmen Cavallaro**
256    Autumn leaves
275    September song
345    Some enchanted evening
609    White Christmas
748    Autumn concerto
        (see also Bing Crosby)
**Page Cavanaugh Trio, The**
(see Doris Day)
**Francisco Cavez and his Orchestra**
686    Arrivederci darling
**Central Band of the RAF, The, conducted by
Wing Comdr. A.E. Sims OBE**
496    Number One (with The RAF Singers)
668    The Dam Busters March
**Frank Chacksfield and his Orchestra**
475    Terry's Theme from 'Limelight'
502    Flirtation waltz (with Roy Plummer –
        guitar)
515    Golden tango
525    Ebb tide
578    Smile
675    Love is a many-splendoured thing (with
        Chorus)
685    The shifting, whispering sands (w. Chorus)
706    Memories of you
**Frank Chacksfield's Tunesmiths**
403    Meet Mr Callaghan
453    Little red monkey (with Jack Jordan –
        clavioline)
**Champs, The**
882    Tequila
**Jeff Chandler**
764    My prayer
**Karen Chandler**
604    Heartbeat
**Chantels, The**
(see Richard Barrett and The Chantels)
**Charles Chaplin**
835    Mandolin serenade
**Paul Chapman**
365    Cry
**Cyd Charisse**
(see Fred Astaire and Cyd Charisse)
**Ray Charles Singers, The**
(see Evelyn Knight; Johnny Desmond; Ella Fitzgerald;
Perry Como)

**Charms, The**
(see Otis Williams and The Charms)
**Cheerleaders, The**
(see Gary Crosby and The Cheerleaders)
**Cherokeys, The**
221    Let's do it again (with Frank Baron Orch)
        (see also Donald Peers)
**Don Cherry**
298    Life's desire
311    I apologise
333    Vanity
334    Belle, Belle, my Liberty Belle
536    Don't leave me now
703    Band of gold
800    Chapel of the roses
        (see also Victor Young and his Orchestra; Eileen
        Wilson and Don Cherry)
**Cherry Sisters, The**
(see Arthur Godfrey)
**Ronald Chesney**
228    Bewitched
243    Mona Lisa
591    The high and the mighty
616    Majorca
929    Volare
**Ronald Chesney and George Elliott**
352    Down yonder
379    Blacksmith blues
406    Delicado
**'Cheerful' Charlie Chester**
27    Let it be soon
142    In a shady nook (with The Singing
        Silhouettes and Edwina Carol)
**Charlie Chester and Edwina Carol**
168    Blue ribbon gal
**Charlie Chester and The Singing Silhouettes**
138    On the 5.45
**Vic Chester**
804    Rock-a-Billy
**Maurice Chevalier**
133    On a slow boat to China
**Children of Dr Barnardo's, The**
983    This old man
        (see also Petula Clark)
**Maureen Childs**
(see Frank Weir and his Orchestra)
**Chipmunks, The**
(see David Seville)
**Chordettes, The**
606    Mr Sandman
746    Lay down your arms
747    Born to be with you
886    Lollipop
        (see also Arthur Godfrey; Arthur Godfrey and
        The Chordettes)
**Chords, The**
584    Sh-boom
**June Christy**
532    My heart belongs to only you
**City Ramblers Skiffle Group, The, with Jimmie
Macgregor**
959/960    Tom Dooley
**Betty Clark**
(see Blue Barron and his Orchestra)
**Buddy Clark**
163    Brush those tears from your eyes (with The
        Modernaires and The Skylarks)
172    I don't see me in your eyes any more

181    You're breaking my heart
        (see also Doris Day and Buddy Clark; Dinah
        Shore and Buddy Clark)
**Petula Clark**
149    Put your shoes on, Lucy
157    I'll always love you
159    Clancy lowered the boom
261    Beloved, be faithful
271    The Tennessee waltz
283    Teasin'
299    May kway o may kway
327    The black note serenade
498    Poppa Piccolino (with The Children of Dr
        Barnardo's Homes)
519    Where did my snowman go? (with The
        Children of Dr Barnardo's Homes)
558    The little shoemaker
578    Smile
614    Somebody
616    Majorca
639    Chee-chee-oo-chee
676    Suddenly there's a valley
688    With your love
700    Memories are made of this
703    Band of gold
821    With all my heart
848    Alone (with The Beryl Stott Group)
857    Long before I knew you
876    Baby lover (with The Beryl Stott Group)
921    Devotion (with The Beryl Stott Chorus)
1025    Suddenly (with The Beryl Stott Group)
**Petula Clark and The Radio Revellers**
646    The pendulum song
648    The Crazy Otto rag
**Clark Sisters, The**
864    Chicago
        (see also Jack Smith and The Clark Sisters)
**Clarke Brothers, The**
(see Max Bygraves)
**Robert Clary**
215    C'est si bon
**Andre Claveau**
324    Mademoiselle de Paris
**Jeff Clay**
(see Sammy Kaye and his Orchestra)
**Jan Clayton and John Raitt**
234    If I loved you
**Steve Clayton**
760    Two different worlds
**Robinson Cleaver and Patricia Rossborough**
339    Love's roundabout
**Larry Clinton and his Orchestra**
133    On a slow boat to China (Helen Lee and The
        Dipsy Doodlers)
**Gail Clooney**
(see Rosemary Clooney)
**Rosemary Clooney**
250    I only saw him once
297    The shot-gun boogie
303    Beautiful brown eyes
325    The Kentucky waltz
343    I wish I wuz
372    Be my life's companion
411    Botch-a-me
412    Half as much
453    Little red monkey
535    Tenderly
589    This ole house (with Thurl Ravenscroft –
        bass voice)

| 601 | Count your blessings instead of sheep (with The Mellomen) |
|---|---|
| 609 | White Christmas (with The Mellomen) |
| 610 | Mambo Italiano (with The Mellomen) |
| 629 | Open up your heart (with Gail Clooney) |
| 638 | Where will the dimple be? (with The Mellomen and Thurl Ravenscroft (bass)) |
| 657 | Learnin' the blues |
| 670 | Hey there |
| 671 | Go on by |
| 796 | Mangos |
| 895 | I could have danced all night |
| 969 | Winter wonderland |
| 979 | Tonight |

(see also Guy Mitchell and Rosemary Clooney; Benny Goodman Trio)

**Cloverleafs, The**
(see Art Mooney's Little Band; Art Mooney and his Orchestra)

**Clubmen, The**
(see Cyril Stapleton and his Orchestra; Jimmy Young)

**Coasters, The**
| 1012 | Charlie Brown |

**Eric Coates and his Concert Orchestra**
| 668 | The Dam Busters March |

**Eddie Cochran**
| 1013 | C'mon everybody |

**Alma Cogan**
| 386 | Blue tango |
|---|---|
| 412 | Half as much |
| 421 | You belong to me (with Jimmy Watson – trumpet) |
| 428 | I went to your wedding |
| 440 | Take me in your arms and hold me |
| 455 | Till I waltz again with you |
| 471 | Hold me, thrill me, kiss me |
| 516 | Ricochet (with Ken Mackintosh Orch) |
| 542 | Bell bottom blues |
| 551 | Make love to me (with Ken Mackintosh Orch) |
| 558 | The little shoemaker |
| 565 | Little things mean a lot |
| 589 | This ole house (with vocal group) |
| 599 | I can't tell a waltz from a tango |
| 610 | Mambo Italiano (with vocal group) |
| 611 | The naughty lady of shady lane (with vocal group) |
| 613 | Softly softly (with choir and organ) |
| 626 | Paper kisses |
| 631 | Tweedle-dee |
| 638 | Where will the dimple be? |
| 639 | Chee-chee-oo-chee (with vocal group) |
| 643 | Dreamboat |
| 669 | Hernando's hideaway |
| 671 | Go on by |
| 673 | Twenty tiny fingers |
| 674 | The banjo's back in town |
| 683 | Never do a tango with an eskimo |
| 692 | Love and marriage |
| 714 | Willie can (with Desmond Lane – penny whistle) |
| 718 | Don't ring-a da bell |
| 736 | Why do fools fall in love? (with vocal group) |
| 737 | The birds and the bees (with vocal group) |
| 757 | In the middle of the house |
| 777 | You, me and us |
| 860 | The story of my life |
| 868 | Sugartime (with The Michael Sammes Singers) |
| 896 | Stairway of love (with The Michael Sammes Singers) |
| 925 | Fly away lovers (with The Michael Sammes Singers) |
| 950 | There's never been a night (with The Michael Sammes Singers) |
| 988 | Last night on the back porch (with The Michael Sammes Singers) |
| 1028 | Pink shoelaces |

(see also Alma Cogan and Larry Day; Frankie Vaughan and Alma Cogan)

**Alma Cogan and Larry Day**
| 388 | The Homing waltz |

**Nat 'King' Cole**
| 115 | Nature boy |
|---|---|
| 243 | Mona Lisa |
| 320 | Too young |
| 362 | Unforgettable |
| 367 | Because of rain |
| 401 | Walkin' my baby back home (with Billy May Orch) |
| 402 | Somewhere along the way |
| 422 | Faith can move mountains |
| 424 | Because you're mine |
| 451 | The ruby and the pearl |
| 461 | Pretend |
| 489 | Can't I? (with Billy May Orch) |
| 491 | Mother Nature and Father Time |
| 509 | Answer me |
| 535 | Tenderly |
| 578 | Smile |
| 586 | Hold my hand |
| 587 | If I give my heart to you |
| 588 | Make her mine |
| 612 | Papa loves mambo |
| 615 | A blossom fell |
| 622 | Teach me tonight (with Billy May Orch) |
| 675 | Love is a many-splendoured thing |
| 699 | Dreams can tell a lie |
| 728 | Too young to go steady |
| 744 | You are my first love |
| 755 | Love me as though there were no tomorrow |
| 808 | When I fall in love |
| 948 | It's all in the game |

(see also The Nat 'King' Cole Trio; Woody Herman and Nat 'King' Cole)

**Nat 'King' Cole Trio, The**
| 144 | Put 'em in a box (Nat 'King' Cole) |
| 257 | Orange coloured sky (Nat 'King' Cole and Stan Kenton Orch) |

**Dorothy Collins**
| 274 | Me and my imagination |
| 692 | Love and marriage |
| 723 | The Italian theme |
| 755 | Love me as though there were no tomorrow |
| 807 | Mr Wonderful |

**Jerry Colonna**
| 525 | Ebb tide |
| 619 | Let me go, lover (with The Three Lovers) |
| 685 | The shifting, whispering sands (with vocal group) |

**Columbians, The**
(see Mindy Carson)

**Norton Colville and his Band for Dancers**
| 363 | Only fools |

**Commanders, The**
| 551 | Make love to me |

**Perry Como**
| 77 | They say it's wonderful |
|---|---|
| 83 | Chi-baba chi-baba |
| 94 | I wonder who's kissing her now (with Ted Weems Orch & Chorus) |
| 94 | I wonder who's kissing her now (with Lloyd Schaefer Orch) |
| 100 | When you were sweet sixteen (with The Satisfyers) |
| 122 | Rambling Rose (with The Satisfyers) |
| 137 | Far away places |
| 154 | Forever and ever |
| 172 | I don't see me in your eyes any more |
| 254 | A dream is a wish your heart makes |
| 270 | If |
| 280 | Patricia |
| 345 | Some enchanted evening |
| 360 | Rollin' stone (with The Fontane Sisters) |
| 373 | Please Mr Sun |
| 423 | My love and devotion |
| 437 | Don't let the stars get in your eyes (with The Ramblers) |
| 451 | The ruby and the pearl |
| 469 | Wild horses |
| 487 | Say you're mine again (with The Ramblers) |
| 506 | You're just in love (w. The Fontane Sisters) |
| 524 | Hello young lovers |
| 563 | Idle gossip |
| 564 | Wanted |
| 609 | White Christmas |
| 612 | Papa loves mambo (with The Ray Charles Singers) |
| 725 | Hot diggity |
| 749 | More (with The Ray Charles Singers) |
| 753 | Glendora |
| 802 | Round and round (with The Ray Charles Singers) |
| 866 | Magic moments (with The Ray Charles Singers) |
| 870 | Catch a falling star (with The Ray Charles Singers) |
| 880 | I may never pass this way again (with The Ray Charles Singers) |
| 898 | Kewpie doll (with The Ray Charles Singers) |
| 933 | Moon talk (with The Ray Charles Singers) |
| 941 | Girl of my dreams |
| 958 | Love makes the world go round (with The Ray Charles Singers) |
| 961 | Mandolins in the moonlight (with The Ray Charles Singers) |
| 969 | Winter wonderland (with The Satisfyers) |
| 1004 | Kiss me and kiss me and kiss me (with The Ray Charles Singers) |
| 1007 | Tomboy (with The Ray Charles Singers) |
| 1045 | I know (with The Ray Charles Singers) |

**Perry Como and The Fontane Sisters**
| 153 | A – you're adorable |
| 251 | Bibbidi bobbidi boo |
| 326 | There's no boat like a rowboat |

**Compagnons de la Chanson, Les**
| 1069 | The three bells |

**Jud Conlon's Rhythmaires**
(see Bing Crosby; Bing Crosby and Evelyn Knight; Bing Crosby and Jane Wyman; Stan Freberg)

**Jud Conlon Singers, The**
| 535 | Tenderly |

(see also Peggy Lee; Jack Smith)

**Edric Connor**
| 825 | Fire down below |

**Continentals, The**
(see Tony Dallara)

**Reginald Conway and his Orchestra**
655   John and Julie (with The Rita Williams Singers)
659   Blue Star (with The Rita Williams Singers)
661   Three galleons

**Russ Conway**
937   Got a match
971   The world outside (with The Rita Williams Singers)
975   Side saddle
1022   Roulette
1041   Pixilated penguin
1044   Trampolina
1058   China tea
1085   Snow coach

**Steve Conway**
5   I can't begin to tell you
24   So would I
44   The stars will remember
46   April showers
47   May I call you sweetheart?
71   Time after time
82   Guilty
86   I'll make up for everything
100   When you were sweet sixteen
128   October twilight
130   Maybe you'll be there (with The Conway Singers)
148   The wedding of Lilli Marlene
178   A shawl of Galway grey
207   Best of all
210   When the world has forgotten
211   My thanks to you
214   My foolish heart
226   Daddy's little girl
254   A dream is a wish your heart makes
256   Autumn leaves
281   Good luck, good health, God bless you (with The Hastings Girls' Choir)
294   Mary Rose
302   Would I love you
320   Too young
331   White wedding
344   At the end of the day (with The Hastings Girls' Choir)

**Steve Conway and The Stargazers**
239   Sentimental me
243   Mona Lisa
245   Ashes of roses

**Conway Singers, The**
(see Steve Conway)

**Sam Cooke**
1057   Only sixteen

**Spade Cooley and his Fiddlin' Friends**
352   Down yonder

**Mae Cooper**
(see Carl Barriteau and his Orchestra)

**Frank Cordell and his Orchestra**
301   List'nin' to the green grass grow (Larry Day)
305   With these hands (Larry Day)
316   My truly, truly fair (Larry Day)
334   Belle, Belle, my Liberty Belle (Larry Day)
341   Allentown Jail (Stella Tanner and Chorus)
406   Delicado
711   The Theme from 'The Threepenny Opera'
900   Little serenade (with The Michael Sammes Singers)

**Roy Cordell**
(see Jan Garber and his Orchestra)

**Annie Cordy**
558   The little shoemaker

**Jill Corey**
(see The Four Lads and Jill Corey)

**Ruggero Cori**
(see Marino Marini and his Quartet)

**Don Cornell**
586   Hold my hand
633   Stranger in paradise
637   Unchained melody
675   Love is a many-splendoured thing
789   All of you
   (see also Sammy Kaye and his Orchestra)

**Coronets, The**
543   The Jones boy
545   Heart of my heart
602   The Mama Doll song
607   The finger of suspicion
673   Twenty tiny fingers
679   Meet me on the corner
   (see also Derrick Francis; Eric Jupp and his Orchestra; The Big Ben Banjo Band; Ray Burns; Benny Hill; Jimmy Parkinson; Lee Lawrence)

**Bob Cort Skiffle Group, The**
781   Don't you rock me, daddy-o
   (see also Liz Winters)

**Bob Cort**
1043   The battle of New Orleans
1051   Waterloo

**Don Costa and his Orchestra and Chorus**
675   Love is a many-splendoured thing

**Billy Cotton – vocal**
(see Billy Cotton and his Band)

**Billy Cotton and his Band**
11   Mary Lou (Alan Breeze)
34   Make-believe world (Alan Breeze)
37   Lilli Marlene (Alan Breeze)
43   Anniversary song (Alan Breeze)
64   Harriett (Alan Breeze)
81   The little old mill (Alan Breeze)
166   Beautiful eyes (Alan Breeze)
200   I've got a lovely bunch of coconuts (Alan Breeze)
208   The French can-can polka (The Bandits)
211   My thanks to you (Doreen Stephens and Alan Breeze)
226   Daddy's little girl (Alan Breeze and The Sentimentalists)
227   Two on a tandem (The Bandits)
230   The night the floor fell in (Alan Breeze and The Bandits)
238   If I were a blackbird (Alan Breeze and Choir)
250   I only saw him once (Doreen Stephens)
265   The thing (Alan Breeze and The Bandits)
266   The petite waltz
268   Flying saucer (Alan Breeze and The Bandits)
271   The Tennessee waltz (Rita and Joyce)
277   My heart cries for you (Doreen Stephens, Alan Breeze and Ensemble)
278   C'n I canoe you up the river? (Alan Breeze and The Bandits)
281   Good luck, good health, God bless you (Doreen Stephens, Alan Breeze and Chorus)
282   Tipperary samba (Alan Breeze and The Bandits)
296   Da-dim, da-dom, da-dim, da-dom (Doreen Stephens, Rita and Joyce)
297   The shot gun boogie (Alan Breeze and The Bandits)
299   May kway o may kway (Billy Cotton, Doreen Stephens and The Bandits)
308   Ivory rag (Alan Breeze and The Bandits)
312   Jezebel (Alan Breeze)
321   Sweet violets (Alan Breeze and The Bandits)
327   The black note serenade (The Bandits)
330   I love the sunshine of your smile (Alan Breeze and The Bandits)
336   Longing for you (Alan Breeze and The Bandits)
340   Rosaline (Alan Breeze and The Bandits)
347   Shrimp boats (Doreen Stephens, Alan Breeze and The Bandits)
350   Why worry (Billy Cotton)
354   There's always room at our house (Alan Breeze and The Bandits)
356   Oodles of noodles (Alan Breeze and The Bandits)
359   I wanna say hello (The Bandits)
368   We won't live in a castle (Doreen Stephens, Alan Breeze and Chorus)
370   Tell me why (Alan Breeze and The Bandits with Charles Smitton – organ)
380   The gandy dancers' ball (Alan Breeze and The Bandits)
383   Auf wiederseh'n sweetheart (Doreen Stephens and Chorus)
388   The homing waltz (Alan Breeze, The Mill Girls and Chorus)
393   Star of Hope (Doreen Stephens and Choir)
394   Trust in me (Alan Breeze and The Bandits)
405   I'll walk alone (Alan Breeze and The Bandits)
407   Rock of Gibraltar (Alan Breeze and The Bandits)
449   In a golden coach (Doreen Stephens with narration by Billy Cotton)
460   I'm walking behind you (Doreen Stephens)
498   Poppa Piccolino (Alan Breeze and The Bandits)
499   Big head (Alan Breeze and Billy Cotton)
507   When you hear Big Ben (Doreen Stephens and Choir)
508   Be mine (Doreen Stephens)
511   I saw mommy kissing Santa Claus (The Mill Girls and The Bandits)
519   Where did my snowman go? (The Mill Girls and The Bandits)
520   When Santa got stuck up the chimney (Billy Cotton and The Bandits)
521   Oh! My pa-pa (Alan Breeze and The Bandits)
543   The Jones boy (The Bandits)
545   Heart of my heart (Alan Breeze, Billy Cotton and The Gang)
552   Friends and neighbours (The Bandits)
566   Bob's yer uncle (Alan Breeze and The Bandits)
589   This ole house (Doreen Stephens and The Bandits)
611   The naughty lady of shady lane (The Bandits)
628   Ready, willing and able (The Mill Girls)
666   The yellow rose of Texas (The Bandits)
668   The Dam Busters March (narration by Billy Cotton)
691   The ballad of Davy Crockett (Billy Cotton)
697   Robin Hood (Doreen Stephens, Alan Breeze and The Bandits)

734 Whatever will be, will be (Billy Cotton)
756 Just walking in the rain (Billy Cotton and Chorus)
773 The Garden of Eden (Alan Breeze and The Bandits)
795 The good companions (Billy Cotton and The Bandits)

**Diana Coupland**
381 A guy is a guy

**Cowboy Church Sunday School, The**
629 Open up your heart
671 Go on by

**Crackerjacks, The**
*(see Jack Parnell and his Orchestra)*

**Francis Craig and his Orchestra**
96 Near you (Bob Lamm)

**Tony Craig**
*(see Guy Lombardo and his Royal Canadians)*

**Cranes Skiffle Group, The**
781 Don't you rock me, daddy-o
797 Cumberland gap
805 Freight train

**Crew Chiefs, The**
*(see Jerry Gray and his Orchestra; Margaret Whiting)*

**Crew Cuts, The**
584 Sh-boom
637 Unchained melody
640 Earth angel
782 Young love

**Crickets, The**
1065 Peggy Sue got married (with David Box)
*(see also Buddy Holly and The Crickets)*

**Bing Crosby**
5 I can't begin to tell you (with Carmen Cavallaro – piano)
6 In the land of beginning again
16 Day by day (with Mel Torme and The Meltones)
24 So would I (with Russ Morgan and his Orchestra)
29 You keep coming back like a song
30 All through the day
37 Lilli Marlene
38 Pretending (with The Les Paul Trio)
43 Anniversary song
49 The things we did last summer (with Jimmy Dorsey and his Orchestra)
65 Try a little tenderness
66 Among my souvenirs (with Russ Morgan and his Orchestra)
67 A gal in calico (with The Calico Kids)
70 People will say we're in love (with Trudy Erwin and The Sportsmen Glee Club)
74 Dear old Donegal (with The Jesters)
77 They say it's wonderful
78 Now is the hour (w. The Ken Darby Choir)
80 Oh, what a beautiful morning (with Trudy Erwin and The Sportsmen Glee Club)
105 Golden earrings
109 Galway Bay
118 Dance, ballerina, dance (with The Rhythmaires)
137 Far away places (with The Ken Darby Choir)
145 How can you buy Killarney?
161 Riders in the sky (with The Ken Darby Singers)
164 Careless hands (with The Ken Darby Singers)

185 The kiss in your eyes
196 The last mile home (with The Ken Lane Singers)
197 Dear hearts and gentle people (with Jud Conlon's Rhythmaires)
198 Mule train
202 We all have a song in our hearts
209 Chattanoogie shoe-shine boy
234 If I loved you
251 Bibbidi bobbidi boo (with Jud Conlon's Rhythmaires)
252 Rudolph, the red-nosed reindeer (with Jud Conlon's Rhythmaires)
253 Home cookin' (with Jud Conlon's Rhythmaires)
256 Autumn leaves
258 Christmas in Killarney (with Jud Conlon's Rhythmaires)
264 All my love (w. The Jeff Alexander Chorus)
269 Marshmallow world (with The Lee Gordon Singers)
275 September song
291 So in love
324 Mademoiselle de Paree
328 Shanghai
345 Some enchanted evening
355 Domino
371 At last! At last!
410 The Isle of Innisfree
450 Keep it a secret (with Jud Conlon's Rhythmaires)
486 I've Never Been In Love Before
517 If you love me
524 Hello young lovers
534 Changing partners (with Jud Conlon's Rhythmaires)
547 Secret love
556 I get so lonely (with Guy Lombardo and his Royal Canadians)
560 Young at heart (with Guy Lombardo and his Royal Canadians)
593 I love Paris
601 Count your blessings instead of sheep
609 White Christmas (with The Ken Darby Singers)
633 Stranger in paradise
663 Love me or leave me
717 No other love
806 Around the world
837 Man on fire
864 Chicago
941 Girl of my dreams
962 I heard the bells on Christmas Day (with The Ken Darby Singers)
992 Gigi

**Bing and Gary Crosby**
242 Sam's song
279 Play a simple melody

**Bing Crosby, Danny Kaye, Peggy Lee and Trudy Stevens**
609 White Christmas

**Bing Crosby and Grace Kelly**
762 True love

**Bing Crosby and Evelyn Knight**
169 Everywhere you go (with Jud Conlon's Rhythmaires)

**Bing Crosby and Carole Richards**
229 Sunshine cake (with The Jeff Alexander Chorus)

**Bing Crosby and Jane Wyman**
337 In the cool, cool, cool of the evening (with The Four Hits and a Miss)
417 Zing a little zong (with Jud Conlon's Rhythmaires)

**Bing Crosby and The Andrews Sisters**
91 South America, take it away
219 Quicksilver
240 Have I told you lately that I love you?
295 Sparrow in the tree top

**Bob Crosby and his Bob-cats**
891 Who's sorry now?
998 Petite fleur

**Bob Crosby and his Orchestra**
36 Five minutes more (Bob Crosby and The Bobolinks)
328 Shanghai (Bob Crosby)

**Gary Crosby and The Cheerleaders**
628 Ready, willing and able
*(see also Bing and Gary Crosby)*

**Larry Cross**
320 Too young
329 Because of you
369 And so to sleep again
405 I'll walk alone
412 Half as much
421 You belong to me
423 My love and devotion
571 Three coins in the fountain
586 Hold my hand
601 Count your blessings instead of sheep
618 Give me your word
640 Earth angel
691 The ballad of Davy Crockett
693 Sixteen tons
709 Chain gang (with The Rita Williams Singers)
728 Too young to go steady
738 Mountain greenery
757 In the middle of the house
*see also Larry Cross and the Song Pedlars; Geraldo and his Orchestra)*

**Larry Cross and The Song Pedlars**
316 My truly, truly fair
321 Sweet violets

**George Crow and the Blue Mariners**
122 Rambling Rose

**Juanita Crowley**
*(see Russ Morgan and his Orchestra)*

**Barry Cryer**
909 The purple people eater
1003 Angelina

**Cubs, The**
*(see Roy Fox and his Band)*

**Xavier Cugat and his Orchestra**
132 Cuanto le gusta (Trio)
174 The wedding samba
264 All my love (Abbe Lane)
488 Say 'si si' (Abbe Lane)
630 Cherry pink and apple blossom white

**Daddy-O's, The**
937 Got a match

**Dan Dailey and The Andrews Sisters**
159 Clancy lowered the boom

**Pete Daily's Chicagoans**
*(see The Castle Jazz Band)*

**Alan Dale**
630 Cherry pink and apple blossom white
697 Robin Hood

**737** The birds and the bees
**929** Volare
**Betty Dale**
(*see Jack Simpson and his Sextet*)
**Bob Dale**
**564** Wanted
**573** The story of Tina
**607** The finger of suspicion
**608** Happy days and lonely nights
**609** White Christmas
**664** The man from Laramie
**666** The yellow rose of Texas
**697** Robin Hood (with The Rita Williams Singers)
**846** Mary's boy child
**854** April love
**855** Kisses sweeter than wine
(*see also Oscar Rabin and his Band; Cyril Stapleton and his Orchestra; Rita Williams and Bob Dale*)
**Jim Dale**
**844** Be my girl
**868** Sugartime
**Cass Daley**
(*see Hoagy Carmichael and Cass Daley*)
**Tony Dallara**
**1001** Ti diro
**1016** Piove (with The Continentals)
**Tony Dalli**
**942** More than ever
**Chappie d'Amato and his Orchestra**
**37** Lilli Marlene
**Vic Damone**
**336** Longing for you
**413** Take my heart
**460** I'm walking behind you
**475** Eternally
**479** April in Portugal
**525** Ebb tide
**633** Stranger in paradise
**651** Mama
**843** An affair to remember
**857** Long before I knew you
**894** On the street where you live
**912** The only man on the island
**992** Gigi
**Dorothy Dandridge**
**335** Blow out the candle (with Phil Moore – piano)
**Billy Daniels**
**275** September song
**358** Charmaine
**578** Smile (with Benny Payne – piano)
**Joe Daniels and his Hot-Shots**
**218** The old piano roll blues
**Joe Daniels Jazz Group, The**
**864** Chicago
**Maxine Daniels**
**739** By the fountains of Rome
**Johnny Dankworth**
**416** Belle of the ball
**Johnny Dankworth and his Orchestra**
**706** Memories of you
**Johnny Dankworth Seven, The**
**242** Sam's song (Marion Williams)
**353** Sin (Cleo Laine)
(*see also Alan Dean*)
**Danny and the Juniors**
**867** At the hop

**Daphne and Benny Lee**
**323** Tulips and heather
**Daphne and David**
**449** In a golden coach
**Ken Darby Choir, The**
(*see Bing Crosby*)
**Ken Darby Singers, The**
(*see Bing Crosby; Danny Kaye*)
**Anita Darian**
(*see The Sauter-Finegan Orchestra*)
**Fred Darian**
(*see Camarata and his Music*)
**Bobby Darin**
**945** Splish splash
**1034** Dream lover
**1073** Mack the knife
**Arthur Darley**
(*see Delia Murphy*)
**Bill Darnel**
**379** Blacksmith blues
**Dany Dauberson**
**286** Be my love
**324** Ma'moiselle de Paris
**339** Love's roundabout
**Harry Davidson and his Orchestra**
**43** Anniversary song
**131** The cuckoo waltz
**466** Side by side
**473** Coronation waltz
**Bob Davie**
(*see Jim Lowe*)
**Beryl Davis**
**19** Do you love me?
**25** The 'Ampstead way
**29** You keep coming back like a song
(*see also Scotty McHarg and Beryl Davis*)
**Marion Davis**
(*see Oscar Rabin and his Band*)
**Sammy Davis Jr.**
**663** Love me or leave me
**670** Hey there
**789** All of you
**857** Long before I knew you
**Marjorie Daw**
(*see Oscar Rabin and his Band*)
**Julie Dawn**
**442** Now
**461** Pretend
**469** Wild horses
**760** Two different worlds (with vocal group)
(*see also Eric Winstone and his Orchestra; Cyril Stapleton and his Orchestra*)
**Harry Dawson**
**185** The kiss in your eyes
**192** Song of Capri
**233** Your heart and my heart
**234** If I loved you
**276** I'll always love you
**298** Life's desire
**306** You are my destiny (with The Mitchell Maids)
**364** Then I'll be there
**549** From the vine came the grape
**Herbert Dawson**
(*see The Luton Girls' Choir*)
**Dennis Day**
**374** Never
**413** Take my heart

**Doris Day**
**144** Put 'em in a box
**150** It's magic
**160** Again
**169** Everywhere you go (with The Mellomen)
**196** The last mile home
**206** Now that I need you (with The Mellomen)
**213** I said my pajamas
**216** Enjoy yourself
**219** Quicksilver (with her Country Cousins)
**228** Bewitched (with The Mellomen)
**231** A load of hay (with The Page Cavanaugh Trio)
**246** I only have eyes for you
**257** Orange coloured sky (with The Page Cavanaugh Trio)
**298** Life's desire
**302** Would I love you (with Harry James and his Orchestra)
**328** Shanghai
**338** Lullaby of Broadway (with The Norman Luboff Choir)
**355** Domino
**381** A guy is a guy
**423** My love and devotion
**425** When I fall in love (with The Norman Luboff Choir)
**486** I've never been in love before
**547** Secret love
**550** Someone else's roses
**557** The Deadwood Stage
**580** The black hills of Dakota (with vocal quartet)
**587** If I give my heart to you (with The Mellomen)
**628** Ready, willing and able
**636** You, my love
**663** Love me or leave me
**672** I'll never stop loving you
**704** Jimmy unknown
**734** Whatever will be, will be
**893** A very precious love
**931** Everybody loves a lover
**Doris Day and Buddy Clark**
**141** Powder your face with sunshine
**188** I'll string along with you
**Doris Day and Frankie Laine**
**404** Sugarbush (w. The Norman Luboff Choir)
**Doris Day and Johnnie Ray**
**493** Let's walk that-a-way
**Jill Day**
**639** Chee-chee-oo-chee
**644** Sincerely
**720** A tear fell
**768** Happiness Street
**776** I dreamed
**780** Give her my love
**796** Mangos (with vocal group)
(*see also Geraldo and his Orchestra*)
**Larry Day**
**294** Mary Rose
**408** Here in my heart
(*see also Frank Cordell and his Orchestra; Alma Cogan and Larry Day*)
**Alan Dean**
**234** If I loved you
**256** Autumn leaves
**291** So in love (with The Johnny Dankworth Seven)

336 Longing for you
342 If you go
384 Be anything (with Leroy Holmes and his Orchestra)
(see also Ambrose and his Orchestra; Jimmy Leach and his New Organolians; Anne Shelton)

**Syd Dean and his Band**
184 Monday, Tuesday, Wednesday (Jill Page and Harry Bolton)
193 The Scottish samba (Harry Bolton)
210 When the world has forgotten (Jill Page)
(see also The Stargazers)

**Larry Deane**
(see Lawrence Welk and his Champagne Music)

**Ronnie Deauville**
(see Ray Anthony and his Orchestra)

**De Castro Sisters, The**
622 Teach me tonight

**Diana Decker**
498 Poppa Piccolino
521 Oh! My papa
539 The happy wanderer
567 The never never land
570 The man with the banjo
574 Jilted
714 Willie can

**Tommy Dee**
(see Carol Kay)

**Deep River Boys, The**
176 Too whit, too whoo
194 Down in the glen
228 Bewitched
245 Ashes of roses
275 September song
320 Too young
353 Sin
617 Shake rattle and roll
635 I wonder
680 Rock around the clock (with Sid Phillips and his Band)

**Buddy de Franco**
472 Song from Moulin Rouge (with Orchestra conducted by Richard Maltby)

**Gloria de Haven**
343 I wish I wuz (with The Lombardo Trio)

**Gloria de Haven and Guy Lombardo**
329 Because of you

**Rich Dehr**
(see Terry Gilkyson and The Easy Riders)

**Roberto del Gado and his Orchestra**
823 Little darling

**Delta Rhythm Boys, The**
335 Blow out the candle
358 Charmaine
(see also Ella Fitzgerald and The Delta Rhythm Boys)

**Terry Dene**
811 A white sport coat
824 Start movin'
896 Stairway of love

**Dene Boys, The**
822 Bye bye love

**Johnny Denis and his Novelty Swing Sextet**
22 And then it's heaven (Johnny Denis and Billie Campbell)

**'Sheriff' Johnny Denis and his Ranchers**
98 The shoemaker's serenade
119 Toolie oolie doolie (with Primo Scala and his Accordion Band)

164 Careless hands (with The Cactus Kids)
197 Dear hearts and gentle people (with The Cactus Kids)
219 Quicksilver
231 A load of hay
325 The Kentucky waltz

**Clark Dennis**
535 Tenderly (with The Walter Gross Trio)

**Denny Dennis**
11 Mary Lou
34 Make-believe world
83 Chi-baba chi-baba (with The Song Pedlars)
84 Danger ahead
157 I'll always love you (with The Keynotes)
179 A rose in a garden of weeds
191 Is it too late?
264 Bolero
695 The tender trap
700 Memories are made of this (with The Canadians)
719 You can't be true to two (with The Rita Williams Singers)
733 The wayward wind
755 Love me as though there were no tomorrow
766 Cindy, oh Cindy
802 Round and round
822 Bye bye love
829 In the middle of an island
842 Let me be loved
861 Love me forever
866 Magic moments
906 Return to me
911 Sugar Moon
(see also Tommy Dorsey and his Orchestra; Sid Phillips and his Band)

**Jackie Dennis**
885 La dee dah
909 The purple people eater
942 More than ever

**Wilbur de Paris and his New Orleans Band**
998 Petite fleur

**Johnny Desmond**
215 C'est si bon (with The Quintones)
267 Sleigh ride
269 Marshmallow world (with The Ray Charles Singers)
320 Too young
329 Because of you
351 I want to be near you (with The Ray Charles Singers)
459 I will never change
591 The high and the mighty
666 The yellow rose of Texas
693 Sixteen tons
811 A white sport coat (with Dick Jacobs and his Skiffle Band)
994 Willingly

**Lorrae Desmond**
586 Hold my hand
596 No one but you
638 Where will the dimple be? (with The Melodaires)
645 Stowaway
759 A house with love in it
901 The secret of happiness
956 Blue, blue day

**Lorrae Desmond and The Johnston Brothers**
599 I can't tell a waltz from a tango

**Frank deVol**
(see Margaret Whiting and Frank deVol)

**Hugh Diamond**
161 Riders in the sky (with Lew Stone and his Orchestra)

**Diamonds, The**
823 Little darlin'

**Diane** (see Oscar Rabin and his Band)

**Franz Dietchmann – zither**
(see Henri Rene and his Orchestra)

**Marlene Dietrich**
37 Lilli Marlene

**Jacques Dieval Quartet, The**
286 Be my love

**Dottie Dillard**
(see Grady Martin and his Slew Foot Five)

**Mike di Napoli**
(see The Frank Petty Trio)

**Lou Dinning**
357 The little white cloud that cried
394 Trust in me (with Quartet)

**Dinning Sisters, The**
127 Buttons and bows
241 Once in a while
(see also Bob Atcher and The Dinning Sisters)

**Dion and The Belmonts**
1036 A teenager in love

**Dipsy Doodlers, The**
(see Larry Clinton and his Orchestra)

**Buddy Di Vito**
(see Harry James and his Orchestra)

**Dixieland All-Stars, The**
(see Teresa Brewer)

**Reg Dixon**
173 Confidentially
397 Heart of a clown

**Reginald Dixon**
35 The green cockatoo
386 Blue tango
(see also Josef Locke)

**Lindy Doherty**
(see Les Baxter and his Orchestra and Chorus)

**Fats Domino**
786 Blueberry Hill

**Lonnie Donegan and his Skiffle Group**
781 Don't you rock me, daddy-o
797 Cumberland Gap
814 Puttin' on the style
845 My Dixie darling
892 Grand Coolie Dam
960 Tom Dooley
995 Does your chewing gum lose its flavour on the bedpost overnight?
1038 Fort Worth Jail
1043 The battle of New Orleans

**Doodlers, The**
(see The Sauter-Finegan Orchestra)

**Evelyne Dorat**
371 L'âmes des poètes

**Nadia Doré**
(see Ambrose and his Orchestra; Geraldo and his Orchestra)

**Jimmy Dorsey and his Orchestra**
51 The whole world is singing my song (Bob Carroll)
60 Hear my song, Violetta (Bob Eberly)
118 Dance, ballerina, dance (Bob Carroll)
(see also Bing Crosby)

**Tommy Dorsey and his Orchestra**
60 Hear my songs, Violetta (Frank Sinatra)

165   While the angelus was ringing (Denny Dennis)

**ommy Dorsey Orchestra, The, directed by**
**arren Covington**
966   Tea for two cha cha

**raig Douglas**
014   Come softly to me
036   A teenager in love
057   Only sixteen

**hnny Douglas and his Orchestra**
661   Three galleons (Chorus)
739   By the fountains of Rome

**eslie Douglas and his Orchestra**
75   Down the old Spanish trail (Leslie Douglas and The Skymasters)

**ew Douglas and his Orchestra**
495   Ruby (with The Jack Halloran Choir)

**lly Douglas**
*e Geraldo and his Orchestra; The Skyrockets conducted Woolf Phillips)*

**hirley Douglas**
*e Chas McDevitt Group)*

**an Dowling**
468   The Windsor waltz
471   Hold me, thrill me, kiss me
494   Is it any wonder?

**ozen and One Lovelies, The**
*e Scotty McHarg and Beryl Davis)*

**armen Dragon**
*e Al Jolson)*

**lfred Drake**
80   Oh, what a beautiful morning

**lfred Drake and Joan Roberts**
70   People will say we're in love

**harlie Drake**
929   Volare
945   Splish splash
980   Tom Thumb's tune

**leen Draper**
455   Till I waltz again with you
477   Tell me you're mine

**usty Draper**
805   Freight train (with The Dick Noel Singers)

**ream Weavers, The**
701   It's almost tomorrow

**ank d'Rone**
850   My special angel

**rifters, The**
*e (a) Reggie Goff, or (b) the later group – Cliff Richard o become The Shadows)*

**etty Driver**
184   Monday, Tuesday, Wednesday
    (see also Sid Phillips and his Band)

**ennie Druss**
*e The Johnny Pate Quintet)*

**rthur Dulay**
*e Charles Williams and his Concert Orchestra)*

**hnny Duncan and his Blue Grass Boys**
827   Last train to San Fernando
037   Kansas City

**ommy Duncan and his Western All-Stars**
209   Chattanoogie shoe-shine boy

**mmy Durante**
251   Bibbidi bobbidi boo
252   Rudolph, the red-nosed reindeer

**im Dusty**
984   The pub with no beer (with Dick Carr and his Bushlanders)

**Johnnie Eager**
*(see Sid Phillips and his Band)*

**Vince Eager**
1082   Makin' love

**Robert Earl**
512   Crying in the chapel (with The Rita Williams Singers)
517   If you love me
538   The Book
590   My son, my son
635   I wonder
661   Three galleons
684   He
688   With your love
707   My September love
745   Believe in me
749   More
791   All
850   My special angel
880   I may never pass this way again
942   More than ever
989   The wonderful secret of love
1092   The key

**Easy Riders, The**
*(see Terry Gilkyson and The Easy Riders; Frankie Laine)*

**Margaret Eaves**
225   I remember the cornfields

**Bob Eberly**
122   Rambling Rose (with Russ Morgan and his Orchestra)
298   Life's desire
374   Never
    (see also Jimmy Dorsey and his Orchestra)

**Ebonaires, The**
*(see John Paris)*

**Eccles, The Famous, and Miss Freda Thing**
707   My September love

**Billy Eckstine**
214   My foolish heart
270   If
286   Be my love
311   I apologise
385   Kiss of fire
424   Because you're mine
486   I've never been in love before
535   Tenderly
596   No one but you
663   Love me or leave me
705   Only you
992   Gigi

**Duane Eddy**
1064   Forty miles of bad road

**Nelson Eddy**
80   Oh, what a beautiful morning

**Nelson Eddy and Jo Stafford**
305   With these hands

**David Ede**
*(see Oscar Rabin and his Band)*

**David Ede Ensemble, The**
*(see Oscar Rabin and his Band)*

**Jimmy Edwards**
*(see Joy Nichols, Dick Bentley and Jimmy Edwards)*

**Roy Edwards**
579   Midnight
    (see also The Squadronaires directed by Ronnie Aldrich; The Squadronaires directed by Jimmy Miller)

**Tommy Edwards**
318   A beggar in love

373   Please Mr Sun
382   My concerto
948   It's all in the game

**Eight Stars, The**
*(see Gracie Fields)*

**Roy Eldridge & Benny Carter Orchestra, The**
662   Close your eyes

**Les Elgart and his Orchestra and Chorus**
606   Mister Sandman

**Elias and his Zig Zag Jive Flutes**
897   Tom Hark

**Mary Ellen Quartet, The**
222   Dearie (Mary Ellen, Bob Scott and Quartet)
236   Candy and cake (Mary Ellen, Bob Scott and Quartet)

**Duke Ellington and his Famous Orchestra**
578   Smile
587   If I give my heart to you

**Duke Ellington and his Orchestra**
139   Twelfth Street rag

**Ray Ellington**
453   Little red monkey
1012   Charlie Brown (with The Beryl Stott Group)
    (see also Ray Ellington and The Stargazers; The Ray Ellington Glee Club; The Ray Ellington Quartet)

**Ray Ellington and The Stargazers**
415   Feet up

**Ray Ellington Glee Club, The**
*(see The Ray Ellington Quartet)*

**Ray Ellington Quartet, The**
135   The Maharajah of Magador (The Ray Ellington Glee Club)
284   Senora (Ray Ellington)
361   Slow coach (Ray Ellington)
446   She wears red feathers (Ray Ellington and the Peter Knight Singers)
581   A sky-blue shirt and a rainbow tie (Ray Ellington)
610   Mambo Italiano (Ray Ellington)
611   The naughty lady of shady lane (Ray Ellington)
640   Earth angel (Ray Ellington)
758   Green door (Ray Ellington)
794   Marianne (Ray Ellington)

**George Elliott**
*(see Ronald Chesney and George Elliott)*

**Peter Elliott**
921   Devotion

**Anita Ellis**
632   Unsuspecting heart
    (see also Fred Astaire, Red Skelton and Anita Ellis)

**Ziggy Elman and his Orchestra**
223   Me and my shadow

**Joan Elms**
*(see Russ Morgan and his Orchestra)*

**George Elrick and The Lumberjacks**
577   Gilly Gilly Ossenfeffer Katzenellen Bogen by the Sea

**Embassy Orchestra, The, directed by Jack Coles**
591   The high and the mighty

**Embassy Singers and Players, The, conducted by Gordon Franks**
992   Gigi
1002   Thank heaven for little girls

**Embassy Singers, The, directed by Jacques Leroy**
996   The little drummer boy

**Embassy Rhythm Group, The**
(see Benny Lee)
**Don Emsley**
(see Billy Ternent and his Orchestra)
**Encores, The**
(see Gene Sheldon)
**Ernie Englund**
  711    The Theme from 'The Threepenny Opera'
**'Enrohtwah'**
(see Red Ingle and The Unnatural Seven)
**Trudy Erwin**
(see Bing Crosby)
**Don Estes**
  384    Be anything
**George Evans**
(see Geraldo and his Orchestra)
**Maureen Evans**
  932    Carolina Moon
  934    Stupid Cupid
  940    Born too late
  953    Hula hoop song
  967    The day the rains came
  970    To know him is to love him
  972    Kiss me, honey honey, kiss me
  976    You always hurt the one you love
1006    May you always
1029    Goodbye, Jimmy, goodbye
1046    Lipstick on your collar
1071    Broken-hearted melody
1080    Plenty good lovin'
**Paul Evans and The Curls**
1090    Seven little girls sitting in the back seat
**Sandy Evans**
(see Gordon Jenkins and his Orchestra)
**Tudor Evans**
(see Sylvia Robin and Tudor Evans)
**Wilbur Evans**
  345    Some enchanted evening
**Everly Brothers, The**
  822    Bye bye love
  849    Wake up little Susie
  905    All I have to do is dream
  944    Bird dog
  991    Problems
1039    Poor Jenny
1040    Take a message to Mary
1070    'Til I kissed you
**Ewing Sisters, The**
(see Gordon MacRae)
**Adam Faith**
1094    What do you want?
**Percy Faith and his Orchestra**
  258    Christmas in Killarney (The Shillelagh
        Singers)
  264    All my love (with Chorus)
  267    Sleigh ride (with Chorus)
  307    On top of Old Smokey (Burl Ives and
        Chorus)
  310    The loveliest night of the year (with Chorus)
  351    I want to be near you (Peter Hanley and
        Chorus)
  406    Delicado
  472    The song from Moulin Rouge (Felicia
        Sanders)
  505    Swedish rhapsody
  572    Dream dream dream
  625    Under the bridges of Paris
**Derry Falligant**
  161    Riders in the sky (w. The Bob Haggart Trio)

  199    Jealous heart
**Harry Farmer**
  380    The gandy dancers' ball
  431    Takes two to tango
  433    Comes along a-love
  509    Answer me
  518    Rags to riches
**Robert Farnon and his Concert Orchestra**
  309    My resistance is low (with The Johnston
        Singers)
**Bob Farnon and his Orchestra**
(see Donald Peers)
**Geraldine Farrar**
  551    Make love to me
        (See also Sid Phillips and his Band)
**Sonny Farrar and his Banjo Band**
(see The Stargazers)
**Bill Farrell**
  277    My heart cries for you
**Billy Farrell**
  954    Someday (you'll want me to want you)
**Wally Fawkes and Sandy Brown Quintet, The**
  998    Petite fleur
**Paul Fenoulhet and his Orchestra**
  101    Once upon a wintertime (Doreen Lundy)
  112    Reflections on the water (Doreen Lundy)
**Tano Ferendinos**
  111    The dream of Olwen
**Lester Ferguson**
  264    All my love
  276    I'll always love you
  291    So in love
  306    You are my destiny
  336    Longing for you
  342    If you go
  344    At the end of the day
  355    Domino
  374    Never
  385    Kiss of fire
**Ferko String Band, The**
  853    Ma, he's making eyes at me (with Chorus)
**Frederick Ferrari**
  111    The dream of Olwen
  125    When you're in love
  126    Take me to your heart again
  181    You're breaking my heart
  243    Mona Lisa
  270    If
  310    The loveliest night of the year
  317    Unless
  332    How can I leave you?
  349    Mistakes
**Mel Ferrer**
(see Leslie Caron and Mel Ferrer)
**Kathleen Ferrier**
  928    I know where I'm going
**Kathran Field**
  389    Singing in the rain (with The Men about
        Town)
(also known as Kathran Oldfield – see also under this
name)
**Benny Fields**
  338    Lullaby of Broadway
**Billy Fields**
  644    Sincerely (with The Naturals)
**George Fields**
(see Victor Young and his Singing Strings)
**Gracie Fields**
  69    Come back to Sorrento

  78    Now is the hour
  89    How are things in Glocca Morra?
  99    Serenade of the bells
  126    La vie en rose
  127    Buttons and bows
  149    Put your shoes on, Lucy
  154    Forever and ever (with The Wardour
        Singers)
  196    The last mile home
  298    Life's desire
  344    At the end of the day (with The Eight Stars)
  437    Don't let the stars get in your eyes
  609    White Christmas
  772    A letter to a soldier
  806    Around the world
  826    Scarlet ribbons (with The Rita Williams
        Singers)
  846    Mary's boy child (with The Rita Williams
        Singers)
1079    Little donkey (with The Rita Williams
        Singers)
**Gracie Fields and The Keynotes**
  212    I'd've baked a cake
**Jack Fina and his Orchestra**
  105    Golden earrings
**Carl Fischer**
(see Frankie Laine)
**Charles Fisher**
(see Blue Barron and his Orchestra)
**Eddie Fisher**
  317    Unless
  370    Tell me why
  375    Any time
  390    I'm yours
  394    Trust in me
  432    Outside of heaven
  460    I'm walking behind you (with Sally
        Sweetland)
  467    Downhearted
  470    Even now
  510    Wish you were here
  521    O my papa
  575    My friend
  600    I need you now
  601    Count your blessings instead of sheep
  609    White Christmas
  634    Wedding bells
  766    Cindy, oh Cindy
**Ella Fitzgerald**
  82    Guilty
  124    My happiness (with The Song Spinners)
  268    Flying saucer
  367    Because of rain
  381    A guy is a guy
  512    Crying in the chapel (with The Ray Charles
        Singers)
  695    The tender trap
  877    The swingin' shepherd blues (with her
        Shepherds)
  997    My happiness (with The Song Spinners)
1073    Mack the knife (with The Paul Smith
        Quartet)
**Ella Fitzgerald and The Delta Rhythm Boys**
  8    It's a pity to say goodnight
  48    For sentimental reasons
**Ella Fitzgerald and The Ink Spots**
  7    Into each life some rain must fall
**Ella Fitzgerald and Louis Jordan**
  182    Baby, it's cold outside

**Five Dallas Boys, The**
856   All the way
908   Big man
992   Gigi
**Five de Marco Sisters, The**
643   Dreamboat
**Five Keys, The**
787   Wisdom of a fool
**Five Smith Brothers, The**
98   The shoemaker's serenade
119   Toolie oolie doolie
122   Rambling Rose
149   Put your shoes on, Lucy
178   A shawl of Galway grey
179   A rose in a garden of weeds
183   Am I wasting my time on you?
186   The hop-scotch polka
187   The Harry Lime theme
222   Dearie .
231   A load of hay
235   Silver dollar
248   Goodnight Irene
265   The thing
279   Play a simple melody
288   So long
337   In the cool, cool, cool of the evening
348   Sweetheart of yesterday
366   Saturday rag
419   Forget-me-not
561   The homecoming waltz
597   Veni vidi vici
641   Don't worry
**Bud Flanagan and Chesney Allen**
237   Hey! Neighbour
**Ralph Flanagan and his Orchestra**
272   Nevertheless (Harry Prime)
481   Hot toddy
**Michael Flanders**
996   The little drummer boy (with The Michael Sammes Singers)
**Fleetwoods, The**
1014   Come softly to me
1081   Mr Blue
**Dusty Fletcher**
56   Open the door, Richard
**Dick Flood**
1069   The three bells
**Red Foley**
209   Chattanoogie shoe-shine boy
437   Don't let the stars get in your eyes
481   Hot toddy
574   Jilted
    *(see also Red Foley and Judy Martin; Red Foley and The Little Foleys; Evelyn Knight and Red Foley; Ernest Tubb and Red Foley)*
**Red Foley and The Little Foleys**
252   Rudolph, the red-nosed reindeer
**Red Foley and Judy Martin**
240   Have I told you lately that I love you?
**Fontane Sisters, The**
149   Put your shoes on, Lucy
151   Candy kisses
271   The Tennessee waltz
608   Happy days and lonely nights
677   Seventeen
785   Banana boat song
976   You always hurt the one you love
    *(see also Perry Como; Perry Como and The Fontane Sisters)*

**Herbert Foote**
*(see Franklyn MacCormack)*
**Patti Forbes**
800   Chapel of the roses
807   Mr Wonderful
    *(see also Oscar Rabin and his Band)*
**Billy Ford's Thunderbirds**
*(see Billie and Lillie)*
**Emile Ford and The Checkmates**
1089   What do you want to make those eyes at me for?
**Tennessee Ernie Ford**
198   Mule train
297   The shot gun boogie
314   Smokey mountain boogie
325   The Kentucky waltz
380   The gandy dancer's ball
618   Give me your word
691   The ballad of Davy Crockett
693   Sixteen tons
829   In the middle of an island (with Quartet)
958   Love makes the world go round
**Helen Forrest**
172   I don't see me in your eyes any more
    *(see also Dick Haymes and Helen Forrest)*
**Jane Forrest**
760   Two different worlds
772   A letter to a soldier
**Charles Forsythe**
*(see Phil Morrow's Music)*
**Ivan Fosello**
*(see Mantovani and his Concert Orchestra)*
**Alan Foster**
*(see Art Mooney's Little Band; Art Mooney and his Orchestra)*
**Stuart Foster**
*(see Bill Snyder and his Orchestra; Gordon Jenkins and his Orchestra)*
**Teddy Foster and his Orchestra**
786   Blueberry Hill (Teddy Foster and The Peter Knight Singers)
**Larry Fotine and his Orchestra**
153   A – you're adorable (Maralyn Marsh and Johnny Goodfellow)
166   Beautiful eyes (Ensemble)
**Four Aces, The, featuring Al Alberts**
370   Tell me why
390   I'm yours
441   Heart and soul
545   Heart of my heart
571   Three coins in the fountain
606   Mister Sandman
633   Stranger in paradise
642   Melody of love
675   Love is a many-splendoured thing
742   The gal with the yaller shoes
750   A woman in love
774   Friendly persuasion
792   Heart
971   The world outside
1000   There goes my heart
**Four Chicks and a Chuck, The**
*(see Mary Mayo)*
**Four Coins, The**
971   The world outside
**Four Esquires, The**
861   Love me forever
**Four Grads, The**
762   True love

**Four Guys, The**
605   Not as a stranger
**Four Hits and a Miss, The**
*(see Charles La Vere; Bing Crosby and Jane Wyman; Dick Haymes; Tony Harper)*
**Four-in-A-Chord, The**
252   Rudolph, the red-nosed reindeer
577   Gilly Gilly Ossenfeffer Katzenellen Bogen by the Sea
583   Sway
584   Sh-boom
597   Veni vidi vici
606   Mister Sandman
610   Mambo Italiano
611   The naughty lady of Shady Lane
617   Shake rattle and roll
631   Tweedle-dee
660   Close the door
673   Twenty tiny fingers
683   Never do a tango with an Eskimo
701   It's almost tomorrow
    *(see also Troise and his Novelty Orchestra; Penny Nicholls and The Four-in-A-Chord; Rita Williams)*
**Four Jones Boys, The**
768   Happiness Street
    *(see also Annette Klooger)*
**Four Knights, The**
330   I love the sunshine of your smile
353   Sin
358   Charmaine
359   I wanna say hello
365   Cry
454   Oh, happy day
556   I get so loney
**Four Lads, The**
522   Istanbul
577   Gilly Gilly Ossenfeffer Katzenellen Bogen by the Sea
747   Born to be with you
759   A house with love in it
802   Round and round
863   Put a light in the window
    *(see also Johnnie Ray; The Four Lads and Jill Corey)*
**The Four Lads and Jill Corey**
568   Cleo and Me-o
**Four Preps, The**
908   Big man
**Four Ramblers, The**
74   Dear old Donegal
258   Christmas in Killarney
282   Tipperary samba
**Four Sensations, The**
414   Raindrops
**Four Shepherd Boys, The**
*(see Michael Holliday)*
**Foursome, The**
*(see Frances Langford)*
**Four Troubadours, The**
164   Careless hands
181   You're breaking my heart
199   Jealous heart
**Don Fox**
844   Be my girl
**Roy Fox and his Band**
33   It's all over now (Bobby Joy)
40   Too many irons in the fire (Jack O'Hagan and Bobby Joy)

48   For sentimental reasons (Jack O'Hagan)
50   The rickety rickshaw man (Beryl Templeman, Bobby Joy, Jack O'Hagan and The Cubs)
51   The whole world is singing my song (Jack O'Hagan)
52   Accordion (Jack O'Hagan)

**Connie Francis**
891   Who's sorry now?
932   Carolina Moon
934   Stupid Cupid
976   You always hurt the one you love
997   My happiness
1046   Lipstick on your collar
1080   Plenty good lovin'

**Derrick Francis**
458   I'd love to fall asleep (with The Coronets)

**Johnny Francis**
603   I still believe
624   Give me the right

**Gordon Franks and his Orchestra**
918   Patricia
952   Hoots mon
966   Tea for two cha cha

**Gordon Franks Sextet, The**
1086   Red river rock

**Johnny Franks and his Rhythm**
617   Shake rattle and roll
631   Tweedle-dee

**John Fraser**
822   Bye bye love (with The Beryl Stott Group)
875   Why don't they understand? (with The Beryl Stott Group)
(see also Janette Scott and John Fraser)

**Morton Fraser's Harmonica Band**
(see Don Cameron)

**Joyce Frazer**
426   Moon above Malaya
428   I went to your wedding
487   Say you're mine again

**Stan Freberg**
584   Sh-boom (with The Toads)
666   The yellow rose of Texas (with Jud Conlon's Rhythmaires and Alvin Stoller (drums))
712   The great pretender (with The Toads)
785   Banana boat (with interruptions by Peter Leeds)

**Freddy**
784   Don't forbid me
785   Banana boat song

**Ernie Freeman**
873   Raunchy

**Frankie Froba and his Boys**
349   Mistakes
(see also Al Morgan)

**Jane Froman**
405   I'll walk alone
465   I believe
607   The finger of suspicion
635   I wonder
741   You'll never walk alone

**Wally Fryer and his Perfect Tempo Dance Orchestra**
320   Too young
329   Because of you
412   Half as much
421   You belong to me
423   My love and devotion
431   Takes two to tango

**Leo Fuld**
177   The windmill song
215   C'est si bon

**Tommy Furtado**
397   The heart of a clown

**David Gailbraith**
979   Tonight

**Sunny Gale**
943   A certain smile
(see also Eddie Wilcox and his Orchestra)

**Bridie Gallagher**
927   Hillside in Scotland

**Frank Gallup**
937   Got a match

**Jan Garber and his Orchestra**
169   Everywhere you go (Tim Reardon)
172   I don't see me in your eyes any more (Tim Reardon)
181   You're breaking my heart (Bob Grabeau)
186   The hop-scotch polka (Ernie Mathias and Roberta Linn)
199   Jealous heart (Bob Grabeau)
218   The old piano roll blues (Ernie Mathias and Frank Macaulay)
270   If (Roy Cordell)
296   A rainy day refrain (Roy Cordell)
374   Never (Roy Cordell)
421   You belong to me (Roy Cordell)
480   Your cheatin' heart (Bill St Claire)

**Freddy Gardner**
246   I only have eyes for you (with Peter Yorke and his Concert Orchestra)

**Kenny Gardner**
(see Guy Lombardo and his Royal Canadians)

**Judy Garland**
741   You'll never walk alone

**Betty Garrett**
127   Buttons and bows
255   Home cookin'

**Betty Garrett and Larry Parks**
466   Side by side

**'Sir Frederick (Frederic) Gas'**
(see Spike Jones and his City Slickers)

**Betsy Gay**
(see Russ Morgan and his Orchestra)

**Gay Sisters, The**
(see Russ Morgan and his Orchestra)

**Jeanne Gayle**
431   Takes two to tango

**Ronnie Gaylord**
594   Santo Natale

**Gaylords, The**
477   Tell me you're mine (with Ronnie Vincent)
549   From the vine came the grape
558   The little shoemaker
597   Veni vidi vici

**Max Geldray**
443   The glow worm
495   Ruby

**Harold Geller and his Orchestra**
173   Confidentially (Anne Lenner and Bob Harvey)
202   We all have a song in our hearts (Bob Harvey)

**Geraldo and his Orchestra**
4   Homesick – that's all (Dick James)
9   Laughing on the outside (Sally Douglas)
12   Money is the root of all evil (The Geraldo Ensemble)
13   Oh, what it seemed to be (Dick James)
16   Day by day (Dick James)
17   Down in the valley (Archie Lewis)
29   You keep coming back like a song (Dick James)
30   All through the day (Sally Douglas)
37   Lilli Marlene (Sally Douglas)
38   Pretending (Archie Lewis)
39   Till then (Archie Lewis)
42   The old lamplighter (Denny Vaughan)
43   Anniversary song (Archie Lewis)
48   For sentimental reasons (Archie Lewis)
49   The things we did last summer (Carole Carr)
50   The rickety rickshaw man (Carole Carr)
53   Don't fall in love (Denny Vaughan)
56   Open the door, Richard (Denny Vaughan and Band)
57   Zip-a-dee-doo-dah (Carole Carr)
64   Harriett (Carole Carr and Denny Vaughan)
66   Among my souvenirs (Denny Vaughan)
67   A gal in calico (The Three Boys and a Girl)
70   People will say we're in love (Carole Carr)
77   They say it's wonderful (Denny Vaughan)
78   Now is the hour (Archie Lewis)
81   The little old mill (Carole Carr)
83   Chi-baba chi-baba (Archie Lewis)
90   Peg o' my heart (Denny Vaughan)
91   South America, take it away (Archie Lewis and Ensemble)
92   The coffee song (Ensemble)
95   Tree in the meadow (Archie Lewis)
96   Near you (Archie Lewis)
99   Serenade of the bells (Archie Lewis)
101   Once upon a winter time (Amru Sani)
105   Golden earrings (Carole Carr)
107   Teresa (Denny Vaughan and Anne Stuart)
120   Woody Woodpecker (Doreen Lundy and George Evans)
123   So tired (George Evans)
124   My happiness (Doreen Lundy)
125   When you're in love (Archie Lewis)
126   Take me to your heart again (Doreen Lundy)
127   Buttons and bows (Doreen Lundy)
128   October twilight (Archie Lewis)
133   On a slow boat to China (Doreen Lundy)
140   Crystal gazer (Denny Vaughan)
143   Lavender blue (Doreen Lundy)
144   Put 'em in a box (Doreen Lundy)
146   A strawberry moon (Neville Williams and Chorus)
147   Red roses for a blue lady (Denny Vaughan)
150   It's magic (Denny Vaughan)
160   Again (Eve Boswell)
162   The echo told me a lie (Denny Vaughan and vocal group)
173   Confidentially (Eve Boswell)
192   Song of Capri (Archie Lewis)
197   Dear hearts and gentle people (Eve Boswell)
202   We all have a song in our hearts (Archie Lewis)
205   Music! Music! Music! (Nadia Doré)
207   Best of all (Eve Boswell)
215   C'est si bon (Cyril Grantham and The Geraldtones)
216   Enjoy yourself (The Geraldtones)
218   The old piano roll blues (Nadia Doré and The Geraldtones)

220  Oh, you sweet one (The Geraldtones)
236  Candy and cake (Nadia Doré)
241  Once in a while
246  I only have eyes for you
257  Orange coloured sky (Nadia Doré)
263  Ferry Boat Inn (The Geraldtones)
264  All my love (Eve Boswell)
270  If (Eve Boswell)
271  The Tennessee waltz
556  I get so lonely (Jill Day, Larry Cross and The Tophatters)
685  The shifting, whispering sands (Chorus)
710  The poor people of Paris

**Geraldo and his New Concert Orchestra**
427  Ecstasy
479  April in Portugal

**Geraldo Ensemble, The**
(see Geraldo and his Orchestra)

**Geraldo Strings, The**
(see Archie Lewis)

**Geraldtones, The**
(see Geraldo and his Orchestra)

**Carroll Gibbons and the Savoy Hotel Orpheans**
3  Chickery chick (Rita Williams)
11  Mary Lou (Denny Vaughan)
36  Five minutes more (Harry Kaye)
77  They say it's wonderful (Edna Kaye)

**Georgia Gibbs**
385  Kiss of fire
484  Seven lonely days (with The Yale Brothers)
492  The Bridge of Sighs
582  Wait for me, darling
593  I love Paris
630  Cherry pink and apple blossom white
631  Tweedle-dee
768  Happiness Street
865  Great balls of fire
953  The hula hoop song

**Don Gibson**
956  Blue, blue day

**Ginny Gibson**
490  Kiss

**Beniamino Gigli**
69  Torna a Surriento
498  Papaveri e Papere
651  Mamma

**Terry Gilkyson**
360  Rollin' stone
(see also The Weavers and Terry Gilkyson; Terry Gilkyson and The Easy Riders)

**Terry Gilkyson and The Easy Riders**
794  Marianne (Rich Dehr)

**Frank Gillespie**
(see Joe Loss and his Orchestra)

**Hermione Gingold and Gilbert Harding**
431  Takes two to tango

**Raymond Girerd**
243  Mona Lisa

**Gladiolas, The**
823  Little darlin'

**Will Glahe and his Musik**
869  Liechtensteiner Polka

**Will Glahe and his Sunshine Sextet**
648  The Crazy Otto rag

**Jackie Gleason and his Orchestra**
475  Terry's Theme from 'Limelight'

**Darrell Glenn**
512  Crying in the chapel

**Gliders, The**
(see LaVern Baker)

**Bernie Glow**
(see Eydie Gorme)

**Susy Goday**
(see Russ Morgan and his Orchestra)

**Arthur Godfrey**
104  Too fat polka
269  Marshmallow world (with The Chordettes and The Cherry Sisters)
278  C'n I canoe you up the river?
387  Dance me loose (with The Chordettes)
(see also Arthur Godfrey and The Chordettes; Mary Martin and Arthur Godfrey)

**Arthur Godfrey and The Chordettes**
236  Candy and cake

**Reggie Goff**
123  So tired (with Felix King, his piano, and his Orchestra)
125  When you're in love
140  Crystal gazer (with The Stapletones and Cyril Stapleton and his Orchestra)
181  You're breaking my heart (with The Velvetones)
183  Am I wasting my time on you?
184  Monday, Tuesday, Wednesday (with The Velvetones)
187  The zither melody (with The Velvetones)
288  So long (with The Drifters and his Waltztimers)
295  Sparrow in the tree top (with The Johnston Brothers)
301  List'nin' to the green grass grow (with The Kingpins)
348  Sweetheart of yesterday (with The Keynotes)
426  Moon above Malaya
492  The Bridge of Sighs
509  Answer me
518  Rags to riches
559  Love me (with The Velvetones and his Sextet)

**Harry Gold and his Pieces of Eight**
168  Blue ribbon gal (Geoff Love)

**Johnny Goodfellow**
(see Larry Fotine and his Orchestra)

**Benny Goodman and his Orchestra**
133  On a slow boat to China (Al Hendrickson)
663  Love me or leave me

**Benny Goodman Sextet, The**
706  Memories of you

**Benny Goodman Trio, The**
706  Memories of you (with Rosemary Clooney)

**Gordon Goodman**
(see Fred Waring and his Pennsylvanians)

**Ron Goodwin and his Concert Orchestra**
425  When I fall in love
472  Song from Moulin Rouge
475  The theme from the film 'Limelight'
503  The Melba waltz
569  Cara mia
571  Three coins in the fountain
578  Smile
636  You, my love
659  Blue star
661  Three galleons
690  The little Laplander
717  No other love
798  I'll find you
(see also Eamonn Andrews)

**Joe Gordon**
1034  Dream lover

**Lee Gordon Singers, The**
(see Danny Kaye; Al Jolson; Evelyn Knight; Bing Crosby)

**Charlie Gore and Ruby Wright**
455  Till I waltz again with you

**Eydie Gorme**
861  Love me forever (with Bernie Glow – trumpet)
889  You need hands
922  Gotta have rain

**Morton Gould and his Orchestra**
139  Twelfth Street rag

**Bob Grabeau**
(see Jan Garber and his Orchestra)

**Charlie Gracie**
801  Butterfly
803  Ninety nine ways
834  Wanderin' eyes

**Gerry Granahan**
941  Girl of my dreams

**Dave Grant**
874  Nairobi

**Earl Grant**
964  The end

**Eddie Grant**
240  Have I told you lately that I love you?
248  Goodnight Irene
264  All my love
266  The petite waltz

**Gerry Grant**
774  Friendly persuasion
778  Moonlight gambler
816  Island in the Sun
837  Man on fire
838  White silver sands
839  Remember you're mine
856  All the way
860  The story of my life
1063  High hopes

**Gogi Grant**
676  Suddenly there's a valley
727  Who are we?
733  The wayward wind
972  Kiss me, honey honey, kiss me

**Johnnie Grant**
(see Ronnie Scott and his Orchestra)

**Norman Grant and his Orchestra for Dancers**
508  Be mine
583  Sway

**Cyril Grantham**
(see Geraldo and his Orchestra)

**Dolores Gray**
121  You can't be true, dear
205  Music! Music! Music!
219  Quicksilver
347  Shrimp boats
487  Say you're mine again

**Jack Gray**
437  Don't let the stars get in your eyes

**Jerry Gray and his Orchestra**
253  Home cookin' (The Crew Chiefs)
302  Would I love you (Tommy Traynor)
330  I love the sunshine of your smile (Tommy Traynor and Ensemble)
378  There's a pawnshop on a corner in Pittsburgh, Pennsylvania (Tommy Traynor)
527  The creep (Linda Lee)

**Johnny Gray**
882    Tequila (with The Ken Jones Orchestra)
**Reg Gray**
*(see Tony Osborne and his Orchestra)*
**Helen Grayco**
287    Red silken stockings
**Joe Graydon**
*(see Gordon Jenkins and his Orchestra; Victor Young and his Orchestra)*
**Carl Grayson**
*(see Spike Jones and his City Slickers)*
**Kathryn Grayson**
993    My heart sings
**Buddy Greco**
587    If I give my heart to you
**Buddy Greco and his Quartet**
894    On the street where you live
**Buddy Greco and his Skiffle Gang**
821    With all my heart
**Johnny Green**
16    Day by day
750    A woman in love
    *(see also Harry Roy and his Orchestra)*
**Larry Green**
*(see The Three Suns)*
**Larry Green and his Orchestra**
96    Near you (Trio)
**Paula Green**
19    Do you love me?
**Philip Green and his Orchestra**
111    The dream of Olwen (with Arthur Sandford)
293    Saloon bar rag (The Beaux and the Belles)
495    Ruby
535    Tenderly
**Jo Ann Greer**
*(see Ray Anthony and his Orchestra)*
**Johnny Gregory Sextet, The**
877    The swingin' shepherd blues
882    Tequila
**Ken Griffin**
121    You can't be true, dear
131    The cuckoo waltz
252    Rudolph, the red-nosed reindeer
266    The petite waltz
420    Walkin' to Missouri
421    You belong to me
453    Little red monkey
455    Till I waltz again with you
478    Have you heard
479    April in Portugal
512    Crying in the chapel
    *(see also Jerry Wayne)*
**David Griffiths**
*(see Joe Loss and his Orchestra)*
**Dan Grissom**
*(see Jimmy Lunceford and his Orchestra)*
**Walter Gross (piano) and his Trio**
*(see Clark Dennis)*
**Walter Gross**
535    Tenderly
**Harry Grove and his Music**
910    Trudie
985    I'll be with you in apple blossom time
**Harry Grove Trio, The**
403    Meet Mister Callaghan
453    Little red monkey
**Georges Guetary**
156    Clopin clopant
264    Bolero

**Bonnie Guitar**
893    A very precious love
**Tony Gumina**
*(see Harry James and his Orchestra)*
**Ruth Haag**
*(see Harry James and his Music Makers)*
**Bob Haggart Trio, The**
*(see Derry Falligant)*
**Dennis Hale**
363    Only fools
375    Any time
444    Why don't you believe me
698    Stealin'
701    It's almost tomorrow
    *(see also Oscar Rabin and his Band; Jack Parnell)*
**Bill Haley and his Comets**
617    Shake rattle and roll
680    Rock around the clock
752    Rockin' through the rye
775    Razzle dazzle
**Adelaide Hall**
333    Vanity
**Roy Hall**
732    Blue suede shoes
**Jack Halloran Choir, The**
*(see Eddy Howard and his Orchestra; Lew Douglas and his Orchestra)*
**Jack Halloran Singers, The**
*(see Richard Hayes)*
**Chris Hamalton**
366    Saturday rag
464    Celebration rag
**Stuart Hamblen**
589    This ole house
671    Go on by
**George Hamilton IV**
875    Why don't they understand?
928    I know where I'm going
**Roy Hamilton**
530    From here to eternity
637    Unchained melody
741    You'll never walk alone
1000    There goes my heart
**Russ Hamilton**
813    We will make love
841    Wedding ring (with The Tonettes)
951    Little one
**Janet Hamilton-Smith and John Hargreaves**
77    They say it's wonderful
**Peter Hanley**
*(see Percy Faith and his Orchestra)*
**Jack Hansen Combo, The**
*(see Buddy Holly)*
**Happy Valley Boys, The**
*(see Dinah Shore)*
**Happy Wanderers Street Band, The**
771    Singing the blues
**Gilbert Harding**
*(see Hermione Gingold and Gilbert Harding)*
**John Hargreaves**
*(see Janet Hamilton-Smith and John Hargreaves)*
**Harmonica Gentlemen, The**
*(see Danny Kaye and The Andrews Sisters)*
**Harmonicats, The**
453    Little red monkey
**I.W. Harper**
*(see Spike Jones and his City Slickers)*
**Janice Harper**
921    Devotion

**Toni Harper**
242    Sam's song (with The Four Hits and a Miss)
    *(see also Harry James and his Orchestra)*
**Betty Harris**
*(see Art Mooney and his Orchestra)*
**Doreen Harris**
10    Let bygones be bygones
28    Sweetheart, we'll never grow old
38    Pretending
613    Softly softly
    *(see also Billy Thorburn's The Organ, the Dance Band and Me)*
**Lester Harris**
*(see The Ray-o-Vacs)*
**Phil Harris**
265    The Thing
    *(see also Phil Harris and his Orchestra)*
**Phil Harris and his Orchestra**
106    He's his own grandpa
203    Is it true what they say about Dixie?
209    Chattanoogie shoe-shine boy
**Ronnie Harris**
573    The story of Tina
586    Hold my hand
593    I love Paris
603    I still believe
633    Stranger in paradise
635    I wonder
759    A house with love in it
842    Let me be loved (with The Rita Williams Singers)
    *(see also Barbara Lyon and Ronnie Harris)*
**Wee Willie Harris**
937    Got a match
**Wilbert Harrison**
1037    Kansas City
**Fred Hartley and his Music**
256    Autumn leaves
**Bob Harvey**
440    Take me in your arms and hold me
    *(see also Harold Geller and his Orchestra)*
**Jack Haskell**
806    Around the world
    *(see also Sy Oliver and his Orchestra)*
**Hastings Girls' Choir, The**
*(see Steve Conway)*
**Tony Hatch**
975    Side saddle
1005    Chick
**Dolores Hawkins**
*(see Blue Barron and his Orchestra)*
**Hawkshaw Hawkins**
361    Slow coach
**Bill Hayes**
392    High noon
691    The ballad of Davy Crockett
**Peter Lind Hayes**
168    Blue ribbon gal
**Richard Hayes**
489    Can't I (with The Jack Halloran Singers)
**Richard Hayman and Jan August**
711    The Theme from 'The Threepenny Opera'
985    I'll be with you in apple blossom time
**Richard Hayman and his Orchestra**
479    April in Portugal
495    Ruby
591    The high and the mighty
831    Tammy

**Dick Haymes**
19 Do you love me?
76 Mam'selle
89 How are things in Glocca Morra?
93 The girl that I marry
99 Serenade of the bells
150 It's magic
165 While the angelus was ringing (with The Jeffrey Alexander Chorus)
249 Count every star (with Artie Shaw and his Strings and Woodwind)
313 Too late now
369 And so to sleep again (with The Four Hits and a Miss)
396 When you're in love
760 Two different worlds
826 Scarlet ribbons
(see also Dick Haymes and Helen Forrest; Dick Haymes and The Andrews Sisters; Dick Haymes and The Song Spinners; Ethel Merman and Dick Haymes and The Troubadours)

**Dick Haymes and Helen Forrrest**
13 Oh, what it seemed to be
30 All through the day

**Dick Haymes and The Andrews Sisters**
107 Teresa
408 Here in my heart

**Dick Haymes and The Song Spinners**
115 Nature boy
121 You can't be true, dear

**Dick Haymes and The Troubadours**
375 Any time

**Ted Heath and his Music**
16 Day by day (Paul Carpenter)
24 So would I (Paul Carpenter)
27 Let it be soon (Paul Carpenter)
29 You keep coming back like a song (Paul Carpenter)
56 Open the door, Richard (Paul Carpenter and Dave Wilkins)
65 Try a little tenderness (Paul Carpenter)
70 People will say we're in love (Paul Carpenter)
242 Sam's song (Dennis Lotis)
243 Mona Lisa (Dickie Valentine)
248 Goodnight Irene (Dennis Lotis)
272 Nevertheless (Dennis Lotis)
338 Lullaby of Broadway (Lita Roza)
379 Blacksmith blues (Lita Roza)
411 Botch-a-me (Lita Roza)
434 That's a-why (Lita Roza and Dennis Lotis)
436 Settin' the woods on fire (Lita Roza and Dennis Lotis)
481 Hot toddy
491 Mother Nature and Father Time (Dickie Valentine)
527 The creep
542 Bell bottom blues (Lita Roza)
612 Papa loves mambo (The Johnston Brothers and Duncan Campbell)
708 The rock and roll waltz (Annette Klooger)
748 Autumn concerto (Bobbie Britton)
762 True love (Bobbie Britton)
873 Raunchy
877 The swingin' shepherd blues
882 Tequila
897 Tom Hark
900 Little serenade

929 Volare
942 More than ever
(see also Lita Roza; Bill Johnson; Les Howard; Dickie Valentine; Anne Shelton; Dennis Lotis; Bobbie Britton; Annette Klooger)

**Heathertones, The**
(see The Korn Kobblers)

**Hefferan Singers, The**
(see Hugo and Luigi)

**Ronnie Height**
1014 Come softly to me

**Ray Heindorf and his Orchestra**
731 Serenade

**Bobby Helms**
850 My special angel (with The Anita Kerr Singers)
1096 Jingle bell rock

**Dickie Henderson**
759 A house with love in it

**Joe 'Mr Piano' Henderson**
578 Smile
711 The Theme from 'The Threepenny Opera'
812 Forgotten dreams
910 Trudie (with The Beryl Stott Chorus)
1005 Chick (with The Beryl Stott Chorus)
1076 Treble chance

**Joe Henderson**
(see Shani Wallis)

**Rikki Henderson**
863 Put a light in the window
868 Sugartime
870 Catch a falling star
887 A wonderful time up there
888 Tulips from Amsterdam
889 You need hands
890 It's too soon to know
898 Kewpie doll
903 Twilight time
921 Devotion
929 Volare
930 Torero
933 Moon talk
935 If dreams came true
958 Love makes the world go round
973 High class baby
986 One night
1007 Tomboy
1016 Ciao ciao bambina
1018 I need your love tonight
1023 Never be anyone else but you
1035 Personality
1036 A teenager in love
1037 Kansas City
1045 I know
1049 Heart of a man
1051 Waterloo
1057 Only sixteen
1065 Peggy Sue got married
1068 Tallahassee Lassie
1069 The three bells
1077 Dynamite

**Skitch Henderson and his Orchestra**
209 Chattanoogie shoe-shine boy (Gregg Lawrence)
226 Daddy's little girl (Gregg Lawrence and Choir)

**Al Hendrickson**
(see Benny Goodman and his Orchestra)

**John Hendrik**
111 The dream of Olwen
192 Song of Capri

**Tom Henry**
(see Cyril Stapleton and his Orchestra; Billy Ternent and his Orchestra)

**Tom Henry and The Tomboys**
13 Oh, what it seemed to be
33 It's all over now

**Herb and Kay**
589 This ole house

**Woody Herman and Nat 'King' Cole**
198 Mule Train (with King Cole's Muleskinners)

**Woody Herman and his Orchestra**
535 Tenderly
675 Love is a many-splendoured thing

**Milt Herth**
139 Twelfth Street rag
(see also Russ Morgan and his Orchestra)

**Milt Herth Trio, The**
81 The little old mill (Bob Johnstone)
139 Twelfth Street rag

**Joe Heyne Players, The**
266 The petite waltz

**Eddie Heywood**
(see Eddie Heywood and his Orchestra)

**Eddie Haywood and his Orchestra**
90 Peg o' my heart (ftg Eddie Heywood – piano)

**Al Hibbler**
637 Unchained melody
684 He

**Colin Hicks**
885 La dee dah (with The Beryl Stott Group)

**Hi Fi Four, The**
703 Band of gold

**High Hatters, The**
(see Lily Ann Carol)

**Irene Hilda**
593 I love Paris

**Benny Hill**
599 I can't tell a waltz from a tango
622 Teach me tonight
700 Memories are made of this (with The Coronets)

**Billy Hill**
(see Bill Hurley)

**David Hill**
818 All shook up

**William Hill-Bowen – harp**
(see The Melachrino Strings)

**William Hill-Bowen – piano**
(see The Melachrino Orchestra)

**Jack Hilliard**
(see Mickey Katz and his Orchestra)

**Hilltoppers, The, featuring Jimmy Sacca**
549 From the vine came the grape
705 Only you
794 Marianne

**Ronnie Hilton**
597 Veni vidi vici
603 I still believe
615 A blossom fell
623 Prize of gold
656 Stars shine in your eyes
666 The yellow rose of Texas
667 Have you ever been lonely?
670 Hey there

| 684 | He |
|---|---|
| 696 | Young and foolish |
| 717 | No other love |
| 727 | Who are we? |
| 750 | A woman in love |
| 760 | Two different worlds |
| 787 | Wisdom of a fool |
| 792 | Heart |
| 806 | Around the world |
| 809 | I'd give you the world |
| 820 | Wonderful, wonderful |
| 866 | Magic moments |
| 880 | I may never pass this way again (with The Michael Sammes Singers) |
| 894 | On the street where you live (with The Michael Sammes Singers) |
| 967 | The day the rains came (with The Michael Sammes Singers) |
| 968 | As I love you (with The Michael Sammes Singers) |
| 971 | The world outside (with The Michael Sammes Singers) |
| 992 | Gigi (with The Michael Sammes Singers) |
| 1050 | The wonder of you (with The Riddelle Singers) |

**Earl Hines Quintet, The**
| 864 | Chicago |
|---|---|

**Valerie Hobson**
| 524 | Hello young lovers |
|---|---|

**Edmund Hockridge**
| 234 | If I loved you |
|---|---|
| 262 | I leave my heart in an English garden |
| 486 | I've never been in love before |
| 575 | My friend |
| 633 | Stranger in paradise |
| 664 | The man from Laramie |
| 670 | Hey there |
| 693 | Sixteen tons (with The Beryl Stott Chorus) |
| 696 | Young and foolish |
| 717 | No other love |
| 739 | By the fountains of Rome (with The Beryl Stott Chorus) |
| 750 | A woman in love |
| 942 | More than ever |
| 979 | Tonight (with The Beryl Stott Chorus) |

**Claire Hogan and Bobby Wayne**
| 242 | Sam's song |
|---|---|

**Louanne Hogan**
*(see Victor Young and his Orchestra)*

**Roy Hogsed**
| 343 | I wish I wuz |
|---|---|

**Billie Holiday**
| 304 | Girls were made to take care of boys (with The Star Dusters) |
|---|---|

**Holidays, The**
| 301 | List'nin' to the green grass grow |
|---|---|

**Betty Holliday**
*(see Ray Anthony and his Orchestra)*

**Michael Holliday**
| 666 | The yellow rose of Texas |
|---|---|
| 693 | Sixteen tons |
| 725 | Hot diggity (with The Four Shepherd Boys) |
| 742 | The gal with the yaller shoes |
| 789 | All of you |
| 860 | The story of my life |
| 896 | Stairway of love |

**Buddy Holly**
| 858 | Peggy Sue |
|---|---|
| 917 | Rave on |

| 1009 | It doesn't matter any more |
|---|---|
| 1065 | Peggy Sue got married (with The Jack Hansen Combo) |

**Buddy Holly and The Crickets**
| 840 | That'll be the day |
|---|---|
| 859 | Oh Boy |
| 884 | Maybe baby |
| 936 | Think it over |

**Frank Holmes**
*(see Paul Adam and his Mayfair Music)*

**Leroy Holmes and his Orchestra**
| 451 | The ruby and the pearl (and Chorus) |
|---|---|
| 591 | The high and the mighty (whistling: Fred Lowery) |
| 637 | Unchained melody (whistling: Fred Lowery) |

**Homer and Jethro**
| 252 | Rudolph, the flat-nosed reindeer |
|---|---|
| 448 | That hound dog in the window |
| 534 | Swappin' partners |
| 1043 | The battle of Kookamonga |
| 1051 | Waterloo |

**Homesteaders, The**
*(see Eve Young)*

**Honky-Tonks, The**
*(see Dorothy Loudon)*

**Larry Hooper**
*(see Lawrence Welk and his Champagne Music)*

**Sol Hoopii and his Novelty Five**
| 139 | Twelfth Street rag |
|---|---|

**Hoosier Hot-Shots, The**
| 457 | The dummy song |
|---|---|

**Bob Hope**
*(see Margaret Whiting and Bob Hope)*

**Lena Horne**
| 663 | Love me or leave me |
|---|---|

**Horsham Girls' Choir, The**
| 194 | Down in the glen |
|---|---|

**Johnny Horton**
| 1043 | The battle of New Orleans |
|---|---|

**Bob Houston**
*(see Jack Pleis and his Orchestra)*

**Don Howard**
| 454 | Oh, happy day |
|---|---|

**Eddy Howard and his Orchestra**
| 353 | Sin (Eddy Howard) |
|---|---|
| 384 | Be anything (Eddy Howard and The Jack Halloran Choir) |
| 524 | Hello young lovers (Eddy Howard) |
| 544 | Bimbo (Eddy Howard) |

**Les Howard**
| 313 | Too late now |
|---|---|
| 320 | Too young |
| 329 | Because of you |
| 331 | White wedding |
| 345 | Some enchanted evening (with Ted Heath and his Music) |
| 367 | Because of rain |
| 375 | Any time |
| 468 | The Windsor waltz |
| 518 | Rags to riches |
| 530 | From here to eternity |
| 548 | Two Easter Sunday sweethearts |
| 582 | Wait for me, darling |
| 659 | Blue star |
| 661 | Three galleons |
| 771 | Singin' the blues |

**Les Howard and The Stargazers**
| 366 | Saturday rag |
|---|---|

**Leslie Howard**
*(see Eric Winstone and his Orchestra)*

**Chris Howland**
| 853 | Ma, he's making eyes at me (with The Boys) |
|---|---|
| 955 | Susie darlin' |

**Floyd Huddleston**
*(see Gordon Jenkins and his Orchestra)*

**David Hughes**
| 305 | With these hands |
|---|---|
| 318 | A beggar in love |
| 363 | Only fools |
| 371 | At last! At last! |
| 374 | Never |
| 384 | Be anything |
| 385 | Kiss of fire |
| 390 | I'm yours |
| 408 | Here in my heart |
| 416 | Belle of the ball (with Chorus) |
| 418 | If I had wings |
| 429 | I'll never forget you |
| 456 | I talk to the trees |
| 469 | Wild horses (w. The Rita Williams Singers) |
| 477 | Tell me you're mine (with The Rita Williams Singers) |
| 492 | The Bridge of Sighs |
| 494 | Is it any wonder |
| 518 | Rags to riches |
| 525 | Ebb tide |
| 582 | Wait for me, darling |
| 594 | Santo Natale |
| 605 | Not as a stranger |
| 624 | Give me the right |
| 649 | Ev'rywhere |
| 650 | Every day of my life |
| 675 | Love is a many-splendoured thing |
| 739 | By the fountains of Rome |
| 760 | Two different worlds |
| 762 | True love |

**Glenn Hughes**
*(see Freddy Martin and his Orchestra)*

**Hugo and Luigi**
| 648 | The Crazy Otto rag (with The Hefferan Singers) |
|---|---|

**Humming Birds, The**
*(see George Browne and his Band)*

**Pee Wee Hunt and his Orchestra**
| 139 | Twelfth Street rag |
|---|---|

**Ivory Joe Hunter**
| 720 | A tear fell |
|---|---|

**Tab Hunter**
| 782 | Young love |
|---|---|
| 803 | Ninety nine ways |

**Bill Hurley**
| 364 | Then I'll be there (with Billy Hill – piano) |
|---|---|
| 371 | Long, long ago |
| 374 | Never |
| 395 | Faith |
| 429 | I'll never forget you |
| 444 | Why don't you believe me |
| 447 | The love of my life |
| 575 | My friend |

**Rusty Hurren**
*(see Lou Preager and his Orchestra)*

**Walter Huston**
| 275 | September song |
|---|---|

**Leslie A. Hutchinson – 'Hutch'**
| 1 | Bless you |
|---|---|
| 19 | Do you love me? |
| 21 | You always hurt the one you love |

29 You keep coming back like a song
30 All through the day
39 Till then
70 People will say we're in love
77 They say it's wonderful
78 Now is the hour
84 Danger ahead
90 Peg o' my heart
95 Tree in the meadow
456 I talk to the trees
472 The song from Moulin Rouge
486 I've never been in love before
588 Make her mine
593 I love Paris

**etty Hutton**
72 I got the sun in the morning
206 Now that I need you
257 Orange coloured sky

**etty Hutton and Howard Keel**
77 They say it's wonderful

**ne Hutton and Axel Stordahl**
450 Keep it a secret (with The Boys Next Door)
472 Song from Moulin Rouge
487 Say you're mine again (with The Boys Next Door)

**at Hutton**
*e Roberto Inglez and his Orchestra)*

**ick Hyman Trio, The**
711 The Theme from 'The Threepenny Opera'

**ford Girls' Choir, The**
*e Dick James)*

**uigi Infantino**
69 Torna a Surriento

**ed Ingle**
*e Red Ingle and the Natural Seven; Red Ingle and the*
*natural Seven; Spike Jones and his City Slickers)*

**ed Ingle and the Natural Seven**
48 For seventy mental reasons (Buttermilk Tussie)
153 A – you're a-dopey-gal (Red Ingle and Karen Tedder)

**ed Ingle and the Unnatural Seven**
115 Serutan yob (Karen Tedder and Enrohtwah)

**oberto Inglez and his Orchestra**
35 The green cockatoo
70 People will say we're in love
76 Mam'selle
83 Chi-bab chi-baba (Roberto Inglez)
98 The shoemaker's serenade
160 Again
167 Have you seen Irene?
174 The wedding samba (Pat Hutton)
180 Our love story
187 The Harry Lime theme
193 The Scottish samba
214 My foolish heart
234 If I loved you
246 I only have eyes for you
256 Autumn leaves
264 All my love – bolero
266 The petite waltz
276 I'll always love you
312 Jezebel
363 Only fools
371 At last! At last!
384 Be anything
396 When you're in love
406 Delicado
441 Heart and soul

453 Little red monkey
479 Coimbra
506 You're just in love
510 Wish you were here

**Roberto Inglez and his Mambo Orchestra**
583 Quien sera

**Ink Spots, The**
1 Bless you
26 To each his own
86 I'll make up for everything
181 You're breaking my heart
270 If
525 Ebb tide
609 White Christmas
642 Melody of love
*(see also Ella Fitzgerald and The Ink Spots)*

**Burl Ives**
143 Lavender blue
161 Riders in the sky
315 The little white duck
391 From the time you say goodbye
691 The ballad of Davy Crockett
*(see also Percy Faith and his Orchestra)*

**Jimmy Jackson**
838 White silver sands

**Stonewall Jackson**
1051 Waterloo

**Dick Jacobs and his Skiffle Band**
*(see Johnny Desmond)*

**Bob Jacqmain Vocal Quartet, The**
*(see Ray Ventura and his Orchestra)*

**Hattie Jacques**
*(see Donald Peers)*

**Illinois Jacquet and his Orchestra**
657 Learnin' the blues

**Dick James**
115 Nature boy
121 You can't be true, dear
158 Till all our dreams come true (with The George Mitchell Choir)
167 Have you seen Irene?
175 Say goodnight but not goodbye (with The Stargazers)
195 Why is it? (with Felix King, his piano, and his Orchestra)
221 Let's do it again (with The Stargazers)
232 Somewhere at the end of the rainbow (with The Stargazers)
255 We'll keep a welcome (with The Ilford Girls' Choir)
270 If
298 Life's desire
302 Would I love you
317 Unless
362 Unforgettable
428 I went to your wedding
442 Now
459 I will never change
478 Have you heard
491 Mother Nature and Father Time
535 Tenderly
537 Don't laugh at me
595 Your heart, my heart
597 Veni vidi vici
637 Unchained melody
684 He
691 The ballad of Davy Crockett
697 Robin Hood (with Stephen James and his Chums)

773 The Garden of Eden
*(see also Geraldo and his Orchestra; Cyril Stapleton and his Orchestra; Stanley Black, his piano, and his Orchestra; Mantovani and his Orchestra; Anne Shelton and Dick James; Dick James and The Stargazers)*

**Dick James and The Stargazers**
316 My truly, truly fair

**Harry James and his Music Makers**
5 I can't begin to tell you (Ruth Haag)

**Harry James and his Orchestra**
19 Do you love me? (Ginnie Powell)
22 And then it's heaven (Buddy Di Vito)
243 Mona Lisa (Dick Williams)
275 September song
379 Blacksmith blues (Toni Harper)
495 Ruby (with Tony Gumina – accordion)
571 Three coins in the fountain
591 The high and the mighty
*(see also Doris Day)*

**Joni James**
421 You belong to me
444 Why don't you believe me
478 Have you heard
480 Your cheatin' heart
494 Is it any wonder
765 Christmas and you
1000 There goes my heart

**Julie James**
821 With all my heart
831 Tammy

**Ricky James**
783 Knee deep in the blues
803 Ninety nine ways

**Sonny James**
782 Young love

**Stephen James**
*(see Dick James)*

**Bob Jaxon**
847 Gotta have something in the bank, Frank

**Jean, Jo, Joy & Penny**
*(see Woolf Phillips and his Orchestra)*

**Jean-ettes, The**
1006 May you always

**Susan Jeans**
*(see The Squadronaires directed by Jimmy Miller)*

**Herb Jeffries**
249 Count every star

**Gordon Jenkins – vocal**
*(see The Weavers and Gordon Jenkins)*

**Gordon Jenkins and his Orchestra**
228 Bewitched (Bonnie Lou Williams)
423 My love and devotion (Don Burke, Betty Mulliner and Elizabeth Rinker)
717 No other love
825 Fire down below

**Gordon Jenkins and his Orchestra and Chorus**
130 Maybe you'll be there (Charles La Vere)
160 Again (Joe Graydon)
190 December (Floyd Huddleston)
214 My foolish heart (Sandy Evans)
244 Tzena tzena tzena (The Weavers)
248 Goodnight Irene (The Weavers)
292 Rose, Rose, I love you (Frisco Ruston)
302 Would I love you (Bob Stevens)
317 Unless (Bob Stevens)
547 Secret love (Stuart Foster)

**'Jennifer'**
*(see Phil Morrow and his Music)*

**Henry Jerome and his Orchestra**
226    Daddy's little girl (Hal Barton)
**Jesters, The**
(see Evelyn Knight; Bing Crosby)
**Johnny & The Hurricanes**
1086    Red River rock
**Johnny's Boys**
1016    Ciao ciao bambina
**Betty Johnson**
776    I dreamed
950    There's never been a night
**Bill Johnson**
60    Hear my song, Violetta
89    How are things in Glocca Morra?
93    The girl that I marry
109    Galway Bay
134    The heart of Loch Lomond
180    Our love story
181    You're breaking my heart
201    Some day my heart will awake
255    We'll keep a welcome
291    So in love
377    Wheel of fortune (with Ted Heath and his Music)
378    There's a pawnshop on a corner in Pittsburgh, Pennsylvania (with Ted Heath and his Music)
**Bryan Johnson**
766    Cindy, oh Cindy
789    All of you
**Bunk Johnson and his New Orleans Band**
976    You always hurt the one you love
**Plas Johnson**
(see Nelson Riddle and his Orchestra)
**Teddy Johnson**
261    Beloved, be faithful
271    The Tennessee waltz
276    I'll always love you
300    Our very own
324    Ma'moiselle de Paris
329    Because of you
336    Longing for you
339    Love's roundabout
340    Rosaline
353    Sin
355    Domino
360    Rollin' stone (with The Peter Knight Singers)
368    We won't live in a castle (with The Peter Knight Singers)
373    Please Mr Sun (with The Peter Knight Singers)
383    Auf wiederseh'n sweetheart
388    The homing waltz
394    Trust in me
400    I'm gonna live till I die
423    My love and devotion
449    In a golden coach
492    The Bridge of Sighs
514    You you you
559    Love me
565    Little things mean a lot
(see Teddy Johnson and Pearl Carr)
**Teddy Johnson and Pearl Carr**
809    I'd give you the world
998    Petite fleur
999    Sing, little birdie
1008    If only I could live my life again

**Johnny Johnston**
(see Roland Shaw and his Orchestra)
**Johnston Brothers, The**
271    The Tennessee waltz
277    My heart cries for you
372    Be my life's companion
414    Raindrops (with Dickie Valentine)
454    Oh, happy day
467    Downhearted
479    April in Portugal (with The Pianotones)
527    The creep
556    I get so lonely
576    West of Zanzibar – Jambo
584    Sh-boom
616    Majorca
631    Tweedle-dee
639    Chee chee-oo chee
643    Dreamboat
669    Hernando's hideaway
670    Hey there
717    No other love
757    In the middle of the house (with The Keynotes)
780    Give her my love
792    Heart
893    A very precious love
900    Little serenade
(see also Reggie Goff; Lita Roza; Edmundo Ros and his Orchestra; Suzi Miller and The Johnston Brothers; Dennis Lotis; Jean Regan; Lorrae Desmond and The Johnston Brothers; Ted Heath and his Music; Lys Assia and The Johnston Brothers)
**Johnston Singers, The**
(see Robert Farnon and his Concert Orchestra; Vera Lynn)
**Bob Johnstone**
(see Milt Herth Trio)
**Al Jolson**
43    Anniversary song
46    April showers (with orchestra directed Carmen Dragon)
46    April showers (with Guy Lombardo and his Royal Canadians)
100    When you were sweet sixteen
117    I'm looking over a four-leaf clover
203    Is it true what they say about Dixie? (with The Lee Gordon Singers)
246    I only have eyes for you
345    Some enchanted evening
982    Baby face
**Al Jolson and The Andrews Sisters**
218    The old piano roll blues
**Al Jolson and The Mills Brothers**
203    Is it true what they say about Dixie?
**Allan Jones**
162    The echo told me a lie
165    While the angelus was ringing (with The Lyrian Singers)
181    You're breaking my heart
214    My foolish heart
239    Sentimental me
243    Mona Lisa
264    All my love
270    If
291    So in love
456    I talk to the trees
465    I believe
498    Poppa Piccolino

**Howard Jones**
(see Joe Loss and his Orchestra)
**Jack Jones**
893    A very precious love
**Jonah Jones Quartet, The**
1063    High hopes
**Ken Jones and his Orchestra**
(see Johnny Gray – tenor sax)
**Spike Jones and his City Slickers**
21    You always hurt the one you love (Carl Grayson and Red Ingle)
161    Riders in the sky (I. W. Harper, Sir Frederick Gas and The Sons of The Sons of the Pioneers)
252    Rudolph, the red-nosed reindeer (Rudolph and The Reindeers)
271    The Tennessee waltz (Sara Berner assisted by Sir Frederick Gas)
428    I went to your wedding (Sir Fredric Gas)
511    I saw mommy kissing Santa Claus (George Rock and The Mitchell Boys' Choir)
547    Secret love (Tony Martinez)
**Teen Jones**
1053    Three stars
**Jones Boys, The**
943    A certain smile
967    The day the rains came
**Dick Jordan**
1073    Mack the knife
1078    Travellin' light
1081    Mr Blue
1088    Put your head on my shoulder
**Jack Jordan**
(see Frank Chacksfield's Tunesmiths)
**Louis Jordan**
(see Ella Fitzgerald and Louis Jordan)
**Louis Jordan and his Tympany Five**
56    Open the door, Richard
**Jordanaires, The**
(see Elvis Presley; Conway Twitty)
**Georges Jouvin and his Ensemble**
967    The day the rains came
**Bobby Joy**
(see Roy Fox and his Band)
**Jubalaires, The**
218    That old piano roll blues
254    A dream is a wish your heart makes
(see also Jack Smith)
**Joe Julian**
975    Side saddle
1022    Roulette
1058    China tea
1085    Snow coach
**Rosemary June**
985    I'll be with you in apple blossom time
1091    The village of St Bernadette
**Junior Chorale, The, conducted by Harold Habberjam**
1079    Little donkey
**Eric Jupp and his Orchestra**
592    They were doin' the mambo (The Coronets
**Bill Justis**
873    Raunchy
**Kalin Twins, The**
915    When
**Kitty Kallen**
565    Little things mean a lot
762    True love

**Dick Kallman**
755  Love me as though there were no tomorrow
760  Two different worlds
**Anton Karas**
187  The Harry Lime theme
217  Cherry stones
(see also Anne Shelton and Dick James)
**Mickey Katz and his Orchestra**
161  Borscht riders in the sky (Mickey Katz)
174  The wedding samba (Jack Hilliard)
198  Yiddish mule train
205  Music! Music! Music! (Mickey Katz)
243  Mona Lisa (Anzio Pizza)
251  The baby, the bubbe and you (Mickey Katz)
347  Herring boats (Mickey Katz)
353  Sin (Mickey Katz)
357  The little white knish that cried (Mickey Katz)
377  I'm a schmiel of fortune (Mickey Katz)
378  There's a pawnshop on a corner in Schvitzburgh, Pennsylvania (Mickey Katz and Chorus)
381  A schmo is a schmo (Mickey Katz)
385  Kiss of Meyer (Mickey Katz)
401  Schleppin' my baby back home (Mickey Katz)
411  Patch-a-me (Mickey Katz)
415  Feet up, pat him on the pipick (Mickey Katz)
421  You belong to me
437  Don't let the schmaltz get in your eyes (Mickey Katz)
444  Why don't you believe me (Sue Allen and Mickey Katz)
691  Duvid Crockett
902  Knish doctor
909  Poiple Kishke eater (Mickey Katz)
**Beatrice Kay and her Kay-Jammers**
218  The old piano roll blues
**Carol Kay**
1053  Three stars (with Tommy Dee and Teen Jones)
**Eric Kay**
996  The little drummer boy
**Kathie Kay**
676  Suddenly there's a valley
699  Dreams can tell a lie
704  Jimmy unknown
759  A house with love in it
813  We will make love
831  Tammy
901  The secret of happiness (with The Michael Sammes Singers)
927  Hillside in Scotland
1029  Goodbye, Jimmy, goodbye
**Norman Kay**
370  Tell me why
**Kaydets, The**
(see Sammy Kaye and his Orchestra)
**Buddy Kaye Quintet, The**
150  It's magic (Artie Malvin and The Tunetimers)
153  A – you're adorable (Artie Malvin)
**Danny Kaye**
94  I wonder who's kissing her now (with The Ken Darby Singers)
129  Ballin' the jack
151  Candy kisses (with The Regalaires)
173  Confidentially (with The Lee Gordon Singers)

200  I've got a lovely bunch of coconuts
215  C'est si bon (with The Lee Gordon Singers)
247  Happy times (with The Lee Gordon Singers)
265  The thing
315  The little white duck
324  Mademoiselle de Paris
438  Wonderful Copenhagen
663  Love me or leave me
(see also Danny Kaye and The Andrews Sisters; Danny Kaye and Patty Andrews; Bing Crosby, Danny Kaye, Peggy Lee and Trudy Stevens)
**Danny Kaye and The Andrews Sisters**
102  Civilisation
120  Woody Woodpecker (with The Harmonica Gentlemen)
144  Put 'em in a box (with The Harmonica Gentlemen)
**Danny Kaye and Patty Andrews**
257  Orange coloured sky
**Dinah Kaye**
(see The Tuneful Twenties Orchestra)
**Edna Kaye**
(see Primo Scala and his Accordion Band; Carroll Gibbons and the Savoy Hotel Orpheans)
**Harry Kaye**
(see Billy Thorburn's The Organ, the Dance Band and Me; Carroll Gibbons and the Savoy Hotel Orpheans)
**Swing and Sway with Sammy Kaye (and his Orchestra)**
164  Careless hands (Don Cornell and The Three Kaydets)
182  Baby, it's cold outside (Don Cornell and Laura Leslie)
266  The petite waltz
280  Patricia (The Kaydets)
428  I went to your wedding (Jeff Clay and Choir)
**Kaye Sisters, The (also known as The Three Kayes, The Three Kaye Sisters)**
724  Mister Cuckoo
729  Ivory tower
746  Lay down your arms
817  Dark Moon
848  Alone
861  Love me forever
872  The Pansy
930  Torero
1029  Goodbye, Jimmy, goodbye
(see also Frankie Vaughan and The Kaye Sisters)
**Howard Keel**
93  The girl that I marry
(see also Betty Hutton and Howard Keel)
**Marion Keene**
829  In the middle of an island
**Greta Keller**
241  Once in a while
402  Somewhere along the way
456  I talk to the trees
**Jerry Keller**
1061  Here comes Summer
**Gene Kelly**
389  Singing in the rain
893  A very precious love
**Grace Kelly**
(see Bing Crosby and Grace Kelly)
**Monte Kelly and his Orchestra**
994  Willingly

**Monty Kelly and his Orchestra**
616  Majorca
**Barry Kendall**
942  More than ever
948  It's all in the game
962  I heard the bells on Christmas Day
979  Tonight
1014  Come softly to me
1072  One more sunrise
1090  Seven little girls sitting in the back seat
**Barry Kendall and June Lowe**
999  Sing, little birdie
**Lou Kennedy**
656  Stars shine in your eyes
**Bill Kenny**
344  At the end of the day (with Male Quartet)
373  Please Mr Sun
**Alan Kent**
745  Believe in me
749  More
**Bill Kent**
881  Oh-oh, I'm falling in love again
**Stan Kenton and his Orchestra**
90  Peg o' my heart
275  September song
406  Delicado
527  The creep
535  Tenderly
882  Tequila
(see also The Nat King Cole Trio)
**Ken-Tones, The**
621  Tomorrow
**Anita Kerr Quartet, The**
(see The Owen Bradley Quintet)
**Anita Kerr Singers, The**
(see Bobby Helms)
**Key Men, The**
(see The Hal McKusick Quintet)
**Keynotes, The**
235  Silver dollar
245  Ashes of roses (with The Keynotes Choir)
466  Side by side (with Primo Scala and his Banjo and Accordion Band)
513  Chicka boom
562  A dime and a dollar
681  Relax-ay-voo
(see also Pearl Carr and The Keynotes; Primo Scala and his Banjo and Accordion Band; Primo Scala and his Accordion Band; Sam Browne; Anne Shelton; Benny Lee and The Keynotes; Joy Nichols and Benny Lee; Denny Dennis; Gracie Fields and The Keynotes; Benny Lee and Lynette Rae; Al Morgan; Harry Roy and his Orchestra; Issy Bonn; Reggie Goff; Mickey Maguire; Bobbie Britton; Dickie Valentine and Joan Regan; Joan Regan; Dickie Valentine; Dave King; The Johnston Brothers)
**Nicky Kidd**
728  Too young to go steady
**Paddy Kierney**
410  The Isle of Innisfree
**Judy Kileen**
756  Just walking in the rain
**Richard Kiley**
(see Doretta Morrow and Richard Kiley)
**Dave King**
700  Memories are made of this (with The Keynotes)
719  You can't be true to two (w. The Keynotes)

737   The birds and the bees (with The Keynotes)
765   Christmas and you
799   Love is a golden ring
821   With all my heart
860   The story of my life
1063   High hopes

**Felix King, his piano, and his Orchestra**
228   Bewitched
241   Once in a while
276   I'll always love you
     (see also Reggie Goff; Dick James)

**Felix King, his piano, and strings**
502   Flirtation waltz

**Pee Wee King and his Golden West Cowboys**
361   Slow coach (Redd Stewart)

**Peter King Singers, The**
405   I'll walk alone
     (see also Dinah Shore)

**King Brothers, The**
792   Heart
794   Marianne
811   A white sport coat
829   In the middle of an island (with The Rita Williams Singers)
849   Wake up, little Susie
863   Put a light in the window
930   Torero (with The Rita Williams Singers)
969   Winter wonderland
1002   Thank heavens for little girls (with The Rita Williams Singers)
1082   Makin' love

**Kingpins, The**
(see Reggie Goff)

**Evelyn Kingsley**
970   To know him is to love him (with The Towers)

**King's Men, The**
349   Mistakes (with The Pianotones)

**Kingston Trio, The**
826   Scarlet ribbons
959   Tom Dooley

**Kingsway Symphony Orchestra, The, conducted by Camarata**
69   Come back to Sorrento

**Kingtones, The**
637   Unchained melody
639   Chee-chee-oo-chee

**Tony Kinsey Quartet, The**
662   Close your eyes
670   Hey there

**Tony Kinsey Trio, The**
631   Tweedle-dee

**Pat Kirby**
831   Tammy

**Basil Kirchin Band, The**
838   White silver sands (with The Moonbeams)

**Kirchin Band, The Ivor and Basil**
631   Tweedle-dee

**Andy Kirk and his Clouds of Joy**
139   Twelfth Street rag

**Eddie Kirk**
151   Candy kisses

**Lisa Kirk**
303   Beautiful brown eyes

**Lisa Kirk and Fran Warren**
222   Dearie

**Ken Kirkham**
701   It's almost tomorrow

**Eartha Kitt**
625   Under the bridges of Paris

**Annette Klooger**
353   Sin
354   There's always room at our house
411   Botch-a-me
521   Oh! My papa
532   My heart belongs to only you
559   Love me
787   Wisdom of a fool (with Ted Heath and his Music)
     (see also Ted Heath and his Music; Annette Klooger and The Four Jones Boys)

**Annette Klooger and The Four Jones Boys**
736   Why do fools fall in love?

**Evelyn Knight**
3   Chickery chick (with The Jesters)
127   Buttons and bows
217   Cherry stones (with The Ray Charles Singers)
225   I remember the cornfields
236   Candy and cake (with The Lee Gordon Singers)
303   Beautiful brown eyes (with The Ray Charles Singers)
430   Snowflakes
     (see also Evelyn Knight and The Star Dusters; Bing Crosby and Evelyn Knight; Evelyn Knight and Red Foley)

**Evelyn Knight and Red Foley**
277   My heart cries for you

**Evelyn Knight and The Star Dusters**
136   A little bird told me
141   Powder your face with sunshine
163   Brush those tears from your eyes

**Peter Knight Singers, The**
(see Teddy Johnson; Ray Ellington and his Quartet; Ken Mackintosh and his Orchestra; Frankie Vaughan; Malcolm Vaughan; Ken Mackintosh (sax); Teddy Foster and his Orchestra)

**Evelyn Bell Knightingales**
(see Art Morton and Evelyn Bell Knightingales)

**Knightsbridge Chorale, The**
1099   Ivy will cling

**Knightsbridge Strings, The**
1054   The windows of Paris

**Moe Koffman Quartet, The**
877   The swinging shepherd blues

**Marie Korchinska**
(see The Bill McGuffie Quartet)

**Kordites, The**
443   The glow worm
     (see also Santiago and his Music; Donald Peers; Joe Loss and his Orchestra; Frankie Vaughan; Anne Shelton)

**Korn Kobblers, The, conducted by Stanley Fritts**
159   Clancy lowered the boom (Frank Saunders and The Heathertones)

**Carlo Krahmer's Chicagoans**
891   Who's sorry now?

**Fred Kreitzer**
(see Guy Lombardo and his Royal Canadians)

**Peter Kreuder**
339   Love's roundabout

**Gene Krupa Quartet, The**
998   Petite fleur

**Charlie Kunz and his Music**
355   Domino

**Dave Kydd**
(see Jack Simpson and his Sextet)

**Kay Kyser and his Orchestra**
120   Woody Woodpecker (Gloria Wood)
133   On a slow boat to China (Harry Babbitt and Gloria Wood)

**Cleo Laine**
(see The Johnny Dankworth Seven)

**Frankie Laine**
198   Mule train
292   Rose, Rose, I love you (with The Norman Luboff Choir)
312   Jezebel (with The Norman Luboff Choir)
380   The gandy dancer's ball (with The Norman Luboff Choir)
392   High noon
396   When you're in love (with The Norman Luboff Choir and Carl Fischer – piano)
400   I'm gonna live till I die
407   Rock of Gibraltar
451   The ruby and the pearl
465   I believe
480   Your cheatin' heart (with The Norman Luboff Choir)
500   Where the winds blow
504   Hey, Joe! (with The Norman Luboff Choir)
509   Answer me (w. The Norman Luboff Choir)
526   Blowing wild
545   Heart of my heart
575   My friend
585   There must be a reason
595   Your heart, my heart (with The Norman Luboff Choir)
658   Cool water (with The Mellomen)
693   Sixteen tons (with The Mellomen)
750   A woman in love
778   Moonlight gambler
799   Love is a golden ring (with The Easy Riders)
     (see also Jo Stafford and Frankie Laine; Frankie Laine and Jimmy Boyd; Doris Day and Frankie Laine)

**Frankie Laine and Jimmy Boyd**
482   Tell me a story (with The Norman Luboff Choir)

**Dawn Lake**
745   Believe in me

**Nappy Lamare and his Dixieland Band**
346   The black and white rag

**Bob Lamm**
(see Francis Craig and his Orchestra)

**Lana Sisters, The, and Al Saxon**
1090   Seven little girls sitting in the back seat
     (see also Al Saxon)

**Lancers, The**
606   Mister Sandman
662   Close your eyes
     (see also Teresa Brewer)

**Abbe Lane**
(see Xavier Cugat and his Orchestra)

**Desmond Lane**
(see Alma Cogan, Cyril Stapleton and his Orchestra)

**Ken Lane Singers, The**
(see Bing Crosby, Frank Sinatra)

**Don Lang**
677   Seventeen

**Don Lang and his Frantic Five**
804   Rock-a-billy
838   White silver sands (with The Norman Quartet)

882 Tequila
902 Witch doctor

**rances Langford**
203 Is it true what they say about Dixie?
241 Once in a while (with The Foursome)

**nooky Lanson**
701 It's almost tomorrow
  *(see also Snooky Lanson and Eve Young; Teresa Brewer and Snooky Lanson)*

**nooky Lanson and Eve Young**
261 Beloved, be faithful

**Mario Lanza**
286 Be my love (with the Jeff Alexander Choir)
310 The loveliest night of the year
424 Because you're mine (with The Jeff Alexander Choir)
731 Serenade
894 On the street where you live (with The Jeff Alexander Chorus)

**lius La Rosa**
571 Three coins in the fountain
620 Mobile
676 Suddenly there's a valley
713 Lipstick and candy and rubber sole shoes
717 No other love
930 Torero

**Charles La Vere**
170 A dreamer with a penny (with The Four Hits and a Miss)
  *(see also Gordon Jenkins and his Orchestra)*

**ertrude Lawrence**
524 Hello young lovers

**regg Lawrence**
*e Skitch Henderson and his Orchestra)*

**ee Lawrence**
145 How can you buy Killarney?
192 Song of Capri
262 I leave my heart in an English garden
280 Patricia
305 With these hands
318 A beggar in love
332 How can I leave you?
333 Vanity
340 Rosaline
363 Only fools
371 At last! At last!
374 Never
386 Blue tango
396 When you're in love
408 Here in my heart
424 Because you're mine
477 Tell me you're mine
489 Can't I?
512 Crying in the chapel
573 The story of Tina
618 Give me your word
641 Don't worry
676 Suddenly there's a valley
696 Young and foolish
790 By you, by you, by you (with The Coronets)
800 Chapel of the roses (with The Bill Shepherd Chorus)
  *(see also Vera Lynn and Lee Lawrence)*

**eve Lawrence**
785 Banana boat song
857 Long before I knew you
003 I don't care only love me

**Turner Layton**
6 In the land of beginning again
9 Laughing on the outside
14 Primrose Hill
17 Down in the valley
37 Lilli Marlene
40 Too many irons in the fire
48 For sentimental reasons
54 How lucky you are
62 Goodnight, you little rascal, you
65 Try a little tenderness
66 Among my souvenirs
94 I wonder who's kissing her now
96 Near you
115 Nature boy
117 I'm looking over a four-leaf clover

**Layton & Johnstone**
941 Girl of my dreams

**Jimmy Leach and his New Organolians**
39 Till then (Cyril Shane)
52 Accordion
81 The little old mill
87 Apple blossom wedding (Alan Dean)
96 Near you (Alan Dean)
107 Teresa (Alan Dean)
136 A little bird told me (Alan Dean)
153 A – you're adorable (Chorus)

**Huddie 'Leadbelly' Ledbetter**
248 Goodnight Irene

**Benny Lee**
216 Enjoy yourself
263 Ferry Boat Inn (with The Stargazers)
319 Fifty years ago (with The Stargazers)
328 Shanghai
463 Pretty little black–eyed Susie
480 Your cheatin' heart
656 Stars shine in your eyes
657 Learnin' the blues (with The Embassy Rhythm Group)
660 Close the door (with Children's Chorus)
669 Hernando's hideaway (with The Three Oscars)
  *(see also Benny Lee and The Keynotes; Joy Nichols and Benny Lee; Benny Lee and Lynette Rae; Benny Lee and Mary; Benny Lee and The Stargazers; Daphne and Benny Lee; Benny Lee, Avril Angers, Janet Brown and Peter Butterworth)*

**Benny Lee, Avril Angers, Janet Brown and Peter Butterworth**
545 Heart of my heart
552 Friends and neighbours

**Benny Lee and Lynette Rae**
220 Oh, you sweet one (with The Keynotes)

**Benny Lee and Mary**
259 I taut I taw a puddy tat (with The Stargazers)

**Benny Lee and The Keynotes**
122 Rambling Rose
147 Red roses for a blue lady
229 Sunshine cake
231 A load of hay
247 Happy times

**Benny Lee and The Stargazers**
292 Rose, Rose, I love you

**Dick Lee**
538 The Book (with Choir)

**Helen Lee**
*(see Larry Clinton and his Orchestra)*

**Miss Hue Lee**
292 Rose, Rose, I love you

**Jackie Lee**
755 Love me as though there were no tomorrow

**Jane Lee**
*(see Ambrose and his Orchestra)*

**Linda Lee**
*(see Jerry Gray and his Orchestra)*

**Peggy Lee**
161 Riders in the sky (with The Jud Conlon Singers)
229 Sunshine cake
384 Be anything
619 Let me go, lover
807 Mr Wonderful

**Roberta Lee**
357 The little white cloud that cried
370 Tell me why
471 Hold me, thrill me, kiss me

**Vanessa Lee**
201 Some day my heart will awake

**Lee Brothers, The**
*(see Jo Stafford)*

**Raymond Le Fevre and his Orchestra**
967 The day the rains came

**Anne Lenner**
*(see Harold Geller and his Orchestra)*

**Lennox Three, The**
*(see Billy Thorburn's The Organ, the Dance Band and Me)*

**Tommy Leonetti**
539 The happy wanderer
1034 Dream lover

**Jacques Leroy and his Orchestra**
998 Petite fleur

**Laura Leslie**
*(see Sammy Kaye and his Orchestra)*

**Frankie Lester**
*(see Buddy Morrow and his Orchestra)*

**Harry Lester and his Hayseeds**
3 Chickery chick

**Charlie Le Vere's Chicago Loopers**
*(see The Castle Jazz Band)*

**Carroll Levis and Mickey Maguire**
482 Tell me a story (with The Stargazers)

**Archie Lewis**
1 Bless you (with The Geraldo Strings)
6 In the land of beginning again (with The Geraldo Strings)
51 The whole world is singing my song (with The Geraldo Strings)
60 Hear my song, Violetta (with The Geraldo Strings)
69 Come back to Sorrento (with The Geraldo Strings)
100 When you were sweet sixteen (with The Geraldo Strings)
114 Time may change (with The Geraldo Strings)
158 Till all our dreams come true (with The Luton Girls' Choir)
165 While the angelus was ringing (with The Luton Girls' Choir)
586 Hold my hand
588 Make her mine
603 I still believe
  *(see also Geraldo and his Orchestra)*

**Jerry Lee Lewis**
865 Great balls of fire

**Monica Lewis**
587   If I give my heart to you
**Patti Lewis**
593   I love Paris
599   I can't tell a waltz from a tango
695   The tender trap
768   Happiness Street
**Robert Q. Lewis and Robert's Quties**
417   Zing a little zong
**Smiley Lewis**
986   One night
**Vic Lewis and his Jazzmen**
129   Ballin' the jack
**Vic Lewis and his Orchestra**
69   Come back to Sorrento
104   Too fat polka (Vic Lewis)
286   Be my love
**Liberace**
637   Unchained melody
992   Gigi
**Gwen Liddel**
349   Mistakes
**Bob Lido**
(see Carmen Cavallaro and his Orchestra)
**Enoch Light and his Vibrant Strings**
826   Scarlet ribbons
**Terry Lightfoot and his Jazzmen**
969   Winter wonderland
**Bobby Limb and his Orchestra**
554   Cross over the bridge (Bobby Limb)
564   Wanted (Johnny O'Connor)
**Kathy Linden**
1029   Goodbye, Jimmy, goodbye
**Roberta Linn**
(see Jan Garber and his Orchestra)
**Little Johnny and The Three Teenagers**
876   Baby lover
**Little Richard and his Band**
982   Baby face
1037   Kansas City
**Little Tinkers, The**
(see Frank Weir and his Orchestra)
**Llon d'Hoo Male Choir, The**
(see Joe Loss and his Orchestra)
**Jimmy Lloyd**
902   Witch doctor
964   The end
1021   I kneel at your throne
**Kathy Lloyd**
622   Teach me tonight
632   Unsuspecting heart
**Josef Locke**
60   Hear my song, Violetta
69   Come back to Sorrento
74   Dear old Donegal
100   When you were sweet sixteen
109   Galway Bay
125   When you're in love
145   How can you buy Killarney?
165   While the angelus was ringing (with Mixed Chorus)
178   A shawl of Galway grey
194   Down in the glen
202   We all have a song in our hearts
238   If I were a blackbird
344   At the end of the day
358   Charmaine
410   The Isle of Innisfree
438   Wonderful Copenhagen

503   The Melba waltz
507   When you hear Big Ben (with Reginald Dixon – organ)
569   Cara mia
594   Santo Natale
**Malcolm Lockyer and his Strict Tempo Music for Dancing**
505   Swedish rhapsody
534   Changing partners
544   Bimbo
547   Secret love
551   Make love to me
552   Friends and neighbours
556   I get so lonely
**Eve Lombard**
734   Whatever will be, will be
737   The birds and the bees
763   St Therese of the Roses
777   You, me and us
817   Dark Moon
848   Alone
(see also Harry Roy and his Band)
**Guy Lombardo – vocal**
(see Gloria de Haven and Guy Lombardo)
**Guy Lombardo and his Royal Canadians**
43   Anniversary song (Kenny Gardner)
46   April showers (Jimmy Brown)
99   Serenade of the bells (Kenny Gardner)
105   Golden earrings (Don Rodney)
106   I'm my own grandpa (The Lombardo Trio)
125   When you're in love (Kenny Gardner)
147   Red roses for a blue lady (Don Rodney)
165   While the angelus was ringing (Kenny Gardner)
174   The wedding samba (Kenny Gardner)
186   The hop-scotch polka (Kenny Gardner and The Lombardo Trio)
187   The Harry Lime theme (ftg Don Rodney – guitar)
216   Enjoy yourself (Kenny Gardner and The Lombardo Trio)
222   Dearie (Kenny Gardner and The Lombardo Trio)
252   Rudolph, the red-nosed reindeer (Kenny Gardner and The Lombardo Trio)
264   All my love (Bill Flanagan)
266   The petite waltz (ftg Fred Kreitzer and Buddy Brennen – two pianos)
270   If (Bill Flanagan)
271   The Tennessee waltz (Kenny Gardner and The Lombardo Trio)
305   With these hands (Bill Flanagan)
315   The little white duck (Kenny Gardner)
348   Sweetheart of yesterday (Kenny Gardner and The Lombardo Trio)
358   Charmaine (Jimmy Brown)
371   At last! At last! (ftg Buddy Brown and Fred Kreitzer – two pianos)
412   Half as much (Kenny Martin and The Lombardo Quartet)
428   I went to your wedding (Kenny Gardner)
444   Why don't you believe me? (Kenny Gardner)
461   Pretend (Kenny Gardner)
467   Downhearted (Kenny Gardner)
484   Seven lonely days (Kenny Gardner)
492   The Bridge of Sighs
501   Vaya con Dios (Kenny Gardner and Bill Flanagan)

516   Ricochet
544   Bimbo (Kenny Gardner and The Lombardo Trio)
609   White Christmas (Tony Craig)
613   Softly softly (The Lombardo Quartet)
630   Cherry pink and apple blossom white (Bill Flanagan)
634   Wedding bells (Kenny Gardner)
652   Hey, Mr Banjo (The Lombardo Trio)
**Lombardo Quartet, The**
(see Guy Lombardo and his Royal Canadians)
**Lombardo Trio, The**
(see Guy Lombardo and his Royal Canadians; Ethel Smith; Gloria de Haven)
**Alice Lon**
(see Lawrence Welk and his Champagne Music)
**Laurie London**
851   He's got the whole world in His hands
**London Community Singers, The, conducted by Glyn Jones**
(see John Rorke)
**Londoners, The**
327   The black note serenade
**London Piano Accordeon Band, The**
123   So tired (Phil Phillips)
126   Take me to your heart again (Phil Phillips)
131   The cuckoo waltz (Phil Phillips)
**Shorty Long**
(see Art Mooney and his Orchestra)
**Denise Lor**
587   If I give my heart to you
650   Every day of my life
**Lord Rockingham's XI**
952   Hoots mon
**Etienne Lorin and his Orchestra**
266   The petite waltz
**Terri Lorraine**
893   A very precious love
**Don Lorusso**
(see The George Mitchell Choir)
**Los Musicos**
406   Delicado
**Joe Loss and his Orchestra**
3   Chickery chick (Howard Jones)
7   Into each life some rain must fall (Howard Jones)
9   Laughing on the outside (Howard Jones)
10   Let bygones be bygones (Chorus)
13   Oh, what it seemed to be (Howard Jones)
15   You can be sure of me (Howard Jones)
28   Sweetheart, we'll never grow old (Howard Jones)
32   Someday (Howard Jones)
33   It's all over now (Elizabeth Batey)
41   Dream again (Howard Jones)
42   The old lamplighter (Howard Jones)
43   Anniversary song (Don Rivers)
44   The stars will remember (Howard Jones)
47   May I call you sweetheart? (Howard Jones)
52   Accordion (Howard Jones)
53   Don't fall in love (Elizabeth Batey)
61   Tell me, Marianne (Don Rivers)
61   A Media Luz
66   Among my souvenirs (Howard Jones)
67   A gal in calico (Elizabeth Batey)
69   Come back to Sorrento (Don Rivers)
70   People will say we're in love (Howard Jones)
72   I got the sun in the morning (Elizabeth Batey)

74    Dear old Donegal (Elizabeth Batey)
77    They say it's wonderful (Howard Jones)
80    Oh, what a beautiful morning
81    The little old mill (Elizabeth Batey)
83    Chi-baba chi-baba (Howard Jones)
85    My first love, my last love for always (Howard Jones)
90    Peg o' my heart (Howard Jones)
91    South America, take it away (Elizabeth Batey)
94    I wonder who's kissing her now (Howard Jones)
95    Tree in the meadow (Howard Jones)
100   When you were sweet sixteen (Howard Jones)
102   Civilisation (Elizabeth Batey)
107   Teresa (Howard Jones)
108   The Silver Wedding waltz (Howard Jones)
109   Galway Bay (The Llon d'Hoo male choir)
112   Reflections on the water (Howard Jones)
114   Time may change (Howard Jones)
115   Nature boy (Elizabeth Batey)
118   Dance, ballerina, dance (Howard Jones)
125   When you're in love (Howard Jones and Don Rivers)
128   October twilight (Howard Jones)
130   Maybe you'll be there (Howard Jones and The Loss Chords)
131   The cuckoo waltz (Howard Jones)
132   Cuanto le gusta (Elizabeth Batey and The Loss Chords)
136   A little bird told me (Elizabeth Batey)
137   Far away places (Howard Jones)
140   Crystal gazer (Howard Jones)
141   Powder your face with sunshine (Howard Jones)
143   Lavender blue (Elizabeth Batey)
144   Put 'em in a box (Elizabeth Batey)
148   The wedding of Lilli Marlene (Howard Jones)
151   Candy kisses (Irene Miller)
152   Behind the clouds (Irene Miller, Elizabeth Batey and Howard Jones)
156   Clopin clopant (Howard Jones)
158   Till all our dreams come true (Howard Jones and David Griffiths)
166   Beautiful eyes (Elizabeth Batey)
174   The wedding samba
177   The windmill song (v)
181   You're breaking my heart
185   The kiss in your eyes
194   Down in the glen
197   Dear hearts and gentle people
199   Jealous heart
205   Music! Music! Music!
209   Chattanoogie shoe-shine boy
212   I'd've baked a cake
214   My foolish heart
215   C'est si bon
216   Enjoy yourself
220   Oh, you sweet one
222   Dearie
234   If I loved you
239   Sentimental me
240   Have I told you lately that I love you?
243   Mona Lisa
247   Happy times
251   Bibbidi bobbidi boo
254   A dream is a wish your heart makes

257   Orange coloured sky
261   Beloved, be faithful
264   All my love
266   The petite waltz
268   Flying saucer (The Loss Chords)
270   If
271   The Tennessee waltz
277   My heart cries for you
278   C'n I canoe you up the river?
279   Play a simple melody
286   Be my love
288   So long
290   Mockin' bird hill
291   So in love
292   Rose, Rose, I love you
294   Mary Rose
302   Would I love you
305   With these hands
310   The loveliest night of the year
311   I apologise
312   Jezebel (Howard Jones and The Loss Chords)
318   A beggar in love
323   Tulips and heather (Rose Brennan and The Loss Chords)
328   Shanghai
329   Because of you
336   Longing for you
340   Rosaline (Howard Jones and The Loss Chords)
341   Allentown Jail
345   Some enchanted evening
353   Sin
360   Rollin' stone
362   Unforgettable
364   Then I'll be there (Rose Brennan and The Loss Chords)
368   We won't live in a castle
372   Be my life's companion
384   Be anything (Howard Jones)
402   Somewhere along the way (Rose Brennan)
410   The Isle of Innisfree (Rose Brennan)
419   Forget-me-not (Howard Jones)
442   Now (Howard Jones)
444   Why don't you believe me? (Rose Brennan)
452   Got you on my mind (Rose Brennan and The Kordites)
484   Seven lonely days (Rose Brennan)
501   Vaya con Dios
505   Swedish rhapsody
506   You're just in love
530   From here to eternity
534   Changing partners
535   Tenderly
540   Luxembourg polka
545   Heart of my heart
547   Secret love
550   Someone else's roses
556   I get so lonely
560   Young at heart
561   The homecoming waltz
562   A dime and a dollar
564   Wanted
565   Little things mean a lot
567   The never never land
570   The man with the banjo
593   I love Paris
597   Veni vidi vici
606   Mister Sandman

608   Happy days and lonely nights
613   Softly softly
614   Somebody
616   Majorca
633   Stranger in paradise
639   Chee-chee-oo-chee
642   Melody of love
643   Dreamboat
647   Evermore
648   The Crazy Otto rag
655   John and Julie
656   Stars shine in your eyes
659   Blue star
665   I'll come when you call
667   Have you ever been lonely?
675   Love is a many-splendoured thing
676   Suddenly there's a valley
695   The tender trap
696   Young and foolish
700   Memories are made of this
701   It's almost tomorrow
702   Zambezi (with Frank Gillespie – sax)
710   The poor people of Paris
712   The great pretender
717   No other love
720   A tear fell
729   Ivory tower
738   Mountain greenery
751   My unfinished symphony
762   True love
774   Friendly persuasion
783   Knee deep in the blues
785   Mambo – the banana boat song
792   Heart
806   Around the world
808   When I fall in love
817   Dark moon
819   Love letters in the sand
831   Tammy
835   Mandolin serenade
838   White silver sands
842   Let me be loved
854   April love
864   Chicago
868   Sugartime
891   Who's sorry now?
894   On the street where you live
895   I could have danced all night
896   Stairway of love
903   Twilight time
924   Wouldn't it be loverly?
929   Volare
931   Everybody loves a lover
932   Carolina Moon
941   Girl of my dreams
942   More than ever
982   Baby face
988   Last night on the back porch
990   Smoke gets in your eyes
992   Gigi
994   Willingly
997   My happiness
1001  Wait for me
1010  Venus
1034  Dream lover
      (see also Rose Brennan)

**Loss Chords, The**
(see Joe Loss and his Orchestra)

**Dennis Lotis**
370   Tell me why
373   Please Mr Sun
408   Here in my heart
413   Take my heart
437   Don't let the stars get in your eyes
469   Wild horses (with Ted Heath and his Music)
553   Such a night (with The Johnston Brothers and Ted Heath and his Music)
592   They were doin' the mambo (with Ted Heath and his Music)
792   Heart (with The Beryl Stott Chorus)
831   Tammy
880   I may never pass this way again (with The Rita Williams Singers)
912   The only man on the island
      *(see also Ted Heath and his Music; Dennis Lotis and the Stargazers)*

**Dennis Lotis and The Stargazers**
493   Let's walk that-a-way
497   Look at that girl
541   The cuff of my shirt

**Bonnie Lou**
484   Seven lonely days
528   Tennessee wig walk
582   Wait for me, darling
607   The finger of suspicion
631   Tweedle-dee (with her Gang)

**Bonnie Lou and Rusty York**
885   La dee dah

**Dorothy Loudon**
359   I wanna say hello (with The Honky-Tonks)
417   Zing a little zong

**Geoff Love – vocal**
*(see Harry Gold and his Pieces of Eight)*

**Geoff Love and his Latin-American Rhythm**
918   Patricia

**Jim Lowe**
660   Close the door
732   Blue suede shoes
758   Green door
790   By you, by you, by you (w. Bob Davie piano)

**June Lowe**
*(see Barry Kendall and June Lowe)*

**Peter Lowe**
785   Banana boat song
787   The wisdom of a fool

**Fred Lowery**
*(see Leroy Holmes and his Orchestra)*

**Jeremy Lubbock**
870   Catch a falling star

**Norman Luboff Choir, The**
*(see Paul Weston and his Orchestra; Frankie Laine; Doris Day; Jo Stafford; Doris Day and Frankie Laine; Jimmy Boyd)*

**Fred Lucas**
774   Friendly persuasion

**Robin Luke**
955   Susie darlin'

**Lulubelle & Scotty**
240   Have I told you lately that I love you?

**Lumberjacks, The**
571   Three coins in the fountain
      *(see also George Elrick and The Lumberjacks)*

**Jimmy Lunceford and his Orchestra**
358   Charmaine (Dan Grissom)

**Art Lund**
90   Peg o' my heart
243   Mona Lisa

337   In the cool, cool, cool of the evening
343   I wish I wuz

**Doreen Lundy**
*(see The Skyrockets conducted by Paul Fenoulhet; The Skyrockets conducted by Woolf Phillips; Paul Fenoulhet and his Orchestra; Geraldo and his Orchestra; Peter Yorke and his Concert Orchestra; Maurice Winnick and his Sweet Music)*

**Nellie Lutcher**
351   I want to be near you
397   The heart of a clown
658   Cool water

**Claude Luter and his Orchestra**
710   The poor people of Paris
967   The day the rains came
      *(see also Sidney Bechet – soprano sax)*

**Luton Girls' Choir, The**
111   The dream of Olwen (with Herbert Dawson)
194   Down in the glen
201   Some day my heart will awake
262   I leave my heart in an English garden

**Frankie Lymon**
*(see The Teenagers featuring Frankie Lymon)*

**Joe Lynch**
769   Davy Crockett is helping Santa Claus

**Tommy Lynn**
*(see Charlie Spivak and his Orchestra)*

**Vera Lynn**
44   The stars will remember
54   How lucky you are (with Ambrose and his Orchestra)
55   The world belongs to you, little man
86   I'll make up for everything
101   Once upon a winter time
108   The silver wedding waltz
121   You can't be true, dear
143   Lavender blue
160   Again
176   Too-whit, too-whoo
180   Our love story
206   Now that I need you
207   Best of all
210   When the world has forgotten
211   My thanks to you
233   Your heart and my heart
296   A rainy day refrain (with The Mayfair Singers)
332   How can I leave you? (with The Mayfair Singers)
342   If you go
357   The little white cloud that cried
365   Cry
369   And so to sleep again
373   Please Mr Sun
383   Auf wiederseh'n sweetheart (with Soldiers and Airmen of HM Forces)
384   Be anything
388   The homing waltz (with Sailors, Soldiers and Airmen of HM Forces)
391   From the time you say goodbye (with Soldiers and Airmen of HM Forces)
419   Forget-me-not (with The Johnston Singers)
432   Outside of heaven
447   The love of my life (with The Johnston Singers)
468   The Windsor waltz (with Chorus of Members of HM Forces)
507   When you hear Big Ben
517   If you love me (with Charles Smart – organ)

536   Don't leave me now
548   Two Easter Sunday sweethearts
561   The homecoming waltz (with Chorus of Men and Women of HM Forces)
575   My friend
585   There must be a reason
590   My son, my son (with Frank Weir, his sax, and his Chorus and Orchestra)
609   White Christmas
650   Ev'ry day of my life
688   With your love
727   Who are we?
735   Walk hand in hand
759   A house with love in it
815   Travellin' home
913   Every hour, every day of my life
1072   Morgen

**Vera Lynn and Sam Browne**
172   I don't see me in your eyes any more

**Vera Lynn and Lee Lawrence**
217   Cherry stones

**Barbara Lyon**
645   Stowaway
646   The pendulum song
670   Hey there
703   Band of gold
737   The birds and the bees
772   A letter to a soldier
825   Fire down below

**Barbara Lyon and Ronnie Harris**
718   Don't ring-a da bell

**Lyrian Singers, The**
255   We'll keep a welcome (with narration by Tom Jones)
      *(see also Allan Jones)*

**Humphrey Lyttleton and his Band**
485   The breeze
593   I love Paris
      *(see also Sidney Bechet – soprano sax)*

**Frank Macaulay**
*(see Jan Garber and his Orchestra)*

**David Macbeth**
1081   Mr Blue (with The Beryl Stott Group)

**Billy McCormack**
632   Unsuspecting heart
656   Stars shine in your eyes
707   My September love
722   I'll be home
750   A woman in love
756   Just walking in the rain
759   A house with love in it
779   Adoration waltz

**Franklyn MacCormack**
642   Melody of love (with Herbert Foote – organ)

**Tiny McDaniel**
*(see Jimmy Palmer and his Orchestra)*

**Chas McDevitt Group, The**
965   Real love (Shirley Douglas)

**Chas McDevitt Skiffle Group, The**
805   Freight train (with Nancy Whiskey)

**Eddie MacDonald**
492   The Bridge of Sighs
507   When you hear Big Ben

**Bill McGuffie**
475   The theme from 'Limelight'
495   Ruby
549   From the vine came the grape
655   John and Julie

669   Hernando's hideaway
670   Hey there

**Bill McGuffie and his Music**
578   Smile
717   No other love
798   I'll find you

**Bill McGuffie Quartet, The**
525   Ebb tide (with Marie Korchinska – harp)

**McGuire Sisters, The**
629   Open up your heart
642   Melody of love
644   Sincerely
678   Christmas alphabet
684   He
696   Young and foolish
792   Heart
868   Sugartime
929   Volare
1006   May you always

**Scotty McHarg**
26   To each his own
44   The stars will remember

**Scotty McHarg and Beryl Davis**
24   So would I (with The Dozen and One Lovelies)

**Kenneth McKellar**
835   Mandolin serenade

**Gisele MacKenzie**
339   Love's roundabout
437   Don't let the stars get in your eyes
455   Till I waltz again with you
484   Seven lonely days (with vocal group)

**Ken Mackintosh – soprano sax**
1072   Morgen

**Ken Mackintosh – saxophone**
716   Come next Spring (with Kenny Bardell and The Peter Knight Singers)

**Ken Mackintosh, his saxophone, and his Orchestra**
330   I love the sunshine of your smile
443   Glow worm
496   Number one (with vocal group)
521   O my papa (with The Peter Knight Singers)
522   Istanbul
527   The creep
584   Sh-boom (The Mackpies)
637   Unchained melody
873   Raunchy
877   Swingin' shepherd blues (with vocal group)
(see also Frankie Vaughan; Alma Cogan; Anne Shelton)

**Hal McKusick Quintet, The**
808   When I fall in love (with The Key Men)

**Joseph McNally**
109   Galway Bay

**Jimmy McPartland and his Orchestra**
129   Ballin' the jack

**Mackpies, The**
(see Ken Mackintosh and his Orchestra)

**Carmen McRae**
968   As I love you

**Gordon MacRae**
150   It's magic
197   Dear hearts and gentle people
198   Mule train
273   Just the way you are (with The Ewing Sisters)
291   So in love
345   Some enchanted evening

601   Count your blessings instead of sheep
633   Stranger in paradise
727   Who are we?
750   A woman in love
(see also Jo Stafford and Gordon MacRae; Gordon MacRae and The Starlighters)

**Gordon MacRae and The Starlighters**
148   The wedding of Lilli Marlene

**Bill Macey and his Orchestra**
379   Blacksmith blues

**Johnny Madara**
844   Be my girl (with vocal group)

**Madcaps, The**
267   Sleigh ride

**Enric Madriguera and his Orchestra**
118   Dance, ballerina, dance (Don Reid)

**Mickey Maguire**
511   I saw mommy kissing Santa Claus (with The Keynotes)
(see also Carroll Levis and Mickey Maguire)

**Ivor Mairants**
(see Wilfrid Thomas)

**Ivor Mairants and his guitar group**
453   Little red monkey

**Bob Mallin**
151   Candy kisses
159   Clancy lowered the boom

**Richard Maltby and his Orchestra**
1072   Morgen (with Chorus)
(see also Buddy de Franco)

**Artie Malvin**
(see The Buddy Kaye Quintet)

**Carl Mann**
1066   Mona Lisa

**Gloria Mann**
736   Why do fools fall in love?

**Lorie Mann**
1034   Dream lover

**Bob Manning**
616   Majorca

**Tony Mansell**
586   Hold my hand
591   The high and the mighty
702   Zambezi

**Mantovani and his Orchestra**
35   The green cockatoo
60   Hear my song, Violetta
61   Tell me, Marianne (Val Merrall)
254   A dream is a wish your heart makes (Dick James)
339   Love's roundabout
345   Some enchanted evening
358   Charmaine
395   Faith
416   Belle of the ball
472   Song from the Moulin Rouge
503   The Melba waltz
505   Swedish rhapsody
540   The Luxembourg polka
555   The shadow waltz
572   Dream dream dream
609   White Christmas
613   Softly softly (Kim Bennett and Chorus)
633   Stranger in paradise
806   Around the world
835   Mandolin serenade
842   Let me be loved (with Stan Newsome – trumpet)
895   I could have danced all night

943   A certain smile
(see also David Whitfield; Mantovani and his Concert Orchestra)

**Mantovani and his Concert Orchestra**
111   The dream of Olwen (with Ivan Fosello – piano)
115   Nature boy (with Arthur Young – piano)

**Maple Leaf Four, The**
365   Cry
641   Don't worry
643   Dreamboat
664   The man from Laramie
758   Green door

**Lucille Mapp**
796   Mangos

**Muzzy Marcellino**
(see Victor Young and his Singing Strings)

**Victor Marchese**
395   Faith

**Janie Marden**
665   I'll come when you call (with Frank Weir, his sax, and his Chorus and Orchestra)

**Charles Margulis**
992   Gigi

**Luis Mariano**
593   I love Paris

**Joe Marine**
575   My friend
(see also Fred Waring and his Pennsylvanians)

**Mariners, The**
639   Chee-chee-oo-chee

**Marino Marini and his Quartet**
821   With all my heart (Ruggero Cori)
872   La Panse (Ruggero Cori)
872   The Pansy
895   I could have danced all night
929   Volare
942   Come prima
1016   Ciao ciao bambina

**Leo Marjane**
156   Clopin clopant

**Marlin Sisters, The, and Don Miles**
290   Mockin' bird hill

**Micki Marlo**
623   Prize of gold

**Rita Marlowe**
(see Ambrose and his Orchestra)

**Maralyn Marsh**
(see Larry Fotine and his Orchestra)

**Ralph Marterie and his Orchestra**
461   Pretend
527   The creep
882   Tequila
930   Torero

**Dean Martin**
141   Powder your face with sunshine
224   Choo'n gum
270   If
276   I'll always love you
337   In the cool, cool, cool of the evening
421   You belong to me
490   Kiss
529   That's amore
583   Sway
610   Mambo Italiano
611   The naughty lady of shady lane
619   Let me go, lover
625   Under the bridges of Paris
639   Chee-chee-oo-chee

| 696 | Young and foolish |
| 700 | Memories are made of this |
| 740 | Watching the world go by |
| 906 | Return to me |
| 929 | Volare |

**Dean Martin and Line Renaud**
| 681 | Relax-ay-voo |

**Denis Martin**
| 100 | When you were sweet sixteen |
| 109 | Galway Bay |
| 145 | How can you buy Killarney? |
| 194 | Down in the glen |
| 196 | The last mile home |
| 225 | I remember the cornfields |
| 294 | Mary Rose |

**Freddy Martin and his Orchestra**
| 133 | On a slow boat to China (Glenn Hughes and The Martin Men) |

**Grady Martin and his Slew Foot Five**
| 421 | You belong to me (Cecil Bayley) |
| 428 | I went to your wedding (Cecil Bayley) |
| 466 | Side by side (Dottie Dillard and Jack Shook) |
| 1015 | A fool such as I (Dottie Dillard and Jack Shook) |
| | (see also Marvin Shiner) |

**Ido Martin and his Latin Band**
| 825 | Fire down below (Beryl Wayne) |

**Judy Martin**
(see Red Foley and Judy Martin)

**Kenny Martin**
(see Guy Lombardo and his Royal Canadians)

**Mary Martin**
| 405 | I'll walk alone |

**Mary Martin and Arthur Godfrey**
| 296 | Dadim, Dadom |

**Ray Martin and his Concert Orchestra**
| 252 | Rudolph, the red-nosed reindeer |
| 362 | Unforgettable |
| 371 | At last! At last! |
| 386 | Blue tango |
| 403 | Meet Mister Callaghan |
| 416 | Belle of the ball |
| 427 | Ecstasy |
| 445 | Hi-Lili, Hi-Lo |
| 505 | Swedish rhapsody |
| 597 | Veni vidi vici |
| 609 | White Christmas |
| 669 | Hernando's hideaway |

**Steve Martin**
| 705 | Only you |
| 842 | Let me be loved |
| 896 | Stairway of love |

**Tony Martin**
| 60 | Hear my song, Violetta |
| 113 | Oh! My achin' heart |
| 150 | It's magic |
| 275 | September song |
| 302 | Would I love you |
| 311 | I apologise |
| 333 | Vanity |
| 355 | Domino |
| 371 | At last! At last! |
| 385 | Kiss of fire |
| 479 | April in Portugal |
| 593 | I love Paris |
| 633 | Stranger in paradise |
| 735 | Walk hand in hand |
| 789 | All of you |

**Tony Martin and Fran Warren**
| 213 | I said my pajamas |

**Tony Martin and Dinah Shore**
| 289 | A penny a kiss – a penny a hug |
| 642 | Melody of love |

**Vince Martin**
| 766 | Cindy, oh Cindy (with The Tarriers) |

**Martin Men, The**
(see Freddy Martin and his Orchestra)

**Tony Martinez**
(see Spike Jones and his City Slickers)

**Al Martino**
| 408 | Here in my heart |
| 413 | Take my heart |
| 442 | Now |
| 508 | Be mine |
| 564 | Wanted |
| 573 | The story of Tina |
| 596 | No one but you |
| 603 | I still believe |
| 605 | Not as a stranger |
| 664 | The man from Laramie |

**Mary**
(see Benny Lee and Mary)

**Glen Mason**
| 570 | The man with the banjo |
| 725 | Hot diggity |
| 753 | Glendora |
| 758 | Green door |
| 784 | Don't forbid me |
| 802 | Round and round |
| 875 | Why don't they understand? |
| 880 | I may never pass this way again |
| 928 | I know where I'm going |
| 964 | The end |
| 1043 | The battle of New Orleans |

**Valerie Masters**
| 901 | The secret of happiness |

**Ernie Mathias**
(see Jan Garber and his Orchestra)

**Johnny Mathis**
| 820 | Wonderful, wonderful |
| 943 | A certain smile |
| 969 | Winter wonderland |
| 1062 | Someone |

**Bobby Maxwell**
| 437 | Don't let the stars get in your eyes (with The Windy City Symphony) |
| 525 | Ebb tide |

**Billy May and his Orchestra**
| 252 | Rudolph, the red-nosed reindeer (Alvin Stoller) |
| 358 | Charmaine |
| 362 | Unforgettable |
| 392 | High noon |
| 409 | When I take my sugar to tea (The Maytimers) |
| 535 | Tenderly |
| 560 | Young at heart |
| 658 | Cool water ('Water' by Bob Morse) |
| 669 | Hernando's hideaway |
| | (see also Nat King Cole) |

**Mayfair Singers, The**
(see Vera Lynn)

**Mary Mayo**
| 289 | A penny a kiss – a penny a hug (with The Four Chicks and a Chuck) |
| 355 | Domino |

**Maytimers, The**
(see Billy May and his Orchestra)

**Joe Medlin**
| 1021 | I kneel at your throne |

**Ronnie Meede**
| 504 | Hey Joe! |

**Melachrino Orchestra, The, conducted by George Melachrino**
| 111 | The dream of Olwen (with William Hill-Bowen – piano) |
| 339 | Love's roundabout |
| 342 | If you go |
| 578 | Smile |
| 748 | Autumn concerto |
| 750 | A woman in love |

**Melachrino Strings, The**
| 126 | La vie en rose |
| 156 | Clopin Clopant |
| 256 | Autumn leaves |
| 275 | September song |
| 320 | Too young |
| 355 | Domino |
| 358 | Charmaine |
| 403 | Meet Mister Callaghan (ftg William Hill-Bowen – harp) |
| 427 | Ecstasy |
| 453 | Little red monkey |
| 475 | The theme from Limelight |
| 479 | April in Portugal |
| 502 | Flirtation waltz |
| 503 | The Melba waltz |
| 535 | Tenderly |
| 623 | Prize of gold |
| 741 | You'll never walk alone |
| | (see also Jean Sablon) |

**Mellomen, The**
(see Doris Day; Rosemary Clooney; Frankie Laine)

**Melodaires, The**
(See Lorrae Desmond)

**Melodeons, The**
| 242 | Sam's song |

**Melody Three, The**
| 570 | The man with the banjo (with Primo Scala and his Band) |

**Men About Town, The**
(see Kathran Field)

**Felix Mendelssohn and his Hawaiian Serenaders**
| 69 | Come back to Sorrento |
| 78 | Now is the hour (George Barclay and The Paradise Island Trio) |
| 126 | La vie en rose |
| 179 | A rose in a garden of weeds (George Barclay) |

**Men Of Song, The**
(see Joy Nichols)

**Johnny Mercer**
| 151 | Candy kisses (with The Starlighters) |
| 443 | Glow worm |
| | (see also Margaret Whiting and Johnny Mercer) |

**Len Mercer and his Magic Strings**
| 656 | Stars shine in your eyes |

**Tommy Mercer**
(see Ray Anthony and his Orchestra)

**Ethel Merman**
| 72 | I got the sun in the morning |

**Ethel Merman and Ray Bolger**
| 212 | I'd've baked a cake |
| 213 | I said my pajamas |
| 222 | Dearie |

**Ethel Merman and Dick Haymes**
| 506 | You're just in love |

**thel Merman and Ray Middleton**
77   They say it's wonderful
**al Merrall**
30   All through the day
    (see also Mantovani and his Orchestra; Ivor
    Moreton and Dave Kaye)
**ob Merrill**
874   Nairobi
**obert Merrill**
992   Gigi
**erry Macs, The**
9   Laughing on the outside
133   On a slow boat to China (with The
    Squadronaires dir. Jimmy Miller)
227   Two on a tandem
    (see also Donald Peers and The Merry Macs)
**erry Melody Makers, The**
116   Heartbreaker
117   I'm looking over a four-leaf clover
**.G.M. Studio Orchestra, The, conducted by**
**harles Wolcott**
680   Rock around the clock
**ichael Twins, The**
(see Frank Weir and his Orchestra)
**bby Mickleburgh's Bob Cats**
891   Who's sorry now?
941   Girl of my dreams
**ay Middleton**
93   The girl that I marry
    (see also Ethel Merman and Ray Middleton)
**mos Milburn and his Orchestra**
941   Girl of my dreams
**on Miles**
(see The Marlin Sisters and Don Miles)
**etty Miller**
727   Who are we? (with The Beryl Stott Chorus)
**huck Miller**
822   Bye bye love
**ary Miller**
391   From the time you say goodbye
455   Till I waltz again with you
460   I'm walking behind you
530   From here to eternity
564   Wanted
586   Hold my hand
591   The high and the mighty
564   The man from Laramie
566   The yellow rose of Texas (with The Beryl
    Stott Chorus)
591   The ballad of Davy Crockett
597   Robin Hood (with The Beryl Stott Chorus)
773   The Garden of Eden (with The Beryl Stott
    Chorus)
819   Love letters in the sand (with The Beryl
    Stott Chorus)
820   Wonderful, wonderful (with The Beryl
    Stott Chorus)
860   The story of my life (with The Beryl Stott
    Group)
863   Put a light in the window (with The Beryl
    Stott Group)
886   Lollipop (with The Beryl Stott Group)
894   On the street where you live (with The
    Beryl Stott Chorus)
**enn Miller and his Orchestra**
90   Peg o' my heart
**ene Miller**
(see Joe Loss and his Orchestra)

**Jimmy Miller**
(see The Squadronaires directed by Jimmy Miller)
**Mandy Miller**
430   Snowflakes
448   That doggie in the window
**Marcie Miller**
(see Ray Anthony and his Orchestra)
**Max Miller**
552   Friends and neighbours
**Mitch Miller and his Orchestra and Chorus**
244   Tzena tzena tzena
256   Autumn leaves
666   The yellow rose of Texas
714   Willie can
983   The children's marching song
**Suzi Miller**
532   My heart belongs to only you
549   From the vine came the grape (with The
    Squadronaires directed Ronnie Aldrich)
631   Tweedle-dee
671   Go on by
674   The banjo's back in town
**Suzi Miller and The Johnston Brothers**
528   Tennessee wig walk
544   Bimbo
608   Happy days and lonely nights
**Mill Girls, The**
(see Billy Cotton and his Band)
**Gary Mills**
1090   Seven little girls sitting in the back seat
**Mills Brothers, The**
21   You always hurt the one you love
32   Someday
39   Till then
40   Too many irons in the fire
100   When you were sweet sixteen (two
    recordings)
113   Oh! My achin' heart
226   Daddy's little girl
272   Nevertheless
372   By my life's companion
443   The glow worm
488   Say 'si si'
543   The Jones boy
676   Suddenly there's a valley
    (see also Al Jolson and The Mills Brothers)
**Sal Mineo**
824   Start movin'
**Carmen Miranda and The Andrews Sisters**
152   Cuanto le gusta
174   The wedding samba
**George Mitchell Choir, The**
255   We'll keep a welcome (with Don Lorusso –
    organ)
262   I leave my heart in an English garden (with
    Don Lorusso – organ)
    (see also Dick James; Stanley Black, his piano,
    and his Orchestra; Anne Shelton)
**Guy Mitchell**
274   Me and my imagination
277   My heart cries for you
285   The roving kind
295   Sparrow in the tree top
316   My truly, truly fair
317   Unless
318   A beggar in love
322   Christopher Columbus
334   Belle, Belle, my liberty Belle
348   Sweetheart of yesterday

354   There's always room at our house
368   We won't live in a castle
378   There's a pawnshop on the corner in
    Pittsburgh, Pennsylvania
398   The day of Jubilo
415   Feet up
446   She wears red feathers
463   Pretty little black-eyed Susie
497   Look at that girl
513   Chicka boom
523   Cloud lucky seven
541   The cuff of my shirt
562   A dime and a dollar
566   Bob's yer uncle
771   Singing the blues
783   Knee deep in the blues
804   Rock-a-Billy
832   In the middle of a dark, dark night
1093   Heartaches by the number
**Guy Mitchell and Mindy Carson**
434   That's a-why
**Guy Mitchell and Rosemary Clooney**
506   You're just in love
**Malcolm Mitchell Trio, The**
292   Rose, Rose, I love you
328   Shanghai
443   The glow worm
493   Let's walk that-a-way
522   Istanbul
543   The Jones boy
568   Cleo and me-o
**Shorty Mitchell**
818   All shook up
**Mitchell Boys' Choir, The**
(see Spike Jones and his City Slickers)
**Mitchell Maids, The**
(see Harry Dawson)
**Modernaires, The, with Paula Kelly**
622   Teach me tonight (with Georgie Auld –
    tenor sax)
    (see also Buddy Clark)
**Domenico Modugno**
929   Volare
942   Come prima
1016   Ciao ciao bambina
**Monotones, The**
904   The book of love
**Matt Monro**
773   The Garden of Eden
**Vaughn Monroe**
592   They were doin' the mambo
606   Mister Sandman
1043   The battle of New Orleans
**Vaughn Monroe and his Orchestra**
32   Someday (Vaughn Monroe and The Moon
    Men)
43   Anniversary song (Vaughn Monroe and
    Chorus)
118   Dance, ballerina, dance (Vaughn Monroe)
135   The Maharajah of Magador (Ziggy Talent)
147   Red roses for a blue lady (Vaughn Monroe
    and The Moon Men)
161   Riders in the sky (Vaughn Monroe and the
    Quartette)
191   Is it too late? (Vaughn Monroe and The
    Moon Maids)
198   Mule train (Vaughn Monroe and The Moon
    Men)
395   Faith (Vaughn Monroe)

495    Ruby (Vaughn Monroe and Chorus)
658    Cool water (Vaughn Monroe and The Sons of the Pioneers)

**Ricardo Montalban**
*(see Esther Williams and Ricardo Montalban)*

**Moonbeams, The**
*(see The Basil Kirchin Band)*

**Art Mooney Choir, The**
*(see Art Mooney and his Orchestra)*

**Art Mooney's Little Band**
488    Say 'si si' (Alan Foster and The Cloverleafs)

**Art Mooney and his Orchestra**
117    I'm looking over a four-leaf clover (Ensemble)
166    Beautiful eyes (Ensemble)
186    The hop-scotch polka (The Art Mooney Choir)
212    I'd've baked a cake (Betty Harris and The Art Mooney Choir)
235    Silver dollar (The Art Mooney Choir)
295    Sparrow in the tree top (Alan Foster)
303    Beautiful brown eyes (Alan Foster, Rosetta Shaw and The Art Mooney Choir)
379    Blacksmith blues (Shorty Long)
502    Flirtation waltz (The Cloverleafs)
527    The creep
673    Twenty tiny fingers (The Cloverleafs)
706    Memories of you (The Cloverleafs)

**Joe Mooney and his Quartet**
275    September song (Joe Mooney)

**Moon Maids, The**
*(see Vaughn Monroe and his Orchestra)*

**Moon Men, The**
*(see Vaughn Monroe and his Orchestra)*

**Phil Moore**
*(see Dorothy Dandridge)*

**Shelley Moore**
687    When you lose the one you love

**Ivor Moreton and Dave Kaye**
308    Ivory rag
350    Why worry (Val Merrall)

**Al Morgan**
199    Jealous heart
277    My heart cries for you (with The Keynotes)
349    Mistakes (with Frankie Froba and his Boys)
353    Sin

**George Morgan**
151    Candy kisses

**Jaye P. Morgan**
667    Have you ever been lonely?

**Jane Morgan**
479    April in Portugal
487    Say you're mine again
806    Around the world
967    The day the rains came
967    Le jour ou la pluie viendra
1008    If only I could live my life again
     *(see Roger Williams and Jane Morgan)*

**Mary Morgan**
704    Jimmy unknown

**Russ Morgan and his Orchestra**
2    Cruising down the river (The Skylarks)
33    It's all over now (Russ Morgan)
117    I'm looking over a four-leaf clover (with Milt Herth – organ, and The Ames Brothers and Ensemble)
123    So tired (Russ Morgan)
149    Put your shoes on, Lucy (Russ Morgan and The Rhythmaires)

154    Forever and ever (The Skylarks)
239    Sentimental me (Russ Morgan and The Morganaires)
261    Beloved, be faithful (The Morganaires)
280    Patricia (Russ Morgan)
290    Mockin' bird hill (Russ Morgan and The Gay Sisters)
316    My truly, truly fair (Russ Morgan and The Morganaires)
336    Longing for you (Russ Morgan and The Morganaires)
387    Dance me loose (Russ Morgan and The Morganaires)
420    Walkin' to Missouri (Russ Morgan and The Morganaires)
455    Till I waltz again with you (Russ Morgan and The Morganaires)
477    Tell me you're mine (Joan Elms)
478    Have you heard (Russ Morgan)
521    Oh! my papa (The Morganaires) (ftg Phil Capicotto – trumpet)
528    Tennessee wig walk (Betsy Gay)
563    Idle gossip (Juanita Crowley)
710    The poor people of Paris
746    Lay down your arms (Susy Goday and The Morganaires)
     *(see also Bing Crosby; Kenny Baker; Bob Eberly; Andrews Sisters)*

**Morganaires, The**
*(see Russ Morgan and his Orchestra)*

**Duncan Morison**
*(see Michael O'Duffy)*

**Patricia Morison**
291    So in love

**Dennis Morley**
*(see Woolf Phillips and his Orchestra)*

**Jeff Morley and his Orchestra**
503    The Melba waltz

**Morris and Mitch**
781    Don't you rock me, daddy-o
797    Cumberland Gap
944    Bird dog

**Buddy Morrow and his Orchestra**
328    Shanghai (Frankie Lester and Quartette)
452    Got you on my mind (Frank Lester and The Quartet)
606    Mister Sandman (vocal quartet)

**Doretta Morrow and Richard Kiley**
633    Stranger in paradise

**Dorothy Morrow Ensemble, The**
124    My happiness

**Phil Morrow and his Music**
265    The thing (Charles Forsythe and The Beaux and The Belles)
268    Flying saucer (Jennifer and The Beaux and The Belles)
282    Tipperary samba

**Ella Mae Morse**
379    Blacksmith blues
494    Is it any wonder?
663    Love me or leave me
677    Seventeen
775    Razzle dazzle

**Art Morton and Evelyn Bell Knightingales**
245    Ashes of roses

**Jelly Roll Morton's New Orleans Jazz Band**
129    Ballin' the jack

**Maureen Morton**
*(see Jack Simpson and his Sextet)*

**Peter Morton**
532    My heart belongs to only you
     *(see also Jack Simpson and his Sextet)*

**Most Brothers, The**
883    Whole lotta woman

**Roger King Mozian (trumpet) and his Orchestr**
796    Mangos
825    Fire down below

**Mudlarks, The**
886    Lollipop
904    The book of love
950    There's never been a night
1051    Waterloo

**Mullan Sisters, The**
*(see Jack Berch and The Mullan Sisters)*

**Gerry Mulligan Quartet, The, with Chet Baker**
663    Love me or leave me

**Betty Mulliner**
*(see Gordon Jenkins and his Orchestra)*

**Hal Munro**
862    Jailhouse rock
879    Don't
899    Wear my ring
1013    C'mon everybody
1026    It's late
1033    Where were you (on our wedding day?)
1034    Dream lover

**Patrice Munsel**
503    The Melba waltz

**Jerry Murad's Harmonicats**
455    Till I waltz again with you

**Delia Murphy**
238    If I were a blackbird (with Arthur Darley – guitar)

**Rose Murphy**
223    Me and my shadow
304    Girls were made to take care of boys
335    Blow out the candle
453    Little red monkey

**Turk Murphy and his Band**
711    The Theme from 'The Threepenny Opera'

**Roy Stuart Murray**
395    Faith

**Ruby Murray**
604    Heartbeat
608    Happy days and lonely nights
613    Softly softly
619    Let me go, lover
627    If anyone finds this, I love you (with Anne Warren)
647    Evermore
665    I'll come when you call
682    The very first Christmas of all
744    You are my first love
762    True love (with The Bill Shepherd Chorus)
792    Heart (with The Bill Shepherd Chorus)
807    Mr Wonderful
826    Scarlet ribbons
951    Little one
965    Real love
1029    Goodbye, Jimmy, goodbye

**Naturals, The**
607    The finger of suspicion
     *(see also Billy Fields and The Naturals)*

**Ricky Nelson**
939    Poor little fool
954    Someday
1023    Never be anyone else but you
1026    It's late

278

1084 Just a little too much

**Anthony Newley**
1027 I've waited so long
1035 Personality

**New Mayfair Dance Orchestra, The**
37 Marlene (Sam Browne)
131 The cuckoo waltz

**Stan Newsome**
*(see Mantovani and his Orchestra)*

**Carole Newton**
*(see Norrie Paramor and his Ragmen)*

**Joy Nichols**
217 Cherry stones
357 The little white cloud that cried (with The Men of Song)
456 I talk to the trees
641 Don't worry
  *(see also Joy Nichols and Benny Lee; Wally Peterson and Joy Nichols; Joy Nichols, Dick Bentley and Jimmy Edwards)*

**Joy Nichols, Dick Bentley and Jimmy Edwards**
453 Little red monkey

**Joy Nichols and Benny Lee**
138 On the 5.45 (with The Keynotes)
146 A strawberry moon (with The Keynotes)

**Red Nichols and his Five Pennies**
90 Peg o' my heart

**Penny Nicholls (also known as Nichols)**
353 Sin
458 I'd love to fall asleep
589 This ole house
648 The Crazy Otto rag
674 The banjo's back in town
718 Don't ring-a da bell
725 Hot diggity
776 I dreamed
783 Knee deep in the blues

**Penny Nicholls and The Canadians**
708 The rock and roll waltz

**Penny Nicholls and The Four-in-a-Chord**
604 Heartbeat
619 Let me go, lover

**Nigerian Union Rhythm Group, The**
959/960 Tom Dooley

**Nina and Frederik**
846 Mary's boy child
1079 Little donkey

**Lisa Noble**
891 Who's sorry now?

**Ray Noble and his Orchestra**
351 I want to be near you (The Noblemen)

**Noble & King**
471 Hold me

**Noblemen, The**
*(see Ray Noble and his Orchestra)*

**Dick Noel**
737 The birds and the bees
  *(see also Ray Anthony and his Orchestra)*

**Dick Noel Singers, The**
*(see Rusty Draper)*

**Lucky Noguez**
1016 Ciao ciao bambina

**Len Nordene**
*(see Billy Vaughn and his Orchestra)*

**Monty Norman**
421 You belong to me
431 Takes two to tango
509 Answer me
530 From here to eternity

547 Secret love
624 Give me the right
685 The shifting, whispering sands (with Chorus)
773 The Garden of Eden

**Norman Quartet, The**
*(see Don Lang and his Frantic Five)*

**Loulie Jean Normon**
*(see Rush Adams)*

**Norrie's Novelties**
*(see Marie Benson)*

**Obernkirchen Children's Choir, The, conducted by Frederick W. Moller**
539 The happy wanderer

**Helen O'Connell**
302 Would I love you
310 The loveliest night of the year
361 Slow coach
375 Any time
384 Be anything
417 Zing a little zong

**Donald O'Connor**
460 I'm walking behind you

**Johnny O'Connor**
615 A blossom fell
624 Give me the right
  *(see also Bobby Limb and his Orchestra)*

**Pat O'Connor**
*(see Billy Butterfield and his Orchestra)*

**Anita O'Day**
271 The Tennessee waltz (with The All-Stars)
311 I apologise

**Pat O'Day**
640 Earth angel

**Michael O'Duffy**
109 Galway Bay (with Duncan Morison – piano)
238 If I were a blackbird

**Jack O'Hagan**
*(see Roy Fox and his Band)*

**Patrick O'Hagan**
194 Down in the glen

**Michael O'Higgins**
109 Galway Bay

**Tessie O'Shea**
25 The 'Ampstead way
27 Let it be soon

**Kathran Oldfield**
249 Count every star
  *(also known as Kathran Field – see also under this name)*

**Johnny Oliver**
709 Chain gang

**Sy Oliver and his Orchestra**
102 Civilisation (Sy Oliver)
251 Bibbidi bobbidi boo (The Aristokats and Ensemble)
254 A dream is a wish your heart makes (Jack Haskell and The Aristokats)
273 Just the way you are (Ralph Young, The Three Beaux and a Peep)
379 Blacksmith blues (Trudy Richards)

**Eileen Orchard**
*(see Lou Preager and his Orchestra)*

**Orioles, The**
471 Hold me, thrill me, kiss me
512 Crying in the chapel

**Cyril Ornadel and his Orchestra**
748 Autumn concerto

**Jon Orvelle**
469 Wild horses

**Kid Ory's Creole Band**
*(see The Castle Jazz Band)*

**Tony Osborne and his Orchestra**
633 Stranger in paradise (Reg Gray)
901 The secret of happiness
1054 The windows of Paris

**Johnny Otis and his Orchestra**
*(see Marie Adams)*

**Johnny Otis Show, The**
853 Ma (he's making eyes at me) (Marie Adams and The Three Tons of Joy)

**Reg Owen and his Orchestra**
1019 Manhattan spiritual

**Jack Owens**
199 Jealous heart

**Oran 'Hot Lips' Page**
*(see Pearl Bailey and Hot Lips Page)*

**Jill Page**
*(see Syd Dean and his Band)*

**Larry Page**
824 Start movin'
840 That'll be the day

**Patti Page**
264 All my love
271 The Tennessee waltz
290 Mockin' bird hill
369 And so to sleep again
421 You belong to me
428 I went to your wedding
444 Why don't you believe me?
448 That doggie in the window
519 Where did my snowman go?
534 Changing partners
554 Cross over the bridge
599 I can't tell a waltz from a tango
602 The Mama doll song
619 Let me go, lover
728 Too young to go steady
747 Born to be with you
926 Left right out of your heart

**Vivien Paget**
*(see Frank Weir and his Orchestra)*

**Jimmy Palmer and his Orchestra**
488 Say 'si si' (Tiny McDaniel and Ensemble)

**Paradise Island Trio, The**
*(see Felix Mendelssohn and his Hawaiian Serenaders)*

**Parakeets, The**
*(see Helen Van Capellen)*

**Norrie Paramor and his Orchestra**
371 At last! At last!
410 The Isle of Innisfree
472 The Song from Moulin Rouge
479 April in Portugal
503 The Melba waltz
540 The Luxembourg polka
591 The high and the mighty
616 Majorca
710 The poor people of Paris
711 The Theme from 'The Threepenny Opera'
748 Autumn concerto
835 Mandolin serenade
895 I could have danced all night (with Chorus)
942 Come prima

**Norrie Paramor and his Ragmen**
308 Ivory rag
327 The black note serenade (Carole Newton)
  *(see also Norrie's Novelties)*

**Norrie Paramor and his Rhythm**
293    Saloon bar rag
**John Paris**
483    The Queen of Tonga (with The Ebonaires)
**Eddie Parker**
755    Love me as though there were no tomorrow
**Fess Parker**
691    The ballad of Davy Crockett
**Jimmy Parkinson**
712    The great pretender
719    You can't be true to two (with The Coronets)
735    Walk hand in hand (with The Bill Shepherd Chorus)
757    In the middle of the house
802    Round and round
**Larry Parks**
(see Betty Garrett and Larry Parks)
**Parlophone Pops Orchestra, The, conducted by Ron Goodwin**
680    Rock around the clock
734    Whatever will be, will be
746    Lay down your arms
**Jack Parnell and his Music Makers**
527    The creep (The Sapphires)
**Jack Parnell and his Orchestra**
526    Blowing wild (Dennis Hale)
581    A sky-blue shirt and a rainbow tie (Jack Parnell)
617    Shake rattle and roll (Jack Parnell and The Crackerjacks)
692    Love and marriage
693    Sixteen tons (Jack Parnell)
**Jack Parnell**
1037    Kansas City
**Mark Pasquin**
685    The shifting, whispering sands (with The Rita Williams Singers)
**Johnny Pate Quintet, The**
877    The swinging shepherd blues (with Lennie Druss – flute)
**Patience and Prudence**
980    Tom Thumb's tune
**Betty Paul**
355    Domino
**Bunny Paul**
553    Such a night
**Les Paul**
403    Meet Mister Callaghan
711    Moritat – from 'The Threepenny Opera'
**Les Paul Trio, The**
(see Bing Crosby)
**Les Paul and Mary Ford**
271    The Tennessee waltz
290    Mockin' bird hill
440    Take me in your arms and hold me
501    Vaya con Dios
606    Mister Sandman
609    White Christmas
**Paulette Sisters, The**
643    Dreamboat
**Benny Payne**
(see Billy Daniels)
**Bob & Alf Pearson**
146    A strawberry Moon
147    Red roses for a blue lady
154    Forever and ever
164    Careless hands
323    Tulips and heather

449    In a golden coach
464    Celebration rag
**Jan Peerce**
329    Because of you
820    Wonderful, wonderful
**Donald Peers**
5    I can't begin to tell you
88    Bow bells (with Bob Farnon and his Orchestra)
137    Far away places
138    On the 5.45
139    Twelfth Street rag
141    Powder your face with sunshine
142    In a shady nook
143    Lavender blue
146    A strawberry moon
155    It happened in Adano
159    Clancy lowered the boom
169    Everywhere you go
179    A rose in a garden of weeds
187    The zither melody
188    I'll string along with you
194    Down in the glen
196    The last mile home
197    Dear hearts and gentle people
204    Out of a clear blue sky
205    Music! Music! Music!
209    Chattanoogie shoe-shine boy
212    I'd've baked a cake
216    Enjoy yourself (with The Cherokeys)
220    Oh, you sweet one
221    Let's do it again (with The Cherokeys)
222    Dearie
225    I remember the cornfields
226    Daddy's little girl (with The Cherokeys)
252    Rudolph, the red-nosed reindeer (with Hattie Jacques)
261    Beloved, be faithful
274    Me and my imagination
290    Mockin' bird hill
343    I wish I wuz
349    Mistakes (with Quartette)
350    Why worry
354    There's always room at our house
368    We won't live in a castle
389    Lullaby of Broadway (with Don Phillips – piano)
446    She wears red feathers (with The Kordites)
449    In a golden coach
464    Celebration rag
480    Your cheatin' heart
494    Is it any wonder?
534    Changing partners
824    Start movin'
881    Oh-oh, I'm falling in love again
**Donald Peers and The Merry Macs**
271    The Tennessee waltz
277    My heart cries for you
**Penguins, The**
640    Earth angel
**People of Hoxton, The**
(see Lily Strange and the People of Hoxton)
**Peppino of Capri Quintet, The**
1016    Ciao ciao bambina
**Carl Perkins**
732    Blue suede shoes
**Mal Perry**
886    Lollipop
994    Willingly

**Ray Peterson**
1050    The wonder of you
**Wally Peterson and Joy Nichols**
394    Trust in me
**Peterson Brothers, The**
214    My foolish heart (with Barry Snow – organ)
**Frank Petty Trio, The**
346    The black and white rag
352    Down yonder
466    Side by side (ftg Mike Di Napoli – piano)
891    Who's sorry now? (ftg Mike Di Napoli – piano)
**Phantoms, The**
(see Johnny Brandon)
**Confrey Phillips**
677    Seventeen
692    Love and marriage
**Don Phillips**
(see Donald Peers)
**Phil Phillips**
(see The London Piano Accordeon Band)
**Phil Phillips with The Twilights**
1074    Sea of love
**Sid Phillips and his Band**
203    Is it true what they say about Dixie?
207    Best of all (The Tanner Sisters)
218    The old piano roll blues (The Tanner Sisters)
235    Silver dollar (Johnnie Eager)
244    Tzena tzena tzena (Johnnie Eager and The Tanner Sisters)
272    Nevertheless (Geraldine Farrar)
285    The roving kind (Johnnie Eager, Geraldine Farrar and The Tanner Sisters)
287    Red silken stockings (Betty Driver)
307    On top of Old Smokey (Johnnie Eager and The Song Pedlars)
308    Ivory rag (Johnnie Eager)
327    The black note serenade (Johnnie Eager)
328    Shanghai (Johnnie Eager)
352    Down yonder (Johnnie Eager)
372    Be my life's companion (Denny Dennis)
379    Blacksmith blues (Denny Dennis)
399    Didja ever (Denny Dennis)
403    Meet Mister Callaghan
404    Sugarbush (Denny Dennis and Chorus)
420    Walkin' to Missouri (Denny Dennis)
551    Make love to me
706    Memories of you
752    Rockin' thru' the rye
891    Who's sorry now?
**Teddy Phillips and his Orchestra**
272    Nevertheless (Billy Sagonn)
**Woolf Phillips and his Orchestra**
595    Your heart, my heart (Dennis Morley)
601    Count your blessings instead of sheep (Jean, Jo, Joy & Penny)
**Edith Piaf**
126    La vie en rose
342    If you go (Si tu partais)
517    Hymne d'amour
**Pianotones, The**
(see The Johnston Brothers; The King's Men)
**Pied Pipers, The**
124    My happiness
**Webb Pierce**
822    Bye bye love
**Dick Pike**
(see Ruby Wright)

**Pilgrim, The**
454 Oh, happy day
**Jacques Pils**
156 Clopin clopant
**Sir Hubert Pimm**
359 I wanna say hello (with Ellen Sutton)
658 Cool water blues
**Pinafores, The**
*(see Gene Autry)*
**Pinky & Perky**
960 Tom Dooley
995 Does your chewing gum lose its flavour on the bedpost overnight?
**Buddy Pipp's Highlifers**
583 Sway
**Anzio Pizza**
*(see Mickey Katz and his Orchestra)*
**Eddie Platt and his Orchestra**
882 Tequila
**Platters, The**
705 Only you
712 The great pretender
764 My prayer
903 Twilight time
990 Smoke gets in your eyes
**Sonny Player**
513 Chicka boom (with The Batsmen)
**Jack Pleis and his Orchestra**
256 Autumn leaves (Bob Houston and Chorus)
266 The petite waltz
**Roy Plummer**
*(see Frank Chacksfield and his Orchestra)*
**Poni-Tails, The**
940 Born too late
**Ginnie Powell**
*(see Harry James and his Orchestra)*
**Jane Powell**
313 Too late now
524 Hello young lovers
762 True love
**Duffy Power**
1034 Dream lover
**Perez 'Prez' Prado and his Orchestra**
591 The high and the mighty
630 Cherry pink and apple blossom white (Billy Regis – trumpet)
918 Patricia
**Lou Preager and his Charm of the Waltz Orchestra**
336 Longing for you (Paul Rich)
339 Love's roundabout
**Lou Preager and his Orchestra**
2 Cruising down the river (Paul Rich)
10 Let bygones be bygones (Rita Williams)
17 Down in the valley (Rita Williams)
19 Do you love me? (Rita Carr)
32 Someday (Paul Rich)
33 It's all over now (Rita Williams)
38 Pretending (Rita Williams)
40 Too many irons in the fire (Paul Rich)
42 The old lamplighter (Paul Rich)
47 May I call you sweetheart? (Paul Rich)
54 How lucky you are (Rita Williams)
55 The world belongs to you, little man (Rita Williams)
58 Hi-jig-a-jig (Paul Rich)
59 When China boy meets China girl (Rita Williams)
62 Goodnight, you little rascal, you (Rita Williams)

63 You went away and left me (Paul Rich)
81 The little old mill (Paul Rich)
85 My first love, my last love for always (Paul Rich)
87 Apple blossom wedding (Paul Rich)
88 Bow Bells (Paul Rich)
90 Peg o' my heart (The Sunnysiders)
98 The shoemaker's serenade (Eileen Orchard)
113 Oh! My achin' heart (Paul Rich)
118 Dance, ballerina, dance (Paul Rich)
119 Toolie oolie doolie (Rusty Hurren)
120 Woody Woodpecker (Eileen Orchard)
122 Rambling Rose (Paul Rich)
129 Ballin' the jack (Paul Rich and The Sunnysiders)
138 On the 5.45 (Rusty Hurren)
148 The wedding of Lilli Marlene (Paul Rich)
163 Brush those tears from your eyes (Rusty Hurren)
174 The wedding samba
176 Too-whit! Too-whoo! (Rusty Hurren and The Sun Spots)
187 The Harry Lime theme
192 Song of Capri (Paul Rich)
208 The French can-can polka (The Sun Spots)
227 Two on a tandem (Paul Rich)
230 The night the floor fell in (Paul Rich)
533 I see the moon (The Ragpickers)
**Elvis Presley**
732 Blue suede shoes
818 All shook up (with The Jordanaires)
862 Jailhouse rock
879 Don't (with The Jordanaires)
899 Wear my ring around your neck (with The Jordanaires)
916 Hard headed woman (with The Jordanaires)
946 King Creole (with The Jordanaires)
981 I got stung
986 One night
1015 A fool such as I (with The Jordanaires)
1018 I need your love tonight (with The Jordanaires)
1052 A big hunk o' love (with The Jordanaires)
1059 My wish came true (with The Jordanaires)
**Cecil Pressling**
*(see Sidney Simone and his Orchestra)*
**Mike Preston**
1081 Mr Blue
**Andre Previn**
338 Lullaby of Broadway
**Lloyd Price**
1017 Stagger Lee
1033 Where were you (on our wedding day)?
1035 Personality
**Rikki Price**
959/960 Tom Dooley
1081 Mr Blue
**Louis Prima and his Orchestra**
539 The happy wanderer (Louis Prima)
**Harry Prime**
*(see Ralph Flanagan and his Orchestra)*
**Arthur Prysock**
353 Sin
377 Wheel of fortune
**Danny Purches**
621 Tomorrow
651 Mama
**Reginald Pursglove and his Music Makers**
1 Bless you

21 You always hurt the one you love
**Quads, The**
*(see The Squadronaires directed by Jimmy Miller)*
**Queen's Hall Light Orchestra, The, conducted by Sidney Torch**
192 Song of Capri
**Quintones, The**
*(see Russ Case and his Orchestra; Johnny Desmond)*
**Oscar Rabin and his Band with Harry Davis or David Ede**
85 My first love, my last love for always (Diane)
89 How are things in Glocca Morra? (Bob Dale)
94 I wonder who's kissing her now (Bob Dale)
110 The wishing waltz
113 Oh! My achin' heart (Bob Dale)
119 Toolie oolie doolie (Diane)
121 You can't be true, dear (Bob Dale)
136 A little bird told me (Marion Davis)
137 Far away places (Bob Dale)
149 Put your shoes on, Lucy (Marion Davis)
171 Leicester Square rag
181 You're breaking my heart (Marjorie Daw)
199 Jealous heart (Marjorie Daw and Marion Davis)
201 Some day my heart will awake
240 Have I told you lately that I love you? (Marion Davis and Marjorie Daw)
242 Sam's song (David Ede)
243 Mona Lisa (Dennis Hale)
280 Patricia (Dennis Hale and the David Ede Ensemble)
301 List'nin' to the green grass grow (Dennis Hale and the David Ede Ensemble)
336 Longing for you (Patti Forbes and Marjorie Daw)
352 Down yonder (David Ede and Ensemble)
379 Blacksmith blues (Patti Forbes)
**Steve Race**
291 So in love
**Steve Race and The Tic-Tac Men**
753 Glendora
**Radio Revellers, The**
56 Open the door, Richard
74 Dear old Donegal
90 Peg o' my heart
98 The shoemaker's serenade
137 Far away places
168 Blue ribbon gal
197 Dear hearts and gentle people
208 The French can can polka
217 Cherry stones
224 Choo'n gum
301 List'nin' to the green grass grow
321 Sweet violets
330 I love the sunshine of your smile
414 Raindrops
521 Oh! my papa
522 Istanbul
531 Don't ever leave me
542 Bell bottom blues
686 Arrivederci darling
*(see also Anthony Steel and The Radio Revellers; The Radio Revellers and Geraldo and his Orchestra; Petula Clark and The Radio Revellers)*
**Radio Revellers, The, and Geraldo and his Orchestra**
361 Slow coach

281

**Jackie Rae**
942    More than ever
**Lynette Rae**
(see Benny Lee and Lynette Rae)
**Ragpickers, The**
(see Lou Preager and his Orchestra)
**Marvin Rainwater**
883    Whole lotta woman
**John Raitt**
424    Because you're mine
      (see also Jan Clayton and John Raitt)
**Ramblers, The**
(see Perry Como)
**Thurl Ravenscroft**
(see Rosemary Clooney)
**Rawicz & Landauer**
266    The petite waltz
**Annita Ray**
772    A letter to a soldier
**Johnnie Ray**
305    With these hands
357    The little white cloud that cried (with The
      Four Lads)
365    Cry
373    Please Mr Sun (with The Four Lads)
401    Walkin' my baby back home
422    Faith can move mountains (w. The Four Lads)
553    Such a night
612    Papa loves mambo
669    Hernando's hideaway
670    Hey there
756    Just walking in the rain
793    Look homeward angel
810    Yes tonight, Josephine
891    Who's sorry now?
1024    I miss you so
**Ted Ray and Kitty Bluett**
222    Dearie
**Tony Raymond**
1071    Broken-hearted melody
**Ray-O-Vacs, The**
239    Sentimental me (Lester Harris)
**Tim Reardon**
(see Jan Garber and his Orchestra)
**Gene Redd and The Globetrotters**
1086    Red River Valley rock
**Jim Reeves**
544    Bimbo
**Regalaires, The**
(see Danny Kaye)
**Joan Regan**
455    Till I waltz again with you
550    Someone else's roses
574    Jilted
582    Wait for me, darling (with The Johnston
      Brothers)
587    If I give my heart to you
589    This ole house (with The Keynotes)
623    Prize of gold
692    Love and marriage
820    Wonderful, wonderful
880    I may never pass this way again
1006    May you always
      (see also Joan Regan and The Squadronaires;
      Dickie Valentine and Joan Regan; Rusty and
      Joan Regan)
**Joan Regan and The Squadronaires directed by
Ronnie Aldrich**
516    Ricochet

**Rusty and Joan Regan**
629    Open up your heart
**Regent Ballroom Orchestra, The**
550    Someone else's roses
555    The shadow waltz
558    The little shoemaker
564    Wanted
569    Cara mia
573    The story of Tina
581    A sky-blue shirt and a rainbow tie
587    If I give my heart to you
593    I love Paris
596    No one but you
602    The Mama Doll song
606    Mister Sandman
607    The finger of suspicion
613    Softly softly
615    A blossom fell
619    Let me go, lover
664    The man from Laramie
666    The yellow rose of Texas
696    Young and foolish
700    Memories are made of this
701    It's almost tomorrow
704    Jimmy unknown
**Billy Regis**
(see Perez Prado and his Orchestra)
**Don Reid**
(see Enric Madriguera and his Orchestra)
**Peggy Reid**
44    The stars will remember
63    You went away and left me
82    Guilty
**Tommy Reilly**
591    The high and the mighty
**Joe Reisman and his Orchestra and Chorus**
697    Robin Hood
**Leo Reisman and his Orchestra**
234    If I loved you (Marshall Young)
**Ken Remo**
514    You you you
**Maria Remusat**
711    The Theme from 'The Threepenny Opera'
**Renato**
479    Coimbra
**Line Renaud**
447    The love of my life
458    I'd love to fall asleep
472    The song from the Moulin Rouge
479    April in Portugal
      (see also Dean Martin and Line Renaud)
**Henri Rene and his Orchestra**
461    Pretend (Franz Dietchmann – zither)
472    Song from Moulin Rouge (Alvy West – sax)
**Don Rennie**
687    When you lose the one you love
727    Who are we?
**Teddy Reno**
1016    Ciao ciao bambina
**Alvino Rey**
187    The Harry Lime theme
**Monte Rey**
28    Sweetheart, we'll never grow old
44    The stars will remember
61    Tell me, Marianne
69    Torna a Surriento
75    Down the old Spanish trail
85    My first love, my last love for always
95    Tree in the meadow

125    When you're in love
192    Song of Capri
195    Why is it?
240    Have I told you lately that I love you?
**Debbie Reynolds**
695    The tender trap
831    Tammy
927    Hillside in Scotland
**Debbie Reynolds and Carleton Carpenter**
399    Didja ever
**Jody Reynolds**
914    Endless sleep
**Rhythmaires, The**
(see Bing Crosby; Russ Morgan and his Orchestra)
**Rhythmettes, The**
705    Only you
985    I'll be with you in apple blossom time
**Paul Rich**
793    Look homeward angel
811    A white sport coat
850    My special angel
858    Peggy Sue
859    Oh boy
867    At the hop
871    You are my destiny
883    Whole lotta woman
884    Maybe baby
885    Le dee dah
894    On the street where you live
902    Witch doctor
904    The book of love
905    All I have to do is dream
909    The purple people eater
912    The only man on the island
914    Endless sleep
916    Hard headed woman
939    Poor little fool
943    A certain smile
944    Bird dog
989    The wonderful secret of love
990    Smoke gets in your eyes
991    Problems
995    Does your chewing gum lose its flavour on
      the bedpost overnight?
1010    Venus
1017    Stagger Lee
1027    I've waited so long
1032    I go ape
1039    Poor Jenny
1040    Take a message to Mary
1043    The battle of New Orleans
1052    A bIg hunk o' love
1066    Mona Lisa
1070    'Til I kissed you
1082    Makin' love
1093    Heartaches by the number
1097    The little white bull
      (see also Lou Preager and his Orchestra)
**Cliff Richard**
949    Move it (with The Drifters)
973    High class baby (with The Drifters)
1031    Mean streak (with The Drifters)
1048    Living doll (with The Drifters)
1077    Dynamite (with The Shadows)
1078    Travellin' light (with The Shadows)
**Carole Richards**
(see Bing Crosby and Carole Richards)
**John Richards**
842    Let me be loved

**Trudy Richards**
485   The breeze
     *(see also Sy Oliver and his Orchestra)*
**Robin Richmond**
427   Ecstasy
527   The creep
**Riddelle Singers, The**
*(see Ronnie Hilton)*
**Nelson Riddle and his Orchestra**
555   Shadow waltz
646   The pendulum song
697   Robin Hood (with vocal group)
929   Volare (ftg Plas Johnson – tenor sax)
**Jackie Riggs**
712   The great pretender
**Shane Rimmer**
1069   The three bells (with The Spinners)
**Elizabeth Rinker**
*(see Gordon Jenkins and his Orchestra)*
**Rita & Joyce**
*(see Billy Cotton and his Band)*
**Tex Ritter**
164   Careless hands
240   Have I told you lately that I love you?
392   High noon (two recordings)
733   Wayward wind
**Don Rivers**
*(see Joe Loss and his Orchestra)*
**Marty Robbins**
811   A white sport coat
860   The story of my life
896   Stairway of love
**Ray Robbins and his Orchestra**
251   Bibbidi bobbidi boo (Ray Robbins)
**Vincent Roberto**
445   Hi-Lili, Hi-Lo
**Andy Roberts**
*(see The Sauter-Finegan Orchestra)*
**Bette Roberts**
*(see Paul Adam and his Mayfair Music)*
**Joan Roberts**
*(see Alfred Drake and Joan Roberts)*
**Don Robertson**
726   The happy whistler
**Lou Ella Robertson**
299   May Kway O May Kway (with The Wanderers)
**Ivo Robic**
1072   Morgen
**Sylvia Robin and Tudor Evans**
194   Down in the glen
**Floyd Robinson**
1082   Makin' love
**Luckie Robinson**
362   Unforgettable
**Sugar 'Chile' Robinson**
252   Rudolph, the red-nosed reindeer
**George Rock**
*(see Spike Jones and his City Slickers)*
**Jimmie Rodgers**
855   Kisses sweeter than wine
881   Oh-oh, I'm falling in love again
**Don Rodney**
*(see Guy Lombardo and his Royal Canadians)*
**Red Rodney New Stars, The**
990   Smoke gets in your eyes
**Eric Rogers and his Music**
980   Tom Thumb's tune

**Eric Rogers Trio, The**
711   The Theme from 'The Threepenny Opera'
**Roy Rogers**
75   Down the old Spanish trail
**Tommy Rogers and his Ballroom Orchestra directed by Harry Gold**
657   Learnin' the blues
667   Have you ever been lonely?
669   Hernando's hideaway
707   My September love
715   Cookie
891   Who's sorry now?
**Ronald & Ruby**
886   Lollipop
**Ronnie Ronalde**
111   The dream of Olwen
125   When you're in love
177   The windmill song (with vocal quartet)
238   If I were a blackbird
262   I leave my heart in an English garden
290   Mockin' bird hill
419   Forget-me-not
465   I believe
691   The ballad of Davy Crockett
697   Robin Hood
726   The happy whistler
**Don Rondo**
760   Two different worlds
838   White silver sands
**Chick Rooster and The Barnyarders**
174   The wedding samba
**John Rorke with The London Community Singers conducted by Glyn Jones**
148   The wedding of Lilli Marlene
175   Say goodnight but not goodbye
255   We'll keep a welcome
**Edmundo Ros and his Orchestra**
174   The wedding samba (Edmundo Ros)
244   Tzena tzena tzena (Edmundo Ros)
406   Delicado
427   Ecstasy
456   I talk to the trees (Edmundo Ros)
479   Coimbra
479   April in Portugal
483   The Queen of Tonga (Edmundo Ros and The Ros-Childs)
522   Istanbul (Edmundo Ros and The Johnston Brothers)
526   Blowing wind (Edmundo Ros and The Johnston Brothers)
630   Cherry pink and apple blossom white
693   Sixteen tons (Edmundo Ros)
697   Robin Hood (Edmundo Ros)
718   Don't ring-a da bell (Edmundo Ros)
724   Mister Cuckoo (Edmundo Ros)
872   The Pansy
**Edmundo Ros and his Rumba Band**
72   I got the sun in the morning
73   A rainy night in Rio (Edmundo Ros and Ensemble)
91   South America, take it away (Edmundo Ros)
92   The coffee song (Edmundo Ros)
132   Cuanto le gusta (Edmundo Ros)
135   The Maharajah of Magador (Edmundo Ros)
193   The Scottish samba (Edmundo Ros)
282   Tipperary samba (Edmundo Ros)
376   A-round the corner (Edmundo Ros)
386   Blue tango

488   Say 'si si' (Edmundo Ros)
**Ros-Childs, The**
*(see Edmundo Ros and his Orchestra)*
**David Rose and his Orchestra**
228   Bewitched
275   September song
535   Tenderly
656   Stars shine in your eyes
675   Love is a many-splendoured thing
717   No other love (ftg Danny Welton – harmonica)
731   Serenade
774   Friendly persuasion
**Rosemary June**
985   I'll be with you in apple blossom time
1091   The village of St Bernadette
**Jan Rosol**
339   Love's roundabout
573   The story of Tina
**Jan Rosol and Gwen Campbell**
593   I love Paris
**Annie Ross**
705   Only you
**David Ross**
749   More
753   Glendora
758   Green door
768   Happiness Street
771   Singing the blues
773   The Garden of Eden
782   Young love
784   Don't forbid me
801   Butterfly
803   Ninety nine ways
819   Love letters in the sand
827   Last train to San Fernando
828   Diana
834   Wanderin' eyes
844   Be my girl
849   Wake up, little Susie
851   He's got the whole world in his hands
852   I love you, baby
**Gene Ross**
914   Endless sleep
**Patricia Rossborough**
*(see Robinson Cleaver and Patricia Rossborough)*
**Derek Roy**
869   Liechtensteiner polka
     *(see also Eve Boswell and Derek Roy)*
**Harry Roy and his Band**
82   Guilty (Eve Lombard)
139   Twelfth Street rag
171   Leicester Square rag (two recordings)
279   Play a simple melody (Johnny Green and The Keynotes)
293   Saloon bar rag (Harry Roy)
373   Please Mr Sun
502   Flirtation waltz
690   The little Laplander
**Lee Roy and his Band**
527   The creep
**Royal Artillery Band, Woolwich, The**
443   The glow worm idyll
**Lita Roza**
341   Allentown Jail (with Ted Heath and his Music)
392   High noon
412   Half as much
420   Walkin' to Missouri (with vocal group)

428     I went to your wedding
444     Why don't you believe me
445     Hi-Lili, Hi-Lo
448     That doggie in the window
478     Have you heard
484     Seven lonely days (with The Johnston Brothers)
525     Ebb tide (with Ted Heath and his Music)
534     Changing partners
547     Secret love
551     Make love to me (with Ted Heath and his Music)
560     Young at heart
563     Idle gossip
578     Smile
602     The Mama doll song
604     Heartbeat
619     Let me go, lover
621     Tomorrow
669     Hernando's hideaway
670     Hey there
704     Jimmy unknown
728     Too young to go steady
895     I could have danced all night
927     Hillside in Scotland
929     Nel blu dipinto di blu (with The Beryl Stott Chorus)
      (see also Ted Heath and his Music)

**Andy Russell**
943     A certain smile
**Connie Russell**
596     No one but you
789     All of you
**Frisco Ruston**
(see Gordon Jenkins and his Orchestra)
**Marion Ryan**
725     Hot diggity
736     Why do fools fall in love?
796     Mangos
807     Mr Wonderful (with The Beryl Stott Chorus)
861     Love me forever (with The Beryl Stott Chorus)
881     Oh-oh, I'm falling in love again (with The Beryl Stott Group)
896     Stairway of love (with The Beryl Stott Group)
907     I need you (with The Beryl Stott Group)
947     The world goes around and around
1001    Wait for me (with The Beryl Stott Chorus)
**Bill St Claire**
(see Jan Garber and his Orchestra)
**Jean Sablon**
214     My foolish heart
215     C'est si bon
472     The song from Moulin Rouge (with The Melachrino Strings)
**Billy Sagonn**
(see Teddy Phillips and his Orchestra)
**Rino Salviati**
686     Arrivederci Roma
**Michael Sammes Singers, The**
996     The little drummer boy
      (see also Jimmy Young; Alma Cogan; Malcolm Vaughan; Ronnie Hilton; Frank Cordell and his Orchestra; Kathie Kay; Michael Flanders)
**Felicia Sanders**
659     Blue star
      (see also Percy Faith and his Orchestra)

**Arthur Sandford**
(see Philip Green and his Orchestra)
**Albert Sandler and his Palm Court Orchestra**
69     Torna a Surriento
**Jodi (Jodie) Sands**
821     With all my heart
954     Someday
**Tommy Sands**
842     Let me be loved
**Amru Sani**
(see Geraldo and his Orchestra; Jack Simpson and his Sextet)
**Santiago and his Music**
174     The wedding samba (The Kordites)
**Sapphires, The**
(see Jack Parnell and his Music Makers)
**Satellites, The**
(see The Three Suns)
**Satisfyers, The**
(see Perry Como; George Towne and his Orchestra)
**Frank Saunders**
(see The Korn Kobblers)
**Sauter–Finegan Orchestra, The**
620     Mobile (Andy Roberts, Anita Darian and The Doodlers)
**Edna Savage**
647     Evermore
656     Stars shine in your eyes
686     Arrivederci darling (with Chorus of Servicemen)
720     A tear fell
764     My prayer
842     Let me be loved
**Joan Savage**
819     Love letters in the sand
821     With all my heart
926     Left right out of my heart
**Saville Brothers, The**
1012    Charlie Brown
**Al Saxon**
967     The day the rains came
1057    Only sixteen
      (see also The Lana Sisters and Al Saxon)
**Primo Scala and his Accordion Band**
2     Cruising down the river (Cyril Shane)
41     Dream again (Edna Kaye)
42     The old lamplighter (Billie Campbell)
45     Go home! (Edna Kaye)
68     The Punch and Judy man (Edna Kaye)
142    In a shady nook (The Keynotes)
710    The poor people of Paris
711    The Theme from 'The Threepenny Opera'
748    Autumn concerto
      (see also Sam Browne; Johnny Denis and his Ranchers)
**Primo Scala and his Banjo and Accordion Band**
141    Powder your face with sunshine (The Keynotes)
162    The echo told me a lie (The Keynotes)
177    The windmill song (The Keynotes)
189    Snowy white snow and jingle bells (The Keynotes)
200    I've got a lovely bunch of coconuts (The Keynotes)
204    Out of a clear blue sky (The Keynotes)
237    Hey! Neighbour (The Keynotes)
252    Rudolph, the red-nosed reindeer (The Keynotes)
290    Mockin' bird hill (The Keynotes)

**Primo Scala and his Band**
(see The Melody Three)
**Scamps, The**
998    Petite fleur
**Lloyd Schaefer and his Orchestra**
(see Perry Como)
**Tito Schipa**
69     Torna a Surriento
**Danny Scholl**
347    Shrimp boats
**Bob Scobey's Jazz Band**
864    Chicago
**Baxter Scott**
423    My love and devotion
**Bob Scott**
(see Mary Ellen Quartet)
**Bobby Scott**
709    Chain gang
**Janette Scott and John Fraser**
795    The good companions (with The Beryl Stott Chorus)
**Jean Scott**
968    As I love you
997    My happiness
**Judy Scott**
821    With all my heart
**Kevin Scott**
1001   Wait for me (with The Rita Williams Singers)
1016   Ciao ciao bambina (with The Rita Williams Singers)
**Marjorie Scott**
175    Say goodnight but not goodbye
**Ronnie Scott**
662    Close your eyes (with The Ronnie Ball Trio)
**Ronnie Scott and his Orchestra**
478    Have you heard (Johnnie Grant)
**Ronnie Scott Quartet, The**
275    September song
990    Smoke gets in your eyes
**John Sebastian**
633    Stranger in paradise
**Harry Secombe**
397    Heart of a clown
408    Here in my heart
422    Faith can move mountains
**Neil Sedaka**
1032   I go ape
1095   Oh, Carol
**Peter Sellers**
567    The never never land
**Semprini**
403    Meet Mister Callaghan
535    Tenderly
812    Forgotten dreams
**Sentimentalists, The, presented by Billy Cotton**
17     Down in the valley
18     There's a harvest moon tonight
49     The things we did last summer
63     You went away and left me
97     My own Darby and Joan
109    Galway Bay
136    A little bird told me
137    Far away places
157    I'll always love you
      (see also Billy Cotton and his Band)
**David Seville**
902    Witch doctor (with The Chipmunks)
**Shadows, The**
(see Cliff Richard)

284

**Cyril Shane**
559 Love me
(See also Primo Scala and his Accordion Band;
Jimmy Leach; Skyrockets Dance Orch
(Fenoulhet))

**Valerie Shane**
919 When the boys talk about the girls

**Jerry Shard and his Music**
545 Heart of my heart

**Sharkey and his Band**
383 Auf wiederseh'n sweetheart

**Sharkey and his Kings of Dixieland**
444 Why don't you believe me (Sharkey)
450 Keep it a secret (Sharkey)

**Ralph Sharon Sextet, The**
441 Heart and soul

**Bob Sharples and his Chorus and Orchestra**
829 In the middle of an island

**Artie Shaw and his Orchestra**
43 Anniversary song
79 I believe (Mel Torme)
256 Autumn leaves

**Artie Shaw and his Strings and Woodwind**
(see Dick Haymes)

**Georgie Shaw**
518 Rags to riches
624 Give me the right
632 Unsuspecting heart

**Roland Shaw and his Orchestra**
591 The high and the mighty (Whistling: Johnny
Johnston)
596 No one but you (Kim Bennett)

**Rosetta Shaw**
(see Art Mooney and his Orchestra)

**Dorothy Shay**
253 Home cookin'

**George Beverly Shea**
851 Got the whole world in His hands

**George Shearing**
535 Tenderly

**George Shearing and his Quintet**
633 Stranger in paradise

**George Shearing and his Trio**
246 I only have eyes for you

**Gene Sheldon**
652 Hey, Mr Banjo (with The Encores)

**Anne Shelton**
37 Lilli Marlene
43 Anniversary song
62 Goodnight, you little rascal, you
73 A rainy night in Rio
109 Galway Bay (with The Wardour Singers)
114 Time may change
120 Woody Woodpecker (with The Keynotes
and Alan Dean)
128 October twilight
134 The heart of Loch Lomond
148 The wedding of Lilli Marlene (with The
Wardour Singers)
149 Put your shoes on, Lucy (with The Keynotes)
155 It happened in Adano
165 While the angelus was ringing (with The
Wardour Singers)
205 Music! Music! Music!
225 I remember the cornfields
238 If I were a blackbird
241 Once in a while
260 My Christmas wish
269 Marshmallow world

310 The loveliest night of the year (with The
George Mitchell Choir)
324 Mademoiselle de Paree (with The George
Mitchell Choir)
382 My concerto
385 Kiss of fire
410 The Isle of Innisfree
456 I talk to the trees
457 Dummy song (with Ted Heath and his
Music)
459 I will never change (with The George
Mitchell Choir)
492 The Bridge of Sighs
509 Answer me (with The George Mitchell
Choir)
536 Don't leave me now
538 The Book (w. The George Mitchell Choir)
554 Cross over the bridge (with The Kordites)
556 I get so lonely
587 If I give my heart to you (with Ken
Mackintosh and his Orchestra)
622 Teach me tonight
686 Arrivederci darling
712 The great pretender
728 Too young to go steady
746 Lay down your arms
780 Give her my love
929 Volare
1091 The village of St Bernadette
(see also Anne Shelton and Dick James; Ambrose
and his Orchestra)

**Anne Shelton and Dick James**
266 The petite waltz (with Anton Karas – zither)

**Bill Shepherd Chorus, The**
(see Jimmy Parkinson; Ruby Murray; Lee Lawrence)

**Bill Shepherd Orchestra, The**
882 Tequila (with The Beryl Stott Group)

**Pauline Shepherd**
667 Have you ever been lonely?
714 Willie can (with the Beryl Stott Chorus)
787 Wisdom of a fool (with The Beryl Stott
Chorus)
790 By you, by you, by you

**Shepherd Sisters, The**
848 Alone

**Shillelagh Singers, The**
(see Percy Faith and his Orchestra)

**Marvin Shiner**
436 Settin' the woods on fire (with Grady
Martin and his Slew Foot Five)

**Joyce Shock**
1035 Personality

**Jack Shook**
(see Grady Martin and his Slew Foot Five)

**Dinah Shore**
9 Laughing on the outside
43 Anniversary song
48 For sentimental reasons
73 A rainy night in Rio
127 Buttons and bows (with her Happy Valley
Boys)
137 Far away places (with Two in Accord)
143 Lavender blue
154 Forever and ever (with Male Quartet)
197 Dear hearts and gentle people
241 Once in a while
247 Happy times
251 Bibbidi-bobbidi-boo
276 I'll always love you

277 My heart cries for you
279 Play a simple melody
291 So in love
313 Too late now
321 Sweet violets
391 From the time you say goodbye (with The
Peter King Singers)
445 Hi-Lili, Hi-Lo
450 Keep it a secret
534 Changing partners
571 Three coins in the fountain
587 If I give my heart to you
645 Stowaway (with The Skylarks)
692 Love and marriage
901 The secret of happiness
(see also Dinah Shore and Buddy Clark; Tony
Martin and Dinah Shore)

**Dinah Shore and Buddy Clark**
182 Baby, it's cold outside

**Victor Silvester and his Ballroom Orchestra**
1 Bless you
7 Into each life some rain must fall
21 You always hurt the one you love
26 To each his own
27 Let it be soon
31 Any time at all
38 Pretending
39 Till then
40 Too many irons in the fire
47 May I call you sweetheart?
61 Tell me, Marianne
65 Try a little tenderness
66 Among my souvenirs
67 A gal in calico
69 Come back to Sorrento
70 People will say we're in love
72 I got the sun in the morning
77 They say it's wonderful
82 Guilty
90 Peg o' my heart
94 I wonder who's kissing her now
96 Near you
105 Golden earrings
110 The wishing waltz
116 Heartbreaker
117 I'm looking over a four-leaf clover
118 Dance, ballerina, dance
126 Take me to your heart again
133 On a slow boat to China
139 Twelfth Street rag
141 Powder your face with sunshine
142 In a shady nook
147 Red roses for a blue lady
150 It's magic
156 Clopin clopant
157 I'll always love you
160 Again
166 Beautiful eyes
167 Have you seen Irene?
180 Our love story
181 You're breaking my heart
183 Am I wasting my time on you?
187 The Harry Lime theme
190 December
194 Down in the glen
196 The last mile home
197 Dear hearts and gentle people
201 Some day my heart will awake
205 Music! Music! Music!

207  Best of all
214  My foolish heart
215  C'est si bon
223  Me and my shadow
228  Bewitched
233  Your heart and my heart
234  If I loved you
246  I only have eyes for you
249  Count every star
254  A dream is a wish your heart makes
256  Autumn leaves
270  If
271  The Tennessee waltz
272  Nevertheless
274  Me and my imagination
286  Be my love
291  So in love
298  Life's desire
300  Our very own
305  With these hands
308  Ivory rag
311  I apologise
313  Too late now
317  Unless
320  Too young
323  Tulips and heather
329  Because of you
338  Lullaby of Broadway
342  If you go
345  Some enchanted evening
349  Mistakes
355  Domino
358  Charmaine
362  Unforgettable
363  Only fools
368  We won't live in a castle
369  And so to sleep again
370  Tell me why
373  Please Mr Sun
375  Any time
377  Wheel of fortune
383  Auf wiederseh'n sweetheart
384  Be anything
388  The homing waltz
390  I'm yours
391  From the time you say goodbye
393  Star of hope
394  Trust in me
395  Faith
402  Somewhere along the way
403  Meet Mister Callaghan
408  Here in my heart
410  The Isle of Innisfree
421  You belong to me
425  When I fall in love
432  Outside of heaven
435  Broken wings
443  The glow worm
447  The love of my life
449  In a golden coach
455  Till I waltz again with you
461  Pretend
465  I believe
467  Downhearted
472  The song from Moulin Rouge
475  The Theme from 'Limelight'
479  April in Portugal
486  I've never been in love before
489  Can't I?

490  Kiss
491  Mother Nature and Father Time
492  The Bridge of Sighs
494  Is it any wonder
497  Look at that girl
501  Vaya con Dios
506  You're just in love
508  Be mine
509  Answer me
510  Wish you were here
525  Ebb tide
534  Changing partners
538  The Book
547  Secret love
550  Someone else's roses
559  Love me
564  Wanted
571  Three coins in the fountain
573  The story of Tina
591  The high and the mighty
593  I love Paris
594  Santo Natale
596  No one but you
603  I still believe
604  Heartbeat
606  Mister Sandman
613  Softly softly
615  A blossom fell
624  Give me the right
625  Under the bridges of Paris
626  Paper kisses
633  Stranger in paradise
636  You, my love
643  Dreamboat
645  Stowaway
649  Ev'rywhere
651  Mama
655  John and Julie
659  Blue star
665  I'll come when you call
667  Have you ever been lonely?
669  Hernando's hideaway
670  Hey there
675  Love is a many-splendoured thing
681  Relax-ay-voo
689  The old pi-anna rag
695  The tender trap
696  Young and foolish
698  Stealin'
705  Only you
707  My September love
710  The poor people of Paris
711  The Theme from 'The Threepenny Opera'
716  Come next Spring
717  No other love
721  Out of town
738  Mountain greenery
739  By the fountains of Rome
744  You are my first love
748  Autumn concerto
749  More
750  A woman in love
760  Two different worlds
762  True love
763  St Therese of the Roses
764  My prayer
776  I dreamed
779  The adoration waltz
789  All of you

791  All
792  Heart
806  Around the world
807  Mr Wonderful
808  When I fall in love
811  A white sport coat
812  Forgotten dreams
819  Love letters in the sand
820  Wonderful, wonderful
821  With all my heart
825  Fire down below
831  Tammy
836  I'm gonna sit right down and write myself a letter
837  Man on fire
842  Let me be loved
843  An affair to remember
848  Alone
850  My special angel
854  April love
856  All the way
857  Long before I knew you
860  The story of my life
861  Love me forever
864  Chicago
866  Magic moments
871  You are my destiny
872  Mandy – the pansy
875  Why don't they understand?
878  To be loved
880  I may never pass this way again
890  It's too soon to know
891  Who's sorry now?
893  A very precious love
894  On the street where you live
895  I could have danced all night
896  Stairway of love
906  Return to me
912  The only man on the island
919  When the boys talk about the girls
921  Devotion
929  Volare
933  Moon talk
942  More than ever
943  A certain smile
947  The world goes around and around
948  It's all in the game
968  As I love you
971  The world outside
979  Tonight
985  I'll be with you in apple blossom time
987  I'll remember tonight
992  Gigi
998  Petite fleur
1001  Wait for me
1002  Thank heaven for little girls
1007  Tomboy
1008  If only I could live my life again
1016  Ciao ciao bambina
1022  Roulette
1054  The windows of Paris
1058  China tea
1062  Someone
1066  Mona Lisa
1072  Morgen
1085  Snow coach
1088  Put your head on my shoulder
1089  What do you want to make those eyes at me for?

**Victor Silvester and his Silver Strings**
385  Kiss of fire
515  Golden tango

**Harry Simeone Chorale, The**
996  The little drummer boy

**Sidney Simone and his Orchestra**
675  Love is a many-splendoured thing (featuring Cecil Pressling – alto sax)

**Jack Simpson and his Sextet**
15  You can be sure of me (Maureen Morton)
20  One-zy, two-zy (Maureen Morton)
28  Sweetheart, you'll never grow old (Maureen Morton)
41  Dream again (Maureen Morton)
52  Accordion (Maureen Morton)
58  Hi-jig-a-jig (Maureen Morton)
63  You went away and left me (Peter Morton)
97  My own Darby and Joan (Betty Dale)
101  Once upon a winter time (Maureen Morton)
109  Galway Bay (Dave Kydd)
114  Time may change (Dave Kydd)
145  How can you buy Killarney? (Dave Kydd)
148  The wedding of Lilli Marlene
176  Too whit, too whoo (Amru Sani)
179  A rose in a garden of weeds (Amru Sani)
191  Is it too late? (Amru Sani)
200  I've got a lovely bunch of cocoanuts (Jack Simpson)
212  I'd've baked a cake (Rita Williams)

**Frank Sinatra**
4  Homesick – that's all
13  Oh, what it seemed to be
16  Day by day
30  All through the day
36  Five minutes more
44  The stars will remember
49  The things we did last Summer
65  Try a little tenderness
66  Souvenirs
70  People will say we're in love
71  Time after time
76  Mam'selle
77  They say it's wonderful
80  Oh, what a beautiful morning
86  I'll make up for everything
92  The coffee song
93  The girl that I marry
165  While the angelus was ringing
209  Chattanoogie shoe-shine boy (with The Jeff Alexander Choir)
234  If I loved you
246  I only have eyes for you
248  Goodnight Irene
272  Nevertheless
275  September song
400  I'm gonna live till I die (with Ray Anthony and his Orchestra)
460  I'm walking behind you
524  Hello young lovers
530  From here to eternity
560  Young at heart
571  Three coins in the fountain
609  White Christmas
636  You, my love
642  Melody of love (with Ray Anthony and his Orchestra)
657  Learnin' the blues
692  Love and marriage
695  The tender trap

741  You'll never walk alone (with The Ken Lane Singers)
856  All the way
864  Chicago
1020  French foreign legion
1063  High hopes (with 'A Bunch of Kids')
(see also Tommy Dorsey and his Orchestra)

**Singing Silhouettes, The**
(see Charlie Chester; Charlie Chester and The Singing Silhouettes)

**Raymond Siozade and his 'Atomic Accordion'**
656  Stars shine in your eyes

**Sir Lancelot**
794  Marianne

**Red Skelton**
(see Fred Astaire, Red Skelton and Anita Ellis)

**Skylarks, The**
(see Russ Morgan and his Orchestra; Buddy Clark; Dinah Shore)

**Skyliners, The**
539  The happy wanderer

**Skyliners, The**
(see Ray Anthony and his Orchestra)

**Skymasters, The**
(see Leslie Douglas and his Orchestra)

**Skyrockets Dance Orchestra, The, Conducted by Paul Fenoulhet**
1  Bless you (Doreen Lundy)
11  Mary Lou (Cyril Shane)
12  Money is the root of all evil (Doreen Lundy)
14  Primrose Hill (Cyril Shane)
16  Day by day (Cyril Shane)
24  So would I (Cyril Shane)
25  The 'Ampstead way (Cyril Shane)
27  Let it be soon (Doreen Lundy)
29  You keep coming back like a song (Cyril Shane)
36  Five minutes more (Doreen Lundy)
50  The rickety rickshaw man (Cyril Shane)
51  The whole world is singing my song (Doreen Lundy)
65  Try a little tenderness (Doreen Lundy)
75  Down the old Spanish trail (Cyril Shane)
82  Guilty (Doreen Lundy)
87  Apple blossom wedding (Doreen Lundy)
88  Bow bells (Dick James)

**Skyrockets Dance Orchestra, The, Conducted by Woolf Phillips**
101  Once upon a winter time (Doreen Lundy)
122  Rambling rose (Doreen Lundy)
134  The heart of Loch Lomond (Sally Douglas)

**John Slater**
448  That doggie in the window
552  Friends and neighbours
566  Bob's yer uncle

**Slim and the Boys**
403  Meet Mister Callaghan

**Joan Small**
716  Come next Spring
748  Autumn concerto

**Mary Small**
355  Domino
399  Didja ever

**Charles Smart**
(see Issy Bonn; Vera Lynn; Charles Smart and Harold Smart)

**Charles Smart (Compton organ) and Harold Smart (Hammond organ)**
502  Flirtation waltz

**Harold Smart (Hammond organ) and his Quartet**
505  Swedish rhapsody

**Arthur 'Guitar Boogie' Smith**
164  Careless hands
198  Mule train (and his Crackerjacks with Arthur Smith – vocal)
556  I get so lonely

**Eddie Smith & The Chief**
352  Down yonder

**Ethel Smith**
35  The green cockatoo
177  The windmill song (with The Travellers)
187  The Harry Lime theme
193  The Scottish samba (with Guy Lombardo and his Royal Canadians with The Lombardo Trio)
208  The French can can polka
267  Sleigh ride
286  Be my love
310  The loveliest night of the year
336  Longing for you
355  Domino
358  Charmaine
460  I'm walking behind you
461  Pretend
465  I believe
472  The Moulin Rouge theme
479  April in Portugal
494  Is it any wonder
495  Ruby
505  Swedish rhapsody
609  White Christmas
669  Hernando's hideaway

**Jack Smith**
168  Blue ribbon gal (with The Jubalaires)
216  Enjoy yourself (with The Jud Conlon Singers)
284  Senora
(see also Jack Smith and The Clark Sisters)

**Jack Smith and The Clark Sisters**
2  Cruising down the river
132  Cuanto le gusta
143  Lavender blue
146  A strawberry moon

**Muriel Smith**
458  I'd love to fall asleep
471  Hold me, thrill me, kiss me
521  Oh! my papa
644  Sincerely

**Paul Smith Quartet, The**
(see Ella Fitzgerald)

**Roy Smith**
684  He

**Tab Smith**
990  Smoke gets in your eyes
997  My happiness cha cha

**Charles Smitton**
(see Billy Cotton and his Band)

**Barry Snow**
(see Petersen Brothers)

**Hank Snow**
428  I went to your wedding

**Bill Snyder, his piano, and his Orchestra**
223  Me and my shadow
228  Bewitched
317  Unless

**Virginia Somers**
554  Cross over the bridge

**Song Pedlars, The**
*(see Denny Dennis; Sid Phillips and his Band; Larry Cross and The Song Pedlars; Billy Thorburn's The Organ, the Dance Band and Me; Max Bygraves)*

**Song Spinners, The**
*(see Dick Haymes and The Song Spinners; Ella Fitzgerald)*

**Sons of the Pioneers, The, with Bob Nolan**
658   Cool water
     *(see also Vaughn Monroe and his Orchestra)*

**Sons of The Sons of The Pioneers, The**
*(see Spike Jones and his City Slickers)*

**Jeri Southern**
425   When I fall in love (with Chorus)
451   The ruby and the pearl
825   Fire down below
826   Scarlet ribbons
990   Smoke gets in your eyes

**Johnny Southern**
813   We will make love (with The Western Rhythm Kings)

**Southlanders, The**
640   Earth angel
648   The Crazy Otto rag
667   Have you ever been lonely?
848   Alone
863   Put a light in the window
930   Torero

**Red Sovine**
693   Sixteen tons

**Fela Sowande Rhythm Group, The**
479   April in Portugal

**Sparklers, The**
*(see Lawrence Welk and his Champagne Music)*

**Spinners, The**
983   This old man
     *(see also Shane Rimmer)*

**Charlie Spivak and his Orchestra**
243   Mona Lisa (Tommy Lynn and The Stardreamers)
300   Our very own (Tommy Lynn)

**Sportsmen, The**
223   Me and my shadow
     *(see also Mel Blanc)*

**Sportsmen Glee Club, The**
*(see Bing Crosby)*

**Squadronaires, The, directed by Ronnie Aldrich**
349   Mistakes (Roy Edwards)
352   Down yonder (featuring Ronnie Aldrich – piano)
361   Slow coach (Roy Edwards)
     *(see also Joan Regan and The Squadronaires, directed by Ronnie Aldrich; Suzi Miller)*

**Squadronaires, The, directed by Jimmy Miller**
11   Mary Lou (Jimmy Miller and The Quads)
12   Money is the root of all evil (Jimmy Miller and The Quads)
20   One-zy, two-zy (The Quads)
26   To each his own (Jimmy Miller)
31   Any time at all (Doreen Stephens)
36   Five minutes more (Jimmy Miller and The Quads)
38   Pretending (Jimmy Miller)
42   The old lamplighter (Jimmy Miller)
66   Among my souvenirs (Doreen Stephens)
98   The shoemaker's serenade (The Quads)
135   The Maharajah of Magador (Jimmy Miller and The Quads)
181   You're breaking my heart (Roy Edwards)

190   December (Roy Edwards)
194   Down in the glen (Firth Archer and The Squads Choir)
199   Jealous heart (Roy Edwards, Susan Jeans and The Squads Choir)
239   Sentimental me (Roy Edwards and Ensemble)
240   Have I told you lately that I love you? (Roy Edwards and The Squads Choir)
274   Me and my imagination (Roy Edwards)
     *(see also Sam Browne and The Squadronaires, directed by Jimmy Miller; The Merry Macs)*

**Squads Choir, The**
*(see The Squadronaires, directed by Jimmy Miller)*

**Dorothy Squires**
8   It's a pity to say goodnight
9   Laughing on the outside
48   For sentimental reasons
59   When China boy meets China girl
84   Danger ahead
85   My first love, my last love for always
95   Tree in the meadow
112   Reflections on the water
123   So tired
175   Say goodnight but not goodbye
176   Too whit, too whoo
180   Our love story
189   Snowy white snow and jingle bells
202   We all have a song in our hearts
225   I remember the cornfields
241   Once in a while
286   Be my love
298   Life's desire
309   My resistance is low
344   At the end of the day
349   Mistakes
357   The little white cloud that cried
362   Unforgettable
369   And so to sleep again
375   Any time
384   Be anything
395   Faith
430   Snowflakes
460   I'm walking behind you
517   If you love me
534   Changing partners
687   When you lose the one you love
770   Come home to my arms (with The Beryl Stott Chorus)
785   Banana boat song (with The Beryl Stott Group)

**Rosemary Squires**
703   Band of gold

**Jo Stafford**
234   If I loved you
247   Happy times
248   Goodnight Irene (with Trio)
256   Autumn leaves
270   If
271   The Tennessee waltz
275   September song
300   Our very own
341   Allentown Jail
345   Some enchanted evening
347   Shrimp boats (with The Norman Luboff Choir)
376   A-round the corner (with The Norman Luboff Choir)
393   Star of hope (with The Lee Brothers)

401   Walkin' my baby back home
421   You belong to me
450   Keep it a secret
551   Make love to me
609   White Christmas
622   Teach me tonight
676   Suddenly there's a valley (with The Norman Luboff Choir)
686   Arrivederci darling
696   Young and foolish
701   It's almost tomorrow
924   Wouldn't it be loverly?
     *(see also Jo Stafford and Gordon MacRae; Gene Autry and Jo Stafford; Jo Stafford and The Starlighters; Nelson Eddy and Jo Stafford; Jo Stafford and Frankie Laine)*

**Jo Stafford and Frankie Laine**
337   In the cool, cool, cool of the evening
436   Settin' the woods on fire

**Jo Stafford and Gordon MacRae**
153   A – you're adorable
184   Monday, Tuesday, Wednesday
188   I'll string along with you
222   Dearie
251   Bibbidi-bobbidi-boo
304   Girls were made to take care of boys

**Jo Stafford and The Starlighters**
196   The last mile home
279   Play a simple melody

**Arnold Stang with The Sunshine Kids**
1009   Ivy will cling

**Staplejacks, The**
*(see Cyril Stapleton and his Orchestra)*

**Cyril Stapleton and his Orchestra**
57   Zip-a-dee-doo-dah (Tom Henry and Quartet)
77   They say it's wonderful (Dick James)
87   Apple blossom wedding (Dick James)
89   How are things in Glocca Morra? (Dick James)
95   Tree in the meadow
163   Brush those tears from your eyes (The Stapletones)
178   A shawl of Galway grey (Bob Dale)
186   The hop-scotch polka (Bob Dale and Jean Campbell)
188   I'll string along with you (Bob Dale)
197   Dear hearts and gentle people (Bob Dale)
236   Candy and cake (Jean Campbell and The Staplejacks)
246   I only have eyes for you (Bob Dale)
257   Orange coloured sky (Jean Campbell)
261   Beloved, be faithful (Bob Dale and The Staplejacks)
264   All my love (Bob Dale)
283   Teasin' (Jean Campbell)
285   The roving kind (David Carey and The Staplejacks)
286   Be my love (Bob Dale)
289   A penny a kiss – a penny a hug (Dave Carey and Jean Campbell)
322   Christopher Columbus (The Stargazers)
334   Belle, Belle, my liberty Belle (Stargazers)
403   Meet Mister Callaghan
443   The glow worm (The Clubmen)
484   Seven lonely days (Jean Campbell and vocal group)
659   Blue star (Julie Dawn)
716   Come next Spring

723   The Italian theme
726   The happy whistler (with Desmond Lane –
      penny whistle)
812   Forgotten dreams
929   Volare
983   Nick nack paddy whack (with Children's
      Chorus)
      (see also Reggie Goff; The Stargazers)

**Stapletones, The**
(see Reggie Goff; Cyril Stapleton and his Orchestra)

**Stardreamers, The**
(see Charlie Spivak and his Orchestra)

**Star Dusters, The**
134   The heart of Loch Lomond (with Sy Oliver
      and his Orchestra)
172   I don't see me in your eyes any more
      (see also Evelyn Knight and The Star Dusters;
      Billie Holiday)

**Stargazers, The**
274   Me and my imagination
287   Red silken stockings (with Cyril Stapleton
      and his Orchestra)
351   I want to be near you
360   Rollin' stone
376   A-round the corner
387   Dance me loose
398   The day of Jubilo
404   Sugarbush
435   Broken wings
439   Make it soon
464   Celebration rag
477   Tell me you're mine
501   Vaya con Dios
514   You you you
533   I see the moon (with Syd Dean and his
      Orchestra)
539   The happy wanderer
570   The man with the banjo
600   I need you now
614   Somebody (with Sonny Farrar and his Banjo
      Band)
648   The Crazy Otto rag
652   Hey, Mr Banjo
660   Close the door
673   Twenty tiny fingers (with Syd Dean and his
      Band)
695   The tender trap
702   Zambezi
725   Hot diggity
796   Mangos
908   Big man
      (see also Dick James; Billy Thorburn's The
      Organ, the Dance Band and Me; Marie Benson
      and The Stargazers; Stanley Black, his Piano
      and his Orchestra; Steve Conway and The
      Stargazers; Benny Lee and Mary; Benny Lee;
      Benny Lee and The Stargazers; Josh White and
      The Stargazers; Dick James and The
      Stargazers; Cyril Stapleton and his Orchestra;
      Les Howard and The Stargazers; Ray Ellington
      and The Stargazers; Carroll Levis and Mickey
      Maguire; Jimmy Young; Dennis Lotis and The
      Stargazers; Dickie Valentine)

**Starlighters, The**
(see Gordon MacRae and The Starlighters; Johnny Mercer;
Jo Stafford and The Starlighters; Margaret Whiting and
Bob Hope)

**Jimmy Starr**
957   It's only make believe

**Kay Starr**
377   Wheel of fortune
433   Comes along a-love
466   Side by side
485   The breeze
517   If you love me
534   Changing partners
598   Am I a toy or treasure?
627   If anyone finds this, I love you
708   The rock and roll waltz
1083  If you love me
      (see also Charlie Barnet and his Orchestra)

**William Starr**
131   The cuckoo waltz

**Station Skiffle Group, The, with Jim Miller**
781   Don't you rock me, daddy-o

**Anthony Steel and The Radio Revellers**
576   West of Zanzibar – jambo
      (see also The Radio Revellers)

**Jon & Sondra Steele**
124   My happiness

**Tommy Steele**
978   Come on, let's go
1068  Tallahassee lassie
1097  The little white bull

**Tommy Steele and the Steelmen**
771   Singing the blues
783   Knee deep in the blues
830   Shiralee
833   A handful of songs
874   Nairobi
912   The only man on the island

**Lou Stein and his Orchestra**
937   Got a match

**Doreen Stephens**
(see The Squadronaires, directed by Jimmy Miller; Billy
Cotton and his Band)

**April Stevens**
369   And so to sleep again

**Bob Stevens**
(see Gordon Jenkins and his Orchestra)

**Dodie Stevens**
1028  Pink shoelaces

**Johnny Stevens**
605   Not as a stranger

**Katie Stevens**
512   Crying in the chapel

**Marti Stevens**
571   Three coins in the fountain

**Roy Stevens**
360   Rollin' stone

**Terri Stevens**
632   Unsuspecting heart

**Trudy Stevens**
(see Bing Crosby, Danny Kaye, Peggy Lee and Trudy
Stevens)

**Ian Stewart and his Music**
345   Some enchanted evening
352   Down yonder
353   Sin
581   A sky-blue shirt and a rainbow tie
586   Hold my hand
601   Count your blessings instead of sheep

**Redd Stewart**
(see Pee Wee King and his Golden West Cowboys)

**Sandy Stewart**
943   A certain smile

**Alvin Stoller**
(see Billy May and his Orchestra; Stan Freberg)

**Butch Stone**
(see Les Brown and his Band of Renown)

**Lew Stone and his Orchestra**
(see Hugh Diamond)

**Axel Stordahl**
(see June Hutton and Axel Stordahl)

**Axel Stordahl and his Orchestra**
572   Dream dream dream

**Gale Storm**
700   Memories are made of this
729   Ivory tower
736   Why do fools fall in love?
817   Dark moon

**Beryl Stott Chorus, The**
(see Gary Miller; Edmund Hockridge; Pauline Shepherd;
Marion Ryan; Joe 'Mr Piano' Henderson; Petula Clark;
Lita Roza; Shani Wallis; Betty Miller; Dorothy Squires;
Dennis Lotis; Janette Scott and John Fraser)

**Beryl Stott Group, The**
(see Dorothy Squires; John Fraser; Frankie Brent; Petula
Clark; Gary Miller; Marion Ryan; The Bill Shepherd
Orchestra; Colin Hicks; Ray Ellington; David Macbeth)

**Wally Stott and his Orchestra**
475   The theme from 'Limelight'
540   The Luxembourg polka
555   The shadow waltz
870   Catch a falling star (with Chorus)
      (see also Murray Campbell – trumpet)

**Ted Straeter and his Orchestra**
371   At last! At last!

**Lily Strange and The People of Hoxton**
449   In a golden coach

**Street Singer, The – Arthur Tracy**
85    My first love, my last love for always

**'Texas' Bill Strength**
666   The yellow rose of Texas

**Benny Strong and his Orchestra**
197   Dear hearts and gentle people (Benny
      Strong)
212   I'd've baked a cake (Benny Strong)
323   Tulips and heather

**Anne Stuart**
(see Geraldo and his Orchestra)

**Sunnysiders, The**
(see Lou Preager and his Orchestra)

**Sunnysiders, The**
652   Hey, Mr Banjo

**Monty Sunshine – clarinet**
(see Chris Barber and his Jazz Band)

**Sunshine Band, The**
643   Dreamboat

**Sun Spots, The**
(see Lou Preager and his Orchestra)

**Ellen Sutton**
(see Sir Hubert Pimm)

**Reinhold Svensson and his Quintet**
241   Once in a while

**Sally Sweetland**
(see Eddie Fisher)

**Sylvia Syms**
895   I could have danced all night

**Ziggy Talent**
(see Vaughn Monroe and his Orchestra)

**Stella Tanner**
(see Frank Cordell and his Orchestra)

**Tanner Sisters, The**
186   The hop-scotch polka
199   Jealous heart
217   Cherry stones (with The Hedley Ward Trio)

219  Quicksilver (with The Hedley Ward Trio)
224  Choo'n gum (with The Hedley Ward Trio)
231  A load of hay (with The Hedley Ward Trio)
240  Have I told you lately that I love you?
248  Goodnight Irene (with The Hedley Ward Trio)
263  Ferry Boat Inn (with The Hedley Ward Trio)
266  The petite waltz
290  Mockin' bird hill
366  Saturday rag
376  A-round the corner
433  Comes a-long a-love
439  Make it soon
527  The creep
643  Dreamboat
756  Just walking in the rain
758  Green door
770  Come home to my arms

**Tarriers, The**
785  Banana boat song
928  I know where I'm going
959/960  Tom Dooley
   *(see also Vince Martin)*

**Phil Tate and his Orchestra**
812  Forgotten dreams

**Richard Tauber**
77  They say it's wonderful
80  Oh, what a beautiful morning

**Burt Taylor**
405  I'll walk alone

**Karen Tedder**
*(see Red Ingle and The Unnatural Seven; Red Ingle and The Natural Seven)*

**Teddy Bears, The**
970  To know him is to love him

**Teenagers, The, featuring Frankie Lymon**
736  Why do fools fall in love?

**Teen Jones**
*(see Carol Kay)*

**Telecast Orchestra, The, conducted by Elliott Mayes**
555  The shadow waltz

**Beryl Templeman**
435  Broken wings
458  I'd love to fall asleep (with The Wondertones)
587  If I give my heart to you
590  My son, my son
593  I love Paris
603  I still believe
667  Have you ever been lonely?
720  A tear fell
746  Lay down your arms
796  Mangos
891  Who's sorry now?
896  Stairway of love
   *(see also Roy Fox and his Band)*

**Billy Ternent and his Orchestra**
156  Clopin clopant (Tom Henry)
163  Brush those tears from your eyes (Eve Beynon)
166  Beautiful eyes (Tom Henry and Eve Beynon)
167  Have you seen Irene? (Don Emsley)
220  Oh, you sweet one (Eva Beynon and Bobby Breen)
222  Dearie (Eva Beynon and Bobby Breen)
234  If I loved you (Bobby Breen)

**Terry, The Irish Minstrel**
239  Sentimental me
258  Christmas in Killarney
410  The Isle of Innisfree

**Pat Terry**
*(see Camarata and his Music)*

**Terry-Thomas and The Band of the WRECS**
746  Lay down your arms (with Chorus)

**Inia Te Wiata**
785  Banana boat song

**Millard Thomas**
*(see Harry Belafonte; Belafonte)*

**Wilfrid Thomas**
392  High noon
500  Where the winds blow (with Ivor Mairants – guitar)

**Carlos Thompson**
596  No one but you

**Sydney Thompson and his Old-Tyme Dance Orchestra**
131  The cuckoo waltz
443  The glow worm
476  A waltz for the Queen

**Billy Thorburn's The Organ, The Dance Band and Me**
1  Bless you
2  Cruising down the river (Rita Williams)
10  Let bygones be bygones (Harry Kaye)
14  Primrose Hill (Harry Kaye)
21  You always hurt the one you love (Rita Williams)
40  Too many irons in the fire
43  Anniversary song
44  The stars will remember (Harry Kaye)
46  April showers (Harry Kaye)
66  Among my souvenirs (Rita Williams)
91  South America, take it away (Harry Kaye)
99  Serenade of the bells (Harry Kaye)
122  Rambling rose (Harry Kaye)
133  On a slow boat to China (Harry Kaye)
134  The heart of Loch Lomond (Harry Kaye)
152  Behind the clouds (Harry Kaye)
153  A – you're adorable (Harry Kaye)
157  I'll always love you (Harry Kaye)
195  Why is it? (The Stargazers)
208  The French can can polka (The Stargazers)
210  When the world has forgotten (Harry Kaye)
231  A load of hay (The Stargazers)
237  Hey! Neighbour (The Stargazers)
245  Ashes of roses (The Stargazers)
248  Goodnight Irene (The Stargazers)
277  My heart cries for you (The Lennox Three)
281  Good luck, good health, God bless you (The Stargazers)
290  Mockin' bird hill (The Bobolinks)
303  Beautiful brown eyes (The Bobolinks)
320  Too young (The Bobolinks)
321  Sweet violets (The Bobolinks)
327  The black note serenade (The Bobolinks)
361  Slow coach (The Bobolinks)
366  Saturday rag (The Bobolinks)
368  We won't live in a castle (The Bobolinks)
383  Auf wiederseh'n sweetheart (The Bobolinks)
391  From the time you say goodbye (The Bobolinks)
403  Meet Mister Callaghan
436  Settin' the woods on fire (The Bobolinks)
447  The love of my life (The Bobolinks)

458  I'd love to fall asleep (The Song Pedlars)
494  Is it any wonder (Doreen Harris)

**Billy Thorburn and his Strict Tempo Music**
514  You you you
516  Ricochet
518  Rags to riches
534  Changing partners
540  The Luxembourg polka
542  Bell bottom blues
544  Bimbo
547  Secret love
574  Jilted
587  If I give my heart to you
594  Santo Natale
608  Happy days and lonely nights
618  Give me your word
627  If anyone finds this, I love you
645  Stowaway
649  Ev'rywhere
655  John and Julie
689  The old pi-anna rag (with vocal group)
704  Jimmy unknown
726  The happy whistler
737  The birds and the bees
748  Autumn concerto
750  A woman in love
762  True love
771  Singing the blues

**Three Beaux and a Peep**
*(see Sy Oliver and his Orchestra)*

**Three Boys and a Girl**
*(see Geraldo and his Orchestra)*

**Three Deuces, The**
667  Have you ever been lonely?

**Three Kaydets, The**
*(see Sammy Kaye and his Orchestra)*

**Three Kayes, The**
*(see under The Kaye Sisters)*

**Three Kaye Sisters, The**
*(see under The Kaye Sisters)*

**Three Lovers, The**
*(see Jerry Colonna)*

**Three Oscars, The**
*(see Benny Lee)*

**Three Suns, The**
266  The petite waltz (with Larry Green – piano)
267  Sleigh ride
686  Arrivederci darling (with The Satellites)

**Three Tons of Joy, The**
*(see The Johnny Otis Show)*

**Dimitri Tiomkin and his Orchestra**
591  The high and the mighty
774  Friendly persuasion

**Toads, The**
*(see Stan Freberg)*

**Art & Dottie Todd**
435  Broken wings

**Dick Todd**
454  Oh, happy day
455  Till I waltz again with you
533  I see the moon
570  The man with the banjo

**Nick Todd**
867  At the hop

**Billy Toffel**
156  Clopin clopant
   *(see also Ray Ventura and his Orchestra)*

**Toralf Tollefsen**
131  The cuckoo waltz
139  Twelfth Street rag

**Tonettes, The**
(see Russ Hamilton)
**Tophatters, The**
(see Geraldo and his Orchestra)
**Sidney Torch and his Orchestra**
266 The petite waltz
296 A rainy day refrain (The Torch Singers)
355 Domino
427 Ecstasy
616 Majorca
668 The dam busters march
**Torch Singers, The**
(see Sidney Torch and his Orchestra)
**Mel Torme**
160 Again
164 Careless hands
228 Bewitched
738 Mountain greenery
789 All of you
(see also Artie Shaw and his Orchestra)
**Mel Torme and The Meltones**
see Bing Crosby)
**Mitchell Torok**
754 When Mexico gave up the rhumba
**Harry Torrani**
131 The cuckoo waltz
**Vico Torriani**
1016 Ciao ciao bambina
**Towers, The**
see Evelyn Knight)
**George Towne and his Orchestra**
209 Chattanoogie shoe-shine boy (The Satisfyers)
222 Dearie (The Satisfyers)
**Cliff Townsend**
637 Unchained melody
**Arthur Tracy**
see The Street Singer)
**Travellers, The**
see Ethel Smith – organ)
**Tommy Traynor**
see Jerry Gray and his Orchestra)
**Paul Tremaine**
see David Carroll and his Orchestra)
**Charles Trenet**
371 At last! At last!
**Bruce Trent**
510 Wish you were here
**Troise and his Novelty Orchestra**
437 Don't let the stars get in your eyes (The Four-in-A-Chord)
**Troubadours, The**
see Dick Haymes and The Troubadours)
**Ernest Tubb and Red Foley**
325 The Kentucky waltz
**Sophie Tucker**
359 I wanna say hello
**Tommy Tucker and his Orchestra**
200 I've got a lovely bunch of cocoanuts
204 Out of a clear blue sky (vocal group)
271 The Tennessee waltz (Don Brown and Trio)
**Tuneful Twenties Orchestra, The, conducted by Tolchard Evans and Ray Terry**
389 Singing in the rain (Dinah Kaye)
**Tunetimers, The**
see Buddy Kaye Quintet)
**Tunettes, The**
792 Heart
794 Marianne

810 Yes tonight, Josephine
823 Little darlin'
836 I'm gonna sit right down and write myself a letter
840 That'll be the day
**Joan Turner**
555 The shadow waltz
561 The homecoming waltz
**Ray Turner**
(see Victor Young and his Singing Strings)
**Jane Turzy**
321 Sweet violets
553 Such a night
**Wesley Tuttle**
512 Crying in the chapel
**Twin Tunes Quintet, The**
876 Baby lover
**Conway Twitty**
957 It's only make believe (with The Jordanaires)
1066 Mona Lisa
**Two in Accord, The**
(see Dinah Shore)
**2.19 Skiffle Group with Mik Lauder and Mike Wallace**
805 Freight train blues
959/960 Tom Dooley
**Leslie Uggams**
1072 One more sunrise
**Ritchie Valens**
978 Come on, let's go
1011 Donna
**Dickie Valentine**
374 Never
388 The homing waltz
421 You belong to me (with Ted Heath and his Music)
435 Broken wings
449 In a golden coach
462 All the time and ev'rywhere
468 The Windsor waltz
536 Don't leave me now
606 Mister Sandman
607 The finger of suspicion (with The Stargazers)
615 A blossom fell
635 I wonder
678 Christmas alphabet
689 The old pi-anna rag
699 Dreams can tell a lie (with The Keynotes)
761 Christmas Island
800 Chapel of roses
814 Puttin' on the style
857 Long before I knew you
1010 Venus
1036 A teenager in love
1072 One more sunrise
(see also Ted Heath and his Music; The Johnston Brothers; Dickie Valentine and Joan Regan)
**Dickie Valentine and Joan Regan**
568 Cleo and me-o (with The Keynotes)
**Joe Valino**
773 The Garden of Eden
**June Valli**
512 Crying in the chapel
**Helen Van Capellen**
567 The never never land (with The Parakeets)
**Denny Vaughan**
735 Walk hand in hand
(see also Carroll Gibbons and the Savoy Hotel Orpheans; Geraldo and his Orchestra)

**Frankie Vaughan**
218 The old piano roll blues
226 Daddy's little girl
497 Look at that girl (with Ken Mackintosh and his Orchestra)
504 Hey, Joe!
522 Istanbul (with The Peter Knight Singers)
523 Cloud lucky seven
541 The cuff of my shirt (with The Kordites and Ken Mackintosh and his Orchestra)
546 Heartless (with The Kordites and Ken Mackintosh and his Orchestra)
549 From the vine came the grape
590 My son, my son
608 Happy days and lonely nights
631 Tweedle-dee (with vocal group)
632 Unsuspecting heart
653 That's how a love song was born
677 Seventeen
679 Meet me on the corner
698 Stealin'
758 Green door
773 The Garden of Eden
834 Wanderin' eyes
837 Man on fire
855 Kisses sweeter than wine
898 Kewpie doll
1049 Heart of a man
1067 Sometime, somewhere
(see also Frankie Vaughan and Alma Cogan; Frankie Vaughan and The Kaye Sisters)
**Frankie Vaughan and Alma Cogan**
574 Jilted
**Frankie Vaughan and The Kaye Sisters**
847 Gotta have something in the bank, Frank
1014 Come softly to me
**Malcolm Vaughan**
650 Every day of my life
651 Mama
654 Take me back again
688 With your love (with The Peter Knight Singers)
705 Only you
755 Love me as though there were no tomorrow
763 St Therese of the Roses
800 Chapel of the roses
850 My special angel
878 To be loved (with The Michael Sammes Singers)
913 Ev'ry hour, ev'ry day of my life (with The Michael Sammes Singers)
942 More than ever (with The Michael Sammes Singers)
994 Willingly
1001 Wait for me
**Sarah Vaughan**
115 Nature boy
150 It's magic
535 Tenderly
785 Banana boat song
1071 Broken-hearted melody
**Billy Vaughn and his Orchestra**
642 Melody of love
685 The shifting, whispering sands (Narrator: Ken Nordene)
711 The Theme from 'The Threepenny Opera'
748 Autumn concerto
873 Raunchy
1072 Morgen

291

**Velvetones, The**
(see Reggie Goff)
**Ray Ventura and his Orchestra**
8     It's a pity to say goodnight (Billy Toffel and Bob Jacqmain Vocal Quartet)
**Ronnie Vincent**
(see The Gaylords)
**Vipers Skiffle Group, The**
781    Don't you rock me, daddy-o
797    Cumberland Gap
**Virtues, The**
1030   Guitar boogie shuffle
**Voices of Walter Schumann, The**
664    The man from Laramie
**Jimmy Wakely**
277    My heart cries for you
303    Beautiful brown eyes (with The Les Baxter Chorus)
428    I went to your wedding
        (see also Margaret Whiting and Jimmy Wakely)
**Anton Walbrook**
339    Love's roundabout
**Fats Waller**
139    Twelfth Street rag
836    I'm gonna sit right down and write myself a letter
**Shani Wallis**
542    Bell bottom blues
545    Heart of my heart
718    Don't ring-a-da bell (with The Beryl Stott Chorus and Joe Henderson – harpsichord)
**Wanderers, The**
(see Lou Ella Robertson)
**Billy Ward and his Dominoes**
518    Rags to riches
571    Three coins in the fountain
763    St Therese of the Roses
**Hedley Ward Trio, The**
216    Enjoy yourself
570    The man with the banjo
581    A sky-blue shirt and a rainbow tie
680    Rock around the clock
891    Who's sorry now?
        (see also The Tanner Sisters)
**Wardour Singers, The**
(see Anne Shelton; Gracie Fields)
**Fred Waring and his Pennsylvanians**
310    The loveliest night of the year (Gordon Goodman)
323    Tulips and heather (The Glee Club)
345    Some enchanted evening (The Glee Club)
432    Outside of heaven (Joe Marine)
741    You'll never walk alone (The Glee Club)
962    I heard the bells on Christmas Day
**Alma Warren**
560    Young at heart
645    Stowaway
698    Stealin'
**Anne Warren**
(see Ruby Murray; Tony Brent)
**Fran Warren**
206    Now that I need you
431    Takes two to tango
436    Settin' the woods on fire
510    Wish you were here
        (see also Tony Martin and Fran Warren; Lisa Kirk and Fran Warren)
**Jeff Warren**
(see Billie Worth and Jeff Warren)

**John Warren's Strictempo Orchestra conducted by Bill Shepherd**
1006   May you always
**Keith Warwick**
633    Stranger in paradise
635    I wonder
651    Mama
675    Love is a many-splendoured thing
676    Suddenly there's a valley
687    When you lose the one you love
716    Come next Spring
**Washboard Joe and his Scrubbers**
626    Paper kisses
629    Open up your heart
**Dinah Washington**
622    Teach me tonight
**Jimmy Watson**
(see Alma Cogan)
**Tommy Watt and his Orchestra**
695    The tender trap
**Lu Watters' Buena Jazz Band**
346    The black and white rag
**Beryl Wayne**
(see Ido Martin and his Latin Band)
**Bobby Wayne**
178    A shawl of Galway grey
348    Sweetheart of yesterday
377    Wheel of fortune
397    Heart of a clown
592    They were doin' the mambo
        (see also Claire Hogan and Bobby Wayne)
**Clive Wayne**
145    How can you buy Killarney?
160    Again
167    Have you seen Irene?
173    Confidentially
175    Say goodnight but not goodbye (with Jackie Brown – organ)
181    You're breaking my heart
190    December
**Jerry Wayne**
121    You can't be true, dear (with Ken Griffin – organ)
486    I've never been in love before
**Judy Wayne**
537    Don't laugh at me
**Weavers, The**
244    Tzena tzena tzena (sung in Hebrew)
285    The roving kind
376    A-round the corner
380    The gandy dancer's ball
855    Kisses sweeter than wine
        (see also Gordon Jenkins and his Orchestra; The Weavers and Gordon Jenkins – vocal; The Weavers and Terry Gilkyson)
**The Weavers and Terry Gilkyson**
307    On top of Old Smokey
**The Weavers and Gordon Jenkins**
288    So long
**Johnny Webb**
753    Glendora
**Lizbeth Webb**
486    I've never been in love before
**Joan Weber**
619    Let me go, lover
**Bert Weedon**
1030   Guitar boogie shuffle
**Bert Weedon and his Music for Dancing**
997    My happiness

998    Petite fleur
999    Sing, little birdie
**Ted Weems and his Orchestra and Chorus**
(see Perry Como)
**Frank Weir and his Orchestra**
30     All through the day (Vivien Paget)
        (see also Lys Assia)
**Frank Weir, his soprano sax, and his Orchestra**
539    The happy wanderer (with Chorus)
558    The little shoemaker (The Michael Twins)
567    The never never land (Maureen Childs and The Little Tinkers)
724    Mister Cuckoo (with Chorus)
        (see also Vera Lynn; Janie Marden)
**Elisabeth Welch**
471    Hold me
**Lawrence Welk and his Champagne Music**
701    It's almost tomorrow (Alice Lon and The Sparklers)
708    The rock and roll waltz
709    Chain gang (Larry Hooper and The Sparklers)
710    The poor people of Paris
806    Around the world
894    On the street where you live (Larry Deane)
895    I could have danced all night (Alice Lon and The Sparklers)
**Lawrence Welk and his Sparkling Sextet**
711    The Theme from 'The Threepenny Opera'
**Danny Welton**
(see Les Baxter and his Orchestra; David Rose and his Orchestra)
**Alvy West**
(see Henri Rene and his Orchestra)
**Western Rhythm Kings, The**
(see Johnny Southern)
**Paul Weston and his Orchestra**
126    La vie en rose
246    I only have eyes for you
256    Autumn leaves
261    Beloved, be faithful (The Norman Luboff Choir)
272    Nevertheless (The Norman Luboff Choir)
288    So long (The Norman Luboff Choir)
345    Some enchanted evening
369    And so to sleep again (The Norman Luboff Choir)
438    Wonderful Copenhagen (The Norman Luboff Choir)
**Nancy Whiskey**
927    Hillside in Scotland
928    I know where I'm going
        (see also The Chas McDevitt Skiffle Group)
**Jack White and his Orchestra**
43     Anniversary song
76     Mam'selle
115    Nature boy
118    Dance, ballerina, dance
121    You can't be true, dear
**Josh White and The Stargazers**
307    On top of Old Smokey
**David Whitfield**
429    I'll never forget you
465    I believe
492    The Bridge of Sighs
509    Answer me
538    The book
578    Smile
594    Santo Natale

649 Ev'rywhere
651 Mama
672 I'll never stop loving you
707 My September love
751 My unfinished symphony
779 Adoration waltz
788 If I lost you
798 I'll find you
809 I'd give you the world
894 On the street where you live
994 Willingly
*(see also David Whitfield and Stanley Black and his Orchestra; David Whitfield and Mantovani and his Orchestra)*

**David Whitfield and Stanley Black and his Orchestra**
518 Rags to riches
**David Whitfield and Mantovani and his Orchestra**
569 Cara mia
687 When you lose the one you love
**June Whitfield**
484 Seven lonely days (with The Rita Williams Singers)
**Margaret Whiting**
46 April showers
137 Far away places (with The Crew Chiefs)
154 Forever and ever
165 While the angelus was ringing
170 A dreamer with a penny
214 My foolish heart
221 Let's do it again (with Joe 'Fingers' Carr and the Carr Hops)
369 And so to sleep again
432 Outside of heaven
486 I've never been in love before
524 Hello young lovers
645 Stowaway
762 True love
*(see also Margaret Whiting and Johnny Mercer; Margaret Whiting and Frank de Vol; Margaret Whiting and Bob Hope; Margaret Whiting and Jimmy Wakely)*

**Margaret Whiting and Bob Hope**
253 Home cookin'
**Margaret Whiting and Frank de Vol**
213 I said my pajamas
**Margaret Whiting and Johnny Mercer**
182 Baby, it's cold outside
**Margaret Whiting and Jimmy Wakely**
393 Star of hope
**Billy Whitlock**
186 Scotch hot (with Harry Bidgood and his Orchestra)
**Slim Whitman**
547 Secret love
672 I'll never stop loving you
731 Serenade
893 A very precious love
**Eddie Wilcox and his Orchestra**
377 Wheel of fortune (Sunny Gale)
**Marty Wilde**
1011 Donna
1036 A teenager in love
1074 Sea of love
**Marty Wilde and The Wildcats**
881 Oh-oh, I'm falling in love again
914 Endless sleep

**Dave Wilkins**
*(see Ted Heath and his Music)*
**Andy Williams**
735 Walk hand in hand
801 Butterfly
1091 The village of St Bernadette
**Billy Williams**
801 Butterfly
836 I'm gonna sit right down and write myself a letter
**Billy Williams Quartet, The**
584 Sh-boom
**Billy Williams Quartette, The**
328 Shanghai
353 Sin
377 Wheel of fortune
**Bonnie Lou Williams**
*(see Gordon Jenkins and his Orchestra)*
**Charles Williams and his Concert Orchestra**
111 The dream of Olwen (with Arthur Dulay – piano)
515 Golden tango
**Dick Williams**
*(see Harry James and his Orchestra)*
**Esther Williams and Ricardo Montalban**
182 Baby, it's cold outside
**Hank Williams and his Drifting Cowboys**
412 Half as much
436 Settin' the woods on fire
**Marion Williams**
*(see The Johnny Dankworth Seven)*
**Neville Williams**
*(see Geraldo and his Orchestra)*
**Otis Williams and The Charms**
729 Ivory tower
**Rita Williams**
33 It's all over now
48 For sentimental reasons
61 Tell me, Marianne
65 Try a little tenderness
70 People will say we're in love
78 Now is the hour
97 My own Darby and Joan
101 Once upon a winter time
110 The wishing waltz
114 Time may change
124 My happiness
126 Take me to your heart again
158 Till all our dreams come true
565 Little things mean a lot
578 Smile
599 I can't tell a waltz from a tango
623 Prize of gold
630 Cherry pink and apple blossom white (with The Four-in-A-Chord)
645 Stowaway (with The Four-in-A-Chord)
670 Hey there
703 Band of gold
714 Willie can (with The Rita Williams Singers)
717 No other love
729 Ivory tower
743 A sweet old-fashioned girl
747 Born to be with you
762 True love
770 Come home to my arms
861 Love me forever
*(see also Billy Thorburn's The Organ, the Dance Band and Me; Carroll Gibbons and the Savoy Hotel Orpheans; Lou Preager and his*

*Orchestra; Ivy Benson and her Girls' Band; Paul Adam and his Mayfair Music; Rita Williams and Bob Dale)*
**Rita Williams and Bob Dale**
681 Relax-ay-voo
692 Love and marriage
**Rita Williams Singers, The**
*(see David Hughes; June Whitfield; Robert Earl; Reginald Conway and his Orchestra; Mark Pasquin; Bob Dale; Larry Cross; Sam Browne; Rita Williams; Denny Dennis; Gracie Fields; The King Brothers; Ronnie Harris; Dennis Lotis; Jeannie Carson; Russ Conway; Kevin Scott; Roberto Cardinali; Shirley Bassey)*
**Roger Williams**
846 Mary's boy child
971 The world outside
*(see also Roger Williams and Jane Morgan)*
**Roger Williams and Jane Morgan**
760 Two different worlds
**Tex Williams**
351 I want to be near you
592 They were doin' the mambo
*(see also Rex Allen and Tex Williams)*
**Foy Willing and his Riders of the Purple Sage**
163 Brush those tears from your eyes (Foy Willing & Trio)
**Eileen Wilson and Don Cherry**
276 I'll always love you
393 Star of hope
*(see also Don Cherry)*
**Jackie Wilson**
878 To be loved
**Robert Wilson**
109 Galway Bay
134 The heart of Loch Lomond
194 Down in the glen
391 From the time you say goodbye
**Shirley Wilson**
636 You, my love
642 Melody of love
**Windy City Symphony, The**
*(see Bobby Maxwell)*
**Franz Winkler Quartet, The**
154 Forever and ever
**Maurice Winnick and his Orchestra**
40 Too many irons in the fire (Sam Browne)
**Maurice Winnick and his Sweet Music**
517 While we love (Doreen Lundy)
**Maurice Winnick and his Sweet Music for Dancing**
357 The little white cloud that cried
**'Winnie the Whistler'**
726 The happy whistler
**Eric Winstone and his Orchestra**
123 So tired (Leslie Howard)
140 Crystal gazer (Julie Dawn)
148 The wedding of Lilli Marlene (Leslie Howard)
168 Blue ribbon gal
182 Baby, it's cold outside (Julie Dawn and Leslie Howard)
363 Only fools (Franklyn Boyd)
**Hugo Winterhalter and his Orchestra**
249 Count every star (with Mixed Chorus)
386 Blue tango
438 Wonderful Copenhagen (with Chorus)
**Liz Winters**
805 Freight train (with The Bob Cort Skiffle Group)

**Norman Wisdom**
397  Heart of a clown
537  Don't laugh at me
560  Young at heart
787  Wisdom of a fool
**Wondertones, The**
(see Beryl Templeman)
**Del Wood**
352  Down yonder
**Gloria Wood**
(see Kay Kyser and his Orchestra)
**Ilene Woods**
251  Bibbidi-bobbidi-boo (with The Woodsmen)
254  A dream is a wish your heart makes
**Woodsmen, The**
(see Ilene Woods)
**Sheb Wooley**
909  Purple people eater
**Miriam Workman**
(see Carmen Cavallaro and his Orchestra)
**Billie Worth and Jeff Warren**
506  You're just in love
**Johnny Worth**
915  When
945  Splish splash
946  King Creole
957  It's only make believe
959  Tom Dooley
977  Chantilly lace
981  I got stung
982  Baby face
984  A pub with no beer
993  My heart sings
1009  It doesn't matter any more
1011  Donna
1015  A fool such as I
1031  Mean streak
1038  Forth Worth Jail
1048  Living doll
1055  Lonely boy
1074  Sea of love
1084  Just a little too much
1089  What do you want to make those eyes at me for?
1094  What do you want?
1095  Oh! Carol
**Ruby Wright**
544  Bimbo
1053  Three stars (with narration by Dick Pike)
(see also Charlie Gore and Ruby Wright)
**Wright Brothers, The**
587  If I give my heart to you
**Jane Wyman**
(see Bing Crosby and Jane Wyman)
**Yale Brothers, The**
(see Georgia Gibbs)
**Yana**
807  Mr Wonderful
907  I need you
**Rusty York**
(see Bonnie Lou and Rusty York)
**Peter Yorke and his Concert Orchestra**
6  In the land of beginning again (Sam Browne)
126  Take me to your heart again
197  Dear hearts and gentle people (Doreen Lundy)
(see also Freddy Gardner)

**Arthur Young**
(see Mantovani and his Concert Orchestra)
**Eve Young**
212  I'd've baked a cake (with The Homesteaders)
235  Silver dollar (with The Homesteaders)
302  Would I love you
(see also Snooky Lanson and Eve Young)
**Jimmy Young**
298  Life's desire
302  Would I love you
320  Too young
329  Because of you
332  How can I leave you?
333  Vanity
353  Sin
357  The little white cloud that cried
363  Only fools
365  Cry
368  We won't live in a castle
369  And so to sleep again
384  Be anything
385  Kiss of fire
395  Faith
410  The Isle of Innisfree
413  Take my heart
418  If I had wings
421  You belong to me
422  Faith can move mountains
423  My love and devotion
426  Moon above Malaya
444  Why don't you believe me
450  Keep it a secret
455  Till I waltz again with you
460  I'm walking behind you
470  Even now (with The Clubmen)
471  Hold me, thrill me, kiss me
475  Eternally
487  Say you're mine again (with The Stargazers)
494  Is it any wonder
510  Wish you were here
525  Ebb tide
565  Little things mean a lot
591  The high and the mighty
618  Give me your word
627  If anyone finds this, I love you
637  Unchained melody
664  The man from Laramie
709  Chain gang
733  The wayward wind
749  More
802  Round and round (with The Michael Sammes Singers)
837  Man on fire
893  A very precious love
929  Volare
**Marshall Young**
(see Leo Reisman and his Orchestra)
**Ralph Young**
664  The man from Laramie
(see also Sy Oliver and his Orchestra)
**Vicki Young**
516  Ricochet
631  Tweedle-dee (with Vocal Group)
**Victor Young and his Orchestra**
243  Mona Lisa (Don Cherry and Chorus)
277  My heart cries for you (Louanne Hogan, Joe Graydon and Chorus)

286  Be my love (Louanne Hogan, Joe Graydon and Chorus)
300  Our very own (Don Cherry and Chorus)
320  Too young (Louanne Hogan)
806  Around the world
**Victor Young and his Singing Strings**
111  The dream of Olwen
126  La vie en rose
410  The Isle of Innisfree
445  Hi-Lili, Hi-Lo
472  The song from Moulin Rouge
475  Terry's Theme from 'Limelight'
495  Ruby (with George Fields – harmonica)
503  The Melba waltz
578  Smile (with Ray Turner – piano)
591  The high and the mighty (Whistling: Muzzy Marcellino)
630  Cherry pink and apple blossom white
636  You, my love
**Florian Zabach**
479  April in Portugal
**Anne Ziegler and Webster Booth**
60  Hear my song, Violetta
78  Now is the hour
201  Some day my heart will awake
(see also Webster Booth)
**Zodiacs, The**
875  Why don't they understand?

# SONG INDEX

## A

Title and first year in charts | Song No.

A – you're adorable (1949) — 153
Accordion (1947) — 52
Adoration waltz (1957) — 779
Affair to remember, An (1957) — 843
Again (1949) — 160
All (1957) — 791
All I have to do is dream (1958) — 905
All my love (1950) — 264
All of you (1957) — 789
All shook up (1957) — 818
All the time and ev'rywhere (1953) — 462
All the way (1958) — 856
All through the day (1946) — 30
Allentown Jail (1951) — 341
Alone (1957) — 848
Am I a toy or treasure? (1954) — 598
Am I wasting my time on you? (1949) — 183
Among my souvenirs (1947) — 66
'Ampstead Way, The (1946) — 25
And so to sleep again (1952) — 369
And then it's heaven (1946) — 22
Angelina (1959) — 1003
Anniversary song, The (1947) — 43
Answer me (1953) — 509
Any time (1952) — 375
Any time at all (1946) — 31
Apple blossom wedding, An (1947) — 87
April in Portugal (1953) — 479
April love (1957) — 854
April showers (1947) — 46
A-round the corner (1952) — 376
Around the world (1957) — 806
Arrivederci darling (1955) — 686
As I love you (1958) — 968
Ashes of roses (1950) — 245
At last! At last! (1952) — 371
At the end of the day (1951) — 344
At the hop (1958) — 867
Auf wiederseh'n sweetheart (1952) — 383
Autumn concerto (1956) — 748
Autumn leaves (1950) — 256

## B

Baby face (1959) — 982
Baby, it's cold outside (1949) — 182
Baby lover (1958) — 876
Ballad of Davy Crockett, The (1956) — 691
Ballin' the Jack (1948) — 129
Banana boat song, The (1957) — 785
Band of gold (1956) — 703
Banjo's back in town, The (1955) — 674
Battle of New Orleans, The (1959) — 1043
Be anything (1952) — 384
Be mine (1953) — 508
Be my girl (1957) — 844
Be my life's companion (1952) — 372
Be my love (1951) — 286
Beautiful brown eyes (1951) — 303
Beautiful eyes (1949) — 166
Because of rain (1952) — 367
Because of you (1951) — 329
Because you're mine (1952) — 424
Beggar in love, A (1951) — 318
Behind the clouds (1949) — 152
Believe in me (1956) — 745
Bell bottom blues (1954) — 542
Belle, Belle, my Liberty Belle (1951) — 334
Belle of the ball (1952) — 416
Beloved, be faithful (1950) — 261
Best of all (1950) — 207
Bewitched (1950) — 228
Bibbidi bobbidi boo (1950) — 251
Big head (1953) — 499
Big hunk o' love, A (1959) — 1052
Big man (1958) — 908
Bimbo (1954) — 544
Bird dog (1958) — 944
Birds and the bees, The (1956) — 737
Black and white rag, The (1951) — 346
Black hills of Dakota, The (1954) — 580
Black note serenade, The (1951) — 327
Blacksmith blues (1952) — 379
Bless you (1946) — 1
Blossom fell, A (1955) — 615
Blow out the candle (1951) — 335
Blowing wild (1954) — 526
Blue, blue day (1958) — 956
Blue ribbon gal (1949) — 168
Blue star (1955) — 659
Blue suede shoes (1956) — 732

Blue tango (1952) — 386
Blueberry Hill (1957) — 786
Bob's yer uncle! (1954) — 566
Book, The (1954) — 538
Book of love, The (1958) — 904
Born to be with you (1956) — 747
Born too late (1958) — 940
Botch-a-me (1952) — 411
Bow bells (1947) — 88
Breeze, The (1953) — 485
Bridge of sighs, The (1953) — 492
Broken-hearted melody (1959) — 1071
Broken wings (1953) — 435
Brush those tears from your eyes (1949) — 163
Butterfly (1957) — 801
Buttons and bows (1948) — 127
By the fountains of Rome (1956) — 739
By you, by you, by you (1957) — 790
Bye bye love (1957) — 822

## C

Candy and cake (1950) — 236
Candy kisses (1949) — 151
Can't I? (1953) — 489
Cara mia (1954) — 569
Careless hands (1949) — 164
Carolina moon (1958) — 932
Catch a falling star (1958) — 870
Celebration rag (1953) — 464
Certain smile, A (1958) — 943
C'est si bon (1950) — 215
Chain gang (1956) — 709
Changing partners (1954) — 534
Chantilly lace (1959) — 977
Chapel of the roses (1957) — 800
Charlie Brown (1959) — 1012
Charmaine (1952) — 358
Chattanoogie shoe-shine boy (1950) — 209
Chee-chee-oo-chee (1955) — 639
Cherry pink and apple blossom white (1955) — 630
Cherry stones (1950) — 217
Chi-baba, chi-baba (1947) — 83
Chicago (1958) — 864
Chick (1959) — 1005
Chicka boom (1953) — 513
Chickery chick (1946) — 3
China tea (1959) — 1058

Choo'n gum (1950) 224
Christmas alphabet (1955) 678
Christmas and you (1956) 765
Christmas in Killarney (1950) 258
Christmas Island (1956) 761
Christopher Columbus (1951) 322
Ciao ciao bambina (1959) 1016
Cindy, oh Cindy (1956) 766
Civilisation (1948) 102
Clancy lowered the boom (1949) 159
Cleo and me-o (1954) 568
Clopin clopant (1949) 156
Close the door (1955) 660
Close your eyes (1955) 662
Cloud lucky seven (1954) 523
C'mon everybody (1959) 1013
C'n I canoe you up the river? (1951) 278
Coffee song, The (1948) 92
Come back to Sorrento (1947) 69
Come home to my arms (1956) 770
Come next Spring (1956) 716
Come on, let's go (1959) 978
Come softly to me (1959) 1014
Comes a-long a-love (1952) 433
Confidentially (1949) 173
Cookie (1956) 715
Cool water (1955) 658
Coronation rag (1953) 474
Coronation waltz (1953) 473
Count every star (1950) 249
Count on me (1959) 1087
Count your blessings instead of sheep
   (1954) 601
Crazy Otto rag, The (1955) 648
Creep, The (1954) 527
Cross over the bridge (1954) 554
Cruising down the river (1946) 2
Cry (1952) 365
Crying in the chapel (1953) 512
Crystal gazer, The (1949) 140
Cuanto le gusta (1948) 132
Cuckoo waltz, The (1948) 131
Cuff of my shirt, The (1954) 541
Cumberland Gap (1957) 797

# D

Daddy's little girl (1950) 226
Dam busters march, The (1955) 668
Dance, ballerina, dance (1948) 118
Dance me loose (1952) 387
Danger ahead (1947) 84
Dark moon (1957) 817
Davy Crockett is helping Santa Claus
   (1956) 769
Day by day (1946) 16
Day of Jubilo, The (1952) 398
Day the rains came, The (1958) 967
Deadwood stage, The (1954) 557

Dear hearts and gentle people (1950) 197
Dear old Donegal (1947) 74
Dearie (1950) 222
December (1949) 190
Delicado (1952) 406
Devotion (1958) 921
Diana (1957) 828
Didja ever (1952) 399
Dime and a dollar, A (1954) 562
Do you love me? (1946) 19
Does your chewing gum lose its flavour?
   (1959) 995
Domino (1952) 355
Donna (1959) 1011
Don't (1958) 879
Don't ever leave me (1954) 531
Don't fall in love (1947) 53
Don't forbid be (1957) 784
Don't laugh at me (1954) 537
Don't leave me now (1954) 536
Don't let the stars get in your eyes (1953) 437
Don't ring-a-da bell (1956) 718
Don't worry (1955) 641
Don't you rock me daddy-o (1957) 781
Down in the glen (1949) 194
Down in the valley (1946) 17
Down the old Spanish trail (1947) 75
Down yonder (1952) 352
Downhearted (1953) 467
Dream again (1947) 41
Dream, dream, dream (1954) 572
Dream is a wish your heart makes, A
   (1950) 254
Dream lover (1959) 1034
Dream of Olwen, The (1948) 111
Dreamboat (1955) 643
Dreamer with a penny, A (1949) 170
Dreams can tell a lie (1956) 699
Dummy song, The (1953) 457
Dynamite (1959) 1077

# E

Earth angel (1955) 640
Ebb tide (1954) 525
Echo told me a lie, The (1949) 162
Ecstasy (1952) 427
Eighteenth century rock (1959) 1100
End, The (1958) 964
Endless sleep (1958) 914
Enjoy yourself (1950) 216
Even now (1953) 470
Evermore (1955) 647
Every day of my life (1955) 650
Everybody loves a lover (1958) 931
Everywhere you go (1949) 169
Ev'ry hour, ev'ry day of my life (1958) 913
Ev'rywhere (1955) 649

# F

Faith (1952) 395
Faith can move mountains (1952) 422
Far away places (1949) 137
Feet up (1952) 415
Ferry Boat Inn (1950) 263
Fifty years ago (1951) 319
Finger of suspicion, The (1954) 607
Fire down below (1957) 825
Five minutes more (1946) 36
Flirtation waltz (1953) 502
Fly away lovers (1958) 925
Flying saucer (1950) 268
Fool such as I, A (1959) 1015
For a penny (1959) 1060
For sentimental reasons (1947) 48
Forever and ever (1949) 154
Forget-me-not (1952) 419
Forgotten dreams (1957) 812
Fort Worth Jail (1959) 1038
Forty miles of bad road (1959) 1064
Freight train (1957) 805
French can-can polka, The (1950) 208
French foreign legion (1959) 1020
Friendly persuasion (1957) 774
Friends and neighbours (1954) 552
From here to eternity (1954) 530
From the time you say goodbye (1952) 391
From the vine came the grape (1954) 549

# G

Gal in calico, A (1947) 67
Gal with the yaller shoes, The (1956) 742
Galway Bay (1948) 109
Gandy dancer's ball, The (1952) 380
Garden of Eden, The (1957) 773
Gigi (1959) 992
Gilly Gilly Ossenfeffer Katzenellen Bogen by
   the sea (1954) 577
Girl of my dreams (1958) 941
Girl that I marry, The (1948) 93
Girls were made to take care of boys
   (1951) 304
Give her my love (1957) 780
Give me the right (1955) 624
Give me your word (1955) 618
Glendora (1956) 753
Glow worm, The (1953) 443
Go home! (1947) 45
Go on by (1955) 671
Golden earrings (1948) 105
Golden tango, The (1953) 515
Good companions, The (1957) 795

Good luck, good health, God bless you
   (1951)   281
Goodbye, Jimmy, goodbye (1959)   1029
Goodnight Irene (1950)   248
Goodnight, you little rascal, you (1947)   62
Got a match? (1958)   937
Got you on my mind (1953)   452
Gotta have rain (1958)   922
Got-ta have something in the bank, Frank
   (1957)   847
Grand Coolie Dam (1958)   892
Great balls of fire (1958)   865
Great pretender, The (1956)   712
Green cockatoo, The (1946)   35
Green door, The (1956)   758
Guilty (1947)   82
Guitar boogie shuffle (1959)   1030
Guy is a guy, A (1952)   381

# H

Half as much (1952)   412
Handful of songs, A (1957)   833
Happiness Street (1956)   768
Happy days and lonely nights (1955)   608
Happy times (1950)   247
Happy wanderer, The (1954)   539
Happy whistler, The (1956)   726
Hard headed woman (1958)   916
Harriett (1947)   64
Harry Lime theme, The (1949)   187
Have I told you lately that I love you?
   (1950)   240
Have you ever been lonely? (1955)   667
Have you heard? (1953)   478
Have you seen Irene? (1949)   167
He (1955)   684
Hear my song, Violetta (1947)   60
Heart (1957)   792
Heart and soul (1953)   441
Heart of a clown (1952)   397
Heart of a man, The (1959)   1049
Heart of Loch Lomond, The (1949)   134
Heart of my heart (1954)   545
Heartaches by the number (1959)   1093
Heartbeat (1954)   604
Heartbreaker (1948)   116
Heartless (1954)   546
Hello young lovers (1954)   524
Here comes Summer (1959)   1061
Here in my heart (1952)   408
Hernando's Hideaway (1955)   669
He's got the whole world in His hands
   (1957)   851
Hey Joe! (1953)   504
Hey, Mr. Banjo (1955)   652
Hey! Neighbour (1950)   237
Hey there (1955)   670
High and the mighty, The (1954)   591

High class baby (1959)   973
High hopes (1959)   1063
High noon (1952)   392
Hi-jig-a-jig, hi-jig-a-jig (1947)   58
Hi-Lili, hi-lo (1953)   445
Hillside in Scotland (1958)   927
Hold me, thrill me, kiss me (1953)   471
Hold my hand (1954)   586
Home cookin' (1950)   253
Homecoming waltz, The (1954)   561
Homesick, that's all (1946)   4
Homing waltz, The (1952)   388
Hoots mon (1958)   952
Hop-Scotch polka, The (1949)   186
Hot diggity (1956)   725
Hot toddy (1953)   481
House with love in it, A (1956)   759
How are things in Glocca Morra? (1947)   89
How can I leave you? (1951)   332
How can you buy Killarney? (1949)   145
How lucky you are (1947)   54
Hula hoop song, The (1958)   953

# I

I apologise (1951)   311
I believe (1947)   79
I believe (1953)   465
I can't begin to tell you (1946)   5
I can't tell a waltz from a tango (1954)   599
I could have danced all night (1958)   895
I don't see me in your eyes any more
   (1949)   172
I dreamed (1957)   776
I get so lonely (1954)   556
I go ape (1959)   1032
I got stung (1959)   981
I got the sun in the morning (1947)   72
I heard the bells on Christmas day (1958)   962
I kneel at your throne (1959)   1021
I know (1959)   1045
I know where I'm going (1958)   928
I leave my heart in an English garden
   (1950)   262
I love Paris (1954)   593
I love the sunshine of your smile (1951)   330
I love you, baby (1957)   852
I may never pass this way again (1958)   880
I miss you so (1959)   1024
I need you (1958)   907
I need you now (1954)   600
I need your love tonight (1959)   1018
I only have eyes for you (1950)   246
I only saw him once (1950)   250
I remember the cornfields (1950)   225
I said my pajamas (1950)   213
I saw mommy kissing Santa Claus (1953)   511
I see the moon (1954)   533
I still believe (1954)   603

I talk to the trees (1953)   456
I taut I taw a puddy tat (1950)   259
I wanna say hello (1952)   359
I want to be near you (1951)   351
I went to your wedding (1952)   428
I will never change (1953)   459
I wish I wuz (1951)   343
I wonder (1955)   635
I wonder who's kissing her now (1948)   94
I'd give you the world (1957)   809
I'd love to fall asleep (1953)   458
Idle gossip (1954)   563
I'd've baked a cake (1950)   212
If (1951)   270
If anyone finds this, I love you (1955)   627
If dreams came true (1958)   935
If I give my heart to you (1954)   587
If I had wings (1952)   418
If I lost you (1957)   788
If I loved you (1950)   234
If I were a blackbird (1950)   238
If only I could live my life again (1959)   1008
If you go (1951)   342
If you love me (1953 & 1959)   517 & 1083
I'll always love you (1949)   157
I'll always love you (1951)   276
I'll be home (1956)   722
I'll be with you in apple blossom time
   (1959)   985
I'll come when you call (1955)   665
I'll find you (1957)   798
I'll make up for everything (1947)   86
I'll never forget you (1952)   429
I'll never stop loving you (1955)   672
I'll remember tonight (1959)   987
I'll string along with you (1949)   188
I'll walk alone (1952)   405
I'm gonna live till I die (1952)   400
I'm gonna sit right down and write
   myself a letter (1957)   836
I'm looking over a four-leaf clover (1948)   117
I'm my own grandpa (1948)   106
I'm walking behind you (1953)   460
I'm yours (1952)   390
In a golden coach (1953)   449
In a shady nook (1949)   142
In the cool, cool, cool of the evening
   (1951)   337
In the land of beginning again (1946)   6
In the middle of a dark, dark
   night (1957)   832
In the middle of an island (1957)   829
In the middle of the house (1956)   757
Into each life some rain must fall (1946)   7
Is it any wonder? (1953)   494
Is it too late? (1949)   191
Is it true what they say about Dixie (1950)   203
Island in the sun (1957)   816
Isle of Innisfree, The (1952)   410
Istanbul (1953)   522
It doesn't matter any more (1959)   1009
It happened in Adano (1949)   155

| | |
|---|---|
| Italian theme, The (1956) | 723 |
| It's a pity to say goodnight (1946) | 8 |
| It's all in the game (1958) | 948 |
| It's all over now (1946) | 33 |
| It's almost tomorrow (1956) | 701 |
| It's late (1959) | 1026 |
| It's magic (1949) | 150 |
| It's only make believe (1958) | 957 |
| It's too soon to know (1958) | 890 |
| I've got a lovely bunch of coconuts (1950) | 200 |
| I've never been in love before (1953) | 486 |
| I've waited so long (1959) | 1027 |
| Ivory rag (1951) | 308 |
| Ivory tower (1956) | 729 |
| Ivy will cling (1959) | 1099 |

# J

| | |
|---|---|
| Jailhouse rock (1958) | 862 |
| Jealous heart (1950) | 199 |
| Jezebel (1951) | 312 |
| Jilted (1954) | 574 |
| Jimmy unknown (1956) | 704 |
| Jingle bell rock (1959) | 1096 |
| John and Julie (1955) | 655 |
| Johnny Fedora (1946) | 23 |
| Jones boy, The (1954) | 543 |
| Just a little too much (1959) | 1084 |
| Just the way you are (1951) | 273 |
| Just walking in the rain (1956) | 756 |

# K

| | |
|---|---|
| Kansas City (1959) | 1037 |
| Keep it a secret (1953) | 450 |
| Kentucky waltz, The (1951) | 325 |
| Kewpie doll (1958) | 898 |
| Key, The (1959) | 1092 |
| King Creole (1958) | 946 |
| Kiss (1953) | 490 |
| Kiss in your eyes, The (1949) | 185 |
| Kiss me and kiss me and kiss me (1959) | 1004 |
| Kiss me, honey honey, kiss me (1959) | 972 |
| Kiss of fire (1952) | 385 |
| Kisses sweeter than wine (1957) | 855 |
| Knee deep in the blues (1957) | 783 |

# L

| | |
|---|---|
| La dee dah (1958) | 885 |
| Last mile home, The (1950) | 196 |
| Last night on the back porch (1959) | 988 |

| | |
|---|---|
| Last train to San Fernando (1957) | 827 |
| Laughing on the outside (1946) | 9 |
| Lavender blue (1949) | 143 |
| Lay down your arms (1956) | 746 |
| Learnin' the blues (1955) | 657 |
| Left right out of my (your) heart (1958) | 926 |
| Leicester Square rag (1949) | 171 |
| Let bygones be bygones (1946) | 10 |
| Let it be soon (1946) | 27 |
| Let me be loved (1957) | 842 |
| Let me go, lover (1955) | 619 |
| Let's do it again (1950) | 221 |
| Let's walk that-a-way (1953) | 493 |
| Letter to a soldier, A (1956) | 772 |
| Liechensteiner polka (1958) | 869 |
| Life's desire (1951) | 298 |
| Lilli Marlene (1946) | 37 |
| Limelight, The theme from (1953) | 475 |
| Lipstick and candy and rubber sole shoes (1956) | 713 |
| Lipstick on your collar (1959) | 1046 |
| List'nin' to the green grass grow (1951) | 301 |
| Little Bernadette (1958) | 920 |
| Little bird told me, A (1949) | 136 |
| Little darlin' (1957) | 823 |
| Little donkey (1959) | 1079 |
| Little drummer boy, The (1959) | 996 |
| Little Laplander, The (1955) | 690 |
| Little old mill, The (1947) | 81 |
| Little one (1958) | 951 |
| Little red monkey (1953) | 453 |
| Little serenade (1958) | 900 |
| Little shoemaker, The (1954) | 558 |
| Little things mean a lot (1954) | 565 |
| Little train (1958) | 923 |
| Little white bull, The (1959) | 1097 |
| Little white cloud that cried, The (1952) | 357 |
| Little white duck, The (1951) | 315 |
| Living doll (1959) | 1048 |
| Load of hay, A (1950) | 231 |
| Lollipop (1958) | 886 |
| Lonely boy (1959) | 1055 |
| Lonesome (1959) | 1075 |
| Long before I knew you (1958) | 857 |
| Longing for you (1951) | 336 |
| Look at that girl (1953) | 497 |
| Look homeward angel (1957) | 793 |
| Love and marriage (1956) | 692 |
| Love is a golden ring (1957) | 799 |
| Love is a many splendoured thing (1955) | 675 |
| Love letters in the sand (1957) | 819 |
| Love makes the world go round (1958) | 958 |
| Love me (1954) | 559 |
| Love me as though there were no tomorrow (1956) | 755 |
| Love me forever (1958) | 861 |
| Love me or leave me (1955) | 663 |
| Love of my life, The (1953) | 447 |
| Loveliest night of the year, The (1951) | 310 |
| Love's roundabout (1951) | 339 |
| Lullaby of Broadway (1951) | 338 |
| Luxembourg polka, The (1954) | 540 |

# M

| | |
|---|---|
| Ma (1957) | 853 |
| Mack the Knife (1959) | 1073 |
| Mad passionate love (1958) | 938 |
| Mademoiselle de Paree (1951) | 324 |
| Magic moments (1958) | 866 |
| Maharajah of Magador, The (1949) | 135 |
| Majorca (1955) | 616 |
| Make her mine (1954) | 588 |
| Make it soon (1953) | 439 |
| Make love to me (1954) | 551 |
| Make-believe world (1946) | 34 |
| Makin' love (1959) | 1082 |
| Mama (1955) | 651 |
| Mama doll song, The (1954) | 602 |
| Mambo Italiano (1955) | 610 |
| Mam'selle (1947) | 76 |
| Man from Laramie, The (1955) | 664 |
| Man on fire (1957) | 837 |
| Man with the banjo, The (1954) | 570 |
| Mandolin serenade (1957) | 835 |
| Mandolins in the moonlight (1958) | 961 |
| Mandy (1958) | 872 |
| Mangos (1957) | 796 |
| Manhattan spiritual (1959) | 1019 |
| Marianne (1957) | 794 |
| Marshmallow world (1951) | 269 |
| Mary Lou (1946) | 11 |
| Mary Rose (1951) | 294 |
| Mary's boy child (1957, 1958 & 1959) | 846 |
| May I call you sweetheart? (1947) | 47 |
| May Kway O May Kway (1951) | 299 |
| May you always (1959) | 1006 |
| Maybe baby (1958) | 884 |
| Maybe you'll be there (1948) | 130 |
| Me and my imagination (1951) | 274 |
| Me and my shadow (1950) | 223 |
| Mean streak (1959) | 1031 |
| Meet me on the corner (1955) | 679 |
| Meet Mister Callaghan (1952) | 403 |
| Melba waltz, The (1953) | 503 |
| Melody of love (1955) | 642 |
| Memories are made of this (1956) | 700 |
| Memories of you (1956) | 706 |
| Midnight (1959) | 579 |
| Mistakes (1951) | 349 |
| Mister (Mr) Blue (1959) | 1081 |
| Mister Cuckoo (1956) | 724 |
| Mister Sandman (1954) | 606 |
| Mister (Mr) Wonderful (1957) | 807 |
| Mobile (1955) | 620 |
| Mockin' bird hill (1951) | 290 |
| Mona Lisa (1950 & 1959) | 243 & 1066 |
| Monday, Tuesday, Wednesday (1949) | 184 |
| Money is the root of all evil (1946) | 12 |
| Moon above Malaya (1952) | 426 |
| Moon talk (1958) | 933 |

Moonlight gambler (1957) 778
More (1956) 749
More than ever (1958) 942
Mother Nature and Father Time (1953) 491
Moulin Rouge theme, The (1953) 472
Mountain greenery (1956) 738
Move it (1958) 949
Mule train (1950) 198
Music! Music! Music! (1950) 205
My Christmas wish (1950) 260
My concerto (1952) 382
My Dixie darling (1957) 845
My first love, my last love for always (1947) 85
My foolish heart (1950) 214
My friend (1954) 575
My happiness (1948 & 1959) 124 & 997
My heart belongs to only you (1954) 532
My heart cries for you (1951) 277
My heart sings (1959) 993
My love and devotion (1952) 423
My own Darby and Joan (1948) 97
My prayer (1956) 764
My resistance is low (1951) 309
My September love (1956) 707
My son, my son (1954) 590
My special angel (1957) 850
My thanks to you (1950) 211
My truly, truly fair (1951) 316
My ukelele (1959) 974
My unfinished symphony (1956) 751
My wish came true (1959) 1059

# N

Nairobi (1958) 874
Nature boy (1948) 115
Naughty lady of Shady Lane, The (1955) 611
Near you (1948) 96
Never (1952) 374
Never be anyone else but you (1959) 1023
Never do a tango with an Eskimo (1955) 683
Never Never Land, The (1954) 567
Nevertheless (1951) 272
Night the floor fell in, The (1950) 230
Ninety nine ways (1957) 803
No one but you (1954) 596
No other love (1956) 717
Not as a stranger (1954) 605
Now (1953) 442
Now is the hour (1947) 78
Now that I need you (1950) 206
Number one (1953) 496

# O

October twilight (1948) 128
Oh boy (1958) 859
Oh, Carol (1959) 1095
Oh, happy day (1953) 454
Oh! My achin' heart (1948) 113
Oh, my papa (1953) 521
Oh, oh, I'm falling in love again (1958) 881
Oh, what a beautiful morning (1947) 80
Oh! What it seemed to be (1946) 13
Oh! You sweet one (1950) 220
Old lamplighter, The (1947) 42
Old pi-anna rag (1955) 689
Old piano roll blues, The (1950) 218
Old postman, The (1948) 103
On a slow boat to China (1949) 133
On the 5.45 (1949) 138
On the street where you live (1958) 894
On top of Old Smoky (1951) 307
Once in a while (1950) 241
Once upon a winter-time (1948) 101
One more sunrise (1959) 1072
One night (1959) 986
One-zy, two-zy (1946) 20
Only fools (1952) 363
Only man on the island, The (1958) 912
Only sixteen (1959) 1057
Only you (1956) 705
Oodles of noodles (1952) 356
Open the door, Richard (1947) 56
Open up your heart (1955) 629
Orange coloured sky (1950) 257
Our love story (1949) 180
Our very own (1951) 300
Out of a clear blue sky (1950) 204
Out of town (1956) 721
Outside of Heaven (1952) 432

# P

Papa loves mambo (1955) 612
Paper kisses (1955) 626
Patricia (1951) 280
Patricia (1958) 918
Peg o' my heart (1947) 90
Peggy Sue (1958) 858
Peggy Sue got married (1959) 1065
Pendulum song, The (1955) 646
Penny a kiss – a penny a hug, A (1951) 289
People will say we're in love (1947) 70
Personality (1959) 1035
Petite fleur (1959) 998
Petite waltz, The (1950) 266
Piano party (1959) 1098

Pickin' a chicken (1956) 694
Pink shoelaces (1959) 1028
Pixilated penguin (1959) 1041
Play a simple melody (1951) 279
Please Mr Sun (1952) 373
Plenty good lovin' (1959) 1080
Poor Jenny (1959) 1039
Poor little fool (1958) 939
Poor people of Paris, The (1956) 710
Poppa Piccolino (1953) 498
Powder your face with sunshine (1949) 141
Pretend (1953) 461
Pretending (1946) 38
Pretty little black-eyed Susie (1953) 463
Primrose Hill (1946) 14
Prize of Gold (1955) 623
Problems (1959) 991
Pub with no beer, A (1959) 984
Punch and Judy man, The (1947) 68
Purple people eater, The (1958) 909
Put a light in the window (1958) 863
Put 'em in a box (1949) 144
Put your head on my shoulder (1959) 1088
Put your shoes on, Lucy (1949) 149
Puttin' on the style (1957) 814

# Q

Queen of Tonga, The (1953) 483
Quicksilver (1950) 219

# R

Rags to riches (1953) 518
Raindrops (1952) 414
Rainy day refrain, A (1951) 296
Rainy night in Rio, A (1947) 73
Rambling rose (1948) 122
Raunchy (1958) 873
Rave on (1958) 917
Razzle dazzle (1957) 775
Ready, willing and able (1955) 628
Real love (1958) 965
Red river rock (1959) 1086
Red roses for a blue lady (1949) 147
Red silken stockings (1951) 287
Reflections on the water (1948) 112
Relax-ay-voo (1955) 681
Remember you're mine (1957) 839
Return to me (1958) 906
Rickety rickshaw man, The (1947) 50
Ricochet (1953) 516
Riders in the sky (1949) 161
Robin Hood (1956) 697
Rock and roll waltz, The (1956) 708
Rock around the clock (1955 & 1956) 680

Rock of Gibraltar, The (1952) 407
Rock-a-billy (1957) 804
Rockin' through the rye (1956) 752
Rollin' stone (1952) 360
Rosaline (1951) 340
Rose in a garden of weeds, A (1949) 179
Rose, Rose, I love you (1951) 292
Roulette (1959) 1022
Round and round (1957) 802
Roving kind, The (1951) 285
Ruby (1953) 495
Ruby and the pearl, The (1953) 451
Rudolph, the red-nosed reindeer (1950, 1951, 1952 & 1953) 252

# S

St Therese of the roses (1956) 763
Saloon bar rag (1951) 293
Sam's song (1950) 242
Santo Natale (1954) 594
Saturday rag, The (1952) 366
Say goodnight but not goodbye (1949) 175
Say 'si si' (1953) 488
Say you're mine again (1953) 487
Scarlet ribbons (1957 & 1959) 826
Scottish samba, The (1949) 193
Sea of love (1959) 1074
Secret love (1954) 547
Secret of happiness, The (1958) 901
Senora (1951) 284
Sentimental me (1950) 239
September song (1951) 275
Serenade (1956) 731
Serenade of the bells (1948) 99
Settin' the woods on fire (1953) 436
Seven little girls sitting in the back seat (1959) 1090
Seven lonely days (1953) 484
Seventeen (1955) 677
Shadow waltz (1954) 555
Shake, rattle and roll (1955) 617
Shanghai (1951) 328
Shawl of Galway grey, A (1949) 178
Sh-boom (1954) 584
She wears red feathers (1953) 446
Shifting, whispering sands, The (1955) 685
Shiralee (1957) 830
Shoemaker's serenade, The (1948) 98
Shot gun boogie, The (1951) 297
Shrimp boats (1951) 347
Side by side (1953) 466
Side saddle (1959) 975
Silver dollar (1950) 235
Silver wedding waltz, The (1948) 108
Sin (1952) 353
Sincerely (1955) 644
Sing, little birdie (1959) 999
Singing in the rain (1952) 389

Singing the blues (1956) 771
Sixteen tons (1956) 693
Sky blue shirt and a rainbow tie, A (1954) 581
Sleigh ride (1950) 267
Slow coach (1952) 361
Smile (1954) 578
Smoke gets in you eyes (1959) 990
Smoky Mountain boogie (1951) 314
Snow coach (1959) 1085
Snowflakes (1952) 430
Snowy white snow and jingle bells (1949) 189
So in love (1951) 291
So long (1951) 288
So tired (1948) 123
So would I (1946) 24
Softly, softly (1955) 613
Some day my heart will awake (1950) 201
Some enchanted evening (1951) 345
Somebody (1955) 614
Someday, you'll want me to want you (1946 & 1958) 32 & 954
Someone (1959) 1062
Someone else's roses (1954) 550
Sometime, somewhere (1959) 1067
Somewhere along the way (1952) 402
Somewhere at the end of the rainbow (1950) 232
Son of Mary (1958) 963
Song of Capri, A (1949) 192
South America, take it away (1947) 91
Sparrow in the tree top (1951) 295
Splish splash (1958) 945
Stagger Lee (1959) 1017
Stairway of love (1958) 896
Star of hope (1952) 393
Stars shine in your eyes (1955) 656
Stars will remember, The (1947) 44
Start movin' (1957) 824
Stealin' (1956) 698
Story of my life, The (1958) 860
Story of Tina, The (1954) 573
Stowaway (1955) 645
Stranger in paradise (1955) 633
Strawberry moon, A (1949) 146
Stupid Cupid (1958) 934
Such a night (1954) 553
Suddenly (1959) 1025
Suddenly there's a valley (1955) 676
Sugar moon (1958) 911
Sugarbush (1952) 404
Sugartime (1958) 868
Summer of the seventeenth doll, The (1959) 1047
Sunshine cake (1950) 229
Susie darlin' (1958) 955
Sway (1954) 583
Swedish rhapsody (1953) 505
Sweet old-fashioned girl, A (1956) 743
Sweet violets (1951) 321
Sweetheart of yesterday (1951) 348
Sweetheart, we'll never grow old (1946) 28
Swingin' shepherd blues (1958) 877

# T

Take a message to Mary (1959) 1040
Take me back again (1955) 654
Take me in your arms and hold me (1953) 440
Take my heart (1952) 413
Takes two to tango (1952) 431
Tallahassee lassie (1959) 1068
Tammy (1957) 831
Tea for two cha cha (1958) 966
Teach me tonight (1955) 622
Tear fell, A (1956) 720
Teasin' (1951) 283
Teenager in love, A (1959) 1036
Tell me a story (1953) 482
Tell me, Marianne (1947) 61
Tell me why (1952) 370
Tell me you're mine (1953) 477
Tender trap, The (1956) 695
Tenderly (1954) 535
Tennessee waltz, The (1951) 271
Tennessee wig walk (1954) 528
Tequila (1958) 882
Teresa (1948) 107
Thank Heaven for little girls (1959) 1002
That dear old gentleman (1956) 767
That doggie in the window (1953) 448
That'll be the day (1957) 840
That's amore (1954) 529
That's a-why (1953) 434
That's how a love song was born (1955) 653
Then I'll be there (1952) 364
There goes my heart (1959) 1000
There must be a reason (1954) 585
There's a harvest moon tonight (1946) 18
There's a pawnshop on a corner in Pittsburg, Pennsylvania (1952) 378
There's always room at our house (1952) 354
There's never been a night (1958) 950
There's no boat like a rowboat (1951) 326
They say it's wonderful (1947) 77
They were doin' the mambo (1954) 592
Thing, The (1950) 265
Things we did last Summer, The (1947) 49
Think it over (1958) 936
This old man (1959) 983
This ole house (1954) 589
Three bells, The (1959) 1069
Three coins in the fountain (1954) 571
Three galleons (1955) 661
Three stars (1959) 1053
Threepenny Opera, Theme from the (1956) 711
'Til I kissed you (1959) 1070
Till all our dreams come true (1949) 158
Till I waltz again with you (1953) 455
Till then (1946) 39
Time after time (1947) 71

Time may change (1948) 114
Tipperary samba (1951) 282
To be loved (1958) 878
To each his own (1946) 26
To know him is to love him (1958) 970
Tom Dooley (Kingston Trio) (1958) 959
Tom Dooley (Lonnie Donegan) (1958) 960
Tom Hark (1958) 897
Tom Thumb's tune (1959) 980
Tomboy (1959) 1007
Tomorrow (1955) 621
Tonight (1959) 979
Too fat polka (1948) 104
Too late now (1951) 313
Too many irons in the fire (1946) 40
Too young (1951) 320
Too young to go steady (1956) 728
Toolie oolie doolie (1948) 119
Too-whit! Too-whoo! (1949) 176
Torero (1958) 930
Trampolina (1959) 1044
Travellin' home (1957) 815
Travellin' light (1959) 1078
Treble chance (1959) 1076
Tree in the meadow, A (1948) 95
Trudie (1958) 910
True love (1956) 762
Trust in me (1952) 394
Try a little tenderness (1947) 65
Try another cherry tree (1956) 730
Tulips and heather (1951) 323
Tulips from Amsterdam (1958) 888
Tweedle-dee (1955) 631
Twelfth Street rag (1949) 139
Twenty tiny fingers (1955) 673
Twilight time (1958) 903
Twixt twelve and twenty (1959) 1056
Two different worlds (1956) 760
Two Easter Sunday sweethearts (1954) 548
Two on a tandem (1950) 227
Tzena tzena tzena (1950) 244

# U

Unchained melody (1955) 637
Under the bridges of Paris (1955) 625
Unforgettable (1952) 362
Unless (1951) 317
Unsuspecting heart (1955) 632

# V

Vanity (1951) 333
Vaya con Dios (1953) 501
Veni-vidi-vici (1954) 597
Venus (1959) 1010

Very first Christmas of all, The (1955) 682
Very precious love, A (1958) 893
Vie en rose, La (1948) 126
Village of St. Bernadette, The (1959) 1091
Volare (1958) 929

# W

Wait for me (1959) 1001
Wait for me, darling (1954) 582
Wake up little Susie (1957) 849
Walk hand in hand (1956) 735
Walkin' my baby back home (1952) 401
Walkin' to Missouri (1952) 420
Waltz for the Queen, A (1953) 476
Wanderin' eyes (1957) 834
Wanted (1954) 564
Watching the world go by (1956) 740
Waterloo (1959) 1051
Wayward wind, The (1956) 733
We all have a song in our hearts (1950) 202
We will make love (1957) 813
We won't live in a castle (1952) 368
Wear my ring (1958) 899
Wedding bells (1955) 634
Wedding of Lilli Marlene, The (1949) 148
Wedding ring (1957) 841
Wedding samba, The (1949) 174
We'll keep a welcome (1950) 255
West of Zanzibar (1954) 576
What do you want? (1959) 1094
What do you want to make those eyes at me for? (1959) 1089
Whatever will be, will be (1956) 734
Wheel of fortune (1952) 377
When (1958) 915
When China boy meets China girl (1947) 59
When I fall in love (1952 & 1957) 425 & 808
When I take my sugar to tea (1952) 409
When Mexico gave up the rhumba (1956) 754
When Santa got stuck up the chimney (1953) 520
When the boys talk about the girls (1958) 919
When the world has forgotten (1950) 210
When you hear Big Ben (1953) 507
When you lose the one you love (1955) 687
When you're in love (1948) 125
When you're in love (1952) 396
When you were sweet sixteen (1948) 100
Where did my snowman go? (1953) 519
Where the winds blow (1953) 500
Where were you? (1959) 1033
Where will the dimple be? (1955) 638
While the angelus was ringing (1949) 165
White Christmas (1955) 609
White silver sands (1957) 838
White sport coat, A. (1957) 811
White wedding (1951) 331
Who are we? (1956) 727

Whole lotta woman (1958) 883
Whole world is singing my song. The (1947) 51
Who's sorry now? (1958) 891
Why do fools fall in love? (1956) 736
Why don't they understand? (1958) 875
Why don't you believe me? (1953) 444
Why is it? (1949) 195
Why should I be lonely? (1959) 1042
Why worry (1951) 350
Wild horses (1953) 469
Willie can (1956) 714
Willingly (1959) 994
Windmill song, The (1949) 177
Windows of Paris, The (1959) 1054
Windsor waltz, The (1953) 468
Winter wonderland (1958) 969
Wisdom of a fool, The (1957) 787
Wish you were here (1953) 510
Wishing waltz, The (1948) 110
Witch doctor (1958) 902
With all my heart (1957) 821
With these hands (1951) 305
With your love (1955) 688
Woman in love, A (1956) 750
Wonder of you, The (1959) 1050
Wonderful Copenhagen (1953) 438
Wonderful secret of love, The (1959) 989
Wonderful time up there, A (1958) 887
Wonderful, wonderful (1957) 820
Woody Woodpecker (1948) 120
World belongs to you, little man, The (1947) 55
World goes around and around, The (1958) 947
World outside, The (1959) 971
Would I love you (1951) 302
Wouldn't it be loverly? (1958) 924

# Y

Yellow rose of Texas, The (1955) 666
Yes tonight, Josephine (1957) 810
You always hurt the one you love (1946 & 1959) 21 & 976
You are my destiny (1951) 306
You are my destiny (1958) 871
You are my first love (1956) 744
You belong to me (1952) 421
You can be sure of me (1946) 15
You can't be true, dear (1948) 121
You can't be true to two (1956) 719
You keep coming back like a song (1946) 29
You, me and us (1957) 777
You, my love (1955) 636
You need hands (1958) 889
You went away and left me (1947) 63
You, you, you (1953) 514
You'll never walk alone (1956) 741

301

Young and foolish (1956)            696
Young at heart (1954)               560
Young love (1957)                   782
Your cheatin' heart (1953)          480
Your heart and my heart (1950)      233
Your heart, my heart (1954)         595
You're breaking my heart (1949)     181
You're just in love (1953)          506

# Z

Zambezi (1956)                      702
Zing a little zong (1952)           417
Zip-a-dee-doo-dah (1947)             57